W9-CQW-259

# Principles of Distributed Database Systems

**M. Tamer Özsu**

*University of Alberta*
*Edmonton, Canada*

**Patrick Valduriez**

*INRIA*
*Paris, France*

**PRENTICE HALL**
Englewood Cliffs, New Jersey 07632

Library of Congress Cataloging-in-Publication Data

Özsu, Tamer M.
   Principles of distributed database systems / M. Tamer Özsu,
   Patrick Valduriez.
       p.   cm.
   Includes bibliographical references.
   ISBN 0-13-691643-0
   1. Distributed data bases.   I. Valduriez, Patrick.   II. Title.
QA76.9.D30956   1991
005.75'8--dc20                                          90-35450
                                                          CIP

Editorial/production supervision: Christina Burghard and Jennifer Wenzel
Cover design: Lundgren Graphics, Ltd.
Manufacturing buyers: Lori Bulwin/Patrice Fraccio

ⓒ1991 by Prentice-Hall, Inc.
A Division of Simon & Schuster
Englewood Cliffs, New Jersey 07632

*To my family
and my parents
M.T.Ö.*

*To Cati, Sarah, and Juliette
P.V.*

Printed in the United States of America

10 9 8 7 6 5 4 3 2

ISBN   0-13-691643-0

PRENTICE-HALL INTERNATIONAL (UK) LIMITED,, *London*
PRENTICE-HALL OF AUSTRALIA PTY. LIMITED, *Sydney*
PRENTICE-HALL CANADA INC., *Toronto*
PRENTICE-HALL HISPANOAMERICANA, S.A., *Mexico*
PRENTICE-HALL OF INDIA PRIVATE LIMITED, *New Delhi*
PRENTICE-HALL OF JAPAN, INC., *Tokyo*
SIMON & SCHUSTER ASIA PTE. LTD., *Singapore*
EDITORA PRENTICE-HALL DO BRASIL, LTDA., *Rio de Janeiro*

# Contents

# Preface

Distributed database system technology is one of the major recent developments in the database systems area. There are claims that in the next ten years centralized database managers will be an "antique curiosity" and most organizations will move toward distributed database managers [Stonebraker, 1988, p. 189]. The intense interest in this subject in both the research community and the commercial marketplace certainly supports this claim. The extensive research activity in the last decade has generated results that now enable the introduction of commercial products into the marketplace.

This book aims to introduce and explain the theory, algorithms, and methods that underly distributed database management systems (distributed DBMS). For the most part, our presentation emphasizes the principles that guide the design of such systems more than their use. However, the issues in designing a distributed database are also addressed.

With its emphasis-on fundamentals, the book is meant to be used as a textbook for a one- or two-semester graduate-level course as well as a reference book. The material is currently being covered in a one-semester graduate course at the University of Alberta. If it is used in a two-semester course, the material can be complemented by current literature. The structure of the text also lends itself to be used as a companion text for undergraduate database courses.

The key features of the text are as follows:

**1.** The book starts by placing the distributed database technology in its proper context vis-à-vis the distributed computing and database management technologies. The introductory chapters are also aimed at providing the necessary background in computer networks and in relational database systems that is necessary for following the subsequent material.

**2.** Coverage of each topic starts by an introductory overview that sets the framework and defines the problems that are addressed. The subsequent discussion elaborates these issues. In certain cases the introductory material is included within one chapter (e.g., Sections 5.1 and 5.2), whereas in others they are separated as independent chapters (e.g., Chapters 7 and 10). It is these parts of the book, in addition to Chapter 1, that can be used to complement the undergraduate courses in database systems.

**3.** In addition to covering matured technology, the book also discusses current research areas such as distributed data servers, distributed object-oriented databases, and distributed knowledge bases. Thus, it serves not only to describe the technology that has been developed during the past decade, but it also provides an introduction to the technology that the researchers will be working on during the next one. Furthermore, there is coverage of issues related to the integration of distributed database systems and distributed operating systems. These issues have to be topics of intense research and experimentation if distributed database managers are to provide the performance, functionality, and extensibility expected of them.

**4.** A database design of an engineering organization is used consistently throughout as an example. This consistency enables the development of topics in a systematic fashion. The only section where a different example is used is in the transaction management chapters (10 through 12), where we opt for an airline reservation system, which is a favorite example of the database community as well as being a major application domain for transaction-based systems.

**5.** The book is structured so that two different uses, as a textbook and as a reference material, can be accommodated. On the one hand, the topics (e.g., distributed database design, semantic data control, distributed query processing and distributed transaction management) are developed systematically with almost no forward referencing. The backward references are few and clearly marked. This enables its use as a textbook where issues can be developed one at a time based on one another. On the other hand, each topic is covered as a self-contained module to the extent that this is possible. Thus, readers who have the background can simply refer to the topics they are interested in. In this mode of use as a reference material, the only important backward references are to previous examples.

**6.** Exercises are at the end of most chapters. However, chapters that serve as an introduction to topics (Chapters 1 through 3, 7, and 10) or which cover discussion of issues (Chapters 4 and 13) do not contain exercises. Where available, the questions are classified with respect to their difficulty. The number of asterisks (*) in front of a question indicates their level of difficulty.

### Organization of the Text

The organization of the book and the dependencies of the chapters are shown in the following figure. The introductory chapter is followed by two chapters that provide an overview of relational database technology and computer networks. If the reader has the background, these chapters can be skipped without any effect on the rest of the book. The only part of Chapter 2 that should be referenced is Example 2.1, which describes the engineering database example.

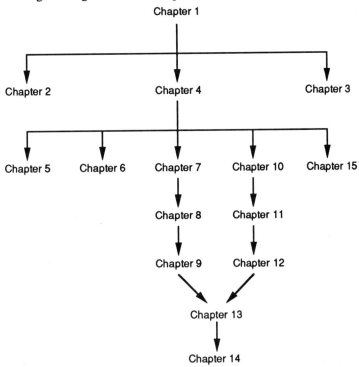

Chapter 4 covers the architectural issues, the types of transparencies that distributed DBMSs are supposed to provide and discusses the differences between what we consider distributed database systems and multidatabase systems. This separation is critical to the rest of the book; thus, this chapter should be covered. Most of the book addresses distributed database system issues; multidatabase issues are covered only in Chapter 14.

Chapter 5 describes the design of a distributed database. It is the only chapter of the book where we emphasize the use of a distributed DBMS rather than its development. A similar discussion relating to multidatabase systems is included in Chapter 14.

Chapter 6 covers a unique issue that is usually omitted from database textbooks—namely, semantic data control. Distributed semantic data control includes security aspects of distributed databases as well as integrity enforcement to ensure that the database is always consistent with respect to a set of semantic consistency rules.

Chapters 7 through 9 are devoted to a discussion of distributed query processing issues. The discussion starts with an introduction to the fundamental issues and the presentation of a methodology for carrying out this process. The following two chapters, on query decomposition and localization and distributed query optimization, discuss the steps of this methodology in more detail.

Chapters 10 through 12 are devoted to transaction management issues. The treatment is organized similar to query processing with an introductory chapter that defines the fundamental terms and presents the goals that transaction managers aim to achieve, and the subsequent chapters cover the two fundamental aspects of distributed transaction management: distributed concurrency control and the reliable execution of distributed transactions.

Chapter 13 is built on previous material, especially the distributed query processing and distributed transaction management issues, and the problems associated with implementing distributed DBMSs on top of distributed operating systems are discussed. This chapter also serves as a short introduction to operating systems issues for database researchers.

As we mentioned before, Chapter 14 is dedicated to a discussion of the issues related to multidatabase systems. They differ from what we call distributed database management environments in the high degree of autonomy that is associated with each data manager and their bottom-up design as opposed to the top-down approach utilized by distributed DBMSs. The treatment assumes knowledge of the related issued and solutions for distributed database systems.

Finally, Chapter 15 covers the current trends in distributed databases. Specifically, we address distributed data servers, distributed object-oriented databases, and distributed knowledge bases.

## Acknowledgments

Sylvia Osborn read the entire manuscript and provided numerous suggestions. Her contributions to the text are invaluable. Janguk Kim reviewed the manuscript as well. A special thanks goes to both of them. Ahmed Kamal reviewed Chapter 3 and helped with the networking terminology. C. Mohan and Ahmed Elmagarmid provided critical comments on the transaction processing chapters. Ahmed, together with Amit Sheth, reviewed the multidatabase chapter and suggested many improvements. Ravi Krishnamurthy provided help on the query processing chapters, and Guy Lohman improved the precision of many aspects of the R* query optimizer. Eric Simon provided invaluable help on the semantic data control chapter.

The notes that form the basis of this book as well as the book's earlier versions were used in a graduate course on distributed database systems at the University of Alberta. The students who took this course in past years have tremendously helped its presentation. They debugged the text thoroughly and found subtle errors that could have otherwise gone unnoticed. We would like to extend to them our sincere appreciation for helping out as well as for putting up with the troubles of using a continuously changing set of notes as a textbook.

The graduate students in the Distributed Database Systems Group of the University of Alberta all made significant contributions to the text. The Ph.D. students, Ken Barker, Tse-Men Koon, Dave Straube and Randal Peters, all read parts of the manuscript and provided critical comments. The thesis of a former Ph.D. student, Abdel Farrag, provided important material for the transaction processing chapters. The works of M.Sc. students Christina Lau, Yan Li, David Meechan, and Mei-Fen Teo found their way into the book, especially in Chapter 13. Another M.Sc. student, Kok-Lung Wong, reviewed the distributed database design chapter and provided exercises for it. We thank them for all this effort over and above their own research.

The language of the text was edited by Suzanne Sauvé. If readers are not completely happy with some of the language in this edition, they should be grateful that they did not see the text before Suzanne went through it. The remaining errors are probably due to our stubbornness in not accepting some of her suggestions.

Throughout this effort, there was one person who maintained interest in the project perhaps even more than we did: our secretary Amanda Collins at the University of Alberta. She not only ably typed the text once, but then converted the full text to LaTeX. On top of all this, she kept pressing us to finish the writing so that she could start typing. We owe her a great deal for maintaining her enthusiasm and good nature even when things were not moving as smoothly as we all wanted.

M. Tamer Özsu would like to thank Lee White not only for creating an exciting environment within the Department of Computing Science at the University of Alberta during the period of writing this book, but also for the continuing friendship and many opportunities that he has provided over the years. Patrick Valduriez would like to thank Haran Boral and Georges Gardarin for their friendship and support as well as his colleagues of the System Architecture Group at MCC and the SABRE group at INRIA for the exceptional working environment.

We would like to thank our families. This project took valuable time away from them during the last four years. We appreciate their understanding and patience during this long period of time.

Another group who had to wait patiently during these years consists of our editors. We would like to thank Rick Williamson, for suggesting the project to us, and the editors at Prentice-Hall, Valerie Ashton, Marcia Horton and Thomas McElwee. They were all very patient and supportive. We would also like to acknowledge the professional help provided by our production editors, Christina Burghard and Jennifer Wenzel, during the production process.

# 1

# Introduction

Distributed database system (DDBS) technology is the union of what appear to be two diametrically opposed approaches to data processing: *database system* and *computer network* technologies. Database systems have taken us from a paradigm of data processing, in which each application defined and maintained its own data (Figure 1.1), to one in which the data is defined and administered centrally (Figure 1.2). This new orientation results in *data independence*, whereby the application programs are immune to changes in the logical or physical organization of the data, and vice versa.

One of the major motivations behind the use of database systems is the desire to integrate the operational data of an enterprise and to provide centralized, thus controlled access to that data. The technology of computer networks, on the other hand, promotes a mode of work that goes against all centralization efforts. At first glance it might be difficult to understand how these two contrasting approaches can possibly be synthesized to produce a technology that is more powerful and more promising than either one alone. The key to this understanding is the realization that the most important objective of the database technology is *integration*, not *centralization*. It is important to realize that either one of these terms does not necessarily imply the other. It is possible to achieve integration without centralization, and that is exactly what the distributed database technology attempts to achieve.

In this chapter we define the fundamental concepts and set the framework for discussing distributed databases. We start by examining distributed systems in general

1

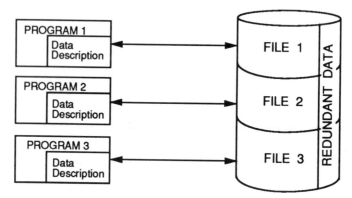

**Figure 1.1**   Traditional File Processing

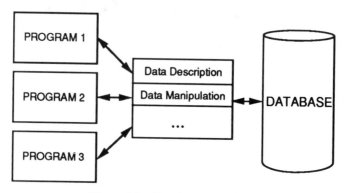

**Figure 1.2**   Database Processing

in order to clarify the role of database technology within distributed data processing, and then move on to topics that are more directly related to DDBS.

## 1.1  DISTRIBUTED DATA PROCESSING

The term *distributed processing* (or *distributed computing*) is probably the most abused term in computer science of the last couple of years. It has been used to refer to such diverse systems as multiprocessor systems, distributed data processing, and computer networks. This abuse has gone on to such an extent that the term *distributed processing* has sometimes been called "a concept in search of a definition and a name." Here are some of the other terms that have been used synonymously with *distributed processing*: distributed function, distributed computers or computing, networks, multiprocessors/multicomputers, satellite processing/satellite computers, backend processing, dedicated/special-purpose computers, time-shared systems, and functionally modular systems.

Obviously, some degree of distributed processing goes on in any computer system, even on single-processor computers. Starting with the second-generation computers, the central processing unit (CPU) and input/output (I/O) functions have been separated and overlapped. This separation and overlap can be considered as one form of distributed processing. However, it should be quite clear that what we would like to refer to as distributed processing, or distributed computing, has nothing to do with this form of distribution of functions in a single-processor computer system.

A term that has caused so much confusion is obviously quite difficult to define precisely. There have been numerous attempts to define what distributed processing is, and almost every researcher has come up with a definition. In this book we define distributed processing in such a way that it leads to a definition of what a distributed database system is. The working definition we use for a *distributed computing system* states that *it is a number of autonomous processing elements (not necessarily homogeneous) that are interconnected by a computer network and that cooperate in performing their assigned tasks.* The "processing element" referred to in this definition is a computing device that can execute a program on its own.

One fundamental question that needs to be asked is: What is being distributed? One of the things that might be distributed is the *processing logic.* In fact, the definition of a distributed computing system given above implicitly assumes that the processing logic or processing elements are distributed. Another possible distribution is according to *function.* Various functions of a computer system could be delegated to various pieces of hardware or software. A third possible mode of distribution is according to *data.* Data used by a number of applications may be distributed to a number of processing sites. Finally, *control* can be distributed. The control of the execution of various tasks might be distributed instead of being performed by one computer system. From the viewpoint of distributed database systems, these modes of distribution are all necessary and important. In the following sections we talk about these in more detail.

Distributed computing systems can be classified with respect to a number of criteria. Some of these criteria are listed by Bochmann as follows: degree of coupling, interconnection structure, interdependence of components, and synchronization between components [Bochmann, 1983]. *Degree of coupling* refers to a measure that determines how closely the processing elements are connected together. This can be measured as the ratio of the amount of data exchanged to the amount of local processing performed in executing a task. If the communication is done over a computer network, there exists *weak coupling* among the processing elements. However, if components are shared, we talk about *strong coupling.* Shared components can be both primary memory or secondary storage devices. As for the *interconnection structure,* one can talk about those cases that have a point-to-point interconnection between processing elements, as opposed to those which use a common interconnection channel. We discuss various interconnection structures in Chapter 3. The processing elements might depend on each other quite strongly in the execution of a task, or this interdependence might be as minimal as passing messages at the beginning of execution and reporting results at the end. *Synchronization* between processing elements might be maintained by synchronous or by asynchronous means. Note that some of these criteria are not entirely independent. For example, if the synchronization between processing elements is synchronous, one would expect the processing elements to be strongly interdependent, and possibly to work in a strongly coupled fashion.

Another reasonable question to ask at this point is: Why do we distribute at all? The classical answers to this question indicate that distributed processing better corresponds to the organizational structure of today's widely distributed enterprises, and that such a system is more reliable and more responsive. Data can be entered and stored where it is generated, without any need for physical (manual) movement. Furthermore, building a distributed system might make economic sense since the costs of memory and processing elements are decreasing continuously. It can provide incremental growth, reduce the impact of change on the data processing functions, and make it possible to share data that is stored at different sites and was previously unsharable. All of these reasons also apply to distributed database systems and are discussed further in Section 1.3.

From a more global perspective, however, it can be stated that the fundamental reason behind distributed processing is to be better able to solve the big and complicated problems that we face today, by using a variation of the well-known divide-and-conquer rule. If the necessary software support for distributed processing can be developed, it might be possible to solve these complicated problems simply by dividing them into smaller pieces and assigning them to different software groups, which work on different computers and produce a system that runs on multiple processing elements but can work efficiently toward the execution of a common task.

This approach has two fundamental advantages from an economics standpoint. First, we are fast approaching the limits of computation speed for a single processing element. The only available route to more computing power, therefore, is to employ multiple processing elements optimally. This requires research in distributed processing as defined earlier, as well as in parallel processing, which is outside the scope of this book. The second economic reason is that by attacking these problems in smaller groups working more or less autonomously, it might be possible to discipline the cost of software development. Indeed, it is well known that the cost of software has been increasing in opposition to the cost trends of hardware.

Distributed database systems should also be viewed within this framework and treated as tools that could make distributed processing easier and more efficient. It is reasonable to draw an analogy between what distributed databases might offer to the data processing world and what the database technology has already provided. There is no doubt that the development of general-purpose, adaptable, efficient distributed database systems will aid greatly in the task of developing distributed software.

## 1.2 WHAT IS A DISTRIBUTED DATABASE SYSTEM?

We can define a *distributed database* as *a collection of multiple, logically interrelated databases distributed over a computer network*. A *distributed database management sys-*

*tem* (distributed DBMS) is then defined as *the software system that permits the management of the DDBS and makes the distribution transparent to the users.* The two important terms in these definitions are *"logically interrelated"* and *"distributed over a computer network."* They help eliminate certain cases that have sometimes been accepted to represent a DDBS.

First, a DDBS is not a "collection of files" that can be individually stored at each node of a computer network. To form a DDBS, files should not only be logically related, but there should be structure among the files, and access should be via a common interface. It has sometimes been assumed that the physical distribution of data is not the most significant issue. The proponents of this view would therefore feel comfortable in labeling as a distributed database two (related) databases that reside in the same computer system. However, the physical distribution of data is very important. It creates problems that are not encountered when the databases reside in the same computer. These difficulties are discussed in Section 1.4. Note that physical distribution does not necessarily imply that the computer systems be geographically far apart; they could actually be in the same room. It simply implies that the communication between them is done over a network instead of through shared memory, with the network as the only shared resource.

This brings us to another point. The definition above also rules out multiprocessor systems as DDBSs. A multiprocessor system is generally considered to be a system where two or more processors share some form of memory, either primary memory, in which case the multiprocessor is called *tightly coupled* (Figure 1.3), or secondary memory, when it is called *loosely coupled* (Figure 1.4)[1]. Sharing memory enables the processors to communicate without exchanging messages. With the improvements in microprocessor and VLSI technologies, other forms of multiprocessors have emerged with a number of microprocessors connected by a switch (Figure 1.5).

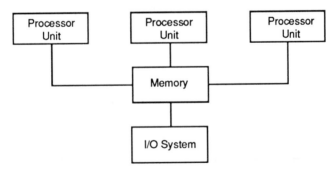

**Figure 1.3**    Tightly-Coupled Multiprocessor

Another distinction that is commonly made in this context is between *shared-everything* and *shared-nothing* architectures. The former architectural model permits

---

[1]Note at this point that our definition of coupling modes is different from that of Bochmann discussed in the preceding section. We refer only to coupling in multiprocessors, not to distributed processing in general.

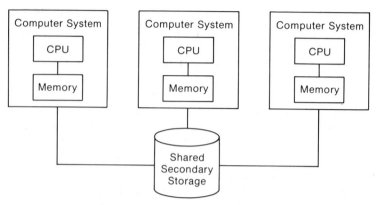

**Figure 1.4**   Loosely-Coupled Multiprocessor

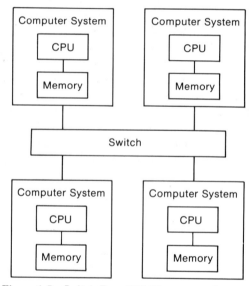

**Figure 1.5**   Switch-Based Multiprocessor System

each processor to access everything (primary and secondary memories, and peripherals) in the system and covers the three models that we described above. The shared-nothing architecture is one where each processor has its own primary and secondary memories as well as peripherals, and communicates with other processors over a very high speed bus. In this sense the shared-nothing multiprocessors are quite similar to the distributed environment that we consider in this book. However, there are differences between the interactions in multiprocessor architectures and the rather loose interaction that is common in distributed computing environments. The fundamental difference is the mode of operation. A multiprocessor system design is rather symmetrical consisting of a number of identical processor and memory components, controlled by one or more copies of the same operating system, which is responsible for a strict control of the task assignment to each processor. This is not true in distributed computing systems, where heterogeneity of the operating system as well as the hardware is quite common.

In addition, a DDBS is not a system where, despite the existence of a network, the database resides at only one node of the network (Figure 1.6). In this case, the problems of database management are no different from the problems encountered in a centralized database environment. The database is centrally managed by one computer system (site 2 in Figure 1.6) and all the requests are routed to that site. The only additional consideration has to do with transmission delays. It is obvious that the existence of a computer network or a collection of "files" is not sufficient to form a distributed database system.

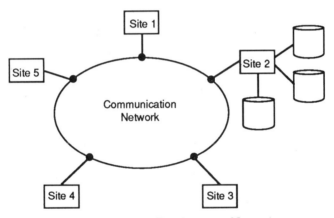

**Figure 1.6**   Central Database on a Network

At this point it might be helpful to look at an example of distributed database application that we can also use to clarify our subsequent discussions. Consider a multinational manufacturing company with its world headquarters in New York, manufacturing plants in Chicago and in Montreal, regional warehouses in Phoenix and Edmonton, European headquarters in Paris, and a research and development facility in San Fransisco. Such an organization will want to keep records on its employees, engineering operations, inventory levels, research projects, marketing operations, and much more. Under such circumstances, it is much more logical to manage the data and information flow as follows:

1. Let each location keep local records about the employees working at that location.

2. Let the research and development facility keep track of the information on projects that are going on at the facility.

3.  Let the manufacturing plants keep data related to their engineering opera-
    tions and give them means to access the information at the research facility.

4.  Let the manufacturing plants keep track of their in-plant inventories. If
    necessary, they can access the inventory data at the warehouse locations.

5.  Let the warehouses maintain their own inventory management systems with
    the necessary record keeping. The manufacturing plants should be allowed
    to access information regarding inventory levels.

6.  The headquarters (both world and European) keep the marketing and sales
    data related to their regions. They can share this data and can access the
    inventory data at the plants and at the warehouses.

Assuming that all the record keeping is done by computers, such an operation is
an ideal candidate for a distributed database application (Figure 1.7). We comment
on this example as we go along.

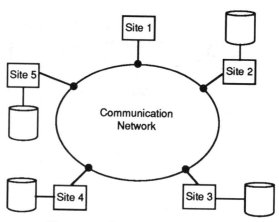

**Figure 1.7**   DDBS Environment

## 1.3 ADVANTAGES AND DISADVANTAGES OF DDBSs

The distribution of data and applications has promising potential advantages. Note
that these are potential advantages which the individual DDBSs aim to achieve. As
such, they may also be considered as the objectives of DDBSs.

### 1.3.1 Advantages

*Local Autonomy.*    Since data is distributed, a group of users that commonly
share such data can have it placed at the site where they work, and thus have local
control. This permits setting and enforcing local policies regarding the use of the data.

There are studies [D'Oliviera, 1977] indicating that the ability to partition the authority and responsibility of information management is the major reason many business organizations consider distributed information systems. This is probably the most important sociological development that we have witnessed in recent years with respect to the use of computers.

Of course, the local autonomy issue is more important in those organizations that are inherently decentralized. For such organizations, implementing the information system in a decentralized manner might also be more suitable. On the other hand, for those organizations with quite a centralized structure and management style, decentralization might not be an overwhelming social or managerial issue.

In the example discussed in the preceding section, the validity of local autonomy is obvious. It would be quite absurd to have an environment where all the record keeping is done locally, as it would be if information were shared among different sites in a manual fashion (either by exchanging hard copies of reports, or by exchanging magnetic tapes, disks, floppies, etc.).

*Improved Performance.*    Again, because the regularly used data is proximate to the users, and given the parallelism inherent in distributed systems, it may be possible to improve the performance of database accesses. On the one hand, since each site handles only a portion of the database, contention for CPU and I/O services is not as severe as for centralized databases. On the other hand, data retrieved by a transaction may be stored at a number of sites, making it possible to execute the transaction in parallel.

Let us assume that in our example the record keeping is done centrally at the world headquarters, with remote access provided to the other sites. This would require the transmission to New York of each request generated in Phoenix inquiring about the inventory level of an item. It would probably be impossible to withstand the low performance of such an operation.

*Improved Reliability/Availability.*    If data is replicated so that it exists at more than one site, a crash of one of the sites, or the failure of a communication link making some of these sites inaccessible, does not necessarily make the data impossible to reach. Furthermore, system crashes or link failures do not cause total system inoperability. Even though some of the data may be inaccessible, the DDBS can still provide limited service.

Obviously, if the inventory information at both warehouses is replicated at both sites, the failure at one of the sites would not make the information inaccessible to the rest of the organization. If proper facilities are set up, it might even be possible to give users at the failed site access to the remote information.

*Economics.*    It is possible to view this from two perspectives. The first is in terms of communication costs. If databases are geographically dispersed and the applications running against them exhibit strong interaction of dispersed data, it may be much more economical to partition the application and do the processing locally at each site. Here the trade-off is between telecommunication costs and data communication costs. The second viewpoint is that it normally costs much less to put together a system of smaller computers with the equivalent power of a single big machine. In the 1960s and early 1970s, it was commonly believed that it would be possible to purchase a fourfold powerful computer if one spent twice as much. This was known as Grosh's law. With the advent of minicomputers, and especially microcomputers, this law is considered invalid.

The case about lower communication costs can easily be demonstrated in the example we have been considering. It is no doubt much cheaper in the long run to maintain a computer system at a site and keep data locally stored instead of having to incur heavy telecommunication costs for each request. The level of use when this becomes true can obviously change depending on the traffic patterns among sites, but it is quite reasonable to expect this to occur.

*Expandability.*    In a distributed environment, it is much easier to accommodate increasing database sizes. Major system overhauls are seldom necessary; expansion can usually be handled by adding processing and storage power to the network. Obviously, it may not be possible to obtain a linear increase in "power," since this also depends on the overhead of distribution. However, significant improvements are still possible.

*Shareability.*    Organizations that have geographically distributed operations normally store data in a distributed fashion as well. However, if the information system is not distributed, it is usually impossible to share these data and resources. A distributed database system therefore makes this sharing feasible.

## 1.3.2 Disadvantages

However, these advantages are offset by several problems arising from the distribution of the database.

*Lack of Experience.*    General-purpose distributed database systems are not yet commonly used. What we have are either prototype systems or systems that are tailored to one application (e.g., airline reservations). This has serious consequences because the solutions that have been proposed for various problems have not been tested in actual operating environments.

*Complexity.*    DDBS problems are inherently more complex than centralized database management ones, as they include not only the problems found in a centralized environment, but also a new set of unresolved problems. We discuss these new issues shortly.

*Cost.*    Distributed systems require additional hardware (communication mechanisms, etc.), thus have increased hardware costs. However, the trend toward decreasing hardware costs does not make this a significant factor. A more important fraction of the cost lies in the fact that additional and more complex software and communication may be necessary to solve some of the technical problems. The development of software engineering techniques (distributed debuggers and the like) should help in this respect.

Perhaps the most important cost component is due to the replication of effort (manpower). When computer facilities are set up at different sites, it becomes necessary to employ people to maintain these facilities. This usually results in an increase in the personnel in the data processing operations. Therefore, the trade-off between increased profitability due to more efficient and timely use of information and the increased personnel costs has to be analyzed carefully.

***Distribution of Control.***    This point was stated previously as an advantage of DDBSs. Unfortunately, distribution creates problems of synchronization and coordination (the reasons for this added complexity are studied in the next section). Distributed control can therefore easily become a liability if care is not taken to adopt adequate policies to deal with these issues.

***Security.***    One of the major benefits of centralized databases has been the control it provides over the access to data. Security can easily be controlled in one central location, with the DBMS enforcing the rules. However, in a distributed database system, a network is involved which is a medium that has its own security requirements. It is well known that there are serious problems in maintaining adequate security over computer networks. Thus the security problems in distributed database systems are by nature more complicated than in centralized ones.

***Difficulty of Change.***    Most businesses have already invested heavily in their database systems, which are not distributed. Currently, no tools or methodologies exist to help these users convert their centralized databases into a DDBS. Research in heterogeneous databases and database integration is expected to overcome these difficulties.

## 1.4 COMPLICATING FACTORS

The problems encountered in database systems take on additional complexity in a distributed environment, even though the basic underlying principles are the same. Furthermore, this additional complexity gives rise to new problems influenced mainly by three factors.

First, data may be replicated in a distributed environment. A distributed database can be designed so that the entire database, or portions of it, reside at different sites of a computer network. It is not essential that every site on the network contain the database; it is only essential that there be more than one site where the database resides. The possible duplication of data items is mainly due to reliability and efficiency considerations. Consequently, the distributed database system is responsible for (1) choosing one of the stored copies of the requested data for access in case of retrievals, and (2) making sure that the effect of an update is reflected on each and every copy of that data item.

Second, if some sites fail (e.g., by either hardware or software malfunction), or if some communication links fail (making some of the sites unreachable) while an update is being executed, the system must make sure that the effects will be reflected on the data residing at the failing or unreachable sites as soon as the system can recover from the failure.

The third point is that since each site cannot have instantaneous information on the actions currently being carried out at the other sites, the synchronization of transactions on multiple sites is considerably harder than for a centralized system.

## 1.5 PROBLEM AREAS

There are several technical problems that need to be solved before the potential benefits of DDBSs can start to be realized. There is active research on most of them. Next we briefly review these problems, which are discussed in detail in the remaining chapters.

### 1.5.1 Distributed Database Design

The question that is being addressed is how the database and the applications that run against it should be placed across the sites. There are two basic alternatives to placing data: *partitioned* (or *nonreplicated*) and *replicated*. In the partitioned scheme the database is divided into a number of disjoint partitions each of which is placed at a different site. Replicated designs can be either *fully replicated* (also called *fully duplicated*) where the entire database is stored at each site, or *partially replicated* (or *partially duplicated*) where each partition of the database is stored at more than one site, but not at all the sites. The two fundamental design issues are *fragmentation*, the separation of the database into partitions called *fragments*, and *distribution*, the optimum distribution of fragments.

The research in this area mostly involves mathematical programming in order to minimize the combined cost of storing the database, processing transactions against it, and communication. The general problem is NP-hard. Therefore, the proposed solutions are based on heuristics.

### 1.5.2 Distributed Query Processing

Query processing deals with designing algorithms that analyze queries and convert them into a series of data manipulation operations. The problem is how to decide on a strategy for executing each query over the network in the most cost-effective way, however cost is defined. The factors to be considered are the distribution of data, communication costs, and lack of sufficient locally available information. The objective is to optimize where the inherent parallelism is used to improve the performance of executing the transaction subject to the above-mentioned constraints. The problem is NP-hard in nature, and the approaches are usually heuristic.

### 1.5.3  Distributed Directory Management

A directory contains information (such as descriptions and locations) about data items in the database. Problems related to directory management are similar in nature to the database placement problem discussed in the preceding section. A directory may be global to the entire DDBS or local to each site; it can be centralized at one site or distributed over several sites; there can be a single copy or multiple copies.

### 1.5.4  Distributed Concurrency Control

Concurrency control involves the synchronization of accesses to the distributed database, such that the integrity of the database is maintained. It is, without any doubt, one of the most extensively studied problems in the DDBS field. The concurrency control problem in a distributed context is somewhat different than in a centralized framework. One not only has to worry about the integrity of a single database, but also about the consistency of multiple copies of the database. The condition that requires all the values of multiple copies of every data item to converge to the same value is called *mutual consistency*.

The alternative solutions are too numerous to discuss here, so we examine them in detail in Chapter 11. Let us only mention that the two general classes are *pessimistic*, synchronizing the execution of user requests before the execution starts, and *optimistic*, executing the requests and then checking if the execution compromised the consistency of the database. Two fundamental primitives that can be used with both approaches are *locking*, which is based on the mutual exclusion of accesses to data items, and *timestamping*, where the transactions are executed in some order. There are variations of these schemes as well as hybrid algorithms that attempt to combine the two basic mechanisms.

### 1.5.5  Distributed Deadlock Management

The deadlock problem in DDBSs is similar in nature to that encountered in operating systems. The competition among users for access to a set of resources (data, in this case) can result in a deadlock if the synchronization mechanism is based on locking. The well-known alternatives of prevention, avoidance, and detection/recovery also apply to DDBSs.

### 1.5.6  Reliability of Distributed DBMS

We mentioned earlier that one of the potential advantages of distributed systems is improved reliability and availability. This, however, is not a feature that comes automatically. It is important that mechanisms be provided to ensure the consistency of the database as well as to detect failures and recover from them. The implication for DDBSs is that when a failure occurs and various sites become either inoperable or inaccessible, the databases at the operational sites remain consistent and up-to-date.

Furthermore, when the computer system or network recovers from the failure, the DDBSs should be able to recover and bring the databases at the failed sites up-to-date. This may be especially difficult in the case of network partitioning, where the sites are divided into two or more groups with no communication among them.

### 1.5.7 Operating System Support

The current implementation of distributed database systems on top of (or under) the conventional operating systems suffers from the performance bottleneck. The support provided by operating systems for database operations does not correspond properly to the requirements of the database management software. The major operating system-related problems in single-processor systems are memory management, file system and access methods, crash recovery, and process management. In distributed environments there is the additional problem of having to deal with multiple layers of network software. The work in this area is on finding solutions to the dichotomy of providing adequate and simple support for distributed database operations, as well as providing general operating system support for other applications.

### 1.5.8 Heterogeneous Databases

When there is no homogeneity among the databases at various sites either in terms of the way data is logically structured (data model) or in terms of the mechanisms provided for accessing it (data language), it becomes necessary to provide a translation mechanism between database systems. This translation mechanism usually involves a canonical form to facilitate data translation, as well as program templates for translating data manipulation instructions.

It turns out that heterogeneity is typically introduced if one is constructing a distributed DBMS from a number of autonomous, centralized DBMSs. In this setting the problems are more general than heterogeneity. In fact, such systems, which we call *multidatabase systems*, should be considered complementary to the distributed DBMSs as defined in this chapter. Thus, all the problems that we have discussed in the preceding sections have complementary specifications for multidatabase systems. We briefly review the related issues in Chapter 14.

### 1.5.9 Relationship among Problems

We should mention at this point that these problems are not isolated from one another. The reasons for studying them in isolation are that (1) problems are difficult enough to study by themselves, and would probably be impossible to present altogether, and that (2) it might be possible to characterize the effect of one problem on another one, through the use of parameters and constraints. In fact, each problem is affected by the solutions found for the others, and in turn affects the set of feasible solutions for them. In this section we discuss how they are related.

The relationship among the components is shown in Figure 1.8. The design of distributed databases affects many areas. It affects directory management, because

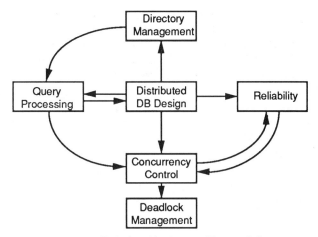

**Figure 1.8**  Relationship Among Research Issues

the definition of fragments and their placement determine the contents of the directory (or directories) as well as the strategies that may be employed to manage them. The same information (i.e., fragment structure and placement) is used by the query processor to determine the query evaluation strategy. On the other hand, the access and usage patterns that are determined by the query processor are used as inputs to the data distribution and fragmentation algorithms. Similarly, directory placement and contents influence the processing of queries.

The replication of fragments when they are distributed affects the concurrency control strategies that might be employed. As we will study in Chapter 11, some concurrency control algorithms cannot be easily used with replicated databases. Similarly, usage and access patterns to the database will influence the concurrency control algorithms. If the environment is update intensive, the necessary precautions are quite different from those in a query-only environment.

There is a strong relationship among the concurrency control problem, the deadlock management problem, and reliability issues. This is to be expected since together they are usually called the *transaction management* problem. The concurrency control algorithm that is employed will determine whether or not a separate deadlock management facility is required. If a locking-based algorithm is used, deadlocks will occur, whereas they will not if timestamping is the chosen alternative.

Reliability mechanisms are implemented on top of a concurrency control algorithm. Therefore, the relationship among them is self-explanatory. It should also be mentioned that the reliability mechanisms being considered have an effect on the choice of the concurrency control algorithm. Techniques to provide reliability also make use of data placement information since the existence of duplicate copies of the data serve as a safeguard to maintain reliable operation.

Two of the problems we discussed in the preceding sections—operating system issues and heterogeneous databases—are not illustrated in Figure 1.8. This is obviously not because they have no bearing on other issues; in fact, exactly the opposite is true. The type of operating system used and the features supported by that operating system greatly influence what solution strategies can be applied in any of the other problem areas. Similarly, the nature of all these problems change considerably when the environment is heterogeneous. The same issues have to be dealt with differently when the machine architecture, the operating systems, and the local database management software vary from site to site.

## 1.6 BIBLIOGRAPHIC NOTES

There are numerous papers as well as chapters in general database books that describe distributed database systems. Chapter 12 of [Ullman, 1982] and Chapter 7 of [Date, 1983] are good introductions, as are the papers [Adiba et al., 1978] and [Rothnie and Goodman, 1977]. [Gray, 1983] is an excellent discussion of general distributed processing issues.

Database design is discussed in an introductory manner in [Levin and Morgan, 1975] and more comprehensively in [Ceri et al., 1987]. A survey of the file distribution algorithms is given in [Dowdy and Foster, 1982]. Directory management has not been considered in detail in the research community, but general techniques can be found in [Chu and Nahouraii, 1975] and [Chu, 1976]. A survey of query processing techniques can be found in [Sacco and Yao, 1982]. Concurrency control algorithms are reviewed in [Bernstein and Goodman, 1981] and [Bernstein et al., 1987], and surveyed in [Hsiao and Özsu, 1981]. Deadlock management has also been the subject of extensive research; an introductory paper is [Isloor and Marsland, 1980], and a widely quoted paper is [Obermarck, 1982]. For deadlock detection, good surveys are [Knapp, 1987] and [Elmagarmid, 1986]. Reliability is one of the issues discussed in [Gray, 1979], which is one of the landmark papers in the field. Other important papers on this topic are [Verhofstadt, 1978] and [Haerder and Reuter, 1983]. [Gray, 1979] is also the first paper discussing the issues of operating system support for distributed databases; the same topic is addressed in [Stonebraker, 1981]. Unfortunately, both papers emphasize centralized database systems. A discussion of the issues in a distributed environment can be found in [Özsu, 1988]. The recent work on heterogeneous databases is summarized in [Barker and Özsu, 1988], [Cardenas, 1987], and [Han and Fisher, 1983].

# 2

# Overview of Relational DBMS

In this chapter we review fundamental relational database concepts. The aim of this chapter is to define the terminology and framework used in subsequent chapters, not to provide substantial background on database systems. Nevertheless, we try to be complete. The reasons for choosing the relational model of data as the underlying formalism are numerous: the mathematical foundation of the relational model makes it a good candidate for theoretical treatment; most of the problems discussed in future chapters are easier to formulate; a large number of relational systems are now on the market (for a survey, see [Valduriez and Gardarin, 1989]); and finally, most distributed database systems are also relational.

The relational model can be characterized by at least three powerful features [Codd, 1982]:

1. Its data structures are simple. They are relations that are two-dimensional tables whose elements are data items. This allows a high degree of independence from the physical data representation (e.g., files and indices).

2. The relational model provides a solid foundation to data consistency. Database design is aided by the normalization process that eliminates data anomalies. Also, consistent states of a database can be uniformly defined and maintained through integrity rules.

3. The relational model allows the set-oriented manipulation of relations. This feature has led to the development of powerful nonprocedural languages based either on set theory (relational algebra) or on logic (relational calculus).

The outline of this chapter is as follows. In Section 2.1 we define fundamental relational database concepts such as a relation, a tuple, a key, and so on. In Section 2.2 the concept of normalization is introduced and different normal forms are discussed. This is followed by a short discussion of integrity rules in Section 2.3. Section 2.4 contains the details of relational data languages (relational algebra and relational calculus), and finally, Section 2.5 presents a short discussion of relational DBMSs. The latter section also serves as a preparation to the architecture discussions of Chapter 4.

## 2.1 RELATIONAL DATABASE CONCEPTS

A *database* is a structured collection of data related to some real-life phenomena that we are trying to model. A *relational database* is one where the database structure is in the form of tables. Formally, a relation $R$ defined over $n$ sets $D_1, D_2, \ldots, D_n$ (not necessarily distinct) is a set of *n-tuples* (or simply *tuples*) $< d_1, d_2, \ldots, d_n >$ such that $d_1 \in D_1, d_2 \in D_2, \ldots, d_n \in D_n$.

### Example 2.1

As an example we will use a database that models an engineering company. The entities to be modeled are the *engineers* (ENG) and *projects* (J). For each engineer, we would like to keep track of the employee number (ENO), name (ENAME), title in the company (TITLE), salary (SAL), identification number of the project(s) the engineer is working on (JNO), responsibility within the project (RESP), and duration of the assignment (DUR) in months. Similarly, for each project we would like to store the project number (JNO), the project name (JNAME), and the project budget (BUDGET).

The *relation schemes* for this database can be defined as follows:

ENG(ENO, ENAME, TITLE, SAL, JNO, RESP, DUR)
J(JNO, JNAME, BUDGET)

In relation scheme ENG, there are seven *attributes*: ENO, ENAME, TITLE, SAL, JNO, RESP, DUR. The values of ENO come from the *domain* of all valid employee numbers, say $D_1$, the values of ENAME come from the domain of all valid names, say $D_2$, and so on. Note that each attribute of each relation does not have to come from a distinct domain. Various attributes within a relation or from a number of relations may be defined over the same domain.

The *key* of a relation scheme is the minimum nonempty subset of its attributes such that the values of the attributes comprising the key uniquely identify each tuple of the relation. The attributes that make up key are called *prime* attributes. The superset of a key is usually called a *superkey*. Thus in our example the key of J is JNO, and that of ENG is the set (ENO, JNO). Each relation has at least one key. Sometimes, there may be more than one possibility for the key. In such cases, each alternative is considered a *candidate key*, and one of the candidate keys is chosen as the *primary key*. The number of attributes of a relation defines its *degree*, whereas the number of tuples of the relation defines its *cardinality*.

In tabular form, the example database consists of two tables, as shown in Figure 2.1. The columns of the tables correspond to the attributes of the relations; if there were any information entered as the rows, they would correspond to the tuples. The empty table, showing the structure of the table, corresponds to the relation scheme; when the table is filled with rows, it corresponds to a *relation instance*. Since the information within a table varies over time, many instances can be generated from one relation scheme. Note that from now on, the term *relation* refers to a relation instance. In Figure 2.2 we depict instances of the relations that are defined in Figure 2.1.

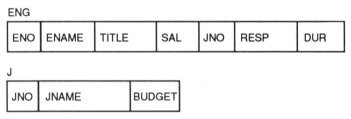

**Figure 2.1**   Sample Database Scheme

An attribute value may be undefined. This lack of definition may have various interpretations, the most common being unknown or not applicable. This special value of the attribute is generally referred to as the *null value*. The representation of a null value must be different from any other domain value, and special care should be given to differentiate it from zero. For example, value "0" for attribute DUR is *known information* (e.g., in the case of a newly hired employee), while value "null" for DUR means unknown in tuple E4 of Figure 2.2. Supporting null values is an important feature necessary to deal with *maybe* queries [Codd, 1979].

## 2.2 NORMALIZATION

"Normalization is a step-by-step reversible process of replacing a given collection of relations by successive collections in which relations have a progressively simpler and more regular structure" [Tsichritzis and Lochovsky, 1977]. The aim of normalization is to eliminate various anomalies (or undesirable aspects) of a relation in order to obtain "better" relations. The following four problems might exist in a relation scheme:

1. *Repetition anomaly.* Certain information may be repeated unnecessarily. Consider, for example, the ENG relation in Figure 2.2. The name, title, and salary of an engineer are repeated for each project on which this person

ENG

| ENO | ENAME | TITLE | SAL | JNO | RESP | DUR |
|-----|-------|-------|-----|-----|------|-----|
| E1 | J. Doe | Elect. Eng. | 40000 | J1 | Manager | 12 |
| E2 | M. Smith | Analyst | 34000 | J1 | Analyst | 24 |
| E2 | M. Smith | Analyst | 34000 | J2 | Analyst | 6 |
| E3 | A. Lee | Mech. Eng. | 27000 | J3 | Consultant | 10 |
| E3 | A. Lee | Mech. Eng. | 27000 | J4 | Engineer | 48 |
| E4 | J. Miller | Programmer | 24000 | J2 | Programmer | 18 |
| E5 | B. Casey | Syst. Anal. | 34000 | J2 | Manager | 24 |
| E6 | L. Chu | Elect. Eng. | 40000 | J4 | Manager | 48 |
| E7 | R. Davis | Mech. Eng. | 27000 | J3 | Engineer | 36 |
| E8 | J. Jones | Syst. Anal. | 34000 | J3 | Manager | 40 |

J

| JNO | JNAME | BUDGET |
|-----|-------|--------|
| J1 | Instrumentation | 150000 |
| J2 | Database Develop. | 135000 |
| J3 | CAD/CAM | 250000 |
| J4 | Maintenance | 310000 |

**Figure 2.2**   Sample Database Instance

serves. This is obviously a waste of storage and is contrary to the spirit of databases.

2. *Update anomaly.* As a consequence of the repetition of data, performing updates may be troublesome. For example, if the salary of an engineer changes, multiple tuples have to be updated to reflect this change.

3. *Insertion anomaly.* It may not be possible to add new information to the database. For example, when a new engineer joins the company, we cannot add personal information (name, title, salary) to the ENG relation unless an appointment to a project is made. This is because the key of ENG includes the attribute JNO, and null values cannot be part of the key.

4. *Deletion anomaly.* This is the converse of the insertion anomaly. If an engineer works on only one project, and that project is terminated, it is not possible to delete the project information from the ENG relation. To do so

would result in deleting the only tuple about the engineer, thereby resulting in the loss of personal information we might want to retain.

Normalization transforms arbitrary relation schemes into ones without these problems. The most popular approach to normalizing a relational database scheme is the *decomposition* approach, where one starts with a single relation, called the *universal relation*, which contains all attributes (and probably anomalies) and iteratively reduces it. At each iteration, a relation is split into two or more relations of a higher *normal form*. A relation is said to be in a normal form if it satisfies the conditions associated with that normal form. Codd initially defined the *first*, *second*, and *third* normal forms (1NF, 2NF, and 3NF, respectively). Boyce and Codd [Codd, 1974] later defined a modified version of the third normal form, commonly known as the *Boyce-Codd normal form (BCNF)*. This was followed by the definition of the *fourth* (4NF) [Fagin, 1977] and *fifth* normal forms (5NF) [Fagin, 1979].

There is a hierarchical relationship among these normal forms. Every normalized relation is in 1NF; some of the relations in 1NF are also in 2NF, some of which are in 3NF, and so on. The higher normal forms have better properties than others with respect to the four anomalies discussed above.

One of the requirements of a normalization process is that the decomposition be lossless. This means that the replacement of a relation by several others should not result in loss of information. If it is possible to join the decomposed relations to obtain the original relation, the process is said to be a *lossless decomposition*.

The join operation is defined formally in Section 2.4.1. Intuitively, it is an operation that takes two relations and concatenates each tuple of the second relation with those tuples of the first relation that satisfy a specified condition. The condition is defined over the attributes of the two relations. For example, it might be specified that the value of an attribute of the first relation should be equal to the value of an attribute of the second relation.

Another requirement of the normalization process is *dependency preservation*. A decomposition is said to be dependency preserving if the union of the dependencies in the decomposed relations is equivalent to the closure (with respect to a set of inference rules) of the dependencies of the original relation.

### 2.2.1 Dependency Structures

The normal forms are based on certain dependency structures. BCNF and lower normal forms are based on *functional dependencies* (FDs), 4NF is based on *multivalued dependencies*, and 5NF is based on *projection-join dependencies*. In this section we define what we mean by dependence.

Let $R$ be a relation defined over the set of attributes $A = \{A_1, A_2, \ldots, A_n\}$ and let $X \subset A$, $Y \subset A$. If for each value of $X$ in $R$, there is only one associated $Y$ value, we say that "*X functionally determines Y*" or that "*Y is functionally dependent* on $X$." Notationally, this is shown as $X \rightarrow Y$. The key of a relation functionally determines the nonkey attributes of the same relation.

**Example 2.2**

For example, in the J relation of Figure 2.2, the valid FD is

$$\text{JNO} \rightarrow (\text{JNAME, BUDGET})$$

In the ENG relation we have

$$(\text{ENO, JNO}) \rightarrow (\text{ENAME,TITLE,SAL,RESP,DUR})$$

This last FD is not the only FD in ENG, however. If each engineer is given unique employee numbers, we can write

$$\text{ENO} \rightarrow (\text{ENAME, TITLE, SAL})$$
$$(\text{ENO, JNO}) \rightarrow (\text{RESP, DUR})$$

It is also reasonable to state that the salary for a given position is fixed, which gives rise to the FD

$$\text{TITLE} \rightarrow \text{SAL}$$

Notice that some of the attributes on the right-hand side of the second FD are also dependent on a subset of the set of attributes at the left-hand side of the same FD. Such attributes (ENAME,TITLE,SAL) are said to be *partially functionally dependent* on (ENO,JNO), whereas the others (RESP, DUR) are said to be *fully functionally dependent*.

Let $R$ be a relation defined over the set of attributes $A = \{A_1, A_2, \ldots, A_n\}$, and let $X \subset A$, $Y \subset A$, $Z \subset A$. If for each value of $Z$ in $R$, there is only one value for the $(X, Y)$-pair, and the value of $Z$ depends only on the value of $X$, we say that "*X multidetermines Z*" or that "*Z is multidependent on X*." This type of dependency is called *multivalued dependency* (MVD) and is denoted as $X \rightarrow\rightarrow Z$.

Intuitively, a MVD represents a situation where the value of one attribute (or a set of attributes) determines a *set of values* of another attribute (or set of attributes). Note that every FD is also an MVD, but the reverse is not necessarily true.

**Example 2.3**

Going back to our example, let us assume that we want to maintain information on the set of engineers and on the set of projects that the company is involved in, as well as the branch office where this project may be carried out. This can be done by defining the relation

$$\text{SKILL(ENO, JNO, PLACE)}$$

Let us assume (probably unrealistically) that (1) each engineer can work on each project, that (2) each engineer is willing to work at any of the branch offices, and that (3) each project can be carried out at any of the branch offices. A sample relation instance satisfying these conditions is illustrated in Figure 2.3.

Notice that there are no FDs in the SKILL relation; the relation consists solely of key attributes. The only dependencies are the two MVDs

$$\text{ENO} \rightarrow\rightarrow \text{JNO}$$
$$\text{ENO} \rightarrow\rightarrow \text{PLACE}$$

SKILL

| ENO | JNO | PLACE |
|-----|-----|-------|
| E1 | J1 | Toronto |
| E1 | J1 | New York |
| E1 | J1 | London |
| E1 | J1 | Toronto |
| E1 | J2 | New York |
| E1 | J2 | London |
| E2 | J1 | Toronto |
| E2 | J1 | New York |
| E2 | J1 | London |
| E2 | J2 | Toronto |
| E2 | J2 | New York |
| E2 | J2 | London |

**Figure 2.3**   Example of MVD

Let $R$ be a relation defined over the set of attributes $A = \{A_1, A_2, \ldots, A_n\}$, and $X \subset A$, $Y \subset A$, $Z \subset A$. Then, if $R$ is equal to the join of $X$, $Y$, and $Z$, $(X, Y, Z)$ constitutes a *projection-join dependency* for $R$. Again, we have not yet defined the join operation formally, but the intuitive discussion that we gave before is sufficient.

There is a set of inference rules based on a set of axioms—known as *Armstrong's axioms* [Armstrong, 1974—that permit the algebraic manipulation of dependencies. They enable the discovery of the minimal cover of a set of FDs that is the minimal set of FDs from which all others can be generated. Given the minimal cover of FDs and a set of attributes, an algorithm can be developed to generate a relational scheme in higher normal forms.

### 2.2.2  Normal Forms

The first normal form states simply that the attributes of the relation contain atomic values only. In other words, the tables should be flat with no repeating groups. The relations ENG and J in Figure 2.2 satisfy this condition, so they both are in 1NF.

Relations in 1NF still suffer from the anomalies discussed earlier. To eliminate some of these anomalies, they should be decomposed into relations in higher normal forms. We are not particularly interested in the second normal form. In fact, it is only of historical importance, since there are algorithms that take a 1NF relation and directly normalize it to 3NF (or higher).

A relation $R$ is in 3NF if for each FD $X \to Y$ where $Y$ is not in $X$, either $X$ is a superkey of $R$ or $Y$ is a prime attribute. There are algorithms that provide a lossless and dependency-preserving decomposition of a 1NF relation into a 3NF relation.

**Example 2.4**

The J relation in the example we are considering is in 3NF, but ENG is not because of FD:

$$TITLE \rightarrow SAL$$

This violates 3NF, because TITLE is not a superkey and SAL is not prime.

The problem with ENG is the following. If we want to insert the fact that a given position (title) earns a specific salary, we cannot do so unless there is at least one employee holding that title. (Similar arguments can be made for the update and deletion anomalies.) Thus we have to decompose ENG into the following two relations:

    EN(ENO, ENAME, TITLE, JNO, RESP, DUR)
    S(TITLE, SAL)

A careful reader will notice that even though S is in 3NF, EN is not due to the FD:

$$ENO \rightarrow (ENAME, TITLE)$$

ENO is not a superkey and ENAME and TITLE are not prime attributes. Therefore, EN needs to be further decomposed into

    E(ENO, ENAME, TITLE)
    G(ENO, JNO, RESP, DUR)

both of which are in 3NF.

Boyce-Codd normal form (BCNF) is a stronger form of 3NF. The definitions are identical except for the last part. For a relation to be in BCNF, for every FD $X \rightarrow Y$, $X$ has to be a superkey. Notice that the clause "or $Y$ is a prime attribute" is deleted from the definition. Given that ENG is not in 3NF, it is clear that it cannot be in BCNF either. Nevertheless, the relations E and S, as well as the relations J and G, are in BCNF.

It is possible to decompose a 1NF relation directly into a set of relations in BCNF. These algorithms are guaranteed to generate lossless decompositions; however, they cannot be guaranteed to preserve dependencies.

A relation $R$ is in 4NF if for each MVD of the type $X \rightarrow\rightarrow Y$ in $R$, $X$ also functionally determines all the attributes of $R$. Thus, if a relation is in BCNF, and all MVDs are also FDs, the relation is in 4NF. The point is that a 4NF relation either does not contain a real MVD (i.e., every MVD is actually a FD) or there is exactly one MVD represented in the attributes and nothing else.

**Example 2.5**

Note that the relations E, S, J, and G are in 4NF since there is no MVD defined on them. However, the SKILL relation discussed previously is not in 4NF. To satisfy the requirements, it needs to be decomposed into two relations:

    EP (ENO, JNO)
    EL (ENO, PLACE)

The careful reader will notice that in all of the previous normal forms, decomposition was into two relations. Fifth normal form deals with those situations where *n*-way decompositions ($n > 2$) may be necessary.

A relation $R$ is in 5NF (also called *projection-join normal form—PJNF*) if every join dependency defined for the relation is implied by the candidate keys of $R$. For a join dependency to be implied by a candidate key of a relation, the subset (or projections) $X$, $Y$, and $Z$ (see definition of join dependency) should be made according to a candidate key.

**Example 2.6**

For relation E we can define the join dependency

$$*((ENO, ENAME), (ENO, TITLE))$$

which is implied by the candidate key ENO (which also happens to be the primary key). It is quite easy to verify that the relations E, S, J, and G are in 5NF. Thus the relation schemes that we end up with after the decompositions are as follows:

E(ENO, ENAME, TITLE)
S(TITLE, SAL)
J(JNO, JNAME, BUDGET)
G(ENO, JNO, RESP, DUR)

The normalized instances of these relations are shown in Figure 2.4.

All NFs presented above are lossless. An important result [Fagin, 1979] is that a 5NF relation cannot be further decomposed without loss of information.

## 2.3 INTEGRITY RULES

Integrity rules are constraints that define consistent states of the database. They are usually expressed as assertions. Integrity constraints can be *structural* or *behavioral*. Structural constraints are inherent to the data model in the sense that they capture information on data relationships that cannot be modeled directly. Behavioral constraints permit the capturing of the semantics of the applications. The dependencies discussed in the preceding section are behavioral constraints. Maintaining integrity constraints is generally expensive in terms of system resources. Ideally, they should be verified at each database update since updates can lead to inconsistent database states. The problem of maintaining distributed integrity constraints is covered in Chapter 6.

According to [Codd, 1982], the two minimal structural constraints of the relational model are the *entity rule* and the *referential integrity rule*. By definition, any relation has a primary key. The entity rule dictates that each attribute of the key is nonnull. In the example of Figure 2.1, attribute JNO of relation J and attributes (ENO, JNO) of relation ENG cannot have null values. This constraint is necessary to enforce the fact that keys are unique.

Referential integrity [Date, 1983] is useful for capturing relationships between objects that the relational model cannot represent. We make use of referential in-

E

| ENO | ENAME | TITLE |
|-----|-------|-------|
| E1 | J. Doe | Elect. Eng. |
| E2 | M. Smith | Syst. Anal. |
| E3 | A. Lee | Mech. Eng. |
| E4 | J. Miller | Programmer |
| E5 | B. Casey | Syst. Anal. |
| E6 | L. Chu | Elect. Eng. |
| E7 | R. Davis | Mech. Eng. |
| E8 | J. Jones | Syst. Anal. |

G

| ENO | JNO | RESP | DUR |
|-----|-----|------|-----|
| E1 | J1 | Manager | 12 |
| E2 | J1 | Analyst | 24 |
| E2 | J2 | Analyst | 6 |
| E3 | J3 | Consultant | 10 |
| E3 | J4 | Engineer | 48 |
| E4 | J2 | Programmer | 18 |
| E5 | J2 | Manager | 24 |
| E6 | J4 | Manager | 48 |
| E7 | J3 | Engineer | 36 |
| E8 | J3 | Manager | 40 |

J

| JNO | JNAME | BUDGET |
|-----|-------|--------|
| J1 | Instrumentation | 150000 |
| J2 | Database Develop. | 135000 |
| J3 | CAD/CAM | 250000 |
| J4 | Maintenance | 310000 |

S

| TITLE | SAL |
|-------|-----|
| Elect. Eng. | 40000 |
| Syst. Anal. | 34000 |
| Mech. Eng. | 27000 |
| Programmer | 24000 |

**Figure 2.4**  Normalized Relations

tegrity in Chapter 5 during our discussion of distributed database design. Other data models, such as the hierarchical model [Tsichritzis and Lochovsky, 1976] or the entity/relationship model [Chen, 1976], can capture this type of information directly. Referential integrity involves two relations and imposes the constraint that a group of attributes in one relation is the key of another relation. In the example of Figure 2.1 there can be a referential integrity constraint between relations J and ENG on attribute JNO. This rule prescribes that each engineer belong to at least one existing project. In other words, the set of JNO values in relation ENG is included in relation J. Thus there cannot be engineers that belong to projects not in relation J.

## 2.4  RELATIONAL DATA LANGUAGES

Data manipulation languages developed for the relational model (commonly called *query languages*) fall into two fundamental groups: *relational algebra*-based languages and *relational calculus*-based languages. The difference between them is based on how the user query is formulated. The relational algebra is procedural in that the user is expected to specify, using certain high-level operators, how the result is to be obtained. The relational calculus, on the other hand, is nonprocedural; the user only specifies the relationships that should hold in the result. Both of these languages were originally proposed by Codd [Codd, 1970], who also proved that they were equivalent in terms of expressive power [Codd, 1972].

Relational algebra is used more than relational calculus in the study of distributed database issues, because it is of lower level and corresponds more directly to the programs exchanged on a network. However, for the sake of completeness, we discuss them both here. Essentially, relational calculus can be translated into relational algebra.

### 2.4.1  Relational Algebra

Relational algebra consists of a set of operators that operate on relations. It is derived from set theory (relations corresponding to sets). Each operator takes one or two relations as operands and produces a result relation, which, in turn, may be an operand to another operator. These operations permit the querying and updating of a relational database.

**Algebra operations.**    There are five fundamental relational algebra operators and five others that can be defined in terms of these. The fundamental operators are *selection, projection, union, set difference*, and *Cartesian product*. The first two of these operators are unary operators, and the last three are binary operators. The additional operators that can be defined in terms of these fundamental operators are *intersection*, *θ-join, natural join, semijoin* and *quotient*. In practice, relational algebra is extended with operators for grouping or sorting the results, and for performing arithmetic and aggregate functions. Other operators, such as *outer join* and *transitive closure*, are sometimes used as well to provide additional functionality. However, they are not discussed here.

The operands of some of the binary relations should be *union compatible*. Two relations $R$ and $S$ are union compatible if and only if they are of the same degree and the $i$th attribute of each is defined over the same domain. The second part of the definition holds, obviously, only when the attributes of a relation are identified by their relative positions within the relation and not by their names. If relative ordering of attributes is not important, it is necessary to replace the second part of the definition by the phrase "the corresponding attributes of the two relations should be defined over the same domain." The correspondence is defined rather loosely here.

*Selection.*    Selection produces a horizontal subset of a given relation. The subset consists of all the tuples that satisfy a formula (condition). The selection from a relation $R$ is

$$\sigma_F(R)$$

where $R$ is the relation and $F$ is a formula.

Since we refer to formulas repeatedly in this chapter, let us define precisely what we mean at this point. We define a formula within the context of first-order predicate calculus ([Stoll, 1963] and [Enderton, 1972]) (since we use that formalism later), and follow the notation of [Gallaire et al., 1984]. First-order predicate calculus is based on a *symbol alphabet* that consists of (1) variables, constants, functions, and predicate symbols; (2) parentheses; (3) the logical connectors $\wedge$ (and), $\vee$ (or), $\neg$ (not), $\rightarrow$ (implication), and $\leftrightarrow$ (equivalence); and (4) quantifiers $\forall$ (for all) and $\exists$ (there exists). A *term* is either a constant or a variable. Recursively, if $f$ is an *n*ary function and $t_1, \ldots, t_n$ are terms, $f(t_1, \ldots, t_n)$ is also a term. An *atomic formula* is of the form $P(t_1, \ldots, t_n)$, where $P$ is an *n*ary predicate symbol and the $t_i$'s are terms. A *well-formed formula* (*wff*) can be defined recursively as follows: If $w_i$ and $w_j$ are wffs, then $(w_i)$, $\neg(w_i)$, $(w_i) \wedge (w_j)$, $(w_i) \vee (w_j)$, $(w_i) \rightarrow (w_j)$, and $(w_i) \leftrightarrow (w_j)$ are all wffs. Variables in a wff may be *free* or they may be *bound* by one of the two quantifiers.

The formula in the selection operation is called a *selection predicate* and is an atomic formula whose terms are of the form $A\theta c$, where $A$ is an attribute of $R$ and $\theta$ is one of the arithmetic comparison operators $<, >, =, \neq, \leq,$ and $\geq$. The terms can be connected by the logical connectors $\wedge, \vee,$ and $\neg$. Furthermore, the selection predicate does not contain any quantifiers.

**Example 2.7**

Consider the relation E shown in Figure 2.4. The result of selecting those tuples for electrical engineers is shown in Figure 2.5.

$$\sigma_{\text{TITLE="Elect. Eng."}}(E)$$

| ENO | ENAME | TITLE |
|-----|-------|-------|
| E1  | J. Doe | Elect. Eng |
| E6  | L. Chu | Elect. Eng. |

**Figure 2.5**   Result of Selection

*Projection.*   Projection produces a vertical subset of a relation. The result relation contains only those attributes of the original relation over which projection is performed. Thus the degree of the result is less than or equal to the degree of the original relation.

The projection of relation $R$ over attributes $A$ and $B$ is denoted as

$$\Pi_{A,B}(R)$$

Note that the result of a projection might contain tuples which are identical. In that case the duplicate tuples may be deleted from the result relation. It is possible to specify projection with or without duplicate elimination.

**Example 2.8**

The projection of relation J shown in Figure 2.4 over attributes JNO and BUDGET is depicted in Figure 2.6.

$$\Pi_{\text{JNO,BUDGET}}\,(\text{J})$$

| JNO | BUDGET |
|-----|--------|
| J1  | 150000 |
| J2  | 135000 |
| J3  | 250000 |
| J4  | 310000 |

**Figure 2.6**    Result of Projection

*Union.*    The union of two relations $R$ and $S$ (denoted as $R \cup S$) is the set of all tuples that are in $R$, or in $S$, or in both. We should note that $R$ and $S$ should be union compatible. As in the case of projection, the duplicate tuples are normally eliminated. Union may be used to insert new tuples into an existing relation, where these tuples form one of the operand relations.

*Set Difference.*    The set difference of two relations $R$ and $S$ ($R - S$) is the set of all tuples that are in $R$ but not in $S$. In this case, not only should $R$ and $S$ be union compatible, but the operation is also asymmetric (i.e., $R - S \neq S - R$). This operation allows the deletion of tuples from a relation. Together with the union operation, we can perform modification of tuples by deletion followed by insertion.

*Cartesian Product.*    The Cartesian product of two relations $R$ of degree $k_1$ and $S$ of degree $k_2$ is the set of $(k_1 + k_2)$-tuples, where each result tuple is a concatenation of one tuple of $R$ with one tuple of $S$, for all tuples of $R$ and $S$. The Cartesian product of $R$ and $S$ is denoted as $R \times S$.

It is possible that the two relations might have attributes with the same name. In this case the attribute names are prefixed with the relation name so as to maintain the uniqueness of the attribute names within a relation.

**Example 2.9**

Consider relations E and S in Figure 2.4. E × S is shown in Figure 2.7. Note that the attribute TITLE, which is common to both relations, appears twice, prefixed with the relation name.

*Intersection.*    Intersection of two relations $R$ and $S$ ($R \cap S$) consists of the set of all tuples that are in both $R$ and $S$. In terms of the basic operators, it can be specified as follows:

$$R \cap S = R - (R - S)$$

E × S

| ENO | ENAME | E.TITLE | S.TITLE | SAL |
|------|-----------|-------------|-------------|-------|
| E1 | J. Doe | Elect. Eng. | Elect. Eng. | 40000 |
| E1 | J. Doe | Elect. Eng. | Syst. Anal. | 34000 |
| E1 | J. Doe | Elect. Eng. | Mech. Eng. | 27000 |
| E1 | J. Doe | Elect. Eng. | Programmer | 24000 |
| E2 | M. Smith | Syst. Anal. | Elect. Eng. | 40000 |
| E2 | M. Smith | Syst. Anal. | Syst. Anal. | 34000 |
| E2 | M. Smith | Syst. Anal. | Mech. Eng. | 27000 |
| E2 | M. Smith | Syst. Anal. | Programmer | 24000 |
| E3 | A. Lee | Mech. Eng. | Elect. Eng. | 40000 |
| E3 | A. Lee | Mech. Eng. | Syst. Anal. | 34000 |
| E3 | A. Lee | Mech. Eng. | Mech. Eng. | 27000 |
| E3 | A. Lee | Mech. Eng. | Programmer | 24000 |
| E8 | J. Jones | Syst. Anal. | Elect. Eng. | 40000 |
| E8 | J. Jones | Syst. Anal. | Syst. Anal. | 34000 |
| E8 | J. Jones | Syst. Anal. | Mech. Eng. | 27000 |
| E8 | J. Jones | Syst. Anal. | Programmer | 24000 |

**Figure 2.7**    Partial Result of Cartesian Product

*θ-Join.*    Join is a derivative of Cartesian product. There are various forms of join, the most general of which is the θ-join, commonly called the join. The θ-join of two relations $R$ and $S$ is denoted as

$$R \bowtie_F S$$

where $F$ is a formula specifying the *join predicate*. A join predicate is specified similar to a selection predicate, except that the terms are of the form $R.A\theta S.B$, where $A$ and $B$ are attributes of $R$ and $S$, respectively.

The join of two relations is equivalent to performing a selection, using the join predicate as the selection formula, over the Cartesian product of the two operand relations. Thus

$$R \bowtie_F S = \sigma_F(R \times S)$$

In the equivalence above, we should note that if $F$ involves attributes of the two relations that are common to both of them, a projection is necessary to make sure that those attributes do not appear twice in the result.

### Example 2.10

Figure 2.8 shows the θ-join of relations E and S in Figure 2.4 over the join predicate E.TITLE=S.TITLE. The same result could have been obtained as

$$\text{E} \bowtie_{\text{E.TITLE=S.TITLE}} \text{S} = \Pi_{\text{ENO, ENAME, TITLE, SAL}}(\sigma_{\text{E.TITLE = S.TITLE}}(\text{E} \times \text{S}))$$

$$E \bowtie_{E.TITLE=S.TITLE} S$$

| ENO | ENAME | TITLE | SAL |
|-----|-------|-------|-----|
| E1 | J. Doe | Elect. Eng. | 40000 |
| E2 | M. Smith | Analyst | 34000 |
| E3 | A. Lee | Mech. Eng. | 27000 |
| E4 | J. Miller | Programmer | 24000 |
| E5 | B. Casey | Syst. Anal. | 34000 |
| E6 | L. Chu | Elect. Eng. | 40000 |
| E7 | R. Davis | Mech. Eng. | 27000 |
| E8 | J. Jones | Syst. Anal. | 34000 |

**Figure 2.8**    The Result of Join

This example demonstrates a special case of $\theta$-join which is called the *equi-join*. This is a case where the formula $F$ only contains equality ($=$) as the arithmetic operator. It should be noted, however, that an equi-join does not have to be specified over a common attribute as the example above might suggest.

*Natural Join.*    A natural join is an equi-join of two relations over a specified attribute, more specifically, over attributes with the same domain. There is a difference, however, in that usually the attributes over which the natural join is performed appear only once in the result. A natural join is denoted as the join without the formula

$$R \bowtie_A S$$

where $A$ is the attribute common to both $R$ and $S$. We should note here that the natural join attribute may have different names in the two relations; what is required is that they come from the same domain. In this case the join is denoted as

$$R_A \bowtie_B S$$

where $B$ is the corresponding join attribute of $S$.

**Example 2.11**

The join of E and S in Example 2.10 is actually a natural join.

*Semijoin.*    The semijoin of relation $R$, defined over the set of attributes $A$, by relation $S$, defined over the set of attributes $B$, is the subset of the tuples of $R$ that participate in the join of $R$ with $S$. It is denoted as $R \ltimes_F S$ (where $F$ is a predicate as defined before) and can be obtained as follows:

$$
\begin{aligned}
R \ltimes_F S &= \Pi_A(R \bowtie_F S) = \Pi_A(R) \bowtie_F \Pi_{A \cap B}(S) \\
&= R \bowtie_F \Pi_{A \cap B}(S)
\end{aligned}
$$

The advantage of semijoin is that it decreases the number of tuples that need to be handled to form the join. In centralized database systems, this is important because it usually results in a decreased number of secondary storage accesses by making better use of the memory. It is even more important in distributed databases since it usually reduces the amount of data that needs to be transmitted between sites in order to evaluate a query. We talk about this in more detail in Chapters 5 and 9. At this point note that the operation is asymmetric (i.e., $R \ltimes_F S \neq S \ltimes_F R$).

**Example 2.12**

To demonstrate the difference between join and semijoin, let us consider the semijoin of E with S over the predicate E.TITLE = S.TITLE, that is,

$$E \ltimes_{E.TITLE \,=\, S.TITLE} S$$

The result of the operation is shown in Figure 2.9. We would like to encourage the reader to compare Figures 2.8 and 2.9 to see the difference between the join and the semijoin operations. Note that the resultant relation does not have the SAL attribute and is therefore smaller.

$$E \ltimes_{E. TITLE=S. TITLE} S$$

| ENO | ENAME | TITLE |
|-----|-------|-------|
| E1 | J. Doe | Elect. Eng. |
| E2 | M. Smith | Analyst |
| E3 | A. Lee | Mech. Eng. |
| E4 | J. Miller | Programmer |
| E5 | B. Casey | Syst. Anal. |
| E6 | L. Chu | Elect. Eng. |
| E7 | R. Davis | Mech. Eng. |
| E8 | J. Jones | Syst. Anal. |

**Figure 2.9**   The Result of Semijoin

*(Division) Quotient.*    The division of relation $R$ of degree $r$ with relation $S$ of degree $s$ (where $r > s$ and $s \neq 0$) is the set of $(r - s)$-tuples $t$ such that for all $s$-tuples $u$ in $S$, the tuple $tu$ is in $R$. The division operation is denoted as $R \div S$ and can be specified in terms of the fundamental operators as follows:

$$R \div S = \Pi_{\bar{A}}(R) - \Pi_{\bar{A}}((\Pi_{\bar{A}}(R) \times S) - R)$$

where $\bar{A}$ is the set of attributes of $R$ that are not in $S$ [i.e., the $(r - s)$-tuples].

**Example 2.13**

Assume that we have a modified version of the G relation (call it $G'$) depicted in Figure 2.10a and defined as follows:

$$G' = \Pi_{ENO,JNO} (G) \bowtie_{JNO} J$$

If one wants to find the employee numbers of those engineers who are assigned to all the projects that have a budget greater than \$200,000, it is necessary to divide $G'$ with a restricted version of J, called $J'$ (see Figure 2.10b). The result of division $(G' \div J')$ is shown in Figure 2.10c.

G'

| ENO | JNO | JNAME | BUDGET |
|------|------|-------------------|--------|
| E1 | J1 | Instrumentation | 150000 |
| E2 | J1 | Instrumentation | 150000 |
| E2 | J2 | Database Develop. | 135000 |
| E3 | J3 | CAD/CAM | 250000 |
| E3 | J4 | Maintenance | 310000 |
| E4 | J2 | Database Develop. | 135000 |
| E5 | J2 | Database Develop. | 135000 |
| E6 | J4 | Maintenance | 310000 |
| E7 | J3 | CAD/CAM | 250000 |
| E8 | J3 | CAD/CAM | 250000 |

(a)

J'

| JNO | JNAME | BUDGET |
|------|-------------|--------|
| J3 | CAD/CAM | 250000 |
| J4 | Maintenance | 310000 |

(b)

$(G' \div J')$

| ENO |
|------|
| E3 |

(c)

**Figure 2.10**    The Result of Division

The keyword in the query above is "*all.*" This rules out the possibility of doing a selection on $G'$ to find the necessary tuples, since that would only give those which correspond to engineers working on *some* project with a budget greater than \$200,000, not those who work on all projects. Note that the result contains only the tuple $< E3 >$ since the tuples $< E3, J3, CAD/CAM, 250000>$ and $< E3, J4, Maintenance, 310000>$ both exist in $G'$. On the other hand, for example, $< E7>$ is not in the result, since even though the tuple $< E7, J3, CAD/CAM, 250000>$ is in $G'$, the tuple $< E7, J4, Maintenance, 310000 >$ is not.

**Relational algebra programs.**     Since all operations take relations as input and produce relations as outputs, we can nest operations using a parenthesized notation and represent relational algebra programs. The parentheses indicate the order of execution. The following are a few examples that demonstrate the issue.

**Example 2.14**

Consider the relations of Figure 2.4. The retrieval query

"Find the names of employees working on the CAD/CAM project"

can be answered by the relational algebra program

$$\Pi_{ENAME}(((\sigma_{JNAME\ =\ \text{``CAD/CAM''}}\ J)\ \bowtie_{JNO}\ G)\ \bowtie_{ENO}\ E)$$

The order of execution is: the selection on J, followed by the join with G, followed by the join with E, and finally the project on ENAME.

An equivalent program where the size of the intermediate relations is smaller is

$$\Pi_{ENAME}\ (E\ \bowtie_{ENO}\ (\Pi_{ENO}\ (G\ \bowtie_{JNO}\ (\sigma_{JNAME=\ \text{``CAD/CAM''}}\ J))))$$

**Example 2.15**

The update query

"Replace the salary of programmers by $25,000"

can be computed by

$$(S - (\sigma_{TITLE\ =\ \text{``Programmer''}}\ S)) \cup (<Programmer, 25000>)$$

## 2.4.2  Relational Calculus

In relational calculus-based languages, instead of specifying *how* to obtain the result, one specifies *what* the result is by stating the relationship that is supposed to hold for the result. Relational calculus languages fall into two groups: *tuple relational calculus* and *domain relational calculus*. The difference between the two is in terms of the primitive variable used in specifying the queries. We briefly review these two types of languages.

Relational calculus languages have a solid theoretical foundation since they are based on first-order predicate logic as we discussed before. Semantics is given to formulas by interpreting them as assertions on the database. A relational database can be viewed as a collection of tuples or a collection of domains. Tuple relational calculus interprets a variable in a formula as a tuple of a relation, whereas domain relational calculus interprets a variable as the value of a domain.

**Tuple relational calculus.**     The primitive variable used in tuple relational calculus is a *tuple variable* which specifies a tuple of a relation. In other words, it ranges over the tuples of a relation. Tuple calculus is the original relational calculus developed by Codd [Codd, 1970].

In tuple relational calculus queries are specified as

$$\{t|F(t)\}$$

where $t$ is a tuple variable and $F$ is a well-formed formula. The atomic formulas are of two forms:

1. *Tuple-variable membership expressions.* If $t$ is a tuple variable ranging over the tuples of relation $R$ (predicate symbol), the expression "tuple $t$ belongs to relation $R$" is an atomic formula, which is usually specified as $R.t$ or $R(t)$.

2. *Conditions.* These can be defined as follows:

   (a) $s[A]\theta t[B]$, where $s$ and $t$ are tuple variables and $A$ and $B$ are components of $s$ and $t$, respectively. $\theta$ is one of the arithmetic comparison operators $<$, $>$, $=$, $\neq$, $\leq$, and $\geq$. This condition specifies that component $A$ of $s$ stands in relation $\theta$ to the $B$ component of $t$: for example, $s[SAL] > t[SAL]$.

   (b) $s[A]\theta c$, where $s$, $A$, and $\theta$ are as defined above and $c$ is a constant. For example, $s[ENAME] =$ "Smith".

Note that $A$ is defined as a component of the tuple variable $s$. Since the range of $s$ is a relation instance, say $S$, it is obvious that component $A$ of $s$ corresponds to attribute $A$ of relation $S$. The same thing is obviously true for $B$.

There are many languages that are based on relational tuple calculus, the most popular ones being SQL[1] [Date, 1987] and QUEL [Stonebraker et al., 1976]. Also, many commercial systems offer variations of the SQL language as their user interface. To illustrate relational tuple calculus language, we use the current version of SQL, which is proposed as a standard and is called SQL/ANS [ANSI, 1986].

SQL provides a uniform approach to data manipulation (retrieval, update), data definition (schema manipulation), and control (authorization, integrity, etc.). We limit ourselves to the expression, in SQL/ANS, of the queries in Examples 2.14 and 2.15.

**Example 2.16**

The query from Example 2.14,

   "Find the names of employees working on the CAD/CAM project"

can be expressed as follows:

```
SELECT      E.ENAME
FROM        E,G,J
```

---

[1]Sometimes SQL is cited as lying somewhere between relational algebra and relational calculus. Its originators called it a "mapping language." However, it follows the tuple calculus definition quite closely; hence we classify it as such.

```
WHERE     E.ENO = G.ENO
AND       G.JNO = J.JNO
AND       J.JNAME = ''CAD/CAM''
```

Note that a retrieval query generates a new relation similar to the relational algebra operations.

**Example 2.17**

The update query of Example 2.15,

"Replace the salary of programmers by $25,000"

is expressed as

```
UPDATE    S
SET       SAL = 25000
WHERE     S.TITLE = ''Programmer''
```

**Domain relational calculus.**  The domain relational calculus was first proposed by [Lacroix and Pirotte, 1977]. The fundamental difference between a tuple relational language and a domain relational language is the use of a *domain variable* in the latter. A domain variable ranges over the values in a domain and specifies a component of a tuple. In other words, the range of a domain variable consists of the domains over which the relation is defined. The wffs are formulated accordingly. The queries are specified in the following form:

$$x_1, x_2, ..., x_n | F(x_1, x_2, ..., x_n)$$

where $F$ is a wff in which $x_1, ..., x_n$ are the free variables.

The success of domain relational calculus languages is due mainly to QBE [Zloof, 1977], which is a visual application of domain calculus. QBE, designed only for interactive use from a visual terminal, is user friendly. The basic concept is an *example*: the user formulates queries by providing a possible example of the answer. Typing relation names triggers the printing, on screen, of their schemes. Then, by supplying keywords into the columns (domains), the user specifies the query. For instance, the attributes of the project relation are given by P, which stands for "Print."

By default, all queries are retrieval. An update query requires the specification of U under the name of the updated relation or in the updated column. The retrieval query corresponding to Example 2.16 is given in Figure 2.11 and the update query of Example 2.17 is given in Figure 2.12. To distinguish examples from constants, examples are underlined.

### 2.4.3 Interface with Programming Languages

Relational data languages are insufficient to write complex application programs. Therefore, interfacing a relational data language to a programming language in which the application is written is usually necessary. We can distinguish between two main approaches in providing this service: the *tightly coupled* and *loosely coupled* approaches.

| E | ENO | ENAME | TITLE |
|---|-----|-------|-------|
|   | E2  | P.    |       |

| G | ENO | JNO | RESP | DUR |
|---|-----|-----|------|-----|
|   | E2  | J3  |      |     |

| J | JNO | JNAME | BUDGET |
|---|-----|-------|--------|
|   | J3  | CAD/CAM |      |

**Figure 2.11**   Retrieval Query in QBE

| S | TITLE | SAL |
|---|-------|-----|
|   | Programmer | U.25000 |

**Figure 2.12**   Update Query in QBE

The tightly coupled approach consists of extending some programming language with data manipulation commands. The loosely coupled approach consists of integrating the data language with a programming language using database calls.

**Tightly coupled approach.**   In this approach the programming language and the database language are merged in a single language. A typical example of this approach is Pascal/R [Schmidt, 1977], in which the language Pascal is extended with a new variable type *relation* that contains several (possibly many) instances of tuples (implemented via Pascal records) and with commands to manipulate relations (e.g., **for each** tuple in relation).

Another typical example of this approach is that of *fourth-generation languages* (4GL) [Martin, 1985]. They are well known because of their commercial success. Fourth-generation languages are new high-level languages that combine relational algebra operators with programming constructs. The possibility of using temporary variables and powerful programming constructs (e.g., loops) makes them "database-oriented programming languages" in which application development is facilitated.

**Example 2.18**

To illustrate this type of language, let us consider the following simple application program (based on relation G in Figure 2.4):

"For the tuples in relation G where DUR > 40, perform a complex subprogram on attribute DUR, and produce a report that uses ENO and the result of the subprogram"

Assuming a generic 4GL, this program can be written as

```
for each G where DUR > 40
do
     perform subprogram X on DUR giving RES
     produce Report on ENO, RES
end
```

where RES is the results of the subprogram and Report is a predefined query to a report generator (often part of a 4GL).

**Loosely coupled approach.**  In this approach the programming language is a high-level language such as COBOL or PL/I which does not know about the database concepts. The programming language is simply extended with special commands that call the database system. These commands are database language constructs simply preceded by a key character (e.g., $) to distinguish them from the constructs of the programming language.

The database languages used with these types of programming languages are usually based on the tuple relational calculus and are set oriented. The programming language, on the other hand, is procedural. The conversion from the set-oriented mode to the procedural mode required by the programming language is generally simple; it is based on the use of a cursor on a set. A cursor can be explicit, as in SQL (embedded primarily in PL/I), or implicit, as in EQUEL (Embedded QUEL).

Two execution modes of such extended languages are possible: interpretation of database calls at run time or precompilation of database calls. The latter mode is more efficient.

**Example 2.19**

We illustrate this approach by considering the same application program as in Example 2.19, but this time writing it in SQL embedded in PL/I, as shown in Figure 2.13. The $ indicates a database command.

## 2.5  RELATIONAL DBMS

A relational DBMS is a software component supporting the relational model and a relational language. It is executed on a general purpose computer, although some systems can run on microcomputers or specialized computers referred to as *database machines*(a topic addressed in Chapter 15).

A DBMS is a reentrant program shared by multiple alive entities, called *transactions*, that run database programs. When running on a general purpose computer, a DBMS is interfaced with two other components: the communication subsystem and the operating system. The generic architecture of a (centralized) DBMS is depicted in Figure 2.14. The communication subsystem permits interfacing the DBMS with other subsystems in order to communicate with applications. For example, the terminal

.

.

.

```
$DCL VARDUR INT;
$DCL VARENO INT;
```

.

.

.

```
$LET C BE { cursor definition }
    SELECT    G.ENO: VARENO, G.DUR: VARDUR
    FROM      G
    WHERE     G.DUR>40
```

.

.

.

```
$OPEN C
DO WHILE "not end C"
BEGIN
   $FETCH C;
   perform subprogram X on DUR giving RES;
   produce Report on ENO, RES
END;
```

**Figure 2.13**   Example PL/I Program

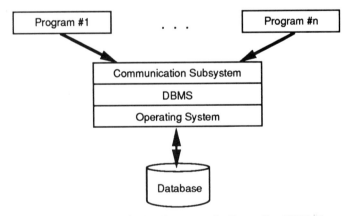

**Figure 2.14**   Generic Architecture of a Centralized DBMS

monitor needs to communicate with the DBMS to run interactive transactions. The operating system provides the interface between the DBMS and computer resources (processor, memory, disk drives, etc.).

The functions performed by a relational DBMS can be layered as in Figure 2.15, where the arrows indicate the direction of the data and the control flow. Taking a top- down approach, the layers are the interface, control, compilation, execution, data access, and consistency management.

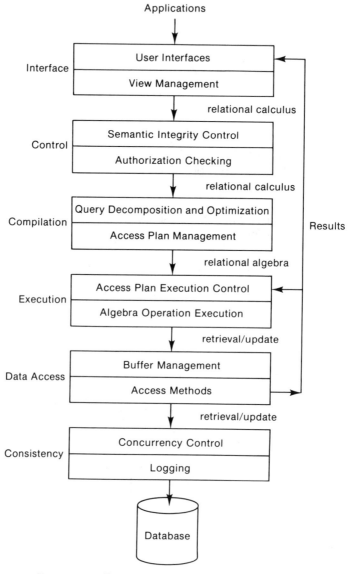

**Figure 2.15**   Functional Layers of a Relational DBMS

The *interface layer* manages the interface to the applications. There can be several interfaces like SQL embedded in COBOL, and QBE (query by example). Database application programs are executed against external *views* of the database. For an application, a view is useful in representing its particular perception of the database (shared by many applications). A relational view is a virtual relation derived from base relations by applying relational algebra operations.[2] View management consists of translating the user query from external data to conceptual data (base relations). If the user query is expressed in relational calculus, the query applied to conceptual data is still in the same form.

The *control layer* controls the query by adding semantic integrity predicates and authorization predicates. Semantic integrity constraints and authorizations are specified in relational calculus, as discussed in Chapter 6. The output of this layer is an enriched query in relational calculus.

The *query processing* layer maps the query into an optimized sequence of lower-level operations. This layer is concerned with performance. It decomposes the query into a tree of relational algebra operations and tries to find the "optimal" ordering of the operations. The result is stored in an access plan. The output of this layer is a query expressed in relational algebra (or in lower-level code).

The *execution layer* directs the execution of the access plans, including transaction management (commit, restart) and synchronization of relational algebra operations. It interprets the relational operations by calling the data access layer through the retrieval and update requests.

The *data access layer* manages the data structures that implement the relations (files, indices). It also manages the buffers by caching the most frequently accessed data. Careful use of this layer minimizes the access to disks to get or write data.

Finally, the *consistency layer* manages concurrency control and logging for update requests. This layer allows transaction, system, and media recovery after failure.

## 2.6  BIBLIOGRAPHIC NOTES

This chapter covered the basic issues related to relational database systems. We chose to go into these concepts in some detail since the discussion in the remainder of the book is based on this data model. For those readers who may need additional coverage of these topics, we refer to a number of excellent database books, such as [Gardarin and Valduriez, 1989], [Ullman, 1982], [Ullman, 1988], [Elmasri and Navathe, 1989], [Korth and Silberschatz, 1986], and [Date, 1986]. A good source for additional information about other data models is [Tsichritzis and Lochovsky, 1981].

---

[2]Note that this does not mean that the real-world views are, or should be, specified in relational algebra. On the contrary, they are specified by some high-level data language such as SQL. The translation from one of these languages to relational algebra is now well understood, and the effects of the view definition can be specified in terms of relational algebra operations.

# 3

# Review of
# Computer Networks

In this chapter we discuss the issues related to computer networks and concentrate on the concepts and issues that are important for distributed database systems. We therefore omit most of the details of the technological and technical issues in favor of these conceptual presentations.

We define a *computer network* as an *interconnected collection of autonomous computers that are capable of exchanging information among them* (Figure 3.1). The keywords in this definition are *interconnected* and *autonomous*. We want the computers to be autonomous so that each computer can execute programs on its own. We also want the computers to be interconnected so that they are capable of exchanging information. Computers on a network are commonly referred to as *nodes*, *hosts*, or *sites*. They form one of the fundamental hardware components of a network. The other fundamental component is the communication path that interconnects the nodes among them. Note that sometimes the terms *host* and *node* are used to refer simply to the equipment, whereas *site* is reserved for the equipment as well as the software that runs on it.

A computer network is a special case of distributed computing environment where computers are the equipment connected to the data communication channel. In a general distributed environment, though, some of this equipment may be terminals or other specialized devices (such as banking machines). The fundamental data communication concepts discussed in Section 3.1 hold in these environments as well.

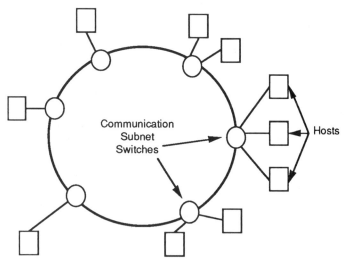

**Figure 3.1**   Computer Network

However, our main interest in this book lies in computer networks since they provide the basic support for distributed database systems.

## 3.1  DATA COMMUNICATION CONCEPTS

Let us first define a few fundamental terms. To quote [Stallings, 1988]: "... *data* [is defined] as entities that convey meaning. *Signals* are electric or electromagnetic encoding of data. *Signaling* is the act of propagating the signal along some suitable medium. Finally, *transmission* is the communication of data by the propagation and processing of signals."

Equipment in a data communication environment is connected by *channels* or *links*. Communication links can carry signals either in digital form or in analog form. Telephone lines, for example, can carry data in analog form, even though such links are slowly being replaced by ones more suitable to digital transmission. Each communication link has a *capacity*, which can be defined as the amount of data that can be transmitted over the link in a given time unit. This capacity is commonly referred to as the *bandwidth* of the channel. In analog transmission channels, the bandwidth is defined as the difference (in hertz) between the lowest and highest frequencies that can be transmitted over the channel per second. In digital links, *bandwidth* refers (less formally) to the number of bits that can be transmitted per second (bps); it is commonly called the *baud rate*[1] of the channel. For example, a channel that transmits at

---

[1]This equality between the baud rate and the bit rate holds if and only if binary signals are used. Strictly speaking, a baud is equal to the number of discrete signal events per second, which might change according to the coding and the modulation methods used. However, we will not be concerned with that detail.

9600 bps is said to have a baud rate of 9600. There are three ranges of communication links, classified according to their bandwidth:

1. *Voice-grade channels*: can carry between 600 to 4800 bps
2. *Sub-voice channels*: can carry less than 1200 bps
3. *Broadband channels*: can carry 50,000 bps and more

If data is transmitted over analog transmission channels, it needs to be *modulated*. This means that the digital data is encoded onto an analog carrier signal by changing one or more of its basic characteristics (amplitude, frequency and phase). The modulated carrier signal propagates to the receiving end, where it is again converted into digital form. The advantage of using higher-bandwidth channels is that the data being transmitted can be *multiplexed*, thereby allowing more than one signal to be transmitted over the same line simultaneously.

For example, in telephone channels the bandwidth required to transmit voice is approximately 3 kilohertz (kHz). If the channel that will carry the voice signal has a bandwidth of, say, 12 kHz, three voice signals can be transmitted over the line at the same time (see Figure 3.2). Each voice transmission is done over one channel, which occupies a 4-kHz band of the available bandwidth. The extra 1 kHz allocated for each voice channel is called a *guard band*. It is used to provide sufficient frequency at each end so that signals from different channels do not interfere with each other. This form of multiplexing is known as *frequency-division multiplexing* (FDM). An alternative to this is to divide the unit transmission time into slots and assign the entire channel (i.e., the entire frequency band) to the transmission of one signal. This form of multiplexing is called *time-division multiplexing* (TDM) and is used more commonly in data communications (Figure 3.3).

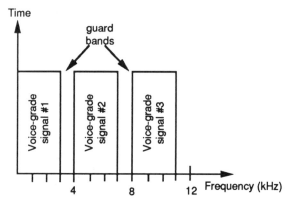

**Figure 3.2**    Frequency Division Multiplexing

We should mention that multiplexing for data transmission may be somewhat different. Depending on the characteristics of the line (i.e., whether the line is working as a digital transmission medium or an analog transmission medium), different forms

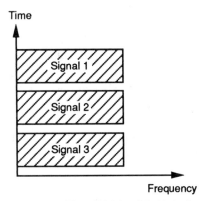

**Figure 3.3**    Time Division Multiplexing

of modulation and multiplexing may be necessary. However, these topics are beyond the scope of our discussion in this chapter. The fundamental point here is that the high-bandwidth channels provide the ability to multiplex many signals onto the same physical line. On the other hand, the higher-bandwidth channels are considerably costlier than their lower-bandwidth counterparts.

Another characteristic of a communication line from the perspective of distributed database systems is its mode of operation. A communication line may operate in a *simplex*, *half-duplex*, or *full-duplex* mode. A line that operates in simplex mode can transmit signals and data in only one direction. Typical application areas of such lines include connection to printers and card readers and real-time control applications where they are used to transmit signals from sensors to a central computer. Such lines are considerably cheap, but they provide no flexibility of use whatsoever. Half-duplex lines can transmit data in both directions, yet they cannot do so simultaneously. The transmission has to proceed first in one direction, then the line has to be "turned around" and the transmission in the reverse direction can begin. Half-duplex lines obviously provide more flexibility than simplex lines, with an added cost. However, there is a delay in turning the line around that may be significant in distributed applications. Full-duplex lines can transmit signals and data in both directions simultaneously. They are the most flexible transmission media and also the most costly. Usually, the dial-up telephone lines operate in half-duplex mode, whereas the leased lines operate in full-duplex mode. However, full duplex operation on telephone lines can be implemented using FDM.

With respect to delays or to getting the user's work done, the bandwidth and the operating mode of a transmission channel are significant factors, but they are not necessarily the only ones that affect how long it takes to transfer data back and forth on a computer network. The other factor in the transmission time is the software employed. There are usually overhead costs involved in data transmission due to the redundancies within the message itself, necessary for error detection and correction. Furthermore, the network software adds headers and trailers to any message, for example, to specify the destination or to check for errors in the entire message. All of these activities contribute to delays in transmitting data. The actual rate at which data is transmitted across the network is known as the *data transfer rate* and this rate is usually less than the actual bandwidth of the transmission channel.

In computer-to-computer communication, data is usually transmitted in *frames*. Usually, upper limits on frame sizes are established for each network and each contains data as well as some control information, such as the destination and source addresses, block error check codes, and so on (Figure 3.4). If a message that is to be sent from a source node to a destination node cannot fit one frame, it is split over a number of frames. This will be discussed further in Section 3.3.

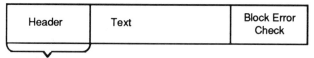

| Header | Text | Block Error Check |

- Source address
- Destination address
- Message number
- Packet number
- Acknowledgment
- Control information

**Figure 3.4**    Typical Frame Format

## 3.2 TYPES OF NETWORKS

There are various criteria by which computer networks can be classified. One criterion is the interconnection structure of computers, another is the mode of transmission, and a third is the geographic distribution.

According to the interconnection structure, which is also called the *topology*, networks can be classified as star, ring, hierarchical, meshed, irregular, and so on. In terms of communication schemes employed, they can be either *point-to-point* networks, or *multi-point* networks. In point-to-point networks, each pair of nodes has a link connecting them, which is not shared by any other node, while in multi-point networks, a common communication channel is utilized by all the nodes in the network. In terms of geographic distribution, there are wide area networks and local area networks. A wide area network is one where the distance between any two nodes is greater than approximately 20 kilometers (km), whereas in a local area network, that distance is less than 20 km. Such distances, however, are not absolute and other features are commonly used to differentiate between the two. In this chapter our primary classification criterion is the geographical distribution. The other two criteria are used to further classify and clarify the types of networks that can exist.

## 3.3  WIDE AREA NETWORKS

### 3.3.1  Topologies

*Wide area* networks (also called *long-haul* networks) can be constructed using either multi-point or point-to-point topologies. The fundamental transmission medium for multi-point type is a *broadcasting* channel such as a radio or satellite. In case of satellite transmission, each site beams its transmission to a satellite which then beams it back at a different frequency (Figure 3.5). Every site on the network listens to the receiving frequency and has to disregard the message if it is not addressed to that site. A network that uses this technique is the SATNET network [Jacobs et al., 1978].

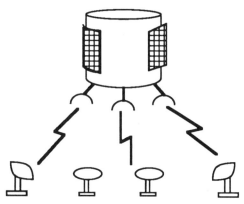

**Figure 3.5**   Satellite-Based Network

*Microwave* transmission is another very popular mode of data communication. Microwave links already form a major portion of most countries' telephone networks. In addition to the public carriers, many companies are making extensive use of private microwave links. In fact, major metropolitan cities face the problem of microwave interference among privately owned and public carrier links. An example of network using microwave transmission as its data communication medium is ALOHA [Abramson, 1973].

A final word on broadcasting topologies is that they have the advantage that it is easier to check for errors and to send messages to more than one site than to do so in point-to-point topologies. On the other hand, since everybody listens in, broadcast networks are not as secure as point-to-point networks.

Most wide area networks are implemented according to a point-to-point topology, with direct interconnections between nodes. Probably the most common form of point-to-point networks is one with an *irregular* connection topology (see Figure 3.6). In such a topology, the interconnection between nodes is not symmetric and does not follow a pattern. It is possible to find a node that is connected to only one other node, as well as nodes that have connections to a number of nodes. Typical examples of wide area networks are ARPANET, TYMENET, CSNET, and DATAPAC.

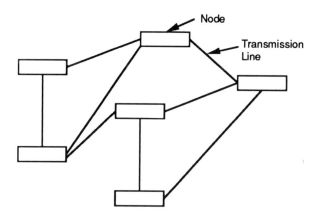

**Figure 3.6** Irregular Point-to-Point Network

Another common type of wide area network topology is the *star* (Figure 3.7). In this case, all the computers are connected to a central computer that coordinates the transmission on the network. Thus if two computers want to communicate, they have to go through the central computer. This type of network is commonly used in organizations that are spread over a large geographical area with a central computer either at headquarters or at the regional centers. In this case local processing is performed at each node and data is eventually transmitted to the central computer. One disadvantage of star-type networks is their unreliability. Since the communication between any two computers depends on the availability of the central computer, a failure at this node will cause transmission over the network to cease completely. Another disadvantage is the excessive load on the central computer; since it has to coordinate the communication that goes on over the network, it has a heavier load to bear than do the other sites. Thus it is common to find a central site that is much more powerful than the satellite computers. Because of these disadvantages, star-type networks are commonly used only where the amount of data transmission between satellite computers is not excessive.

Even though the star and irregular topologies are the most common point-to-point network structures, it is possible to design point-to-point wide area networks that employ other structuring topologies. For example, the interconnection among the nodes can be in the form of a *hierarchy*, or *tree* (Figure 3.8). In this case, all transmission among the nodes at the same level has to proceed upward until a common node can be found, after which it proceeds down to the other node. Such a connection might be suitable where there is a geographical or functional grouping among the sites.

Another interconnection scheme is a *complete (meshed)* interconnection, where each node is interconnected to every other node (Figure 3.9). Such an interconnection structure obviously provides more reliability and the possibility of better performance than that of the structures noted previously. However, it is also the costliest.

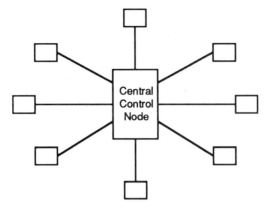

**Figure 3.7**   Star Network

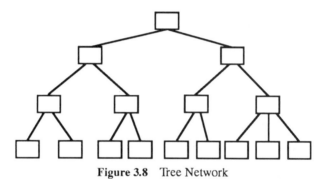

**Figure 3.8**   Tree Network

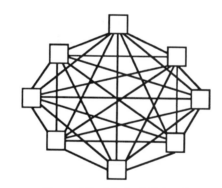

**Figure 3.9**   Meshed Network

   In point-to-point connections a complete (meshed) interconnection scheme is not very realistic, as indicated earlier. Even if the number of computers on the network is small, the fact that they are geographically distributed makes this unfeasible. Furthermore, most long-distance data communication is over telephone networks, and it is unreasonable to expect a complete connection among the available telephones. In North America there are approximately 20 million telephones, and providing linkages among any pair of telephones (i.e., complete connection of telephones) would require approximately $(20,000,000)^2$ links.[2] Therefore, a number of intermediate switches are used to facilitate the interconnection (Figure 3.10).

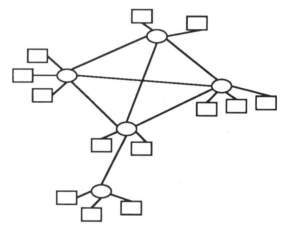

**Figure 3.10**   Switching

There are various possible forms of switching that can connect two sites. It is possible to establish a connection such that a dedicated channel exists between them during the period of transmission. This is called *circuit switching* and is commonly used in telephone connections. When a subscriber dials the number of another subscriber, a circuit is established between the two phones by means of various switches. The circuit is maintained during the period of conversation and is broken when one side hangs up.

Another form of switching used in computer communication is *packet switching*, where a message is broken up into packets and each packet transmitted individually. Packets for the same message may travel independently of each other and may, in fact, take different routes. Thus the software at the destination site should be able to sort them into their original order to reconstruct the message.

There is a relationship between packets and frames that we discussed previously. These terms refer to more or less the same thing, but at different layers of the communication protocol. Specifically, in the ISO/OSI nomenclature that we discuss in the next section, the term packet refers to a unit of transmission at the network layer while frame refers to a unit of transmission at the data link layer. From a practical perspective, the difference between the two have to do with their formats. A packet format differs from a frame format as depicted in Figure 3.4 in that the former does not have a trailer field (i.e., block error check) and the header information is different.

---

[2]The general form of the equation is $n(n-1)/2$, where $n$ is the number of nodes on the network.

The advantages of packet switching are many. First, packet-switching networks provide higher channel utilization since each channel is not dedicated to a pair of communicating equipment and can be shared by many. This is especially useful in computer communication due to its bursty nature. Typically, a terminal user will type in a command, wait for it to be executed and responded to, and then will spend some time thinking before typing in the next request. In such an environment, data transmission over the network is not continuous, but rather, bursty. The channel can be used by others when the user is waiting for an answer or is thinking. Another reason is that packetizing may permit the parallel transmission of data. There is usually no requirement that various packets belonging to the same message travel the same route through the network. In such a case, they may be sent in parallel via different routes to improve the total data transmission time.

## 3.3.2 ISO/OSI Architecture

Wide area networks commonly have to accommodate equipment that has been manufactured by different companies. This requires that the transmission media be able to handle the *heterogeneity* of equipment. There might be differences in equipment in terms of speed, word length, coding scheme used to represent information, or any other criteria. If such heterogeneous machines are to be interconnected and are to support transmission of data among them, some standardization is obviously necessary. This standardization for wide area networks is provided by the open systems interconnection architecture of the International Standards Organization (commonly referred to as the *ISO/OSI architecture*) [ISO, 1983].

The ISO/OSI architecture specifies that the network is to be built in a layered fashion. Between layers at a given node, *interfaces* that facilitate the passing of information between the layers of software and hardware need to be clearly defined. Between the corresponding layers at different sites, *protocols* are defined to specify how the two nodes, more specifically, the same layers at different nodes present messages to each other. The ISO/OSI architecture, whose structure is shown in Figure 3.11, consists of seven layers. Starting from the lowest layer, these are the physical layer, the data link layer, the network layer, the transport layer, the session layer, the presentation layer, and the application layer. The lowest three layers, the physical, data link, and network layers, are together known as the *communication subnet*. The communication subnet is fundamentally responsible for providing a reliable physical communication between two sites. In the remainder of this section we look at each layer in somewhat more detail. Our fundamental emphasis is on the layers that constitute the communication subnet since the distributed DBMS expects a reasonable degree of service from these layers.

The *physical layer* is concerned with transmitting raw bits of data over a communication channel between two switches. The only physical connection between the two sites is in this layer. This means that a message originating, let's say, in an application program that resides in the application layer at one site has to go downward in the layered architecture at that site until it gets to the physical layer. It is then trans-

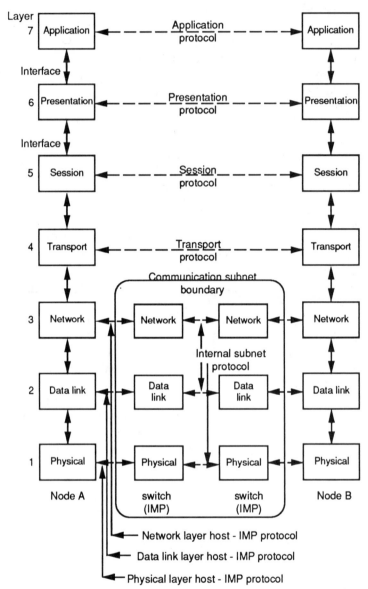

**Figure 3.11**   ISO/OSI Architecture (From: A.S. Tanenbaum, COMPUTER NETWORKS 2/E, ©1988, p. 15. Reprinted by permission of Prentice-Hall, Inc., Englewood Cliffs, NJ.)

mitted over the physical channel to the destination site, where it moves upward to the application to which it is addressed. As the original message moves downward, it is modified by adding headers and trailers, as well as redundant bits for error detection and correction. At the destination site, while it goes upward in the layered structure, the added bits and fields are stripped off so that what gets handed to the destination application is the original message sent by the source application.

The physical layer addresses physical problems such as the type of transmission medium to be used (i.e., coaxial, twisted wire, satellite, etc.), the channel operation mode (i.e., half-duplex versus full-duplex), the voltage levels for the 0 and 1 bits, the bit durations, the structure of the hardware connections (in other words, the interfaces), and finally, the type of hardware bit-error-handling mechanism to be employed (i.e., the type of parity checks, as well as cyclic redundancy checks or forward error recovery). Note that the data communication issues discussed in the preceding section are all concerns of the physical layer.

The *data link layer* consists of a set of protocols whose aim is to maintain error-free, reliable, efficient transmission between adjacent sites. One of the problems addressed at this layer is framing: in other words, how many bits of data will constitute each frame transmitted to the destination site. If the original message consists of more information than can be accommodated in one frame, it may be necessary to split it into multiple frames. Another problem is the error-handling mechanism, which at this level has more to do with software than with hardware. Protocols need to be developed to handle cases where messages might reach the destination with error. When an error is detected, the source can be asked to retransmit the message, or the error-correcting codes can be used to recover it. Furthermore, to provide reliable transmission, the protocols must deal with the problems of lost or duplicate messages. If messages get lost in the network, some means have to be provided to enable the retransmission of the message without intervention by the user. If this eventually fails, a notice needs to be given to the user to that effect. Similarly, if the source falsely believes that a message is not received at its destination, it might attempt to retransmit. In that case the message might be received at the destination more than once. The algorithms at the receiving end therefore have to be able to detect the duplicate message and eliminate it from the buffered messages that will eventually be handed over to the higher-level protocols. Finally, the data link layer is responsible for delivering packets sequentially to the higher layers if they are received out of sequence.

The *network layer* ensures the transparent transfer of data between transport entities. In other words, it establishes, maintains, and terminates the connections across the communications facility, so that the source site can communicate with the destination site as if no other layers were involved (i.e., the transparency of the communication subnet). The most important function of the network layer is routing, which is the function of controlling how the messages are sent from the source site to the destination site. The various alternative routing methods are as follows:

1. *Predetermined routing.* The path that the message will follow from each source to each destination is determined when the system is set up.

2. *Calculated routing.* The path to be followed is somehow calculated from the address in the header of the message.

3. *Static directory routing.* Each site determines the next node of transmission for each possible destination site.

4. *Dynamic directory routing.* The path that the message follows is determined dynamically as it moves from one site to the other.

5. *Adaptive routing.* The route is determined according to the current network conditions. The sites inform each other periodically how long it takes for a message to be transmitted in either direction and set up their routing tables accordingly. The route is not determined dynamically, as in dynamic directory routing, but the table is updated periodically.

In addition to routing, the network layer shares responsibility with data link layer in maintaining flow control. Flow control is the process by which the receiver prevents the sender from sending frames at a rate which is faster than the receiver can handle.

The *transport layer* of the ISO/OSI architecture is responsible for providing a reliable mechanism for the exchange of data between different sites. The transport layer is intended to add more reliability to the communication network when necessary. If the network layer is already reliable, not much is required from the transport layer.

The *session layer* provides a mechanism for controlling the dialogue between applications at the source and destination sites. In general, there are two fundamental ways of communicating. One method is called a *datagram*, where the source application simply sends a message to the destination application and there is no need for extensive two-way communication. The other method is called a *session*, where a virtual link is established between the applications at the source and destination sites, and an extensive dialogue goes on between the two applications. The session layer is responsible for maintaining this second mode of communication, which uses different types of dialogues, such as one-way, two-way alternate, or two-way simultaneous.

The *presentation layer* is concerned with the syntax of the data exchanged between application entities. This is the interface between the actual applications and the rest of the network. It consists of algorithms that resolve differences in format and data representation between the applications at the source and the destination.

Finally, the *application layer* is the layer where all user applications are developed. It provides a means by which user applications can access the OSI environment. It is at this layer that the distributed database manager resides.

The first three layers of the ISO/OSI architecture (i.e., physical, data link, and network) are defined precisely in terms of international standards. Attempts at defining the higher-level protocols continue.

## 3.4  LOCAL AREA NETWORKS

Local area networks (LANs) are typically packet communication networks that are limited in geographic scope. They provide high-bandwidth communication over inexpensive transmission media. The types of transmission media employed in local area networks are usually coaxial cables, twisted-wire pairs, or optical fibers. A comparison of local area and wide area networks reveals the following differences:

1. In wide area networks, the cost of communication is quite high, whereas in local area networks, it is relatively low. There are various reasons for this difference, an obvious one being that the transmission distance is considerably shorter in local area networks than in wide area networks.

2. Wide area networks usually have a limited bandwidth of about 50 kbps, whereas local area networks have a larger bandwidth, typically about 10 Mbps (but potentially much higher).

3. Owing to the distances that need to be traveled, long delays are involved in wide area data transmission. For example, via satellite, there is a minimum delay of half a second for data to be transmitted from the source to the destination. This is because the speed with which signals can be transmitted is limited to the speed of light, and the distances that need to be spanned are great (19,200 miles from an earth station to a satellite). In contrast, the delays in local area networks are very short.

4. To connect to wide area networks, large computers are required for switching. In local area networks, the interface consists of large-scale integrated (LSI) or very large-scale integrated (VSLI) circuits, which are very cheap, often with the entire interface on a single board.

5. The transmission in wide area networks is usually in analog form, so modulation is required for data transmission. In local area networks, the transmission is usually in digital baseband form and no modulation is necessary although (analog) broadband transmission is sometimes used. This is another reason for the simplicity of the interfaces in local area networks.

6. Owing to the heterogeneity of the transmission media, the computers, and the user community involved, as well as the low noise quality of the lines being used, elaborate protocols are required in wide area networks to guarantee reliable data transmission. In local area networks the lines are much cleaner, the heterogeneity among the computers that are connected is easier to manage, and a common transmission medium is used. Therefore, simpler protocols are generally sufficient.

7. Local area networks are owned and used by a single organization. However, wide area networks are rarely owned by their users. Thus, LAN users purchase a product while WAN users purchase a service.

LANs also provide additional opportunities, such as office automation applications, distributed process control applications, and central file servers, which could possibly decrease the cost of secondary storage on the system. Furthermore, local area networks are commonly broadcast type and therefore enjoy their associated advantages.

One of the problems that have to be addressed in broadcast networks is: Who can transmit? This problem of determining who can access the network at any given time is controlled by the link control mechanism. As we will see in the remainder of this section, different types of local area networks employ different link control mechanisms. In this section we also discuss the two common topologies used in local area networks: *ring* or *loop* networks and *bus* networks.

### 3.4.1 Ring Networks

In ring networks, the computers are connected to the transmission medium, which is in the form of a loop (Figure 3.12). Data transmission around the ring is usually unidirectional, with each station (actually the interface to which each station is connected) serving as an active repeater which receives a message, checks the address, copies the message if it is addressed to that station, and retransmits it.

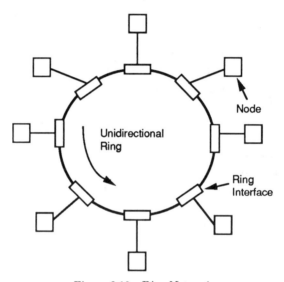

**Figure 3.12**    Ring Network

Networks that have a single ring-type transmission medium can be unreliable simply because breakage in the link at any point, or the failure of one of the stations, may disable the network. To provide more reliability, a double-loop topology may be employed [Wolf et al., 1979]. In such a network, the failure of one tap does not necessarily make the remaining portions of the network inaccessible since the damaged station can be bypassed by routing the transmission over the second ring (Figure 3.13).

An alternative mode of providing reliability is to use a central switch (Figure 3.14). The connections between the stations are made via a switching center. If a station fails, or if a link breakage occurs, that portion of the network can very easily be bypassed within the central switch. This architecture was developed at the IBM Zurich Laboratory [Bux et al., 1983] and is implemented in the IBM token ring LAN.

The most prominent advantage of ring-type LANs is that since the message eventually has to come back to the sender, there is no necessity for a separate acknowl-

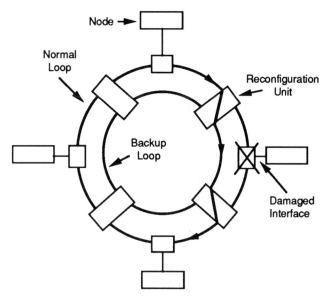

**Figure 3.13**   Double Loop Network

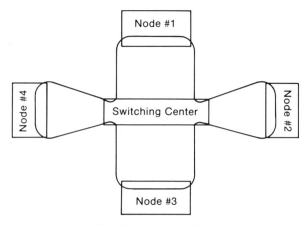

**Figure 3.14**   Ring Network with Switching Center

edgment message to be sent from the receiver to the sender as they can be piggybacked on the original message. The mere fact that the message is received by the sender in correct form signifies that it has also reached the intended receiver in correct form.

For ring networks, there are three alternative link control mechanisms: slotted, register insertion, and control token. In *slotted* ring control, a number of fixed-length message slots travel continuously around the ring (Figure 3.15). Each slot has an indicator which signals whether the slot is full or empty. A slot is full if there is a message in the data portion of the slot. If a node wants to transmit a message, it checks the indicators of the slots as they pass by. When it finds an empty slot, it places the message in the data portion of the slot and changes the indicator to full. Each site checks the header portion of each slot to see if there is a message directed to it. If so, it buffers the message and lets the message go around the network. When the slot reaches back to the site where it originated, its indicator is reset to empty.

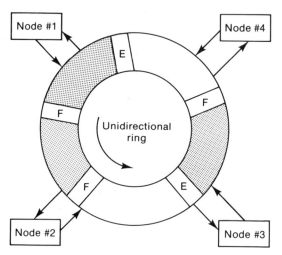

**Figure 3.15**   Slotted Ring Control. E and F indicate empty and full slots, respectively.

A fundamental disadvantage of the slotted ring control mechanism is that one has to cope with fixed-length slots and has to divide the message into more than one piece if it does not fit into a given message slot.

The second form of ring control is *register insertion*. Each site maintains two registers, one for keeping the incoming messages and one for placing new messages. Every message is read from the network into the site's incoming register and checked to see if it is addressed to that site. If it is, it is read, but if not, it is again placed on the network. When a site wants to transmit a new message, it places the message in its new message register (Figure 3.16a). This message in its message register is then inserted into the ring either when the ring is idle, or in between two incoming packets (Figure 3.16b). In other words, when a site reads an incoming message into its incoming packet register, it holds it there and places the outgoing message in its new packet register onto the ring, and then releases the incoming message back onto the ring. When the destination site receives a message, it can either remove it from the network, or, as in the slotted control mechanism, it can simply copy the message and let it circulate back to the sender [Martin and Chapman, 1989].

The third and probably the most popular type of ring control is the *control to-ken*. In the simplest type of control token networks, a token, which has one bit pattern to indicate that the network is free and a different bit pattern to indicate that it is in

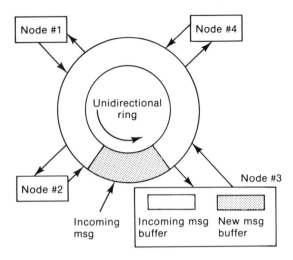

(a) Incoming message is buffered at node #3

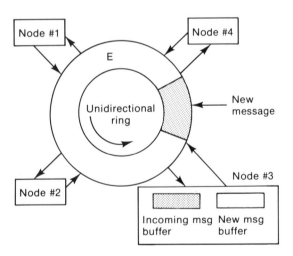

(b) Node #3 transmits new message

**Figure 3.16**   Register Insertion Control

use, is circulated around the network (Figure 3.17a). Any site wanting to transmit a message waits for the token. When the token arrives, the site checks the token's bit pattern to see if the network is free or in use. If it is free, the site changes the bit pattern to indicate that the network is in use and then places the message on the ring (Figure 3.17b). Again the message is circulated around the ring and eventually comes back to the sender, who then changes the bit pattern of the token to free. Obviously, circulating a single token around the network is going to reduce the efficiency of the network since only one message can be transmitted at any one time. Therefore, usually, a number of tokens are circulated around the ring. There is, however, a trade-off

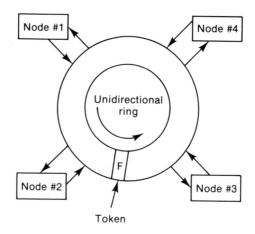

(a) Node #3 wants to transmit
(F: token free)

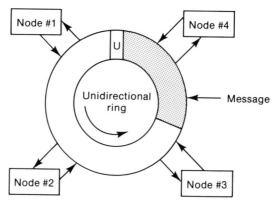

**Figure 3.17**   Token Ring Network

between using a single token and multiple tokens. In a single-token mechanism, entire network is devoted to the transmission of a single message; therefore, there is no reason to restrict the length of the messages. This is not the case in multiple-token schemes, where there is usually a need to limit the size of the messages.

### 3.4.2 Bus Networks

Another popular topology for local area networks is the bus, where a common channel used to transmit data is tapped by computers and terminals (Figure 3.18). In this type of network, the link control is performed in two fundamental ways. One scheme is called *carrier sense multiple access* (CSMA), and the other, *carrier sense multiple access with collision detection* (CSMA/CD). In addition to these two fundamental link control mechanisms, the bus can also be controlled by the use of a token. If this scheme is used, the bus is assumed to form a logical ring. In what follows, we concentrate on the CSMA and the CSMA/CD control mechanisms.

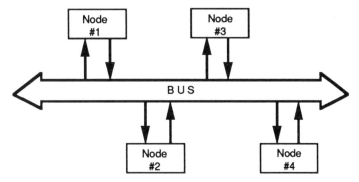

**Figure 3.18**    Bus Network

The CSMA bus control mechanism can best be described as a "listen before you transmit" scheme. The fundamental point is that each site listens continuously to what occurs on the bus. When a message is being transmitted, the site checks the header of the message to see if that message is addressed to it, and takes the appropriate action. If it wants to transmit, it waits until it detects no more activity on the bus and then places its message on the network. There are a number of variations of this basic scheme. One version, *basic CSMA*, or *one-persistent CSMA*, transmits if the channel is idle; if it is busy, it waits until it finds the bus free. A second version, *nonpersistent CSMA*, transmits if the channel is idle; however, if the channel is busy, it waits a random amount of time before retrying. A third version, *t-persistent CSMA*, uses fixed-size packets and time slots and synchronizes packet transmission with time slots. If a site wants to transmit a message and the channel is idle, it will transmit with a predetermined probability $t$ and will defer to the next time slot with probability $1 - t$.

The CSMA/CD bus control mechanism, on the other hand, can best be described as a "listen while you transmit" scheme. The *basic CSMA/CD* operates in the following fashion. The sites function as in the CSMA scheme, except that they keep listening to the bus even after they transmit their message. The purpose of listening during transmission is to detect if collisions occur. There is a collision when two sites transmit messages concurrently (a site starts transmission while another is transmitting). In such a case, and when the collision is detected, the sites abort the transmission, wait a random amount of time, and then retransmit the message. The basic CSMA/CD scheme is used in the Ethernet local area network.

There are other versions of the CSMA/CD mechanism. One version uses dynamic priorities and is called *CSMA/CD-DP*. It assigns a unique priority to each site and operates in the basic CSMA/CD mode when the network load is light. However, when a collision occurs, it waits $n$ time slots, where $n$ is its own priority at that moment. After it transmits its message correctly, the priorities are recycled in order to be fair to all the sites on the network. Another version, the *priority CSMA (p-CSMA)* scheme, uses two priority levels which are not assigned to sites but rather, to workloads. The higher priority is given to interactive data, and lower priority to file transfer. Again, it operates in the basic CSMA/CD mode when the network load is light, but when a collision occurs, the transmission with the higher priority is handled first. A third variation of the scheme is *CSMA/CD with deterministic contention resolution (CSMA/CD-DCR)*. This scheme also operates as the basic CSMA/CD when the network load is light. However, there is some notion of left-to-right ordering among the sites on the network. When a collision is detected, the system enters what is called a resolution phase. In this phase, the nodes transmit from left to right, and this transmission takes place sequentially until the end of the resolution phase. The fundamental idea is to give a chance to every site to transmit its message while eliminating the high load that caused the collision in the first place.

### 3.4.3 Comparison of Ring and Bus LANs

Based on the discussions of the two LAN technologies in previous sections, it is possible to draw some comparative solutions. Note that, unless otherwise indicated, our comments on bus networks are based on CSMA/CD buses.

1. It is possible to bound the message transmission delay in ring networks. However, due to the occurrences of collisions and retransmissions, delays are unbounded in CSMA/CD bus networks. In token buses, on the other hand, delays can be bounded.

2. On the other hand, the average delay in ring networks is higher than in bus networks. The reason for this is that even though the possibility of collision exists in bus LANs, in actual use the percentage of collisions is not high.

3. In ring networks, there is an implicit priority among the sites, depending on where they are connected to the ring. In bus LANs, each site has the same priority.

4. Since there are no collisions in ring LANs, they operate with regulated decentralized control. However, in bus LANs, there is no regulation; they operate with unregulated decentralized control.

5. The sites in the ring networks are active, whereas they are passive in bus networks. This means that the failure of a site is more serious in ring networks than in bus networks, thus implying slightly lower reliability for ring networks.

### 3.4.4  LAN Standards

Development of standards for local area networks has proved to be quite difficult. With the invention of CSMA/CD link control mechanisms for bus networks, a number of companies announced their support for such an approach. More important, Digital, Intel, and Xerox announced their joint efforts to manufacture and market products supporting this approach. On the other hand, IBM announced that it would support a token-passing ring network and Burroughs provided a token bus network. The standardization efforts therefore had to take into account all of these approaches. Today there are products that support each of these local area network versions.

The standardization in this area is spearheaded by the Institute of Electrical and Electronics Engineers (IEEE), specifically their Committee No. 802. This committee has established a standard that has two or three layers. The number of layers depends somewhat on how each layer is viewed. The fundamental requirements that were specified for this standard, known as the IEEE 802 Standard, are as follows. LANs are designed for commercial and light industrial applications, and to support reasonable reliability. The networks can transmit up to 2 km at a data rate of 1 to 10 Mbps.[3] These specifications indicate that networks developed according to the standard are not to be used in heavy industrial applications for example, in real-time control. The IEEE 802 standard requires that the protocols allow peer-to-peer communication. The latter specification eliminates star-type networks where a central node monitors and controls access to the transmission channel. The three layers of the IEEE 802 local area network standard are the physical layer, the medium access control layer, and the logical link control layer. Their structure and their relationship to the ISO standard appear in Figure 3.19.

The physical layer of the local area network standard handles the same sort of functions as the physical layer of the ISO standard, described earlier. The medium access control layer manages the communication over the link. It therefore performs part of the functions of the data link layer in ISO networks. Some of the other functions of the ISO data link layer are performed by the third layer of the IEEE standard, the logical link control layer. In addition to assembling data into frames upon transmission and disassembling frames upon receipt, the logical link control layer provides one or more service access points to user-level applications.

To enable it to cover a variety of the products on the market, the 802 local area network standard is actually a number of standards rather than a single one. As shown

---

[3]However, the new version of the IBM token ring operates at 16 Mbps and discussions are under way to include this within the standard.

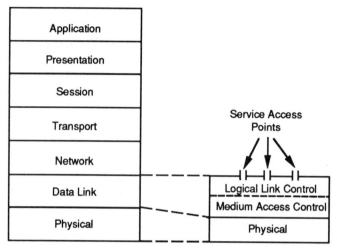

**Figure 3.19**   ISO/OSI–IEEE 802 Relationship (From: LOCAL AREA & MULTIPLE AC-CESS NETWORKS, by William Stallings, edited by Raymond L. Pickholtz. Copyright ©1986 by Computer Science Press. Reprinted by permission of W.H. Freeman and Company.)

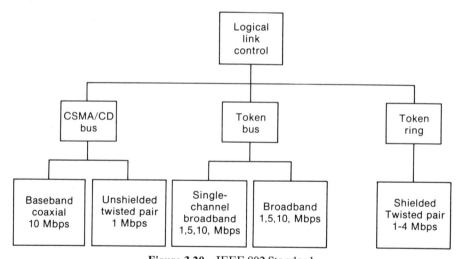

**Figure 3.20**   IEEE 802 Standard

in Figure 3.20 [Stallings, 1988], at the medium access control level, it supports three mechanisms: the CSMA/CD mechanism, token ring, and token access mechanism for bus networks. Provision has also been made to accommodate higher-speed networks in the future. Note that there are other standardization efforts in addition to those by IEEE. For example, the U.S. Department of Defense has released the standard MIL-STD-1533 for military applications, and General Motors has defined the Manufacturing and Automation Protocol (MAP) standard for LANs in integrated manufacturing control and the Boeing Company developed the Technical and Office Protocols (TOP) standard for office automation. Both MAP and TOP are based on the IEEE 802 standard specifications and build on top of them.

## 3.5  BIBLIOGRAPHIC NOTES

Details on data communication issues can be found in many books such as [Sherman, 1985], [Stallings, 1988], and [Halsall, 1988]. An excellent discussion of computer networks is presented in [Tanenbaum, 1987a]. Local networking issues are discussed in detail in [Stallings, 1984].

As of this writing, the IEEE 802 Standard is still in draft form, awaiting approval of the necessary agencies. The draft protocol is described in detail in the four volumes [IEEE, 1985a], [IEEE, 1985b], [IEEE, 1985c], and [IEEE, 1985d].

# 4

# Distributed DBMS Architecture

The architecture of a system defines its structure. This means that the components of the system are identified, the function of each component is specified, and the interrelationships and interactions among these components are defined. This general framework also holds true for computer systems in general and software systems in particular. The specification of the architecture of a software system requires identification of the various modules, with their interfaces and interrelationships, in terms of the data and control flow through the system. From a software engineering perspective, the task of developing individual modules is called *programming-in-the-small*, whereas the task of integrating them into a complete system is referred to as *programming-in-the-large*.

Since we are treating distributed DBMSs as large-scale software systems, we can define their architecture in a similar manner. In this chapter we develop a "reference" architecture for a distributed DBMS. It is an "idealized" view of the system in that many of the commercially available systems may deviate from it; however, it will serve as a reasonable framework within which the issues related to distributed DBMS can be discussed. A reference architecture is commonly created by standards developers since it clearly defines the interfaces that need to be standardized. For example, the ISO/OSI model discussed in Chapter 3 is a reference architecture for wide area computer networks.

We started discussing the architectural features of relational DBMSs in Chapter 2. In this chapter we extend the discussion to nonrelational systems by studying generic architectures. We start by looking at various transparency issues that constitute the ultimate goals of centralized and distributed DBMSs (Section 4.1). These issues are important from an architectural point of view, because the structure of a system should match the level of transparency one wants to provide. We then discuss the DBMS standardization efforts (Section 4.2) and present a well-known reference architecture for centralized DBMSs. This is followed (Section 4.3) by a study of the reference architecture for distributed DBMSs that is used in the remainder of this book. Finally, in Section 4.4, global directory issues are dealt with.

## 4.1 TRANSPARENCIES IN A DISTRIBUTED DBMS

Transparency in a distributed DBMS refers to separation of the higher-level semantics of a system from lower-level implementation issues. In other words, a transparent system "hides" the implementation details from users. The advantage of a fully transparent DBMS is the high level of support that it provides for the development of complex applications. It is obvious that we would like to make all DBMSs (centralized or distributed) fully transparent. In fact, in Chapter 1 we have alluded to this under the topic of data independence, which is one form of transparency. In the remainder of this section we consider the various forms of transparency that a designer aims to provide within centralized or distributed DBMS.

### 4.1.1 Data Independence

Data independence is a fundamental form of transparency that we look for within a DBMS. It is also the only type that is important within the context of a centralized DBMS. To reiterate the definition given in Chapter 1, data independence refers to the immunity of user applications to changes in the definition and organization of data, and vice versa.

As we will see in Section 4.2, data definition can occur at two levels. At one level the logical structure of the data is specified, and at the other level the physical structure of the data is defined. The former is commonly known as the *schema definition*, whereas the latter is referred to as the *physical data description*. We can therefore talk about two types of data independence: logical data independence and physical data independence. *Logical data independence* refers to the immunity of user applications to changes in the logical structure of the database. In general, if a user application operates on a subset of the attributes of a relation, it should not be affected later when new attributes are added to the same relation. For example, let us consider the engineer relation discussed in Chapter 2. If a user application deals with only the address fields of this relation (it might be a simple mailing program), the later additions to the relation of say, skill, would not and should not affect the mailing application.

*Physical data independence* deals with hiding the details of the storage structure from user applications. When a user application is written, it should not be concerned with the details of physical data organization. The data might be organized on different disk types, parts of it might be organized differently (e.g., random versus indexed-sequential access) or might even be distributed across different storage hierarchies (e.g., disk storage and tape storage). The application should not be involved with these issues since, conceptually, there is no difference in the operations carried out against the data. Therefore, the user application should not need to be modified when data organizational changes occur with respect to these issues. Nevertheless, it is common knowledge that these changes may be necessary for performance considerations.

Of course, as indicated in Chapter 1, data independence is more of a goal than a standard feature commonly provided by most of today's DBMSs. Some commercial products provide better data independence than others. Specifically, most of the microcomputer DBMSs do not provide high levels of data independence. Adding a new attribute to a relation (i.e., logical data independence) very often requires unloading the database, changing the relation definition, and then reloading the database.

### 4.1.2  Network Transparency

In centralized database systems, the only available resource that needs to be shielded from the user is the data (i.e., the storage system). In a distributed database management environment, however, there is a second resource that needs to be managed in much the same manner: the network. Preferably, the user should be protected from the operational details of the network. Furthermore, it is desirable to hide even the existence of the network, if possible. Then there would be no difference between database applications that would run on a centralized database and those that would run on a distributed database. This type of transparency is referred to as *network transparency* or *distribution transparency*.

One can consider network transparency from the viewpoint of either the services provided or the data. From the former perspective, it is desirable to have uniform means by which services are accessed. To give an example, let us talk for the moment not at the database level but at the operating system level in a network environment. If we want to copy a file, the command needed should be the same whether the file is being copied within one machine or across two machines connected by the network. Unfortunately, however, most commercially available operating systems that run on networks do not provide this transparency. For example, the UNIX[1] command for copying in one machine is

```
cp <source file> <target file>
```

whereas the same command, if the source and the target files are on different machines, takes the form

```
rcp <machine_name:source file> <machine_name:target file>
```

Note how it is now necessary to name the machine on which the file resides and to use a different operating system command to perform the copy function. If

---

[1]UNIX is a trademark of AT&T Bell Laboratories.

the same discussion is carried over to the database level, we would see that different user interfaces (i.e., query languages and data manipulation languages) need to be designed for both centralized and distributed database environments. Clearly, this is not very desirable.

The example above demonstrates two things: location transparency and naming transparency (or the lack of these). *Location transparency* refers to the fact that the command used is independent of both the location of the data and the system on which an operation is carried out. *Naming transparency* means that a unique name is provided for each object in the database. It is obvious that in a system such as the one described above, the task of providing unique names for different objects falls on the user rather than the system. The way the system handles naming transparency is by requiring the user to embed the location name (or an identifier) as part of the object name.

It is unfortunate that some distributed database systems (R*, for example [Williams et al., 1982]) do indeed embed the location names within the name of each database object. Furthermore, they require the user to specify the full name for access to the object. Obviously, it is possible to set up aliases for these long names if the operating system provides such a facility. However, user-defined aliases are not real solutions to the problem in as much as they are attempts to avoid addressing them within the distributed DBMS. The system, not the user, should be responsible for assigning unique names to objects and for translating user-known names to these unique internal object names.

Besides these semantic considerations, there is also a very pragmatic problem associated with embedding location names within object names. Such an approach makes it very difficult to move objects across machines for performance optimization or other purposes. Every such move will require users to change their access names for the affected objects, which is clearly undesirable.

### 4.1.3  Replication Transparency

The issue of replicating data within a distributed database is discussed in quite some detail in Chapter 5. At this point, let us just mention that for performance, reliability, and availability reasons, it is usually desirable to be able to distribute data in a replicated fashion across the machines on a network. Such replication helps performance since diverse and conflicting user requirements can be more easily accommodated. For example, data that is commonly accessed by one user can be placed on that user's local machine as well as on the machine of another user with the same access requirements. This increases the locality of reference. Furthermore, if one of the machines fail, a copy of the data is still available on another machine on the network. Of course, this is a very simpleminded description of the situation. In fact, the decision as to whether to replicate or not, and how many copies of any database object to have, depends to a considerable degree on user applications. Note that replication causes problems in updating databases. Therefore, if the user applications are predominantly update oriented, it may not be a good idea to have too many copies of the data. As this discussion is the subject matter of Chapter 5, we will not dwell further here on the pros and cons of replication.

Assuming that data is replicated, the issue related to transparency that needs to be addressed is whether the users should be aware of the existence of copies or whether the system should handle the management of copies and the user should act as if there is a single copy of the data (note that we are not referring to the placement of copies, only their existence). From a user's perspective the answer is obvious. It is preferable not to be involved with handling copies and having to specify the fact that a certain action can and/or should be taken on multiple copies. From a systems point of view, however, the answer is not that simple. As we will see in Chapter 11, when the responsibility of specifying that an action needs to be executed on multiple copies is delegated to the user, it makes transaction management simpler for distributed DBMSs. On the other hand, doing so inevitably results in the loss of some flexibility. It is not the system that decides whether or not to have copies and how many copies to have, but the user application. Any change in these decisions because of various considerations definitely affects the user application and therefore reduces data independence considerably. Given these considerations, it is desirable that replication transparency be provided as a standard feature of DBMSs. Remember that replication transparency refers only to the existence of replicas, not to their actual location. Note also that distributing these replicas across the network in a transparent manner is the domain of network transparency.

### 4.1.4 Fragmentation Transparency

The final form of transparency that needs to be addressed within the context of a distributed database system is that of fragmentation transparency. In Chapter 5 we discuss and justify the fact that it is commonly desirable to divide each database relation into smaller fragments and treat each fragment as a separate database object (i.e., another relation). This is commonly done for reasons of performance, availability, and reliability. Furthermore, fragmentation can reduce the negative effects of replication. Each replica is not the full relation but only a subset of it; thus less space is required and fewer data items need be managed.

When database objects are fragmented, we have to deal with the problem of handling user queries that were specified on entire relations but now have to be performed on subrelations. In other words, the issue is one of finding a query processing strategy based on the fragments rather than the relations, even though the queries are specified on the latter. Typically, this requires a translation from what is called a *global query* to several *fragment queries*. Since the fundamental issue of dealing with fragmentation transparency is one of query processing, we defer the discussion of techniques by which this translation can be performed until Chapter 8.

### 4.1.5 Who Should Provide Transparency?

In previous sections we discussed various possible forms of transparency within a distributed computing environment. Obviously, to provide easy and efficient access by novice users to the services of the DBMS, one would want to have full transparency, involving all the various types that we discussed. Nevertheless, the level of transparency is inevitably a compromise between ease of use and the difficulty and overhead cost of providing high levels of transparency.

What has not yet been discussed is who is responsible for providing these services. It is possible to identify three distinct layers at which the services of transparency can be provided. It is quite common to treat these as mutually exclusive means of providing the service, although it is more appropriate to view them as complementary.

We could leave the responsibility of providing transparent access to data resources to the access layer. The transparency features can be built into the user language, which then translates the requested services into required operations. In other words, the compiler or the interpreter takes over the task and no transparent service is provided to the implementer of the compiler or the interpreter.

The second layer at which transparency can be provided is the operating system level. State-of-the-art operating systems provide some level of transparency to system users. For example, the device drivers within the operating system handle the minute details of getting each piece of peripheral equipment to do what is requested. The typical computer user, or even an application programmer, does not normally write device drivers to interact with individual peripheral equipment; that operation is transparent to the user.

Providing transparent access to resources at the operating system level can obviously be extended to the distributed environment, where the management of the network resource is taken over by the distributed operating system. This is a good level at which to provide network transparency if it can be accomplished. The unfortunate aspect is that not all commercially available distributed operating systems provide a reasonable level of transparency in network management.

The third layer at which transparency can be supported is within the DBMS. In such a case one might talk about different modes of operation. In database machines (see Chapter 15; see also [Ozkarahan, 1986]), for example, the DBMS generally does not expect any transparent service from the operating system; in fact, there is no identifiable operating system other than a monitor and some device drivers. The DBMS acts as the integrated operating and database management system. A more typical environment is the development of a DBMS on a general-purpose computer running some operating systems. In this type of environment, the transparency and support for database functions provided to the DBMS designers is minimal and typically limited to very fundamental operations for performing certain tasks. It is the responsibility of the DBMS to make all the necessary translations from the operating system to the higher-level user interface. This mode of operation is the most common method today. There are, however, various problems associated with leaving the task of providing full transparency to the DBMS. These have to do with the interaction of the operating system with the distributed DBMS and are the topics of Chapter 13.

It is therefore quite important to realize that reasonable levels of transparency depend on different components within the data management environment. Network transparency can easily be handled by the distributed operating system as part of its responsibilities for providing replication and fragmentation transparencies (especially those aspects dealing with transaction management and recovery). The DBMS should be responsible for providing a high level of data independence together with replication and fragmentation transparencies. Finally, the user interface can support a higher level of transparency not only in terms of a uniform access method to the data resources from within a language, but also in terms of structure constructs that permit the user to deal with objects in his or her environment rather than focusing on the details of database description. Specifically, it should be noted that the interface to a distributed DBMS does not need to be a programming language but can be a graphical user interface, a natural language interface, and even a voice system.

A hierarchy of these transparencies is shown in Figure 4.1. It is not always easy to delineate clearly the levels of transparency, but such a figure serves an important instructional purpose even if it is not fully correct. To complete the picture we have added a "language transparency" layer, although it is not discussed in this chapter. With this generic layer, users have high-level access to the data (e.g., fourth-generation languages, graphical user interfaces, natural language access, etc.).

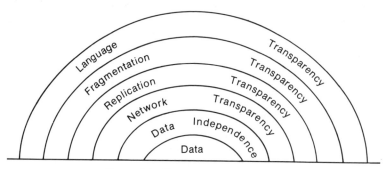

**Figure 4.1**  Layers of Transparency

## 4.2  DBMS STANDARDIZATION

In this section we discuss the standardization efforts related to DBMSs because of the close relationship between the architecture of a system and the reference model of that system, which is developed as a precursor to any standardization activity. For all practical purposes, the reference model can be thought of as an idealized architectural model of the system. It is defined as "a conceptual framework whose purpose is to divide standardization work into manageable pieces, and to show at a general level how these pieces are related with each other" [DAFTG, 1986]. Even though there is some controversy as to the desirability of standardization of DBMSs, it is a useful activity to the extent that it can establish uniform interfaces to the users and to other higher-level software developers. A reference model (and therefore a system architecture) can be described according to three different approaches [Kangassalo, 1983]:

1. Based on *components*. The components of the system are defined together with the interrelationships between components. Thus a DBMS consists of a number of components, each of which provides some functionality. Their orderly and well-defined interaction provides total system functionality. This is a desirable approach if the ultimate objective is to design and implement the system under consideration. On the other hand, it is difficult to determine the functionality of a system by examining its components. The DBMS standard proposals prepared by the Computer Corporation of America for the National Bureau of Standards ([CCA, 1980] and [CCA, 1982]) fall within this category.

2. Based on *functions*. The different classes of users are identified and the functions that the system will perform for each class are defined. The system specifications within this category typically specify a hierarchical structure for user classes. This results in a hierarchical system architecture with well-defined interfaces between the functionalities of different layers. The ISO/OSI architecture discussed in Chapter 3 [ISO, 1983] fall in this category. The advantage of the functional approach is the clarity with which the objectives of the system are specified. However, it gives very little insight into how these objectives will be attained or the level of complexity of the system.

3. Based on *data*. The different types of data are identified, and an architectural framework is specified which defines the functional units that will realize or use data according to these different views. Since data is the central resource that a DBMS manages, this approach is claimed to be the preferable choice for standardization activities [DAFTG, 1986]. The advantage of the data approach is the central importance it associates with the data resource. This is significant from the DBMS viewpoint since the fundamental resource that a DBMS manages is data. On the other hand, it is impossible to specify an architectural model fully unless the functional modules are also described. The ANSI/SPARC architecture [Tsichritzis and Klug, 1978] discussed in the next section belongs in this category.

Even though three distinct approaches are identified, one should never lose sight of the interplay among them. As indicated in a report of the Database Architecture Framework Task Group of ANSI [DAFTG, 1986], all three approaches need to be used together to define an architectural model, with each point of view serving to focus our attention on different aspects of an architectural model.

A more important issue is the orthogonality of the foregoing classification schemes and the DBMS objectives (e.g., functionality, performance, etc.). Regardless of how we choose to view a DBMS, these objectives have to be taken into account. For example, in the functional approach, the objectives have to be addressed within each functional unit (e.g., query processor, transaction manager, etc.). In the remainder of this section we concentrate on a reference architecture that has generated considerable interest and is the basis of our reference model, described in Section 4.3.

### 4.2.1 ANSI/SPARC Architecture

Two important events in the late 1960s and early 1970s influenced the standardization activities in database management. The Database Task Group (DBTG) of the CO-DASYL Systems Committee issued two reports, one providing a survey of DBMSs [CODASYL, 1969], and the second describing the features of a network DBMS [CO-DASYL, 1971]. The second event is the publication of Codd's initial papers on the relational data model ([Codd, 1970] and [Codd, 1972]). The existence of two alternative data models competing for dominance created considerable discussion not only of the merits of each, but also of the features of the next generation DBMSs.

In late 1972, the Computer and Information Processing Committee (X3) of the American National Standards Institute (ANSI) established a Study Group on Database Management Systems under the auspices of its Standards Planning and Requirements Committee (SPARC). The mission of the study group was to study the *feasibility* of setting up standards in this area, as well as determining which aspects should be standardized if it was feasible. The study group issued its interim report in 1975 [SPARC, 1975], and its final report in 1977 [Tsichritzis and Klug, 1978]. The architectural framework proposed in these reports came to be known as the "ANSI/SPARC architecture," its full title being "ANSI/X3/SPARC DBMS Framework." The study group proposed that the interfaces be standardized, and defined an architectural framework that contained 43 interfaces, 14 of which would deal with the physical storage subsystem of the computer and therefore not be considered essential parts of the DBMS architecture.

With respect to our earlier discussion on alternative approaches to standardization, the ANSI/SPARC architecture is claimed to be based on the data organization. It recognizes three views of data: the *external view*, which is that of the user, who might be a programmer; the *internal view*, that of the system or machine; and the *conceptual view*, that of the enterprise. For each of these views, an appropriate schema definition is required. Figure 4.2 depicts the ANSI/SPARC architecture from the data organization perspective.

At the lowest level of the architecture is the internal view, which deals with the physical definition and organization of data. The location of data on different storage devices and the access mechanisms used to reach and manipulate data are the issues dealt with at this level. At the other extreme is the external view, which is concerned with how users view the database. An individual user's view represents the portion of the database that will be accessed by that user as well as the relationships that the user would like to see among the data. A view can be shared among a number of users, with the collection of user views making up the external schema. In between these two extremes is the conceptual schema, which is an abstract definition of the database. It is the "real world" view of the enterprise being modeled in the database [Yormark, 1977]. As such, it is supposed to represent the data and the relationships among data without considering the requirements of individual applications or the restrictions of the physical storage media. In reality, however, it is not possible to ignore these requirements completely, due to performance reasons. The transformation between

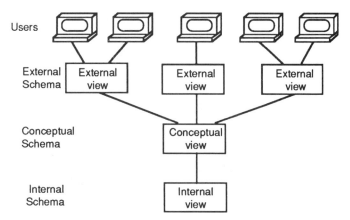

**Figure 4.2**   The ANSI/SPARC Architecture

these three levels is accomplished by mappings that specify how a definition at one level can be obtained from a definition at another level.

**Example 4.1**

Let us consider the engineering database example we have been using and indicate how it can be described using a fictitious DBMS that conforms to the ANSI/SPARC architecture. Remember that we have four relations: E, S, J, and G. The conceptual schema should describe each relation with respect to its attributes and its key. The description might look like the following:[2]

```
RELATION EMPLOYEE [
   KEY =  {EMPLOYEE_NUMBER}
   ATTRIBUTES = {
         EMPLOYEE_NUMBER  : CHARACTER(9)
         EMPLOYEE_NAME    : CHARACTER(15)
         TITLE            : CHARACTER(10)
         }
   ]
RELATION TITLE_SALARY [
   KEY = {TITLE}
   ATTRIBUTES = {
         TITLE            : CHARACTER(10)
         SALARY           : NUMERIC(6)
         }
   ]
RELATION PROJECT [
   KEY = {PROJECT_NUMBER}
   ATTRIBUTES = {
```

---

[2]Two points to note here. First, we are using the relational representation for the conceptual schema, but by no means do we suggest that the relational model is the only suitable formalism at the conceptual level. Second, the syntax of the description does not conform to any programming language.

```
            PROJECT_NUMBER    : CHARACTER(7)
            PROJECT_NAME      : CHARACTER(20)
            BUDGET            : NUMERIC(7)
            }
     ]
RELATION ASSIGNMENT [
     KEY = {EMPLOYEE_NUMBER,PROJECT_NUMBER}
     ATTRIBUTES = {
            EMPLOYEE_NUMBER   : CHARACTER(9)
            PROJECT_NUMBER    : CHARACTER(7)
            RESPONSIBILITY    : CHARACTER(10)
            DURATION          : NUMERIC(3)
            }
     ]
```

We used more descriptive names for the relations and the attributes. This is not the essential issue; a more important aspect is that these names can be different at all three levels, as we demonstrate below.

At the internal level, the storage details of these relations are described. Let us assume that the EMPLOYEE relation is stored in an indexed file, where the index is defined on the key attribute (i.e., the EMPLOYEE_NUMBER) called EMINX.[3] Let us also assume that we associate a HEADER field which might contain flags (delete, update, etc.) and other control information. Then the internal schema definition of the relation may be as follows:

```
INTERNAL_REL EMP [
     INDEX ON E# CALL EMINX
     FIELD = {
            E#          : BYTE(9)
            E:NAME      : BYTE(15)
            TIT         : BYTE(10)
            }
     ]
```

We have used similar syntaxes for both the conceptual and the internal descriptions. This is done for convenience only and does not imply the true nature of languages for these functions.

Finally, let us consider the external views, which we will describe using SQL notation. We consider two applications: one that calculates the payroll payments for engineers, and a second that produces a report on the budget of each project.[4] Notice that for the first application, we need attributes from both the EMPLOYEE and the TITLE_SALARY relations. In other words, the view consists of a join, which can be defined as

---

[3]To keep the presentation simple, we will not concern ourselves with the details of indexing. Consider EMINX to be a primary index.

[4]For simplicity, we will ignore semantic data control aspects of external view generation. These issues are discussed in Chapter 6

```
CREATE    VIEW      PAYROLL (ENO, ENAME, SAL)
AS        SELECT    EMPLOYEE.EMPLOYEE_NUMBER,
                    EMPLOYEE.EMPLOYEE_NAME,
                    TITLE_SALARY.SALARY
          FROM      EMPLOYEE, TITLE_SALARY
          WHERE     EMPLOYEE.TITLE=TITLE_SALARY.TITLE
```

The second application is simply a projection of the PROJECT relation, which can be specified as

```
CREATE    VIEW      BUDGET(PNAME, BUD)
AS        SELECT    PROJECT_NAME, BUDGET
          FROM      PROJECT
```

The investigation of the ANSI/SPARC architecture with respect to its functions results in a considerably more complicated view, as depicted in Figure 4.3.[5] The square boxes represent processing functions, whereas the hexagons are administrative roles. The arrows indicate data, command, program, and description flow, whereas the "I"-shaped bars on them represent interfaces.

The major component that permits mapping between different data organizational views is the data dictionary/directory (depicted as a triangle), which is a meta-database. It should at least contain schema and mapping definitions. It may also contain usage statistics, access control information, and the like. It is clearly seen that the data dictionary/directory serves as the central component in both processing different schemas and in providing mappings among them.

We also see in Figure 4.3 a number of administrator roles, which might help to define a functional interpretation of the ANSI/SPARC architecture. The three roles are the database administrator, the enterprise administrator, and the application administrator. The database administrator is responsible for defining the internal schema definition. The enterprise administrator's role is to prepare the conceptual schema definition. The person in this role is the focal point of the use of information within an enterprise. Finally, the application administrator is responsible for preparing the external schema for applications. Note that these are roles that might be fulfilled by one particular person or by several people. Hopefully, the system will provide sufficient support for these roles.

In addition to these three classes of administrative user defined by the roles, there are two more, the application programmer and the system programmer. Two more user classes can be defined, namely casual users and novice end users. Casual users occasionally access the database to retrieve and possibly to update information. Such users are aided by the definition of external schemas and by an easy-to-use query language. Novice users typically have no knowledge of databases and access information by means of predefined menus and transactions (e.g., banking machines).

---

[5]This is only a part of the system schematic that is provided in [Tsichritzis and Klug, 1978].

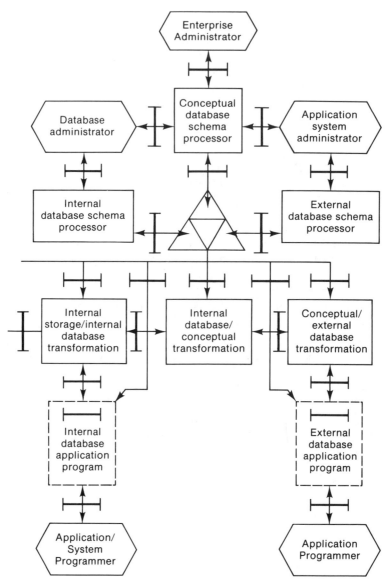

**Figure 4.3** Partial Schematic of the ANSI/SPARC Architectural Model (Adapted from [Tsichritzis and Klug, 1978])

## 4.3  ARCHITECTURAL MODELS FOR DISTRIBUTED DBMSs

The intuitive and logical nature of the ANSI/SPARC architecture has prompted many researchers to investigate ways of extending it to the distributed environment. The proposals range from simple extensions, such as that described by [Mohan and Yeh, 1978], to very complicated ones, such as Shreiber's model [Schreiber, 1977], and anything in between [Adiba et al., 1978]. In this book we use a simple extension of the ANSI/SPARC architecture.

Before discussing the specific architecture, however, we need to discuss the possible ways in which multiple databases may be put together for sharing by multiple DBMSs. We use a classification (Figure 4.4) that organizes the systems as characterized with respect to (1) the autonomy of local systems, (2) their distribution, and (3) their heterogeneity.

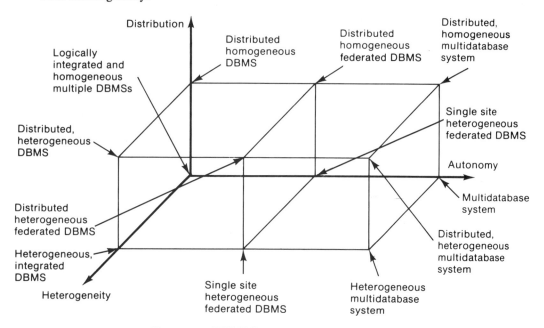

**Figure 4.4**   DBMS Implementation Alternatives

*Autonomy* refers to the distribution of control, not of data. It indicates the degree to which individual DBMSs can operate independently. Autonomy is a function of a number of factors such as whether the component systems exchange information, whether they can independently execute transactions, and whether one is allowed to modify them. Requirements of an autonomous system have been specified in a variety of ways. For example, [Gligor and Popescu-Zeletin, 1986] lists these requirements as follows:

1. The local operations of the individual DBMSs are not affected by their participation in the multidatabase system.

2. The manner in which the individual DBMSs process queries and optimize them should not be affected by the execution of global queries that access multiple databases.

3. System consistency or operation should not be compromised when individual DBMSs join or leave the multidatabase confederation.

On the other hand, [Du and Elmagarmid, 1989] specifies the dimensions of autonomy as:

1. Design autonomy: Individual DBMSs are free to use the data models and transaction management techniques that they prefer.

2. Communication autonomy: Each of the individual DBMSs is free to make its own decision as to what type of information it wants to provide to the other DBMSs or to the software that controls their global execution.

3. Execution autonomy: Each DBMS can execute the transactions that are submitted to it in any way that it wants to.

In the taxonomy that we consider in the book, we will use a classification that covers the important aspects of these features. One alternative is *tight integration*, where a single-image of the entire database is available to any user who wants to share the information, which may reside in multiple databases. From the users' perspective, the data is logically centralized in one database. In these tightly integrated systems, the data managers are implemented so that one of them is in control of the processing of each user request even if that request is serviced by more than one data manager. The data managers do not typically operate as independent DBMSs even though they usually have the funcationality to do so.

Next we identify *semiautonomous* systems that consist of DBMSs that can (and usually do) operate independently, but have decided to participate in a federation to make their local data sharable. Each of these DBMSs determine what parts of their own database they will make accessible to users of other DBMSs. They are not fully autonomous systems because they need to be modified to enable them to exchange information with one another.

The last alternative that we consider is *total isolation*, where the individual systems are stand-alone DBMSs, which know neither of the existence of other DBMSs nor how to communicate with them. In such systems, the processing of user transactions that access multiple databases is especially difficult since there is no global control over the execution of individual DBMSs.

It is important to note at this point that the three alternatives that we consider for autonomous systems are not the only possibilities. We simply highlight the three most popular ones.

Whereas autonomy refers to the distribution of control, the distribution dimension of the taxonomy deals with data. We consider two cases, namely, either the data is physically distributed over multiple sites that communicate with each other over some form of communication medium or it is stored at only one site.

Heterogeneity may occur in various forms in distributed systems, ranging from hardware heterogeneity and differences in networking protocols to variations in data managers. The important ones from the perspective of this book relate to data models, query languages, and transaction management protocols. Representing data with different modeling tools creates heterogeneity because of the inherent expressive powers and limitations of individual data models. Heterogeneity in query languages not only involves the use of completely different data access paradigms in different data models (set-at-a-time access in relational systems versus record-at-a-time access in network and hierarchical systems), but also covers differences in languages even when the individual systems use the same data model. Different query languages that use the same data model often select very different methods for expressing identical requests (e.g., DB2 uses SQL, while INGRES uses QUEL).[6]

Let us consider the architectural alternatives starting at the origin in Figure 4.4 and moving along the autonomy dimension. The first class of systems are those which are logically integrated. Such systems can be given the generic name *composite systems* [Heimbigner and McLeod, 1985]. If there is no distribution or heterogeneity, the system is a set of multiple DBMSs that are logically integrated. There are not many examples of such systems, but they may be suitable for shared-everything multiprocessor systems. If heterogeneity is introduced, one has multiple data managers that are heterogeneous but provide an integrated view to the user. In the past, some work was done in this class where systems were designed to provide integrated access to network, hierarchical, and relational databases residing on a single machine (see, e.g., [Dogac and Ozkarahan, 1980]). The more interesting case is where the database is distributed even though an integrated view of the data is provided to users. Recall from Chapter 1 that this is exactly the definition of what we have called a *distributed DBMS*, which can be homogeneous or heterogeneous.

Next in the autonomy dimension are semiautonomous systems, which are commonly termed *federated DBMS* [Heimbigner and McLeod, 1985]. As specified before, the component systems in a federated environment have significant autonomy in their execution, but their participation in a federation indicate that they are willing to cooperate with others in executing user requests that access multiple databases. Similar to logically integrated systems discussed above, federated systems can be distributed or single-site, homogeneous or heterogeneous.

If we move to full autonomy, we get what we call the class of *multidatabase system* (MDBS) architectures. Without heterogeneity or distribution, an MDBS is an interconnected collection of autonomous databases. A multidatabase management system (multi-DBMS) is the software that provides for the management of this collection of autonomous databases and transparent access to it. If the individual databases that make up the MDBS are distributed over a number of sites, we have a *distributed MDBS*. The organization of a distributed MDBS as well as its management is quite different from that of a distributed DBMS. We discuss this issue in more detail in the upcoming sections. At this point it suffices to point out that the fundamental difference is one of the level of autonomy of the local data managers. Centralized or distributed multidatabase systems can be homogeneous or heterogeneous.

---

[6]For completeness, note that INGRES may also support SQL.

The fundamental point of the foregoing discussion is that the distribution of databases, their possible heterogeneity, and their autonomy are orthogonal issues. Since our concern in this book is on distributed systems, it is more important to note the orthogonality between autonomy and heterogeneity. Thus it is possible to have autonomous distributed databases that are not heterogeneous. In that sense, the more important issue is the autonomy of the databases rather than their heterogeneity. In other words, if the issues related to the design of a distributed multidatabase are resolved, introducing heterogeneity may not involve significant additional difficulty. This, of course, is true only from the perspective of database management; there may still be significant heterogeneity problems from the perspective of the operating system and the underlying hardware.

It is fair to claim that the fundamental issues related to multidatabase systems can be investigated without reference to their distribution. The additional considerations that distribution brings, in this case, are no different from those of logically integrated distributed database systems. Therefore, in this chapter we consider architectural models of logically integrated distributed DBMSs and multidatabase systems.

## 4.3.1 Distributed DBMS Architecture

Let us start the description of the architecture by looking at the data organizational view. We first note that the physical data organization on each machine may be, and probably is, different. This means that there needs to be an individual internal schema definition at each site, which we call the *local internal schema* (LIS). The enterprise view of the data is described by the *global conceptual schema* (GCS), which is global because it describes the logical structure of the data at all the sites.

As we discussed briefly in Chapter 1, data in a distributed database is usually fragmented and replicated. To handle this phenomenon of fragmentation and replication, the logical organization of data at each site needs to be described. Therefore, there needs to be a third layer in the architecture, the *local conceptual schema* (LCS). In the architectural model we have chosen, then, the global conceptual schema is the union of the local conceptual schemas. Finally, user applications and user access to the database is supported by *external schemas* (ESs), defined as being above the global conceptual schema.

This architecture model, depicted in Figure 4.5, provides the levels of transparency discussed in Section 4.1. Data independence is supported since the model is an extension of ANSI/SPARC, which provides such independence naturally. Location and replication transparencies are supported by the definition of the local and global conceptual schemas and the mapping in between. Network transparency, on the other hand, is supported by the definition of the global conceptual schema. The user queries data irrespective of its location or of which local component of the distributed database system will service it. As mentioned before, the distributed DBMS translates global queries into a group of local queries, which are executed by distributed DBMS components at different sites that communicate with one another.

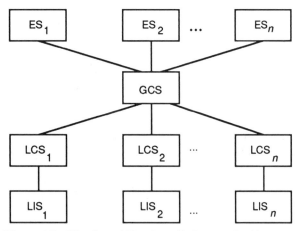

**Figure 4.5**   Distributed Database Reference Architecture

In terms of the detailed functional description of our model, the ANSI/SPARC model is extended by the addition of a *global directory/dictionary* (GD/D) that permits the required global mappings. The local mappings are still performed by a *local directory/dictionary* (LD/D). Thus the local database management components are integrated by means of global DBMS functions (Figure 4.6).

As we can see in Figure 4.6, the local conceptual schemas are mappings of the global schema onto each site. Furthermore, such databases are typically designed in a top-down fashion, and therefore, all external view definitions are made globally. We have also depicted, in Figure 4.6, a local database administrator at each site. The existence of such a role may be controversial. However, remember that one of the primary motivations of distributed processing is the desire to have local control over the administration of data.

The detailed components of a distributed DBMS are shown in Figure 4.7. One component handles the interaction with users, and another deals with the storage. The first major component, which we call the *user processor*, consists of four elements:

1.  The *user interface handler* is responsible for interpreting user commands as they come in, and formatting the result data as it is sent to the user.

2.  The *semantic data controller* uses the integrity constraints and authorizations that are defined as part of the global conceptual schema to check if the user query can be processed. This component, which is studied in detail in Chapter 6, is also responsible for authorization and other functions.

3.  The *global query optimizer and decomposer* determines an execution strategy to minimize a cost function, and translates the global queries into local ones using the global and local conceptual schemas as well as the global directory/dictionary. The global query optimizer is responsible, among other things, for generating the best strategy to execute distributed join operations. These issues are discussed in Chapters 7 through 9.

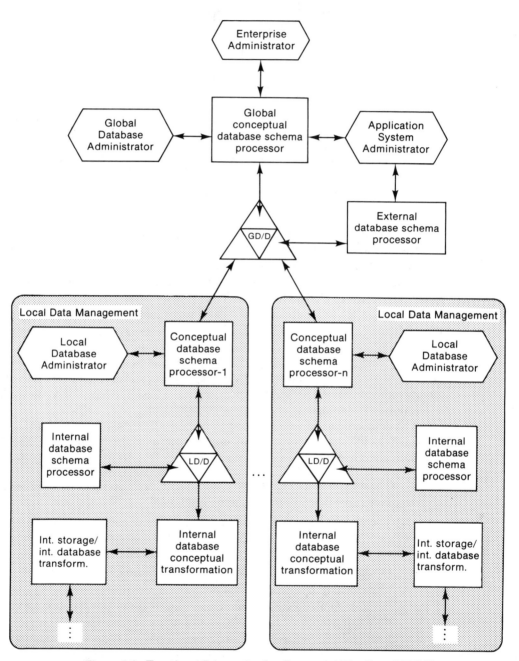

**Figure 4.6**   Functional Schematic of an Integrated Distributed DBMS

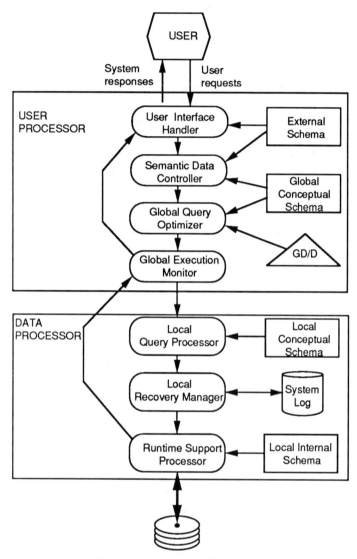

**Figure 4.7**   Components of a Distributed DBMS

4. The *distributed execution monitor* coordinates the distributed execution of the user request. The execution monitor is also called the *distributed transaction manager*. In executing queries in a distributed fashion, the execution monitors at various sites may, and usually do, communicate with one another.

The second major component of a distributed DBMS is the *data processor* and consists of three elements:

1.  The *local query optimizer*, which actually acts as the *access path selector*, is responsible for choosing the best access path[7] to access any data item (touched upon briefly in Chapter 9).

2.  The *local recovery manager* is responsible for making sure that the local database remains consistent even when failures occur (Chapter 12).

3.  The *run-time support processor* physically accesses the database according to the physical commands in the schedule generated by the query optimizer. The run-time support processor is the interface to the operating system and contains the *database buffer* (or *cache*) *manager*, which is responsible for maintaining the main memory buffers (Chapter 13) and managing the data accesses.

### 4.3.2  MDBS Architecture

The differences in the level of autonomy between the distributed multi-DBMSs and distributed DBMSs are also reflected in their architectural models. The fundamental difference relates to the definition of the global conceptual schema. In the case of logically integrated distributed DBMSs, the global conceptual schema defines the conceptual view of the *entire* database, while in the case of distributed multi-DBMSs, it represents only the collection of *some* of the local databases that each local DBMS wants to share. Thus the definition of a *global database* is different in MDBSs than in distributed DBMSs. In the latter, the global database is equal to the union of local databases, whereas in the former it is only a subset of the same union. There are even arguments as to whether the global conceptual schema should even exist in multidatabase systems. This question forms the basis of our architectural discussions in this section.

**Models using a global conceptual schema.**   In a MDBS, the GCS is defined by integrating either the external schemas of local autonomous databases or parts of their local conceptual schemas (Figure 4.8). Furthermore, users of a local DBMS define their own views on the local database and do not need to change their applications if they do not want to access data from another database. This is again an issue of autonomy.

Designing the global conceptual schema in multidatabase systems involves the integration of either the local global conceptual schemas or the local external schemas. A major difference between the design of the GCS in multi-DBMSs and in logically integrated distributed DBMSs is that in the former the mapping is from local conceptual schemas to a global schema. In the latter, however, mapping is in the reverse

---

[7]The term *access path* refers to the data structures and the algorithms that are used to access the data. A typical access path, for example, is an index on one or more attributes of a relation.

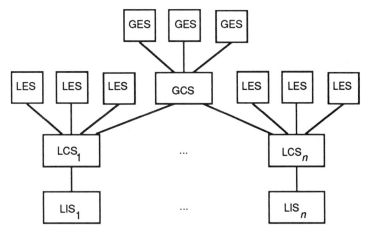

**Figure 4.8**    MDBS Architecture with a GCS

direction. As we discuss in Chapter 5, this is because the design in the former is usually a bottom-up process, whereas in the latter it is usually a top-down procedure. Furthermore, if heterogeneity exists in the multidatabase system, a canonical data model has to be found to define the GCS.

Once the GCS has been designed, views over the global schema can be defined for users who require global access. It is not necessary for the GES and GCS to be defined using the same data model and language; whether they do or not determines whether the system is homogeneous or heterogeneous.

If heterogeneity exists in the system, then two implementation alternatives exist: unilingual and multilingual. A *unilingual* multi-DBMS requires the users to utilize possibly different data models and languages when both a local database and the global database are accessed. The identifying characteristic of unilingual systems is that any application that accesses data from multiple databases must do so by means of an external view that is defined on the global conceptual schema. This means that the user of the global database is effectively a different user than those who access only a local database, utilizing a different data model and a different data language. Thus, one application may have a *local external schema* (LES) defined on the local conceptual schema as well as a *global external schema* (GES) defined on the global conceptual schema. The different external view definitions may require the use of different access languages. Figure 4.8 actually depicts the datalogical model of a unilingual database system that integrates the local conceptual schemas (or parts of them) into a global conceptual schema. Examples of such an architecture are the MULTIBASE system ([Landers and Rosenberg, 1982] and [Smith et al., 1981]) Mermaid [Templeton et al., 1987] and DDTS [Dwyer et al., 1986].

An alternative is *multilingual* architecture, where the basic philosophy is to permit each user to access the global database (i.e., data from other databases) by means of an external schema, defined using the language of the user's local DBMS. The GCS definition is quite similar in the multilingual architecture and the unilingual approach, the major difference being the definition of the external schemas, which are described in the language of the external schemas of the local database. Assuming that the definition is purely local, a query issued according to a particular schema is handled exactly as any query in the centralized DBMSs. Queries against the global database are made using the language of the local DBMS, but they generally require some processing to be mapped to the global conceptual schema.

The multilingual approach obviously makes querying the databases easier from the user's perspective. However, it is more complicated because we must deal with translation of queries at run time. The multilingual approach is used in Sirius-Delta [Ferrier and Stangret, 1982] and in the HD-DBMS project [Cardenas, 1987].

**Models without a global conceptual schema.**    The existence of a global conceptual schema in a multidatabase system is a controversial issue. There are researchers who even define a multidatabase management system as one that manages "several databases without a global schema" [Litwin, 1988]. It is argued that the absence of a GCS is a significant advantage of multidatabase systems over distributed database systems. One prototype system that has used this architectural model is the MRDSM project ([Litwin and Abdellatif, 1987], [Litwin and Abdellatif, 1986]). The architecture depicted in Figure 4.9, identifies two layers: the local system layer and the multidatabase layer on top of it. The local system layer consists of a number of DBMSs, which present to the multidatabase layer the part of their local database they are willing to share with users of other databases. This shared data is presented either as the actual local conceptual schema or as a local external schema definition. (Figure 4.9 shows this layer as a collection of local conceptual schemas.) If heterogeneity is involved, each of these schemas, $LCS_i$, may use a different data model.

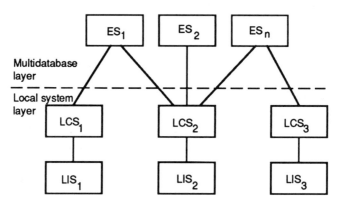

**Figure 4.9**    MDBS Architecture Without a GCS (From [Litwin, 1988])

Above this layer, external views are constructed where each view may be defined on one local conceptual schema or on multiple conceptual schemas. Thus the responsibility of providing access to multiple (and maybe heterogeneous) databases is delegated to the mapping between the external schemas and the local conceptual schemas. This is fundamentally different from architectural models that use a global conceptual schema, where this responsibility is taken over by the mapping between the global conceptual schema and the local ones. This shift in responsibility has a practical consequence. Access to multiple databases is provided by means of a powerful language in which user applications are written [Siegel, 1987].

Federated database architectures, which we discussed briefly, do not use a global conceptual schema either. In the specific system described in [Heimbigner and McLeod, 1985], each local DBMS defines an *export schema*, which describes the data it is willing to share with others. In the terminology that we have been using, the global database is the union of all the export schemas. Each application that accesses the global database does so by the definition of an *import schema*, which is simply a global external view.

The component-based architectural model of a multi-DBMS is significantly different from a distributed DBMS. The fundamental difference is the existence of full-fledged DBMSs, each of which manages a different database. The MDBS provides a layer of software that runs on top of these individual DBMSs and provides users with the facilities of accessing various databases (Figure 4.10). Depending on the existence (or lack) of the global conceptual schema or the existence of heterogeneity (or lack of it), the contents of this layer of software would change significantly. Note that Figure 4.10 represents a nondistributed multi-DBMS. If the system is distributed, we would need to replicate the multidatabase layer to each site where there is a local DBMS that participates in the system. Also note that as far as the individual DBMSs are concerned, the MDBS layer is simply another application that submits requests and receives answers.

## 4.4  GLOBAL DIRECTORY ISSUES

The discussion of the global directory issues is relevant only if one talks about a distributed DBMS or a multi-DBMS that uses a global conceptual schema. Otherwise, there is no concept of a global directory. If it exists, the global directory is an extension of the dictionary as described in the ANSI/SPARC report. It includes information about the location of the fragments as well as the makeup of the fragments.

As stated earlier, the directory is itself a database that contains *meta-data* about the actual data stored in the database. Therefore, the techniques we discuss in Chapter 5 with respect to distributed database design also apply to directory management. Briefly, a directory may be either *global* to the entire database or *local* to each site. In other words, there might be a single directory containing information about all the data in the database, or a number of directories, each containing the information stored at one site. In the latter case, we might either build hierarchies of directories to facilitate searches, or implement a distributed search strategy that involves considerable communication among the sites holding the directories.

The second issue has to do with location. The directory may be maintained *centrally* at one site, or in a *distributed* fashion by distributing it over a number of sites.

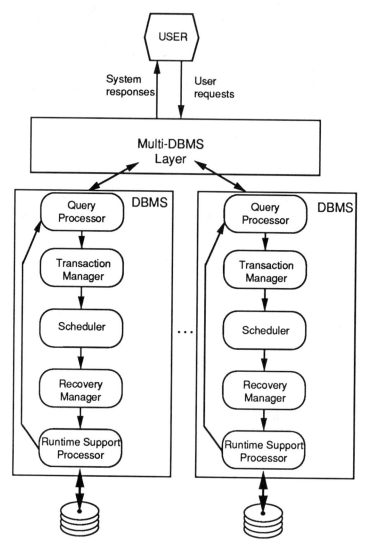

**Figure 4.10**   Components of an MDBS

Keeping the directory at one site might increase the load at that site, thereby causing a bottleneck as well as increasing message traffic around that site. Distributing it over a number of sites, on the other hand, increases the complexity of managing directories. In the case of multi-DBMSs, the choice is dependent on whether or not the system is distributed. If it is, the directory is always distributed; otherwise of course, it is maintained centrally.

The final issue is replication. There may be a *single* copy of the directory or *multiple* copies. Multiple copies would provide more reliability, since the probability of reaching one copy of the directory would be higher. Furthermore, the delays in accessing the directory would be lower, due to less contention and the relative proximity of the directory copies. On the other hand, keeping the directory up to date would be considerably more difficult, since multiple copies would need to be updated. Therefore, the choice should depend on the environment in which the system operates and should be made by balancing such factors as the response-time requirements, the size of the directory, the machine capacities at the sites, the reliability requirements, and the volatility of the directory (i.e., the amount of change experienced by the database, which would cause a change to the directory). Of course, these choices are valid only in the case of a distributed DBMS. A nondistributed multi-DBMS always maintains a single copy of the directory, while a distributed one typically maintains multiple copies, one at each site.

These three dimensions are orthogonal to one another (Figure 4.11). Even though some combinations may not be realistic, a large number of them are. In Figure 4.11 we have designated the unrealistic combinations by a question mark. Note that the choice of an appropriate directory management scheme should also depend on the query processing and the transaction management techniques that will be used in subsequent chapters. We will come back to this issue again.

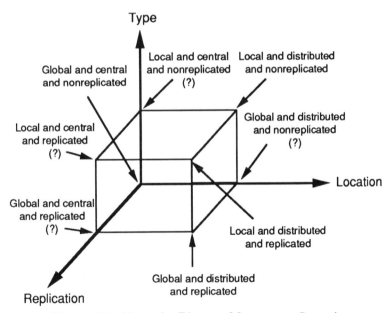

**Figure 4.11**    Alternative Directory Management Strategies

## 4.5 CONCLUSION

In this chapter we have considered the architectural issues in designing distributed
database systems. Specifically, we considered two alternative design approaches which
can be differentiated according to the degree of local autonomy that they provide for
the management of local databases. The purposes of discussing the generic reference architectures are twofold: (1) to present the issues that need to be addressed
in designing a distributed DBMS or a distributed multi-DBMS, and (2) to present a
framework within which the design and implementation issues of such systems can be
discussed. We should note that these are only abstract architectural models that we
use in this book. There may not be (and probably is not) any distributed DBMS that
adopts exactly this organization of components. Nevertheless, these models provide a
pedagogically useful framework within which we can discuss the issues covered in the
book.

We should indicate at this point that most of this book is devoted to a discussion of the issues related to logically integrated distributed database rather than mu-
tidatabase systems. The reason for this emphasis is simple. Most research results
obtained to date emphasize distributed DBMSs; research in multidatabase systems
is relatively new and has not yet generated general-purpose solutions. For example,
there is no transaction management theory for multidatabase systems, which in most
cases prevents global updates of local databases. The material is simply not available
to provide an in-depth and detailed analysis of solutions to problems. The notable exception is schema integration; most of this research has started with interest in heterogeneous database systems and several methodologies have been developed to design
the global conceptual schema by integrating local conceptual schemas. Therefore, we
devote Chapter 14 to a summary of the issues in designing multi-DBMSs.

The standardization activity on database systems is an ongoing activity. Numerous other architectural proposals have been reported in the literature, some of which
are discussed in detail in Chapter 13.

## 4.6 BIBLIOGRAPHIC NOTES

In addition to the early CODASYL reports and the ANSI/SPARC proposal, each
of which defined new architectural models, recent activity has included reports by
the Relational Database Task Group [Brodie and Schmidt, 1981] and the report of
the Database Architecture Framework Task Group [DAFTG, 1986] of the ANSI/X3/
SPARC Database System Study Group. International DBMS standardization activity
as of 1982 is described in detail in [Locke, 1982] and [Steel, 1982].

Among other architectural frameworks, the following are the most interesting.
Schreiber [Schrieber, 1977] describes a quite detailed extension of the ANSI/SPARC
framework which attempts to accommodate heterogeneity of the data models. The
proposal by Mohan and Yeh [Mohan and Yeh, 1978] is quite similar to ours. The
detailed component-wise system architecture given in Figure 4.7 also derives from

[Rahimi, 1987]. An alternative to the classification that we provide in Figure 4.4 can be found in [Sheth, 1989].

Most of the discussion on architectural models for multi-DBMSs is from [Barker and Özsu, 1988] and [Özsu and Barker, 1990]. Other architectural discussions on multi-DBMSs are given in [Gilgor and Luckenbaugh, 1984], [Litwin, 1988], and [Sheth and Larson, 1990]. All of these papers provide overview discussions of various prototype and commercial systems.

# 5

# Distributed
# Database Design

The design of a distributed computer system involves making decisions on the placement of *data* and *programs* across the sites of a computer network, as well as possibly designing the network itself. In the case of distributed DBMSs, the distribution of applications involves two things: the distribution of the distributed DBMS software and the distribution of the application programs that run on it. The former is not a significant problem, since we assume that a copy of the distributed DBMS software exists at each site where data is stored. In this chapter we do not concern ourselves with application program placement either. Furthermore, we assume that the network has already been designed, or will be designed at a later stage, according to the decisions related to the distributed database design. We concentrate on distribution of data.

It has been suggested that the organization of distributed systems can be investigated along three orthogonal dimensions [Levin and Morgan, 1975]:

1. Level of sharing
2. Behavior of access patterns
3. Level of knowledge on access pattern behavior

Figure 5.1 depicts the alternatives along these dimensions. In terms of the level of sharing, there are three possibilities. First, there is *no sharing*: each application and

94

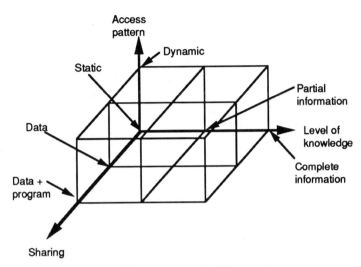

**Figure 5.1**    Framework of Distribution

its data execute at one site, and there is no communication with any other program or access to any data file at other sites. This characterizes the very early days of networking and is probably not very common today. We then find the level of *data sharing*; all the programs are replicated at all the sites, but data files are not. Accordingly, user requests are handled at the site where they originate and the necessary data files are moved around the network. Finally, in *data-plus-program sharing*, both data and programs may be shared, meaning that a program at a given site can request a service from another program at a second site, which, in turn, may have to access a data file located at a third site.

Levin and Morgan draw a distinction between data sharing and data-plus-program sharing to illustrate the differences between homogeneous and heterogeneous distributed computer systems. They indicate, correctly, that in a heterogeneous environment it is usually very difficult, if not impossible, to execute a given program on different hardware under a different operating system. It might, however, be possible to move data around relatively easily.

Along the second dimension of access pattern behavior, it is possible to identify two alternatives. The access patterns of user requests may be *static*, so that they do not change over time, or *dynamic*. It is obviously considerably easier to plan for and manage the static environments than would be the case for dynamic distributed systems. Unfortunately, it is difficult to find many real-life distributed applications that would be classified as static. The significant question, then, is not whether a system is static or dynamic, but how dynamic it is. Incidentally, it is along this dimension that the relationship between the distributed database design and query processing is established (refer to Figure 1.8).

The third dimension of classification is the level of knowledge about the access pattern behavior. One possibility, of course, is that the designers do not have any information about how users will access the database. This is a theoretical possibility, but it is very difficult, if not impossible, to design a distributed DBMS that can effectively cope with this situation. The more practical alternatives are that the designers have *complete information*, where the access patterns can reasonably be predicted and do not deviate significantly from these predictions, and *partial information*, where there are deviations from the predictions.

The distributed database design problem should be considered within this general framework. In all the cases discussed, except in the no-sharing alternative, new problems are introduced in the distributed environment which are not relevant in a centralized setting. In this chapter it is our objective to focus on these unique problems. The outline of this chapter is as follows. In Section 5.1 we discuss briefly two approaches to distributed database design: the top-down and the bottom-up design strategies. The details of the top-down approach are given in Sections 5.3 and 5.4, while the details of the bottom-up approach are postponed to another chapter (Chapter 14). Prior to the discussion of these alternatives, in Section 5.2 we present the issues in distribution design.

## 5.1 ALTERNATIVE DESIGN STRATEGIES

Two major strategies that have been identified [Ceri et al., 1987] for designing distributed databases are the *top-down approach* and the *bottom-up approach*. As the names indicate, they constitute very different approaches to the design process. But as any software designer knows, real applications are rarely simple enough to fit nicely in either of these alternatives. It is therefore important to keep in mind that in most database designs, the two approaches may need to be applied to complement one another.

We should also indicate that the issue addressed here is one of designing a database system using a distributed DBMS within the framework discussed in Section 4.3. This activity is a joint function of the database, enterprise, and application system administrators (or of the administrator performing all three roles).

### 5.1.1 Top-Down Design Process

A framework for this process is shown in Figure 5.2. The activity begins with a requirements analysis that defines the environment of the system and "elicits both the data and processing needs of all potential database users" [Yao et al., 1982a]. The requirements study also specifies where the final system is expected to stand with respect to the objectives of a distributed DBMS as identified in Section 1.3. To reiterate, these objectives are defined with respect to performance, reliability and availability, economics, and expandability (flexibility).

The requirements document is input to two parallel activities: view design and conceptual design. The *view design* activity deals with defining the interfaces for end

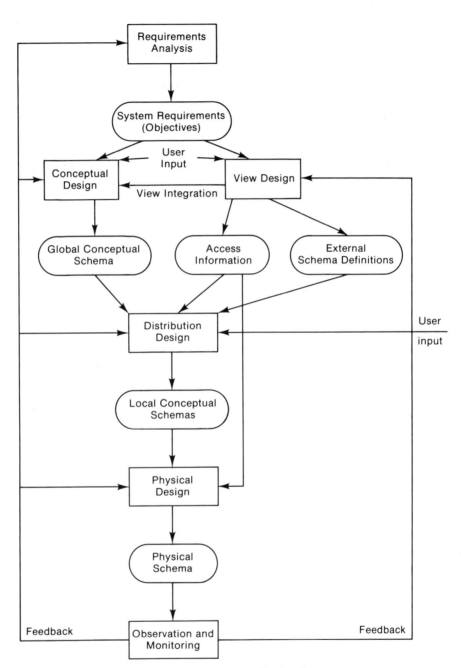

**Figure 5.2**    Top-Down Design Process

users. The *conceptual design*, on the other hand, is the process by which the enterprise is examined to determine entity types and relationships among these entities. One can possibly divide this process into two related activity groups [Davenport, 1981]: entity analysis and functional analysis. *Entity analysis* is concerned with determining the entities, their attributes, and the relationships among them. *Functional analysis*, on the other hand, is concerned with determining the fundamental functions with which the modeled enterprise is involved. The results of these two steps need to be cross-referenced to get a better understanding of which functions deal with which entities.

There is a relationship between the conceptual design and the view design. In one sense, the conceptual design can be interpreted as being an integration of user views. Even though this *view integration* activity is very important, the conceptual model should support not only the existing applications, but also future applications. View integration should be used to ensure that entity and relationship requirements for all the views are covered in the conceptual schema.

In conceptual design and view design activities the user needs to specify the data entities and must determine the applications that will run on the database as well as statistical information about these applications. Statistical information includes the specification of the frequency of user applications, the volume of various information, and the like. Note that from the conceptual design step comes the definition of global conceptual schema discussed in Section 4.3. We have not yet considered the implications of the distributed environment; in fact, up to this point, the process is identical to that in a centralized database design.

The global conceptual schema (GCS) and access pattern information collected as a result of view design are inputs to the *distribution design* step. The objective at this stage, which is the focus of this chapter, is to design the local conceptual schemas (LCSs) by distributing the entities over the sites of the distributed system. It is possible, of course, to treat each entity as a unit of distribution. Given that we use the relational model as the basis of discussion in this book, the entities correspond to relations.

Rather than distributing relations, it is quite common to divide them into subrelations, called *fragments*, which are then distributed. Thus the distribution design activity consists of two steps: *fragmentation* and *allocation*. These are the major issues that are treated in this chapter, so we delay discussing them until later sections.

The last step in the design process is the physical design, which maps the local conceptual schemas to the physical storage devices available at the corresponding sites. The inputs to this process are the local conceptual schema and access pattern information about the fragments in these.

It is well known that the design and development activity of any kind is an ongoing process requiring constant monitoring and periodic adjustment and tuning. We have therefore included observation and monitoring as a major activity in this process. Note that one does not monitor only the behavior of the database implementation but also the suitability of user views. The result is some form of feedback, which may result in backing up to one of the earlier steps in the design.

### 5.1.2 Bottom-Up Design Process

Top-down design is a suitable approach when a database system is being designed from scratch. Commonly, however, a number of databases already exist, and the design task involves integrating them into one database. The bottom-up approach is suitable for this type of environment. The starting point of bottom-up design is the individual local conceptual schemas. The process consists of integrating local schemas into the global conceptual schema.

This type of environment exists primarily in the context of heterogeneous databases. Significant research has been conducted within this context as well. We will, therefore, defer the discussion of the bottom-up design process until Chapter 14. The rest of this chapter concentrates on the two fundamental issues in top-down design: fragmentation and allocation.

## 5.2 DISTRIBUTION DESIGN ISSUES

In the preceding section we indicated that the relations in a database schema are usually decomposed into smaller fragments, but we did not offer any justification or details for this process. The objective of this section is to fill in these details.

The following set of interrelated questions covers the entire issue. We will therefore seek to answer them in the remainder of this section.

- Why fragment at all?
- How should we fragment?
- How much should we fragment?
- Is there any way to test the correctness of decomposition?
- How should we allocate?
- What is the necessary information for fragmentation and allocation?

### 5.2.1 Reasons for Fragmentation

From a data distribution viewpoint, there is really no reason to fragment data. After all, in distributed file systems, the distribution is performed on the basis of entire files. In fact, the earlier work dealt specifically with the allocation of files to nodes on a computer network. We consider earlier models in Section 5.4.

With respect to fragmentation, the important issue is the appropriate unit of distribution. A relation is not a suitable unit, for a number of reasons. First, application views are usually subsets of relations. Therefore, the locality of accesses of applications is defined not on entire relations but on their subsets. Hence it is only natural to consider subsets of relations as distribution units.

Second, if the applications that have views defined on a given relation reside at different sites, two alternatives can be followed, with the entire relation being the unit of distribution. Either the relation is not replicated and is stored at only one site, or it is replicated at all or some of the sites where the applications reside. The former results in an unnecessarily high volume of remote data accesses. The latter, on the other hand, has unnecessary replication, which causes problems in executing updates (to be discussed later) and may not be desirable if storage is limited.

Finally, the decomposition of a relation into fragments, each being treated as a unit, permits a number of transactions to execute concurrently. In addition, the fragmentation of relations typically results in the parallel execution of a single query by dividing it into a set of subqueries that operate on fragments. Thus fragmentation typically increases the level of concurrency and therefore the system throughput. This form of concurrency, which we choose to refer to as *intraquery concurrency*, is dealt with mainly in Chapters 8 and 9, under query processing.

For the sake of completeness, we should also indicate the disadvantages of fragmentation. If the applications have conflicting requirements which prevent decomposition of the relation into mutually exclusive fragments, those applications whose views are defined on more than one fragment may suffer performance degradation. It might, for example, be necessary to retrieve data from two fragments and then take either their union or their join, which is costly. Avoiding this is a fundamental fragmentation issue.

The second problem is related to semantic data control, specifically to integrity checking. As a result of fragmentation, attributes participating in a dependency may be decomposed into different fragments which might be allocated to different sites. In this case, even the simpler task of checking for dependencies would result in chasing after data in a number of sites. In Chapter 6 we return to the issue of semantic data control.

### 5.2.2 Fragmentation Alternatives

Relation instances are essentially tables, so the issue is one of finding alternative ways of dividing a table into smaller ones. There are clearly two alternatives for this: dividing it *horizontally* or dividing it *vertically*.

#### Example 5.1

In this chapter we use a modified version of the relational database scheme developed in Chapter 2. We have added to the J relation a new attribute (LOC) that indicates the place of each project. Figure 5.3 depicts the database schema instance we will use. Figure 5.4 shows the J relation of Figure 5.3 divided horizontally into two relations. Subrelation $J_1$ contains information about projects whose budgets are less than $200,000, whereas $J_2$ stores information about projects with larger budgets.

#### Example 5.2

Figure 5.5 shows the J relation of Figure 5.3 partitioned vertically into two subrelations, $J_1$ and $J_2$. $J_1$ contains only the information about project budgets, whereas $J_2$ contains project names and locations. It is important to notice that the key to the relation (JNO) is included in both fragments.

E

| ENO | ENAME | TITLE |
|-----|-------|-------|
| E1 | J. Doe | Elect. Eng |
| E2 | M. Smith | Syst. Anal. |
| E3 | A. Lee | Mech. Eng. |
| E4 | J. Miller | Programmer |
| E5 | B. Casey | Syst. Anal. |
| E6 | L. Chu | Elect. Eng. |
| E7 | R. Davis | Mech. Eng. |
| E8 | J. Jones | Syst. Anal. |

G

| ENO | JNO | RESP | DUR |
|-----|-----|------|-----|
| E1 | J1 | Manager | 12 |
| E2 | J1 | Analyst | 24 |
| E2 | J2 | Analyst | 6 |
| E3 | J3 | Consultant | 10 |
| E3 | J4 | Engineer | 48 |
| E4 | J2 | Programmer | 18 |
| E5 | J2 | Manager | 24 |
| E6 | J4 | Manager | 48 |
| E7 | J3 | Engineer | 36 |
| E8 | J3 | Manager | 40 |

J

| JNO | JNAME | BUDGET | LOC |
|-----|-------|--------|-----|
| J1 | Instrumentation | 150000 | Montreal |
| J2 | Database Develop. | 135000 | New York |
| J3 | CAD/CAM | 250000 | New York |
| J4 | Maintenance | 310000 | Paris |

S

| TITLE | SAL |
|-------|-----|
| Elect. Eng. | 40000 |
| Syst. Anal. | 34000 |
| Mech. Eng. | 27000 |
| Programmer | 24000 |

**Figure 5.3**    Modified Example Database

$J_1$

| JNO | JNAME | BUDGET | LOC |
|-----|-------|--------|-----|
| J1 | Instrumentation | 150000 | Montreal |
| J2 | Database Develop. | 135000 | New York |

$J_2$

| JNO | JNAME | BUDGET | LOC |
|-----|-------|--------|-----|
| J3 | CAD/CAM | 255000 | New York |
| J4 | Maintenance | 310000 | Paris |

**Figure 5.4**    Example of Horizontal Partitioning

| J₁ | |
|---|---|
| JNO | BUDGET |
| J1 | 150000 |
| J2 | 135000 |
| J3 | 250000 |
| J4 | 310000 |

| J₂ | | |
|---|---|---|
| JNO | JNAME | LOC |
| J1 | Instrumentation | Montreal |
| J2 | Database Develop. | New York |
| J3 | CAD/CAM | New York |
| J4 | Maintenance | Paris |

**Figure 5.5**   Example of Vertical Partitioning

The fragmentation may, of course, be nested. If the nestings are of different types, one gets *hybrid* fragmentation. Even though we do not treat hybrid fragmentation as a primitive type of fragmentation strategies, it is quite obvious that many real-life partitionings may be hybrid.

### 5.2.3 Degree of Fragmentation

The extent to which the database should be fragmented is an important decision that affects the performance of query execution. In fact, the issues in Section 5.2.1 concerning the reasons for fragmentation constitute a subset of the answers to the question we are addressing here. The degree of fragmentation goes from one extreme, that is, not to fragment at all, to the other extreme, to fragment to the level of individual tuples (in the case of horizontal fragmentation) or to the level of individual attributes (in the case of vertical fragmentation).

We have already addressed the adverse effects of very large and very small units of fragmentation. What we need, then, is to find a suitable level of fragmentation which is a compromise between the two extremes. Such a level can only be defined with respect to the applications that will run on the database. The issue is, how? In general, the applications need to be characterized with respect to a number of parameters. According to the values of these parameters, individual fragments can be identified. In Section 5.3 we describe how this characterization can be carried out for alternative fragmentations.

### 5.2.4 Correctness Rules of Fragmentation

When we looked at normalization in Chapter 2, we mentioned a number of rules to ensure the consistency of the database. It is important to note the similarity between the fragmentation of data for distribution (specifically, vertical fragmentation) and the normalization of relations. Thus fragmentation rules similar to the normalization principles can be defined.

We will enforce the following three rules during fragmentation, which, together, ensure that the database does not undergo semantic change during fragmentation.

1. *Completeness.* If a relation instance $R$ is decomposed into fragments $R_1, R_2,$ $\ldots, R_n$, each data item that can be found in $R$ can also be found in one or more of $R_i$'s. This property, which is identical to the *lossless decomposition* property of normalization (Chapter 2), is also important in fragmentation since it ensures that the data in a global relation is mapped into fragments without any loss [Grant, 1984]. Note that in the case of horizontal fragmentation, the "item" typically refers to a tuple, while in the case of vertical fragmentation, it refers to an attribute.

2. *Reconstruction.* If a relation $R$ is decomposed into fragments $R_1, R_2, \ldots,$ $R_n$, it should be possible to define a relational operator $\bigtriangledown$ such that

$$R = \bigtriangledown R_i, \quad \forall R_i \in F_R$$

The operator $\bigtriangledown$ will be different for the different forms of fragmentation; it is important, however, that it can be identified. The reconstructability of the relation from its fragments ensures that constraints defined on the data in the form of dependencies are preserved.

3. *Disjointness.* If a relation $R$ is horizontally decomposed into fragments $R_1, R_2, \ldots, R_n$ and data item $d_i$ is in $R_j$, it is not in any other fragment $R_k$ $(k \neq j)$. This criterion ensures that the horizontal fragments are disjoint. If relation $R$ is vertically decomposed, its primary key attributes are typically repeated in all its fragments. Therefore, in case of vertical partitioning, disjointness is defined only on the nonprimary key attributes of a relation.

### 5.2.5 Allocation Alternatives

Assuming that the database is fragmented properly, one has to decide on the allocation of the fragments to various sites on the network. When data is allocated, it may either be replicated or maintained as a single copy. The reasons for replication are reliability and efficiency of read-only queries. If there are multiple copies of a data item, there is a good chance that some copy of the data will be accessible somewhere even when system failures occur. Furthermore, read-only queries that access the same data items can be executed in parallel since copies exist on multiple sites. On the other hand, the execution of update queries cause trouble since the system has to ensure that all the copies of the data are updated properly. Hence the decision regarding replication is a trade-off which depends on the ratio of the read-only queries to the update queries. This decision affects almost all of the distributed DBMS algorithms and control functions.

A nonreplicated database (commonly called a *partitioned* database) contains fragments that are allocated to sites, and there is only one copy of any fragment on the network. In case of replication, either the database exists in its entirety at each site (*fully replicated* database), or fragments are distributed to the sites in such a way that copies of a fragment may reside in multiple sites (*partially replicated* database). In the latter the number of copies of a fragment may be an input to the allocation algorithm or a decision variable whose value is determined by the algorithm. Figure 5.6 compares these three replication alternatives with respect to various distributed DBMS functions.

|  | Full replication | Partial replication | Partitioning |
|---|---|---|---|
| QUERY PROCESSING | Easy | Same difficulty ← → | |
| DIRECTORY MANAGEMENT | Easy or nonexistent | Same difficulty ← → | |
| CONCURRENCY CONTROL | Moderate | Difficult | Easy |
| RELIABILITY | Very high | High | Low |
| REALITY | Possible application | Realistic | Possible application |

**Figure 5.6**   Comparison of Replication Alternatives

### 5.2.6 Information Requirements

One aspect of distribution design is that too many factors contribute to an optimal design. The logical organization of the database, the location of the applications, the access characteristics of the applications to the database, and the properties of the computer systems at each site all have an influence on distribution decisions. This makes it very complicated to formulate a distribution problem.

The information needed for distribution design can be divided into four categories: database information, application information, communication network information, and computer system information. The latter two categories are completely quantitative in nature and are used in allocation models rather than in fragmentation algorithms. We do not consider them in detail here. Instead, the detailed information requirements of the fragmentation and allocation algorithms are discussed in their respective sections.

## 5.3 FRAGMENTATION

In this section we present the various fragmentation strategies and algorithms. As mentioned previously, there are two fundamental fragmentation strategies: horizontal and vertical. Furthermore, there is a possibility of nesting fragments in a hybrid fashion.

### 5.3.1 Horizontal Fragmentation

As we explained earlier, horizontal fragmentation partitions a relation along its tuples. Thus each fragment has a subset of the tuples of the relation. There are two versions of horizontal partitioning: primary and derived. *Primary horizontal fragmentation* of a relation is performed using predicates that are defined on that relation. *Derived horizontal fragmentation*, on the other hand, is the partitioning of a relation that results from predicates being defined on another relation.

Later in this section we consider an algorithm for performing both of these fragmentations. However, first we investigate the information needed to carry out horizontal fragmentation activity.

#### Information requirements of horizontal fragmentation

*Database Information.*    The database information concerns the global conceptual schema. In this context it is important to note how the database relations are connected to one another, especially with joins. In the relational model, these relationships are also depicted as relations. However, in other data models, such as the entity-relationship (E–R) model [Chen, 1976], these relationships between database objects are depicted explicitly. In [Ceri et al., 1983] the relationship is also modeled explicitly, within the relational framework, for purposes of the distribution design. In the latter notation, directed *links* are drawn between relations that are related to each other by an equijoin operation.

**Example 5.3**

Figure 5.7 shows the expression of links among the database relations given in Figure 2.4. Note that the direction of the link shows a one-to-many relationship. For example, for each title there are multiple employees with that title; thus there is a link between the S and E relations. Along the same lines, the many-to-many relationship between the E and J relations is expressed with two links to the G relation.

The links between database objects (i.e., relations in our case) should be quite familiar to those who have dealt with network models of data. In the relational model they are introduced as join graphs, which we discuss in detail in subsequent chapters on query processing. We introduce them here because they help to simplify the presentation of the distribution models we discuss later.

The relation at the tail of a link is called the *owner* of the link and the relation at the head is called the *member* [Ceri et al., 1983]. More commonly used terms, within the relational framework, are *source* relation for owner and *target* relation for member. Let us define two functions: *owner* and *member*, both of which provide mappings from the set of links to the set of relations. Therefore, given a link, they return the member or owner relations of the link, respectively.

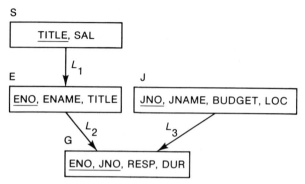

**Figure 5.7**    Expression of Relationships Among Relations Using Links

**Example 5.4**

Given link L₁ of Figure 5.7, the *owner and member* functions have the following values:

$$owner(L_1) \quad = \quad S$$
$$member(L_1) \quad = \quad E$$

The quantitative information required about the database is the cardinality of each relation $R$, denoted $card(R)$.

***Application Information.***    As indicated previously in relation to Figure 5.2, both qualitative and quantitative information is required about applications. The qualitative information guides the fragmentation activity, whereas the quantitative information is incorporated primarily into the allocation models.

The fundamental qualitative information consists of the predicates used in user queries. If it is not possible to analyze all of the user applications to determine these predicates, one should at least investigate the most "important" ones. It has been suggested that as a rule of thumb, the most active 20% of user queries account for 80% of the total data accesses [Wiederhold, 1982]. This "80/20 rule" may be used as a guideline in carrying out this analysis.

At this point we are interested in determining *simple predicates*. Given a relation $R(A_1, A_2, \ldots, A_n)$, where $A_i$ is an attribute defined over domain $D_i$, a simple predicate $p_j$ defined on $R$ has the form

$$p_j : A_i \ \theta \ Value$$

where $\theta \in \{=, <, \neq, \leq, >, \geq\}$ and *Value* is chosen from the domain of $A_i$ ($Value \in D_i$). We use $Pr_i$ to denote the set of all simple predicates defined on a relation $R_i$. The members of $Pr_i$ are denoted by $p_{ij}$.

**Example 5.5**

Given the relation instance J of Figure 5.3,

$$PNAME = \text{"Maintenance"}$$

is a simple predicate, as well as

$$BUDGET \le 200000$$

Even though simple predicates are quite elegant to deal with, user queries quite often include more complicated predicates, which are Boolean combinations of simple predicates. One combination that we are particularly interested in, called a *minterm predicate*, is the conjunction of simple predicates. Since it is always possible to transform a Boolean expression into conjunctive normal form, the use of minterm predicates in the design algorithms does not cause any loss of generality.

Given a set $Pr_i = \{p_{i1}, p_{i2}, \ldots, p_{im}\}$ of simple predicates for relation $R_i$, the set of minterm predicates $M_i = \{m_{i1}, m_{i2}, \ldots, m_{iz}\}$ is defined as

$$M_i = \{m_{ij} | m_{ij} = \bigwedge_{p_{ik} \in Pr_i} p_{ik}^*\}, \ 1 \le k \le m, \ 1 \le j \le z$$

where $p_{ik}^* = p_{ik}$ or $p_{ik}^* = \neg p_{ik}$. So each simple predicate can occur in a minterm predicate either in its natural form or its negated form.

It is important to note one point here. The reference to the negation of a predicate is meaningful for equality predicates of the form

$$Attribute = Value$$

For inequality predicates, the negation should be treated as the complement. For example, the negation of the simple predicate

$$Attribute \le Value$$

is

$$Attribute > Value$$

Besides theoretical problems of complementation in infinite sets, there is also the practical problem that the complement may be difficult to define. For example, if two simple predicates of the form

$$Lower\_bound \ \le \ Attribute\_1$$
$$Attribute\_1 \ \le \ Upper\_bound$$

are defined, their complements are

$$\neg(Lower\_bound \le Attribute\_1)$$

and

$$\neg(Attribute\_1 \le Upper\_bound)$$

However, the original two simple predicates can be written as

$$Lower\_bound \leq Attribute\_1 \leq Upper\_bound$$

with a complement,

$$\neg(Lower\_bound \leq Attribute\_1 \leq Upper\_bound)$$

that may not be easy to define. Therefore, the research in this area typically considers only simple equality predicates ([Ceri et al., 1982a] and [Ceri and Pelagatti, 1984]).

**Example 5.6**

Consider relation S of Figure 5.3. The following are some of the possible simple predicates that can be defined on S.

$$p_1: \quad \text{TITLE} = \text{"Elect. Eng."}$$
$$p_2: \quad \text{TITLE} = \text{"Syst. Anal."}$$
$$p_3: \quad \text{TITLE} = \text{"Mech. Eng."}$$
$$p_4: \quad \text{TITLE} = \text{"Programmer"}$$
$$p_5: \quad \text{SAL} \leq 30000$$
$$p_6: \quad \text{SAL} > 30000$$

The following are *some* of the minterm predicates that can be defined based on these simple predicates.

$$m_1: \quad \text{TITLE} = \text{"Elect. Eng."} \wedge \text{SAL} \leq 30000$$
$$m_2: \quad \text{TITLE} = \text{"Elect. Eng."} \wedge \text{SAL} > 30000$$
$$m_3: \quad \neg(\text{TITLE} = \text{"Elect. Eng."}) \wedge \text{SAL} \leq 30000$$
$$m_4: \quad \neg(\text{TITLE} = \text{"Elect. Eng."}) \wedge \text{SAL} > 30000$$
$$m_5: \quad \text{TITLE} = \text{"Programmer"} \wedge \text{SAL} \leq 30000$$
$$m_6: \quad \text{TITLE} = \text{"Programmer"} \wedge \text{SAL} > 30000$$

There are two points to mention here. First, these are not all the minterm predicates that can be defined; we are presenting only a representative sample. Second, some of these may be meaningless given the semantics of relation S. We are not addressing that issue here either. In addition, note that $m_3$ can also be rewritten as

$$m_3: \quad \text{TITLE} \neq \text{"Elect. Eng."} \wedge \text{SAL} \leq 30000$$

In terms of quantitative information about user applications, we need to have two sets of data.

1. *Minterm selectivity*: number of tuples of the relation that would be accessed by a user query specified according to a given minterm predicate. For example, the selectivity of $m_1$ of Example 5.6 is 0 since there are no tuples in S that satisfy the minterm predicate. The selectivity of $m_2$, on the other hand, is 1. We denote the selectivity of a minterm $m_i$ as $sel(m_i)$.

**2.** *Access frequency*: frequency with which user applications access data. If $Q = \{q_1, q_2, \ldots, q_q\}$ is a set of user queries, $acc(q_i)$ indicates the access frequency of query $q_i$ in a given period.

Note that minterm access frequencies can be determined from the query frequencies. We refer to the access frequency of a minterm $m_i$ as $acc(m_i)$.

**Primary horizontal fragmentation.**    Before we present a formal algorithm for horizontal fragmentation, we should intuitively discuss the process for both primary and derived horizontal fragmentation. A *primary horizontal fragmentation* is defined by a selection operation on the owner relations of a database schema. Therefore, given relation $R_i$, its horizontal fragments are given by

$$R_i^j = \sigma_{F_j}(R_i), \; 1 \leq j \leq w$$

where $F_j$ is the selection formula used to obtain fragment $R_i^j$. Note that if $F_j$ is in conjunctive normal form, it is a minterm predicate ($m_{ij}$). The algorithm we discuss will, in fact, insist that $F_j$ be a minterm predicate.

**Example 5.7**

The decomposition of relation J into horizontal fragments $J_1$ and $J_2$ in Example 5.1 is defined as follows:[1]

$$J_1 \quad = \quad \sigma_{\text{BUDGET} \leq 200000} \, (J)$$
$$J_2 \quad = \quad \sigma_{\text{BUDGET} > 200000} \, (J)$$

Example 5.7 demonstrates one of the problems of horizontal partitioning. If the domain of the attributes participating in the selection formulas are continuous and infinite, as in Example 5.7, it is quite difficult to define the set of formulas $F = \{F_1, F_2, \ldots, F_n\}$ that would fragment the relation properly. One possible course of action is to define ranges as we have done in Example 5.7. However, there is always the problem of handling the two endpoints. For example, if a new tuple with a BUDGET value of, say, $600,000 were to be inserted into J, one would have had to review the fragmentation to decide if the new tuple is to go into $J_2$ or if the fragments need to be revised and a new fragment needs to be defined as

$$J_2 \quad = \quad \sigma_{200000 < \text{BUDGET} \leq 400000} \, (J)$$
$$J_3 \quad = \quad \sigma_{\text{BUDGET} > 400000} \, (J)$$

This issue can obviously be resolved in practice by limiting the domain of the attribute(s) according to the requirements of the application.

---

[1]We assume that the nonnegativity of the BUDGET values is a feature of the relation that is enforced by an integrity constraint. Otherwise, a simple predicate of the form $0 \leq$ BUDGET also needs to be included in $Pr$. We assume this to be true in all our examples and discussions in this chapter.

**Example 5.8**

Consider relation J of Figure 5.3. We can define the following horizontal fragments based on the project location. The resulting fragments are shown in Figure 5.8.

$$J_1 = \sigma_{LOC=\text{"Montreal"}} (J)$$
$$J_2 = \sigma_{LOC=\text{"New York"}} (J)$$
$$J_3 = \sigma_{LOC=\text{"Paris"}} (J)$$

$J_1$

| JNO | JNAME | BUDGET | LOC |
|-----|-------|--------|-----|
| J1 | Instrumentation | 150000 | Montreal |

$J_2$

| JNO | JNAME | BUDGET | LOC |
|-----|-------|--------|-----|
| J2 | Database Develop. | 135000 | New York |
| J3 | CAD/CAM | 250000 | New York |

$J_3$

| JNO | JNAME | BUDGET | LOC |
|-----|-------|--------|-----|
| J4 | Maintenance | 310000 | Paris |

**Figure 5.8**   Primary Horizontal Fragmentation of Relation J

Now we can define a horizontal fragment more carefully. A horizontal fragment $R_i$ of relation $R$ consists of all the tuples of $R$ that satisfy a minterm predicate $m_i$. Hence, given a set of minterm predicates $M$, there are as many horizontal fragments of relation $R$ as there are minterm predicates. This set of horizontal fragments is also commonly referred to as the set of *minterm fragments*.

We have presented examples of primary horizontal fragmentation but have not yet given an algorithm that can provide such a fragmentation given a relation $R$ and a set of applications that will run on it. From the foregoing discussion it is obvious that the definition of the horizontal fragments depends on minterm predicates. Therefore, the first step of any fragmentation algorithm is to determine a set of simple predicates with certain properties.

An important aspect of simple predicates is their *completeness*; another is their *minimality*. A set of simple predicates $Pr$ is said to be *complete* if and only if there is an equal probability of access by every application to any two tuples belonging to any minterm fragment that is defined according to $Pr$. Hence it is clear that the definition of completeness of a set of simple predicates is different from the completeness rule of fragmentation given in Section 5.2.4.

**Example 5.9**

Consider the fragmentation of relation J given in Example 5.8. If the only application that accesses J wants to access the tuples according to the location, the set is complete since each tuple of each fragment $J_i$ (Example 5.8) has the same probability of being accessed. If, however, there is a second application which accesses only those project tuples where the budget is less than $200,000, then $Pr$ is not complete. Some of the tuples within each $J_i$ have a higher probability of being accessed due to this second application. To make the set of predicates complete, we need to add (BUDGET $\leq$ 200000, BUDGET $>$ 200000) to $Pr$:

$$Pr \quad = \quad \{\text{LOC="Montreal",LOC="New York",LOC="Paris"},$$
$$\text{BUDGET} \leq 200000, \text{BUDGET} \geq 200000\}$$

The reason completeness is a desirable property is because a complete set of predicates enables us to define a set of minterm predicates according to which primary horizontal fragmentation can be carried out. Fragments obtained this way are not only logically uniform in that they all satisfy the minterm predicate, but statistically homogeneous.

It is possible to define completeness more formally so that a complete set of predicates can be obtained automatically. However, this would require the designer to specify the access probabilities for *each* tuple of a relation for *each* application under consideration. This is considerably more work than appealing to the common sense and experience of the designer to come up with a complete set. Shortly, we will present an algorithmic way of obtaining this set.

The second desirable property of the set of predicates, according to which minterm predicates and in turn fragments are to be defined, is minimality, which is very intuitive. It simply states that if a predicate influences how fragmentation is performed (i.e., causes a fragment $f$ to be further fragmented into, say, $f_i$ and $f_j$), there should be at least one application that accesses $f_i$ and $f_j$ differently. In other words, the simple predicate should be *relevant* in determining a fragmentation. If all the predicates of a set $Pr$ are relevant, $Pr$ is *minimal*.

A formal definition of relevance can be given as follows [Ceri et al., 1982a]. Let $m_i$ and $m_j$ be two minterm predicates that are identical in their definition, except that $m_i$ contains the simple predicate $p_i$ in its natural form while $m_j$ contains $\neg p_i$. Also, let $f_i$ and $f_j$ be two fragments defined according to $m_i$ and $m_j$, respectively. Then $p_i$ is *relevant* if and only if

$$\frac{acc(m_i)}{card(f_i)} \quad \neq \quad \frac{acc(m_j)}{card(f_j)}$$

Once again, we appeal to the intuition and expertise of the designer rather than employing the formal definition.

**Example 5.10**

The set $Pr$ defined in Example 5.9 is complete and minimal. If, however, we were to add the predicate

JNAME = "Instrumentation"

to $Pr$, the resulting set would not be minimal since the new predicate is not relevant with respect to $Pr$. There is no application that would access the resulting fragments any differently.

We can now present an iterative algorithm that would generate a complete and minimal set of predicates $Pr'$ given a set of simple predicates $Pr$. This algorithm, called COM_MIN, is given in Algorithm 5.1. To avoid lengthy wording, we have adopted the following notation:

$Rule1$: fundamental rule of completeness and minimality, which states that a relation or fragment is partitioned "into at least two parts which are accessed differently by at least one application."

$f_i$ *of* $Pr'$: fragment $f_i$ defined according to a minterm predicate defined over the predicates of $Pr'$.

**Algorithm 5.1** *COM_MIN*

  **input:** $R$: relation; $Pr$: set of simple predicates
  **output:** $Pr'$: set of simple predicates
  **declare**
    $F$: set of minterm fragments
  **begin**
    find a $p_i \in Pr$ such that $p_i$ partitions $R$ according to *Rule* 1
    $Pr' \leftarrow p_i$
    $Pr \leftarrow Pr - p_i$
    $F \leftarrow f_i$                  {$f_i$ is the minterm fragment according to $p_i$}
    **do**
      **begin**
        find a $p_j \in Pr$ such that $p_j$ partitions some $f_k$ of $Pr'$ according
          to *Rule* 1
        $Pr' \leftarrow Pr' \cup p_j$
        $Pr \leftarrow Pr - p_j$
        $F \leftarrow F \cup f_j$
        **if** $\exists p_k \in Pr'$ which is nonrelevant **then**
        **begin**
          $Pr' \leftarrow Pr' - p_k$
          $F \leftarrow F - f_k$
        **end-if**
      **end-begin**
    **until** $Pr'$ is complete
  **end.** {COM_MIN}

The algorithm begins by finding a predicate that is relevant and that partitions the input relation. The **do-until** loop iteratively adds predicates to this set, ensuring minimality at each step. Therefore, at the end the set $Pr'$ is both minimal and complete.[2]

The second step in the primary horizontal design process is to derive the set of minterm predicates that can be defined on the predicates in set $Pr'$. These minterm predicates determine the fragments that are used as candidates in the allocation step. Determination of individual minterm predicates is trivial; the difficulty is that the set of minterm predicates may be quite large (in fact, exponential on the number of simple predicates). In the next step we look at ways of reducing the number of minterm predicates that need to be considered in fragmentation.

The third step of the design process is the elimination of some of the minterm fragments that may be meaningless. This elimination is performed by identifying those minterms that might be contradictory to a set of implications $I$. For example, if $Pr' = \{p_1, p_2\}$, where

$$p_1 : \quad att = value\_1$$
$$p_2 : \quad att = value\_2$$

and the domain of $att$ is $\{value\_1, value\_2\}$, it is obvious that $I$ contains two implications, which state

$$i_1 : \quad (att = value\_1) \Rightarrow \neg(att = value\_2)$$
$$i_2 : \quad \neg(att = value_1) \Rightarrow (att = value\_2)$$

The following four minterm predicates are defined according to $Pr'$:

$$m_1 : \quad (att = value\_1) \wedge (att = value\_2)$$
$$m_2 : \quad (att = value\_1) \wedge \neg(att = value\_2)$$
$$m_3 : \quad \neg(att = value\_1) \wedge (att = value\_2)$$
$$m_4 : \quad \neg(att = value\_1) \wedge \neg(att = value\_2)$$

In this case the minterm predicates $m_1$ and $m_4$ are contradictory to the implications $I$ and can therefore be eliminated from $M$.

The algorithm for primary horizontal fragmentation is given in Algorithm 5.2. The input to the algorithm PHORIZONTAL is a relation $R_i$ that is subject to primary horizontal fragmentation, and $Pr_i$, which is the set of simple predicates that have been determined according to applications defined on relation $R_i$.

**Algorithm 5.2**   $PHORIZONTAL$

**input:** $R_i$: relation; $Pr_i$: set of simple predicates
**output:** $M_i$: set of minterm fragments
**begin**
    $Pr_i' \leftarrow$ COM_MIN($R_i, Pr_i$)

---

[2]Note that a minimal set is always complete. The converse is not true, however.

> determine the set $M_i$ of minterm predicates
> determine the set $I_i$ of implications among $p_i \in Pr_i'$
> **for each** $m_i \in M_i$ **do**
>   **if** $m_i$ is contradictory according to $I$ **then**
>       $M_i \leftarrow M_i - m_i$
>   **end-if**
> **end-for**
> **end.** {PHORIZONTAL}

**Example 5.11**

We now consider the design of the database scheme given in Figure 5.7. The first thing to note is that there are two relations that are the subject of primary horizontal fragmentation: the S and J relations.

Suppose that there is only one application that accesses S. That application checks the salary information and determines a raise accordingly. Assume that employee records are managed in two places, one handling the records of those with salaries less than or equal to $30,000, and the other handling the records of those who earn more than $30,000. Therefore, the query is issued at two sites.

The simple predicates that would be used to partition relation S are

$$p_1: \quad \text{SAL} \leq 30000$$
$$p_2: \quad \text{SAL} > 30000$$

thus giving the initial set of simple predicates $Pr = \{p_1, p_2\}$. Applying the COM_MIN algorithm demonstrates that $Pr$ is indeed complete and minimal. Therefore, $Pr' = Pr$.

We can form the following minterm predicates as members of $M$:

$$m_1: \quad (\text{SAL} \leq 30000) \wedge (\text{SAL} > 30000)$$
$$m_2: \quad (\text{SAL} \leq 30000) \wedge \neg(\text{SAL} > 30000)$$
$$m_3: \quad \neg(\text{SAL} \leq 30000) \wedge (\text{SAL} > 30000)$$
$$m_4: \quad \neg(\text{SAL} \leq 30000) \wedge \neg(\text{SAL} > 30000)$$

Assuming that the domain of SALARY can indeed be partitioned in two, as suggested by $p_1$ and $p_2$, the following implications are obvious:

$$i_1: \quad (\text{SAL} \leq 30000) \Rightarrow \neg(\text{SAL} > 30000)$$
$$i_2: \quad \neg(\text{SAL} \leq 30000) \Rightarrow (\text{SAL} > 30000)$$
$$i_3: \quad (\text{SAL} > 30000) \Rightarrow \neg(\text{SAL} \leq 30000)$$
$$i_4: \quad \neg(\text{SAL} > 30000) \Rightarrow (\text{SAL} \leq 30000)$$

According to $i_1$, minterm predicate $m_1$ is contradictory; according to $i_2$, $m_4$ is contradictory. Therefore, we are left with $M = \{m_2, m_3\}$.

Together, $i_1$ and $i_4$ reduce the specification of $m_2$ into $p_1$, and similarly for the reduction of $m_3$ to $p_2$ due to $i_2$ and $i_3$. Therefore, we define two fragments $F_s = \{S_1, S_2\}$ according to $M$ (Figure 5.9).

S₁

| TITLE | SAL |
|---|---|
| Mech. Eng. | 27000 |
| Programmer | 24000 |

S₂

| TITLE | SAL |
|---|---|
| Elect. Eng. | 40000 |
| Syst. Anal. | 34000 |

**Figure 5.9**   Horizontal Fragmentation of Relation S

Let us next consider relation J. Assume that there are two applications. The first is issued at three sites and finds the names and budgets of projects given their number. In SQL notation, the query is

```
SELECT     JNAME, BUDGET
FROM       J
WHERE      JNO=Value
```

For this application, the simple predicates that would be used are the following:

$$p_1: \quad \text{LOC} = \text{"Montreal"}$$
$$p_2: \quad \text{LOC} = \text{"New York"}$$
$$p_3: \quad \text{LOC} = \text{"Paris"}$$

The second application is issued at two sites and has to do with the management of the projects. Those projects that have a budget of less than \$200,000 are managed at one site, whereas those with larger budgets are managed at a second site. Thus the simple predicates that should be used to fragment according to the second application are

$$p_4: \quad \text{BUDGET} \leq 200000$$
$$p_5: \quad \text{BUDGET} > 200000$$

If the algorithm COM_MIN is followed, the set $Pr' = \{p_1, p_2, p_3, p_4, p_5\}$ is obviously complete and minimal.

Based on $Pr'$, the following six minterm predicates that form $M$ can be defined:

$$m_1: \quad (\text{LOC} = \text{"Montreal"}) \wedge (\text{BUDGET} \leq 200000)$$
$$m_2: \quad (\text{LOC} = \text{"Montreal"}) \wedge (\text{BUDGET} > 200000)$$
$$m_3: \quad (\text{LOC} = \text{"New York"}) \wedge (\text{BUDGET} \leq 200000)$$
$$m_4: \quad (\text{LOC} = \text{"New York"}) \wedge (\text{BUDGET} > 200000)$$
$$m_5: \quad (\text{LOC} = \text{"Paris"}) \wedge (\text{BUDGET} \leq 200000)$$
$$m_6: \quad (\text{LOC} = \text{"Paris"}) \wedge (\text{BUDGET} > 200000)$$

These are not the only minterm predicates that can be generated. It is, for example, possible to specify predicates of the form

$$p_1 \wedge p_2 \wedge p_3 \wedge p_4 \wedge p_5$$

However, the obvious implications

$$
\begin{aligned}
i_1: & \quad p_1 \Rightarrow \neg p_2 \wedge \neg p_3 \\
i_2: & \quad p_2 \Rightarrow \neg p_1 \wedge \neg p_3 \\
i_3: & \quad p_3 \Rightarrow \neg p_1 \wedge \neg p_2 \\
i_4: & \quad p_4 \Rightarrow \neg p_5 \\
i_5: & \quad p_5 \Rightarrow \neg p_4 \\
i_6: & \quad \neg p_4 \Rightarrow p_5 \\
i_7: & \quad \neg p_5 \Rightarrow p_4
\end{aligned}
$$

eliminate these minterm predicates and we are left with $m_1$ to $m_6$.

Looking at the database instance in Figure 5.3, one may be tempted to claim that the following implications hold:

$$
\begin{aligned}
i_8: & \quad \text{LOC = “Montreal”} \Rightarrow \neg \, (\text{BUDGET} > 200000) \\
i_9: & \quad \text{LOC = “Paris”} \Rightarrow \neg \, (\text{BUDGET} \leq 200000) \\
i_{10}: & \quad \neg \, (\text{LOC = “Montreal”}) \Rightarrow \text{BUDGET} \leq 200000 \\
i_{11}: & \quad \neg \, (\text{LOC = “Paris”}) \Rightarrow \text{BUDGET} > 200000
\end{aligned}
$$

However, remember that implications should be defined according to the semantics of the database, not according to the current values. Some of the fragments defined according to $M = \{m_1, \ldots, m_6\}$ may be empty, but they are, nevertheless, fragments. There is nothing in the database semantics that suggest that the implications $i_8$ through $i_{11}$ hold.

The result of the primary horizontal fragmentation of J is to form six fragments $F_J = \{J_1, J_2, J_3, J_4, J_5, J_6\}$ of relation J according to the minterm predicates $M$ (Figure 5.10). We should also note that some of these fragments are empty and therefore are not depicted in Figure 5.10.

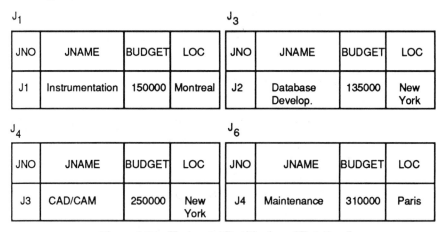

**Figure 5.10**   Horizontal Partitioning of Relation J

**Derived horizontal fragmentation.**     A derived horizontal fragmentation is defined on a member relation of a link according to a selection operation specified on its owner. It is important to remember two points. First, the link between the owner and the member relations is defined as an equi-join. Second, an equi-join can be implemented by means of semijoins. This second point is especially important for our purposes, since we want to partition a member relation according to the fragmentation of its owner, but we also want the resulting fragment to be defined *only* on the attributes of the member relation.

Accordingly, given a link $L$ where $owner(L) = S$ and $member(L) = R$, the derived horizontal fragments of $R$ are defined as

$$R_i = R \ltimes S_i, 1 \leq i \leq w$$

where $w$ is the maximum number of fragments that will be defined on $R$, and $S_i = \sigma_{F_i}(S)$, where $F_i$ is the formula according to which the primary horizontal fragment $S_i$ is defined.

**Example 5.12**

Consider link $L_1$ in Figure 5.7, where $owner(L_1) = S$ and $member(L_1) = E$. Then we can group engineers into two groups according to their salary: those making less than or equal to \$30,000, and those making more than \$30,000. The two fragments $E_1$ and $E_2$ are defined as follows:

$$E_1 = E \ltimes S_1$$
$$E_2 = E \ltimes S_2$$

where

$$S_1 = \sigma_{SAL \leq 30000}(S)$$
$$S_2 = \sigma_{SAL > 30000}(S)$$

The result of this fragmentation is depicted in Figure 5.11.

$E_1$

| ENO | ENAME | TITLE |
|-----|-------|-------|
| E3 | A. Lee | Mech. Eng. |
| E4 | J. Miller | Programmer |
| E7 | R. Davis | Mech. Eng. |

$E_2$

| ENO | ENAME | TITLE |
|-----|-------|-------|
| E1 | J. Doe | Elect. Eng. |
| E2 | M. Smith | Syst. Anal. |
| E5 | B. Casey | Syst. Anal. |
| E6 | L. Chu | Elect. Eng. |
| E8 | J. Jones | Syst. Anal. |

**Figure 5.11**    Derived Horizontal Fragmentation of Relation E

To carry out a derived horizontal fragmentation, three inputs are needed: the set of partitions of the owner relation (e.g., $S_1$ and $S_2$ in Example 5.12), the member relation, and the set of semijoin predicates between the owner and the member (e.g., E.TITLE = S.TITLE in Example 5.12). The fragmentation algorithm, then, is quite trivial, so we will not present it in any detail.

There is one potential complication that deserves some attention. In a database schema, it is common that there are more than two links into a relation $R$ (e.g., in Figure 5.7, G has two incoming links). In this case there is more than one possible derived horizontal fragmentation of $R$. The decision as to which candidate fragmentation to choose is based on two criteria:

1. The fragmentation with better join characteristics
2. The fragmentation used in more applications

Let us discuss the second criterion first. This is quite straightforward if we take into consideration the frequency with which applications access some data. If possible, one should try to facilitate the accesses of the "heavy" users so that their total impact on system performance is minimized.

Applying the first criterion, however, is not that straightforward. Consider, for example, the fragmentation we discussed in Example 5.12. The effect (and the objective) of this fragmentation is that the join of the E and S relations to answer the query is assisted (1) by performing it on smaller relations (i.e., fragments), and (2) by potentially performing joins in a distributed fashion.

The first point is obvious. The fragments of E are smaller than E itself. Therefore, it will be faster to join any fragment of S with any fragment of E than to work with the relations themselves. The second point, however, is more important and is at the heart of distributed databases. If, besides executing a number of queries at different sites, we can execute one query in parallel, the response time or throughput of the system can be expected to improve. In the case of joins, this is possible under certain circumstances. Consider, for example, the join graph (i.e., the links) between the fragments of E and S derived in Example 5.10 (Figure 5.12). There is only one link coming in or going out of a fragment. Such a join graph is called a *simple* graph. The advantage of a design where the join relationship between fragments is simple is that the member and owner of a link can be allocated to one site and the joins between different pairs of fragments can proceed independently and in parallel.

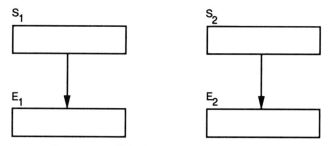

**Figure 5.12**   Join Graph Between Fragments

Unfortunately, obtaining simple join graphs may not always be possible. In that case, the next desirable alternative is to have a design that results in a *partitioned* join graph. A partitioned graph consists of two or more subgraphs with no links between them. Fragments so obtained may not be distributed for parallel execution as easily as those obtained via simple join graphs, but the allocation is still possible.

**Example 5.13**

Let us continue with the distribution design of the database we started in Example 5.11. We already decided on the fragmentation of relation E according to the fragmentation of S (Example 5.12). Let us now consider G. Assume that there are the following two applications:

1. The first application finds the names of engineers who work at certain places. It runs on all three sites and accesses the information about the engineers who work on local projects with higher probability than those of projects at other locations.

2. At each administrative site where employee records are managed, users would like to access the projects that these employees work on and learn how long they will work on those projects.

The first application results in a fragmentation of G according to the fragments $J_1, J_3, J_4$ and $J_6$ of J obtained in Example 5.11. Remember that

$$J_1: \quad \sigma_{LOC=\text{"Montreal"}} \wedge BUDGET \leq 200000 \, (J)$$
$$J_3: \quad \sigma_{LOC=\text{"New York"}} \wedge BUDGET \leq 200000 \, (J)$$
$$J_4: \quad \sigma_{LOC=\text{"New York"}} \wedge BUDGET > 200000 \, (J)$$
$$J_6: \quad \sigma_{LOC=\text{"Paris"}} \wedge BUDGET > 200000 \, (J)$$

Therefore, the derived fragmentation of G according to $\{J_1, J_2, J_3\}$ is defined as follows:

$$G_1 = G \ltimes J_1$$
$$G_2 = G \ltimes J_3$$
$$G_3 = G \ltimes J_4$$
$$G_4 = G \ltimes J_6$$

These fragment instances are shown in Figure 5.13.

The second query can be specified in SQL as

```
SELECT    RESP, DUR
FROM      G, Eᵢ
WHERE     G.ENO = Eᵢ.ENO
```

where $i = 1$ or $i = 2$, depending on which site the query is issued at. The derived fragmentation of G according to the fragmentation of E is defined below and depicted in Figure 5.14.

$$G_1 = G \ltimes E_1$$
$$G_2 = G \ltimes E_2$$

This example demonstrates two things:

1. Derived fragmentation may follow a chain where one relation is fragmented as a result of another one's design and it, in turn, causes the fragmentation of another relation (e.g., the chain S–E–G).

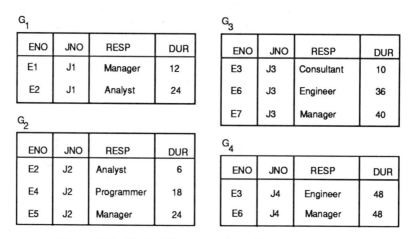

**G₁**

| ENO | JNO | RESP | DUR |
|-----|-----|------|-----|
| E1 | J1 | Manager | 12 |
| E2 | J1 | Analyst | 24 |

**G₂**

| ENO | JNO | RESP | DUR |
|-----|-----|------|-----|
| E2 | J2 | Analyst | 6 |
| E4 | J2 | Programmer | 18 |
| E5 | J2 | Manager | 24 |

**G₃**

| ENO | JNO | RESP | DUR |
|-----|-----|------|-----|
| E3 | J3 | Consultant | 10 |
| E6 | J3 | Engineer | 36 |
| E7 | J3 | Manager | 40 |

**G₄**

| ENO | JNO | RESP | DUR |
|-----|-----|------|-----|
| E3 | J4 | Engineer | 48 |
| E6 | J4 | Manager | 48 |

**Figure 5.13**   Derived Fragmentation of G with respect to J

**G₁**

| ENO | JNO | RESP | DUR |
|-----|-----|------|-----|
| E3 | J3 | Consultant | 10 |
| E3 | J4 | Engineer | 48 |
| E4 | J2 | Programmer | 18 |
| E7 | J3 | Engineer | 36 |

**G₂**

| ENO | JNO | RESP | DUR |
|-----|-----|------|-----|
| E1 | J1 | Manager | 12 |
| E2 | J1 | Analyst | 24 |
| E3 | J2 | Analyst | 6 |
| E4 | J2 | Manager | 24 |
| E5 | J4 | Manager | 48 |
| E6 | J3 | Manager | 40 |

**Figure 5.14**   Derived Fragmentation of G with respect to E

2. Typically, there will be more than one candidate fragmentation for a relation (e.g., relation G). The final choice of the fragmentation scheme may be a decision problem addressed during allocation.

**Checking for correctness.**   We should now check the fragmentation algorithms discussed so far with respect to the three correctness criteria presented in Section 5.2.4.

*Completeness.*   The completeness of a primary horizontal fragmentation is based on the selection predicates used. As long as the selection predicates are complete, the resulting fragmentation is guaranteed to be complete as well. Since the basis of the fragmentation algorithm is a set of *complete* and *minimal* predicates, $Pr'$, completeness is guaranteed as long as no mistakes are made in defining $Pr'$.

The completeness of a derived horizontal fragmentation is somewhat more difficult to define. The difficulty is due to the fact that the predicate determining the fragmentation involves two relations. Let us first define the completeness rule formally and then look at an example.

Let $R$ be the member relation of a link whose owner is relation $S$, which is fragmented as $F_S = \{S_1, S_2, \ldots, S_w\}$. Furthermore, let $A$ be the join attribute between $R$ and $S$. Then for each tuple $t$ of $R$, there should be a tuple $t'$ of $S$ such that

$$t[A] = t'[A].$$

For example, there should be no G tuple which has a project number that is not also contained in J. Similarly, there should be no E tuples with TITLE values where the same TITLE value does not appear in S as well. This rule is known as *referential integrity* and ensures that the tuples of any fragment of the member relation are also in the owner relation.

***Reconstruction.***    Reconstruction of a global relation from its fragments is performed by the union operator in both the primary and the derived horizontal fragmentation. Thus, for a relation $R$ with fragmentation $F_R = \{R_1, R_2, \ldots, R_w\}$,

$$R = \bigcup R_i, \quad \forall R_i \in F_R$$

***Disjointness.***    It is easier to establish disjointness of fragmentation for primary than for derived horizontal fragmentation. In the former case, disjointness is guaranteed as long as the minterm predicates determining the fragmentation are mutually exclusive.

In derived fragmentation, however, there is a semijoin involved that adds considerable complexity. Disjointness can be guaranteed if the join graph is simple. If it is not simple, it is necessary to investigate actual tuple values. In general, we do not want a tuple of a member relation to join with two or more tuples of the owner relation when these tuples are in different fragments of the owner. This may not be very easy to establish, and illustrates why derived fragmentation schemes that generate a simple join graph are always desirable.

**Example 5.14**

In fragmenting relation S (Example 5.11), the minterm predicates $M = \{m_1, m_2\}$ were

$$m_1: \quad \text{SAL} \leq 30000$$
$$m_2: \quad \text{SAL} > 30000$$

Since $m_1$ and $m_2$ are mutually exclusive, the fragmentation of S is disjoint.

For relation E, however, we require that

1.  Each engineer have a single title.
2.  Each title have a single salary value associated with it.

Since these two rules follow from the semantics of the database, the fragmentation of E with respect to S is also disjoint.

## 5.3.2 Vertical Fragmentation

Remember that a vertical fragmentation of a relation $R$ produces fragments $R_1, R_2,$ $\ldots, R_r$, each of which contains a subset of $R$'s attributes as well as the primary key of $R$. The objective of vertical fragmentation is to partition a relation into a set of smaller relations so that many of the user applications will run on only one fragment. In this context, an "optimal" fragmentation is one that produces a fragmentation scheme which minimizes the execution time of user applications that run on these fragments.

Vertical fragmentation has been investigated within the context of centralized database systems as well as distributed ones. Its motivation within the centralized context is as a design tool, which allows the user queries to deal with smaller relations, thus causing a smaller number of page accesses [Navathe et al., 1984]. It has also been suggested that the most active subrelations can be identified and placed in a faster memory subsystem in those cases where memory hierarchies are supported [Eisner and Severance, 1976].

Vertical partitioning is inherently more complicated than horizontal partitioning. This is due to the total number of alternatives that are available. For example, in horizontal partitioning, if the total number of simple predicates in $Pr$ is $n$, there are $2^n$ possible minterm predicates that can be defined on it. In addition, we know that some of these will contradict the existing implications, further reducing the candidate fragments that need to be considered. In the case of vertical partitioning, however, if a relation has $m$ nonprimary key attributes, the number of possible fragments is equal to $B(m)$, which is the $m$th Bell number [Niamir, 1978]. For large values of $m, B(m) \approx m^m$; for example, for $m=10$, $B(m) \approx 115,000$, for $m=15$, $B(m) \approx 10^9$, for $m=30$, $B(m) = 10^{23}$ ([Hammer and Niamir, 1979] and [Navathe et al., 1984]).

These values indicate that it is futile to attempt to obtain optimal solutions to the vertical partitioning problem; one has to resort to heuristics. Two types of heuristic approaches exist for the vertical fragmentation of global relations:

1. *Grouping:* starts by assigning each attribute to one fragment, and at each step, joins some of the fragments until some criteria is satisfied. Grouping was first suggested in [Hammer and Niamir, 1979] for centralized databases, and was used later in [Sacca and Wiederhold, 1985] for distributed databases.

2. *Splitting:* starts with a relation and decides on beneficial partitionings based on the access behavior of applications to the attributes. The technique was first discussed for centralized database design in [Hoffer and Severance, 1975]. It was then extended to the distributed environment in [Navathe et al., 1984].

In what follows we discuss only the splitting technique, since it fits more naturally within the top-down design methodology, and as stated in [Navathe et al., 1984], since the "optimal" solution is probably closer to the full relation than to a set of fragments each of which consists of a single attribute. Furthermore, splitting generates nonoverlapping fragments whereas grouping typically results in overlapping fragments. Within the context of distributed database systems, we are concerned with nonoverlapping fragments, for obvious reasons. Of course, nonoverlapping refers only to nonprimary key attributes.

Before we proceed, let us clarify an issue that we only mentioned in Example 5.2, namely, the replication of the global relation's key in the fragments. This is a characteristic of vertical fragmentation that allows the reconstruction of the global relation. Therefore, splitting is considered only for those attributes that do not participate in the primary key.

There is a strong advantage to replicating the key attributes despite the obvious problems it causes. This advantage has to do with semantic integrity enforcement, to be discussed in Chapter 6. Note that every dependency presented in Chapter 2 is, in fact, a constraint that has to hold among the attribute values of the respective relations at all times. Remember also that most of these dependencies involve the key attributes of a relation. If we now design the database so that the key attributes are part of one fragment that is allocated to one site, and the implied attributes are part of another fragment that is allocated to a second site, every update request that causes an integrity check will necessitate communication among sites. Replication of the key attributes at each fragment reduces the chances of this occurring but does not eliminate it completely, since such communication may be necessary due to integrity constraints that do not involve the primary key, as well as due to concurrency control.

One alternative to the replication of the key attributes is the use of *tuple identifiers* (TIDs), which are system-assigned unique values to the tuples of a relation. Since TIDs are maintained by the system, the fragments are disjoint as far as the user is concerned.

**Information requirements of vertical fragmentation.**   The major information required for vertical fragmentation is related to applications. The following discussion, therefore, is exclusively on what needs to be determined about applications that will run against the distributed database. Since vertical partitioning places in one fragment those attributes usually accessed together, there is a need for some measure that would define more precisely the notion of "togetherness." This measure is the *affinity* of attributes, which indicates how closely related the attributes are. Unfortunately, it is not realistic to expect the designer or the users to be able to easily specify these values. We now present one way by which they can be obtained from more primitive data.

The major data requirement related to applications is their access frequencies. Let $Q = \{q_1, q_2, \ldots, q_q\}$ be the set of user queries (applications) that will run on relation $R(A_1, A_2, \ldots, A_n)$. Then, for each query $q_i$ and each attribute $A_j$, we associate an *attribute usage value*, denoted as $use(q_i, A_j)$, and defined as follows:

$$use(q_i, A_j) = \begin{cases} 1 & \text{if attribute } A_j \text{ is referenced by query } q_i \\ 0 & \text{otherwise} \end{cases}$$

The $use(q_i, \bullet)$ vectors for each application are easy to define if the designer knows the applications that will run on the database. Again, remember that the 80-20 rule discussed in Section 5.3.1 should be helpful in this task.

**Example 5.15**

Consider relation J of Figure 5.3. Assume that the following applications are defined to run on this relation. In each case we also give the SQL specification.

$q_1$: Find the budget of a project, given its identification number.

```
SELECT    BUDGET
FROM      J
WHERE     JNO=Value
```

$q_2$: Find the names and budgets of all projects.

```
SELECT    JNAME, BUDGET
FROM      J
```

$q_3$: Find the names of projects located at a given city.

```
SELECT    JNAME
FROM      J
WHERE     LOC=Value
```

$q_4$: Find the total project budgets for each city.

```
SELECT    SUM(BUDGET)
FROM      J
WHERE     LOC=Value
```

According to these four applications, the attribute usage values can be defined. As a notational convenience, we let $A_1 = $ JNO, $A_2 = $ JNAME, $A_3 = $ BUDGET, and $A_4 = $ LOC. The usage values are defined in matrix form (Figure 5.15), where entry $(i, j)$ denotes $use(q_i, A_j)$.

$$
\begin{array}{c}
 & A_1 & A_2 & A_3 & A_4 \\
q_1 & 1 & 0 & 1 & 0 \\
q_2 & 0 & 1 & 1 & 0 \\
q_3 & 0 & 1 & 0 & 1 \\
q_4 & 0 & 0 & 1 & 1
\end{array}
$$

**Figure 5.15**  Example Attribute Usage Matrix

Attribute usage values are not sufficiently general to form the basis of attribute splitting and fragmentation. This is because these values do not represent the weight of application frequencies. The frequency measure can be included in the definition of the attribute affinity measure $aff(A_i, A_j)$, which measures the bond between two attributes of a relation according to how they are accessed by applications.

The measure of attribute affinity between two attributes $A_i$ and $A_j$ of a relation $R(A_1, A_2, \ldots, A_n)$ with respect to the set of applications $Q = \{q_1, q_2, \ldots, q_q\}$ is defined as

$$aff(A_i, A_j) = \sum_{k|use(q_k,A_i)=1 \wedge use(q_k,A_j)=1} \sum_{\forall S_l} ref_l(q_k)acc_l(q_k)$$

where $ref_l(q_k)$ is the number of accesses to attributes $(A_i, A_j)$ for each execution of application $q_k$ at site $S_l$ and $acc_l(q_k)$ is the application access frequency measure previously defined and modified to include frequencies at different sites.

The result of this computation is an $n \times n$ matrix, each element of which is one of the measures defined above. We call this matrix the *attribute affinity matrix* ($AA$).

**Example 5.16**

Let us continue with the case that we examined in Example 5.15. For simplicity, let us assume that $ref_l(q_k) = 1$ for all $q_k$ and $S_l$. If the application frequencies are

$$
\begin{array}{lll}
acc_1(q_1) = 15 & acc_2(q_1) = 20 & acc_3(q_1) = 10 \\
acc_1(q_2) = 5 & acc_2(q_2) = 0 & acc_3(q_2) = 0 \\
acc_1(q_3) = 25 & acc_2(q_3) = 25 & acc_3(q_3) = 25 \\
acc_1(q_4) = 3 & acc_2(q_4) = 0 & acc_3(q_4) = 0
\end{array}
$$

then the affinity measure between attributes $A_1$ and $A_3$ can be measured as

$$aff(A_1, A_3) = \sum_{k=1}^{1} \sum_{l=1}^{3} acc_l(q_k) = acc_1(q_1) + acc_2(q_1) + acc_3(q_1) = 45$$

since the only application that accesses both of the attributes is $q_1$. The complete attribute affinity matrix is shown in Figure 5.16. Note that for completeness the diagonal values are also computed even though they are meaningless.

|       | $A_1$ | $A_2$ | $A_3$ | $A_4$ |
|-------|-------|-------|-------|-------|
| $A_1$ | 45    | 0     | 45    | 0     |
| $A_2$ | 0     | 80    | 5     | 75    |
| $A_3$ | 45    | 5     | 53    | 3     |
| $A_4$ | 0     | 75    | 3     | 78    |

**Figure 5.16**   Attribute Affinity Matrix

The attribute affinity matrix will be used in the rest of this chapter to guide the fragmentation effort. The process involves first clustering together the attributes with high affinity for each other, and then splitting the relation accordingly.

**Clustering algorithm.**   The fundamental task in designing a vertical fragmentation algorithm is to find some means of grouping the attributes of a relation based on the attribute affinity values in $AA$. It has been suggested by [Hoffer and Severance, 1975] and [Navathe et al., 1984] that the bond energy algorithm (BEA) [McCormick et al., 1972] should be used for this purpose. It is considered appropriate for the following reasons [Hoffer and Severance, 1975]:

1. It is designed specifically to determine groups of similar items as opposed to, say, a linear ordering of the items (i.e., it clusters the attributes with larger affinity values together, and the ones with smaller values together).

2. The final groupings are insensitive to the order in which items are presented to the algorithm.

3. The computation time of the algorithm is reasonable [$O(n^2)$, where $n$ is the number of attributes].

4. Secondary interrelationships between clustered attribute groups are identifiable.

The bond energy algorithm takes as input the attribute affinity matrix, permutes its rows and columns, and generates a *clustered affinity matrix* ($CA$). The permutation is done in such a way as to *maximize* the following *global affinity measure* ($AM$):

$$AM = \sum_{i=1}^{n} \sum_{j=1}^{n} aff(A_i, A_j)[aff(A_i, A_{j-1}) + aff(A_i, A_{j+1})$$
$$+ \ aff(A_{i-1}, A_j) + aff(A_{i+1}, A_j)]$$

where

$$aff(A_0, A_j) = aff(A_i, A_0) = aff(A_{n+1}, A_j) = aff(A_i, A_{n+1}) = 0$$

The last set of conditions takes care of the cases where an attribute is being placed in $CA$ to the left of the leftmost attribute or to the right of the rightmost attribute during column permutations, and prior to the topmost row and following the last row during row permutations. In these cases, we take 0 to be the *aff* values between the attribute being considered for placement and its left or right (top or bottom) neighbors, which do not exist in $CA$.

The maximization function considers the nearest neighbors only, thereby resulting in the grouping of large values with large ones, and small values with small ones. Also, the attribute affinity matrix ($AA$) is symmetric, which reduces the objective function of the formulation above to

$$AM = \sum_{i=1}^{n} \sum_{j=1}^{n} aff(A_i, A_j)[aff(A_i, A_{j-1}) + aff(A_i, A_{j+1})]$$

The details of the bond energy algorithm are given in Algorithm 5.3. Generation of the clustered affinity matrix ($CA$) is done in three steps:

1. *Initialization.* Place and fix one of the columns of $AA$ arbitrarily into $CA$. Column 1 was chosen in the algorithm.

2. *Iteration.* Pick each of the remaining $n-i$ columns (where $i$ is the number of columns already placed in $CA$) and try to place them in the remaining $i+1$ positions in the $CA$ matrix. Choose the placement that makes the greatest contribution to the global affinity measure described above. Continue this step until no more columns remain to be placed.

3. *Row ordering.* Once the column ordering is determined, the placement of the rows should also be changed so that their relative positions match the relative positions of the columns.[3]

**Algorithm 5.3**    *BEA*

**input:** $AA$: attribute affinity matrix
**output:** $CA$: clustered affinity matrix
**begin**
    {initialize; remember that $AA$ is an $n \times n$ matrix}
    $CA(\bullet, 1) \leftarrow AA(\bullet, 1)$
    $CA(\bullet, 2) \leftarrow AA(\bullet, 2)$
    $index \leftarrow 3$
    **while** $index \leq n$ **do** {choose the "best" location for attribute $AA_{index}$}
    **begin**
        **for** $i$ **from** 1 **to** $index - 1$ **by** 1 **do**
            calculate $cont(A_{i-1}, A_{index}, A_i)$
        **end-for**
        calculate $cont(A_{index-1}, A_{index}, A_{index+1})$   {boundary condition}
        $loc \leftarrow$ placement given by maximum $cont$ value
        **for** $j$ **from** $index$ **to** $loc$ **by** $-1$ **do**         {shuffle the two matrices}
            $CA(\bullet, j) \leftarrow CA(\bullet, j-1)$
        **end-for**
        $CA(\bullet, loc) \leftarrow AA(\bullet, index)$
        $index \leftarrow index + 1$
    **end-while**
    order the rows according to the relative ordering of columns
**end.** {BEA}

---

[3]From now on, we may refer to elements of the $AA$ and $CA$ matrices as $AA(i,j)$ and $CA(i,j)$, respectively. This is done for notational convenience only. The mapping to the affinity measures is $AA(i,j) = aff(A_i, A_j)$ and $CA(i,j) = aff$(attribute placed at column $i$ in $CA$, attribute placed at column $j$ in $CA$). Even though $AA$ and $CA$ matrices are identical except for the ordering of attributes, since the algorithm orders all the $CA$ columns before it orders the rows, the affinity measure of $CA$ is specified with respect to columns. Note that the endpoint condition for the calculation of the affinity measure $(AM)$ can be specified, using this notation, as $CA(0,j) = CA(i,0) = CA(n+1,j) = CA(i,n+1) = 0$.

For the second step of the algorithm to work, we need to define what is meant by the contribution of an attribute to the affinity measure. This contribution can be derived as follows. Recall that the global affinity measure $AM$ was previously defined as

$$AM = \sum_{i=1}^{n}\sum_{j=1}^{n} aff(A_i, A_j)[aff(A_i, A_{j-1}) + aff(A_i, A_{j+1})]$$

which can be rewritten as

$$
\begin{aligned}
AM &= \sum_{i=1}^{n}\sum_{j=1}^{n}[aff(A_i, A_j)aff(A_i, A_{j-1}) + aff(A_i, A_j)aff(A_i, A_{j+1})]\\
&= \sum_{j=1}^{n}\left[\sum_{i=1}^{n} aff(A_i, A_j)aff(A_i, A_{j-1}) + \sum_{i=1}^{n} aff(A_i, A_j)aff(A_i, A_{j+1})\right]
\end{aligned}
$$

Let us define the *bond* between two attributes $A_x$ and $A_y$ as

$$bond(A_x, A_y) = \sum_{z=1}^{n} aff(A_z, A_x)aff(A_z, A_y)$$

Then $AM$ can be written as

$$AM = \sum_{j=1}^{n}[bond(A_j, A_{j-1}) + bond(A_j, A_{j+1})]$$

Now consider the following $n$ attributes

$$\underbrace{A_1\ A_2\ \ldots\ A_{i-1}}_{AM'}\ A_i\ A_j\ \underbrace{A_{j+1}\ \ldots\ A_n}_{AM''}$$

The global affinity measure for these attributes can be written as

$$
\begin{aligned}
AM_{old} &= AM' + AM'' + bond(A_i, A_j) + bond(A_j, A_i)\\
&= \sum_{l=1}^{n}[bond(A_l, A_{l-1}) + bond(A_l, A_{l+1})]\\
&\quad + \sum_{l=i+2}^{n}[bond(A_l, A_{l-1}) + bond(A_l, A_{l+1})]\\
&\quad + 2bond(A_i, A_j)
\end{aligned}
$$

Now consider placing a new attribute $A_k$ between attributes $A_i$ and $A_j$ in the clustered affinity matrix. The new global affinity measure can be similarly written as

$$AM_{new} \;=\; AM' + AM'' + bond(A_i, A_k) + bond(A_k, A_i)$$
$$+bond(A_k, A_j) + bond(A_j, A_k)$$
$$=\; AM' + AM'' + 2bond(A_i, A_k) + 2bond(A_k, A_j)$$

Thus, the net *contribution*[4] to the global affinity measure of placing attribute $A_k$ between $A_i$ and $A_j$ is

$$cont(A_i, A_k, A_j) \;=\; AM_{new} - AM_{old}$$
$$=\; 2bond(A_i, A_k) + 2bond(A_k, A_j) - 2bond(A_i, A_j)$$

**Example 5.17**

Let us consider the $AA$ matrix given in Figure 5.16 and study the contribution of moving attribute $A_4$ between attributes $A_1$ and $A_2$, given by the formula

$$cont(A_1, A_4, A_2) = 2bond(A_1, A_4) + 2bond(A_4, A_2) - 2bond(A_1, A_2)$$

Computing each term, we get

$$bond(A_1, A_4) \;=\; 45 * 0 + 0 * 75 + 45 * 3 + 0 * 78 = 135$$
$$bond(A_4, A_2) \;=\; 11865$$
$$bond(A_1, A_2) \;=\; 225$$

Therefore,

$$cont(A_1, A_4, A_2) = 2 * 135 + 2 * 11865 - 2 * 225 = 23550$$

Note that the calculation of the bond between two attributes requires the multiplication of the respective elements of the two columns representing these attributes and taking the row-wise sum.

The algorithm and our discussion so far have both concentrated on the columns of the attribute affinity matrix. We can make the same arguments and redesign the algorithm to operate on the rows as well. Since the $AA$ matrix is symmetric, both of these approaches will generate the same result.

Another point about Algorithm 5.3 is that to improve the efficiency, the second column is also fixed and placed next to the first one during the initialization step. This is acceptable since, according to the algorithm, $A_2$ can be placed either to the left of $A_1$ or to its right. The bond between the two, however, is independent of their positions relative to one another.

Finally, we should indicate the problem of computing *cont* at the endpoints. If an attribute $A_i$ is being considered for placement to the left of the leftmost attribute, one of the bond equations to be calculated is between a nonexistent left element and $A_k$ [i.e., $bond(A_0, A_k)$]. Thus we need to refer to the conditions imposed on the definition

---

[4]In literature [Hoffer and Severance, 1975] this measure is specified as $bond(A_i, A_k) + bond(A_k, A_j) - 2bond(A_i, A_j)$. However, this is a pessimistic measure which does not follow from the definition of $AM$.

of the global affinity measure $AM$, where $CA(0, k) = 0$. The other extreme is if $A_j$ is the rightmost attribute that is already placed in the $CA$ matrix and we are checking for the contribution of placing attribute $A_k$ to the right of $A_j$. In this case the $bond(k, k + 1)$ needs to be calculated. However, since no attribute is yet placed in column $k + 1$ of $CA$, the affinity measure is not defined. Therefore, according to the endpoint conditions, this $bond$ value is also 0.

**Example 5.18**

We consider the clustering of the J relation attributes and use the attribute affinity matrix $AA$ of Figure 5.16.

According to the initialization step, we copy columns 1 and 2 of the $AA$ matrix to the $CA$ matrix (Figure 5.17a) and start with column 3 (i.e., attribute $A_3$). There are three alternative places where column 3 can be placed: to the left of column 1, resulting in the ordering (3-1-2), in between columns 1 and 2, giving (1-3-2), and to the right of 2, resulting in (1-2-3). Note that to compute the contribution of the last ordering we have to compute $cont(A_2, A_3, A_4)$ rather than $cont(A_1, A_2, A_3)$. Furthermore, in this context $A_4$ refers to the fourth index position in the $CA$ matrix, which is empty (Figure 5.17c), not to the attribute column $A_4$ of the $AA$ matrix. Let us calculate the contribution to the global affinity measure of each alternative.

Ordering (0-3-1):

$$cont(A_0, A_3, A_1) = 2bond(A_0, A_3) + 2bond(A_3, A_1) - 2bond(A_0, A_1)$$

We know that

$$
\begin{aligned}
bond(A_0, A_1) &= bond(A_0, A_3) = 0 \\
bond(A_3, A_1) &= 45*45 + 5*0 + 53*45 + 3*0 = 4410
\end{aligned}
$$

Thus

$$cont(A_0, A_3, A_1) = 8820$$

Ordering (1-3-2):

$$
\begin{aligned}
cont(A_1, A_3, A_2) &= 2bond(A_1, A_3) + 2bond(A_3, A_2) - 2bond(A_1, A_2) \\
bond(A_1, A_3) &= bond(A_3, A_1) = 4410 \\
bond(A_3, A_2) &= 890 \\
bond(A_1, A_2) &= 225
\end{aligned}
$$

Thus

$$cont(A_1, A_3, A_2) = 10150$$

Ordering (2-3-4):

$$
\begin{aligned}
cont(A_2, A_3, A_4) &= 2bond(A_2, A_3) + 2bond(A_3, A_4) - 2bond(A_2, A_4) \\
bond(A_2, A_3) &= 890 \\
bond(A_3, A_4) &= 0 \\
bond(A_2, A_4) &= 0
\end{aligned}
$$

Thus

$$cont(A_2, A_3, A_4) = 1780$$

Since the contribution of the ordering (1-3-2) is the largest, we select to place $A_3$ to the right of $A_1$ (Figure 5.17b). Similar calculations for $A_4$ indicate that it should be placed to the right of $A_2$ (Figure 5.17c).

Finally, the rows are organized in the same order as the columns and the result is shown in Figure 5.17d.

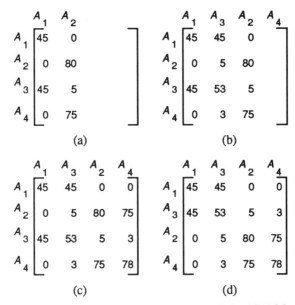

**Figure 5.17**    Calculation of the Clustered Affinity (CA) Matrix

In Figure 5.17d we see the creation of two clusters: one is in the upper left corner and contains the smaller affinity values and the other is in the lower right corner and contains the larger affinity values. This clustering indicates how the attributes of relation J should be split. However, in general the border for this split is not this clear-cut. When the $CA$ matrix is big, usually more than two clusters are formed and there are more than one candidate partitionings. Thus there is a need to approach this problem more systematically.

**Partitioning algorithm.**    The objective of the splitting activity is to find sets of attributes that are accessed solely, or for the most part, by distinct sets of applications. For example, if it is possible to identify two attributes, $A_1$ and $A_2$, which are accessed only by application $q_1$, and attributes $A_3$ and $A_4$, which are accessed by, say, two applications $q_2$ and $q_3$, it would be quite straightforward to decide on the fragments. The task lies in finding an algorithmic method of identifying these groups.

Consider the clustered attribute matrix of Figure 5.18. If a point along the diagonal is fixed, two sets of attributes are identified. One set $\{A_1, A_2, \ldots, A_i\}$ is at the upper left-hand corner and the second set $\{A_{i+1}, \ldots, A_n\}$ is to the right and to the bottom of this point. We call the former set *top* and the latter set *bottom* and denote the attribute sets as $TA$ and $BA$, respectively.

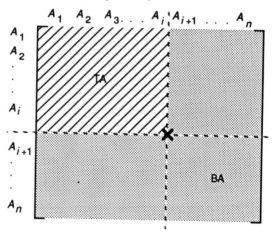

**Figure 5.18**    Locating a Splitting Point

We now turn to the set of applications $Q = \{q_1, q_2, \ldots, q_q\}$ and define the set of applications that access only $TA$, only $BA$, or both. These sets are defined as follows:

$$
\begin{aligned}
AQ(q_i) &= \{A_j | use(q_i, A_j) = 1\} \\
TQ &= \{q_i | AQ(q_i) \subseteq TA\} \\
BQ &= \{q_i | AQ(q_i) \subseteq BA\} \\
OQ &= Q - \{TQ \cup BQ\}
\end{aligned}
$$

The first of these equations defines the set of attributes accessed by application $q_i$; $TQ$ and $BQ$ are the sets of applications that only access $TA$ or $BA$, respectively, and $OQ$ is the set of applications that access both.

There is an optimization problem here. If there are $n$ attributes of a relation, there are $n - 1$ possible positions where the dividing point can be placed along the diagonal of the clustered attribute matrix for that relation. The best position for division is one which produces the sets $TQ$ and $BQ$ such that the total accesses to *only one* fragment are maximized while the total accesses to *both* fragments are minimized. We therefore define the following cost equations:

$$
CQ = \sum_{q_i \in Q} \sum_{\forall S_j} ref_j(q_i) acc_j(q_i)
$$

$$
CTQ = \sum_{q_i \in TQ} \sum_{\forall S_j} ref_j(q_i) acc_j(q_i)
$$

$$CBQ = \sum_{q_i \in BQ} \sum_{\forall S_j} ref_j(q_i) acc_j(q_i)$$

$$COQ = \sum_{q_i \in OQ} \sum_{\forall S_j} ref_j(q_i) acc_j(q_i)$$

Each of the equations above counts the total number of accesses to attributes by applications in their respective classes. Based on these measures, the optimization problem is defined as finding the point $x$ ($1 \le x \le n$) such that the expression

$$z = CTQ * CBQ - COQ^2$$

is maximized [Navathe et al., 1984]. The important feature of this expression is that it defines two fragments such that the values of $CTQ$ and $CBQ$ are as nearly equal as possible. This enables the balancing of processing loads when the fragments are distributed to various sites. It is clear that the partitioning algorithm has linear complexity in terms of the number of attributes of the relation, that is, $O(n)$.

There are two complications that need to be addressed. The first is with respect to the splitting. The careful reader should have noticed that the procedure splits the set of attributes two-way. For larger sets of attributes, it is quite likely that $m$-way partitioning may be necessary.

Designing an $n$-way partitioning is possible but computationally expensive. Along the diagonal of the $CA$ matrix, it is necessary to try $1, 2, \ldots, n-1$ split points, and for each of these, it is necessary to check which place maximizes $z$. Thus the complexity of such an algorithm is $O(2^n)$. Of course, the definition of $z$ has to be modified for those cases where there are multiple split points. The alternative solution is to recursively apply the binary partitioning algorithm to each of the fragments obtained during the previous iteration. One would compute $TQ$, $BQ$, and $OQ$, as well as the associated access measures for each of the fragments, and partition them further.

The second complication relates to the location of the block of attributes that should form one fragment. Our discussion so far assumed that the split point is unique and single and divides the $CA$ matrix into an upper left-hand partition and a second partition formed by the rest of the attributes. The partition, however, may also be formed in the middle of the matrix. In this case we need to modify the algorithm slightly. The leftmost column of the $CA$ matrix is shifted to become the rightmost column and the topmost row is shifted to the bottom. The shift operation is followed by checking the $n-1$ diagonal positions to find the maximum $z$. The idea behind shifting is to move the block of attributes that should form a cluster to the topmost left corner of the matrix, where it can easily be identified. With the addition of the shift operation, the complexity of the partitioning algorithm increases by a factor of $n$ and becomes $O(n^2)$.

Assuming that a shift procedure, called SHIFT, has already been implemented, the partitioning algorithm is given in Algorithm 5.4. The input of the PARTITION is the clustered affinity matrix $CA$ and the relation $R$ to be fragmented. The output is a set of fragments $F_R = \{R_1, R_2\}$, where $R_i \subseteq \{A_1, A_2 \ldots, A_n\}$ and $R_1 \cap R_2 =$ the key attributes of relation $R$. Note that for $n$-way partitioning, this routine should either be invoked iteratively, or implemented as a recursive procedure that iterates itself.

**Algorithm 5.4**  *PARTITION*

> **input:** $CA$: clustered affinity matrix; $R$: relation
> **output:** $F$: set of fragments
> **begin**
> > {determine the z value for the first column}
> > {the subscripts in the cost equations indicate the split point}
> > calculate $CTQ_{n-1}$
> > calculate $CBQ_{n-1}$
> > calculate $COQ_{n-1}$
> > $best \leftarrow CTQ_{n-1} * CBQ_{n-1} - (COQ_{n-1})^2$
> > **do**                                    {determine the best partitioning}
> > > **begin**
> > > > **for i from** $n-2$ **to 1 by** $-1$ **do**
> > > > **begin**
> > > > > calculate $CTQ_i$
> > > > > calculate $CBQ_i$
> > > > > calculate $COQ_i$
> > > > > $z \leftarrow CTQ * CBQ_i - COQ_i^2$
> > > > > **if** $z > best$ **then**
> > > > > **begin**
> > > > > > $best \leftarrow z$
> > > > > > record the shift position
> > > > > **end-if**
> > > > **end-for**
> > > > call SHIFT($CA$)
> > > **end-begin**
> > **until** no more SHIFT is possible
> > reconstruct the matrix according to the shift position
> > $R_1 \leftarrow \Pi_{TA}(R) \cup K$ {$K$ is the set of primary key attributes of $R$}
> > $R_2 \leftarrow \Pi_{BA}(R) \cup K$
> > $F \leftarrow \{R_1, R_2\}$
> **end.** {PARTITION}

**Example 5.19**

When the PARTITION algorithm is applied to the $CA$ matrix obtained for relation J (Example 5.18), the result is the definition of fragments $F_J = \{J_1, J_2\}$, where $J_1 = \{A_1, A_3\}$ and $J_2 = \{A_1, A_2, A_4\}$. Thus

$$J_1 \quad = \quad \{\text{JNO, BUDGET}\}$$
$$J_2 \quad = \quad \{\text{JNO, JNAME, LOC}\}$$

Note that in this exercise we performed the fragmentation over the entire set of attributes rather than only on the nonkey ones. The reason for this is the simplicity of the example. For that reason, we included JNO, which is the key of J in J $_2$ as well as in J $_1$.

**Checking for correctness.**    We follow arguments similar to those of horizontal partitioning to prove that the PARTITION algorithm yields a correct vertical fragmentation.

*Completeness.*    Completeness is guaranteed by the PARTITION algorithm since each attribute of the global relation is assigned to one of the fragments. As long as the set of attributes $A$ over which the relation $R$ is defined consists of

$$A = TA \cup TB$$

completeness of vertical fragmentation is ensured.

*Reconstruction.*    We have already mentioned that the reconstruction of the original global relation is made possible by the join operation. Thus, for a relation $R$ with vertical fragmentation $F_R = \{R_1, R_2, \ldots, R_r\}$ and key attribute(s) $K$,

$$R = \bowtie_K R_i, \forall R_i \in F_R$$

Therefore, as long as each $R_i$ is complete, the join operation will properly reconstruct $R$. Another important point is that either each $R_i$ should contain the key attribute(s) of $R$, or it should contain the system assigned tuple IDs (TIDs).

*Disjointness.*    As we indicated before, the disjointness of fragments is not as important in vertical fragmentation as it is in horizontal fragmentation. There are two cases here:

1.  TIDs are used, in which case the fragments are disjoint since the TIDs that are replicated in each fragment are system assigned and managed entities, totally invisible to the users.

2.  The key attributes are replicated in each fragment, in which case one cannot claim that they are disjoint in the strict sense of the term. However, it is important to realize that this duplication of the key attributes is known and managed by the system and does not have the same implications as tuple duplication in horizontally partitioned fragments. In other words, as long as the fragments are disjoint except for the key attributes, we can be satisfied and call them disjoint.

### 5.3.3 Hybrid Fragmentation

In most cases a simple horizontal or vertical fragmentation of a database schema will not be sufficient to satisfy the requirements of user applications. In this case a vertical fragmentation may be followed by a horizontal one, or vice versa, producing a tree-structured partitioning (Figure 5.19). Since the two types of partitioning strategies are applied one after the other, this alternative is called *hybrid* fragmentation. It has also been named *mixed* fragmentation or *nested* fragmentation.

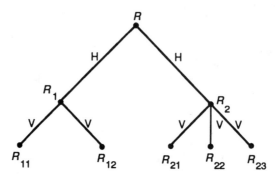

**Figure 5.19**    Hybrid Fragmentation

A good example for the necessity of hybrid fragmentation is relation J, which we have been working with. In Example 5.11 we partitioned it into six horizontal fragments based on two applications. In Example 5.19 we partitioned the same relation vertically into two. What we have, therefore, is a set of horizontal fragments, each of which is further partitioned into two vertical fragments.

The number of levels of nesting can be large, but it is certainly finite. In the case of horizontal fragmentation, one has to stop when each fragment consists of only one tuple, whereas the termination point for vertical fragmentation is one attribute per fragment. These limits are quite academic, however, since the levels of nesting in most practical applications do not exceed 2. This is due to the fact that normalized global relations already have small degrees and one cannot perform too many vertical fragmentations before the cost of joins becomes very high.

We will not discuss in detail the correctness rules and conditions for hybrid fragmentation, since they follow naturally from those for vertical and horizontal fragmentations. For example, to reconstruct the original global relation in case of hybrid fragmentation, one starts at the leaves of the partitioning tree and moves upward by performing joins and unions (Figure 5.20). The fragmentation is complete if the intermediate and leaf fragments are complete. Similarly, disjointness is guaranteed if intermediate and leaf fragments are disjoint.

## 5.4 ALLOCATION

The allocation of resources across the nodes of a computer network is a problem that has been studied extensively. Most of this work, however, does not address the problem of distributed database design, but rather that of placing individual files on a com-

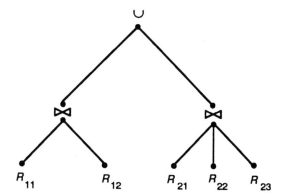

**Figure 5.20**   Reconstruction of Hybrid Fragmentation

puter network. We will examine the differences between the two shortly. We first need to define the allocation problem more precisely.

### 5.4.1 Allocation Problem

Assume that there are a set of fragments $F = \{F_1, F_2, \ldots, F_n\}$ and a network consisting of sites $S = \{S_1, S_2, \ldots, S_m\}$ on which a set of applications $Q = \{q_1, q_2, \ldots, q_q\}$ is running. The allocation problem involves finding the "optimal" distribution of $F$ to $S$.

One of the important issues that needs to be discussed is the definition of optimality. The optimality can be defined with respect to two measures [Dowdy and Foster, 1982]:

1. *Minimal cost.* The cost function consists of the cost of storing each $F_i$ at a site $S_j$, the cost of querying $F_i$ at site $S_j$, the cost of updating $F_i$ at all sites where it is stored, and the cost of data communication. The allocation problem, then, attempts to find an allocation scheme that minimizes a combined cost function.

2. *Performance.* The allocation strategy is designed to maintain a performance metric. Two well-known ones are to minimize the response time and to maximize the system throughput at each site.

Most of the models that have been proposed to date make this distinction of optimality. However, if one really examines the problem in depth, it is apparent that the "optimality" measure should include both the performance and the cost factors. In other words, one should be looking for an allocation scheme that, for example, answers user queries in minimal time while keeping the cost of processing minimal. A similar statement can be made for throughput maximization. One can then ask why such models have not been developed. The answer is quite simple: complexity.

Let us consider a *very* simple formulation of the problem. Let $F$ and $S$ be defined as before. For the time being, we consider only a single fragment, $F_k$. We make a number of assumptions and definitions that will enable us to model the allocation problem.

1. Assume that $Q$ can be modified so that it is possible to identify the update and the retrieval-only queries, and to define the following for a *single* fragment $F_k$:

$$T = \{t_1, t_2, \ldots, t_m\}$$

where $t_i$ is the read-only traffic generated at site $S_i$ for $F_k$, and

$$U = \{u_1, u_2, \ldots, u_m\}$$

where $u_i$ is the update traffic generated at site $S_i$ for $F_k$.

2. Assume that the communication cost between any two pair of sites $S_i$ and $S_j$ is fixed for a unit of transmission. Furthermore, assume that it is different for updates and retrievals in order that the following can be defined:

$$\begin{aligned} C(T) &= \{c_{12}, c_{13}, \ldots, c_{1m}, \ldots, c_{m-1,m}\} \\ C'(U) &= \{c'_{12}, c'_{13}, \ldots, c'_{1m}, \ldots, c'_{m-1,m}\} \end{aligned}$$

where $c_{ij}$ is the unit communication cost for retrieval requests between sites $S_i$ and $S_j$, and $c'_{ij}$ is the unit communication cost for update requests between sites $S_i$ and $S_j$.

3. Let the cost of storing the fragment at site $S_i$ be $d_i$. Thus we can define $D = \{d_1, d_2, \ldots, d_m\}$ for the storage cost of fragment $F_k$ at all the sites.

4. Assume that there are no capacity constraints for either the sites or the communication links.

Then the allocation problem can be specified as a cost-minimization problem where we are trying to find the set $I \subseteq S$ that specifies where the copies of the fragment will be stored. In the following, $x_j$ denotes the decision variable for the placement such that

$$x_j = \begin{cases} 1 & \text{if the fragment } F_k \text{ is assigned to site } S_j \\ 0 & \text{otherwise} \end{cases}$$

The precise specification is as follows:

$$\min \left[ \sum_{i=1}^{m} \left( \sum_{j|S_j \in I} x_j u_j c'_{ij} + t_j \min_{j|S_j \in I} c_{ij} \right) + \sum_{j|S_j \in I} x_j d_j \right]$$

subject to

$$x_j = 0 \ or \ 1$$

The second term of the objective function calculates the total cost of storing all the duplicate copies of the fragment. The first term, on the other hand, corresponds to the cost of transmitting the updates to all the sites that hold the replicas of the fragment, and to the cost of executing the retrieval-only requests at the site, which will result in minimal data transmission cost.

This is a very simplistic formulation that is not suitable for distributed database design. But even if it were, there is another problem. This formulation, which comes from [Casey, 1972], has been proven to be NP-complete [Eswaran, 1974]. Various different formulations of the problem have been proven to be just as hard over the years (e.g., [Sacca and Wiederhold, 1985] and [Lam and Yu, 1980]). The implication is, of course, that for large problems (i.e., large number of fragments and sites), obtaining optimal solutions is probably not computationally feasible. Considerable research has therefore been devoted to finding good heuristics that provide suboptimal solutions.

There are a number of reasons why simplistic formulations such as the one we have discussed are not suitable for distributed database design. These are inherent to all the early file allocation models for computer networks.

1. One cannot treat fragments as individual files that can be allocated one at a time, in isolation. The placement of one fragment usually has an impact on the placement decisions about the other fragments which are accessed together since the access costs to the the remaining fragments may change (e.g., due to distributed join). Therefore, the relationship between fragments should be taken into account.

2. The access to data by applications is modeled very simply. A user request is issued at one site and all the data to answer it is transferred to that site. In distributed database systems, access to data is more complicated than this simple "remote file access" model suggests. Therefore, the relationship between the allocation and query processing should be properly modeled.

3. These models do not take into consideration the cost of integrity enforcement, yet locating two fragments involved in the same integrity constraint at two different sites can be costly.

4. Similarly, the cost of enforcing concurrency control mechanisms should be considered [Rothnie and Goodman, 1977].

In summary, let us remember the interrelationship between the distributed database problems as depicted in Figure 1.8. Since the allocation is so central, its relationship with algorithms that are implemented for other problem areas needs to be represented in the allocation model. However, this is exactly what makes it quite difficult to solve these models. To separate the traditional problem of file allocation from the fragment allocation in distributed database design, we refer to the former as the *file allocation problem* (FAP) and to the latter as the *database allocation problem* (DAP).

There are no general heuristic models that take as input a set of fragments and produce a near-optimal allocation subject to the types of constraints discussed here.

The models developed to date make a number of simplifying assumptions and are applicable to certain specific formulations. Therefore, instead of presenting one or more of these allocation algorithms, we present a relatively general model and then discuss a number of possible heuristics that might be employed to solve it.

### 5.4.2 Information Requirements

It is at the allocation stage that we need the quantitative data about the database, the applications that run on it, the communication network, the processing capabilities, and storage limitations of each site on the network. We will discuss each of these in detail.

**Database information.**   To perform horizontal fragmentation, we defined the selectivity of minterms. We now need to extend that definition to fragments, and define the selectivity of a fragment $F_j$ with respect to query $q_i$. This is the number of tuples of $F_j$ that need to be accessed in order to process $q_i$. This value will be denoted as $sel_i(F_j)$.

Another piece of necessary information on the database fragments is their size. The size of a fragment $F_j$ is given by

$$size(F_j) = card(F_j) * length(F_j)$$

where $length(F_j)$ is the length (in bytes) of a tuple of fragment $F_j$.

**Application information.**   Most of the application-related information is already compiled during the fragmentation activity, but a few more are required by the allocation model. The two important measures are the number of read accesses that a query $q_i$ makes to a fragment $F_j$ during its execution (denoted as $RR_{ij}$), and its counterpart for the update accesses ($UR_{ij}$). These may, for example, count the number of block accesses required by the query.

We also need to define two matrices $UM$ and $RM$, with elements $u_{ij}$ and $r_{ij}$, respectively, which are specified as follows:

$$u_{ij} = \begin{cases} 1 & \text{if query } q_i \text{ updates fragment } F_j \\ 0 & \text{otherwise} \end{cases}$$

$$r_{ij} = \begin{cases} 1 & \text{if query } q_i \text{ retrieves from fragment } F_j \\ 0 & \text{otherwise} \end{cases}$$

A vector $O$ of values $o(i)$ is also defined, where $o(i)$ specifies the originating site of query $q_i$. Finally, to define the response-time constraint, the maximum allowable response time of each application should be specified.

**Site information.**   For each computer site, we need to know about its storage and processing capacity. Obviously, these values can be computed by means of elaborate functions or by simple estimates. The unit cost of storing data at site $S_k$ will be denoted as $USC_k$. There is also a need to specify a cost measure $LPC_k$ as the cost of processing one unit of work at site $S_k$. The work unit should be identical to that of the $RR$ and $UR$ measures.

**Network information.**    In our model we assume the existence of a simple network where the cost of communication is defined in terms of one frame of data. Thus $g_{ij}$ denotes the communication cost per frame between sites $S_i$ and $S_j$. To enable the calculation of the number of messages, we use $fsize$ as the size (in bytes) of one frame. There is no question that there are more elaborate network models which take into consideration the channel capacities, distances between sites, protocol overhead, and so on. However, the derivation of those equations is beyond the scope of this chapter.

### 5.4.3  Allocation Model

We discuss an allocation model that attempts to minimize the total cost of processing and storage while trying to meet certain response time restrictions. The model we use has the following form:

   min(Total Cost)

subject to

   response-time constraint
   storage constraint
   processing constraint

In the remainder of this section we expand the components of this model based on the information requirements discussed in Section 5.4.2. The decision variable is $x_{ij}$, which is defined as

$$x_{ij} = \begin{cases} 1 & \text{if the fragment } F_i \text{ is stored at site } S_j \\ 0 & \text{otherwise} \end{cases}$$

**Total cost.**    The total cost function has two components: query processing and storage. Thus it can be expressed as

$$TOC = \sum_{\forall q_i \in Q} QPC_i + \sum_{\forall S_k \in S} \sum_{\forall F_j \in F} STC_{jk}$$

where $QPC_i$ is the query processing cost of application $q_i$, and $STC_{jk}$ is the cost of storing fragment $F_j$ at site $S_k$.

Let us consider the storage cost first. It is simply given by

$$STC_{jk} = USC_k * size(F_j) * x_{jk}$$

and the two summations find the total storage costs at all the sites for all the fragments.

The query processing cost is more difficult to specify. Most models of the file allocation problem (FAP) separate it into two components: the retrieval-only processing cost, and the update processing cost. We choose a different approach in our model of the database allocation problem (DAP) and specify it as consisting of the processing cost ($PC$) and the transmission cost ($TC$). Thus the query processing cost ($QPC$) for application $q_i$ is

$$QPC_i = PC_i + TC_i$$

According to the guidelines presented in Section 5.4.1, the processing component, $PC$, consists of three cost factors, the access cost ($AC$), the integrity enforcement cost ($IE$), and the concurrency control cost ($CC$):

$$PC_i = AC_i + IE_i + CC_i$$

The detailed specification of each of these cost factors depends on the algorithms used to accomplish these tasks. However, to demonstrate the point, we specify $AC$ in some detail.

$$AC_i = \sum_{\forall S_k \in S} \sum_{\forall F_j \in F} (u_{ij} * UR_{ij} + r_{ij} * RR_{ij}) * x_{jk} * LPC_k$$

The first two terms in the formula above calculate the number of accesses of user query $q_i$ to fragment $F_j$. Note that $(UR_{ij} + RR_{ij})$ gives the total number of update and retrieval accesses. We assume that the local costs of processing them are identical. The summation gives the total number of accesses for all the fragments referenced by $q_i$. Multiplication by $LPC_k$ gives the cost of this access at site $S_k$. We again use $x_{jk}$ to select only those cost values for the sites where fragments are stored.

A very important issue needs to be pointed out here. The access cost function assumes that processing a query involves decomposing it into a set of subqueries, each of which works on a fragment stored at the site, followed by transmitting the results back to the site where the query has originated. As we discussed earlier, this is a very simplistic view which does not take into consideration the complexities of database processing. For example, the cost function does not take into account the cost of performing joins (if necessary), which may be executed in a number of ways, studied in Chapter 9. In a model that is more realistic than the generic model we are considering, these issues should not be omitted.

The integrity enforcement cost factor can be specified much like the processing component, except that the unit local processing cost would probably change to reflect the true cost of integrity enforcement. Since the integrity checking and concurrency control methods are discussed later in the book, we do not need to study these cost components further here. The reader should refer back to this section after reading Chapters 6 and 11 to be convinced that the cost functions can indeed be derived.

The transmission cost function can be formulated along the lines of the access cost function. However, the data transmission overhead for update and that for retrieval requests are quite different. In update queries it is necessary to inform all the sites where replicas exist, while in retrieval queries, it is sufficient to access only one of the copies. In addition, at the end of an update request, there is no data transmission back to the originating site other than a confirmation message, whereas the retrieval-only queries may result in significant data transmission.

The update component of the transmission function is

$$TCU_i = \sum_{\forall S_k \in S} \sum_{\forall F_j \in F} u_{ij} * x_{jk} * g_{o(i),k} + \sum_{\forall S_k \in S} \sum_{\forall F_j \in F} u_{ij} * x_{jk} * g_{k,o(i)}$$

The first term is for sending the update message from the originating site $o(i)$ of $q_i$ to all the fragment replicas that need to be updated. The second term is for the confirmation.

The retrieval cost can be specified as

$$TCR_i = \sum_{\forall F_j \in F} \min_{S_k \in S} \left( u_{ij} * x_{jk} * g_{o(i),k} + r_{ij} * x_{jk} * \frac{sel_i(F_j)}{fsize} * g_{k,o(i)} \right)$$

The first term in $TCR$ represents the cost of transmitting the retrieval request to those sites which have copies of fragments that need to be accessed. The second term accounts for the transmission of the results from these sites to the originating site. The equation states that among all the sites with copies of the same fragment, only the site that yields the minimum total transmission cost should be selected for the execution of the operation.

Now the transmission cost function for query $q_i$ can be specified as

$$TC_i = TCU_i + TCR_i$$

which fully specifies the total cost function.

**Constraints.**    The constraint functions can be specified in similar detail. However, instead of describing these functions in depth, we will simply indicate what they should look like. The response-time constraint should be specified as

execution time of $q_i \leq$ maximum response time of $q_i, \forall q_i \in Q$

Preferably, the cost measure in the objective function should be specified in terms of time, as it makes the specification of the execution-time constraint relatively straightforward.

The storage constraint is

$$\sum_{\forall F_j \in F} STC_{jk} \leq \text{storage capacity at site } S_k, \forall S_k \in S$$

whereas the processing constraint is

$$\sum_{\forall q_i \in Q} \text{processing load of } q_i \text{ at site } S_k \leq \text{processing capacity of } S_k, \forall S_k \in S$$

This completes our development of the allocation model. Even though we have not developed it entirely, the precision in some of the terms indicates how one goes about formulating such a problem. In addition to this aspect, we have indicated the important issues that need to be addressed in allocation models.

### 5.4.4 Solution Methods

In the preceding section we developed a generic allocation model which is considerably more complex than the FAP model presented in Section 5.4.1. Since the FAP model is NP-complete, one would expect the solution of this formulation of the database allocation problem (DAP) also to be NP-complete. Even though we will not prove this conjecture, it is indeed true. Thus one has to look for heuristic methods that yield suboptimal solutions. The test of "goodness" in this case is, obviously, how close the results of the heuristic algorithm are to the optimal allocation.

A number of different heuristics have been applied to the solution of FAP and DAP models. It was observed early on that there is a correspondence between FAP and the plant location problem that has been studied in operations research. In fact, the isomorphism of the simple FAP and the single commodity warehouse location problem has been shown [Ramamoorthy and Wah, 1983]. Thus heuristics developed by operations researchers have commonly been adopted to solve the FAP and DAP problems. Examples are the knapsack problem solution [Ceri et al., 1982b], branch-and-bound techniques [Fisher and Hochbaum, 1980], and network flow algorithms [Chang and Liu, 1982].

There has been other attempts to reduce the complexity of the problem. One strategy has been to assume that all the candidate partitionings have been determined together with their associated costs and benefits in terms of query processing. The problem, then, is modeled so as to choose the optimal partitioning and placement for each relation [Ceri et al., 1983]. Another simplification frequently employed is to ignore replication at first and find an optimal nonreplicated solution. Replication is handled at the second step by applying a greedy algorithm which starts with the nonreplicated solution as the initial feasible solution, and tries to improve upon it ([Ceri et al., 1983] and [Ceri and Pernici, 1985]). For these heuristics, however, there is not enough data to determine how close the results are to the optimal.

## 5.5 CONCLUSION

In this chapter we presented the techniques that can be used for distributed database design with special emphasis on the fragmentation and allocation issues. There are a number of lines of research that have been followed in distributed database design. For example, Chang has independently developed a theory of fragmentation [Chang and Cheng, 1980], and allocation [Chang and Liu, 1982]. However, for its maturity of development, we have chosen to develop this chapter along the track developed by Ceri, Pelagatti, Navathe, and Wiederhold. Our references to the literature by these authors reflect this quite clearly.

There is a considerable body of literature on the allocation problem, focusing mostly on the simpler file allocation issue. We still do not have sufficiently general models that take into consideration all the aspects of data distribution. The model presented in Section 5.4 highlights the types of issues that need to be taken into account. Within this context, it might be worthwhile to take a somewhat different approach to the solution of the distributed allocation problem. One might develop a set of heuristic rules that might accompany the mathematical formulation and reduce the solution space, thus making the solution feasible.

One very interesting line of research in database design that has not been investigated fully is the use of simulation techniques. There is some work along these lines which analyzes the effects on the database performance of file redundancy ([Muro et al., 1983] and [Muro et al., 1985]) and of allocation decisions [Yoshida et al., 1985]. However, there has not yet been work that uses simulation as a design tool rather than an analysis one.

## 5.6  BIBLIOGRAPHIC NOTES

Most of the known results about fragmentation have been covered in this chapter. Work on fragmentation in distributed databases initially concentrated on horizontal fragmentation. Most of the literature on this has been cited in the appropriate section. The topic of vertical fragmentation for distribution design has been addressed in several recent papers ([Navathe et al., 1984] and [Sacca and Wiederhold, 1985]). The original work on vertical fragmentation goes back to Hoffer's dissertation [Hoffer, 1975] and to Hammer and Niamir's work ([Niamir, 1978] and [Hammer and Niamir, 1979]). Parts of Hoffer's dissertation were reported in [Hoffer and Severance, 1975].

It is not possible to be as exhaustive when discussing allocation as we have been for fragmentation, given there is no limit to the literature on the subject. The investigation of FAP on wide area networks goes back to [Chu, 1969] and [Chu, 1973]. Most of the early work on FAP has been covered in the excellent survey by [Dowdy and Foster, 1982]. Some theoretical results about FAP are reported in [Grapa and Belford, 1977] and in [Kollias and Hatzopoulos, 1981].

The DAP work dates back to the mid-1970s to the works of [Eswaran, 1974] and others. In their earlier work, Levin and Morgan [1975] concentrated on data allocation, but later they considered program and data allocation together [Morgan and Levin, 1977]. The DAP has been studied in many specialized settings as well. Work has been done to determine the placement of computers and data in a wide area network design [Gavish and Pirkul, 1986]. Channel capacities have been examined along with data placement [Mahmoud and Riordon, 1976] and data allocation on supercomputer systems [Irani and Khabbaz, 1982] as well as on a cluster of processors [Sacca and Wiederhold, 1985]. An interesting work is the one by Apers, where the relations are optimally placed on the nodes of a virtual network, and then the best matching between the virtual network nodes and the physical network are found [Apers, 1981].

Some of the allocation work has also touched upon physical design. The assignment of files to various levels of a memory hierarchy has been studied in [Foster and Browne, 1976] and in [Navathe et al., 1984]. These are outside the scope of this chapter, as are those that deal with general resource and task allocation in distributed systems (e.g., [Bucci and Golinelli, 1977], [Ceri and Pelagatti, 1982], and [Haessig and Jenny, 1980]).

We should finally point out that some effort was spent to develop a general methodology for distributed database design along the lines that we presented (Figure 5.2). Ours is similar to the DATAID-D methodology discussed in [Ceri and Navathe, 1983] and [Ceri et al., 1987]. Other attempts to develop a methodology are reported in [Fisher et al., 1980], [Dawson, 1980], [Hevner and Schneider, 1980] and [Mohan, 1979].

## 5.7 EXERCISES

**\*5.1** Consider relation G in Figure 5.3. Suppose there are two applications that access G. The first is issued at four sites and attempts to find the duration of assignment of employees given their numbers. Assume that managers, consultants, engineers, and programmers are located at four different sites. The second application is issued at two sites where the employees with an assignment duration of less than 20 months are managed at one site, whereas those with longer duration are managed at a second site. Derive the primary horizontal fragmentation of G using the foregoing information.

**5.2** Consider relations E and S in Figure 5.3. E and S are horizontally fragmented as follows:

$$
\begin{aligned}
E_1 &= \sigma_{\text{TITLE}=\text{"Elect.Eng."}}(E) \\
E_2 &= \sigma_{\text{TITLE}=\text{"Syst.Anal."}}(E) \\
E_3 &= \sigma_{\text{TITLE}=\text{"Mech.Eng."}}(E) \\
E_4 &= \sigma_{\text{TITLE}=\text{"Programmer"}}(E) \\
\\
S_1 &= \sigma_{\text{SAL}\geq 30000}(S) \\
S_2 &= \sigma_{\text{SAL}<30000}(S)
\end{aligned}
$$

Draw the join graph of E $\bowtie_{\text{TITLE}}$ S. Is the graph simple or partitioned? If it is partitioned, modify the fragmentation of either E or S so that the join graph of E $\bowtie_{\text{TITLE}}$ S is simple.

**5.3** Give an example of a $CA$ matrix where the split point is not unique and the partition is in the middle of the matrix. Show the number of shift operations required to obtain a single, unique split point.

**\*\*5.4** Let $Q = \{q_1, q_2, q_3, q_4, q_5\}$ be a set of queries, $A = \{A_1, A_2, A_3, A_4, A_5\}$ be a set of attributes, and $S = \{S_1, S_2, S_3\}$ be a set of sites. The matrix of Figure 5.21a describes the attribute usage values and the matrix of Figure 5.21b gives the application access frequencies. Assume that $ref_i(q_k) = 1$ for all $q_k$ and $S_i$ and that $A_1$ is the key attribute. Use the bond energy and vertical partitioning algorithms to obtain a vertical fragmentation of the set of attributes in $A$.

**\*\*5.5** Write an algorithm for derived horizontal fragmentation.

**\*\*5.6** Formally define the three correctness criteria for derived horizontal fragmentation.

**\*5.7** Show that the bond energy algorithm generates the same results using either row or column operation.

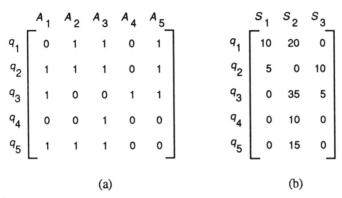

**Figure 5.21**    Attribute Usage Values and Application Access Frequencies in Exercise 5.4

**\*\*5.8**    Modify algorithm PARTITION to allow $n$-way partitioning, and compute the complexity of the resulting algorithm.

**\*\*5.9**    Formally define the three correctness criteria for hybrid fragmentation.

**5.10**    Discuss how the order in which the two basic fragmentation schemas are applied in hybrid fragmentation affects the final fragmentation.

**\*\*5.11**    Describe how the following can be properly modeled in the database allocation problem.

    **(a)**    Relationships among fragments
    **(b)**    Query processing
    **(c)**    Integrity enforcement
    **(d)**    Concurrency control mechanisms

**\*\*5.12**    Consider the various heuristic algorithms for the database allocation problem.

    **(a)**    What are some of the reasonable criteria for comparing these heuristics? Discuss.
    **(b)**    Compare the heuristic algorithms with respect to these criteria.

**\*5.13**    Pick one of the heuristic algorithms used to solve the DAP, and write a program for it.

# 6

# Semantic Data Control

An important requirement of a centralized or a distributed DBMS is the ability to support semantic data control. Semantic data control typically includes view management, security control, and semantic integrity control. Informally, these functions must ensure that *authorized* users perform *correct* operations on the database, contributing to the maintenance of database integrity. The functions necessary for maintaining the physical integrity of the database in the presence of concurrent accesses and failures are studied separately in Chapters 10 through 12. In the relational framework, semantic data control can be achieved in a uniform fashion. Views, security constraints, and semantic integrity constraints can be defined as rules that the system automatically enforces. The violation of some such rule by a user program (a set of database operations) generally implies the rejection of the effects of that program.

The definition of the rules for controlling data manipulation is part of the administration of the database, a function generally performed by a database administrator (DBA). This person is also in charge of applying the organizational policies. Well-known solutions for semantic data control have been proposed for centralized DBMSs. In this chapter we briefly review the centralized solution to semantic data control, and present the problems incurred in a distributed environment and solutions to these problems. The cost of enforcing semantic data control, which is high in terms of resource utilization in a centralized DBMS, can be prohibitive in a distributed environment.

Since the rules for semantic data control must be stored in a catalog, the management of a distributed directory (also called a catalog) is also relevant in this chapter. We discussed directories in Chapter 4. Remember that the directory of a distributed DBMS is itself a distributed database. There are several ways to store semantic data control definitions, according to the way the directory is managed. Directory information can be stored differently according to its type; in other words, some information might be fully duplicated whereas other information might be distributed. For example, information that is useful at compile time, such as security control information, could be duplicated. In this chapter we emphasize the impact of directory management on the performance of semantic data control mechanisms.

This chapter is organized as follows. View management is the subject of Section 6.1. Security control is presented in Section 6.2. Finally, semantic integrity control is treated in Section 6.3. For each section we first outline the solution in a centralized DBMS and then give the distributed solution, which is often an extension of the centralized one, although more difficult.

## 6.1 VIEW MANAGEMENT

One of the main advantages of the relational model is that it provides full logical data independence. As introduced in Chapter 4, external schemas enable user groups to have their particular *view* of the database. In a relational system, a view is a *virtual relation*, defined as the result of a query on *base relations* (or real relations), but not materialized like a base relation, which is stored in the database. A view is a dynamic window in the sense that it reflects all updates to the database. An external schema can be defined as a set of views and/or base relations. Besides their use in external schemas, views are useful for ensuring data security in a simple way. By selecting a subset of the database, views *hide* some data. If users may only access the database through views, they cannot see or manipulate the hidden data, which are therefore secure.

In the remainder of this section we look at view management in centralized and distributed systems as well as the problems of updating views. Note that in a distributed DBMS, a view can be derived from distributed relations, and the access to a view requires the execution of the distributed query corresponding to the view definition. An important issue in a distributed DBMS is to make view materialization efficient. We will see how the concept of snapshots helps to solve this problem, but first let us concentrate on centralized DBMSs.

### 6.1.1  Views in Centralized DBMSs

Most relational DBMSs use a view mechanism similar to those of INGRES [Stonebraker, 1975] and System R [Chamberline et al., 1975]. In this context a view is a relation derived from base relations as the result of a relational query. It is defined by associating the name of the view with the retrieval query that specifies it.

**Example 6.1**

The view SYSAN (system analysts) derived from relation E(ENO,ENAME,TITLE), can be defined by the following SQL query:

```
CREATE    VIEW    SYSAN(ENO, ENAME)
AS        SELECT  ENO, ENAME
          FROM    E
          WHERE   TITLE = ''Syst. Anal.''
```

The single effect of this statement is the storage of the view definition in the catalog. No other information needs to be recorded. Therefore, the result to the query defining the view (i.e., a relation having the attributes ENO and ENAME for the system analysts as shown in Figure 6.1) is *not* produced. However, the view SYSAN can be manipulated as a base relation.

SYSAN

| ENO | ENAME |
|-----|---------|
| E2  | M.Smith |
| E5  | B.Casey |
| E8  | J.Jones |

**Figure 6.1**    Relation Corresponding to the View SYSAN

**Example 6.2**

The query

> "Find the names of all the system analysts with their project number and responsibility(ies)"

involving the view SYSAN and relation G(ENO,JNO,RESP,DUR) can be expressed as

```
SELECT    ENAME, JNO, RESP
FROM      SYSAN, G
WHERE     SYSAN.ENO = G.ENO
```

Mapping a query expressed on views into a query expressed on base relations can be done by *query modification* [Stonebraker, 1975]. With this technique the variables are changed to range on base relations and the query qualification is merged (ANDed) with the view qualification.

**Example 6.3**

The preceding query can be modified to

```
SELECT    ENAME, JNO, RESP
FROM      E, G
WHERE     E.ENO = G.ENO
AND       TITLE = ''Syst. Anal.''
```

The result of this query is illustrated in Figure 6.2.

| ENAME | JNO | RESP |
|-------|-----|------|
| M.Smith | J1 | Analyst |
| M.Smith | J2 | Analyst |
| B.Casey | J3 | Manager |
| J.Jones | J4 | Manager |

**Figure 6.2**    Result of Query involving View SYSAN

The modified query is expressed on base relations and can therefore be processed by the query processor. It is important to note that view processing can be done at compile time. The view mechanism can also be used for refining the access controls to include subsets of objects. To specify any user from whom one wants to hide data, the key word USER generally refers to the logged-on user identifier.

**Example 6.4**

The view ESAME restricts the access by any user to those employees having the same title:

```
CREATE    VIEW    ESAME
AS        SELECT  *
          FROM    E E1, E E2
          WHERE   E1.TITLE = E2.TITLE
          AND     E1.ENO = USER
```

In the view definition above, * stands for "all attributes" and the two tuple variables (E1 and E2) ranging over relation E are required to express the join of one tuple of E (the one corresponding to the logged-on user) with all tuples of E based on the same title. For example, the following query issued by the user J. Doe,

```
SELECT    *
FROM      ESAME
```

returns the relation of Figure 6.3. Note that the user J. Doe also appears in the result. If the user who creates ESAME is an electrical engineer, as in this case, the view represents the set of all electrical engineers.

## 6.1.2  Updates through Views

Views can be defined using arbitrarily complex relational queries involving selection, projection, join, aggregate functions, and so on. All views can be interrogated as base relations, but not all views can be manipulated as such. Updates through views can be handled automatically only if they can be propagated correctly to the base relations.

| ENO | ENAME | TITLE |
|-----|-------|-------|
| E1 | J. Doe | Elect. Eng |
| E2 | L. Chu | Elect. Eng |

**Figure 6.3**   Result of Query on View ESAME

We can classify views as being updatable and not updatable. A view is updatable only if the updates to the view can be propagated to the base relations without ambiguity.

The view SYSAN above is updatable; the insertion, for example, of a new system analyst <201, Smith> will be mapped into the insertion of a new employee <201, Smith, Syst. Anal.>. If attributes other than TITLE were hidden by the view, they would be assigned *null values*. The following view, however, is not updatable:

```
CREATE    VIEW    EG(ENAME, RESP)
AS        SELECT  ENAME, RESP
          FROM    E, G
          WHERE   E.ENO = G.ENO
```

The deletion, for example, of the tuple <Smith, Analyst> cannot be propagated, since it is ambiguous. Deletions of Smith in relation E or analyst in relation G are both meaningful, but the system does not know which is correct.

Current systems are very restrictive about supporting updates through views. Views can be updated only if they are derived from a single relation by selection and projection. This precludes views defined by joins, aggregates, and so on. However, it is theoretically possible to automatically support updates of a larger class of views ([Bancilhon and Spyratos, 1981], [Dayal and Bernstein, 1978], and [Keller, 1982]). It is interesting to note that views derived by join are updatable if they include the keys of the base relations.

### 6.1.3 Views in Distributed DBMSs

The definition of a view is similar in a distributed DBMS and in centralized systems. However, a view in a distributed system may be derived from fragmented relations stored at different sites. When a view is defined, its name and its retrieval query are stored in the catalog.

Since views may be used as base relations by application programs, their definition should be stored in the directory in the same way as the base relation descriptions. Depending on the degree of site autonomy offered by the system [Williams et al., 1982], view definitions can be centralized at one site, partially duplicated, or fully duplicated. In any case, the information associating a view name to its definition site should be duplicated. If the view definition is not present at the site where the query is issued, remote access to the view definition site is necessary.

The mapping of a query expressed on views into a query expressed on base relations (which can potentially be fragmented) can also be done in the same way as in centralized systems, that is, through query modification. With this technique, the qualification defining the view is found in the distributed database catalog and then merged with the query to provide a query on base relations. Such a modified query is a *distributed query*, which can be processed by the distributed query processor (see Chapter 7). The query processor maps the distributed query into a query on physical fragments.

In Chapter 5 we presented alternative ways of fragmenting base relations. The definition of fragmentation is, in fact, very similar to the definition of particular views. In [Adiba, 1981], a unified mechanism for managing views and fragments is proposed. It is based on the observation that views in a distributed DBMS can be defined with rules similar to fragment definition rules. Furthermore, replicated data can be handled in the same way. The value of such a unified mechanism is to facilitate distributed database administration. The objects manipulated by the database administrator can be seen as a hierarchy where the leaves are the fragments from which relations and views can be derived. Therefore, the DBA may increase locality of reference by making views in one-to-one correspondence with fragments. For example, it is possible to implement the view SYSAN illustrated in Example 6.1 by a fragment at a given site, provided that most users accessing the view SYSAN are at the same site.

Views derived from distributed relations may be costly to evaluate. Since in a given organization it is likely that many users access the same views, some proposals have been made to optimize view derivation. We saw in Section 6.1.1 that view derivation is done by merging the view qualification with the query qualification. An alternative solution proposed in [Adiba and Lindsay, 1980] is to avoid view derivation by maintaining actual versions of the views, called *snapshots*. A snapshot represents a particular state of the database and is therefore *static*, meaning that it does not reflect updates to base relations. Snapshots are useful when users are not particularly interested in seeing the most recent version of the database. They are managed as temporary relations in the sense that they do not have access methods other than sequential scanning. Therefore, a query expressed on a snapshot will not exploit indices available on the base relations from which it is derived. Access through snapshots seems more adequate for queries that have bad selectivity and scan the entire snapshot. In this case a snapshot behaves more like a predefined answer to a query. It is necessary to recalculate snapshots periodically. However, this can be done when the system is idle. In addition, for snapshots derived by selection and projection, only the difference needs to be calculated [Blakeley et al., 1986].

## 6.2  DATA SECURITY

Data security is an important function of a database system that protects data against unauthorized access. Data security includes two aspects: *data protection* and *authorization control*.

Data protection is required to prevent unauthorized users from understanding the physical content of data. This function is typically provided by file systems in the context of centralized and distributed operating systems. The main data protection approach is data encryption [Fernandez et al., 1981], which is useful both for information stored on disk and for information exchanged on a network. Encrypted (encoded) data can be decrypted (decoded) only by authorized users who "know" the code. The two main schemes are the Data Encryption Standard [NBS, 1977] and the public-key encryption schemes ([Diffie and Hellman, 1976] and [Rivest et al., 1978]). In this section we concentrate on the second aspect of data security, which is more specific to database systems. A complete presentation of protection techniques can be found in [Fernandez et al., 1981].

Authorization control must guarantee that only authorized users perform operations they are allowed to perform on the database. Many different users may have access to a large collection of data under the control of a single centralized or distributed system. The centralized or distributed DBMS must thus be able to restrict the access of a subset of the database to a subset of the users. Authorization control has long been provided by operating systems, and more recently, by distributed operating systems [Tannenbaum and van Renesse, 1985] as services of the file system. In this context, a centralized control is offered. Indeed, the central controller creates objects, and this person may allow particular users to perform particular operations (read, write, execute) on these objects. Also, objects are identified by their external names.

Authorization control in database systems differs in several aspects from that in traditional file systems. Authorizations must be refined so that different users have different rights on the same database objects. This requirement implies the ability to specify subsets of objects more precisely than by name and to distinguish between groups of users. In addition, the decentralized control of authorizations is of particular importance in a distributed context. In relational systems, authorizations can be uniformly controlled by database administrators using high-level constructs. For example, controlled objects can be specified by predicates in the same way as is a query qualification.

From solutions to authorization control in centralized systems, we derive those for distributed DBMSs. However, there is the additional complexity which stems from the fact that objects and users can be distributed. In what follows we first present authorization control in centralized systems and then the additional problems and their solutions in distributed systems.

### 6.2.1 Centralized Authorization Control

Three main actors are involved in authorization control: the *users*, who trigger the execution of application programs; the *operations*, which are embedded in application programs; and the *database objects*, on which the operations are performed [Hoffman, 1977]. Authorization control consists of checking whether a given triple (user, operation, object) can be allowed to proceed (i.e., the user can execute the operation on the object). An authorization can be viewed as a triple (user, operation type, object definition) which specifies that the user has the right to perform an operation of operation type on a object. To control authorizations properly, the DBMS requires users, objects, and rights to be defined.

The introduction of a user (a person or a group of persons) in the system is typically done by a pair (user name, password). The user name uniquely *identifies* the users of that name in the system, while the password, known only to the users of that name, *authenticates* the users. Both user name and password must be supplied in order to log in the system. This prevents people who do not know the password to enter the system with only the user name.

The objects to protect are subsets of the database. Relational systems provide finer and more general protection granularity than do earlier systems. In a file system, the protection granule is the file, while in the network or hierarchical DBMS ([Taylor and Frank, 1976] and [Tsichritzis and Lochovsky, 1976]), it is the object type (e.g., record, file). In a relational system, objects can be defined by their type (view, relation, tuple, attribute) as well as by their content using selection predicates. Furthermore, the view mechanism as introduced in Section 6.1 permits the protection of objects simply by hiding subsets of relations (attributes or tuples) to unauthorized users.

A right expresses a relationship between a user and an object for a particular set of operations. In an SQL-based relational DBMS, an operation is a high-level statement such as SELECT, INSERT, UPDATE, or DELETE, and rights are defined (granted or revoked) using the following statements:

GRANT <operation type(s)> ON <object> TO <user(s)>

REVOKE <operation type(s)> FROM <object> TO <user(s)>

The keyword *public* can be used to mean all users. Authorization control can be characterized based on who (the grantors) can grant the rights. In its simplest form, the control is centralized: a single user or user class, the database administrators, has all privileges on the database objects and is the only one allowed to use the GRANT and REVOKE statements.

A more flexible but complex form of control is decentralized [Griffiths and Wade, 1976]: the creator of an object becomes its owner and is granted all privileges on it. In particular, there is the additional operation type GRANT. Granting the GRANT privilege means that all the rights of the grantor performing the statement are given to the specified users. Therefore, the person receiving the right (the grantee) may subsequently grant privileges on that object. The main difficulty with this approach is that the revoking process must be recursive. For example, if A, who granted B who granted C the GRANT privilege on object O, wants to revoke all the privileges of B on O, all the privileges of C on O must also be revoked. To perform revocation, the system must maintain a hierarchy of grants per object where the creator of the object is the root. A complete scheme for handling revocation is proposed in [Fagin, 1978].

The privileges of the subjects over objects are recorded in the catalog (directory) as authorization rules. There are several ways to store the authorizations. The most convenient approach is to consider all the privileges as an *authorization matrix*, in which a row defines a subject, a column an object, and a matrix entry (for a pair <subject, object>), the authorized operations. The authorized operations are specified by their operation type (e.g., SELECT, UPDATE). It is also customary to associate with the operation type a predicate that further restricts the access to the object. The latter option is provided when the objects must be base relations and cannot be views. For example, one authorized operation for the pair <Jones, relation E> could be

```
SELECT WHERE TITLE = ''Syst. Anal.''
```

which authorizes Jones to access only the employee tuples for system analysts. Figure 6.4 gives an example of an authorization matrix where objects are either relations (E and G) or attributes (ENAME).

|        | E      | ENAME  | G                           |
|--------|--------|--------|-----------------------------|
| Casey  | UPDATE | UPDATE | UPDATE                      |
| Jones  | SELECT | SELECT | SELECT WHERE RESP ≠ "Manager" |
| Smith  | NONE   | SELECT | NONE                        |

**Figure 6.4**   Example of Authorization Matrix

The authorization matrix can be stored in three ways: by row, by column, or by element. When the matrix is stored by *row*, each subject is associated with the list of objects that may be accessed together with the related access rights. This approach makes the enforcement of authorizations efficient, since all the rights of the logged-on user are together (in the user profile). However, the manipulation of access rights per object (e.g., making an object public) is not efficient since all subject profiles must be accessed. When the matrix is stored by *column*, each object is associated with the list of subjects who may access it with the corresponding access rights. The advantages and disadvantages of this approach are the disadvantages and advantages of the previous approach.

The respective advantages of the two approaches can be combined in the third approach, in which the matrix is stored by *element*, that is, by relation (subject, object, right). This relation can have indices on both subject and object, thereby providing fast-access right manipulation per subject and per object.

### 6.2.2 Distributed Authorization Control

The additional problems of authorization control in a distributed environment stem from the fact that objects and subjects are distributed. These problems are: remote user authentication, management of distributed authorization rules, as well as handling of views and of user groups.

Remote user authentication is necessary since any site of a distributed DBMS may accept programs initiated, and authorized, at remote sites. To prevent remote access by unauthorized users (e.g., from a site that is not part of the distributed DBMS), users must also be identified and authenticated at the accessed site. Two solutions are possible:

1. The information for authenticating users (user name and password) is replicated at all sites in the catalog. Local programs, initiated at a remote site, must also indicate the user name and password.

2. All sites of the distributed DBMS identify and authenticate themselves similar to the way users do. Intersite communication is thus protected by the use of the site password. Once the initiating site has been authenticated, there is no need for authenticating their remote users.

The first solution is more costly in terms of directory management given that the introduction of a new user is a distributed operation. However, users can access the distributed database from any site. The second solution is necessary if user information is not replicated. Nevertheless, it can also be used if there is replication of the user information. In this case it makes remote authentication more efficient. If user names and passwords are not replicated, they should be stored at the sites where the users accessed the system (i.e., the home site). The latter solution is based on the realistic assumption that users are more static, or at least they always access the distributed database from the same site.

Distributed authorization rules are expressed in the same way as centralized ones. Like view definitions, they must be stored in the catalog. They can be either fully replicated at each site or stored at the sites of the referenced objects. In the latter case the rules are duplicated only at the sites where the referenced objects are distributed. The main advantage of the fully replicated approach is that authorization can be processed by query modification [Stonebraker, 1975] at compile time. However, directory management is more costly because of data duplication. The second solution is better if locality of reference is very high. However, distributed authorization cannot be controlled at compile time.

Views may be considered to be objects by the authorization mechanism. Views are composite objects, that is, composed of other underlying objects. Therefore, granting access to a view translates into granting access to underlying objects. If view definition and authorization rules for all objects are fully replicated (as in many systems), this translation is rather simple and can be done locally. The translation is harder when the view definition and its underlying objects are all stored separately [Wilms and Lindsay, 1981], as is the case with site autonomy assumption. In this situation, the translation is a totally distributed operation. The authorizations granted on views depend on the access rights of the view creator on the underlying objects. A solution is to record the association information at the site of each underlying object.

Handling user groups for the purpose of authorization simplifies distributed database administration. In a centralized DBMS, "all users" can be referred to as *public*. In a distributed DBMS, the same notion is useful, the public denoting all the users of the system. However an intermediate level is often introduced to specify the public at a particular site, denoted by public@site_s, in [Wilms and Lindsay, 1981]. The public is a particular user group. More precise groups can be defined by the command

```
DEFINE GROUP <group_id> AS <list of subject ids>
```

The management of groups in a distributed environment poses some problems since the subjects of a group can be located at various sites and access to an object may be granted to several groups, which are themselves distributed. If group information as well as authorization rules are fully replicated at all sites, the enforcement of access rights is similar to that of a centralized system. However, maintaining this replication is quite expensive. The problem is more difficult if site autonomy (with decentralized control) must be maintained. Several solutions to this problem are identified in [Wilms and Lindsay, 1981]. One solution enforces access rights by performing a remote query to the nodes holding the group definition. Another solution replicates a group definition at each node containing an object that may be accessed by subjects of that group. These solutions tend to decrease the degree of site autonomy.

In conclusion, full replication of authorization information has two strong advantages: authorization control is much simpler and can be done at compile time. However, the overhead cost incurred for managing the distributed catalog can be significant if there are many sites in the system.

## 6.3 SEMANTIC INTEGRITY CONTROL

Another important and difficult problem for a database system is how to guarantee *database consistency*. A database state is said to be consistent if the database satisfies a set of constraints, called *semantic integrity constraints*. Maintaining a consistent database requires various mechanisms such as concurrency control, reliability, protection, and semantic integrity control. Semantic integrity control ensures database consistency by rejecting update programs which lead to inconsistent database states, or by activating specific actions on the database state, which compensate for the effects of the update programs. Note that the updated database must satisfy the set of integrity constraints.

In general, semantic integrity constraints are rules that represent the *knowledge* about the properties of an application. They define static or dynamic application properties which cannot be directly captured by the object and operation concepts of a data model. Thus the concept of an integrity rule is strongly connected with that of a data model in the sense that more semantic information about the application can be captured by means of these rules.

Two main types of integrity constraints can be distinguished: structural constraints and behavioral constraints. *Structural constraints* express basic semantic properties inherent to a model. Examples of such constraints are unique key constraints in the relational model, or one-to-many associations between objects in the network model. *Behavioral constraints*, on the other hand, regulate the application behavior. Thus they are essential in the database design process. They can express associations between objects, such as inclusion dependency in the relational model, or describe object properties and structures. The increasing variety of database applications and the recent development of database design aid tools call for powerful integrity constraints which can enrich the data model.

Integrity control appeared with data processing and evolved from procedural methods (in which the controls were embedded in application programs) to declarative methods. Declarative methods have emerged with the relational model to alleviate the problems of program/data dependency, code redundancy, and poor performance of the procedural methods. The idea, formerly suggested in [Florentin, 1974], is to express integrity constraints using assertions of predicate calculus. Thus a set of semantic integrity assertions defines database consistency. This approach easily allows one to declare and modify complex integrity assertions.

The main problem in supporting automatic semantic integrity control is that the cost of checking assertions can be prohibitive. Enforcing integrity assertions is costly because it generally requires access to a large amount of data which is not involved in the database updates. The problem is more difficult when assertions are defined over a distributed database.

Various solutions have been investigated to design an integrity subsystem by combining optimization strategies. Their purpose is to (1) limit the number of assertions that need to be enforced, (2) decrease the number of data accesses to enforce a given assertion in the presence of an update program, (3) define a preventive strategy that detects inconsistencies in a way that avoids undoing updates, (4) perform as much integrity control as possible at compile time. A few of these solutions have been implemented, but they suffer from a lack of generality. Either they are restricted to a small set of assertions (more general constraints would have a prohibitive checking cost) or they only support restricted programs (e.g., single-tuple updates).

In this section we present the solutions for semantic integrity control first in centralized systems and then in distributed systems. Since our context is the relational model, we consider only declarative methods. The content of this section is strongly based on the work on semantic integrity control for centralized systems reported in [Simon and Valduriez, 1984] and [Simon and Valduriez, 1987] and for distributed systems [Simon and Valduriez, 1986]. In addition, the relational integrity subsystem proposed in [Simon and Valduriez, 1987] offers a rich functionality, by supporting a large subset of multivariable, multirelation assertions with aggregates, and general database programs.

### 6.3.1 Centralized Semantic Integrity Control

A semantic integrity subsystem has two main components: a language for expressing and manipulating integrity assertions, and an enforcement mechanism that performs specific actions to enforce database integrity at updates.

**Specification of integrity constraints.**   Integrity constraints should be manipulated by the database administrator using a high level language. In this section we illustrate a declarative language for specifying integrity constraints, defined in [Simon and Valduriez, 1987]. This language is much in the spirit of the standard SQL language [ANSI, 1986], but with more generality. It allows one to specify, read, or drop integrity constraints. These constraints can be defined either at relation creation time, or at any time, even if the relation already contains tuples. In both cases, however, the syntax is almost the same.

In relational database systems, integrity constraints are defined as assertions. An assertion is a particular expression of tuple relational calculus (see Chapter 2), in which each variable is either universally ($\forall$) or existentially ($\exists$) quantified. Thus an assertion can be seen as a query qualification that is either true or false for each tuple in the Cartesian product of the relations determined by the tuple variables. We can distinguish between three types of integrity constraints: predefined, precompiled, or general constraints.

Examples of integrity constraints will be given on the following database:

E(ENO, ENAME, TITLE)

J(JNO, JNAME, BUDGET)

G(ENO, JNO, RESP, DUR)

Predefined constraints are based on simple keywords. Through them, it is possible to express concisely the more common constraints of the relational model, such as nonnull attribute, unique key, foreign key, or functional dependency [Fagin and Vardi, 1984]. Examples 6.5 through 6.8 demonstrate predefined constraints.

**Example 6.5**   *Nonnull Attribute*

Employee number in relation E cannot be null.

```
ENO NOT NULL IN E
```

**Example 6.6**   *Unique Key*

The pair (ENO, JNO) is the unique key in relation G.

```
(ENO, JNO) UNIQUE IN G
```

**Example 6.7**   *Foreign Key*

The project number JNO in relation G is a foreign key matching the primary key JNO of relation J. In other words, a project referred to in relation G must exist in relation J.

```
JNO IN G REFERENCES JNO IN J
```

**Example 6.8**   *Functional Dependency*

The employee number functionally determines the employee name.

```
ENO IN E DETERMINES ENAME
```

Precompiled constraints express preconditions that must be satisfied by all tuples in a relation for a given update type. The update type, which might be INSERT, DELETE, or MODIFY, permits restricting the integrity control. To identify in the constraint definition the tuples that are subject to update, two variables, NEW and OLD, are implicitly defined. They range over new tuples (to be inserted) and old tuples (to be deleted), respectively [Astrahan et al., 1976]. Precompiled constraints can be expressed with the SQL CHECK statement enriched with the ability to specify the update type. The syntax of the CHECK statement is

```
CHECK ON   < relation name > WHEN < update type >
           ( < qualification over relation name >)
```

Examples of precompiled constraints are the following:

**Example 6.9**  *Domain Constraint*

The budget of a project is between 500K and 1000K.

```
CHECK ON J (BUDGET ≥ 500000 AND BUDGET ≤ 1000000)
```

**Example 6.10**  *Domain Constraint on Deletion*

Only the tuples whose budget is 0 may be deleted.

```
CHECK ON J WHEN DELETE (BUDGET = 0)
```

**Example 6.11**  *Transition Constraint*

The budget of a project can only increase.

```
CHECK ON J (NEW.BUDGET > OLD.BUDGET AND NEW.JNO = OLD.JNO)
```

General constraints are formulas of tuple relational calculus where all variables are quantified. The database system must ensure that those formulas are always true. General constraints are more concise than precompiled constraints since the former may involve more than one relation. For instance, at least three precompiled constraints are necessary to express a general constraint on three relations. A general constraint may be expressed with the following syntax:

```
CHECK ON list of <variable name> : <relation name>, (<qualification>)
```

Examples of general constraints are given below.

**Example 6.12**  *Functional Dependency*

The constraint of Example 6.8 may also be expressed as

```
CHECK ON e1:E, e2:E
        (e1.ENAME = e2.ENAME IF e1.ENO = e2.ENO)
```

**Example 6.13**  *Constraint with Aggregate Function*

The total duration for all employees in the CAD project is less than 100.

```
CHECK ON g:G, j:J (SUM(g.DUR WHERE g.JNO=j.JNO)<100
        IF j.JNAME=''CAD/CAM'')
```

**Integrity enforcement.**    Enforcing semantic integrity consists of rejecting update programs that violate some integrity constraints. A constraint is violated when it becomes false in the new database state produced by the update. A major difficulty in designing an integrity subsystem is finding efficient enforcement algorithms. Two basic methods permit the rejection of inconsistent updates. The first one is based on the *detection* of inconsistencies. The update $u$ is executed, causing a change of the database state $D$ to $D_u$. The enforcement algorithm verifies, by applying tests derived from these constraints, that all relevant constraints hold in state $D_u$. If state $D_u$ is inconsistent, the DBMS can try either to reach another consistent state, $D'_u$, by modifying $D_u$ with compensation actions, or to restore state $D$ by undoing $u$. Since these tests are applied *after* having changed the database state, they are generally called *posttests*. This approach may be inefficient if a large amount of work (the update of $D$) must be undone in the case of an integrity failure.

The second method is based on the *prevention* of inconsistencies. An update is executed only if it changes the database state to a consistent state. The tuples subject to the update are either directly available (in the case of insert) or must be retrieved from the database (in the case of deletion or modification). The enforcement algorithm verifies that all relevant constraints will hold after updating those tuples. This is generally done by applying to those tuples tests that are derived from the integrity constraints. Given that these tests are applied *before* the database state is changed, they are generally called *pretests*. The preventive approach is more efficient than the detection approach since updates never need to be undone because of integrity violation.

The query modification algorithm [Stonebraker, 1975] is an example of a preventive method that is particularly efficient at enforcing domain constraints. It adds the assertion qualification to the query qualification by an AND operator so that the modified query can enforce integrity.

### Example 6.14

The query for increasing the budget of the CAD/CAM project by 10%, which would be specified as

```
UPDATE    J
SET       BUDGET = BUDGET*1.1
WHERE     JNAME= ''CAD/CAM''
```

will be transformed into the following query in order to enforce the domain constraint discussed in Example 6.9.

```
UPDATE    J
SET       BUDGET = BUDGET * 1.1
WHERE     JNAME= ''CAD/CAM''
          AND NEW.BUDGET ≥ 500000
          AND NEW.BUDGET ≤ 1000000
```

The query modification algorithm, which is well known for its elegance, produces pretests at run time by ANDing the assertion predicates with the update predicates of each instruction of the transaction. However, the algorithm only applies to tuple calculus formulas and can be specified as follows. Consider the assertion $(\forall x \in R) F(x)$, where $F$ is a tuple calculus expression in which $x$ is the only free variable. An update of $R$ can be written as $(\forall x \in R)(Q(x) \Rightarrow update(x))$, where $Q$ is a tuple calculus expression whose only free variable is $x$. Roughly speaking, the query modification consists in generating the update $(\forall x \in R)((Q(x)$ and $F(x)) \Rightarrow update(x))$. Thus $x$ needs to be universally quantified.

**Example 6.15**

The foreign key assertion of Example 6.7 that can be rewritten as

$$\forall\, g \in G,\, \exists\, j \in J : g.JNO = j.JNO$$

could not be processed by query modification because the variable j is not universally quantified.

To handle more general assertions, pretests can be generated at assertion definition time, and enforced at run time when updates occur ([Bernstein et al., 1980a], [Bernstein and Blaustein, 1982], [Blaustein, 1981], and [Nicolas, 1982]). The method described in [Nicolas, 1982] is restricted to updates that insert or delete a *single* tuple of a single relation. The algorithm proposed in [Bernstein et al., 1980a] and [Blaustein, 1981] is an improvement over the one in [Nicolas, 1982]. Updates are also single tuple. The algorithm builds a pretest at assertion definition time for each assertion and each update type (insert, delete). These pretests are enforced at run time. This method accepts multirelation, monovariable assertions, possibly with aggregates. The principle is the substitution of the tuple variables in the assertion by constants from an updated tuple. Despite its important contribution to research, the method is hardly usable in a real environment because of the restriction on updates.

In the rest of this section, we present the method reported in [Simon and Valduriez, 1986] and [Simon and Valduriez, 1987], which combines the generality of updates supported in [Stonebraker, 1975] with at least the generality of assertions for which pretests can be produced in [Blaustein, 1981]. This method is based on the production, at assertion definition time, of *compiled assertions* which are used subsequently to prevent the introduction of inconsistencies in the database. This is a general preventive method that handles the entire set of assertions introduced in the preceding section. It significantly reduces the proportion of the database that must be checked when enforcing assertions in the presence of updates.

The definition of compiled assertions is based on the notion of differential relations. Let $u$ be an update of relation $R$. $R^+$ and $R^-$ are *differential relations* of $R$ by $u$, where $R^+$ contains the tuples inserted by $u$ into $R$, and $R^-$ contains the tuples of $R$ deleted by $u$. If $u$ is an insertion, $R^-$ is empty. If $u$ is a deletion, $R^+$ is empty. Finally, if $u$ is a modification, relation $R$ after modification is equal to $R^+ \cup (R - R^-)$.

A *compiled assertion* is a triple $(R, T, C)$ in which $R$ is a relation, $T$ is an update type, and $C$ is an assertion ranging over the differential relation(s) involved in an update of type $T$. When an integrity constraint $I$ is defined, a set of compiled assertions may be produced for the relations used by $I$. Whenever a relation involved in $I$ is updated by a program $u$, the compiled assertions that must be checked to enforce $I$ are only those defined on $I$ for the update type of $u$. The performance advantage of this approach is twofold. First, the number of assertions to enforce is minimized since only the compiled assertions of type $u$ need be checked. Second, the cost of enforcing a compiled assertion is less than that of enforcing $I$ since differential relations are, in general, much smaller than the base relations.

Compiled assertions may be obtained by applying transformation rules to the original assertion. These rules are based on a syntactic analysis of the assertion and quantifier permutations. They permit the substitution of differential relations for base relation. Since the compiled assertions are simpler than the original ones, the process that generates them is called *simplification*.

**Example 6.16**

Consider the modified expression of the foreign key constraint in Example 6.15. The compiled assertions associated with this constraint are

$$(\text{G}, \textbf{INSERT}, C_1), (\text{J}, \textbf{DELETE}, C_2) \text{ and } (\text{J}, \textbf{MODIFY}, C_3)$$

where $C_1$ is

$$\forall \textbf{NEW} \in \text{G}^+, \exists j \in \text{J}: \textbf{NEW}.\text{JNO} = j.\text{JNO}$$

$C_2$ is

$$\forall g \in \text{G}, \forall \textbf{OLD} \in \text{J}^- : g.\text{JNO} \neq \textbf{OLD}.\text{JNO}$$

and $C_3$ is

$$\forall g \in \text{G}, \forall \textbf{OLD} \in \text{J}^-, \exists \textbf{NEW} \in \text{J}^+ :$$
$$g.\text{JNO} \neq \textbf{OLD}.\text{JNO} \text{ OR } \textbf{OLD}.\text{JNO} = \textbf{NEW}.\text{JNO}$$

The advantage provided by such compiled assertions is obvious. For instance, a deletion on relation G does not incur any assertion checking.

The enforcement algorithm described in [Simon and Valduriez, 1984] makes use of compiled assertions and is specialized according to the class of the assertions. Three classes of assertions are distinguished: the single-relation and multirelation assertions, and assertions involving aggregate functions.

Let us now summarize the enforcement algorithm. We recall that an update program updates all tuples of relation $R$ that satisfy some qualification. The algorithm acts in two steps. The first step generates the differential relations $R^+$ and $R^-$ from $R$. The second step simply consists of retrieving the tuples of $R^+$ and $R^-$, which do not satisfy the compiled assertions. If no tuples are retrieved, the assertion is valid.

**Example 6.17**

Suppose there is a deletion on J. Enforcing (J, **DELETE**, $C_2$) consists in generating the following statement:

$$result \leftarrow \text{retrieve all tuples of J}^- \text{ where } \neg(C_2)$$

Then, if the result is empty, the assertion is verified by the update.

## 6.3.2  Distributed Semantic Integrity Control

In this section we present algorithms for ensuring the semantic integrity of distributed databases. They are extensions of the simplification method discussed previously. In what follows we assume site autonomy, meaning that each site processes local queries and performs data control as a centralized DBMS. This assumption simplifies the description of the method. However, the method obviously works with replicated directories. The two main problems of designing an integrity subsystem for a distributed DBMS are the definition and storage of assertions, and the enforcement of these assertions.

**Definition of distributed integrity assertions.**    An integrity assertion is supposed to be expressed in tuple relational calculus. Each assertion is seen as a query qualification which is either true or false for each tuple in the Cartesian product of the relations determined by tuple variables. Since assertions can involve data stored at different sites, their storage must be decided so as to minimize the cost of integrity checking. There is a strategy based on a taxonomy of integrity assertions that distinguishes three classes of assertions:

1. *Individual assertions*: single-relation single-variable assertions. They refer only to tuples to be updated independently of the rest of the database. For instance, domain constraint of Example 6.9 is an individual assertion.

2. *Set-oriented assertions*: include single-relation multivariable constraints such as functional dependency (Example 6.8) and multirelation multivariable constraints such as foreign key constraints (Example 6.7).

3. *Assertions involving aggregates*: require special processing because of the cost of evaluating the aggregates. The assertion in Example 6.13 is representative of an assertion of this class.

The definition of a new integrity assertion can be started at one of the sites that store the relations involved in the assertion. Remember that the relations can be fragmented. A fragmentation predicate is a particular case of assertion of class 1. Different fragments of the same relation can be located at different sites. Thus, defining an integrity assertion becomes a distributed operation, which is done in two steps. The first step is to transform the high-level assertions into compiled assertions, using the techniques discussed in the preceding section. The next step is to store compiled assertions according to the class of assertion. Assertions of class 3 are treated like those of class 1 or 2, depending on whether they are individual or set oriented.

*Individual Assertions.*    The assertion definition is sent to all other sites that contain fragments of the relation involved in the assertion. The assertion must be compatible with the relation data at each site. Compatibility can be checked at two levels: predicate and data. First, predicate compatibility is verified by comparing the assertion predicate with the fragment predicate. An assertion $C$ is not compatible with a fragment predicate $p$ if "$C$ is true" implies that "$p$ is false," and is compatible with $p$ otherwise. If noncompatibility is found at one of the sites, the assertion definition is globally rejected because tuples of that fragment do not satisfy the integrity constraints. Second, if predicate compatibility has been found, the assertion is tested against the instance of the fragment. If it is not satisfied by that instance, the assertion is also globally rejected. If compatibility is found, the assertion is stored at each site. Note that the compatibility checks are performed only for compiled assertions whose update type is "insert" (the tuples in the fragments are considered "inserted").

**Example 6.18**

Consider relation E, horizontally fragmented across three sites using the predicates

$$p_1: \quad 0 \leq \text{ENO} < \text{"E3"}$$

$$p_2: \quad \text{"E3"} \leq \text{ENO} \leq \text{"E6"}$$

$$p_3: \quad \text{ENO} > \text{"E6"}$$

and the domain assertion $C$: ENO < "E4". Assertion $C$ is compatible with $p_1$ (if $C$ is true, $p_1$ is true) and $p_2$ (if $C$ is true, $p_2$ is not necessarily false), but is not with $p_3$ (if $C$ is true, then $p_3$ is false). Therefore, assertion $C$ should be globally rejected because the tuples at site 3 cannot satisfy $C$, and thus relation E does not satisfy $C$.

***Set-Oriented Assertions.***  Set-oriented assertions are multivariable; that is, they involve join predicates. Although the assertion predicate may be multirelation, a compiled assertion is associated with a single relation. Therefore, the assertion definition can be sent to all the sites that store a fragment referenced by these variables. Compatibility checking also involves fragments of the relation used in the join predicate. Predicate compatibility is useless here because it is impossible to infer that a fragment predicate $p$ is false, if the assertion $C$ (based on a join predicate) is true. Therefore $C$ must be checked for compatibility against the data. This compatibility check basically requires joining each fragment of the relation, say $R$, with all fragments of the other relation, say $S$, involved in the assertion predicate. This operation may be expensive and, as any join, should be optimized by the distributed query processor. Three cases, given in increasing cost of checking, can occur:

1. The fragmentation of $R$ is derived (see Chapter 5) from that of $S$ based on a semijoin on the attribute used in the assertion join predicate.
2. $S$ is fragmented on join attribute.
3. $S$ is not fragmented on join attribute.

In the first case, compatibility checking is cheap since the tuple of $S$ matching with a tuple of $R$ is at the same site. In the second case, each tuple of $R$ must be compared with at most one fragment of $S$, because the join attribute value of the tuple of $R$ can be used to find the site of the corresponding fragment of $S$. In the third case, each tuple of $R$ must be compared with all fragments of $S$. If compatibility is found for all tuples of $R$, the assertion is stored at each site.

**Example 6.19**

Consider the set-oriented compiled assertion (G, **INSERT**, $C_1$) defined in Example 6.16, where $C_1$ is

$$\forall \textbf{NEW} \in G^+, \exists j \in J : \textbf{NEW.JNO} = j.\text{JNO}$$

Let us consider the three following cases:

1.  G is fragmented using the predicate

    $$G \bowtie_{\text{JNO}} J_i$$

    where $J_i$ is a fragment of relation J. In this case each tuple **NEW** of G has been placed at the same site as tuple j such that **NEW.JNO** = j.JNO. Since the fragmentation predicate is identical to that of $C_1$, compatibility checking does not incur communication.

2.  J is horizontally fragmented based on the two predicates

    $$p_1 : \quad \text{JNO} < \text{``J3''}$$
    $$p_2 : \quad \text{JNO} \geq \text{``J3''}$$

    In this case each tuple **NEW** of G is compared with either fragment $J_1$, if **NEW.JNO** < "J3", or fragment $J_2$ if **NEW.JNO** ≥ "J3".

3.  J is horizontally fragmented based on the two predicates

    $$p_1 : \quad \text{JNAME} = \text{``CAD/CAM''}$$
    $$p_2 : \quad \text{JNAME} \neq \text{``CAD/CAM''}$$

    In this case each tuple of G must be compared with both fragments $J_1$ and $J_2$.

**Enforcement of distributed integrity assertions.** Enforcing distributed integrity assertions is more complex than needed in centralized DBMSs. The main problem is to decide where (at which site) to enforce the integrity assertions. The choice depends on the class of the assertion, the type of update, and the nature of the site where the update is issued (called the *query master site*). This site may, or may not, store the updated relation or some of the relations involved in the integrity assertions. The critical parameter we consider is the cost of transferring data, including messages, from one site to another. We now discuss the different types of strategies according to these criteria.

*Individual Assertions.* Two cases are considered. If the update is an insert statement, all the tuples to be inserted are explicitly provided by the user. In this case, all individual assertions can be enforced at the site where the update is submitted. If the update is a qualified update (delete or modify statements), it is sent to the sites storing the relation that will be updated. The query processor executes the update qualification for each fragment. The resulting tuples at each site are combined into one temporary relation in the case of a delete statement, or two, in the case of a modify statement (i.e., $R^+$ and $R^-$). Each site involved in the distributed update enforces the assertions relevant at that site (e.g., domain constraints when it is a delete).

*Set-Oriented Assertions.* We first study single-relation constraints by means of an example. Consider the functional dependency of Example 6.8. The compiled assertion associated with update type INSERT is

$$(\text{E, INSERT, } C)$$

where $C$ is

$$(\forall e \in \text{E})(\forall \text{NEW1} \in \text{E})(\forall \text{NEW2} \in \text{E}) \tag{1}$$

$$(\text{NEW1.ENO} = e.\text{ENO} \Rightarrow \text{NEW1.ENAME} = e.\text{ENAME}) \wedge \tag{2}$$

$$(\text{NEW1.ENO} = \text{NEW2.ENO} \Rightarrow \text{NEW1.ENAME} = \text{NEW2.ENAME}) \tag{3}$$

The second line in the definition of $C$ checks the constraint between the inserted tuples (NEW1) and the existing ones ($e$), while the third checks it between the inserted tuples themselves. That is why two variables (NEW1 and NEW2) are declared in the first line.

Consider now an update of E. First, the update qualification is executed by the query processor and returns one or two temporary relations, as in the case of individual assertions. These temporary relations are then sent to all sites storing E. Assume that the update is an INSERT statement. Then each site storing a fragment of E will enforce assertion $C$ described above. Because $e$ in $C$ is universally quantified, $C$ must be satisfied by the local data of each site. This is due to the fact that $\forall x \in \{a_1, \ldots, a_n\} f(x)$ is equivalent to $[f(a_1) \wedge f(a_2) \wedge \cdots \wedge f(a_n)]$. Thus the site where the update is submitted must receive for each site a message indicating that this assertion is satisfied and that it is a condition for all sites. If the assertion is not true for one site, this site sends an error message indicating that the assertion has been violated. The update is then invalid, and it is the responsibility of the integrity subsystem to decide if the entire program must be rejected.

Let us now consider multirelation assertions. For the sake of clarity, we assume that the integrity assertions do not have more than one tuple variable ranging over the same relation. Note that this is likely to be the most frequent case. As with single-relation assertions, the update is computed at the site where it was submitted. The enforcement is done at the query master site, using the ENFORCE algorithm given in Algorithm 6.1.

> **Algorithm 6.1**   *ENFORCE*
> **input:** $T$: update type; $R$: relation
> **begin**
>     retrieve all compiled assertions $(R, T, C_i)$
>     *inconsistency* $\leftarrow$ **false**
>     **for each** compiled assertion **do**
>     **begin**
>         *result* $\leftarrow$ retrieve all new (respectively old), tuples of $R$ where $\neg(C_i)$
>         **if** *card(result)* $\neq$ 0 **then**

        **begin**
           *inconsistency* ← **true**
           **exit**
        **end-if**
      **end-for**
      **if not** *(inconsistency)* **then**
        send the tuples to update to all the sites storing fragments of $R$
      **else** reject the update
      **end-if**
    **end.** {ENFORCE}

**Example 6.20**

We illustrate this algorithm through an example based on the foreign key assertion of Example 6.7. Let $u$ be an insertion of a new tuple into G. The previous algorithm uses the compiled assertion (G, **INSERT**, $C$), where $C$ is

$$\forall \text{NEW} \in G^+, \exists j \in J : \text{NEW.JNO} = j.\text{JNO}$$

For this assertion, the retrieval statement is to retrieve all new tuples in $G^+$ where $C$ is not true.

This statement can be expressed in SQL as

```
SELECT  NEW.*
FROM    G+ NEW, J
WHERE   COUNT(J.JNO WHERE NEW.JNO = J.JNO)=0
```

Note that **NEW.*** denotes all the attributes of $G^+$.

Thus the strategy is to send new tuples to sites storing relation J in order to perform the joins, and then to centralize all results at the query master site. For each site storing a fragment of J, the site joins the fragment with $G^+$ and sends the result to the query master site, which performs the union of all results. If the union is empty, the database is consistent. Otherwise, the update leads to an inconsistent state. The rejection of the program depends on the strategy chosen by the program manager of the distributed DBMS.

*Assertions involving Aggregates.* These assertions are among the most costly to test because they require the calculation of the aggregate functions. The aggregate functions generally manipulated are MIN, MAX, SUM, and COUNT. Each aggregate function contains a projection part and a selection part. To enforce these assertions efficiently, it is possible to produce compiled assertions that isolate redundant data which can be stored at each site storing the associated relation [Bernstein and Blaustein, 1982]. This data is called *concrete views*.

**Summary of distributed integrity control.** The main problem of distributed integrity control is that the communication and processing costs of enforcing distributed assertions can be prohibitive. The two main issues in designing a distributed integrity subsystem are the definition of the distributed assertions and of the enforcement algorithms, which minimize the cost of distributed integrity checking. We have shown that distributed integrity control can be completely achieved, by extending a preventive method based on the compilation of semantic integrity assertions. The method is general since all types of assertions expressed in first-order predicate logic can be handled. It is compatible with fragment definition and minimizes intersite communication. A better performance of distributed integrity enforcement can be obtained if fragments are defined carefully. Therefore, the specification of distributed integrity constraints is an important aspect of the distributed database design process.

## 6.4 CONCLUSION

Semantic data control includes view management, security control, and semantic integrity control. In the relational framework, these functions can be uniformly achieved by enforcing rules that specify data manipulation control. Well known solutions exist for handling these functions in centralized systems. However, few solutions exist for distributed systems. The main reason is that semantic data control is costly in centralized systems and can be prohibitive in distributed systems. The two main issues for efficiently performing data control are the definition and storage of the rules (site selection) and the design of enforcement algorithms which minimize communication costs. The problem is difficult since increased functionality (and generality) tends to increase site communication. Solutions for distributed semantic data control are extensions of centralized solutions. The problem is simplified if control rules are fully replicated at all sites and harder if site autonomy is to be preserved. In addition, specific optimizations can be done to minimize the cost of data control but with extra overhead such as managing snapshots or redundant data. Thus the specification of distributed data control must be included in the distributed database design so that the cost of control for update programs is also considered.

## 6.5 BIBLIOGRAPHIC NOTES

A few papers deal with semantic data control in distributed databases. Generally, the problems of view management, authorization control, and semantic integrity control are treated separately in a distributed context. However, more references are available for centralized systems [Gardarin and Valduriez, 1989].

The two basic papers on centralized view management are [Chamberlin et al., 1975] and [Stonebraker, 1975]. The first reference presents an integrated solution for view and authorization management in System R. The second reference describes IN-GRES's query modification technique for uniformly handling views, authorizations, and semantic integrity control. This method was presented in Section 6.1.

Theoretical solutions to the problem of view updates are given in [Bancilhon and Spyratos, 1981], [Dayal and Bernstein, 1978], and [Keller, 1982]. Semantic information about the base relations is particularly useful for finding unique propagation of updates. The current commercial systems are very restrictive in supporting updates through views.

The notion of snapshot for optimizing view derivation in distributed database systems is due to [Adiba and Lindsay, 1980]. [Adiba, 1981] generalizes the notion of snapshot by that of derived relation in a distributed context. He also proposes a unified mechanism for managing views, and snapshots, as well as fragmented and replicated data.

[Fernandez et al., 1981] deals with security and integrity in database systems, mainly in a centralized context. Authorization and protection are extensively treated, while only physical integrity (not semantic integrity) is described. [Hoffman, 1977] describes security and protection in computer systems in general. The authorization mechanism of System R is presented in [Griffiths and Wade, 1976] in a more complete way than in [Chamberlin et al., 1975]. In [Wilms and Lindsay, 1981] the authorization mechanism of System R is extended to handle groups of users and to run in a distributed environment.

The content of Section 6.3 comes largely from the work on semantic integrity control described in [Simon and Valduriez, 1984], [Simon and Valduriez, 1986] and [Simon and Valduriez, 1987]. In particular, [Simon and Valduriez, 1986] extends a preventive strategy for centralized integrity control based on compiled assertions to run in a distributed environment. The initial idea of declarative methods, that is, to use assertions of predicate logic to specify integrity constraints, is due to [Florentin, 1974]. The most important declarative methods are in [Bernstein et al., 1980a], [Blaustein, 1981], [Nicolas, 1982], [Simon and Valduriez, 1984], and [Stonebraker, 1975]. The notion of concrete views for storing redundant data is described in [Bernstein and Blaustein, 1982]. Note that concrete views are useful in optimizing the enforcement of assertions involving aggregates. [Civelek et al., 1988], [Sheth et al., 1988b] and [Sheth et al., 1988a] describe systems and tools for semantic data control, particularly view management.

## 6.6 EXERCISES

**6.1**  Define in SQL-like syntax a view of the engineering database V(ENO, ENAME, JNO, RESP), where the duration is 24. Is view V updatable? Assume that relations E and G are horizontally fragmented based on access frequencies as follows:

| Site 1 | Site 2 | Site 3 |
|--------|--------|--------|
| $E_1$  | $E_2$  |        |
|        | $G_1$  | $G_2$  |

where

$$
\begin{aligned}
E_1 &= \sigma_{TITLE \neq \text{"Engineer"}}(E) \\
E_2 &= \sigma_{TITLE = \text{"Engineer"}}(E) \\
G_1 &= \sigma_{0 < DUR < 36}(G) \\
G_2 &= \sigma_{DUR \geq 36}(G)
\end{aligned}
$$

At which site(s) should the definition of V be stored without being fully replicated, to increase locality of reference?

**6.2** Express the following query: names of employees in view V who work on the CAD project.

**\*6.3** Assume that relation J is horizontally fragmented as

$$J_1 = \sigma_{\text{JNAME} = \text{``CAD''}}(J)$$
$$J_2 = \sigma_{\text{JNAME} \neq \text{``CAD''}}(J)$$

Modify the query obtained in Exercise 6.2 to a query expressed on fragments.

**\*\*6.4** Propose an algorithm to efficiently update a snapshot derived by projection from horizontally fragmented relations.

**6.5** Propose a relation schema for storing the access rights associated with user groups in a distributed database catalog, and give a fragmentation scheme for that relation, assuming that all members of a group are at the same site.

**\*\*6.6** Give an algorithm for executing the REVOKE statement in a distributed DBMS, assuming that the GRANT privilege can be granted only to a group of users where all its members are at the same site.

**6.7** Using the assertion specification language of this chapter, express an integrity constraint which states that the duration spent in a project cannot exceed 48 months.

**\*6.8** Define the compiled assertions associated with integrity constraints covered in Examples 6.5 to 6.8.

**6.9** Assume the following vertical fragmentation of relations E, G and J:

| Site 1 | Site 2 | Site 3 | Site 4 |
|--------|--------|--------|--------|
| $E_1$ | $E_2$ | | |
| | $J_1$ | $J_2$ | |
| | | $G_1$ | $G_2$ |

where

$$E_1 = \Pi_{\text{ENO, ENAME}}(E)$$
$$E_2 = \Pi_{\text{ENO, TITLE}}(E)$$
$$J_1 = \Pi_{\text{JNO, JNAME}}(J)$$
$$J_2 = \Pi_{\text{JNO, BUDGET}}(J)$$
$$G_1 = \Pi_{\text{ENO, JNO, RESP}}(G)$$
$$G_2 = \Pi_{\text{ENO, JNO, DUR}}(G)$$

Where should the compiled assertions obtained in Exercise 6.8 be stored assuming site autonomy?

**\*\*6.10** Apply algorithm ENFORCE for distributed integrity assertions for the compiled assertions derived from assertion (b).

# 7

# Overview of
# Query Processing

The increasing success of relational database technology in data processing is due, in part, to the availability of nonprocedural languages, which can significantly improve application development and end-user productivity. By hiding the low-level details about the physical organization of the data, relational database languages (see Chapter 2) allow the expression of complex queries in a concise and simple fashion. In particular, to construct the answer to the query, the user does not precisely specify the procedure to follow. This procedure is actually devised by a DBMS module, usually called a *query processor*. This also relieves the user from query optimization, a time-consuming task that is best handled by the query processor, since it can exploit a large amount of useful information about the data.

Because it is a critical performance issue, query processing has received considerable attention in the context of both centralized and distributed DBMSs. However, the query processing problem is much more difficult in distributed environments than in centralized ones, because a larger number of parameters affect the performance of distributed queries. In particular, the relations involved in a distributed query may be fragmented and/or replicated, thereby inducing communication overhead costs.

In this chapter we give an overview of query processing in distributed DBMSs, leaving the details of the important aspects of distributed query processing to the next two chapters. The context chosen is that of relational calculus and relational algebra, because of their generality and wide use in distributed DBMSs. As we saw in Chapter

5, distributed relations are implemented by fragments. Distributed database design is of major importance for query processing since the definition of fragments is based on the objective of increasing reference locality, and sometimes parallel execution for the most important queries. The role of a distributed query processor is to map a high-level query (assumed to be expressed in relational calculus) on a distributed database (i.e., a set of global relations) into a sequence of database operations (of relational algebra) on relation fragments. Several important functions characterize this mapping. First, the *calculus query* must be *decomposed* into a sequence of relational operations called an *algebraic query*. Second, the data accessed by the query must be *localized* so that the operations on relations are translated to bear on local data (fragments). Finally, the algebraic query on fragments must be extended with communication operations and *optimized* with respect to a cost function to be minimized. This cost function typically refers to computing resources such as disk I/Os, CPUs, and communication networks.

The chapter is organized as follows. In Section 7.1 we illustrate the query processing problem. In Section 7.2 we define precisely the objectives of query processing algorithms. The complexity of relational algebra operations, which affect mainly the performance of query processing, is given in Section 7.3. In Section 7.4 we provide a characterization of query processors based on their implementation choices. Finally, in Section 7.5 we introduce the different layers of query processing starting from a distributed query down to the execution of operations on local sites and communication between sites. The layers introduced in Section 7.5 are described in detail in the next two chapters.

## 7.1  QUERY PROCESSING PROBLEM

The main function of a relational query processor is to transform a high-level query (typically, in relational calculus) into an equivalent lower-level query (typically, in some variation of relational algebra). The low-level query actually implements the execution strategy for the query. The transformation must achieve both correctness and efficiency. It is correct if the low-level query has the same semantics as the original query, that is, if both queries produce the same result. The well-defined mapping from relational calculus to relational algebra (see Chapter 2) makes the correctness issue easy. But producing an efficient execution strategy is more involved. A relational calculus query may have many equivalent and correct transformations into relational algebra. Since each equivalent execution strategy can lead to very different consumptions of computer resources, the main difficulty is to select the execution strategy that minimizes resource consumption.

**Example 7.1**

We consider the following subset of the engineering database scheme given in Figure 2.4:

E(ENO, ENAME, TITLE)
G(ENO, JNO, RESP, DUR)

and the following simple user query:

"Find the names of employees who are managing a project"

The expression of the query in relational calculus using the SQL syntax is

```
SELECT   ENAME
FROM     E,G
WHERE    E.ENO = G.ENO
AND      G.RESP = ''Manager''
```

Two equivalent relational algebra queries that are correct transformations of the query above are

$$\Pi_{ENAME}(\sigma_{RESP="Manager" \wedge E.ENO=G.ENO} (E \times G))$$

and

$$\Pi_{ENAME}(E \bowtie_{ENO} (\sigma_{RESP="Manager"} (G)))$$

It is intuitively obvious that the second query, which avoids the Cartesian product of E and G, consumes much less computing resource than the first and thus should be retained.

In a centralized context, query execution strategies can be well expressed in an extension of relational algebra. The main role of a centralized query processor is to choose, for a given query, the best relational algebra query among all equivalent ones. Since the problem is computationally intractable with a large number of relations [Ibaraki and Kameda, 1984], it is generally reduced to choosing a solution close to the optimum.

In a distributed system, relational algebra is not enough to express execution strategies. It must be supplemented with operations for exchanging data between sites. Besides the choice of ordering relational algebra operations, the distributed query processor must also select the best sites to process data, and possibly the way data should be transformed. This increases the solution space from which to choose the distributed execution strategy, making distributed query processing significantly more difficult.

**Example 7.2**

This example illustrates the importance of site selection and communication for a chosen relational algebra query against a fragmented database. We consider the following query of Example 7.1:

$$\Pi_{ENAME} (E \bowtie_{ENO} (\sigma_{RESP="Manager"} (G)))$$

We assume that relations E and G are horizontally fragmented as follows:

$$E_1 = \sigma_{ENO \leq "E3"} (E)$$
$$E_2 = \sigma_{ENO > "E3"} (E)$$
$$G_1 = \sigma_{ENO \leq "E3"} (G)$$
$$G_2 = \sigma_{ENO > "E3"} (G)$$

Fragments $G_1$, $G_2$, $E_1$, and $E_2$ are stored at sites 1, 2, 3, and 4, respectively, and the result is expected at site 5.

For the sake of pedagogical simplicity, we ignore the project operation in the following. Two equivalent distributed execution strategies for the above query are shown in Figure 7.1. An arrow from site $i$ to site $j$ labeled with $R$ indicates that relation $R$ is transferred from site $i$ to site $j$. Strategy A exploits the fact that relations E and G are fragmented the same way in order to perform the select and join operation in parallel. Strategy B centralizes all the operand data at the result site before processing the query.

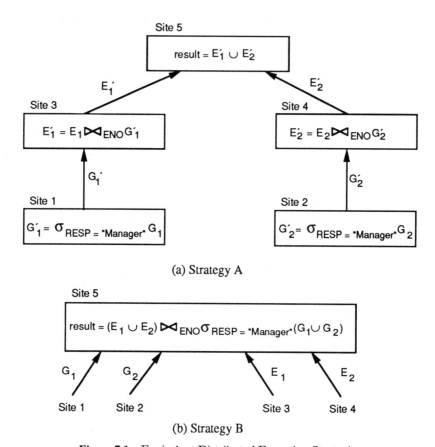

(a) Strategy A

(b) Strategy B

**Figure 7.1**   Equivalent Distributed Execution Strategies

To evaluate the resource consumption of these two strategies, we use a simple cost model. We assume that a tuple access, denoted *tupacc*, is 1 unit (which we leave unspecified) and a tuple transfer, denoted *tuptrans*, is 10 units. We assume that relations E and G have 400 and 1000 tuples, respectively, and that there are 20 managers in relation G. We also assume that data is uniformly distributed among sites. Finally, we assume that relations G and E are locally clustered on attributes RESP and ENO, respectively. Therefore, there is direct access to tuples of G (respectively, E) based on the value of attribute RESP (respectively, ENO).

The cost of strategy A can be derived as follows:

1. Produce G' by selecting G requires 20 ∗ *tupacc*                   =         20
2. Transfer G' to the sites of E requires 20 ∗ *tuptrans*           =        200
3. Produce E' by joining G' and E requires (10 ∗ 10) ∗ *tupacc* ∗ 2  =     200
4. Transfer E' to result site requires 20 ∗ *tuptrans*              =        200

   The total cost is                                                    $\overline{620}$

The cost of strategy B can be derived as follows:

1. Transfer E to site 5 requires 400 ∗ *tuptrans*                   =      4,000
2. Transfer G to site 5 requires 1000 ∗ *tuptrans*                  =     10,000
3. Produce G' by selecting G requires 1000 ∗ *tupacc*               =      1,000
4. Join E and G' requires 400 ∗ 20 ∗ *tupacc*                       =      8,000

   The total cost is                                                   $\overline{23,000}$

In strategy B we assumed that the access methods to relations E and G based on attributes RESP and ENO are lost because of data transfer. This is a reasonable assumption in practice. Strategy A is better by a factor of 37, which is quite significant. Furthermore, it provides better distribution of work among sites. The difference would be even higher if we assumed slower communication and/or higher degree of fragmentation.

## 7.2  OBJECTIVES OF QUERY PROCESSING

As stated before, the objective of query processing in a distributed context is to transform a high-level query on a distributed database, which is seen as a single database by the users, into an efficient execution strategy expressed in a low-level language on local databases. We assume that the high-level language is relational calculus, while the low-level language is an extension of relational algebra with communication operations. The different layers involved in the query transformation are detailed in Section 7.5. An important aspect of query processing is query optimization. Because many execution strategies are correct transformations of the same high-level query, the one that optimizes (minimizes) resource consumption should be retained.

A good measure of resource consumption is the *total cost* that will be incurred in processing the query [Sacco and Yao, 1982]. Total cost is the sum of all times incurred in processing the operations of the query at various sites and in intersite communication. Another good measure is the *response time* of the query [Epstein et al., 1978], which is the time elapsed for executing the query. Since operations can be executed in parallel at different sites, the response time of a query may be significantly less than its total cost.

In a distributed database system, the total cost to be minimized includes CPU, I/O, and communication costs. The CPU cost is incurred when performing operations on data in main memory. The I/O cost is the time necessary for disk input/output operations. This cost can be minimized by reducing the number of I/O operations through fast access methods to the data and efficient use of main memory (buffer management). The communication cost is the time needed for exchanging data between sites participating in the execution of the query. This cost is incurred in processing the messages (formatting/deformatting), and in transmitting the data on the communication network.

The first two cost components (I/O and CPU cost) are the only factors considered by centralized DBMSs. The communication cost component is probably the most important factor considered in distributed databases. Most of the early proposals for distributed query optimization assume that the communication cost largely dominates local processing cost (I/O and CPU cost), and thus ignore the latter. This assumption is based on very slow communication networks (e.g., wide area networks with a bandwidth of a few kilobytes per second) rather than on networks with disk bandwidths. Therefore, the aim of distributed query optimization is simplified to the problem of minimizing communication costs generally at the expense of local processing. The advantage is that local optimization can be done independently using the known methods for centralized systems. However, distributed processing environments now exist where the communication network is much faster (e.g., local area networks) and that can have a bandwidth comparable to that of disks. Therefore, more recent research efforts consider a weighted combination of these three cost components since they all contribute significantly to the total cost of evaluating a query [Page and Popek, 1985]. Nevertheless, in distributed environments with high bandwidths, the overhead cost incurred for communication between sites (e.g., software protocols) makes communication cost still an important factor—as important as I/O cost [Valduriez and Gardarin, 1984]. For completeness, let us consider the methods that minimize all cost components.

## 7.3 COMPLEXITY OF RELATIONAL ALGEBRA OPERATIONS

In this chapter we consider relational algebra as a basis to express the output of query processing. Therefore, the complexity of relational algebra operations, which directly affects their execution time, dictates some principles useful to a query processor. These principles can help in choosing the final execution tree.

The simplest way of defining complexity is in terms of relation cardinalities independent of physical implementation details such as fragmentation and storage structures. Figure 7.2 shows the complexity of unary and binary operations in the order of increasing complexity, and thus of increasing execution time. Complexity is $O(n)$ for unary operations, where $n$ denotes the relation cardinality, if the resulting tuples may be obtained independent of each other. Complexity is $O(n * \log n)$ for binary operations if each tuple of one relation must be compared with each tuple of the other on the basis of the equality of selected attributes. This complexity assumes that tuples of each relation must be sorted on the comparison attributes. Projects with duplicate elimination and group operations require that each tuple of the relation be compared with each other tuple, and thus have $O(n * \log n)$ complexity. Finally, complexity is $O(n^2)$ for the Cartesian product of two relations because each tuple of one relation must be combined with each tuple of the other.

| Operation | Complexity |
|---|---|
| Select<br>Project<br>(without duplicate elimination) | $O(n)$ |
| Project<br>(with duplicate elimination)<br>Group | $O(n^* \log n)$ |
| Join<br><br>Semijoin<br><br>Division<br><br>Set Operators | $O(n^* \log n)$ |
| Cartesian Product | $O(n^2)$ |

**Figure 7.2**   Complexity of Relational Algebra Operations

This simple look at operation complexity suggests two principles. First, because complexity is relative to relation cardinalities, the most selective operations that reduce cardinalities (e.g., selection) should be performed first. Second, operations should be ordered by increasing complexity so that Cartesian products can be avoided or delayed.

## 7.4 CHARACTERIZATION OF QUERY PROCESSORS

It is quite difficult to evaluate and compare query processors in the context of both centralized systems [Jarke and Koch, 1984] and distributed systems ([Sacco and Yao,

1982] and [Apers et al., 1983]) because they may differ in many aspects. In what follows, we list important characteristics of query processors that can be used as a basis for comparison. The first four characteristics hold for both centralized and distributed query processors, while the next four characteristics are particular to distributed query processors. This characterization is used in Chapter 9 to compare various algorithms.

### 7.4.1 Languages

Initially, most work on query processing was done in the context of relational databases because their high-level languages give the system many opportunities for optimization. The input language to the query processor can be based on relational calculus or relational algebra. The former requires an additional phase to decompose a query expressed in relational calculus into relational algebra. In a distributed context, the output language is generally some internal form of relational algebra augmented with communication primitives. The operations of the output language are implemented directly in the system. Query processing must perform efficient mapping from the input language to the output language.

### 7.4.2 Types of Optimization

Conceptually, query optimization aims at choosing the best point in the solution space of all possible execution strategies. An immediate method for query optimization is to search the solution space, exhaustively predict the cost of each strategy, and select the strategy with minimum cost. Although this method is effective in selecting the best strategy, it may incur a significant processing cost for the optimization itself. The problem is that the solution space can be large; that is, there may be many equivalent strategies, even with a small number of relations. The problem becomes worse as the number of relations increases. Having high optimization cost is not necessarily bad, particularly if query optimization is done once for many subsequent executions of the query. Therefore, the exhaustive search approach is often used [Selinger et al., 1979].

One popular way of reducing the cost of exhaustive search is the use of heuristics, whose effect is to restrict the solution space so that only a few strategies are considered. In both centralized and distributed systems, a common heuristic is to minimize the size of intermediate relations. This can be done by performing unary operations first, and ordering the binary operations by the increasing sizes of their intermediate relations. An important heuristic in distributed systems is to replace join operations by combinations of semijoins to minimize data communication.

### 7.4.3 Optimization Timing

A query may be optimized at different times relative to the actual time of query execution. Optimization can be done *statically* before executing the query or *dynamically* as the query is executed. Static query optimization is done at query compilation time. Thus the cost of optimization may be amortized over multiple query executions.

Therefore, this timing is appropriate for use with the exhaustive search method. Since the sizes of the intermediate relations of a strategy are not known until run time, they must be estimated using database statistics. Errors in these estimates can lead to the choice of suboptimal strategies.

Dynamic query optimization proceeds at query execution time. At any point of execution, the choice of the best next operation can be based on accurate knowledge of the results of the operations executed previously. Therefore, database statistics are not needed to estimate the size of intermediate results. However, they may still be useful in choosing the first operations. The main advantage over static query optimization is that the actual sizes of intermediate relations are available to the query processor, thereby minimizing the probability of a bad choice. The main shortcoming is that query optimization, an expensive task, must be repeated for each execution of the query.

Hybrid query optimization attempts to provide the advantages of static query optimization while avoiding the issues generated by inaccurate estimates. The approach is basically static, but dynamic query optimization may take place at run time when a high difference between predicted sizes and actual size of intermediate relations is detected.

### 7.4.4  Statistics

The effectiveness of query optimization relies on *statistics* on the database. Dynamic query optimization requires statistics in order to choose which operations should be done first. Static query optimization is even more demanding since the size of intermediate relations must also be estimated based on statistical information. In a distributed database, statistics for query optimization typically bear on fragments, and include fragment cardinality and size as well as the size and number of distinct values of each attribute. To minimize the probability of error, more detailed statistics such as histograms of attribute values are sometimes used at the expense of higher management cost. The accuracy of statistics is achieved by periodic updating. With static optimization, significant changes in statistics used to optimize a query might result in query reoptimization.

### 7.4.5  Decision Sites

When static optimization is used, either a single site or several sites may participate in the selection of the strategy to be applied for answering the query. Most systems use the centralized decision approach, in which a single site generates the strategy. However, the decision process could be distributed among various sites participating in the elaboration of the best strategy. The centralized approach is simpler but requires knowledge of the entire distributed database, while the distributed approach requires only local information. Hybrid approaches where one site makes the major decisions and other sites can make local decisions are also frequent. For example, R* [Williams et al., 1982] uses a hybrid approach.

### 7.4.6  Exploitation of the Network Topology

The network topology is generally exploited by the distributed query processor. With wide area networks, the cost function to be minimized can be restricted to the data communication cost, which is considered to be the dominant factor. This assumption greatly simplifies distributed query optimization, which can be divided into two separate problems: selection of the global execution strategy, based on intersite communication, and selection of each local execution strategy, based on a centralized query processing algorithm.

With local area networks, communication costs are comparable to I/O costs. Therefore, it is reasonable for the distributed query processor to increase parallel execution at the expense of communication cost. The broadcasting capability of some local area networks can be exploited successfully to optimize the processing of join operations ([Özsoyoglu and Zhou, 1987] and [Wah and Lien, 1985]). Other algorithms specialized to take advantage of the network topology are presented in [Kerschberg et al., 1982] for star networks and in [LaChimia, 1984] for satellite networks.

### 7.4.7  Exploitation of Replicated Fragments

A distributed relation is usually divided into relation fragments as described in Chapter 5. Distributed queries expressed on global relations are mapped into queries on physical fragments of relations by translating relations into fragments. We call this process *localization* because its main function is to localize the data involved in the query. For reliability purposes it is useful to have fragments replicated at different sites. Most optimization algorithms consider the localization process independently of optimization. However, some algorithms exploit the existence of replicated fragments at run time in order to minimize communication times. The optimization algorithm is then more complex because there are a larger number of possible strategies.

### 7.4.8  Use of Semijoins

The semijoin operation has the important property of reducing the size of the operand relation. When the main cost component considered by the query processor is communication, a semijoin is particularly useful for improving the processing of distributed join operations as it reduces the size of data exchanged between sites. However, using semijoins may result in an increase in the number of messages and in the local processing time. The early distributed DBMSs, such as SDD-1 [Bernstein et al., 1981], which were designed for slow wide area networks, make extensive use of semijoins. Some recent systems, such as R* [Williams et al., 1982], assume faster networks and do not employ semijoins. Rather, they perform joins directly since using joins leads to lower local processing costs. Nevertheless, semijoins are still beneficial in the context of fast networks when they induce a strong reduction of the join operand. Therefore, some recent query processing algorithms aim at selecting an optimal combination of joins and semijoins ([Özsoyoglu and Zhou, 1987] and [Wah and Lien, 1985]).

## 7.5  LAYERS OF QUERY PROCESSING

In Chapter 4 we have seen where query processing fits within the distributed DBMS architecture. The problem of query processing can itself be decomposed into several subproblems, corresponding to various layers. In Figure 7.3 a generic layering scheme for query processing is shown where each layer solves a well-defined subproblem. To simplify the discussion, let us assume a static and semicentralized query processor that does not exploit replicated fragments. The input is a query on distributed data expressed in relational calculus. This distributed query is posed on global (distributed) relations, meaning that data distribution is hidden. Four main layers are involved to map the distributed query into an optimized sequence of local operations, each acting on a local database. These layers perform the functions of *query decomposition*, *data localization*, *global query optimization*, and *local query optimization*. The first three layers are performed by a central site and use global information; the fourth is done by the local sites. The first two layers are treated extensively in Chapter 8, while the two last layers are detailed in Chapter 9. In the remainder of this chapter we present an overview of the layers.

### 7.5.1  Query Decomposition

The first layer decomposes the distributed calculus query into an algebraic query on global relations. The information needed for this transformation is found in the global conceptual schema describing the global relations. However, the information about data distribution is not used here but in the next layer. Thus the techniques used by this layer are those of a centralized DBMS.

Query decomposition can be viewed as four successive steps. First, the calculus query is rewritten in a *normalized* form that is suitable for subsequent manipulation. Normalization of a query generally involves the manipulation of the query quantifiers and of the query qualification by applying logical operator priority.

Second, the normalized query is *analyzed* semantically so that incorrect queries are detected and rejected as early as possible. Techniques to detect incorrect queries exist only for a subset of relational calculus. Typically, they use some sort of graph that captures the semantics of the query.

Third, the correct query (still expressed in relational calculus) is *simplified*. One way to simplify a query is to eliminate redundant predicates. Note that redundant queries are likely to arise when a query is the result of system transformations applied to the user query. As seen in Chapter 6, such transformations are used for performing semantic data control (views, protection, and semantic integrity control).

Fourth, the calculus query is *restructured* as an algebraic query. Recall from Section 7.1 that several algebraic queries can be derived from the same calculus query, and that some algebraic queries are "better" than others. The quality of an algebraic query is defined in terms of expected performance. The traditional way to do this transformation toward a "better" algebraic specification is to start with an initial algebraic query and transform it in order to find a "good" one. The initial algebraic query

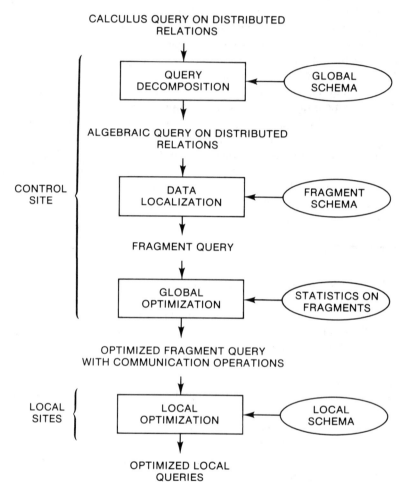

**Figure 7.3**   Generic Layering Scheme for Distributed Query Processing

is derived immediately from the calculus query by translating the predicates and the target statement into relational operations as they appear in the query. This directly translated algebra query is then restructured through transformation rules. The algebraic query generated by this layer is good in the sense that the worse executions are avoided. For instance, a relation will be accessed only once, even if there are several select predicates. However, this query is generally far from providing an optimal execution, since information about data distribution and local fragments is not used at this layer.

## 7.5.2  Data Localization

The input to the second layer is an algebraic query on distributed relations. The main role of the second layer is to localize the query's data using data distribution information. In Chapter 5 we saw that relations are fragmented and stored in disjoint subsets, called fragments, each being stored at a different site. This layer determines which fragments are involved in the query and transforms the distributed query into a fragment query. Fragmentation is defined through fragmentation rules which can be expressed as relational operations. A distributed relation can be reconstructed by applying the fragmentation rules, and then deriving a program, called a *localization program*, of relational algebra operations which then acts on fragments. Generating a fragment query is done in two steps. First, the distributed query is mapped into a fragment query by substituting each distributed relation by its reconstruction program (also called *materialization program*), discussed in Chapter 5. Second, the fragment query is simplified and restructured to produce another "good" query. Simplification and restructuring may be done according to the same rules used in the decomposition layer. As in the decomposition layer, the final fragment query is generally far from optimal because information regarding fragments is not utilized.

## 7.5.3  Global Query Optimization

The input to the third layer is a fragment query, that is, an algebraic query on fragments. The goal of query optimization is to find an execution strategy for the query which is close to optimal. Remember that finding the optimal solution is computationally intractable. An execution strategy for a distributed query can be described with relational algebra operations and *communication primitives* (send/receive operations) for transferring data between sites. The previous layers have already optimized the query, for example, by eliminating redundant expressions. However, this optimization is independent of fragment characteristics such as cardinalities. In addition, communication operations are not yet specified. By permuting the ordering of operations within one fragment query, many equivalent queries may be found.

Query optimization consists of finding the "best" ordering of operations in the fragment query, including communication operations which minimize a cost function. The cost function, often defined in terms of time units, refers to computing resources such as disk space, disk I/Os, buffer space, CPU cost, communication cost, and so on. Generally, it is a weighted combination of I/O, CPU, and communication costs. Nevertheless, a typical simplification made by distributed DBMSs, as we mentioned before, is to consider communication cost as the most significant factor. This is valid for wide area networks, where the limited bandwidth makes communication much more costly than local processing. To select the ordering of operations it is necessary to predict execution costs of alternative candidate orderings. Determining execution costs before query execution (i.e., static optimization) is based on fragment statistics and the formulas for estimating the cardinalities of results of relational operations. Thus the optimization decisions depend on the available statistics on fragments.

An important aspect of query optimization is *join ordering*, since permutations of the joins within the query may lead to improvements of orders of magnitude. One basic technique for optimizing a sequence of distributed join operations is through the semijoin operator. The main value of the semijoin in a distributed system is to reduce the size of the join operands and then the communication cost. However, more recent techniques, which consider local processing costs as well as communication costs, do not use semijoins because they might increase local processing costs. The output of the query optimization layer is an optimized algebraic query with communication operations included on fragments.

### 7.5.4 Local Query Optimization

The last layer is performed by all the sites having fragments involved in the query. Each subquery executing at one site, called a *local query*, is then optimized using the local schema of the site. At this time, the algorithms to perform the relational operations may be chosen. Local optimization uses the algorithms of centralized systems (see Chapter 9).

## 7.6 CONCLUSION

In this chapter we provided an overview of query processing in distributed DBMSs. We first introduced the function and objectives of query processing. The main assumption is that the distributed query is expressed in relational calculus since that is the case with most current distributed DBMS. The complexity of the problem is proportional to the expressive power and the abstraction capability of the query language. For instance, the problem is even harder with logic-based languages for deductive databases ([Gallaire et al., 1984] and [Valduriez and Boral, 1986]).

The goal of distributed query processing may be summarized as follows: given a calculus query on a distributed database, find a corresponding execution strategy that minimizes a system cost function that includes I/O, CPU, and communication costs. An execution strategy is specified in terms of relational algebra operations and communication primitives (send/receive) applied to the local databases (i.e., the relation fragments). Therefore, complexity of relational operations that affect the performance of query execution is of major importance in the design of a query processor.

We gave a characterization of query processors based on their implementation choices. Query processors may differ in various aspects such as type of algorithm, optimization granularity, optimization timing, use of statistics, choice of decision site(s), exploitation of the network topology, exploitation of replicated fragments, and use of semijoins. This characterization is useful for comparing alternative query processor designs and to understand the trade-offs between efficiency and complexity.

The query processing problem is very difficult to understand in distributed environments because many elements are involved. However, the problem may be divided into several subproblems which are easier to solve individually. Therefore, we have proposed a generic layering scheme for describing distributed query processing. Four main functions have been isolated: query decomposition, data localization, query optimization, and local query optimization. These functions successively refine the query by adding more details about the processing environment. Query decomposition and data localization are treated in detail in Chapter 8. Distributed and local query optimization is the topic of Chapter 9.

## 7.7  BIBLIOGRAPHIC NOTES

[Kim et al., 1985] provides a comprehensive set of papers presenting the results of research and development in query processing within the context of the relational model. After a survey of the state of the art in query processing, the book treats most of the important topics in the area. In particular, there are three papers on distributed query processing. [Gardarin and Valduriez, 1989] includes a chapter on query processing in centralized DBMSs.

[Ceri and Pelagatti, 1984] deals extensively with distributed query processing by treating the problem of localization and optimization separately in two chapters. The main assumption is that the query is expressed in relational algebra, so the decomposition phase that maps a calculus query into an algebraic query is ignored.

There are several survey papers on query processing and query optimization in the context of the relational model. A detailed survey is available in [Jarke and Koch, 1984]. Its main emphasis is on centralized query processing and a short section deals with distributed query processing. It also treats the general problem of mapping a relational calculus query into an optimal execution strategy. Many solutions to distributed query processing are extensively compiled in [Sacco and Yao, 1982] and [Yu and Chang, 1984].

In [Ibaraki and Kameda, 1984] it is formally shown that finding the optimal execution strategy for a query is computationally intractable. Assuming a simplified cost function including the number of page accesses, it is proven that the minimization of this cost function for a multiple-join query is NP-complete.

# 8

# Query Decomposition and Data Localization

In Chapter 7 we discussed a generic layering scheme for distributed query processing in which the first two layers are responsible for query decomposition and data localization. These two functions are applied successively to transform a calculus query specified on distributed relations (i.e., global relations) into an algebraic query defined on relation fragments. In this chapter we present the techniques for query decomposition and data localization.

Query decomposition maps a distributed calculus query into an algebraic query on global relations. The techniques used at this layer are those of the centralized DBMS since relation distribution is not yet considered at this point. The resultant algebraic query is "good" in the sense that even if the subsequent layers apply a straightforward algorithm, the worst executions will be avoided. However, the subsequent layers usually perform important optimizations, as they add to the query increasing detail about the processing environment.

Data localization takes as input the decomposed query on global relations and applies data distribution information to the query in order to localize its data. In Chapter 5 we have seen that to increase the locality of reference and/or parallel execution, relations are fragmented and then stored in disjoint subsets, called fragments, each being placed at a different site. Data localization determines which fragments are involved in the query and thereby transforms the distributed query into a fragment query. Similar to the decomposition layer, the final fragment query is generally far from optimal because quantitative information regarding fragments is not exploited at this point. Quantitative information is used by the query optimization layer that will be presented in Chapter 9.

This chapter is organized as follows. In Section 8.1 we present the four successive phases of query decomposition: normalization, semantic analysis, simplification, and restructuring of the query. In Section 8.2 we describe data localization, with emphasis on reduction and simplification techniques for the four following types of fragmentation: horizontal, vertical, derived, and hybrid.

## 8.1 QUERY DECOMPOSITION

Query decomposition (see Figure 7.3) is the first phase of query processing that transforms a relational calculus query into a relational algebra query. Both input and output queries refer to global relations, without knowledge of the distribution of data. Therefore, query decomposition is the same for centralized and distributed systems [Gardarin and Valduriez, 1989]. In this section the input query is assumed to be syntactically correct. When this phase is completed successfully the output query is semantically correct and good in the sense that redundant work is avoided. The successive steps of query decomposition are (1) normalization, (2) analysis, (3) elimination of redundancy, and (4) rewriting. Steps 1, 3, and 4 rely on the fact that various transformations are equivalent for a given query, and some can have better performance than others. We present the first three steps in the context of tuple relational calculus (e.g., SQL). Only the last step rewrites the query into relational algebra.

### 8.1.1 Normalization

The input query may be arbitrarily complex, depending on the facilities provided by the language. It is the goal of normalization to transform the query to a normalized form to facilitate further processing. With relational languages such as SQL, the most important transformation is that of the query qualification (the WHERE clause), which may be an arbitrarily complex, quantifier-free predicate, preceded by all necessary quantifiers ($\forall$ or $\exists$). There are two possible normal forms for the predicate, one giving precedence to the AND ($\wedge$) and the other to the OR ($\vee$). The *conjunctive normal form* is a conjunction ($\wedge$ predicate) of disjunctions ($\vee$ predicates) as follows:

$$(p_{11} \vee p_{12} \vee \cdots \vee p_{1n}) \wedge \cdots \wedge (p_{m1} \vee p_{m2} \vee \cdots \vee p_{mn})$$

where $p_{ij}$ is a simple predicate. A qualification in *disjunctive normal form*, on the other hand, is as follows:

$$(p_{11} \wedge p_{12} \wedge \cdots \wedge p_{1n}) \vee \cdots \vee (p_{m1} \wedge p_{m2} \wedge \cdots \wedge p_{mn})$$

The transformation of the quantifier-free predicate is straightforward using the well-known equivalence rules for logical operations ($\wedge$, $\vee$, and $\neg$):

1. $p_1 \land p_2 \Leftrightarrow p_2 \land p_1$

2. $p_1 \lor p_2 \Leftrightarrow p_2 \lor p_1$

3. $p_1 \land (p_2 \land p_3) \Leftrightarrow (p_1 \land p_2) \land p_3$

4. $p_1 \lor (p_2 \lor p_3) \Leftrightarrow (p_1 \lor p_2) \lor p_3$

5. $p_1 \land (p_2 \lor p_3) \Leftrightarrow (p_1 \land p_2) \lor (p_1 \land p_3)$

6. $p_1 \lor (p_2 \land p_3) \Leftrightarrow (p_1 \lor p_2) \land (p_1 \lor p_3)$

7. $\neg(p_1 \land p_2) \Leftrightarrow \neg p_1 \lor \neg p_2$

8. $\neg(p_1 \lor p_2) \Leftrightarrow \neg p_1 \land \neg p_2$

9. $\neg(\neg p) \Leftrightarrow p$

In the disjunctive normal form, the query can be processed as independent conjunctive subqueries linked by unions (corresponding to the disjunctions). However, this form may lead to replicated join and select predicates, as shown in the following example. The reason is that predicates are very often linked with the other predicates by AND. The use of rule 5 mentioned above, with $p_1$ as a join or select predicate, would result in replicating $p_1$. The conjunctive normal form is more practical since query qualifications typically include more AND than OR predicates. However, it leads to predicate replication for queries involving many disjunctions and few conjunctions, a rare case.

### Example 8.1

Let us consider the following query on the engineering database that we have been referring to:

"Find the names of employees who have been working on project J1 for 12 or 24 months"

The query expressed in SQL is

```
SELECT    ENAME
FROM      E, G
WHERE     E.ENO = G.ENO
AND       G.JNO = ''J1''
AND       DUR = 12 OR DUR = 24
```

The qualification in conjunctive normal form is

$$E.ENO = G.ENO \land G.JNO = \text{"J1"} \land (DUR = 12 \lor DUR = 24)$$

while the qualification in disjunctive normal form is

$$(E.ENO = G.ENO \land G.JNO = \text{"J1"} \land DUR = 12) \lor$$
$$(E.ENO = G.ENO \land G.JNO = \text{"J1"} \land DUR = 24)$$

In the latter form, treating the two conjunctions independently may lead to redundant work if common subexpressions are not eliminated.

### 8.1.2 Analysis

Query analysis enables rejection of normalized queries for which further processing is either impossible or unnecessary. The main reasons for rejection are that the query is *type incorrect* or *semantically incorrect*. When one of these cases is detected, the query is simply returned to the user with an explanation. Otherwise, query processing is continued. Below we present techniques to detect these incorrect queries.

A query is type incorrect if any of its attribute or relation names are not defined in the global schema, or if operations are being applied to attributes of the wrong type. The technique used to detect type incorrect queries is similar to type checking for programming languages. However, the type declarations are part of the global schema rather than of the query, since a relational query does not produce new types.

**Example 8.2**

The following SQL query on the engineering database

```
SELECT    E#
FROM      E
WHERE     ENAME > 200
```

is type incorrect for two reasons. First, attribute E# is not declared in the schema. Second, the operation ">200" is incompatible with the type string of ENAME.

A query is semantically incorrect if components of it do not contribute in any way to the generation of the result. In the context of relational calculus, it is not possible to determine the semantic correctness of general queries. However, it is possible to do so for a large class of relational queries, those which do not contain disjunction and negation [Rosenkrantz and Hunt, 1980]. This is based on the representation of the query as a graph, called a *query graph* or *connection graph* [Ullman, 1982]. We define this graph for the most useful kinds of queries involving select, project, and join operations. In a query graph, one node indicates the result relation, and any other node indicates an operand relation. An edge between two nodes that are not results represents a join, whereas an edge whose destination node is the result represents a project. Furthermore, a nonresult node may be labeled by a select or a self-join (join of the relation with itself) predicate. An important subgraph of the relation connection graph is the *join graph*, in which only the joins are considered. The join graph is particularly useful in the query optimization phase.

**Example 8.3**

Let us consider the following query:

"Find the names and responsibilities of programmers who have been working on the CAD/CAM project for more than 3 years, and their manager's name"

The query expressed in SQL is

```
SELECT    ENAME, RESP
FROM      E, G, J
WHERE     E.ENO = G.ENO
```

```
AND   G.JNO = J.JNO
AND   JNAME = ''CAD/CAM''
AND   DUR ≥ 36
AND   TITLE = ''Programmer''
```

The query graph for the query above is shown in Figure 8.1a. Figure 8.1b shows the join graph for the graph in Figure 8.1a.

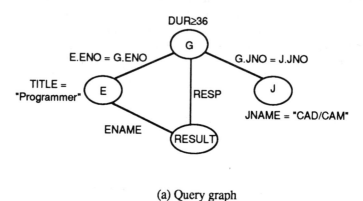

(a) Query graph

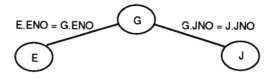

(b) Corresponding join graph

**Figure 8.1**   Relation Graphs

The query graph is useful to determine the semantic correctness of a conjunctive multivariable query without negation. Such a query is semantically incorrect if its query graph is not connected. In this case one or more subgraphs (corresponding to subqueries) are disconnected from the graph that contains the result relation, and therefore are useless. The query could be considered correct (which some systems do) by eliminating the useless portions. But, in general, the problem is that join predicates are missing and the query should be rejected.

**Example 8.4**

Let us consider the following SQL query:

```
SELECT   ENAME, RESP
FROM     E, G, J
WHERE    E.ENO = G.ENO
AND      JNAME = ''CAD/CAM''
```

AND   DUR $\geq$ 36
AND   TITLE = ''Programmer''

Its query graph, shown in Figure 8.2, is disconnected, which tells us that the query is semantically incorrect. There are basically three solutions to the problem: (1) reject the query, (2) assume that the access to relation J is useless and remove the predicate JNAME = "CAD/CAM" from the query, or (3) infer (using the schema) the missing join predicate G.JNO = J.JNO which transforms the query into that of Example 8.3.

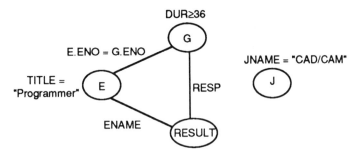

**Figure 8.2**   Disconnected Query Graph

### 8.1.3 Elimination of Redundancy

As we saw in Chapter 6, relational languages can be used uniformly for semantic data control. In particular, a user query typically expressed on a view may be enriched with several predicates to achieve view-relation correspondence, and ensure semantic integrity and security. The enriched query qualification may then contain redundant predicates. A naive evaluation of a qualification with redundancy can well lead to duplicated work. Such redundancy and thus redundant work may be eliminated by simplifying the qualification with the following well-known idempotency rules:

1. $p \wedge p \Leftrightarrow p$
2. $p \vee p \Leftrightarrow p$
3. $p \wedge true \Leftrightarrow p$
4. $p \vee false \Leftrightarrow p$
5. $p \wedge false \Leftrightarrow false$
6. $p \vee true \Leftrightarrow true$
7. $p \wedge \neg p \Leftrightarrow false$
8. $p \vee \neg p \Leftrightarrow true$
9. $p_1 \wedge (p_1 \vee p_2) \Leftrightarrow p_1$
10. $p_1 \vee (p_1 \wedge p_2) \Leftrightarrow p_1$

**Example 8.5**

The SQL query

```
SELECT    TITLE
FROM      E
WHERE     (NOT (TITLE = ''Programmer'')
AND       (TITLE = ''Programmer''
OR        TITLE = ''Elect. Eng.'')
AND       NOT (TITLE = ''Elect. Eng.''))
OR        ENAME = ''J. Doe''
```

can be simplified using the previous rules to become

```
SELECT    TITLE
FROM      E
WHERE     ENAME = ''J. Doe''
```

The simplification proceeds as follows. Let $p_1$ be <TITLE = "Programmer">, $p_2$ be <TITLE = "Elect. Eng.">, and $p_3$ be < ENAME = "J. Doe">. The query qualification is

$$(\neg p_1 \land (p_1 \lor p_2) \land \neg p_2) \lor p_3$$

The disjunctive normal form for this qualification is obtained by applying rules 3 and 5 defined in Section 8.1.1, which yields

$$(\neg p_1 \land p_1 \land \neg p_2) \lor (\neg p_1 \land p_2 \land \neg p_2) \lor p_3$$

By applying rule 7 defined above, we obtain

$$(false \land \neg p_2) \lor (\neg p_1 \land false) \lor p_3$$

By applying the same rule, we get

$$false \lor false \lor p_3$$

which is equivalent to $p_3$ by rule 4 above.

### 8.1.4 Rewriting

The last step of query decomposition rewrites the query in relational algebra. This is typically divided into the following two substeps: (1) straightforward transformation of the query from relational calculus into relational algebra, and (2) restructuring of the relational algebra query to improve performance. For the sake of clarity it is customary to represent the relational algebra query graphically by a *relational algebra tree*. A relational algebra tree is a tree in which a leaf node is a relation stored in the database, and a nonleaf node is an intermediate relation produced by a relational algebra operation. The sequence of operations is directed from the leaves to the root, which represents the answer to the query.

The transformation of a tuple relational calculus query into a relational algebra tree can easily be achieved as follows. First, a different leaf is created for each different tuple variable (corresponding to a relation). In SQL, the leaves are immediately available in the FROM clause. Second, the root node is created as a project operation involving the result attributes. These are found in the SELECT clause in SQL. Third, the qualification (SQL WHERE clause) is translated into the appropriate sequence of relational operations (select, join, union, etc.) going from the leaves to the root. The sequence can be given directly by the order of appearance of the predicates and operators.

**Example 8.6**

The query

> "Find the names of employees other than J. Doe who worked on the CAD/CAM project for either one or two years" whose SQL expression is

```
SELECT   ENAME
FROM     J, G, E
WHERE    G.ENO = E.ENO
AND      G.JNO = J.JNO
AND      ENAME ≠ ''J. Doe''
AND      J.NAME = ''CAD/CAM''
AND      (DUR = 12 OR DUR = 24)
```

can be mapped in a straightforward way in the tree in Figure 8.3. The predicates have been transformed in order of appearance as join and then select operations.

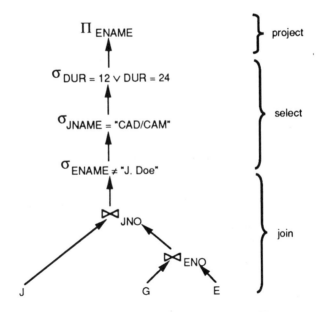

**Figure 8.3**  Example of Relational Algebra Tree

By applying *transformation rules*, many different trees may be found equivalent to the one produced by the method described above [Smith and Chang, 1975]. The six most useful equivalence rules, which concern the basic relational algebra operations, are now presented. The correctness of these rules is given in [Ullman, 1982].

In the remainder of this section, $R$, $S$, and $T$ are relations where $R$ is defined over attributes $A = \{A_1, A_2, \ldots, A_n\}$ and $S$ is defined over $B = \{B_1, B_2, \ldots, B_n\}$.

**1. Commutativity of binary operations.** The Cartesian product of two relations $R$ and $S$ is commutative:

$$R \times S \Leftrightarrow S \times R$$

Similarly, the join of two relations is commutative:

$$R \bowtie S \Leftrightarrow S \bowtie R$$

This rule also applies to union but not to set difference or semijoin.

**2. Associativity of binary operations.** The Cartesian product and the join are associative operations:

$$(R \times S) \times T \;\; \Leftrightarrow \;\; R \times (S \times T)$$
$$(R \bowtie S) \bowtie T \;\; \Leftrightarrow \;\; R \bowtie (S \bowtie T)$$

**3. Idempotence of unary operations.** Several subsequent projections on the same relation may be grouped. Conversely, a single projection on several attributes may be separated into several subsequent projections. If $R$ is defined over the attribute set $A$, and $A' \subseteq A, A'' \subseteq A$, and $A' \subseteq A''$, then

$$\Pi_{A'}(\Pi_{A''}(R)) \Leftrightarrow \Pi_{A'}(R)$$

Several subsequent selections $\sigma_{p_i(A_i)}$ on the same relation, where $p_i$ is a predicate applied to attribute $A_i$, may be grouped as follows:

$$\sigma_{p_1(A_1)}(\sigma_{p_2(A_2)}(R)) = \sigma_{p_1(A_1) \wedge p_2(A_2)}(R)$$

Conversely, a single selection with a conjunction of predicates may be separated into several subsequent selections.

**4. Commuting selection with projection.** Selection and projection on the same relation can be commuted as follows:

$$\Pi_{A_1, \ldots, A_n}(\sigma_{p(A_p)}(R)) \Leftrightarrow \Pi_{A_1, \ldots, A_n}(\sigma_{p(A_p)}(\Pi_{A_1, \ldots, A_n, A_p}(R)))$$

Note that if $A_p$ is already a member of $\{A_1, \ldots, A_n\}$, the last projection on $[A_1, \ldots, A_n]$ on the right-hand side of the equality is useless.

**5. Commuting selection with binary operations.** Selection and Cartesian product can be commuted using the following rule (remember that attribute $A_i$ belongs to relation $R$):

$$\sigma_{p(A_i)}(R \times S) \Leftrightarrow (\sigma_{p(A_i)}(R)) \times S$$

Selection and join can be commuted:

$$\sigma_{p(A_i)}(R \bowtie_{p(A_j, B_k)} S) \Leftrightarrow \sigma_{p(A_i)}(R) \bowtie_{p(A_j, B_k)} S$$

Selection and union can be commuted if $R$ and $T$ are union compatible (have the same schema):

$$\sigma_{p(A_i)}(R \cup T) \Leftrightarrow \sigma_{p(A_i)}(R) \cup \sigma_{p(A_i)}(T)$$

Selection and difference can be commuted in a similar fashion.

**6. Commuting projection with binary operations.** Projection and Cartesian product can be commuted. If $C = A' \cup B'$, where $A' \subseteq A$, $B' \subseteq B$, and $A$ and $B$ are the sets of attributes over which relations $R$ and $S$, respectively, are defined, we have

$$\Pi_C(R \times S) \Leftrightarrow \Pi_{A'}(R) \times \Pi_{B'}(S)$$

Projection and join can also be commuted.

$$\Pi_C(R \bowtie_{p(A_i, B_j)} S) \Leftrightarrow \Pi_{A'}(R) \bowtie_{p(A_i, B_j)} \Pi_{B'}(S)$$

For the join on the right-hand side of the implication to hold we need to have $A_i \in A'$ and $B_i \in B'$. Since $C = A' \cup B'$, $A_i$ and $B_i$ are in $C$ and therefore we don't need a projection over $C$ once the projections over $A'$ and $B'$ are performed. Projection and union can be commuted as follows:

$$\Pi_C(R \cup S) \Leftrightarrow \Pi_C(R) \cup \Pi_C(S)$$

Projection and difference can be commuted similarly.

   The application of these six rules enables the generation of many equivalent trees. For instance, the tree in Figure 8.4 is equivalent to the one in Figure 8.3. However, the one in Figure 8.4 requires a Cartesian product of relations E and J, and may lead to a higher execution cost than the original tree. In the optimization phase, one can imagine comparing all possible trees based on their predicted cost. However, the excessively large number of possible trees makes this approach unrealistic. The rules presented above can be used to restructure the tree in a systematic way so that the "bad" relational algebra trees are eliminated. These rules can be used in four different ways. First, they allow the separation of the unary operations, simplifying the query expression. Second, unary operations on the same relation may be grouped so that access to a relation for performing unary operations can be done only once. Third, unary operations can be commuted with binary operations so that some operations (e.g., selection) may be done first. Fourth, the binary operations can be ordered. This last rule is used extensively in query optimization. A simple restructuring algorithm, presented in [Ullman, 1982], uses a single heuristic that consists of applying unary operations (select/project) as soon as possible to reduce the size of intermediate relations.

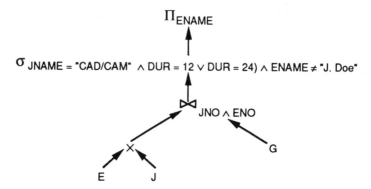

**Figure 8.4** Equivalent Relational Algebra Tree

**Example 8.7**

The restructuring of the tree in Figure 8.3 leads to the tree in Figure 8.5. The resulting tree is good in the sense that repeated access to the same relation (as in Figure 8.3) is avoided and that the most selective operations are done first. However, this tree is far from optimal. For example, the select operation on E is not very useful before the join because it does not greatly reduce the size of the operand relation.

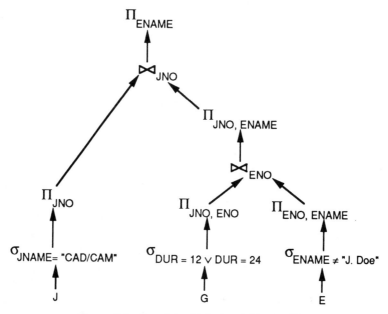

**Figure 8.5** Rewritten Relational Algebra Tree

## 8.2 LOCALIZATION OF DISTRIBUTED DATA

In Section 8.1 we presented general techniques for decomposing and restructuring queries expressed in relational calculus. These global techniques apply to both centralized and distributed DBMSs and do not take into account the distribution of data. This is the role of the localization layer. As shown in the generic layering scheme of query processing described in Chapter 7, the localization layer translates an algebraic query on global relations into an algebraic query expressed on physical fragments. Localization uses information stored in the fragment schema.

Fragmentation is defined through fragmentation rules, which can be expressed as relational queries. As we discussed in Chapter 5, a global relation can be reconstructed by applying the reconstruction (or reverse fragmentation) rules and deriving a relational algebra program whose operands are the fragments. We call this a *localization program*. To simplify this section, we do not consider the fact that data fragments may be replicated, although this can improve performance. Replication is considered in Chapter 9.

A naive way to localize a distributed query is to generate a query where each global relation is substituted by its localization program. This can be viewed as replacing the leaves of the relational algebra tree of the distributed query with subtrees corresponding to the localization programs. We call the query obtained this way the *generic query*. In general, this approach is inefficient because important restructurings and simplifications of the generic query can still be made ([Ceri and Pelagatti, 1983] and [Ceri et al., 1986]). In the remainder of this section, for each type of fragmentation we present *reduction techniques* that generate simpler and optimized queries. We use the transformation rules and the heuristics, such as pushing unary operations down the tree, that were introduced in Section 8.1.4.

### 8.2.1  Reduction for Primary Horizontal Fragmentation

The horizontal fragmentation function distributes a relation based on selection predicates. The following example is used in subsequent discussions.

**Example 8.8**

Relation E(ENO, ENAME, TITLE) of Figure 2.4 can be split into three horizontal fragments $E_1$, $E_2$, and $E_3$, defined as follows:

$$
\begin{aligned}
E_1 &= \sigma_{ENO \leq \text{"E3"}}(E) \\
E_2 &= \sigma_{\text{"E3"} < ENO \leq \text{"E6"}}(E) \\
E_3 &= \sigma_{ENO > \text{"E6"}}(E)
\end{aligned}
$$

Note that this fragmentation of the E relation is different from the one discussed in Example 5.12.

The localization program for an horizontally fragmented relation is the union of the fragments. In our example we have

$$E = E_1 \cup E_2 \cup E_3$$

Thus the generic form of any query specified on E is obtained by replacing it by ($E_1 \cup E_2 \cup E_3$).

The reduction of queries on horizontally fragmented relations consists primarily of determining, after restructuring the subtrees, those that will produce empty relations, and removing them. Horizontal fragmentation can be exploited to simplify both selection and join operations.

**Reduction with selection.**   Selections on fragments that have a qualification contradicting the qualification of the fragmentation rule generate empty relations. Given a relation $R$ that has been horizontally fragmented as $R_1$, $R_2$, ..., $R_w$, where $R_j = \sigma_{p_j}(R)$, the rule can be stated formally as follows:

**Rule 1:**

$$\sigma_{p_i}(R_j) = \phi \text{ if } \forall x \text{ in } R : \neg(p_i(x) \wedge p_j(x))$$

where $p_i$ and $p_j$ are selection predicates, $x$ denotes a tuple, and $p(x)$ denotes "predicate $p$ holds for $x$."

For example, the selection predicate ENO="E1" conflicts with the predicates of fragments $E_2$ and $E_3$ of Example 8.8 (i.e., no tuple in $E_2$ and $E_3$ can satisfy this predicate). Determining the contradicting predicates requires theorem-proving techniques if the predicates are quite general [Hunt and Rosenkrantz, 1979]. However, DBMSs generally simplify predicate comparison by supporting only simple predicates for defining fragmentation rules (by the database administrator).

**Example 8.9**

We now illustrate reduction by horizontal fragmentation using the following example query

```
SELECT    *
FROM      E
WHERE     ENO = ''E5''
```

Applying the naive approach to localize E from $E_1$, $E_2$, and $E_3$ gives the generic query of Figure 8.6a. By commuting the selection with the union operation, it is easy to detect that the selection predicate contradicts the predicates of $E_1$ and $E_3$, thereby producing empty relations. The reduced query is simply applied to $E_2$ as shown in Figure 8.6b.

**Reduction with join.**   Joins on horizontally fragmented relations can be simplified when the joined relations are fragmented according to the join attribute. The simplification consists of distributing joins over unions and eliminating useless joins. The distribution of join over union can be stated as

$$(R_1 \cup R_2) \bowtie R_3 = (R_1 \bowtie R_3) \cup (R_2 \bowtie R_3)$$

where $R_i$ are fragments.

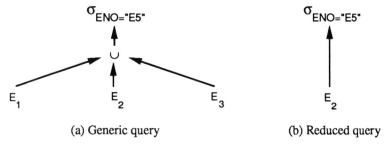

(a) Generic query                    (b) Reduced query

**Figure 8.6**   Reduction for Horizontal Fragmentation (with Selection)

With this transformation, unions can be moved up in the query tree so that all possible joins of fragments are exhibited. Useless joins of fragments can be determined when the qualifications of the joined fragments are contradicting. Assuming that fragments $R_i$ and $R_j$ are defined, respectively, according to predicates $p_i$ and $p_j$ on the same attribute, the simplification rule can be stated as follows:

**Rule 2:**

$$R_i \bowtie R_j = \phi \text{ if } \forall x \text{ in } R_i, \forall y \text{ in } R_j : \neg(p_i(x) \land p_j(y))$$

The determination of useless joins can thus be performed by looking only at the fragment predicates. The application of this rule permits the join of two relations to be implemented as parallel partial joins of fragments [Ceri et al., 1986]. It is not always the case that the reduced query is better (i.e., simpler) than the generic query. The generic query is better when there are a large number of partial joins in the reduced query. This case arises when there are few contradicting fragmentation predicates. The worst case occurs when each fragment of one relation must be joined with each fragment of the other relation. This is tantamount to the Cartesian product of the two sets of fragments, with each set corresponding to one relation. The reduced query is better when the number of partial joins is small. For example, if both relations are fragmented using the same predicates, the number of partial joins is equal to the number of fragments of each relation. One advantage of the reduced query is that the partial joins can be done in parallel, and thus increase response time.

**Example 8.10**

Assume that relation E is fragmented between $E_1$, $E_2$, and $E_3$, as above, and that relation G is fragmented as

$$\begin{aligned} G_1 &= \sigma_{\text{ENO} \leq \text{"E3"}}(G) \\ G_2 &= \sigma_{\text{ENO} > \text{"E3"}}(G) \end{aligned}$$

$E_1$ and $G_1$ are defined by the same predicate. Furthermore, the predicate defining $G_2$ is the union of the predicates defining $E_2$ and $E_3$. Now consider the join query

```
SELECT    *
FROM      E, G
WHERE     E.ENO = G.ENO
```

The equivalent generic query is given in Figure 8.7a. The query reduced by distributing joins over unions and applying rule 2 can be implemented as a union of three partial joins that can be done in parallel (Figure 8.7b).

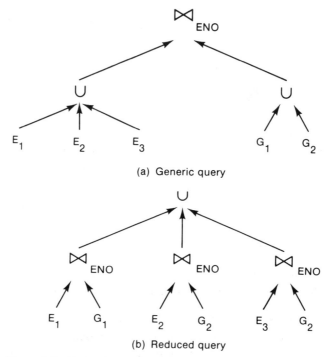

**Figure 8.7**   Reduction by Horizontal Fragmentation (with Join)

## 8.2 2  Reduction for Vertical Fragmentation

The vertical fragmentation function distributes a relation based on projection attributes. Since the reconstruction operator for vertical fragmentation is the join, the localization program for a vertically fragmented relation consists of the join of the fragments on the common attribute. For vertical fragmentation, we use the following example.

**Example 8.11**

Relation E can be divided into two vertical fragments where the key attribute ENO is duplicated:

$$E_1 = \Pi_{ENO,ENAME}(E)$$
$$E_2 = \Pi_{ENO,TITLE}(E)$$

The localization program is

$$E = E_1 \bowtie_{ENO} E_2$$

Similar to horizontal fragmentation, queries on vertical fragments can be reduced by determining the useless intermediate relations and removing the subtrees that produce them. Projections on a vertical fragment that has no attributes in common with the projection attributes (except the key of the relation) produce useless, though not empty relations. Given a relation $R$, defined over attributes $A = \{A_1, \ldots, A_n\}$, which is vertically fragmented as $R_i = \Pi_{A'}(R)$, where $A' \subseteq A$, the rule can be formally stated as follows:

**Rule 3:**    $\Pi_{D,K}(R_i)$ is useless if the set of projection attributes $D$ is not in $A'$.

**Example 8.12**

Let us illustrate the application of this rule using the following example query in SQL:

```
SELECT     ENAME
FROM       E
```

The equivalent generic query on $E_1$ and $E_2$ (as obtained in Example 8.10) is given in Figure 8.8a. By commuting the projection with the join (i.e., projecting on ENO, ENAME), we can see that the projection on $E_2$ is useless because ENAME is not in $E_2$. Therefore, the projection needs to apply only to $E_1$, as shown in Figure 8.8b.

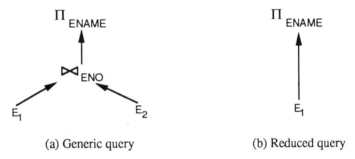

(a) Generic query                        (b) Reduced query

**Figure 8.8**    Reduction for Vertical Fragmentation

## 8.2.3  Reduction for Derived Fragmentation

As we saw in previous sections, the join operation, which is probably the most important operation because it is both frequent and expensive, can be optimized using primary horizontal fragmentation when the joined relations are fragmented according to the join attributes. In this case the join of two relations is implemented as a union of partial joins. However, this method precludes one of the relations from being fragmented on a different attribute used for selection. Derived horizontal fragmentation is another way of distributing two relations so that the joint processing of select and join is improved. Typically, if relation $R$ is subject to derived horizontal fragmentation due to relation $S$, the fragments of $R$ and $S$ that have the same join attribute values are located at the same site. In addition, $S$ can be fragmented according to a selection predicate.

Since tuples of $R$ are placed according to the tuples of $S$, derived fragmentation should be used only for one-to-many (hierarchical) relationships of the form $S \rightarrow R$, where a tuple of $S$ can match with $n$ tuples of $R$, but a tuple of $R$ matches with exactly one tuple of $S$. Note that derived fragmentation could be used for many-to-many relationships provided that tuples of $S$ (that match with $n$ tuples of $R$) are replicated. Such replication is difficult to maintain consistently. For simplicity, we assume and advise that derived fragmentation be used only for hierarchical relationships.

**Example 8.13**

Given a one-to-many relationship from E to G, relation G(ENO, JNO, RESP, DUR) can be indirectly fragmented according to the following rules:

$$G_1 \quad = \quad G \ltimes_{ENO} E_1$$
$$G_2 \quad = \quad G \ltimes_{ENO} E_2$$

Recall from Chapter 5 that the predicate on relation E is used to define the fragments, where relation E is itself horizontally fragmented as

$$E_1 \quad = \quad \sigma_{TITLE = \text{"Programmer"}}(E)$$
$$E_2 \quad = \quad \sigma_{TITLE \neq \text{"Programmer"}}(E)$$

The localization program for a horizontally fragmented relation is the union of the fragments. In our example, we have

$$G = G_1 \cup G_2$$

Queries on derived fragments can also be reduced. Since this type of fragmentation is useful for optimizing join queries, a useful transformation is to distribute joins over unions (used in the localization programs) and to apply rule 2 introduced earlier. Because the fragmentation rules indicate what the matching tuples are, certain joins will produce empty relations if the fragmentation predicates conflict. For example, the predicates of $G_1$ and $E_2$ conflict; thus we have

$$G_1 \bowtie E_2 = \phi$$

Contrary to the reduction with join discussed previously, the reduced query is always preferable to the generic query because the number of partial joins usually equals the number of fragments of $R$.

**Example 8.14**

The reduction by derived fragmentation is illustrated by applying it to the following SQL query, which retrieves all attributes of tuples from E and G that have the same value of ENO and the title "Mech. Eng.":

```
SELECT    *
FROM      E, G
WHERE     G.ENO = E.ENO
AND       TITLE = ''Mech. Eng.''
```

The generic query on fragments $E_1$, $E_2$, $G_1$, and $G_2$, defined previously is given in Figure 8.9a. By pushing selection down to fragments $E_1$ and $E_2$, the query reduces to that of Figure 8.9b. This is because the selection predicate conflicts with that of $E_1$, and thus $E_1$ can be removed. In order to discover conflicting join predicates, we distribute joins over unions. This produces the tree of Figure 8.9c. The left subtree joins two fragments, $G_1$ and $E_2$, whose qualifications conflict because of predicates TITLE = "Programmer" in $G_1$, and TITLE $\neq$ "Programmer" in $E_2$. Therefore the left subtree which produces an empty relation can be removed, and the reduced query of Figure 8.9d is obtained. This example illustrates the value of fragmentation in improving the execution performance of distributed queries.

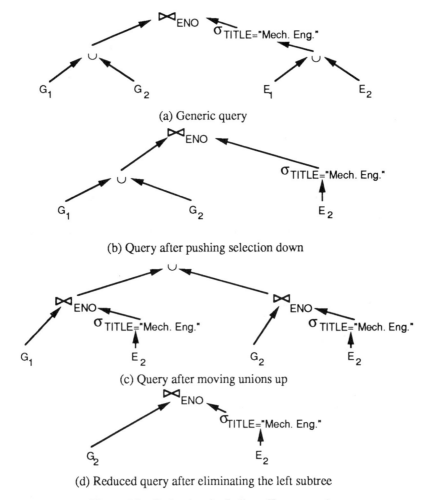

(a) Generic query

(b) Query after pushing selection down

(c) Query after moving unions up

(d) Reduced query after eliminating the left subtree

**Figure 8.9**    Reduction for Indirect Fragmentation

### 8.2.4 Reduction for Hybrid Fragmentation

Hybrid fragmentation is obtained by combining the fragmentation functions discussed above. The goal of hybrid fragmentation is to support, efficiently, queries involving projection, selection, and join. Note that the optimization of an operation or of a combination of operations is always done at the expense of other operations. For example, hybrid fragmentation based on selection-projection will make selection only, or projection only, less efficient than with horizontal fragmentation (or vertical fragmentation). The localization program for a hybrid fragmented relation uses unions and joins of fragments.

**Example 8.15**

Here is an example of hybrid fragmentation of relation E:

$$E_1 \quad = \quad \sigma_{ENO \leq \text{``E4''}}(\Pi_{ENO,ENAME}(E))$$
$$E_2 \quad = \quad \sigma_{ENO > \text{``E4''}}(\Pi_{ENO,ENAME}(E))$$
$$E_3 \quad = \quad \Pi_{ENO,TITLE}(E)$$

In our example, the localization program is

$$E = (E_1 \cup E_2) \bowtie_{ENO} E_3$$

Queries on hybrid fragments can be reduced by combining the rules used, respectively, in primary horizontal, vertical, and derived horizontal fragmentation. These rules can be summarized as follows:

1. Remove empty relations generated by contradicting selections on horizontal fragments.

2. Remove useless relations generated by projections on vertical fragments.

3. Distribute joins over unions in order to isolate and remove useless joins.

**Example 8.16**

The following example query in SQL illustrates the application of rules (1) and (2) to the horizontal-vertical fragmentation of relation E into $E_1$, $E_2$ and $E_3$ given above:

```
SELECT    ENAME
FROM      E
WHERE     ENO=''E5''
```

The generic query of Figure 8.10a can be reduced by first pushing selection down, eliminating fragment $E_1$, and then pushing projection down, eliminating fragment $E_3$. The reduced query is given in Figure 8.10b.

## 8.3 CONCLUSION

In this chapter we focused on the techniques for query decomposition and data localization layers of the generic query processing scheme that was introduced in Chapter 7.

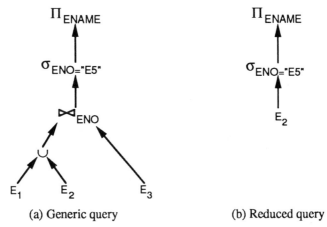

(a) Generic query                    (b) Reduced query

**Figure 8.10**   Reduction for Hybrid Fragmentation

Query decomposition and data localization are the two successive functions that map a calculus query, expressed on distributed relations, into an algebraic query (query decomposition), expressed on relation fragments (data localization).

These two layers can produce a generic query corresponding to the input query in a naive way. Query decomposition can generate an algebraic query simply by translating into relational operations the predicates and the target statement as they appear. Data localization can, in turn, express this algebraic query on relation fragments, by substituting for each distributed relation an algebraic query corresponding to its fragmentation rules.

Many algebraic queries may be equivalent to the same input query. The queries produced with the naive approach are inefficient in general, since important simplifications and optimizations have been missed. Therefore, a generic query expression is restructured using a few transformation rules and heuristics. The rules enable separation of unary operations, grouping of unary operations on the same relation, commuting of unary operations with binary operations, and permutation of the binary operations. Examples of heuristics are to push selections down the tree and do projection as early as possible. In addition to the transformation rules, data localization uses reduction rules to simplify the query further, and therefore optimize it. Two main types of rules may be used. The first one avoids the production of empty relations which are generated by contradicting predicates on the same relation(s). The second type of rule determines which fragments yield useless attributes.

The query produced by the query decomposition and data localization layers is good in the sense that the worse executions are avoided. However, the subsequent layers usually perform important optimizations, as they add to the query, increasing detail about the processing environment. In particular, quantitative information regarding fragments has not yet been exploited. This information will be used by the query optimization layer for selecting an "optimal" strategy to execute the query. Query optimization is the subject of Chapter 9.

## 8.4 BIBLIOGRAPHIC NOTES

Traditional techniques for query decomposition are surveyed in [Jarke and Koch, 1984] and [Gardarin and Valduriez, 1989]. Techniques for semantic analysis and simplification of queries have their origins in [Rosenkrantz and Hunt, 1980]. The notion of query graph or connection graph is introduced in [Ullman, 1982]. The notion of query tree, which we called relational algebra tree in this chapter, and the transformation rules to manipulate algebraic expressions have been introduced in [Smith and Chang, 1975] and developed in [Ullman, 1982]. Proofs of completeness and correctness of the rules are given in the latter reference.

Data localization is treated in detail in [Ceri and Pelagatti, 1983] for horizontally partitioned relations which are referred to as multirelations. In particular, an algebra of qualified relations is defined as an extension of relation algebra, where a qualified relation is a relation name and the qualification of the fragment. Proofs of correctness and completeness of equivalence transformations between expressions of algebra of qualified relations are also given. The formal properties of horizontal and vertical fragmentation are used in [Ceri et al., 1986] to characterize distributed joins over fragmented relations.

## 8.5 EXERCISES

**8.1**   Simplify the following query, expressed in SQL, on our example database using idempotency rules:

```
SELECT   ENO
FROM     G
WHERE    RESP = ''Analyst''
AND      NOT(JNO=''J2'' OR DUR=12)
AND      JNO ≠ ''J2''
AND      DUR=12
```

**8.2**   Give the query graph of the following query, expressed in SQL, on our example database:

```
SELECT   ENAME, JNAME
FROM     E, G, J
WHERE    DUR > 12
AND      E.ENO = G.ENO
```

and map it into a relational algebra tree.

**\*8.3**   Simplify the following query:

```
SELECT   ENAME, JNAME
FROM     E, G, J
WHERE    DUR > 12
AND      E.ENO = G.ENO
AND      (TITLE = ''Elect. Eng.''
```

```
OR         G.JNO < ''J3'')
AND        G.JNO = J.JNO
```

and transform it into an optimized relational algebra tree using the restructuring algorithm.

**8.4**  Assume that relation J of the sample database is horizontally fragmented in

$$J_1 \quad = \quad \sigma_{JNO \leq \text{"J2"}}(J)$$
$$J_2 \quad = \quad \sigma_{JNO > \text{"J2"}}(J)$$

Transform the following query into a reduced query on fragments:

```
SELECT     BUDGET
FROM       J,G
WHERE      J.JNO = G.JNO
AND        G.JNO = ''J4''
```

**\*8.5**  Assume that relation J is horizontally fragmented as in Exercise 8.4, and that relation G is horizontally fragmented as

$$G_1 \quad = \quad \sigma_{JNO \leq \text{"J2"}}(G)$$
$$G_2 \quad = \quad \sigma_{\text{"J2"} < JNO \leq \text{"J3"}}(G)$$
$$G_3 \quad = \quad \sigma_{JNO > \text{"J3"}}(G)$$

Transform the following query into a reduced query on fragments, and determine whether it is better than the generic query:

```
SELECT     RESP, BUDGET
FROM       G, J
WHERE      G.JNO = J.JNO
AND        JNAME = ''CAD/CAM''
```

**\*\*8.6**  Assume that relation J is fragmented as in Exercise 8.4. Furthermore, relation G is indirectly fragmented as

$$G_1 \quad = \quad G \bowtie_{JNO} J_1$$
$$G_2 \quad = \quad G \bowtie_{JNO} J_2$$

and relation E is vertically fragmented as

$$E_1 \quad = \quad \Pi_{ENO,ENAME}(E)$$
$$E_2 \quad = \quad \Pi_{ENO,TITLE}(E)$$

Transform the following query into a reduced query on fragments:

```
SELECT     ENAME
FROM       E,G,J
WHERE      J.JNO = G.JNO
AND        JNAME = ''Instrumentation ''
AND        E.ENO = G.ENO
```

# 9

# Optimization of Distributed Queries

Chapter 8 shows how a calculus query expressed on distributed relations can be mapped into a query on relation fragments by decomposition and data localization. This mapping uses the fragment schema. During this process, the application of transformation rules permits the simplification of the query by eliminating common subexpressions and useless expressions. This type of optimization is independent of fragment characteristics such as cardinalities. The query resulting from decomposition and localization can be executed in that form simply by adding communication primitives in a systematic way. However, the permutation of the ordering of operations within the query can provide many equivalent strategies to execute it. Finding an "optimal" ordering of operations for a given query is the main role of the query optimization layer, or *optimizer* for short.

Since the selection of the optimal ordering for a query is computationally intractable [Ibaraki and Kameda, 1984], the actual objective of the optimizer is to find a strategy close to optimal and, perhaps more important, to avoid bad strategies. In this chapter we refer to the strategy (or operation ordering) produced by the optimizer as the *optimal strategy* (or *optimal ordering*). The output of the optimizer is an optimized schedule consisting of the algebraic query specified on fragments and the communication operations to support the execution of the query over the fragment sites.

The selection of the optimal strategy generally requires the prediction of execution costs of the alternative candidate orderings prior to actually executing the query.

The execution cost is expressed as a weighted combination of I/O, CPU, and communication costs. However, a typical simplification is to ignore local processing cost (I/O and CPU costs) by assuming that the communication cost is dominant. Important inputs to the optimizer for estimating execution costs are fragment statistics and formulas for estimating the cardinalities of results of relational operations. In this chapter we focus mostly on the ordering of join operations for two reasons; it is a well-understood problem, and queries involving joins, selections, and projections are usually considered to be the most frequent type. Furthermore, it is easier to generalize the basic algorithm for other binary operations, such as unions. We also discuss how semijoin operations can help to process a join efficiently.

This chapter is organized as follows. In Section 9.1 we introduce the main inputs to query optimization, including the cost model, the database statistics, and the formulas for estimating the size of the intermediate results. Centralized query optimization is described in Section 9.2 as a prerequisite to understand distributed query optimization, which is more complex. In Section 9.3 we discuss the major optimization issue, which deals with the join ordering in fragment queries. We also examine alternative join strategies based on semijoin. In Section 9.4 we illustrate the use of the techniques and concepts in four important distributed query optimization algorithms.

## 9.1  INPUTS TO QUERY OPTIMIZATION

### 9.1.1  Cost Model

The cost of a distributed execution strategy can be expressed with respect to either the total cost (time) or the response time. The total cost is the sum of all cost components, while the response time is the elapsed time from the initiation to the completion of the query. A general formula for determining the total cost can be specified as follows [Lohman et al., 1985]:

$$Total\_cost = C_{CPU} * \#insts + C_{I/O} * \#I/Os + C_{MSG} * \#msgs + C_{TR} * \#bytes$$

The two first cost components measure the local processing time, where $C_{CPU}$ is the cost of a CPU instruction and $C_{I/O}$ is the cost of a disk I/O. The communication cost is depicted by the two last components. $C_{MSG}$ is the fixed cost of initiating and receiving a message, while $C_{TR}$ is the cost of transmitting a data unit from one site to another. The data unit is given here in terms of bytes ($\#bytes$ is the sum of the sizes of all messages), but could be in different units (e.g., packets). A typical assumption is that $C_{TR}$ is constant. This might not be true for wide area networks, where some sites are farther away than others. However, this assumption greatly simplifies query optimization. Thus the communication cost of transferring $\#bytes$ of data from one site to another is assumed to be a linear function of $\#bytes$:

$$CC(\#bytes) = C_{MSG} + C_{TR} * \#bytes$$

Costs are generally expressed in terms of time units, which in turn, can be translated into other units (e.g., dollars).

The relative values of the cost coefficients characterize the distributed database environment. The topology of the network greatly influences the ratio between the cost components. In a wide area network such as the ARPANET (on the order of 10 kbps), the communication cost is clearly the dominant factor since communication is slower than local processing by more than an order of magnitude. A typical ratio of communication cost to I/O cost for one page is about 20:1 [Selinger and Adiba, 1980]. Hence most distributed DBMSs designed for wide area networks ignore the local processing cost and concentrate on minimizing the communication cost. In a local area network such as the Ethernet (10 Mbps) local processing costs contribute significantly to the total cost. A typical ratio of communication cost to I/O cost is 1:1.6 [Page and Popek, 1985]. Furthermore, this ratio will improve in favor of the communication cost with higher-speed local area networks such as the FDDI (100 Mbps) [Ross, 1986]. Hence, distributed DBMSs designed for local area networks consider all three cost components.

When the response time of the query is the objective function of the optimizer, parallel local processing and parallel communications must be considered [Khoshafian and Valduriez, 1987]. A general formula for response time is

$$
\begin{aligned}
Response\_time \;=\; & C_{CPU} * seq\_\#insts + C_{I/O} * seq\_\#I/Os \\
+\; & C_{MSG} * seq\_\#msgs + C_{TR} * seq\_\#bytes
\end{aligned}
$$

where $seq\_\#x$, in which $x$ can be instructions ($insts$), $I/O$, messages ($msgs$) or $bytes$, is the maximum number of $x$ which must be done sequentially for the execution of the query. Thus any processing and communication done in parallel is ignored.

**Example 9.1**

Let us illustrate the difference between total cost and response time using the example of Figure 9.1, which computes the answer to a query at site 3 with data from sites 1 and 2. For simplicity, we assume that only communication cost is considered.

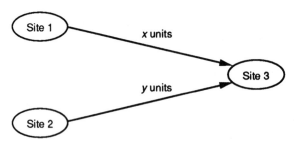

**Figure 9.1**   Example of Data Transfers for a Query

Assume that $C_{MSG}$ and $C_{TR}$ are expressed in time units. The total cost of transferring $x$ data units from site 1 to site 3 and $y$ data units from site 2 to site 3 is

$$Total\_time = 2\ C_{MSG} + C_{TR} * (x + y)$$

The response time of the same query can be approximated as

$$Response\_time = max\{C_{MSG} + C_{TR} * x, C_{MSG} + C_{TR} * y\}$$

since the transfers can be done in parallel.

Minimizing response time is achieved by increasing the degree of parallel execution. This does not, however, imply that the total cost is also minimized. On the contrary, it can increase the total cost, for example, by having more parallel local processing and transmissions. Minimizing the total cost implies that the utilization of the resources improves, thus increasing the system throughput. In practice, a compromise between the two is desired. In Section 9.4 we present algorithms that can optimize a combination of total cost and response time, with more weight on one of them.

### 9.1.2  Database Statistics

The main factor affecting the performance of an execution strategy is the size of the intermediate relations that are produced during the execution. When a subsequent operation is located at a different site, the intermediate relation must be transmitted over the network. Therefore, it is of prime interest to estimate the size of the intermediate results of relational algebra operations in order to minimize the size of data transfers. This estimation is based on statistical information about the base relations and formulas to predict the cardinalities of the results of the relational operations. There is a direct trade-off between the precision of the statistics and the cost of managing them, the more precise statistics being the more costly [Piatetsky and Connell, 1984]. For a relation $R$ defined over the attributes $A = \{A_1, A_2, \ldots, A_n\}$ and fragmented as $R_1, R_2, \ldots, R_r$, the statistical data typically are the following:

1.  For each attribute $A_i$, its length (in number of bytes), denoted by $length(A_i)$, and for each attribute $A_i$ of each fragment $R_j$, the number of distinct values of $A_i$, with the cardinality of the projection of fragment $R_j$ on $A_i$, denoted by $card(\Pi_{A_i}(R_j))$.

2.  For the domain of each attribute $A_i$, which is defined on a set of values that can be ordered (e.g., integers or reals), the minimum and maximum possible values, denoted by $min(A_i)$ and $max(A_i)$.

3.  For the domain of each attribute $A_i$, the cardinality of the domain of $A_i$, denoted by $card(dom[A_i])$. This value gives the number of unique values in the $dom[A_i]$.

4.  The number of tuples in each fragment $R_j$, denoted by $card(R_j)$.

Sometimes, the statistical data also include the join selectivity factor for some pairs of relations, that is the proportion of tuples participating in the join. The *join selectivity factor*, denoted $SF_J$, of relations $R$ and $S$ is a real value between 0 and 1:

$$SF_J(R, S) = \frac{card(R \bowtie S)}{card(R) * card(S)}$$

For example, a join selectivity factor of 0.5 corresponds to a very large joined relation, while 0.001 corresponds to a small one. We say that the join has bad selectivity in the former case and good selectivity in the latter case.

These statistics are useful to predict the size of intermediate relations. Remember that in Chapter 5 we defined the size of an intermediate relation $R$ as follows:

$$size(R) = card(R) * length(R)$$

where $length(R)$ is the length (in bytes) of a tuple of $R$, computed from the lengths of its attributes. The estimation of $card(R)$, the number of tuples in $R$, requires the use of the formulas given in the following section.

### 9.1.3 Cardinalities of Intermediate Results

Database statistics are useful in evaluating the cardinalities of the intermediate results of queries. Two simplifying assumptions are commonly made about the database. The distribution of attribute values in a relation is supposed to be uniform, and all attributes are independent, meaning that the value of an attribute does not affect the value of any other attribute. These two assumptions are often wrong in practice, but they make the problem tractable. In what follows we give the formulas for estimating the cardinalities of the results of the basic relational algebra operations (selection, projection, Cartesian product, join, semijoin, union, and difference). The operand relations are denoted by $R$ and $S$. The *selectivity factor* of an operation, that is, the proportion of tuples of an operand relation that participate in the result of that operation, is denoted $SF_{OP}$, where $OP$ denotes the operation.

**Selection.**    The cardinality of selection is

$$card(\sigma_F(R)) = SF_S(F) * card(R)$$

where $SF_S(F)$ is dependent on the selection formula and can be computed as follows [Selinger et al., 1979], where $p(A_i)$ and $p(A_j)$ indicate predicates over attributes $A_i$ and $A_j$, respectively:

$$SF_S(A = value) = \frac{1}{card(\Pi_A(R))}$$

$$SF_S(A > value) = \frac{max(A) - value}{max(A) - min(A)}$$

$$SF_S(A < value) = \frac{value - min(A)}{max(A) - min(A)}$$

$$SF_S(p(A_i) \wedge p(A_j)) = SF_S(p(A_i)) * SF_S(p(A_j))$$

$$SF_S(p(A_i) \vee p(A_j)) = SF_S(p(A_i)) + SF_S(p(A_j)) - (SF_S(p(A_i)) * SF_S(p(A_j)))$$

$$SF_S(A \in \{values\}) = SF_S(A = value) * card(\{values\})$$

**Projection.**    As indicated in Chapter 2, projection can be with or without duplicate elimination. We consider projection with duplicate elimination. An arbitrary projection is difficult to evaluate precisely because the correlations between projected attributes are usually unknown [Gelenbe and Gardy, 1982]. However, there are two particularly useful cases where it is trivial. If the projection of relation $R$ is based on a single attribute $A$, the cardinality is simply the number of tuples when the projection is performed. If one of the projected attributes is a key of $R$, then

$$card(\Pi_A(R)) = card(R)$$

**Cartesian product.**    The cardinality of the Cartesian product of $R$ and $S$ is simply

$$card(R \times S) = card(R) * card(S)$$

**Join.**    There is no general way to estimate the cardinality of a join without additional information. The upper bound of the join cardinality is the cardinality of the Cartesian product. Some systems, such as Distributed INGRES [Epstein et al., 1978], use this upper bound, which is quite pessimistic. R* [Selinger and Adiba, 1980] uses this upper bound divided by a constant to reflect the fact that the join result is smaller than that of the Cartesian product. However, there is a case, which occurs frequently, where the estimation is simple. If relation $R$ is equijoined with $S$ over attribute $A$ from $R$, and $B$ from $S$, where $A$ is a key of relation $R$, and $B$ is a foreign key of relation $S$, the cardinality of the result can be approximated as

$$card(R \bowtie_{A=B} S) = card(S)$$

because each tuple of $S$ matches with at most one tuple of $R$. Obviously, the same thing is true if $B$ is a key of $S$ and $A$ is a foreign key of $R$. However, this estimation is an upper bound since it assumes that each tuple of $R$ participates in the join. For other important joins, it is worthwhile to maintain their join selectivity factor $SF_J$ as part of statistical information. In that case the result cardinality is simply

$$card(R \bowtie S) = SF_J * card(R) * card(S)$$

**Semijoin.**    The selectivity factor of the semijoin of $R$ by $S$ gives the fraction (percentage) of tuples of $R$ that join with tuples of $S$. An approximation for the semijoin selectivity factor is given in [Hevner and Yao, 1979] as

$$SF_{SJ}(R \ltimes_A S) = \frac{card(\Pi_A(S))}{card(dom[A])}$$

This formula depends only on attribute $A$ of $S$. Thus it is often called the selectivity factor of attribute $A$ of $S$, denoted $SF_{SJ}(S.A)$, and is the selectivity factor of $S.A$ on any other joinable attribute. Therefore, the cardinality of the semijoin is given by

$$card(R \ltimes_A S) = SF_{SJ}(S.A) * card(R)$$

**Union.** It is quite difficult to estimate the cardinality of the union of $R$ and $S$ because the duplicates between $R$ and $S$ are removed by the union. We give only the simple formulas for the upper and lower bounds, which are, respectively,

$$card(R) + card(S)$$
$$max\{card(R), card(S)\}$$

Note that these formulas assume that $R$ and $S$ do not contain duplicate tuples.

**Difference.** Like the union, we give only the upper and lower bounds. The upper bound of $card(R - S)$ is $card(R)$, whereas the lower bound is 0.

## 9.2 CENTRALIZED QUERY OPTIMIZATION

In this section we present two of the most popular query optimization techniques for centralized systems. This presentation is a prerequisite to understanding distributed query optimization for three reasons. First, a distributed query is translated into local queries, each of which is processed in a centralized way. Second, distributed query optimization techniques are often extensions of the techniques for centralized systems. Finally, centralized query optimization is a simpler problem; the minimization of communication costs makes distributed query optimization more complex. Since we discussed in Chapter 8 some common techniques for query decomposition, we will concentrate on the optimization aspects used by two popular relational database systems: INGRES [Stonebraker et al., 1976] and System R [Astrahan et al., 1976]. Furthermore, both systems have distributed versions (see Section 9.4) whose optimization algorithms are extensions of the centralized version.

The optimization techniques of these systems differ significantly (see [Gardarin and Valduriez, 1989] for more details). INGRES employs a dynamic optimization algorithm and System R uses a static optimization algorithm based on exhaustive search using statistics about the database. We note that most commercial relational DBMSs (see [Valduriez and Gardarin, 1989] for a survey) implement variants of the exhaustive search approach for its efficiency and compatibility with query compilation.

### 9.2.1 INGRES Algorithm

INGRES uses a dynamic query optimization algorithm [Wong and Youssefi, 1976] that recursively breaks up a calculus query into smaller pieces. It combines the two phases of calculus-algebra decomposition and optimization. A multivariable[1] query is first decomposed into a sequence of queries having a unique variable in common. Then each monovariable query is processed by a "one-variable query processor" (OVQP). The OVQP optimizes the access to a single relation involved in the one-variable query

---

[1]A variable in INGRES is a tuple variable, discussed in Chapter 2. Thus a multivariable query is one that refers to more than one relation or refers to a relation more than once.

by selecting, based on the one-variable predicate, the best access method to that relation (e.g., index, sequential scan). For example, if the predicate is of the form $< A = value >$, an index available on attribute $A$ would be used. However, if the predicate is of the form $< A \neq value >$, an index on $A$ would not help, and sequential scan should be used.

We concentrate our presentation on the main query type, which is the "retrieve" command of the QUEL language [Stonebraker et al., 1976], which is used by INGRES and is similar to the "select" command of SQL. However, to maintain uniformity throughout the book, we use SQL to express our examples. The algorithm executes first the unary (monovariable) operations and tries to minimize the sizes of intermediate results in ordering binary (multivariable) operations.

Let us denote by $q_{i-1} \rightarrow q_i$ a query $q$ decomposed into two subqueries, $q_{i-1}$ and $q_i$, where $q_{i-1}$ is executed first and its result is consumed by $q_i$. Given an $n$-variable query $q$, the INGRES query processor decomposes $q$ into $n$ subqueries $q_1 \rightarrow q_2 \rightarrow \cdots \rightarrow q_n$. This decomposition uses two basic techniques: detachment and substitution. These techniques are presented and illustrated in the rest of this section.

Detachment is the first technique employed by the query processor. It breaks a query $q$ into $q' \rightarrow q''$, based on a common variable that is the result of $q'$. If the query $q$ expressed in SQL is of the form

```
SELECT   V_2.A_2, V_3.A_3, ..., V_n.A_n
FROM     R_1 V_1, R_2 V_2, ..., R_n V_n
WHERE    P_1(V_1.A'_1)
AND      P_2(V_1.A_1, V_2.A_2, ..., V_n.A_n)
```

where the FROM statement defines tuple variables (e.g., $V_1$) over relations (e.g., $R_1$), $A_i$ and $A'_i$ are lists of attributes of relation $R_i$, $P_1$ is a single-variable predicate involving attributes from relation $R_1$, and $P_2$ is a multivariable predicate involving attributes of relations $R_1, R_2, \ldots, R_n$. Such a query may be decomposed into two subqueries, $q'$ followed by $q''$, by detachment of the common variable $V_1$:

```
q' :  SELECT   V_1.A_1 INTO R'_1
      FROM     R_1 V_1
      WHERE    P_1(V_1.A'_1)
```

where $R'_1$ is a temporary relation containing the information necessary for the continuation of the query:

```
q'' :  SELECT   V_2.A_2, ..., V_n.A_n
       FROM     R'_1 V_1, R_2 V_2, ..., R_n V_n
       WHERE    P_2(V_1.A_1, ..., V_n.A_n)
```

This step has the effect of reducing the size of the relation on which the variable $V_1$ of the query $q''$ is defined. Furthermore, the created relation $R'_1$ may be stored in a particular structure to speed up the following subqueries. For example, the storage of $R'_1$ in a hashed file on the join attributes of $q''$ will make the processing of the join more efficient. Detachment extracts the select operations, which are usually the most selective ones. Therefore, detachment is systematically done whenever possible. Note that this can have adverse effects on performance if the selection has bad selectivity.

**Example 9.2**

To illustrate the detachment technique, we apply it to the following query:

"Names of employees working on the CAD/CAM project"

This query can be expressed in SQL by the following query $q_1$ on the engineering database of Chapter 2:

```
q₁:    SELECT    E.ENAME
       FROM      E, G, J
       WHERE     E.ENO=G.ENO
       AND       G.JNO=J.JNO
       AND       JNAME=''CAD/CAM''
```

After detachment of the selections, query $q_1$ is replaced by $q_{11}$ followed by $q'$, where JVAR is an intermediate relation.

```
q₁₁:   SELECT    J.JNO INTO JVAR
       FROM      J
       WHERE     JNAME=''CAD/CAM''
q':    SELECT    E.ENAME
       FROM      E, G, JVAR
       WHERE     E.ENO=G.ENO
       AND       G.JNO=JVAR.JNO
```

The successive detachments of $q'$ may generate

```
q₁₂:   SELECT    G.ENO INTO GVAR
       FROM      G, JVAR
       WHERE     G.JNO=JVAR.JNO
q₁₃:   SELECT    E.ENAME
       FROM      E, GVAR
       WHERE     E.ENO=GVAR.ENO
```

Note that other subqueries are also possible.

Thus query $q_1$ has been reduced to the subsequent queries $q_{11} \rightarrow q_{12} \rightarrow q_{13}$. Query $q_{11}$ is monovariable and can be performed by the OVQP. However, $q_{12}$ and $q_{13}$ are not monovariable and cannot be reduced by detachment.

Multivariable queries, which cannot be further detached (e.g., $q_{12}$ and $q_{13}$ in Example 9.2), are converted into monovariable queries by tuple substitution. Given an $n$-variable query $q$, the tuples of one variable are substituted by their values, thereby producing a set of $(n-1)$-variable queries. Tuple substitution proceeds as follows. First, one variable in $q$ is chosen for tuple substitution. Let $V_1$, ranging over relation $R_1$, be that variable. Then for each tuple $t_{1i}$ in $R_1$, the attributes referred to by $V_1$ in $q$ are replaced by their actual values in $t_{1i}$, thereby generating a query $q'$ with $n-1$

variables. Therefore, the total number of queries $q'$ produced by tuple substitution is $card(R_1)$. Tuple substitution can be summarized as follows:

$$q(V_1, V_2, \ldots, V_n) \text{ is replaced by } \{q'(t_{1i}, V_2, V_3, \ldots, V_n), t_{1i} \in R_1\}$$

For each tuple thus obtained, the subquery is recursively processed by substitution if it is not yet irreducible.

**Example 9.3**

Let us consider the query $q_{13}$:

```
SELECT    E.ENAME
FROM      E, GVAR
WHERE     E.ENO=GVAR.ENO
```

The relation defined by the variable GVAR is over a single attribute (ENO). Assume that it contains only two tuples: <E1> and <E2>. The substitution of GVAR generates two one-variable subqueries:

```
q131:    SELECT    E.ENAME
         FROM      E
         WHERE     E.ENO=''E1''

q132:    SELECT    E.ENAME
         FROM      E
         WHERE     E.ENO=''E2''
```

These queries may then be processed by the OVQP.

The query optimization algorithm of INGRES (called INGRES-QOA) is depicted in Algorithm 9.1. The algorithm works recursively until there remains no more monovariable queries to be processed. It consists of applying the selections and projections as soon as possible by detachment. The results of the monovariable queries are stored in data structures that are capable of optimizing the later queries (such as joins) and will be used by the OVQP. The irreducible queries that remain after detachment must be processed by tuple substitution. For the irreducible query, denoted by $MVQ'$, the variable that is associated with the smallest relation whose cardinality is known from the result of the preceding query is chosen for substitution. This simple method enables one to generate the smallest number of subqueries. Monovariable queries generated by the reduction algorithm are processed by the OVQP that chooses the best existing access path to the relation, according to the query qualification.

**Algorithm 9.1    *INGRES-QOA***

  **input:**    *MVQ*:    multivariable query with $n$ variables
  **output:**  *output*:   result of execution
  **begin**
     *output* $\leftarrow \phi$

```
if n = 1 then
    output ← run(MVQ)                    {execute the one variable query}
else begin
    {detach MVQ into m one-variable queries and one multivariable query}
    OVQ₁, ..., OVQₘ, MVQ' ← MVQ
    for i ← 1 to m do
    begin
        output' ← run(OVQᵢ)                           {execute OVQᵢ}
        output ← output ∪ output'                     {merge all results}
    end-for
    V ← CHOOSE_VARIABLE(MVQ')   {V chosen for tuple substitution}
    for each tuple t ∈ V do
    begin
        MVQ" ← substitute values for t in MVQ'
        output' ← INGRES-QOA(MVQ")                    {recursive call}
        output ← output ∪ output'                     {merge all results}
    end-for
end-if
end. { INGRES-QOA }
```

### 9.2.2  System R Algorithm

System R performs static query optimization based on the exhaustive search of the solution space [Selinger et al., 1979]. The input to the optimizer of System R is a relational algebra tree resulting from the decomposition of an SQL query. The output is an execution plan that implements the "optimal" relational algebra tree.

Instead of systematically executing the select operations before the joins as in INGRES, System R does so only if this leads to a better strategy. The optimizer assigns a cost to every candidate tree and retains the one with the smallest cost. The candidate trees are obtained by a permutation of the join orders of the $n$ relations of the query using the commutativity and associativity rules. To limit the cost of optimization, the number of alternative trees is reduced using dynamic programming. The set of alternative strategies is constructed dynamically so that, when two joins are equivalent by commutativity, only the cheapest one is kept. Furthermore, the strategies that include Cartesian products are eliminated whenever possible.

The cost of a candidate strategy is a weighted combination of I/O and CPU costs. The estimation of such costs (at compile time) is based on a cost model that provides a cost formula for each low-level operation (e.g., select using a B-tree index with a range predicate). For most operations (except exact match select), these cost formulas are based on the cardinalities of the operands. The cardinality information for the relations stored in the database is found in the database statistics, automatically managed by System R. The cardinality of the intermediate results is estimated based on the operation selectivity factors (see Section 9.1.3).

The optimization algorithm consists of two major steps. First, the best access method to each individual relation based on a select predicate is predicted (this is the one with least cost). Second, for each relation $R$, the best join ordering is estimated, where $R$ is first accessed using its best single-relation access method. The cheapest ordering becomes the basis for the best execution plan.

In considering the joins, there are two algorithms available, with one of them being optimal in a given context. For the join of two relations, the relation whose tuples are read first is called the *external*, while the other, whose tuples are found according to the values obtained from the external relation, is called the *internal relation*. An important decision with either join method is to determine the cheapest access path to the internal relation.

The first method, called *nested loops*, composes the product of the two relations. For each tuple of the external relation, the tuples of the internal relation that satisfy the join predicate are retrieved one by one to form the resulting relation. An index on the join attribute is a very efficient access path for the internal relation. In the absence of an index, for relations of $n_1$ and $n_2$ pages, respectively, this algorithm has a cost proportional to $n_1 * n_2$, which may be prohibitive if $n_1$ and $n_2$ are high.

The second method, called *merge join*, consists of merging two sorted relations on the join attribute. Indices on the join attribute may be used as access paths. If the join criterion is equality, the cost of joining two relations of $n_1$ and $n_2$ pages, respectively, is proportional to $n_1 + n_2$. Therefore, this method is always chosen when there is an equijoin, and when the relations are previously sorted. If only one or neither of the relations are sorted, the cost of the nested loop algorithm is to be compared with the combined cost of the merge join and of the sorting. The cost of sorting $n$ pages is proportional to $n \log n$. In general, it is useful to sort and apply the merge join algorithm when large relations are considered.

The simplified version of the System R optimization algorithm, for a select-project-join query, is shown in Algorithm 9.2. It consists of two loops, the first of which selects the best single-relation access method to each relation in the query, while the second examines all possible permutations of join orders (there are $n!$ permutations with $n$ relations) and selects the best access strategy for the query. The permutations are produced by the dynamic construction of a tree of alternative strategies. First, the join of each relation with every other relation is considered, followed by joins of three relations. This continues until joins of $n$ relations are optimized. Actually, the algorithm does not generate all possible permutations since some of them are useless. As we discussed earlier, permutations involving Cartesian products are eliminated, as are the commutatively equivalent strategies with the highest cost. With these two heuristics, the number of strategies examined has an upper bound of $2^n$ rather than $n!$.

### Algorithm 9.2    *R-QOA*

**input:** $QT$: query tree with $n$ relations
**output:** *output*: the result of execution

**begin**
  **for each** relation $R_i \in QT$ **do**
  **begin**
    **for each** access path $AP_{ij}$ to $R_i$ **do**
      determine $cost(AP_{ij})$
    **end-for**
    $best\_AP_i \leftarrow AP_{ij}$ with minimum cost
  **end-for**
  **for each** order $(R_{i1}, R_{i2}, \cdots, R_{in})$ with $i=1, \cdots, n!$ **do**
  **begin**
    build strategy $(\ldots((\text{ best } AP_{i1} \bowtie R_{i2}) \bowtie R_{i3}) \bowtie \ldots \bowtie R_{in})$
    compute the cost of strategy
  **end-for**
  $output \leftarrow$ strategy with minimum cost
**end.** { R-QOA }

**Example 9.4**

Let us illustrate this algorithm with the query $q_1$ (see Example 9.2) on the engineering database. The join graph of $q_1$ is given in Figure 9.2. For short, the label ENO on edge E–G stands for the predicate E.ENO=G.ENO and the label JNO on edge G–J stands for the predicate G.JNO=J.JNO. We assume the following indices:

    E has an index on ENO
    G has an index on JNO
    J has an index on JNO and an index on JNAME

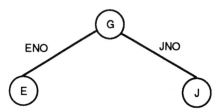

**Figure 9.2**   Join Graph of Query $q_1$

We assume that the first loop of the algorithm selects the following best single-relation access paths:

    E:   sequential scan (because there is no selection on E)
    G:   sequential scan (because there is no selection on G)
    J:   index on JNAME (because there is a selection on J
          based on JNAME)

The dynamic construction of the tree of alternative strategies is illustrated in Figure 9.3. Note that the maximum number of join orders is 3!; dynamic search considers fewer alternatives, as depicted in Figure 9.3. The operations marked "pruned" are dynamically eliminated. The first level of the tree indicates the best single-relation access method. The second level indicates, for each of these, the best join method with any other relation. Strategies (E × J) and (J × E) are pruned because they are Cartesian products that can be avoided (by other strategies). We assume that (E ⋈ G) and (G ⋈ J) have a cost higher than (G ⋈ E) and (J ⋈ G), respectively. Thus they can be pruned because there are better join orders equivalent by commutativity. The two remaining possibilities are given at the third level of the tree. The best total join order is the least costly of ((G ⋈ E) ⋈ J) and ((J ⋈ G) ⋈ E). The latter is the only one that has a useful index on the select attribute and direct access to the joining tuples of G and E. Therefore, it is chosen with the following access methods:

Select J using index on JNAME

Then join with G using index on JNO

Then join with E using index on ENO

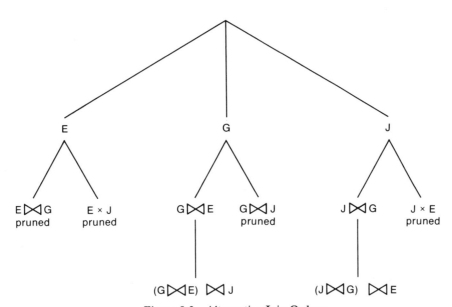

**Figure 9.3** Alternative Join Orders

The performance measurement of System R [Mackert and Lohman, 1986] substantiates the important contribution of the CPU cost to the total cost of the query. The accuracy of the optimizer's estimations is generally good when the relations can be contained in the main memory buffers, but degrades as the relations increase in size and are written to disk. An important performance parameter that should also be considered for better predictions is buffer utilization.

## 9.3 JOIN ORDERING IN FRAGMENT QUERIES

As we have seen in Section 9.2, ordering joins is an important aspect of centralized query optimization. Join ordering in a distributed context is even more important since joins between fragments may increase the communication cost. Two basic approaches exist to order joins in fragment queries. One tries to optimize the ordering of joins directly, whereas the other replaces joins by combinations of semijoins in order to minimize communication costs.

### 9.3.1 Join Ordering

Some algorithms optimize the ordering of joins directly without using semijoins. Distributed INGRES and R* algorithms are representative of algorithms that use joins rather than semijoins. The purpose of this section is to stress the difficulty that join ordering presents and to motivate the subsequent section, which deals with the use of semijoins to optimize join queries.

A number of assumptions are necessary to concentrate on the main issues. Since the query is localized and expressed on fragments, we do not need to distinguish between fragments of the same relation and fragments of different relations. To simplify notation, we use the term *relation* to designate a fragment stored at a particular site. Also, to concentrate on join ordering, we ignore local processing cost, assuming that reducers (selection, projection) are executed locally either before or during the join (remember that doing selection first is not always efficient). Therefore, we consider only join queries whose operand relations are stored at different sites. We assume that relation transfers are done in a set-at-a-time mode rather than in a tuple-at-a-time mode. Finally, we ignore the transfer cost for producing the data at a result site.

Let us first concentrate on the simpler problem of operand transfer in a single join. The query is $R \bowtie S$, where $R$ and $S$ are relations stored at different sites. The obvious choice of the relation to transfer is to send the smaller relation to the site of the larger one, which gives rise to two possibilities, as shown in Figure 9.4. To make this choice we need to evaluate the size of $R$ and of $S$. We now consider the case where there are more than two relations to join. As in the case of a single join, the objective of the join-ordering algorithm is to transmit smaller operands. The difficulty stems from the fact that the join operations may reduce or increase the size of the intermediate results. Thus, estimating the size of join results is mandatory, but also difficult. A solution is to estimate the communication costs of all alternative strategies and to choose the best one. However, the number of strategies grows rapidly with the number of relations. This approach, used by System R*, makes optimization costly, although this overhead is amortized rapidly if the query is executed frequently.

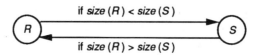

**Figure 9.4**   Transfer of Operands in Binary Operation

**Example 9.5**

Consider the following query expressed in relational algebra:

$$J \bowtie_{JNO} E \bowtie_{ENO} G$$

whose join graph is given in Figure 9.5. Note that we have made certain assumptions about the locations of the three relations. This query can be executed in at least five different ways. We describe these strategies by the following programs, where (R → site *j*) stands for "relation *R* is transferred to site *j*."

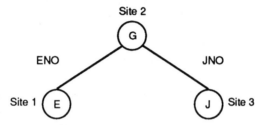

**Figure 9.5**  Join Graph of Distributed Query

1.  E → site 2
    Site 2 computes E′ = E ⋈ G
    E′ → site 3
    Site 3 computes E′ ⋈ J

2.  G → site 1
    Site 1 computes E′ = E ⋈ G
    E′ → site 3
    Site 3 computes E′ ⋈ J

3.  G → site 3
    Site 3 computes G′ = G ⋈ J
    G′ → site 1
    Site 1 computes G′ ⋈ E

4.  J → site 2
    Site 2 computes J′ = J ⋈ G
    J′ → site 1
    Site 1 computes J′ ⋈ E

5.  E → site 2
    J → site 2
    Site 2 computes E ⋈ J ⋈ G

To select one of these programs, the following sizes must be known or predicted: $size(E)$, $size(G)$, $size(J)$, $size(E \bowtie G)$, and $size(G \bowtie J)$. Furthermore, if it is the response time that is being considered, the optimization must take into account the fact that transfers can be done in parallel with strategy 5. An alternative to enumerating all the solutions is to use heuristics that consider only the sizes of the operand relations by assuming, for example, that the cardinality of the resulting join is the product of cardinalities. In this case, relations are ordered by increasing sizes and the order of execution is given by this ordering and the join graph. For instance, the order $(E, G, J)$ could use strategy 1, while the order $(J, G, E)$ could use strategy 4.

### 9.3.2 Semijoin Based Algorithms

In this section we show how the semijoin operation can be used to decrease the total cost of join queries. The theory of semijoins is defined in [Bernstein and Chiu, 1981]. We are making the same assumptions as in Section 9.3.1. The main shortcoming of the join approach described in the preceding section is that entire operand relations must be transferred between sites. The semijoin acts as a size reducer for a relation much as a selection does.

The join of two relations $R$ and $S$ over attribute $A$, stored at sites 1 and 2, respectively, can be computed by replacing one or both operand relations by a semijoin with the other relation, using the following rules:

$$R \bowtie_A S \Leftrightarrow (R \ltimes_A S) \bowtie_A S$$
$$\Leftrightarrow R \bowtie_A (S \ltimes_A R)$$
$$\Leftrightarrow (R \ltimes_A S) \bowtie_A (S \ltimes_A R)$$

The choice between one of the three semijoin strategies requires estimating their respective costs.

The use of the semijoin is beneficial if the cost to produce and send it to the other site is less than the cost of sending the whole operand relation and of doing the actual join. To illustrate the potential benefit of the semijoin, let us compare the costs of the two alternatives: $R \bowtie_A S$ versus $(R \ltimes_A S) \bowtie_A S$, assuming that $size(R) < size(S)$.

The following program, using the notation of Section 9.3.1, uses the semijoin operation:

1. $\Pi_A(S) \to$ site 1
2. Site 1 computes $R' = R \ltimes_A S$
3. $R' \to$ site 2
4. Site 2 computes $R' \bowtie_A S$

For the sake of simplicity, let us ignore the constant $C_{MSG}$ in the communication cost assuming that the term $C_{TR} * size(R)$ is much larger. We can then compare the two alternatives in terms of the amount of transmitted data. The cost of the join-based algorithm is that of transferring relation $R$ to site 2. The cost of the semijoin-based algorithm is the cost of steps 1 and 3 above. Therefore, the semijoin approach is better if

$$size(\Pi_A(S)) + size(R \ltimes_A S) < size(R)$$

The semijoin approach is better if the semijoin acts as a sufficient reducer, that is, if a few tuples of $R$ participate in the join. The join approach is better if almost all tuples of $R$ participate in the join, because the semijoin approach requires an additional transfer of a projection on the join attribute. The cost of the projection step can be minimized by encoding the result of the projection in bit arrays [Valduriez, 1982], thereby reducing the cost of transferring the joined attribute values. It is important to note that neither approach is systematically the best; they should be considered as complementary.

More generally, the semijoin can be useful in reducing the size of the operand relations involved in multiple join queries. However, query optimization becomes more complex in these cases. Consider again the join graph of relations E, G, and J given in Figure 9.5. We can apply the previous join algorithm using semijoins to each individual join. Thus an example of a program to compute E $\bowtie$ G $\bowtie$ J is E' $\bowtie$ G' $\bowtie$ J, where E' = E $\ltimes$ G and G' = G $\ltimes$ J.

However, we may further reduce the size of an operand relation by using more than one semijoin. For example, E' can be replaced in the preceding program by E'' derived as

$$E'' = E \ltimes (G \ltimes J)$$

since if $size(G \ltimes J) \leq size(G)$, we have $size(E'') \leq size(E')$. In this way, E can be reduced by the sequence of semijoins: E $\ltimes$ (G $\ltimes$ J). Such a sequence of semijoins is called a *semijoin program* for E. Similarly, semijoin programs can be found for any relation in a query. For example, J could be reduced by the semijoin program J $\ltimes$ (G $\ltimes$ E). However, not all of the relations involved in a query need to be reduced; in particular, we can ignore those relations that are not involved in the final joins.

For a given relation, there exist several potential semijoin programs. The number of possibilities is in fact exponential in the number of relations. But there is one optimal semijoin program, called the *full reducer*, which for each relation $R$ reduces $R$ more than the others [Chiu and Ho, 1980]. The problem is to find the full reducer. A simple method is to evaluate the size reduction of all possible semijoin programs and to select the best one. The problems with the enumerative method are twofold:

1. There is a class of queries, called *cyclic queries*, that have cycles in their join graph and for which full reducers cannot be found.
2. For other queries, called *tree queries*, full reducers exist, but the number of candidate semijoin programs is exponential in the numbers of relations, which makes the enumerative approach NP-hard.

In what follows we discuss solutions to these problems.

**Example 9.6**

Consider the following relations, where attribute CITY has been added to relations E (renamed ET) and J (renamed JT) of the engineering database:

  ET(ENO, ENAME, TITLE, CITY)
  G(ENO, JNO, RESP, DUR)
  JT(JNO, JNAME, BUDGET, CITY)

The following SQL query retrieves the names of all employees living in the city in which their project is located.

```
SELECT    ET.ENAME
FROM      ET, G, JT
WHERE     ET.ENO = G.ENO
AND       G.ENO = JT.ENO
AND       ET.CITY = JT.CITY
```

As illustrated in Figure 9.6a, this query is cyclic.

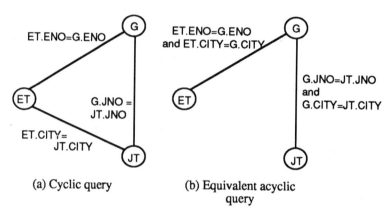

(a) Cyclic query          (b) Equivalent acyclic
                              query

**Figure 9.6**　Transformation of Cyclic Query

No full reducer exists for the query in Example 9.6. In fact, it is possible to derive semijoin programs for reducing it, but the number of operations is multiplied by the number of tuples in each relation, making the approach inefficient. One solution consists of transforming the cyclic graph into a tree by removing one arc of the graph and by adding appropriate predicates to the other arcs such that the removed predicate is preserved by transitivity [Kambayashi et al., 1982].

In the example of Figure 9.6b, where the arc (ET,JT) is removed, the additional predicate ET.CITY = G.CITY and G.CITY = JT.CITY imply ET.CITY = JT.CITY by transitivity. Thus the acyclic query is equivalent to the cyclic query. The addition of these predicates implies the addition of attribute CITY in relation G. Hence, the values for attribute CITY must be sent from either ET or G.

Although full reducers for tree queries exist, the problem of finding them is NP-hard. However, there is an important class of queries, called *chained queries*, for which a polynomial algorithm exists ([Chiu and Ho, 1980] and [Ullman, 1982]). A chained query has a join graph where relations can be ordered, and each relation joins only with the next relation in the order. Furthermore, the result of the query is at the end of the chain. For instance, the query in Figure 9.5 is a chain query. Because of the difficulty of implementing an algorithm with full reducers, most systems use single semijoins to reduce the relation size.

### 9.3.3  Join versus Semijoin

Compared with the join, the semijoin induces more operations but possibly on smaller operands. Figure 9.7 illustrates these differences with an equivalent pair of join and semijoin strategies for the query whose join graph is given in Figure 9.5. The join of two relations, E ⋈ G in Figure 9.5, is done by sending one relation, G, to the site of the other one, E, to complete the join locally. When a semijoin is used, however, the transfer of relation G is avoided. Instead, it is replaced by the transfer of the join attribute values of relation E to the site of relation G, followed by the transfer of the matching tuples of relation G to the site of relation E, where the join is completed. If the join attribute length is smaller than the length of an entire tuple and the semijoin has good selectivity, then the semijoin approach can result in significant savings in communication cost. Using semijoins may well increase the local processing cost, since one of the two joined relations must be accessed twice. For example, relations E and J are accessed twice in Figure 9.7. Furthermore, the join of two intermediate relations produced by semijoins cannot exploit the indices that were available on the base relations. Therefore, using semijoins might not be a good idea if the communication cost is not the dominant factor, as is the case with local area networks [Lu and Carey, 1985].

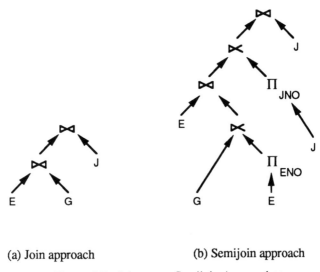

(a) Join approach                    (b) Semijoin approach

**Figure 9.7**   Join versus Semijoin Approaches

Semijoins can still be beneficial with fast networks if they have very good selectivity and are implemented with bit arrays [Valduriez, 1982]. A bit array $BA[1:n]$ is useful in encoding the join attribute values present in one relation. Let us consider the semijoin $R \ltimes S$. Then $BA[i]$ is set to 1 if there exists a join attribute value $A = val$ in relation $S$ such that $h(val) = i$, where $h$ is a hash function. Otherwise, $BA[i]$ is set to 0. Such a bit array is much smaller than a list of join attribute values. Therefore, transferring the bit array instead of the join attribute values to the site of relation $R$ saves communication cost. The semijoin can be completed as follows. Each tuple of relation $R$, whose join attribute value is $val$, belongs to the semijoin if $BA[h(val)] = 1$.

## 9.4 DISTRIBUTED QUERY OPTIMIZATION ALGORITHMS

In this section we illustrate the use of the techniques presented previously in the following four query optimization algorithms: the reduction algorithm of Distributed INGRES [Epstein et al., 1978], System R* algorithm [Selinger et al., 1979], SDD-1 algorithm [Bernstein et al., 1981], and family of algorithms of Apers, Hevner, and Yao [Apers et al., 1983], which we will refer to as AHY. We describe them because they are representative of different classes of algorithms and are therefore often used as paradigms. The differences among them can be specified in terms of the features introduced in Chapter 7 (specifically, Section 7.4):

1. The optimization timing is dynamic for distributed INGRES, while it is static for the others.

2. The objective function of SDD-1 and R* is to minimize total cost, while distributed INGRES and AHY aim at decreasing a combination of response time and total cost.

3. The optimization factors of the cost function are the message size for SDD-1. AHY uses message size and number of messages. System R*, which takes into account local processing cost, uses message size, number of messages, I/O, and CPU costs. Distributed INGRES considers both message size and local processing time (I/O + CPU cost).

4. The network topology is assumed to be a wide area point-to-point network by SDD-1 and AHY. The algorithms of distributed INGRES and R* can work in both local and wide area networks.

5. The use of semijoins as a query optimization technique is employed by SDD-1 and AHY. Distributed INGRES and R* perform joins in a fashion similar to that of the centralized query optimization algorithms of their counterparts: INGRES and System R.

6. Each algorithm assumes statistical information about the data. As shown in Figure 9.8, semijoin algorithms typically use more information.

7. INGRES can handle fragments.

The differences between these four algorithms are summarized in Figure 9.8. In the rest of this section we detail each of these algorithms.

### 9.4.1 Distributed INGRES Algorithm

The query optimization algorithm of Distributed INGRES [Epstein et al., 1978] is derived from the algorithm used in centralized INGRES (see Section 9.2.1). Therefore,

| Algorithms | Optm. Timing | Objective Function | Optm. Factors | Network Topology | Semi Joins | Stats† | Fragments |
|---|---|---|---|---|---|---|---|
| Dist. INGRES | Dynamic | Response time or total cost | Msg size, proc. cost | General or broadcast | No | 1 | Horizontal |
| R* | Static | Total Cost | #Msg, Msg size, IO, CPU | General or local | No | 1, 2 | No |
| SDD—1 | Static | Total cost | Msg size, | General | Yes | 1, 3, 4, 5 | No |
| AHY | Static | Response time or total cost | #Msg, Msg size | General | Yes | 1, 3, 5 | No |

† 1 = relation cardinality, 2 = number of unique values per attribute, 3 = join selectivity factor,
  4 = size of projection on each join attribute, 5 = attribute size and tuple size.

**Figure 9.8**   Comparison of Query Optimization Algorithms

it consists of dynamically optimizing the processing strategy of a given query. The objective function of the algorithm is to minimize a combination of both the communication cost and the response time. Because these two objectives are conflicting (increasing communication cost may well decrease response time), the function can give a greater weight to one or the other. Note that this query optimization algorithm ignores the cost of transmitting the data to the result site. The algorithm also takes advantage of fragmentation, but only horizontal fragmentation is handled for simplicity.

Since both general and broadcast networks are considered, the query processing algorithm takes into account the network topology. In broadcast networks, the same data unit can be transmitted from one site to all the other sites in a single transfer, and the algorithm explicitly takes advantage of this capability. For example, broadcasting is used to replicate fragments and then to maximize the degree of parallelism.

The input to the query processing algorithm is a query expressed in tuple relational calculus (in conjunctive normal form) and schema information (the network type, as well as the location and size of each fragment). As in the centralized version, we describe the distributed query optimization algorithm for the case of a retrieval query. This algorithm is executed by the site, called the *master site*, where the query is initiated. The algorithm, which we call D-INGRES-QOA, is given in Algorithm 9.3.

**Algorithm 9.3**   *D-INGRES-QOA*

**input:** $MVQ$: multivariable query
**output:** result of the last multivariable query
**begin**

   **for** each detachable $OVQ_i$ in $MVQ$ **do** {run all one-variable queries}
      run($OVQ_i$);                                                    (1)
   **end-for**
   $MVQ'\_list \leftarrow$ REDUCE($MVQ$)         {replace MVQ by $n$
                                          irreducible queries} (2)
   **while** $n \neq 0$ **do**          {$n$ is the number of irreducible queries} (3)
   **begin**
      {choose next irreducible query involving the smallest fragments}
      $MVQ' \leftarrow$ SELECT_QUERY($MVQ'\_list$)                 (3.1)
      {determine fragments to transfer and processing site for $MVQ'$}
      Fragment-site-list $\leftarrow$ SELECT_STRATEGY($MVQ'$)       (3.2)
      {move the selected fragments to the selected sites}
      **for** each pair $(F, S)$ in Fragment-site-list **do**           (3.3)
         move fragment $F$ to site $S$
      **end-for**
      run($MVQ'$)                                                  (3.4)
      $n \leftarrow n - 1$
   **end-while**     {output of the algorithm is the result of the last $MVQ'$}
   **end.**{ D-INGRES-QOA }

All one-variable queries (e.g., selection and projection) that can be detached are first processed locally [Step (1)]. Then a reduction algorithm [Wong and Youssefi, 1976] is applied to the original query [Step (2)]. Reduction is a technique that isolates all irreducible subqueries and one-variable subqueries by detachment (see Section 9.2.1). One-variable subqueries are ignored because they have already been processed in step (1). Based on the list of irreducible queries isolated in step (2) and the size of each fragment, the next subquery, $MVQ'$, which has at least two variables, is chosen at step (3.1) and steps (3.2), (3.3), and (3.4) are applied to it. Steps (3.1) and (3.2) are discussed below. Step (3.2) selects the best strategy to process the query $MVQ'$. This strategy is described by a list of pairs $(F, S)$, in which $F$ is a fragment to transfer to the processing site $S$. Step (3.3) transfers all the fragments to their processing sites. Finally, step (3.4) executes the query $MVQ'$. If there are remaining subqueries, the algorithm goes back to step (3) and performs the next iteration. Otherwise, the algorithm terminates.

Optimization occurs in steps (3.1) and (3.2). The algorithm has produced subqueries with several components and their dependency order (similar to the one given by a relational algebra tree). At step (3.1) a simple choice for the next subquery is to take the next one having no predecessor and involving the smaller fragments. This minimizes the size of the intermediate results. For example, if a query $q$ has the subqueries $q_1$, $q_2$, and $q_3$, with dependencies $q_1 \rightarrow q_3, q_2 \rightarrow q_3$, and if the fragments referred to by $q_1$ are smaller than those referred to by $q_2$, then $q_1$ is selected. Depending on the network, this choice can also be affected by the number of sites having relevant fragments. [Epstein et al., 1978] provides more details about this choice.

The $n$-variable subquery selected must then be executed. An example of such query that cannot be reduced (with detachment) is given in Figure 9.2a. Since the relation involved in a subquery may be stored at different sites and even fragmented, the subquery may nevertheless be further subdivided.

**Example 9.7**

Assume that relations E, G, and J of the query of Example 9.2 are stored as follows, where relation E is fragmented.

| Site 1 | Site 2 |
|:------:|:------:|
| $E_1$  | $E_2$  |
| G      | J      |

There are several possible strategies, including the following:

1. Execute the entire query (E $\bowtie$ G $\bowtie$ J) by moving $E_1$ and G to site 2.
2. Execute (E $\bowtie$ G) $\bowtie$ J by moving ($E_1$ $\bowtie$ G) and G to site 2, and so on.

The choice between the possible strategies requires an estimate of the size of the intermediate results. For example, if $size(E_1 \bowtie G) > size (E_1)$, strategy 1 is preferred to strategy 2. Therefore, an estimate of the size of joins is required.

At step (3.2), the next optimization problem is to determine how to execute the subquery by selecting the fragments that will be moved and the sites where the processing will take place. For an $n$-variable subquery, fragments from $n-1$ relations must be moved to the site(s) of fragments of the remaining relation, say $R_p$, and then replicated there. Also, the remaining relation may be further partitioned into $k$ "equalized" fragments in order to increase parallelism. This method is called *fragment-and-replicate* and performs a substitution of fragments rather than of tuples as in centralized IN-GRES. The selection of the remaining relation and of the number of processing sites $k$ on which it should be partitioned is based on the objective function and the topology of the network. Remember that replication is cheaper in broadcast networks than in point-to-point networks. Furthermore, the choice of the number of processing sites involves a trade-off between response time and total cost. A larger number of sites decreases response time (by parallel processing) but increases total cost, in particular increasing communication costs.

In [Epstein et al., 1978], formulas are given to minimize either communication cost or processing time. These formulas use as input the location of fragments, their size, and the network type. They can minimize both costs but with a priority to one. To illustrate these formulas, we give the rules for minimizing communication cost. The rule for minimizing response time is even more complex (see [Epstein et al., 1978] for details). We use the following assumptions. There are $n$ relations $R_1, R_2, \ldots, R_n$ involved in the $n$-variable query. $R_i^j$ denotes the fragment of $R_i$ stored at site $j$. There are $m$ sites in the network. Finally, $CC_k(\#bytes)$ denotes the communication cost of transferring $\#bytes$ to $k$ sites, with $1 \leq k \leq m$.

The rule for minimizing communication cost considers the types of networks separately. Let us first concentrate on a broadcast network. In this case we have

$$CC_k(\#bytes) = CC_1(\#bytes)$$

The rule can be stated as

**if** $\max_{j=1,m}(\sum_{i=1}^{n} size(R_i^j)) > \max_{i=1,n}(size(R_i))$
**then**
    the processing site is $j$ which has the largest amount of data
**else**
    $R_p$ is the largest relation and site of $R_p$ is the processing site

If the inequality predicate is satisfied, one site contains an amount of data useful to the query larger than the size of the largest relation. Therefore, this site should be the processing site. If the predicate is not satisfied, one relation is larger than the maximum useful amount of data at one site. Therefore, this relation should be the $R_p$, and the processing sites are those which have its fragments.

Let us now consider the case of the point-to-point networks. In this case we have

$$CC_k(\#bytes) = k * CC_1(\#bytes)$$

The choice of $R_p$ that minimizes communication is obviously the largest relation. Assuming that the sites are arranged by decreasing order of amounts of useful data for the query, that is,

$$\sum_{i=1}^{n} size(R_j^i) > \sum_{i=1}^{n} size(R_i^{j+1})$$

the choice of $k$, the number of sites at which processing needs to be done, is given as

**if** $\sum_{i \neq p}(size(R_i) - size(R_i^1)) > size(R_p^1)$
**then**
    $k = 1$
**else**
    $k$ is the largest $j$ such that $\sum_{i \neq p}(size(R_i) - size(R_i^j)) \leq size(R_p^j)$

This rule chooses a site as the processing site only if the amount of data it must receive is smaller than the additional amount of data it would have to send if it were not a processing site. Obviously, the then-part of the rule assumes that site 1 stores a fragment of $R_p$.

**Example 9.8**

Let us consider the query J $\bowtie$ G, where J and G are fragmented. Assume that the allocation of fragments and their sizes are as follows (in kilobytes):

|   | Site 1 | Site 2 | Site 3 | Site 4 |
|---|--------|--------|--------|--------|
| J | 1000 | 1000 | 1000 | 1000 |
| G |      |      | 2000 |      |

With a point–to–point network, the best strategy is to send each $J_i$ to site 3, which requires a transfer of 3000 kbytes, versus 6000 kbytes if G is sent to sites 1, 2, and 4. However, with a broadcast network, the best strategy is to send G (in a single transfer) to sites 1, 2, and 4, which incurs a transfer of 2000 kbytes. The latter strategy is faster and maximizes response time because the joins can be done in parallel.

The algorithm of Distributed INGRES is characterized by a limited search of the solution space, where an optimization decision is taken for each step without concerning itself with the consequences of that decision on global optimization. However, the algorithm is able to correct a local decision that proves to be incorrect. An alternative to the limited search is the exhaustive search approach (used by R*), where all possible strategies are evaluated to find the best one. In [Epstein and Stonebraker, 1980], the two approaches are simulated and compared on the basis of the size of data transfers. An important conclusion of this study is that exhaustive search significantly outperforms limited search as soon as the query accesses more than three relations. Another conclusion is that dynamic optimization is beneficial because the exact sizes of the intermediate results are known.

### 9.4.2  R* Algorithm

The distributed query optimization algorithm of R* ([Selinger and Adiba, 1980] and [Lohman et al., 1985]) is a substantial extension of the techniques developed for System R's optimizer (see Section 9.2.2). Therefore, it uses a compilation approach where an exhaustive search of all alternative strategies is performed in order to choose the one with the least cost. Although predicting and enumerating these strategies is costly, the overhead of exhaustive search is rapidly amortized if the query is executed frequently. Although the algorithm described in [Selinger and Adiba, 1980] deals with fragmentation, the implemented version of R* supports neither fragmentation nor replication. Therefore, the R* query processing algorithm deals only with relations as basic units. Query compilation is a distributed task in R*, coordinated by a *master site*, where the query is initiated. The optimizer of the master site makes all intersite decisions, such as the selection of the execution sites and the fragments as well as the method for transferring data. The *apprentice sites*, which are the other sites that have relations involved in the query, make the remaining local decisions (such as the ordering of joins at a site) and generate local access plans for the query. The objective function of the System R*'s optimizer is the general total cost function, including local processing and communications costs (see Section 9.1.1).

We now summarize the query optimization algorithm of R*. The input to the algorithm is a localized query expressed as a relational algebra tree (the query tree), the location of relations, and their statistics. The algorithm is described by the procedure R*-QOA in Algorithm 9.4.

Algorithm 9.4    *R\*-QOA*

**input:**$QT$: query tree
**output:**$strat$: minimum cost strategy
**begin**
    **for** each relation $R_i \in QT$ **do**
    **begin**
        **for each** access path $AP_{ij}$ to $R_i$ **do**
            determine $cost(AP_{ij})$
        **end-for**
        $best\_AP_i \leftarrow AP_{ij}$ with minimum cost
    **end**
    **for** each order $(R_{i1}, R_{i2}, \cdots, R_{in})$ with $i = 1, \cdots, n!$ **do**
    **begin**
        build strategy $(\ldots(( \text{ best } AP_{i1} \bowtie R_{i2}) \bowtie R_{i3}) \bowtie \ldots \bowtie R_{in})$
        compute the cost of strategy
    **end-for**
    $strat \leftarrow$ strategy with minimum cost
    **for** each site $k$ storing a relation involved in $QT$ **do**
    **begin**
        $LS_k \leftarrow$ local strategy (strategy, $k$)
        send $(LS_k,$ site $k)$       {each local strategy is optimized at site $k$}
    **end-for**
**end.** { R*-QOA }

As in the centralized case, the optimizer must select the join ordering, the join algorithm (nested loop or merge join), and the access path for each fragment (e.g., clustered index, sequential scan, etc.). These decisions are based on statistics and formulas used to estimate the size of intermediate results and access path information. In addition, the optimizer must select the sites of join results and the method of transferring data between sites. To join two relations, there are three candidate sites: the site of the first relation, the site of the second relation, or a third site (e.g., the site of a third relation to be joined with). In R*, two methods are supported for intersite data transfers.

   **1.** *Ship-whole.* The entire relation is shipped to the join site and stored in a temporary relation before being joined. If the join algorithm is merge join, the relation does not need to be stored, and the join site can process incoming tuples in a pipeline mode, as they arrive.

2. *Fetch-as-needed*. The external relation is sequentially scanned, and for each tuple the join value is sent to the site of the internal relation, which selects the internal tuples matching the value and sends the selected tuples to the site of the external relation. This method is equivalent to the semijoin of the internal relation with each external tuple.

The trade-off between these two methods is obvious. Ship-whole generates a larger data transfer but fewer messages than fetch-as-needed. It is intuitively better to ship whole relations when they are small. On the contrary, if the relation is large and the join has good selectivity (only a few matching tuples), the relevant tuples should be fetched as needed. R* does not consider all possible combinations of join methods with transfer methods since some of them are not worthwhile. For example, it would be useless to transfer the external relation using fetch-as-needed in the nested-loop join algorithm, because all the outer tuples must be processed anyway and therefore should be transferred as a whole.

Given the join of an external relation $R$ with an internal relation $S$ on attribute $A$, there are four join strategies. In what follows we describe each strategy in detail and provide a simplified cost formula for each, where $LC$ denotes local processing cost (I/O + CPU time) and $CC$ denotes communication cost. For simplicity, we ignore the cost of producing the result. For convenience, we denote by $s$ the average number of tuples of $S$ that match one tuple of $R$:

$$s = \frac{card(S \bowtie_A R)}{card(R)}$$

***Strategy 1.*** *Ship the entire external relation to the site of the internal relation.* In this case the external tuples can be joined with $S$ as they arrive. Thus we have

$$
\begin{aligned}
Total\_cost \;=\;& LC(\text{retrieve } card(R) \text{ tuples from } R) \\
+\;& CC(size(R)) \\
+\;& LC(\text{retrieve } s \text{ tuples from } S) * card(R)
\end{aligned}
$$

***Strategy 2.*** *Ship the entire internal relation to the site of the external relation.* In this case, the internal tuples cannot be joined as they arrive, and they need to be stored in a temporary relation $T$. Thus we have

$$
\begin{aligned}
Total\_cost \;=\;& LC(\text{retrieve } card(S) \text{ tuples from } S) \\
+\;& CC(size(S)) \\
+\;& LC(\text{store } card(S) \text{ tuples in } T) \\
+\;& LC(\text{retrieve } card(R) \text{ tuples from } R) \\
+\;& LC(\text{retrieve } s \text{ tuples from } T) * card(R)
\end{aligned}
$$

*Strategy 3.* *Fetch tuples of the internal relation as needed for each tuple of the external relation.* In this case, for each tuple in $R$, the join attribute value is sent to the site of $S$. Then the $s$ tuples of $S$ which match that value are retrieved and sent to the site of $R$ to be joined as they arrive. Thus we have

$$
\begin{aligned}
Total\_cost \ = \ & LC(\text{retrieve } card(R) \text{ tuples from } R) \\
+ \ & CC(length(A)) * card(R) \\
+ \ & LC(\text{retrieve } s \text{ tuples from } S) * card(R) \\
+ \ & CC(s * length(S)) * card(R)
\end{aligned}
$$

*Strategy 4.* *Move both relations to a third site and compute the join there.* In this case the internal relation is first moved to a third site and stored in a temporary relation $T$. Then the external relation is moved to the third site and its tuples are joined with $T$ as they arrive. Thus we have

$$
\begin{aligned}
Total\_cost \ = \ & LC(\text{retrieve } card(S) \text{ tuples from } S) \\
+ \ & CC(size(S)) \\
+ \ & LC(\text{store } card(S) \text{ tuples in } T) \\
+ \ & LC(\text{retrieve } card(R) \text{ tuples from } R) \\
+ \ & CC(size(R)) \\
+ \ & LC(\text{retrieve } s \text{ tuples from } T) * card(R)
\end{aligned}
$$

**Example 9.9**

Let us consider a query that consists of the join of relations J, the external relation, and G, the internal relation, on attribute JNO. We assume that J and G are stored at two different sites and that there is an index on attribute JNO for relation G. The possible execution strategies for the query are as follows :

1. Ship whole J to site of G.
2. Ship whole G to site of J.
3. Fetch G tuples as needed for each tuple of J.
4. Move G and J to a third site.

The R* algorithm predicts the total cost of each strategy and selects the cheapest. Given that there is no operation following the join J $\bowtie$ G, strategy 4 obviously incurs the highest cost since both relations must be transferred. If $size(\text{J})$ is much larger than $size(\text{G})$, strategy 2 minimizes the communication cost and is likely to be the best if local processing cost is not too high compared to strategies 1 and 3. Note that the local processing cost of strategies 1 and 3 is probably much better than that of strategy 2 since they exploit the index on the join attribute.

If strategy 2 is not the best, the choice is between strategies 1 and 3. Local processing costs in both of these alternatives are identical. If J is large and only a few tuples of G match, strategy 3 probably incurs the least communication cost and is the best. Otherwise, that is, if J is small or many tuples of G match, strategy 1 should be the best.

Conceptually, the algorithm can be viewed as an exhaustive search among all alternatives that are defined by the permutation of the relation join order, join methods (including the selection of the join algorithm), result site, access path to the internal relation, and intersite transfer mode. Such an algorithm has a combinatorial complexity in the number of relations involved. Actually, the R* algorithm significantly reduces the number of alternatives by using dynamic programming and the heuristics, as does the System R's optimizer (see Section 9.2.2). With dynamic programming, the tree of alternatives is dynamically constructed and pruned by eliminating the inefficient choices.

In [Lohman and Mackert, 1986] and [Mackert and Lohman, 1986], an instructive performance evaluation of the R* optimizer is described in the context of both high-speed networks (similar to local networks) and medium-speed wide area networks. The tests confirm the significant contribution of local processing costs, even for wide area networks. It is shown in particular that for the distributed join, transferring the entire internal relation outperforms the fetch-as-needed method.

### 9.4.3 SDD-1 Algorithm

The query optimization algorithm of SDD-1 [Bernstein et al., 1981] is derived from an earlier method called the "hill-climbing" algorithm [Wong, 1977], which has the distinction of being the first distributed query processing algorithm. In this algorithm, refinements of an initial feasible solution are recursively computed until no more cost improvements can be made. The algorithm does not use semijoins, nor does it assume data replication and fragmentation. It is devised for wide area point-to-point networks. The cost of transferring the result to the final site is ignored. This algorithm is quite general in that it can minimize an arbitrary objective function, including the total cost and response time.

The hill-climbing algorithm proceeds as follows. The input to the algorithm includes the query graph, location of relations, and relation statistics. Following the completion of initial local processing, an initial feasible solution is selected which is a global execution schedule that includes all intersite communication. It is obtained by computing the cost of all the execution strategies that transfer all the required relations to a single candidate result site, and then choosing the least costly strategy. Let us denote this initial strategy as $ES_0$. Then the optimizer splits $ES_0$ into two strategies, $ES_1$ followed by $ES_2$, where $ES_1$ consists of sending one of the relations involved in the join to the site of the other relation. The two relations are joined locally and the resulting relation is transmitted to the chosen result site (specified as schedule $ES_2$). If the cost of executing strategies $ES_1$ and $ES_2$, plus the cost of local join processing, is less than that of $ES_0$, then $ES_0$ is replaced in the schedule by $ES_1$ and $ES_2$. The process is then applied recursively to $ES_1$ and $ES_2$ until no more benefit can be gained. Notice that if $n$-way joins are involved, $ES_0$ will be divided into $n$ subschedules instead of just two.

The hill-climbing algorithm is in the class of greedy algorithms, which start with an initial feasible solution and iteratively improve it. The main problem is that strategies with higher initial cost, which could nevertheless produce better overall benefits, are ignored. Furthermore, the algorithm may get stuck at a local minimum cost solution and fail to reach the global minimum.

**Example 9.10**

Let us illustrate the hill-climbing algorithm using the following query involving relations E, S, J, and G of the engineering database:

"Find the salaries of engineers who work on the CAD/CAM project"

The query in relational algebra is

$$\Pi_{SAL} (S \bowtie_{TITLE} (E \bowtie_{ENO} (G \bowtie_{JNO}(\sigma_{JNAME = \text{"CAD/CAM"}}(J)))))$$

We assume that $C_{MSG} = 0$ and $C_{TR} = 1$. Furthermore, we ignore the local processing, following which the database is

| Relation | Size | Site |
|----------|------|------|
| E | 8 | 1 |
| S | 4 | 2 |
| J | 1 | 3 |
| G | 10 | 4 |

To simplify this example, we assume that the length of a tuple (of every relation) is 1, which means that the size of a relation is equal to its cardinality. Furthermore, the placement of the relation is arbitrary. Based on join selectivities, we know that $size(E \bowtie S) = size(E)$, $size(J \bowtie G) = 2 * size(J)$, and $size(G \bowtie E) = size(G)$.

Considering only data transfers, the initial feasible solution is to choose site 4 as the result site, producing the schedule

$$ES_0 : \quad E \rightarrow \text{site 4}$$
$$S \rightarrow \text{site 4}$$
$$J \rightarrow \text{site 4}$$
$$Total\_cost(ES_0) = 4 + 8 + 1 = 13$$

This is true because the cost of any other solution is greater than the foregoing alternative. For example, if one chooses site 2 as the result site and transmits all the relations to that site, the total cost will be

$$Total\_cost \quad = \quad cost(E \rightarrow \text{site 2}) + cost(G \rightarrow \text{site 2}) + cost(J \rightarrow \text{site 2})$$
$$= \quad 19$$

Similarly, the total cost of choosing either site 1 or site 3 as the result site is 15 and 22, respectively.

One way of splitting this schedule (call it $ES'$) is the following:

$$ES_1 : \quad E \rightarrow \text{site 2}$$
$$ES_2 : \quad (E \bowtie S) \rightarrow \text{site 4}$$
$$ES_3 : \quad J \rightarrow \text{site 4}$$
$$Total\_cost(ES') = 8 + 8 + 1 = 17$$

A second splitting alternative $(ES'')$ is as follows:

$$ES_1: \quad S \rightarrow \text{site 1}$$
$$ES_2: \quad (S \bowtie E) \rightarrow \text{site 4}$$
$$ES_3: \quad J \rightarrow \text{site 4}$$
$$Total\_cost(ES'') = 4 + 8 + 1 = 13$$

Since the cost of either of the alternatives is greater than or equal to the cost of $ES_0$, $ES_0$ is kept as the final solution. A better solution (ignored by the algorithm) is

$$B: \quad J \rightarrow \text{site 4}$$
$$G' = (J \bowtie G) \rightarrow \text{site 1}$$
$$(G' \bowtie E) \rightarrow \text{site 2}$$
$$Total\_cost(B) = 1 + 2 + 2 = 5$$

The hill-climbing algorithm has been substantially improved in SDD-1 [Bernstein et al., 1981] in a number of ways. The improved version makes extensive use of semijoins. The objective function is expressed in terms of total communication cost (local cost and response time are not considered). Finally, the algorithm uses statistics on the database, called *database profiles*, where a profile is associated with a relation. The improved version also selects an initial feasible solution that is iteratively refined. Furthermore, a postoptimization step is added to improve the total cost of the solution selected. The main step of the algorithm consists of determining and ordering beneficial semijoins, that is semijoins whose cost is less than their benefit.

The communication cost of a semijoin (see Section 9.3.2) is that of transferring the semijoin attributes $A$,

$$Cost(R \ltimes_A S) = C_{MSG} + C_{TR} * size(\Pi_A(S))$$

while its benefit is the cost of transferring irrelevant tuples of $R$ (which is avoided by the semijoin):

$$Benefit(R \ltimes_A S) = (1 - SF_{SJ}(S.A)) * size(R) * C_{TR}$$

The SDD-1 algorithm proceeds in four phases: initialization, selection of beneficial semijoins, assembly site selection, and postoptimization. The output of the algorithm is a global strategy for executing the query. The algorithm is detailed in Algorithm 9.5 by the procedure SDD-1-QOA.

**Algorithm 9.5    *SDD-1-QOA***

**input:** $QG$: query graph with $n$ relations; statistics for each relation
**output:** $ES$: execution strategy
**begin**
    ES $\leftarrow$ local-operations $(QG)$;
    modify statistics to reflect the effect of local processing
    BS $\leftarrow \phi$                           {set of beneficial semijoins}
    **for** each semijoin $SJ$ in $QG$ **do**

**if** $cost(SJ) < benefit(SJ)$ **then**
    $BS \leftarrow BS \cup SJ$
**end-if**
**end-for**
**while** $BS \neq \phi$ **do**                        {selection of beneficial semijoins}
**begin**
    $SJ \leftarrow most\_beneficial(BS)$ {$SJ$: semijoin with $max(benefit - cost)$}
    $BS \leftarrow BS - SJ$                          {remove $SJ$ from $BS$}
    $ES \leftarrow ES + SJ$                   {append $SJ$ to execution strategy}
    modify statistics to reflect the effect of incorporating $SJ$
    $BS \leftarrow BS-$ nonbeneficial semijoins
    $BS \leftarrow BS\cup$ new beneficial semijoins
**end-while**
{assembly site selection}
$AS(ES) \leftarrow$ select site $i$ such that $i$ stores the largest amount
    of data after all local operations
$ES \leftarrow ES \cup$ transfers of intermediate relations to $AS(ES)$
{postoptimization}
**for** each relation $R_i$ at $AS(ES)$ **do**
    **for** each semijoin $SJ$ of $R_i$ by $R_j$ **do**
        **if** $cost(ES) > cost(ES - SJ)$ **then**
            $ES \leftarrow ES - SJ$
        **end-if**
    **end-for**
**end-for**
**end.** { SDD-1-QOA }

The initialization phase generates a set of beneficial semijoins, $BS = \{SJ_1, SJ_2, \ldots, SJ_k\}$, and an execution strategy $ES$ that includes only local processing. The next phase selects the beneficial semijoins from $BS$ by iteratively choosing the most beneficial semijoin, $SJ_i$, and modifying the database statistics and $BS$ accordingly. The modification affects the statistics of relation $R$ involved in $SJ_i$ and the remaining semijoins in $BS$ that use relation $R$. The iterative phase terminates when all semijoins in $BS$ have been appended to the execution strategy. The order in which semijoins are appended to $ES$ will be the execution order of the semijoins.

The next phase selects the assembly site by evaluating, for each candidate site, the cost of transferring to it all the required data and taking the one with the least cost. Finally, a postoptimization phase permits the removal from the execution strategy of those semijoins that affect only relations stored at the assembly site. This phase is necessary because the assembly site is chosen after all the semijoins have been ordered. The SDD-1 optimizer is based on the assumption that relations can be transmitted to another site. This is true for all relations except those stored at the assembly site, which is selected after beneficial semijoins are considered. Therefore, some semijoins may incorrectly be considered beneficial. It is the role of postoptimization to remove them from the execution strategy.

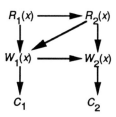

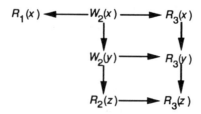

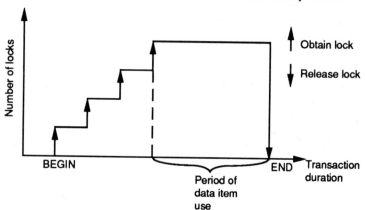

**Figure 11.8** Strict 2PL Lock Graph

we present the strict 2PL algorithm in its entirety in Algorithm 11.2. The transaction manager algorithm for 2PL scheduling is given in Algorithm 11.3.

> **Algorithm 11.2**    *S2PL-LM*
>
> **declare-var**
>     *msg* : *Message*
>     *dop* : *Dbop*
>     *Op* : *Operation*
>     *x* : *DataItem*
>     *T* : *TransactionId*
>     *pm* : *Dpmsg*
>     *res* : *DataVal*
>     *SOP* : *OpSet*
> **begin**
>     **repeat**
>         WAIT(*msg*)
>         **case of** *msg*
>             *Dbop* :
>             **begin**
>                 *Op* ← *dop.opn*
>                 *x* ← *dop.data*
>                 *T* ← *dop.tid*
>                 **case of** *Op*
>                     Begin_transaction:
>                     **begin**
>                         send *dop* to the data processor
>                     **end**
>                     Read **or** Write:                                   {requires locking}

that have written (updated) $x$. It is now sufficient to compare the timestamp of an operation with the read and write timestamps of the data item that it wants to access to determine if any transaction with a larger timestamp has already accessed the same data item.

Architecturally (see Figure 10.4), the transaction manager is responsible for assigning a timestamp to each new transaction and attaching this timestamp to each database operation that it passes on to the scheduler. The latter component is responsible for keeping track of read and write timestamps as well as performing the serializability check.

### 11.4.1  Basic TO Algorithm

The basic TO algorithm is a straightforward implementation of the TO rule. The coordinating transaction manager assigns the timestamp to each transaction, determines the sites where each data item is stored, and sends the relevant operations to these sites. The basic TO transaction manager algorithm (BTO-TM) is depicted in Algorithm 11.6. The schedulers at each site simply enforce the TO rule. The scheduler algorithm is given in Algorithm 11.7.

> **Algorithm 11.6**    *BTO-TM*
>
> **declare-var**
>     $T : Transaction$
>     $Op : Operation$
>     $x : DataItem$
>     $msg : Message$
>     $O : Dbop$
>     $pm : Dpmsg$
>     $res : DataVal$
>     $S : SiteSet$
> **begin**
>     **repeat**
>         WAIT($msg$)
>         **case of** $msg$
>             $Dbop$ :              {database operation from the application program}
>             **begin**
>                 $Op \leftarrow O.opn$
>                 $x \leftarrow O.data$
>                 $T \leftarrow O.tid$
>                 **case of** $Op$
>                     Begin_Transaction:
>                     **begin**
>                         $S \leftarrow \phi$
>                         assign a timestamp to $T$ $[ts(T)]$

theory and concentrates almost exclusively on concurrency control. A good collection of papers that focus on the concurrency control and reliability aspects of distributed systems is [Bhargava, 1987]. Distributed concurrency control is the topic of [Cellary et al., 1988].

A very important work is a set of notes on database operating systems by Jim Gray [Gray, 1979]. These notes contain valuable information on transaction management, among other things. The same author now has a set of videotaped lectures and accompanying tutorial notes which contain considerable updated information about the same issues [Gray and Reuter, 1987]. The discussion concerning transaction classification at the end of Section 10.3 is from [Farrag, 1986].

There are numerous papers dealing with various transaction management issues. The ones referred to in this chapter are those that deal with the concept of a transaction. More detailed references on their management are left to Chapters 11 and 12.

# 11

# Distributed
# Concurrency Control

As we discussed in Chapter 10, concurrency control deals with the isolation and consistency properties of transactions. The distributed concurrency control mechanism of a distributed DBMS ensures that the consistency of the database, as defined in Section 10.2.2, is maintained in a multiuser distributed environment. If transactions are internally consistent (i.e., do not violate any consistency constraints), the simplest way of achieving this objective is to execute each transaction alone, one after another. It is obvious that such an alternative is only of theoretical interest and cannot be implemented in any practical system, since it minimizes the system throughput. The level of concurrency (i.e., the number of concurrent transactions) is probably the most important parameter in distributed systems [Balter et al., 1982]. Therefore, the concurrency control mechanism attempts to find a suitable trade-off between maintaining the consistency of the database and maintaining a high level of concurrency.

In this chapter we make one major assumption: the distributed system is fully reliable and does not experience any failures (of hardware or software). Even though this is an entirely unrealistic assumption, there is a reason for making it. It permits us to delineate the issues related to the management of concurrency from those related to the operation of a reliable distributed system. In Chapter 12, we discuss how the algorithms that are presented in this chapter need to be revised to operate in an unreliable environment. We start our discussion of concurrency control with a presentation of serializability theory in Section 11.1. Serializability is the most widely accepted correctness criterion for concurrency control algorithms. In Section 11.2 we present a taxonomy of algorithms that will form the basis for most of the discussion in the remainder of the chapter. Sections 11.3 and 11.4 cover the two major classes of algorithms: locking-based and timestamp ordering-based. Both locking and time-stamp ordering classes cover what is called pessimistic algorithms; optimistic concurrency control is discussed in Section 11.5. Any locking-based algorithm may result in deadlocks, requiring special management methods. Various deadlock management techniques are therefore the topic of Section 11.6.

## 11.1  SERIALIZABILITY THEORY

In Section 10.2.3 we discussed the issue of isolating transactions from one another in terms of their effects on the database. We also pointed out that if the concurrent execution of transactions leaves the database in a state that can be achieved by their serial execution in some order, problems such as lost updates will be resolved. This is exactly the point of the serializability argument. The remainder of this section addresses serializability issues more formally.

A *schedule S* (also called a *history*) is defined over a set of transactions $T = \{T_1, T_2, \ldots, T_n\}$ and specifies an interleaved order of execution of these transactions' operations. Based on the definition of a transaction introduced in Section 10.1, the schedule can be specified as a partial order over $T$. We need a few preliminaries, though, before we present the formal definition.

Recall the definition of conflicting operations that we gave in Chapter 10. Two operations $O_{ij}(x)$ and $O_{kl}(x)$ ($i$ and $k$ not necessarily distinct) accessing the same database entity $x$ are said to be in *conflict* if at least one of them is a write. Note two things in this definition. First, read operations do not conflict with each other. We can, therefore, talk about two types of conflicts: *read-write* (or *write-read*), and *write-write*. Second, the two operations can belong to the same transaction or to two different transactions. In the latter case, the two transactions are said to be *conflicting*. Intuitively, the existence of a conflict between two operations indicate that their order of execution is important. The ordering of two read operations is insignificant.

We first define a *complete schedule,* which defines the execution order of all operations in its domain. We will then define a schedule as a prefix of a complete schedule. Formally, a complete schedule $S_T^c$ defined over a set of transactions $T = \{T_1, T_2, \ldots, T_n\}$ is a partial order $S_T^c = \{\Sigma_T, \prec_T\}$ where

1. $\Sigma_T = \bigcup_{i=1}^{n} \Sigma_i$.
2. $\prec_T \supseteq \bigcup_{i=1}^{n} \prec_i$.
3. For any two conflicting operations $O_{ij}, O_{kl} \in \Sigma_T$, either $O_{ij} \prec_T O_{kl}$, or $O_{kl} \prec_T O_{ij}$.

The first condition simply states that the domain of the schedule is the union of the domains of individual transactions. The second condition defines the ordering relation as a superset of the ordering relations of individual transactions. This maintains the ordering of operations within each transaction. The final condition simply defines the execution order among conflicting operations.

**Example 11.1**

Consider the two transactions from Example 10.8. They were specified as

$$
\begin{array}{llll}
T_1: & \text{Read}(x) & T_2: & \text{Read}(x) \\
     & x \leftarrow x + 1 & & x \leftarrow x + 1 \\
     & \text{Write}(x) & & \text{Write}(x) \\
     & \text{Commit} & & \text{Commit}
\end{array}
$$

A possible complete schedule $S_T^c$ over $T = \{T_1, T_2\}$ can be written as the following partial order (where the subscripts indicate the transactions):

$$S_T^c = \{\Sigma_T, \prec_T\}$$

where

$$
\begin{array}{lll}
\Sigma_1 & = & \{R_1(x), W_1(x), C_1\} \\
\Sigma_2 & = & \{R_2(x), W_2(x), C_2\}
\end{array}
$$

Thus

$$\Sigma_T = \Sigma_1 \cup \Sigma_2 = \{R_1(x), W_1(x), C_1, R_2(x), W_2(x), C_2\}$$

and

$$
\begin{array}{lll}
\prec_T & = & \{(R_1, R_2), (R_1, W_1), (R_1, C_1), (R_1, W_2), (R_1, C_2), (R_2, W_1), \\
& & (R_2, C_1), (R_2, W_2), (R_2, C_2), (W_1, C_1), (W_1, W_2), (W_1, C_2), \\
& & (C_1, W_2), (C_1, C_2), (W_2, C_2)\}
\end{array}
$$

which can be specified as a DAG as depicted in Figure 11.1. Note that consistent with our earlier adopted convention (see Example 10.7), we do not draw the arcs that are implied by transitivity [e.g., $(R_1, C_1)$]. Also note that we omit the data items that these operations operate on since this is obvious from the context.

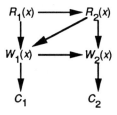

**Figure 11.1** DAG Representation of a Complete Schedule

At this point we should mention a convention that is commonly employed to simplify the notation of a schedule. It is often specified as a listing of the operations in $\Sigma_T$, where their execution order is relative to their order in this list. Thus $S_T^c$ can be specified as

$$S_T^c = \{R_1(x), R_2(x), W_1(x), C_1, W_2(x), C_2\}$$

Because of its simplicity, we use the latter notation in the remainder of this chapter.

A schedule is defined as a prefix of a complete schedule. A prefix of a partial order can be defined as follows. Given a partial order $P = \{\Sigma, \prec\}$, $P' = \{\Sigma', \prec'\}$ is a *prefix* of $P$ if

1. $\Sigma' \subseteq \Sigma$;
2. $\forall e_i \in \Sigma', e_1 \prec' e_2$ if and only if $e_1 \prec e_2$; and
3. $\forall e_i \in \Sigma'$, if $\exists e_j \in \Sigma$ and $e_j \prec e_i$, then $e_j \in \Sigma'$.

The first two conditions define $P'$ as a *restriction* of $P$ on domain $\Sigma'$, whereby the ordering relations in $P$ are maintained in $P'$. The last condition indicates that for any element of $\Sigma'$, all its predecessors in $\Sigma$ have to be included in $\Sigma'$ as well.

The real question that needs to be asked is: What does this definition of a schedule as a prefix of a partial order provide for us? The answer is simply that we can now deal with incomplete schedules. This is useful for a number of reasons. From the perspective of the serializability theory, we deal only with those operations of transactions that conflict rather than with all operations. Furthermore, and perhaps more important, when we introduce failures, we need to be able to deal with incomplete schedules, which is what a prefix enables us to do.

The schedule discussed in Example 11.1 is special in that it is complete. It needs to be complete in order to talk about the execution order of these two transactions' operations. The following example demonstrates a schedule that is not complete.

**Example 11.2**

Consider the following three transactions:

| $T_1$: | Read($x$)  | $T_2$: | Write($x$) | $T_3$: | Read($x$)  |
|--------|------------|--------|------------|--------|------------|
|        | Write($x$) |        | Write($y$) |        | Read($y$)  |
|        | Commit     |        | Read($z$)  |        | Read($z$)  |
|        |            |        | Commit     |        | Commit     |

A complete schedule $S^c$ for these transactions is given in Figure 11.2, and a schedule $S$ (as a prefix of $S^c$) is depicted in Figure 11.3.

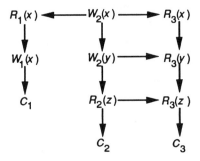

**Figure 11.2**   A Complete Schedule

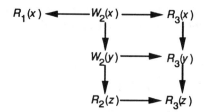

**Figure 11.3**   Prefix of Complete Schedule in Figure 11.2

If in a schedule $S$, the operations of various transactions are not interleaved (i.e., the operations of each transaction occur consecutively), the schedule is said to be *serial*. As we indicated before, the serial execution of a set of transactions maintains the consistency of the database. This follows naturally from the consistency property of transactions: each transaction, when executed alone on a consistent database, will produce a consistent database.

**Example 11.3**

Consider the three transactions of Example 11.2. The following schedule,

$$S = \{W_2(x), W_2(y), R_2(z), C_2, R_1(x), W_1(x), C_1, R_3(x), R_3(y), R_3(z), C_3\}$$

is serial since all the operations of $T_2$ are executed before all the operations of $T_1$ and all operations of $T_1$ are executed before all operations of $T_3$. One common way to denote this precedence relationship between transaction executions is $T_2 \prec_S T_1 \prec_S T_3$ or $T_2 \rightarrow T_1 \rightarrow T_3$.

Based on the precedence relationship introduced by the partial order, it is possible to discuss the equivalence of schedules with respect to their effects on the database. Intuitively, two schedules $S_1$ and $S_2$, defined over the same set of transactions $T$, are *equivalent* if they have the same effect on the database. More formally, two schedules, $S_1$ and $S_2$, defined over the same set of transactions $T$, are said to be *equivalent* if for each pair of conflicting operations $O_{ij}$ and $O_{kl}$ $(i \neq k)$, whenever $O_{ij} \prec_1 O_{kl}$, then $O_{ij} \prec_2 O_{kl}$. This is called *conflict equivalence* since it defines equivalence of two schedules in terms of the relative order of execution of the conflicting operations in those schedules. In the definition above, for the sake of simplicity, we assume that $T$ does not include any aborted transaction. Otherwise, the definition needs to be modified to specify only those conflicting operations that belong to unaborted transactions.[1]

**Example 11.4**

Again consider the three transactions of Example 11.2. The following schedule $S'$ defined over them is conflict equivalent to $S$ given in Example 11.3:

$$S' = \{W_2(x), R_1(x), R_3(x), W_1(x), C_1, W_2(y), R_3(y), R_2(z), C_2, R_3(z), C_3\}$$

---

[1]For the sake of completeness, we should also point out that there is another form of equivalence, called *view equivalence*. The concept of serializability can also be defined based on view equivalence. We will not dwell on this point further since conflict equivalence is a more useful concept to work with in concurrency control.

We are now ready to define serializability more formally. A schedule $S$ is said to be *serializable* if and only if it is conflict equivalent to a serial schedule. Note that serializability roughly corresponds to degree 3 consistency, which we defined in Section 10.2.2. Serializability so defined is also known as *conflict-based serializability* since it is defined according to conflict equivalence.

**Example 11.5**

Schedule $S'$ in Example 11.4 is serializable since it is equivalent to the serial schedule $S$ of Example 11.3. Also note that the problem with the uncontrolled execution of transactions $T_1$ and $T_2$ in Example 10.8 was that they could generate an unserializable schedule.

Now that we have formally defined serializability, we can indicate that the primary function of a concurrency controller is to generate a serializable schedule for the execution of pending transactions. The issue, then, is to devise algorithms that are guaranteed to generate only serializable schedules.

Serializability theory extends in a straightforward manner to the nonreplicated (or partitioned) distributed databases. The schedule of transaction execution at each site is called a *local schedule*. If the database is not replicated and each local schedule is serializable, their union (called the *global schedule*) is also serializable as long as local serialization orders are identical. In a replicated distributed database, however, the extension of the serializability theory requires more care. It is possible that the local schedules are serializable, but the mutual consistency of the database is still compromised.

**Example 11.6**

We will give a very simple example to demonstrate the point. Consider two sites and one data item ($x$) that is duplicated in both sites. Further consider the following two transactions:

$T_1$:    Read($x$)        $T_2$:    Read($x$)

         $x \leftarrow x + 5$              $x \leftarrow x * 10$

         Write($x$)              Write($x$)

         Commit                Commit

Obviously, both of these transactions need to run at both sites. Consider the following two schedules that may be generated locally at the two sites:

$$S_1 = \{R_1(x), W_1(x), C_1, R_2(x), W_2(x), C_2\}$$
$$S_2 = \{R_2(x), W_2(x), C_2, R_1(x), W_1(x), C_1\}$$

Note that both of these schedules are serializable; indeed, they are serial. Therefore, each represents a correct execution order. However, observe that they serialize $T_1$ and $T_2$ in reverse order. Assume that the value of $x$ prior to the execution of these transactions was 1. At the end of the execution of these schedules, the value of $x$ is 60 at site 1 while it is 15 at site 2. This violates the mutual consistency of the two local databases.

Mutual consistency requires that all the values of all replicated data items be identical. Schedules that can maintain mutual consistency are called *one-copy serializable* [Bernstein and Goodman, 1985]. Intuitively, a one-copy serializable global schedule has to meet the following conditions:

1. Each local schedule should be serializable.

2. Two conflicting operations should be in the same relative order in all of the local schedules where they appear together.

The second condition simply ensures that the serialization order be the same at all the sites where the conflicting transactions execute together. Recall that concurrency control algorithms ensure serializability by synchronizing conflicting accesses to the database. In replicated databases, the additional task of ensuring one-copy serializability is usually the responsibility of the *replica control protocol*.

Let us assume the existence of a data item $x$ with copies $x_1, x_2, \ldots, x_n$. We will refer to $x$ as the *logical data* item and to its copies as *physical data* items. If replication transparency is to be provided, user transactions will issue read and write operations on the logical data item $x$. The replica control protocol is responsible for mapping each read on the logical data item $x$ [Read($x$)] to a read on one of the physical data item copies $x_j$ [Read($x_j$)]. Each write on the logical data item $x$, on the other hand, is mapped to a set of writes on a (possibly proper) subset of the physical data item copies of $x$. Whether this mapping is to the full set of physical data item copies or to a subset is the basis of classifying replica control algorithms. In this chapter, and for the most part in this book, we consider replica control protocols that map a read on a logical data item to only *one* copy of the data item, but map a write on a logical data item to a set of writes on *all* physical data item copies. Such a protocol is commonly known as the *read-once/write-all* (ROWA) protocol.

The common complaint about the ROWA protocol is that it reduces the availability of the database in case of failures since the transaction may not complete unless it reflects the effects of the write operation on all the copies (more on this in Chapter 12). Therefore, there have been a number of algorithms that have attempted to maintain mutual consistency without employing the ROWA protocol. They are all based on the premise that one can continue processing an operation as long as the operation can be scheduled at a subset of the sites which correspond to a majority of the sites where copies are stored [Thomas, 1979] or to all sites that can be reached (i.e., available) [Bernstein and Goodman, 1984] and [Goodman et al., 1983].

## 11.2 TAXONOMY OF CONCURRENCY CONTROL MECHANISMS

There are a number of ways that the concurrency control approaches can be classified. One obvious classification criterion is the mode of database distribution. Some algorithms that have been proposed require a fully replicated database, while others can operate on partially replicated or partitioned databases. The concurrency control algorithms may also be classified according to network topology, such as those requiring a communication subnet with broadcasting capability or those working in a star-type network or a circularly connected network.

The most common classification criterion, however, is the synchronization primitive. The corresponding breakdown of the concurrency control algorithms results in two classes: those algorithms that are based on mutually exclusive access to shared data (locking), and those that attempt to order the execution of the transactions according to a set of rules (protocols). However, these primitives may be used in algorithms with two different viewpoints: the pessimistic view that many transactions will conflict with each other, or the optimistic view that not too many transactions will conflict with one another.

We will thus group the concurrency control mechanisms into two broad classes: pessimistic concurrency control methods and optimistic concurrency control methods. *Pessimistic* algorithms synchronize the concurrent execution of transactions early in their execution life cycle, whereas *optimistic* algorithms delay the synchronization of transactions until their termination. The pessimistic group consists of *locking-based* algorithms, *timestamp ordering* (or *transaction ordering*) *based* algorithms, and *hybrid* algorithms. The optimistic group can, similarly, be classified as locking-based or timestamp ordering-based. This classification is depicted in Figure 11.4.

In the *locking-based* approach, the synchronization of transactions is achieved by employing physical or logical locks on some portion or granule of the database. The size of these portions (usually called *locking granularity*) is an important issue. However, for the time being, we will ignore it and refer to the chosen granule as a *lock unit*. This class is subdivided further according to where the lock management activities are performed:

1. In *centralized locking*, one of the sites in the network is designated as the primary site where the lock tables for the entire database are stored and is charged with the responsibility of granting locks to transactions.

2. In *primary copy locking*, on the other hand, one of the copies (if there are multiple copies) of each lock unit is designated as the primary copy, and it is this copy that has to be locked for the purpose of accessing that particular unit. For example, if lock unit $x$ is replicated at sites 1, 2, and 3, one of these sites (say, 1) is selected as the primary site for $x$. All transactions desiring access to $x$ obtain their lock at site 1 before they can access a copy of $x$. If the database is not replicated (i.e., there is only one copy of each lock unit), the primary copy locking mechanisms distribute the lock management responsibility among a number of sites.

3. In *decentralized locking*, the lock management duty is shared by all the sites of a network. In this case, the execution of a transaction involves the participation and coordination of schedulers at more than one site. Each local scheduler is responsible for the lock units local to that site. Using the same example as above, entities accessing $x$ must obtain locks at all three sites.

The *timestamp ordering* (TO) class involves organizing the execution order of transactions so that they maintain mutual and interconsistency. This ordering is maintained by assigning timestamps to both the transactions and the data items that are stored in the database. These algorithms can be *basic TO, multiversion TO,* or *conservative TO*.

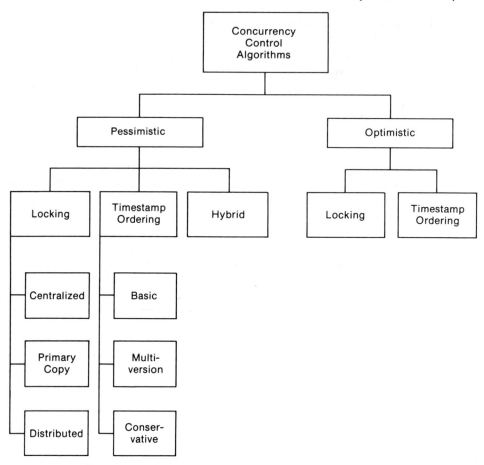

**Figure 11.4**   Classification of Concurrency Control Algorithms

We should indicate that in some locking-based algorithms, timestamps are also used. This is done primarily to improve efficiency and the level of concurrency. We call this class the *hybrid* algorithm. We will not discuss these algorithms in this chapter since they have not been implemented in any commercial or research prototype distributed DBMS. The rules for integrating locking and timestamp ordering protocols are given in [Bernstein and Goodman, 1981].

## 11.3 LOCKING-BASED CONCURRENCY CONTROL ALGORITHMS

The main idea of locking-based concurrency control is to ensure that the data that is shared by conflicting operations is accessed by one operation at a time. This is accomplished by associating a "lock" with each lock unit. This lock is set by a transaction before it is accessed and is reset at the end of its use. Obviously a lock unit cannot be accessed by an operation if it is already locked by another. Thus a lock request by a transaction is granted only if the associated lock is not being held by any other transaction.

Since we are concerned with synchronizing the conflicting operations of conflicting transactions, there are two types of locks (commonly called *lock modes*) associated with each lock unit: *read lock* (*rl*) and *write lock* (*wl*). A transaction $T_i$ that wants to read a data item contained in lock unit $x$ obtains a read lock on $x$ [denoted $rl_i(x)$]. The same happens for write operations. It is common to talk about the *compatibility* of lock modes. Two lock modes are compatible if two transactions which access the same data item can obtain these locks on that data item at the same time. As Figure 11.5 shows, read locks are compatible, whereas read-write or write-write locks are not. Therefore, it is possible, for example, for two transactions to read the same data item concurrently.

|            | $rl_i(x)$         | $wl_i(x)$         |
|------------|-------------------|-------------------|
| $rl_j(x)$  | compatible        | not compatible    |
| $wl_j(x)$  | not compatible    | not compatible    |

**Figure 11.5**    Compatibility of Lock Modes

The distributed DBMS not only manages locks but also handles the lock management responsibilities on behalf of the transactions. In other words, the users do not need to specify when data needs to be locked; the distributed DBMS takes care of that every time the transaction issues a read or write operation.

In locking-based systems, the scheduler (see Figure 10.4) is a *lock manager* (LM). The transaction manager passes to the lock manager the database operation (read or write) and associated information (such as the item that is accessed and the identifier of the transaction that issues the database operation). The lock manager then checks if the lock unit that contains the data item is already locked. If so, and if the existing lock mode is incompatible with that of the current transaction, the current operation is delayed. Otherwise, the lock is set in the desired mode and the database operation is passed on to the data processor for actual database access. The transaction manager is then informed of the results of the operation. The termination of a transaction results in the release of its locks and the initiation of another transaction that might be waiting for access to the same data item.

The basic locking algorithm is given in Algorithm 11.1. In Figure 11.6 we give the type declarations and the procedure definitions that we use in the algorithms of this chapter. Note that the definitions in Figure 11.6 are at a high level of abstraction. Also, in Algorithm 11.1, we do not yet pay any attention to how the commit and abort operations of transactions are serviced. Those complications are not added until Chapter 12.

**declare-type**

*Operation*: one of Read, Write, Abort, or Commit
*DataItem*: a data item in the distributed database
*TransactionId*: a unique identifier assigned to each transaction
*DataVal*: a primitive data-type value (i.e., integer, real, etc.)
*SiteId*: a unique site identifier

*Dbop*: a 3-tuple of {a database operation from the application program}
  *opn* : *Operation*
  *data* : *DataItem*
  *tid* : *TransactionId*

*Dpmsg*: a 3-tuple of                    {a message from the data processor}
  *opn* : *Operation*
  *tid* : *TransactionId*
  *res* : *DataVal*

*Scmsg*: a 3-tuple of                    {a message from the scheduler}
  *opn* : *Operation*
  *tid* : *TransactionId*
  *res* : *DataVal*

*Transaction* ← a 2-tuple of
  *tid* : *TransactionId*
  *body* : a transaction body as defined in Chapter 10

*Message* ← a string of characters that are to be transmitted

*OpSet*: a set of *DbOp*'s

*SiteSet*: a set of *SiteId*'s

WAIT(*msg* : *Message*)
**begin**
   {wait until a message arrives}
**end**

**Figure 11.6**   Preliminary Definitions for the Upcoming Algorithms

**Algorithm 11.1**   *Basic LM*

**declare-var**
  *msg* : *Message*
  *dop* : *Dbop*
  *Op* : *Operation*
  *x* : *DataItem*
  *T* : *TransactionId*
  *pm* : *Dpmsg*

$res : DataVal$
$SOP : OpSet$
**begin**
  **repeat**
    WAIT($msg$)
    **case of** $msg$
      $Dbop$ :
      **begin**
        $Op \leftarrow dop.opn$
        $x \leftarrow dop.data$
        $T \leftarrow dop.tid$
        **case of** $Op$
        Begin_transaction:
        **begin**
          send $dop$ to the data processor
        **end**
        Read **or** Write:                                              {requires locking}
        **begin**
          find the lock unit $lu$ such that $x \subseteq lu$
          **if** $lu$ is unlocked **or** lock mode of $lu$ is compatible with $Op$ **then**
          **begin**
            set lock on $lu$ in appropriate mode
            send $dop$ to the data processor
          **end**
          **else**
            put $dop$ on a queue for $lu$
          **end-if**
        **end**
        Abort **or** Commit:
        **begin**
          send $dop$ to the data processor
        **end**
      **end-case**
      $Dpmsg$ :                                    {acknowledgment from the data processor}
      **begin**                                                        {requires unlocking}
        $Op \leftarrow pm.opn$
        $res \leftarrow pm.result$
        $T \leftarrow pm.tid$
        find lock unit $lu$ such that $x \subseteq lu$
        release lock on $lu$ held by $T$
        **if** there are no more locks on $lu$ **and**
          there are operations waiting in queue to lock $lu$ **then**
        **begin**
          $SOP \leftarrow$ first operation from the queue

$SOP \leftarrow SOP \cup \{O|O$ is a operation on queue that can lock $lu$
      in a compatible mode with the current operations in SOP$\}$
      set the locks on $lu$ on behalf of operations in $SOP$
      **for** all the operations in $SOP$ **do**
         send each operation to the data processor
      **end-for**
    **end-if**
  **end**
  **end-case**
**until** $forever$
**end.** {Basic LM}

The locking algorithm that is given in Algorithm 11.1 will not, unfortunately, properly synchronize transaction executions. This is because to generate serializable schedules, the locking and releasing operations of transactions also need to be coordinated. We demonstrate this by an example.

**Example 11.7**

Consider the following two transactions:

$$T_1: \quad \text{Read}(x) \qquad T_2: \quad \text{Read}(x)$$
$$x \leftarrow x + 1 \qquad\qquad x \leftarrow x * 2$$
$$\text{Write}(x) \qquad\qquad \text{Write}(x)$$
$$\text{Read}(y) \qquad\qquad \text{Read}(y)$$
$$y \leftarrow y - 1 \qquad\qquad y \leftarrow y * 2$$
$$\text{Write}(y) \qquad\qquad \text{Write}(y)$$
$$\text{Commit} \qquad\qquad\quad \text{Commit}$$

The following is a valid schedule that a lock manager employing the algorithm of Algorithm 11.1 may generate:

$$S \;=\; \{wl_1(x), R_1(x), W_1(x), lr_1(x), wl_2(x), R_2(x), w_2(x), lr_2(x), wl_2(y),$$
$$R_2(y), W_2(y), lr_2(y), C_2, wl_1(y), R_1(y), W_1(y), lr_1(y), C_1\}$$

Here, $lr_i(z)$ indicates the release of the lock on $z$ that transaction $T_i$ holds.

Note that $S$ is not a serializable schedule. For example, if prior to the execution of these transactions, the values of $x$ and $y$ are 50 and 20, respectively, one would expect their values following execution to be, respectively, either 102 and 38 if $T_1$ executes before $T_2$, or 101 and 39 if $T_2$ executes before $T_1$. However, the result of executing $S$ would give $x$ and $y$ the values 102 and 39. Obviously, $S$ is not serializable.

The problem with schedule $S$ in Example 11.7 is the following. The locking algorithm releases the locks that are held by a transaction (say, $T_i$) as soon as the associated database command (read or write) is executed, and that lock unit (say $x$) no longer needs to be accessed. However, the transaction itself is locking other items (say, $y$), after it releases its lock on $x$. Even though this may seem to be advantageous from the viewpoint of increased concurrency, it permits transactions to interfere with one another, resulting in the loss of total isolation and atomicity. Hence the argument for *two-phase locking* (2PL).

The two-phase locking rule simply states that no transaction should request a lock after it releases one of its locks. Alternatively, a transaction should not release a lock until it is certain that it will not request another lock. 2PL algorithms execute transactions in two phases. Each transaction has a *growing phase*, where it obtains locks and accesses data items, and a *shrinking phase*, during which it releases locks (Figure 11.7). The *lock point* is the moment when the transaction has achieved all its locks but has not yet started to release any of them. Thus the lock point determines the end of the growing phase and the beginning of the shrinking phase of a transaction. It is a well-known theorem [Eswaran et al., 1976] that any schedule generated by a concurrency control algorithm that obeys the 2PL rule is serializable.

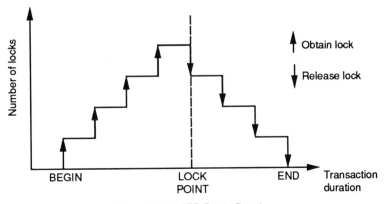

**Figure 11.7**    2PL Lock Graph

Figure 11.7 indicates that the lock manager releases locks as soon as access to that data item has been completed. This permits other transactions awaiting access to go ahead and lock it, thereby increasing the degree of concurrency. However, this is difficult to implement since the lock manager has to know that the transaction has obtained all its locks and will not need to lock another data item. The lock manager also needs to know that the transaction no longer needs to access the data item in question, so that the lock can be released. Finally, if the transaction aborts after it releases a lock, it may cause other transactions that may have accessed the unlocked data item to abort as well. This is known as *cascading aborts*. Because of these difficulties, most 2PL schedulers implement what is called *strict two-phase locking*, which releases all the locks together when the transaction terminates (commits or aborts). Thus the lock graph is as shown in Figure 11.8.

The strict 2PL lock manager requires minimal modification of the algorithm of Algorithm 11.1. In fact, the only modification that is necessary is to change the section that handles the responses from the data processor. This is necessary to ensure that the locks are released only if the operation is a commit or abort. For completeness,

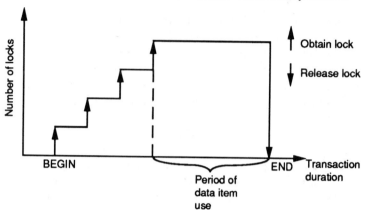

**Figure 11.8**   Strict 2PL Lock Graph

we present the strict 2PL algorithm in its entirety in Algorithm 11.2. The transaction manager algorithm for 2PL scheduling is given in Algorithm 11.3.

     **Algorithm 11.2**   *S2PL-LM*

        **declare-var**
           $msg : Message$
           $dop : Dbop$
           $Op : Operation$
           $x : DataItem$
           $T : TransactionId$
           $pm : Dpmsg$
           $res : DataVal$
           $SOP : OpSet$
        **begin**
          **repeat**
            WAIT($msg$)
            **case of** $msg$
              $Dbop$ :
             **begin**
               $Op \leftarrow dop.opn$
               $x \leftarrow dop.data$
               $T \leftarrow dop.tid$
               **case of** $Op$
                 Begin_transaction:
                 **begin**
                   send $dop$ to the data processor
                 **end**
                 Read **or** Write:                          {requires locking}

```
                begin
                    find the lock unit lu such that x ⊆ lu
                    if lu is unlocked or lock mode of lu is compatible with Op then
                    begin
                        set lock on lu in appropriate mode
                        send dop to the data processor
                    end
                    else
                        put dop on a queue for lu
                    end-if
                end
                Abort or Commit:
                begin
                    send dop to the data processor
                end
            end-case
        Dpmsg :
        begin
            Op ← pm.opn
            res ← pm.result
            T ← pm.tid
            if Op=Abort or Op=Commit then
            begin
                for each lock unit lu locked by T do
                begin
                    release lock on lu held by T
                    if there are no more locks on lu and
                        there are operations waiting in queue for lu then
                    begin
                        SOP ← first operation from the queue
                        SOP ← SOP ∪ {O|O is an operation on queue that
                                    can lock lu in a compatible mode with
                                    the current operations in SOP}
                        set the locks on lu on behalf of operations in SOP
                        for all the operations in SOP do
                            send each operation to the data processor
                        end-for
                    end-if
                end-for
            end-if
        end
        end-case
    until forever
end. {S2PL-LM}
```

**Algorithm 11.3**    *2PL-TM*

**declare-var**
   $msg$ : *Message*
   $Op$ : *Operation*
   $x$ : *DataItem*
   $T$ : *TransactionId*
   $O$ : *Dbop*
   $sm$ : *Scmsg*
   $res$ : *DataVal*
   $SOP$ : *OpSet*
**begin**
  **repeat**
    WAIT($msg$)
    **case of** $msg$
      $Dbop$ :
      **begin**
        send $O$ to the lock manager
      **end**
      $Scmsg$ :                   {acknowledgment from the lock manager}
      **begin**
        $Op \leftarrow sm.opn$
        $res \leftarrow sm.result$
        $T \leftarrow sm.tid$
        **case of** $Op$
          Read:
          **begin**
            return $res$ to the user application (i.e., the transaction)
          **end**
          Write:
          **begin**
            inform user application of completion of the write
            return res to the user application
          **end**
          Commit:
          **begin**
            destroy $T$'s workspace
            inform user application of successful completion of transaction
          **end**
          Abort:
          **begin**
            inform user application of completion of the abort of $T$
          **end**
        **end-case**

> **end**
> **end-case**
> **until** *forever*
> **end.** {2PL-TM}

### 11.3.1 Centralized 2PL

The 2PL algorithm discussed in the preceding section can easily be extended to the (replicated or partitioned) distributed DBMS environment. One way of doing this is to delegate lock management responsibility to a single site only. This means that only one of the sites has a lock manager; the transaction managers at the other sites communicate with it rather than with their own lock managers. This approach is also known as the *primary site* 2PL algorithm [Alsberg and Day, 1976].

The communication between the cooperating sites in executing a transaction according to a centralized 2PL (C2PL) algorithm is depicted in Figure 11.9. This communication is between the transaction manager at the site where the transaction is initiated (called the *coordinating* TM), the lock manager at the central site, and the data processors (DP) at the other participating sites. The participating sites are those at which the operation is to be carried out. The order of messages is denoted in the figure.

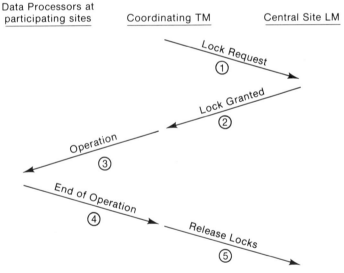

**Figure 11.9**   Communication Structure of Centralized 2PL

An important difference between the centralized TM algorithm and the TM algorithm of Algorithm 11.3 is that the distributed TM has to implement the replica control protocol if the database is replicated. The C2PL-LM algorithm also differs from the strict 2PL lock manager in one major way. The central lock manager does not send the operations to the respective data processors; that is done by the coordinating TM.

The centralized 2PL transaction management algorithm (C2PL-TM) that incorporates these changes is given in Algorithm 11.4, while the centralized 2PL lock management algorithm (C2PL-LM) is shown in Algorithm 11.5.

**Algorithm 11.4    C2PL-TM**

**declare-var**
   $T$ : $Transaction$
   $Op$ : $Operation$
   $x$ : $DataItem$
   $msg$ : $Message$
   $O$ : $Dbop$
   $pm$ : $Dpmsg$
   $res$ : $DataVal$
   $S$ : $SiteSet$
**begin**
  **repeat**
    WAIT($msg$)
    **case of** $msg$
      $Dbop$ :
      **begin**
        $Op \leftarrow O.opn$
        $x \leftarrow O.data$
        $T \leftarrow O.tid$
        **case of** $Op$
          Begin_Transaction:
          **begin**
            $S \leftarrow \emptyset$
          **end**
          Read:
          **begin**
            $S \leftarrow S\cup$ {the site that stores $x$ and has the lowest
                         access cost to it}
            send $O$ to the central lock manager
          **end**
          Write:
          **begin**
            $S \leftarrow S \cup \{S_i | x$ is stored at site $S_i\}$
            send $O$ to the central lock manager
          **end**
          Abort or Commit:
          **begin**

   send $O$ to the central lock manager
  **end**
 **end-case**
**end**
*Scmsg* :       {lock request granted on locks released}
**begin**
 **if** lock request granted **then**
  send $O$ to the data processors in $S$
 **else**
  inform user about the termination of transaction
 **end-if**
**end**
*Dpmsg* :
**begin**
 $Op \leftarrow pm.opn$
 $res \leftarrow pm.result$
 $T \leftarrow pm.tid$
 **case of** $Op$
  Read:
  **begin**
   return $res$ to the user application (i.e., the transaction)
  **end**
  Write:
  **begin**
   inform user application of completion of the write
  **end**
  Commit:
  **begin**
   **if** commit msg has been received from all participants **then**
   **begin**
    inform user application of successful completion of
     transaction
    send $pm$ to the central lock manager
   **else**     {wait until commit msg comes from all}
    record the arrival of the commit message
   **end-if**
  **end**
  Abort:
  **begin**
   inform user application of completion of the abort of $T$
   send $pm$ to the central lock manager
  **end**
 **end-case**
**end**

**end-case**
**until** *forever*
**end.** {C2PL-TM}

Algorithm 11.5　*C2PL-LM*

**declare-var**
　*msg* : *Message*
　*dop* : *SingleOp*
　*Op* : *Operation*
　*x* : *DataItem*
　*T* : *TransactionId*
　*SOP* : *OpSet*
**begin**
　**repeat**
　　WAIT(*msg*)　　　{The only msg that can arrive is from coordinating TM }
　　*Op* ← *dop.opn*
　　*x* ← *dop.data*
　　*T* ← *dop.tid*
　　**case of** *Op*
　　　Read **or** Write:
　　　**begin**
　　　　find the lock unit *lu* such that *x* ⊆ *lu*
　　　　**if** *lu* is unlocked **or** lock mode of *lu* is compatible with *Op* **then**
　　　　**begin**
　　　　　set lock on *lu* in appropriate mode
　　　　　*msg* ← "Lock granted for operation *dop*"
　　　　　send *msg* to the coordinating TM of *T*
　　　　**end**
　　　　**else**
　　　　　put *Op* on a queue for *lu*
　　　　**end-if**
　　　**end**
　　　Commit **or** Abort:
　　　**begin**
　　　　**for** each lock unit *lu* locked by *T* **do**
　　　　**begin**
　　　　　release lock on *lu* held by *T*
　　　　　**if** there are operations waiting in queue for *lu* **then**
　　　　　**begin**
　　　　　　*SOP* ← first operation (call *O*) from the queue
　　　　　　*SOP* ← *SOP* ∪ {*O*|*O* is a operation on queue that can lock *lu*

in a compatible mode with the current operations in $SOP$}
set the locks on $lu$ on behalf of operations in $SOP$
**for** all the operations $O$ in $SOP$ **do**
**begin**
          $msg \leftarrow$ "Lock granted for operation $O$"
          send $msg$ to all the coordinating TM's
      **end-for**
    **end-if**
  **end-for**
  $msg \leftarrow$ "Locks of $T$ released"
  send $msg$ to the coordinating TM of $T$
     **end**
   **end-case**
 **until** $forever$
**end.** {C2PL-LM}

One common criticism of C2PL algorithms is that a bottleneck may quickly form around the central site. Furthermore, the system may be less reliable since the failure or inaccessibility of the central site would cause major system failures. There are studies that indicate that the bottleneck will indeed form as the transaction rate increases, but is insignificant at low transaction rates ([Özsu, 1985a] and [Koon and Özsu, 1986]). Furthermore, sharp performance degradation at high loads is observed in other locking-based algorithms as well.

### 11.3.2  Primary Copy 2PL

Primary copy 2PL (PC2PL) is a straightforward extension of centralized 2PL in an attempt to counter the latter's potential performance problems, discussed above. Basically, it implements lock managers at a number of sites and makes each lock manager responsible for managing the locks for a given set of lock units. The transaction managers then send their lock and unlock requests to the lock managers that are responsible for that specific lock unit. Thus the algorithm treats one copy of each data item as its primary copy.

We do not give the detailed primary copy 2PL algorithm since the changes from centralized 2PL are minimal. Basically, the only change is that the primary copy locations have to be determined for each data item prior to sending a lock or unlock request to the lock manager at that site. This is a directory design and management issue that we discussed in Chapter 4.

Primary copy 2PL was proposed for the prototype distributed version of INGRES [Stonebraker and Neuhold, 1977]. Even though it demands a more sophisticated directory at each site, it also reduces the load of the central site without causing a large amount of communication among the transaction managers and lock managers. In one sense it is an intermediate step between the centralized 2PL that we discussed in the preceding section and the distributed 2PL that we will cover next.

### 11.3.3  Distributed 2PL

Distributed 2PL (D2PL) expects the availability of lock managers at each site. If the database is not replicated, distributed 2PL degenerates into the primary copy 2PL algorithm. If data is replicated, the transaction implements the ROWA replica control protocol.

The communication between cooperating sites that execute a transaction according to the distributed 2PL protocol is depicted in Figure 11.10. Notice that Figure 11.10 does not show application of the ROWA rule.

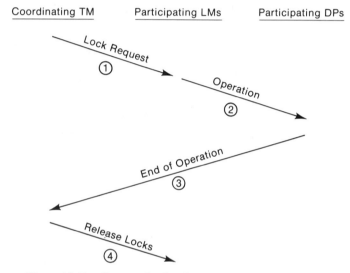

**Figure 11.10**   Communication Structure of Distributed 2PL

The distributed 2PL transaction management algorithm is similar to the C2PL-TM, with two major modifications. The messages that are sent to the central site lock manager in C2PL-TM are sent to the lock managers at all participating sites in D2PL-TM. The second difference is that the operations are not passed to the data processors by the coordinating transaction manager, but by the participating lock managers. This means that the coordinating transaction manager does not wait for a "lock request granted" message. Another point about Figure 11.10 is the following. The participating data processors send the "end of operation" message to the coordinating TM. The alternative is for each DP to send it to its own lock manager who can then release the locks and inform the coordinating TM. We have chosen to describe the former since it uses an LM algorithm identical to the strict 2PL lock manager that we have already discussed and it makes the discussion of the commit protocols simpler (see Chapter 12). Owing to these similarities, we do not give the distributed TM and LM algorithms here. Distributed 2PL algorithms are used in System R* [Mohan et al., 1986] and in NonStop SQL ([Tandem, 1987], [Tandem, 1988] and [Borr, 1988]).

## 11.4  TIMESTAMP-BASED CONCURRENCY CONTROL ALGORITHMS

Unlike the locking-based algorithms, timestamp-based concurrency control algorithms do not attempt to maintain serializability by mutual exclusion. Instead, they select, a priori a serialization order and execute transactions accordingly. To establish this ordering, the transaction manager assigns each transaction $T_i$ a unique *timestamp* $ts(T_i)$ at its initiation.

A timestamp is a simple identifier that serves to identify each transaction uniquely and to permit ordering. *Uniqueness* is only one of the properties of timestamp generation. The second property is *monotonicity*. Two timestamps generated by the same transaction manager should be monotonically increasing. Thus timestamps are values derived from a totally ordered domain. It is this second property that differentiates a timestamp from a transaction identifier.

There are a number of ways that timestamps can be assigned. One method is to use a global (systemwide) monotonically increasing counter. However, the maintenance of global counters is a problem in distributed systems. Therefore, it is preferable that each site autonomously assign timestamps based on its local counter. To maintain uniqueness, each site appends its own identifier to the counter value. Thus the timestamp is a two-tuple of the form <local counter value, site identifier>. Note that the site identifier is appended in the least significant position. Hence it serves only to order the timestamps of two transactions that might have been assigned the same local counter value. If each system can access its own system clock, it is possible to use system clock values instead of counter values.

With this information, it is simple to order the execution of the transactions' operations according to their timestamps. Formally, the timestamp ordering (TO) rule can be specified as follows:

**TO Rule.**  Given two conflicting operations $O_{ij}$ and $O_{kl}$ belonging, respectively, to transactions $T_i$ and $T_k$, $O_{ij}$ is executed before $O_{kl}$ if and only if $ts(T_i) < ts(T_k)$. In this case $T_i$ is said to be the *older* transaction and $T_k$ is said to be the *younger* one.

A scheduler that enforces the TO rule checks each new operation against conflicting operations that have already been scheduled. If the new operation belongs to a transaction that is younger than all the conflicting ones that have already been scheduled, the operation is accepted; otherwise, it is rejected, causing the entire transaction to restart with a *new* timestamp.

A timestamp ordering scheduler that operates in this fashion is guaranteed to generate serializable schedules. However, this comparison between the transaction timestamps can be performed only if the scheduler has received all the operations to be scheduled. If operations come to the scheduler one at a time (which is the realistic case), it is necessary to be able to detect if an operation has arrived out of sequence. To facilitate this check, each data item $x$ is assigned two timestamps: a *read timestamp* $[rts(x)]$, which is the largest of the timestamps of the transactions that have read $x$, and a *write timestamp* $[wts(x)]$, which is the largest of the timestamps of the transactions that have written (updated) $x$. It is now sufficient to compare the timestamp of an operation with the read and write timestamps of the data item that it wants to access to determine if any transaction with a larger timestamp has already accessed the same data item.

Architecturally (see Figure 10.4), the transaction manager is responsible for assigning a timestamp to each new transaction and attaching this timestamp to each database operation that it passes on to the scheduler. The latter component is responsible for keeping track of read and write timestamps as well as performing the serializability check.

### 11.4.1 Basic TO Algorithm

The basic TO algorithm is a straightforward implementation of the TO rule. The coordinating transaction manager assigns the timestamp to each transaction, determines the sites where each data item is stored, and sends the relevant operations to these sites. The basic TO transaction manager algorithm (BTO-TM) is depicted in Algorithm 11.6. The schedulers at each site simply enforce the TO rule. The scheduler algorithm is given in Algorithm 11.7.

    **Algorithm 11.6**   *BTO-TM*

     **declare-var**
       $T : Transaction$
       $Op : Operation$
       $x : DataItem$
       $msg : Message$
       $O : Dbop$
       $pm : Dpmsg$
       $res : DataVal$
       $S : SiteSet$
     **begin**
      **repeat**
        WAIT($msg$)
        **case of** $msg$
          $Dbop$ :         {database operation from the application program}
          **begin**
            $Op \leftarrow O.opn$
            $x \leftarrow O.data$
            $T \leftarrow O.tid$
            **case of** $Op$
              Begin_Transaction:
              **begin**
                $S \leftarrow \phi$
                assign a timestamp to $T$ $[ts(T)]$

**end**
Read:
**begin**
$\quad$ $S \leftarrow S \cup$ {the site that stores $x$ and has the lowest access cost to it}
$\quad$ send $O$ and $ts(T)$ to the scheduler at $S$
**end**
Write:
**begin**
$\quad$ $S \leftarrow S \cup \{S_i \mid x$ is stored at site $S_i\}$
$\quad$ send $O$ and $ts(T)$ to the schedulers at $S$
**end**
Abort or Commit:
**begin**
$\quad$ send $O$ to the schedulers in $S$
**end**
**end-case**
$Scmsg:$ $\qquad$ {the operation must have been rejected by a scheduler}
**begin**
$\quad$ $msg \leftarrow$ "Abort $T$"
$\quad$ send $msg$ to schedulers in $S$
$\quad$ restart $T$ $\qquad$ {will assign a new timestamp}
**end**
$Dpmsg:$
**begin**
$\quad$ $Op \leftarrow pm.opn$
$\quad$ $res \leftarrow pm.result$
$\quad$ $T \leftarrow pm.tid$
$\quad$ **case of** $Op$
$\quad\quad$ Read:
$\quad\quad$ **begin**
$\quad\quad\quad$ return $res$ to the user application (i.e., the transaction)
$\quad\quad$ **end**
$\quad\quad$ Write:
$\quad\quad$ **begin**
$\quad\quad\quad$ inform user application of completion of the write
$\quad\quad$ **end**
$\quad\quad$ Commit:
$\quad\quad$ **begin**
$\quad\quad\quad$ inform user application of successful completion of transaction
$\quad\quad$ **end**
$\quad\quad$ Abort:
$\quad\quad$ **begin**
$\quad\quad\quad$ inform user application of completion of the abort of $T$
$\quad\quad$ **end**

```
                    end-case
                end
              end-case
          until forever
        end. {BTO-TM}
```


Algorithm 11.7     *BTO-SC*

```
declare-var
    msg : Message
    dop : SingleOp
    Op : Operation
    x : DataItem
    T : TransactionId
    SOP : OpSet
begin
  repeat
    WAIT(msg)
    case of msg
        Dbop :    {database operation passed from the transaction manager}
        begin
            Op ← dop.opn
            x ← dop.data
            T ← dop.tid
            save initial rts(x) and wts(x)
            case of Op
              Read:
              begin
                if ts(T) > rts(x) then
                begin
                    send dop to the data processor
                    rts(x) ← ts(T)
                end
                else begin
                    msg ← "Reject T"
                    send msg to the coordinating TM
                end
                end-if
              end {of Read case}
              Write:
              begin
                if ts(T) > rts(x) and ts(T) > wts(x) then
                begin
```

```
            send dop to the data processor
            rts(x) ← ts(T)
            wts(x) ← ts(T)
        end
        else begin
            msg ← "Reject T"
            send msg to the coordinating TM
        end
        end-if
    end {of Write case}
    Commit:
    begin
        send dop to the data processor
    end {of Commit case}
    Abort:
    begin
        for all x that has been accessed by T do
            reset rts(x) and wts(x) to their initial values
        end-for
        send dop to the data processor
    end {of Abort case}
    end-case
end
end-case
until forever
end. {BTO-SC}
```

As indicated before, a transaction which contains an operation that is rejected by a scheduler is restarted by the transaction manager with a new timestamp. This ensures that the transaction has a chance to execute in its next try. Since the transactions never wait while they hold access rights to data items, the basic TO algorithm never causes deadlocks. However, the penalty of deadlock freedom is potential restart of a transaction numerous times. There is an alternative to the basic TO algorithm that reduces the number of restarts, which we consider in the next section.

Another detail that needs to be considered relates to the communication between the scheduler and the data processor. When an accepted operation is passed on to the data processor, the scheduler needs to refrain from sending another incompatible, but acceptable operation to the data processor until the first is processed and acknowledged. This is a requirement to ensure that the data processor execute the operations in the same order in which the scheduler passes them on. Otherwise, the read and write timestamp values for the accessed data item would not be accurate.

**Example 11.8**

Assume that the TO scheduler first receives $W_i(x)$ and then receives $W_j(x)$, where $ts(T_i) < ts(T_j)$. The scheduler would accept both operations and pass them on to the data processor. The result of these two operations is that $wts(x) = ts(T_j)$, and we then expect the effect of $W_j(x)$ to be represented in the database. However, if the data processor does not execute them in that order, the effects on the database will be wrong.

The scheduler can enforce the ordering by maintaining a queue for each data item that is used to delay the transfer of the accepted operation until an acknowledgment is received from the data processor regarding the previous operation on the same data item. This detail is not shown in Algorithm 11.7.

Such a complication does not arise in 2PL-based algorithms because the lock manager effectively orders the operations by releasing the locks only after the operation is executed. In one sense the queue that the TO scheduler maintains may be thought of as a lock. However, this does not imply that the schedule generated by a TO scheduler and a 2PL scheduler would always be equivalent. There are some schedules that a TO scheduler would generate that would not be admissible by a 2PL schedule.

Remember that in the case of strict 2PL algorithms, the releasing of locks is delayed further, until the commit or abort of a transaction. It is possible to develop a strict TO algorithm by using a similar scheme. For example, if $W_i(x)$ is accepted and released to the data processor, the scheduler delays all $R_j(x)$ and $W_j(x)$ operations (for all $T_j$) until $T_i$ terminates (commits or aborts).

### 11.4.2 Conservative TO Algorithm

We indicated in the preceding section that the basic TO algorithm never causes operations to wait, but instead, restarts them. We also pointed out that even though this is an advantage due to deadlock freedom, it is also a disadvantage, because numerous restarts would have adverse performance implications. The conservative TO algorithms attempt to lower this system overhead by reducing the number of transaction restarts.

Let us first present a technique that is commonly used to reduce the probability of restarts. Remember that a TO scheduler restarts a transaction if a younger conflicting transaction is already scheduled or has been executed. Note that such occurrences increase significantly if, for example, one site is comparatively inactive relative to the others and does not issue transactions for an extended period. In this case its timestamp counter indicates a value that is considerably smaller than the counters of other sites. If the TM at this site then receives a transaction, the operations that are sent to the schedulers at the other sites will almost certainly be rejected, causing the transaction to restart. Furthermore, the same transaction will restart repeatedly until the timestamp counter value at its originating site reaches a level of parity with the counters of other sites.

The foregoing scenario indicates that it is useful to keep the counters at each site synchronized. However, total synchronization is not only costly—since it requires exchange of messages every time a counter changes—but also unnecessary. Instead, each transaction manager can send its remote operations to the transaction managers at the other sites, instead of to the schedulers. The receiving transaction managers can then compare their own counter values with that of the incoming operation. Any manager whose counter value is smaller than the incoming one adjusts its own counter to one more than the incoming one. This ensures that none of the counters in the system run away or lag behind significantly. Of course, if system clocks are used instead of counters, this approximate synchronization may be achieved automatically as long as the clocks are of comparable speeds.

We can now return to our discussion of conservative TO algorithms. The "conservative" nature of these algorithms relates to the way they execute each operation. The basic TO algorithm tries to execute an operation as soon as it is accepted; it is therefore "aggressive" or "progressive." Conservative algorithms, on the other hand, delay each operation until there is an assurance that no operation with a smaller timestamp can arrive at that scheduler. If this condition can be guaranteed, the scheduler will never reject an operation. However, this delay introduces the possibility of deadlocks.

The basic technique that is used in conservative TO algorithms is based on the following idea: the operations of each transaction are buffered until an ordering can be established so that rejections are not possible, and they are executed in that order. We will consider one possible implementation of the conservative TO algorithm. Our discussion follows that of [Herman and Verjus, 1979].

Assume that each scheduler maintains one queue for each transaction manager in the system. The scheduler at site $i$ stores all the operations that it receives from the transaction manager at site $j$ in queue $Q_{ij}$. Scheduler $i$ has one such queue for each $j$. When an operation is received from a transaction manager, it is placed in its appropriate queue in increasing timestamp order. The schedulers at each site execute the operations from these queues in increasing timestamp order.

This scheme will reduce the number of restarts, but it will not guarantee that they will be eliminated completely. Consider the case where at site $i$ the queue for site $j$ $(Q_{ij})$ is empty. The scheduler at site $i$ will choose an operation [say, $R(x)$] with the smallest timestamp and pass it on to the data processor. However, site $j$ may have sent to $i$ an operation [say, $W(x)$] with a smaller timestamp which may still be in transit in the network. When this operation reaches site $i$, it will be rejected since it violates the TO rule: it wants to access a data item that is currently being accessed (in an incompatible mode) by another operation with a higher timestamp.

It is possible to design an extremely conservative TO algorithm by insisting that the scheduler choose an operation to be sent to the data processor only if there is at least one operation in each queue. This guarantees that every operation that the scheduler receives in the future will have timestamps greater than or equal to those currently in the queues. Of course, if a transaction manager does not have a transaction to process, it needs to send dummy messages periodically to every scheduler in the system, informing them that the operations that it will send in the future will have timestamps greater than that of the dummy message.

The careful reader will realize that the extremely conservative timestamp ordering scheduler actually executes transactions serially at each site. This is very restrictive.

One method that has been employed to overcome this restriction is to group transactions into classes. Transaction classes are defined with respect to their read sets and write sets. It is therefore sufficient to determine the class that a transaction belongs to by comparing the transaction's read set and write set, respectively, with the read set and write set of each class. Thus the conservative TO algorithm can be modified so that instead of requiring the existence, at each site, of one queue for each transaction manager, it is only necessary to have one queue for each transaction class. Alternatively, one might mark each queue with the class to which it belongs. With either of these modifications, the conditions for sending an operation to the data processor are changed. It is no longer necessary to wait until there is at least one operation in each queue; it is sufficient to wait until there is at least one operation in each class to which the transaction belongs. This and other weaker conditions that reduce the waiting delay can be defined and are sufficient. A variant of this method is used in the SDD-1 prototype system [Bernstein et al., 1980b].

### 11.4.3 Multiversion TO Algorithm

Multiversion TO is another attempt at eliminating the restart overhead cost of transactions. Most of the work on multiversion TO has concentrated on centralized databases, so we present only a brief overview. However, we should indicate that multiversion TO algorithm would be a suitable concurrency control mechanism for DBMSs that are designed to support applications which inherently have a notion of versions of database objects (e.g., engineering databases).

In multiversion TO, the updates do not modify the database; each write operation creates a new version of that data item. Each version is marked by the timestamp of the transaction that creates it. Thus the multiversion TO algorithm trades storage space for time. In doing so, it processes each transaction on a state of the database that it would have seen if the transactions were executed serially in timestamp order.

The existence of versions is transparent to users who issue transactions simply by referring to data items, not to any specific version. The transaction manager assigns a timestamp to each transaction which is also used to keep track of the timestamps of each version. The operations are processed by the schedulers as follows:

1. A $R_i(x)$ is translated into a read on one version of $x$. This is done by finding a version of $x$ (say, $x_v$) such that $ts(x_v)$ is the largest timestamp less than $ts(T_i)$. $R_i(x_v)$ is then sent to the data processor.

2. A $W_i(x)$ is translated into $W_i(x_w)$ so that $ts(x_w) = ts(T_i)$ and sent to the data processor if and only if no other transaction with a timestamp greater than $ts(T_i)$ has read the value of a version of $x$ (say, $x_r$) such that $ts(x_r) > ts(x_w)$. In other words, if the scheduler has already processed a $R_j(x_r)$ such that

$$ts(T_i) < ts(x_r) < ts(T_j)$$

then $W_i(x)$ is rejected.

A scheduler that processes the read and the write requests of transactions according to the rules noted above is guaranteed to generate serializable schedules. To save space, the versions of the database may be purged from time to time. This should be done when the distributed DBMS is certain that it will no longer receive a transaction that needs to access the purged versions.

## 11.5  OPTIMISTIC CONCURRENCY CONTROL ALGORITHMS

The concurrency control algorithms discussed in Sections 11.3 and 11.4 are pessimistic in nature. In other words, they assume that the conflicts between transactions are quite frequent and do not permit a transaction to access a data item if there is a conflicting transaction that accesses that data item. Thus the execution of any operation of a transaction follows the sequence of phases: validation (V), read (R), computation (C), write (W) (Figure 11.11).[2] Generally, this sequence is valid for an update transaction as well as for each of its operations.

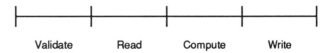

Validate        Read        Compute        Write

**Figure 11.11**    Phases of Pessimistic Transaction Execution

Optimistic algorithms, on the other hand, delay the validation phase until just before the write phase (Figure 11.12). Thus an operation submitted to an optimistic scheduler is never delayed. The read, compute, and write operations of each transaction are processed freely without updating the actual database. Each transaction initially makes its updates on local copies of data items. The validation phase consists of checking if these updates would maintain the consistency of the database. If the answer is affirmative, the changes are made global (i.e., written into the actual database). Otherwise, the transaction is aborted and has to restart.

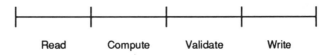

Read        Compute        Validate        Write

**Figure 11.12**    Phases of Optimistic Transaction Execution

It is possible to design locking-based optimistic concurrency control algorithms (see [Bernstein et al., 1987]). However, the original optimistic proposals ([Kung and Robinson, 1981] and [Thomas, 1979]) are based on timestamp ordering. Therefore, we describe only the optimistic approach using timestamps. Our discussion is brief

---

[2]We consider only the update transactions in this discussion because they are the ones that cause consistency problems. Read-only actions do not have the computation and write phases. Furthermore, we assume that the write phase includes the commit action.

and emphasizes concepts rather than implementation details. The reasons for this are twofold. First, most of the current work on optimistic methods concentrates on centralized rather than distributed DBMSs. Second, optimistic algorithms have not been implemented in any commercial or prototype DBMS. Therefore, the information regarding their implementation trade-offs is insufficient. As a matter of fact, the only centralized implementation of optimistic concepts (not the full algorithm) is in IBM's IMS-FASTPATH, which provides primitives that permit the programmer to access the database in an optimistic manner.

The algorithm that we discuss was proposed in [Kung and Robinson, 1981] and was later extended for distributed DBMS [Ceri and Owicki, 1982]. This is not the only extension of the model to distributed databases, however (see, for e.g., [Sinha et al., 1985]). It differs from pessimistic TO-based algorithms not only by being optimistic but also in its assignment of timestamps. Timestamps are associated only with transactions, not with data items (i.e., there are no read or write timestamps). Furthermore, timestamps are not assigned to transactions at their initiation but at the beginning of their validation step. This is because the timestamps are needed only during the validation phase, and as we will see shortly, their early assignment may cause unnecessary transaction rejections.

Each transaction $T_i$ is subdivided (by the transaction manager at the originating site) into a number of subtransactions, each of which can execute at many sites. Notationally, let us denote by $T_{ij}$ a subtransaction of $T_i$ that executes at site $j$. Until the validation phase, each local execution follows the sequence depicted in Figure 11.12. At that point a timestamp is assigned to the transaction which is copied to all its subtransactions. The local validation of $T_{ij}$ is performed according to the following rules, which are mutually exclusive.

**Rule 1.** If all transactions $T_k$, where $ts(T_k) < ts(T_{ij})$ have completed their write phase before $T_{ij}$ has started its read phase (Figure 11.13a),[3] validation succeeds, because transaction executions are in serial order.

**Rule 2.** If there is any transaction $T_k$ such that $ts(T_k) < ts(T_{ij})$ which completes its write phase while $T_{ij}$ is in its read phase (Figure 11.13b), the validation succeeds if $WS(T_k) \cap RS(T_{ij}) = \emptyset$.

**Rule 3.** If there is any transaction $T_k$ such that $ts(T_k) < ts(T_{ij})$ which completes its read phase before $T_{ij}$ completes its read phase (Figure 11.13c), the validation succeeds if $WS(T_k) \cap RS(T_{ij}) = \emptyset$, and $WS(T_k) \cap WS(T_{ij}) = \emptyset$.

Rule 1 is obvious; it indicates that the transactions are actually executed serially in their timestamp order. Rule 2 ensures that none of the data items updated by $T_k$ are read by $T_{ij}$ and that $T_k$ finishes writing its updates into the database before $T_{ij}$

---

[3]Following the convention we have adopted, we omit the computation step in this figure and in the subsequent discussion. Thus timestamps are assigned at the end of the read phase.

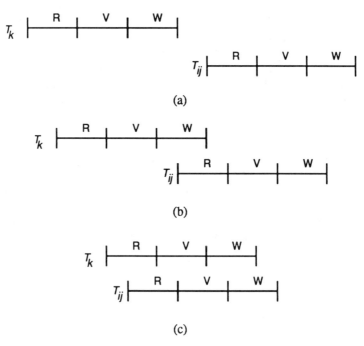

**Figure 11.13**    Possible Execution Scenarios

starts writing. Thus the updates of $T_{ij}$ will not be overwritten by the updates of $T_k$. Rule 3 is similar to Rule 2, but does not require that $T_k$ finish writing before $T_{ij}$ starts writing. It simply requires that the updates of $T_k$ not affect the read phase or the write phase of $T_{ij}$.

Once a transaction is locally validated to ensure that the local database consistency is maintained, it also needs to be globally validated to ensure that the mutual consistency rule is obeyed. Unfortunately, there is no known optimistic method of doing this. A transaction is globally validated if all the transactions that precede it in the serialization order (at that site) terminate (either by committing or aborting). This is a pessimistic method since it performs global validation early and delays a transaction. However, it guarantees that transactions execute in the same order at each site.

An advantage of the optimistic concurrency control algorithms is their potential to allow a higher level of concurrency. It has been shown [Kung and Robinson, 1981] that when transaction conflicts are very rare, the optimistic mechanism performs better than locking. A major problem with optimistic algorithms is the higher storage cost. To validate a transaction, the optimistic mechanism has to store the read and the write sets of several other terminated transactions. Specifically, the read and write sets of terminated transactions that were in progress when transaction $T_{ij}$ arrived at site $j$ need to be stored in order to validate $T_{ij}$. Obviously, this increases the storage cost.

Another problem is starvation. Consider a situation in which the validation phase of a long transaction fails. In subsequent trials it is still possible that the validation will fail repeatedly. Of course, it is possible to solve this problem by permitting the transaction exclusive access to the database after a specified number of trials. However, this reduces the level of concurrency to a single transaction. The exact "mix" of transactions that would cause an intolerable level of restarts is an issue that remains to be studied.

## 11.6  DEADLOCK MANAGEMENT

As we indicated before, any locking-based concurrency control algorithm may result in deadlocks, since there is mutual exclusion of access to shared resources (data) and transactions may wait on locks. Furthermore, we have seen that some TO-based algorithms that require the waiting of transactions (e.g., strict TO) may also cause deadlocks. Therefore, the distributed DBMS requires special procedures to handle them.

A deadlock can occur because transactions wait for one another. Informally, a deadlock situation is a set of requests that can never be granted by the concurrency control mechanism.

**Example 11.9**

Consider two transactions $T_i$ and $T_j$ that hold write locks on two entities $x$ and $y$ [i.e., $wl_i(x)$ and $wl_j(y)$]. Suppose that $T_i$ now issues a $rl_i(y)$ or a $wl_i(y)$. Since $y$ is currently locked by transaction $T_j$, $T_i$ will have to wait until $T_j$ releases its write lock on $y$. However, if during this waiting period, $T_j$ now requests a lock (read or write) on $x$, there will be a deadlock. This is because, $T_i$ will be blocked waiting for $T_j$ to release its lock on $y$ while $T_j$ will be waiting for $T_i$ to release its lock on $x$. In this case, the two transactions $T_i$ and $T_j$ will wait indefinitely for each other to release their respective locks.

A deadlock is a permanent phenomenon. If one exists in a system, it will not go away unless outside intervention takes place. This outside interference may come from the user, the system operator, or the software system (the operating system or the distributed DBMS).

A useful tool in analyzing deadlocks is a *wait-for graph* (WFG). A WFG is a directed graph that represents the wait-for relationship among transactions. The nodes of this graph represent the concurrent transactions in the system. An arc $T_i \rightarrow T_j$ exists in the WFG if transaction $T_i$ is waiting for $T_j$ to release a lock on some entity. Figure 11.14 depicts the WFG for Example 11.9.

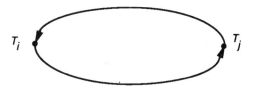

**Figure 11.14**   A WFG Example

Using the WFG, it is easier to indicate the condition for the occurrence of a deadlock. A deadlock occurs when the WFG contains a cycle. We should indicate that the formation of the WFG is more complicated in distributed systems, since two transactions that participate in a deadlock condition may be running at different sites. We call this situation a *global deadlock*. In distributed systems, then, it is not sufficient that each local distributed DBMS form a *local wait-for graph* (LWFG) at each site; it is also necessary to form a *global wait-for graph* (GWFG), which is the union of all the LWFGs.

**Example 11.10**

Consider four transactions $T_1, T_2, T_3$, and $T_4$ with the following wait-for relationship among them: $T_1 \rightarrow T_2 \rightarrow T_3 \rightarrow T_4 \rightarrow T_1$. If $T_1$ and $T_2$ run at site 1 while $T_3$ and $T_4$ run at site 2, the LWFGs for the two sites are shown in Figure 11.15a. Notice that it is not possible to detect a deadlock simply by examining the two LWFGs, because the deadlock is global. The deadlock can easily be detected, however, by examining the GWFG where intersite waiting is shown by dashed lines (Figure 11.15b).

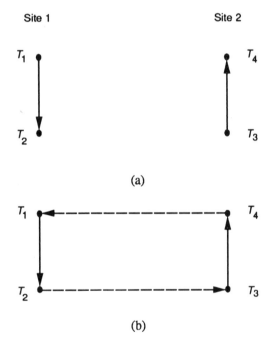

**Figure 11.15**    Difference between LWFG and GWFG

There are three known methods for handling deadlocks: prevention, avoidance, and detection and resolution.[4] In the remainder of this section we discuss each approach in more detail.

---

[4]Of course, there is a fourth alternative that the system ignore deadlocks and require either that the application programmer deal with it or that the system be restarted. However, we obviously do not consider this to be a serious alternative.

### 11.6.1 Deadlock Prevention

Deadlock prevention methods guarantee that deadlocks cannot occur in the first place. Thus the transaction manager checks a transaction when it is first initiated and does not permit it to proceed if it may cause a deadlock. To perform this check, it is required that all of the data items that will be accessed by a transaction be predeclared. The transaction manager then permits a transaction to proceed if all the data items that it will access are available. Otherwise, the transaction is not permitted to proceed. The transaction manager reserves all the data items that are predeclared by a transaction that it allows to proceed.

Unfortunately, such systems are not very suitable for database environments. The fundamental problem is that it is usually difficult to know precisely which data items will be accessed by a transaction. Access to certain data items may depend on conditions that may not be resolved until run time. For example, in the reservation transaction that we developed in Example 10.3, access to CID and CNAME is conditional upon the availability of free seats. To be safe, the system would thus need to consider the maximum set of data items, even if they end up not being accessed. This would certainly reduce concurrency. Furthermore, there is additional overhead in evaluating whether a transaction can proceed safely. On the other hand, such systems require no run-time support, which reduces the overhead. It has the additional advantage that it is not necessary to abort and restart a transaction due to deadlocks. This not only reduces the overhead but also makes such methods suitable for systems that have no provisions for undoing processes.[5]

### 11.6.2 Deadlock Avoidance

Deadlock avoidance schemes either employ concurrency control techniques that will never result in deadlocks or require that schedulers detect potential deadlock situations in advance and ensure that they will not occur. We consider both of these cases.

The simplest means of avoiding deadlocks is to order the resources and insist that each process request access to these resources in that order. This solution was long ago proposed for operating systems. A revised version has been proposed for database systems as well [Garcia-Molina, 1979]. Accordingly, the lock units in the distributed database are ordered and transactions always request locks in that order. This ordering of lock units may be done either globally or locally at each site. In the latter case, it is also necessary to order the sites and require that transactions which access data items at multiple sites request their locks by visiting the sites in the predefined order.

Another alternative is to make use of transaction timestamps to prioritize transactions and resolve deadlocks by aborting transactions with higher (or lower) priorities. To implement this type of prevention method, the lock manager is modified as follows. If a lock request of a transaction $T_i$ is denied, the lock manager does not

---

[5]This is not a significant advantage since most systems have to be able to undo transactions for reliability purposes, as we will see in Chapter 12.

automatically force $T_i$ to wait. Instead, it applies a prevention test to the requesting transaction and the transaction that currently holds the lock (say $T_j$). If the test is passed, $T_i$ is permitted to wait for $T_j$; otherwise, one transaction or the other is aborted.

A well-known algorithm that uses this approach is the WAIT-DIE and WOUND-WAIT algorithms [Rosenkrantz et al., 1978], also used in the MADMAN DBMS [GE, 1976]. These algorithms are based on the assignment of timestamps to transactions. WAIT-DIE is a nonpreemptive algorithm in that if the lock request of $T_i$ is denied because the lock is held by $T_j$, it never preempts $T_j$. The rule is as follows:

**WAIT-DIE Rule.** If $T_i$ requests a lock on a data item that is already locked by $T_j$, $T_i$ is permitted to wait if and only if $T_i$ is older than $T_j$. If $T_i$ is younger than $T_j$, then $T_i$ is aborted and restarted with the same timestamp.

A preemptive version of the same idea is the WOUND-WAIT algorithm, which can be stated as follows:

**WOUND-WAIT Rule.** If $T_i$ requests a lock on a data item that is already locked by $T_j$, then $T_i$ is permitted to wait if only if it is younger than $T_j$; otherwise, $T_j$ is aborted and the lock is granted to $T_i$.

The rules are specified from the viewpoint of $T_i$: $T_i$ waits, $T_i$ dies, and $T_i$ wounds $T_j$. In fact, the result of wounding and dying are the same: the affected transaction is aborted and restarted. With this perspective, the two rules can be specified as follows:

$$\textbf{if } ts(T_i) < ts(T_j) \textbf{ then } T_i \text{ waits } \textbf{else } T_i \text{ dies} \qquad \text{(WAIT-DIE)}$$
$$\textbf{if } ts(T_i) < ts(T_j) \textbf{ then } T_j \text{ is wounded } \textbf{else } T_i \text{ waits} \qquad \text{(WOUND-WAIT)}$$

Notice that in both algorithms the younger transaction is aborted. The difference between the two algorithms is whether or not they preempt active transactions. Also note that the WAIT-DIE algorithm prefers younger transactions and kills older ones. Thus an older transaction tends to wait longer and longer as it gets older. By contrast, the WOUND-WAIT rule prefers the older transaction since it never waits for a younger one. One of these methods, or a combination, may be selected in implementing a deadlock prevention algorithm.

Deadlock avoidance methods are more suitable than prevention schemes for database environments. Their fundamental drawback is that they require run-time support for deadlock management, which adds to the run-time overhead of transaction execution.

### 11.6.3  Deadlock Detection and Resolution

Detection and resolution is the most popular and best-studied deadlock management method. Detection is done by studying the GWFG for the formation of cycles. We will discuss means of doing this in considerable detail. Resolution of deadlocks is typically done by the selection of one or more *victim* transaction(s) that will be preempted and aborted in order to break the cycles in the GWFG. Under the assumption that the cost of preempting each member of a set of deadlocked transactions is known, the problem of selecting the minimum total-cost set for breaking the deadlock cycle has been shown to be a difficult (NP-complete) problem [Leung and Lai, 1979]. However, there are some factors that affect this choice [Bernstein et al., 1987]:

1. The amount of effort that has already been invested in the transaction. This effort will be lost if the transaction is aborted.

2. The cost of aborting the transaction. This cost generally depends on the number of updates that the transaction has already performed.

3. The amount of effort it will take to finish executing the transaction. The scheduler wants to avoid aborting a transaction that is almost finished. To do this, it must be able to predict the future behavior of active transactions (e.g., based on the transaction's type).

4. The number of cycles that contain the transaction. Since aborting a transaction breaks all cycles that contain it, it is best to abort transactions that are part of more than one cycle (if such transactions exist).

Now we can return to deadlock detection. We should first indicate that there are three fundamental methods of detecting distributed deadlocks. These are commonly called *centralized, distributed*, and *hierarchical deadlock detection*.

**Centralized deadlock detection.** In the centralized deadlock detection approach, one site is designated as the deadlock detector for the entire system. Periodically, each lock manager transmits its LWFG to the deadlock detector, which then forms the GWFG and looks for cycles in it. Actually, the lock managers need only send changes in their graphs (i.e., the newly created or deleted edges) to the deadlock detector. The length of intervals for transmitting this information is a system design decision: the smaller the interval, the smaller the delays due to undetected deadlocks, but the larger the communication cost.

Centralized deadlock detection has been proposed for distributed INGRES. This method is simple and would be a very natural choice if the concurrency control algorithm were centralized 2PL. However, the issues of vulnerability to failure, and high communication overhead, must also be considered.

**Hierarchical deadlock detection.** An alternative to centralized deadlock detection is the building of a hierarchy of deadlock detectors [Menasce and Muntz, 1979] (see Figure 11.16). Deadlocks that are local to a single site would be detected at that site using the local WFG. Each site also sends its local WFG to the deadlock detector at the next level. Thus, distributed deadlocks involving two or more sites would be detected by a deadlock detector in the next lowest level that has control over these sites. For example, a deadlock at site 1 would be detected by the local deadlock detector $(DD)$ at site 1 (denoted $DD_{21}$, 2 for level 2, 1 for site 1). If, however, the deadlock involves sites 1 and 2, then $DD_{11}$ detects it. Finally, if the deadlock involves sites 1 and 4, $DD_{0x}$ detects it, where $x$ is either one of 1, 2, 3, or 4.

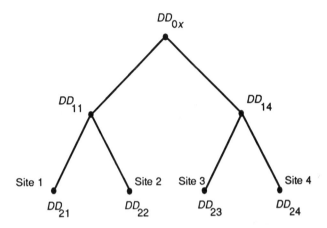

**Figure 11.16**    Hierarchical Deadlock Detection

The hierarchical deadlock detection method reduces the dependence on the central site, thus reducing the communication cost. It is, however, considerably more complicated to implement and would involve nontrivial modifications to the lock and transaction manager algorithms.

**Distributed deadlock detection.**    Distributed deadlock detection algorithms delegate the responsibility of detecting deadlocks to each site. Thus, as in the hierarchical deadlock detection, there are local deadlock detectors at each site which communicate their local WFGs with one another (in fact, only the potential deadlock cycles are transmitted). Among the various distributed deadlock detection algorithms, the one implemented in System R seems to be the more widely known and referenced. We therefore briefly outline that method. This discussion is based on [Obermarck, 1982]. A similar distributed deadlock management algorithm that is used in System R* is described in [Mohan et al., 1986].

The local WFG at each site is formed and is modified as follows:

1. Since each site receives the potential deadlock cycles from other sites, these edges are added to the local WFGs.
2. The edges in the local WFG which show that local transactions are waiting for transactions at other sites are joined with edges in the local WFGs which show that remote transactions are waiting for local ones.

**Example 11.11**

Consider the example depicted in Figure 11.15. The local WFG for the two sites are modified as shown in Figure 11.17.

**Figure 11.17**   Modified LWFGs

Local deadlock detectors look for two things. If there is a cycle that does not include the external edges, there is a local deadlock that can be handled locally. If, on the other hand, there is a cycle involving these external edges, there is a potential distributed deadlock and this cycle information has to be communicated to other deadlock detectors. In the case of Example 11.11, the possibility of such a distributed deadlock is detected by both sites.

A question that needs to be answered at this point is to whom to transmit the information. Obviously, it can be transmitted to all deadlock detectors in the system. In the absence of any more information, this is the only alternative, but it incurs a high overhead. If, however, one knows whether the transaction is ahead or behind in the deadlock cycle, the information can be transmitted forward or backward along the sites in this cycle. The receiving site then modifies its LWFG as discussed above, and checks for deadlocks. Obviously, there is no need to transmit along the deadlock cycle in both the forward and backward directions. In the case of Example 11.11, site 1 would send it to site 2 in both forward and backward transmission along the deadlock cycle.

The distributed deadlock detection algorithms require uniform modification to the lock managers at each site. This uniformity makes them easier to implement. However, there is the potential for excessive message transmission. This happens, for example, in the case of Example 11.11: site 1 sends its potential deadlock information to site 2, and site 2 sends its information to site 1. In this case the deadlock detectors at both sites will detect the deadlock. Besides causing unnecessary message transmission, there is the additional problem that each site may choose a different victim to abort. The algorithm proposed in [Obermarck, 1982] solves the problem by using transaction timestamps as well as the following rule. Let the path that has the potential of causing a distributed deadlock in the local WFG of a site be $T_i \rightarrow \cdots \rightarrow T_j$. A local deadlock detector forwards the cycle information only if $ts(T_i) < ts(T_j)$. This reduces the average number of message transmissions by one-half. In the case of Example 11.11, site 1 has a path $T_1 \rightarrow T_2 \rightarrow T_3$, whereas site 2 has a path $T_3 \rightarrow T_4 \rightarrow T_1$. Therefore, assuming that the subscripts of each transaction denote their timestamp, only site 1 will send information to site 2.

## 11.7 CONCLUSION

In this chapter we discussed distributed currency control algorithms that provide the isolation and consistency properties of transactions. The distributed concurrency control mechanism of a distributed DBMS ensures that the consistency of the distributed database is maintained and is therefore one of the fundamental components of a distributed DBMS. This is evidenced by the significant amount of research that has been conducted in this area. In Section 11.8 we point to some of the literature.

Our discussion in this chapter assumed that both the hardware and the software components of the computer systems were totally reliable. Even though this assumption is completely unrealistic, it has served a didactic purpose. It has permitted us to focus only on the concurrency control aspects, leaving to another chapter the features that need to be added to a distributed DBMS to make it reliable in an unreliable environment.

There are a few issues that we have omitted from this chapter. We mention them here for the benefit of the interested reader.

**1.** *Performance evaluation of concurrency control algorithms.* We have not explicitly included performance analysis results or methodologies. This may be somewhat surprising given the significant number of papers that have appeared in the literature. However, the reasons for this omission are numerous. First, there is no single comprehensive performance study of concurrency control algorithms. The performance studies have developed rather haphazardly and for specific purposes. Therefore, each has made different assumptions and has measured different parameters. It is quite difficult, if not impossible, to make meaningful generalizations that extend beyond the obvious. Second, the analytical methods for conducting these performance analysis studies have not been developed sufficiently. Some attempts have been made at developing this theoretical basis, and results of this work look promising.

**2.** *Different transaction models.* We have considered only the flat transaction model in this chapter. More recent studies on topics such as nested transactions or concurrency control in object-oriented systems have not been included as they are still in their infancy.

**3.** *Other concurrency control methods.* There is another class of concurrency control algorithms, called "serializability graph testing methods," which we have not mentioned in this chapter. Such mechanisms work by explicitly building a *dependency* (or *serializability*) *graph* and checking it for cycles. The dependency (serializability) graph of a schedule $S$, denoted $DG(S)$, is a directed graph representing the conflict relations among the transactions in $S$. The nodes of this graph are the set of transactions in $S$ [i.e., each transaction $T_i$ in $S$ is represented by a node in $DG(S)$]. An arc $(T_i, T_j)$ exists in $DG(S)$ if and only if there is an operation in $T_i$ that conflicts with and precedes another operation in $T_j$.

### Example 11.12

The dependency graph of schedule $S_1$ discussed in Example 11.6 is given in Figure 11.18.

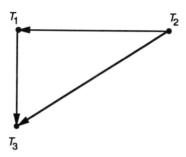

**Figure 11.18**   Dependency Graph

Schedulers update their dependency graphs whenever one of the following conditions is fulfilled: (1) a new transaction starts in the system, (2) a read or a write operation is received by the scheduler, (3) a transaction terminates, or (4) a transaction aborts.

It is now possible to talk about "correct" concurrency control algorithms based on the dependency graph. Given a schedule $S$, if its dependency graph $DG(S)$ is acyclic, then $S$ is serializable. In the distributed case we may use a global dependency graph, which can be formed by taking the union of the local dependency graphs and further annotating each transaction by the identifier of the site where it is executed. It is then necessary to show that the global dependency graph is acyclic.

**4.** *Assumptions about transactions.* It is known that concurrency control algorithms which produce serializable schedules are the best we can do if all that is known about transactions consists of the data items they access (i.e., syntactic knowledge). However, if we also know the semantics of the transaction, the level of concurrency can be increased significantly. There is some work on finding concurrency control algorithms that make use of semantic knowledge about transactions. These studies attempt to go beyond serializability theory as a correctness criterion and provide higher levels of concurrency. They are quite recent and have only dealt with centralized systems.

Similar to the above is the treatment of read-only transactions. It is possible to improve significantly the performance of transactions that read only data items, or of systems with a high ratio of read-only transactions to update transactions. We have not discussed these issues either since they have not yet been fully developed.

Finally, we have treated read and write locks in an identical fashion. It is possible to differentiate between them and develop concurrency control algorithms that permit "lock conversion," whereby transactions can obtain locks in one mode and then modify their lock modes as they change their requirements. Typically, the conversion is from read locks to write locks.

**5.** *More "general" algorithms.* There are some indications which suggest that it should be possible to study the two fundamental concurrency control primitives (i.e., locking and timestamp ordering) using a unifying framework. Three major indications are worth mentioning. First, it is possible to develop both pessimistic and optimistic algorithms based on either one of the primitives. Second, a strict TO algorithm performs similar to a locking algorithm since it delays the acceptance of a transaction until all older ones are terminated. This does not mean that all schedules which can be generated by a strict TO scheduler would be permitted by a 2PL scheduler. However, this similarity is interesting. Finally, it is possible to develop hybrid algorithms that use both timestamp ordering and locking. Furthermore, it is possible to state precisely rules for their interaction.

One study ([Farrag, 1986], [Farrag and Özsu, 1985] and [Farrag and Özsu, 1987]) that has resulted in the development of a theoretical framework for the uniform treatment of both of these primitives. Based on this theoretical foundation, it was shown that 2PL and TO algorithms are two endpoints of a range of algorithms that can be generated by a more general concurrency control algorithm. This study, which is only for centralized database systems, is significant not only because it indicates that locking and timestamp ordering are related, but also because it would be interesting to study the nature and characteristics of the algorithms that lie between these two endpoints. In addition, such a uniform framework may be helpful in conducting comprehensive and internally consistent performance studies.

**6.** *Transaction execution models.* The algorithms that we have described all assume a computational model where the transaction manager at the originating site of a transaction coordinates the execution of each database operation of that transaction. This is called *centralized execution* [Carey and Livny, 1988]. It is also possible to consider a *distributed execution* model where a transaction is decomposed into a set of subtransactions each of which is allocated to one site where the transaction manager coordinates its execution. This is intuitively more attractive because it may permit load balancing across the multiple sites of a distributed database. However, the performance studies indicate that distributed computation performs better only under light load.

## 11.8 BIBLIOGRAPHIC NOTES

As indicated earlier, distributed concurrency control has been a very popular area of study. [Bernstein and Goodman, 1981] is a comprehensive study of the fundamental primitives which also lays down the rules for building hybrid algorithms. A survey of algorithms that have been proposed until the end of 1980 is included in [Hsiao and Özsu, 1981]. The issues that are addressed in this chapter are discussed in much more detail in [Cellary et al., 1988], [Bernstein et al., 1987], and [Papadimitriou, 1986].

Nested transaction models and their specific concurrency control algorithms have been subjects of some study. Specific results can be found in [Moss, 1985], [Lynch, 1983a], [Lynch and Merritt, 1986], [Fekete et al., 1987a], [Fekete et al., 1987b], [Goldman, 1987], [Beeri et al., 1989], and more recently in [Fekete et al., 1989].

Concurrency control techniques on different database models have also been studied. Specifically, transaction management on more complex database structures involving abstract data types and other object models has been described in [Weihl,

1988], [Weihl and Liskov, 1985], [Weihl, 1989], [Allchin and McKendry, 1983], [Badrinath and Ramamritham, 1988], [Roesler and Burkhard, 1988], and [Aspnes et al., 1988]. Serializability graph testing algorithms are discussed in [Schlageter, 1978], [Badal, 1979], and in [Hadzilacos and Yannakakis, 1986].

The work on transaction management with semantic knowledge is presented in [Lynch, 1983b], [Garcia-Molina, 1983], and [Farrag and Özsu, 1989]. The processing of read-only transactions is discussed in [Garcia-Molina and Wiederhold, 1982]. Concurrency control methods for complex objects referred to above also make use of semantic information. Furthermore, work on the Aries system ([Mohan et al., 1989], [Rothermel and Mohan, 1989]) is also within this class of algorithms. An algorithm based on ordering transactions using "serialization numbers" is discussed in [Halici and Dogac, 1989].

There are a number of papers that discuss results of performance evaluation studies on distributed concurrency control algorithms. These include [Gelenbe and Sevcik, 1978], [Garcia-Molina, 1979], [Potier and LeBlanc, 1980], [Menasce and Nakanishi, 1982a], [Menasce and Nakanishi, 1982b], [Lin, 1981], [Lin and Nolte, 1982], [Lin and Nolte, 1983], [Goodman et al., 1983], [Sevcik, 1983], [Carey and Stonebraker, 1984], [Merrett and Rallis, 1985], [Özsu, 1985a], [Özsu, 1985b], [Koon and Özsu, 1986], [Tsuchiya et al., 1986], [Li, 1987], [Agrawal et al., 1987], [Bhide, 1988], and [Carey and Livny, 1988].

An early but comprehensive review of deadlock management is [Isloor and Marsland, 1980]. Most of the work on distributed deadlock management has been on detection and resolution (see, e.g., [Obermarck, 1982] and [Elmagarmid et al., 1988]). Two surveys of the important algorithms are included in [Elmagarmid, 1986] and [Knapp, 1987]. There are two annotated bibliographies on the deadlock problem, which do not emphasize the database issues but consider the problem in general: [Newton, 1979] and [Zobel, 1983].

## 11.9 EXERCISES

**11.1** Which of the following schedules are conflict equivalent?

$$S_1 = W_2(x), W_1(x), R_3(x), R_1(x), W_2(y), R_3(y), R_3(z), R_2(x)$$
$$S_2 = R_3(z), R_3(y), W_2(y), R_2(z), W_1(x), R_3(x), W_2(x), R_1(x)$$
$$S_3 = R_3(z), W_2(x), W_2(y), R_1(x), R_3(x), R_2(z), R_3(y), W_1(x)$$
$$S_4 = R_2(z), W_2(x), W_2(y), W_1(x), R_1(x), R_3(x), R_3(z), R_3(y)$$

**\*\*11.2** The distributed 2PL algorithm requires that all transaction managers and lock managers follow the ROWA rule. Assuming unit communication cost between any pair of sites, show (as a graph) the behavior of the total communication cost as a function of the transaction mix (percentage of read-only queries versus the percentage of updates) and the number of sites involved. Assume full replication of data. (Hint: Just show the trend, do not try to derive actual values.)

**\*11.3** Give the algorithms for the transaction managers and the lock managers for the distributed two-phase locking approach.

**\*\*11.4**  Modify the centralized 2PL algorithm to handle phantoms. (See Chapter 10 for a definition of phantoms.)

**11.5**  Timestamp ordering-based concurrency control algorithms depend on either an accurate clock at each site or a global clock that all sites can access (the clock can be a counter). Assume that each site has its own clock which "ticks" every 0.1 second. If all local clocks are resynchronized every 24 hours, what is the maximum drift in seconds per 24 hours permissible at any local site to ensure that a timestamp-based mechanism will successfully synchronize transactions?

**\*\*11.6**  Incorporate the distributed deadlock strategy described in this chapter into the distributed 2PL algorithms that you designed in Exercise 11.3.

**11.7**  Explain the relationship between transaction manager storage requirement and transaction size (number of operations per transaction) for a transaction manager using an optimistic timestamp ordering for concurrency control.

**\*11.8**  Give the scheduler and transaction manager algorithms for the distributed optimistic concurrency controller described in this chapter.

**11.9**  Recall from the discussion in Section 11.7 that the computational model that is used in our descriptions in this chapter is a centralized one. How would the distributed 2PL transaction manager and lock manager algorithms change if a distributed execution model were to be used?

**11.10**  It is sometimes claimed that serializability is quite a restrictive correctness criterion. Can you give examples of distributed schedules that are correct (i.e., maintain the consistency of the local databases as well as their mutual consistency) but are not serializable?

# 12

# Distributed DBMS Reliability

We have referred to "reliability" and "availability" of the database a number of times so far without defining these terms precisely. Specifically, we mentioned these terms in conjunction with data replication. It should come as no surprise to the reader that the distribution of the database or the replication of data items is not sufficient to make the distributed DBMS reliable. A number of protocols need to be implemented within the DBMS to exploit this distribution and replication in order to make operations more reliable.

A reliable distributed database management system is one that can continue to process user requests even when the underlying system is unreliable. In other words, even when components of the distributed computing environment fail, a reliable distributed DBMS should be able to continue executing user requests without violating database consistency.

The purpose of this chapter is to discuss the reliability features of a distributed DBMS. From Chapter 10 the reader will recall that the reliability of a distributed DBMS refers to the atomicity and durability properties of transactions. Two specific aspects of reliability protocols that need to be discussed in relation to these properties are the commit the recovery protocols. In that sense, in this chapter we relax the major assumption of Chapter 11 that the underlying distributed system is fully reliable and does not experience any hardware or software failures. Furthermore, the commit protocols discussed in this chapter constitute the support provided by the distributed DBMS for the execution of commit commands which we have placed in transactions.

It is possible to discuss database reliability in isolation. However, the distributed DBMS is only one component of a distributed computing system. Its reliability is strongly dependent on the reliability of the hardware and software components that make up the distributed environment. Therefore, our discussion in this chapter starts with a general presentation of the reliability issues in distributed computing systems, and then focuses on the reliability aspects of distributed databases.

The organization of this chapter is as follows. As mentioned above, we start with a definition of the fundamental reliability concepts and reliability measures. In Section 12.2 we discuss the reasons for failures in distributed systems as well as an overview of some of the fundamental techniques that are used in designing reliable distributed computing systems. In Section 12.3 we extend the discussion of Section 12.2 to the types of failures in distributed DBMSs. Section 12.4 focuses on the functions of the local recovery manager and provides an overview of reliability measures in centralized DBMS. This discussion forms the foundation for the distributed commit and recovery protocols, which are introduced in Section 12.5. In Sections 12.6 and 12.7 we present detailed protocols for dealing with site failures and network partitioning, respectively. Implementation of these protocols within our architectural model is the topic of Section 12.8.

## 12.1 RELIABILITY CONCEPTS AND MEASURES

Too often, the terms *reliability* and *availability* are used loosely in literature. Even among the researchers in the area of reliable computer systems, there is no consensus on the definitions of these terms. In this section we give precise definitions of a number of concepts that are fundamental to an understanding and study of reliable systems. Our definitions follow those of [Anderson and Lee, 1985] and [Randell et al., 1978]. Nevertheless, we indicate where these definitions might differ from other usage of the terms.

### 12.1.1 System, State, and Failure

In the context of reliability, *system* refers to a mechanism that consists of a collection of components and interacts with its environment by responding to stimuli from the environment with a recognizable pattern of behavior (Figure 12.1). Each component of a system is itself a system, commonly called a *subsystem*. The environment of a component is the system of which it is a part. The way the components of a system are put together is called the *design* of the system. For example, Figure 4.7 depicts a distributed DBMS with all its components and the design of the DBMS, which indicates the interactions between these components. Note in Figure 4.7 that we have depicted only the software components. The only hardware component that is shown is the disk drive. It is, however, possible and even necessary to define the hardware components if one has to reason about the reliability of the entire DBMS.

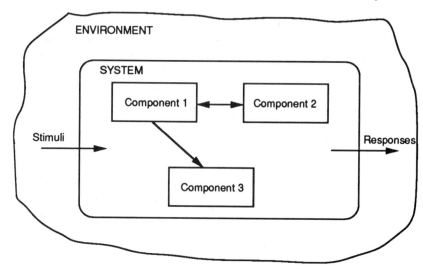

**Figure 12.1**   Schematic of a System

There are a number of ways of modeling the interaction between the software and the hardware in a computer system. One possible modeling method is to treat the program text as the design of an abstract system whose components are the hardware and software objects that are manipulated during the execution of the program. Figure 12.2 depicts this type of interaction. Another modeling alternative is to specify each software and hardware component explicitly, and let the design represent the way these components interact with one another (similar to Figure 4.7).

An *external state* of a system can be defined as the response that a system gives to an external stimulus. It is therefore possible to talk about a system changing external states according to repeated stimuli from the environment. We can define the *internal state* of the system similarly. It is convenient to define the internal state as the union of the external states of the components that make up the system. Again, the system changes its internal state in response to stimuli from the environment.

The behavior of the system in providing response to all the possible stimuli from the environment needs to be laid out in an authoritative *specification* of its behavior. The specification indicates the valid behavior of each system state. Such a specification is not only necessary for a successful system design but is also essential to define the following reliability concepts.

Any deviation of a system from the behavior described in the specification is considered a *failure*. For example, in a distributed transaction manager the specification would state that only serializable schedules for the execution of concurrent transactions should be generated. If the transaction manager generates a nonserializable schedule, we say that it has failed.

Each failure obviously needs to be traced back to its cause. Failures in a system can be attributed to deficiencies either in the components that make it up, or in the

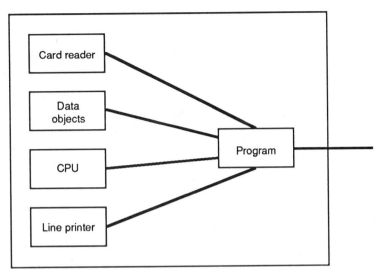

**Figure 12.2**   Reliability Modeling of the Interaction Between Software and Hardware Components of a Computer System (From: T. Anderson and P.A. Lee, FAULT TOLERANCE-PRINCIPLES AND PRACTICE, ©1981. Reprinted by permission of Prentice Hall, Inc., Englewood Cliffs, NJ.)

design, that is, how these components are put together. Each state a reliable system goes through is valid in the sense that the state fully meets its specification. However, in an unreliable system, it is possible that the system may get to an internal state that may not obey its specification. Further transitions from this state would eventually cause a system failure. Such internal states are called *erroneous states*; the part of the state that is incorrect is called an *error* in the system. Any error in the internal states of the components of a system or in the design of a system is called a *fault* in the system. Thus a fault causes an error that results in a system failure (Figure 12.3).

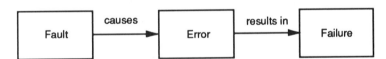

**Figure 12.3**   Chain of Events Leading to System Failure

We differentiate between errors (or faults and failures) that are permanent and those that are not permanent. Permanence can apply to a failure, a fault, or an error, although we typically use the term with respect to faults. A *permanent fault*, also commonly called a *hard fault*, is one that reflects an irreversible change in the behavior of the system. Permanent faults cause permanent errors that result in permanent failures. The characteristics of these failures is that recovery from them requires intervention to "repair" the fault. Systems also experience *intermittent* and *transient faults*.

In the literature, these two are typically not differentiated; they are jointly called *soft faults*. The dividing line in this differentiation is the repairability of the system that has experienced the fault [Siewiorek and Swarz, 1982]. An intermittent fault refers to a fault that demonstrates itself occasionally due to unstable hardware or varying hardware or software states. A typical example is the faults that systems may demonstrate when the load becomes too heavy. On the other hand, a transient fault describes a fault that results from temporary environmental conditions. A transient fault might occur, for example, due to a sudden increase in the room temperature. The transient fault is therefore the result of environmental conditions that may be impossible to repair. An intermittent fault, on the other hand, can be repaired since the fault can be traced to a component of the system.

Remember that we have also indicated that system failures can be due to design faults. Design faults together with unstable hardware cause intermittent errors which result in system failure. A final source of system failure that may not be attributable to a component fault or a design fault is operator mistakes. These are the sources of a significant number of errors as the statistics included further in this section demonstrate. The relationship between various types of faults and failures is depicted in Figure 12.4.

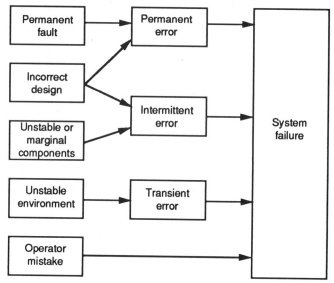

**Figure 12.4**  Sources of System Failure (Reprinted with permission from THE THEORY AND PRACTICE OF RELIABLE SYSTEM DESIGN, by Daniel P. Siewiorek and Robert S. Swarz, copyright ©Digital Press/Digital Equipment Corporation;, 12 Crosby Drive, Bedform, MA 01730.)

As indicated previously, there are a number of different definitions of the fundamental reliability terms that we discussed. For example, the terms *fault* and *failure* are used interchangeably in the fault tolerance literature, whereas the terms *failure* and *error* are used interchangeably in the coding theory literature [Elkind, 1982]. Alternatively, a *fault* may be defined as "an erroneous state of hardware or software resulting from failures of components" and an *error* as "a manifestation of a fault within a program or data structure." *Failure* is defined as a "physical change in hardware" [Avizienis, 1977]. These definitions are specific to hardware systems and represent a rather different view as to what causes what. According to these definitions, a failure causes a fault that results in an error.

### 12.1.2  Reliability and Availability

*Reliability* refers to the probability that the system under consideration does not experience any failures in a given time interval. It is typically used to describe systems that cannot be repaired (as in space-based computers), or where the operation of the system is so critical that no downtime for repair can be tolerated.

Formally, the reliability of a system, $R(t)$, is defined as the following conditional probability:

$$R(t) = \Pr\{0 \text{ failures in time } [0,t] \,|\, \text{no failures at } t = 0\}$$

Reliability theory, as it applies to hardware systems, has been developed significantly. Let us therefore illustrate the foregoing formula for hardware components, for which it is customary to assume that failures follow a Poisson distribution. In this case

$$R(t) = \Pr\{0 \text{ failures in time } [0,t]\}$$

Under the same assumptions it is possible to derive that

$$\Pr\{k \text{ failures in time } [0,\ t]\} = \frac{e^{-m(t)}[m(t)]^k}{k!}$$

where $m(t) = \int_0^t z(x)\,dx$. Here $z(t)$ is known as the *hazard function*, which gives the time-dependent failure rate of the specific hardware component under consideration. The probability distribution for $z(t)$ may be different for different electronic components.

The expected (mean) number of failures in time $[0, t]$ can then be computed as

$$E[k] = \sum_{k=0}^{\infty} k \, \frac{e^{-m(t)}[m(t)]^k}{k!} = m(t)$$

and the variance as

$$Var[k] = E[k^2] - (E[k])^2 = m(t)$$

Given these values, $R(t)$ can be written as

$$R(t) = e^{-m(t)}$$

Note that the reliability equation above is written for one component of the system. For a system that consists of $n$ nonredundant components (i.e., they all have to function properly for the system to work) whose failures are independent, the overall system reliability can be written as

$$R_{sys}(t) = \Pi_{i=1}^n R_i(t)$$

*Availability*, $A(t)$, refers to the probability that the system is operational according to its specification at a given point in time $t$. A number of failures may have occurred prior to time $t$, but if they have all been repaired, the system is available at time $t$. It is apparent that availability refers to systems that can be repaired.

If one looks at the limit of availability as time goes to infinity, it refers to the expected percentage of time that the system under consideration is available to perform useful computations. Availability can be used as some measure of "goodness" for those systems that can be repaired and which can be out of service for short periods of time during repair. Reliability and availability of a system are considered to be contradictory objectives [Siewiorek and Swarz, 1982]. It is usually accepted that it is easier to develop highly available systems as opposed to highly reliable systems.

If we assume that failures follow a Poisson distribution with a failure rate $\lambda$, and that repair time is exponential with a mean repair time of $1/\mu$, the steady-state availability of a system can be written as

$$A = \frac{\mu}{\lambda + \mu}$$

### 12.1.3  Mean Time between Failures/Mean Time to Repair

Calculation of the reliability and the availability functions is quite tedious. It is therefore customary to use two single-parameter metrics to model the behavior of systems. The two measures used are *mean time between failures* (MTBF) and *mean time to repair* (MTTR). MTBF is the expected time between subsequent failures in a system with repair.[1] MTBF can be calculated either from empirical data or from the reliability function as

$$\text{MTBF} = \int_0^\infty R(t)\, dt$$

Since $R(t)$ is related to the system failure rate, there is a direct relationship between MTBF and the failure rate of a system. MTTR is the expected time to repair a failed system. It is related to the repair rate as MTBF is related to the failure rate. Using these two metrics, the steady-state availability of a system with exponential failure and repair rates can be specified as

$$A = \frac{\text{MTBF}}{\text{MTBF} + \text{MTTR}}$$

---

[1]A distinction is sometimes made between MTBF and MTTF (mean time to fail). MTTF is defined as the expected time of the first system failure given a successful startup at time 0. MTBF is then defined only for systems that can be repaired. An approximation for MTBF is given as MTBF = MTTF + MTTR [McConnel and Siewiorek, 1982]. We do not make this distinction in this book.

## 12.2  FAILURES AND FAULT TOLERANCE IN DISTRIBUTED SYSTEMS

In this section we consider the reasons for failures in distributed systems as well as the basic fault-tolerance techniques that are used to cope with them. This discussion is based on empirical statistics and is not meant to be complete and exhaustive. It is aimed only at providing a general framework for the distributed database reliability issues.

### 12.2.1  Reasons for Failures

Let us first take a look at soft and hard failures. Soft failures make up more than 90% of all hardware system failures. It is interesting to note that this percentage has not changed significantly since the early days of computing. A 1967 study of the U.S. Air Force indicates that 80% of electronic failures in computers are intermittent [Roth et al., 1967]. A study performed by IBM during the same year concludes that over 90% of all failures are intermittent [Ball and Hardie, 1967]. More recent studies indicate that the occurrence of soft failures is significantly higher than that of hard failures ([Longbottom, 1980] and [Gray, 1987]). Gray [1987] also mentions that most of the software failures are transient—and therefore soft—suggesting that a dump and restart may be sufficient to recover without any need to "repair" the software.

Another way of looking at the causes of errors is to investigate various computer system error statistics. A study of the reliability of the IBM/XA operating system indicates that 57% of all system failures are due to hardware, 12% to software, 14% to operations, and 17% to environmental conditions [Mourad and Andres, 1985] (Figure 12.5a). This study was conducted at the Stanford linear accelerator (SLAC). Another study of Tandem computers [Gray, 1985] based on early warning reports indicates that hardware failures make up 18% of the failures, software is responsible for 25%, maintenance for 25%, operations for 17%, and environment for 14% (Figure 12.5b). Finally, a performance study of the AT&T 5ESS digital switch indicates that as a percentage of total system failures, hardware accounts for 32.3% of failures, software for 44.3%, and operations for 17.5% (Figure 12.5c). The causes of the remaining 5.9% of failures were unknown [Yeager, 1987]. Unfortunately, the environmental causes for failures that cannot be attributable specifically to the 5ESS switch are not included in these figures, so they are not directly comparable to the previous two.

When one investigates hardware causes of failures in more detail, the Tandem data suggest that about 49% of hardware failures are disk failures, 23% are due to communication, 17% to processor failure, 9% to wiring, and 1% to the failure of spares. The latter category is unique to fault tolerant or nonstop computer systems such as Tandem since they use spare modules to achieve fault tolerance. In the case of the 5ESS switch, 32.5% of the hardware failures are due to disk failures, 9.3% are due to electromagnetic interference due to insufficient isolation of wires, and the remaining 58.2% are due to defective components, circuit packs, or cables.

Software failures are more difficult to discuss because there is no agreement on a classification scheme. The Tandem data again suggests that software failures due to

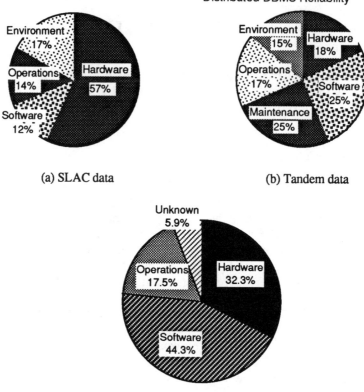

(a) SLAC data                        (b) Tandem data

(c) 5ESS switch data

**Figure 12.5**    Reasons for Computer System Failures

communication and database are by far the dominant causes. These are followed by operating system failures, which are then followed by failures in the application code and in the transaction management software.

Software failures are typically caused by "bugs" in the code. The estimates for the number of bugs in software vary considerably. Figures such as 0.25 bug per 1000 instructions to 10 bugs per 1000 instructions have been reported. As stated before, most of the software failures are soft failures. The statistics for software failure are comparable to those we have previously reported on hardware failures. The fundamental reason for the dominance of soft failures in software is the significant amount of design review and code inspection that a typical software project goes through before it gets to the testing stage. Furthermore, most commercial software goes through extensive alpha and beta testing before being released for field use.

An interesting classification for software bugs which derives from physics can also be provided [Gray, 1985]. The classification divides software bugs into Heisenbugs and Bohrbugs. Bohrbugs cause hard faults; they are solid like a Bohr atom and will continue to cause faults at retry. Heisenbugs, on the other hand, behave according to the Heisenberg uncertainty principle in physics, which states that it is not possible to measure both the position and the velocity of an electron accurately and simultaneously. The measurement procedure for one of these will cause a change in the other one. The implication of this principle for software bugs is that the testing process to find a bug may cause sufficient perturbation for the bug to disappear. Thus Heisenbugs cause soft faults and are more challenging to detect. They are sensitive to time of execution, system load, and other similar factors and the system may work on retry.

## 12.2.2 Basic Fault Tolerance Approaches and Techniques

The two fundamental approaches to constructing a reliable system are fault tolerance and fault prevention. *Fault tolerance* refers to a system design approach which recognizes that faults will occur; it tries to build mechanisms into the system so that the faults can be detected and removed or compensated for before they can result in a system failure. *Fault prevention* techniques, on the other hand, aim at ensuring that the implemented system will not contain any faults. Fault prevention has two aspects. The first is *fault avoidance*, which refers to the techniques used to make sure that faults are not introduced into the system. These techniques involve detailed design methodologies (such as design walkthroughs, design inspections, etc.) and quality control. The second aspect of fault prevention is *fault removal*, which refers to the techniques that are employed to detect any faults that might have remained in the system despite the application of fault avoidance and removes these faults. Typical techniques that are used in this area are extensive testing and validation procedures. Note that these fault removal techniques apply during system implementation prior to field use of the system.

The terms *fault prevention* and *fault avoidance* are used interchangably. Another common name for these approaches is *fault intolerance* [Avizienis, 1976] since they cannot withstand faults that show up during system use. These techniques concentrate on designing systems using high-reliability components and refinement of the packaging techniques followed by extensive testing. Such measures are expected to reduce the occurrence of system failures to a minimum so that the features may then be handled by manual maintenance. Unfortunately, there are a number of environments where manual maintenance and repair is impossible, or the downtime needed for repair would be intolerable. In those environments fault tolerant system designs are the preferred alternative.

It is possible to talk about a third approach to constructing reliable systems. This is *fault detection* [Myers, 1976]. Specification of fault detection as a separate approach may be challenged since detection has to be included in any fault tolerance technique. However, if fault detection techniques are not coupled with fault tolerance features, they issue a warning when a failure occurs but do not provide any means of tolerating the failure. Therefore, it might be appropriate to separate fault detection from strictly fault tolerant approaches.

It is important to note at this point that system failures may be *latent*. A latent failure is one that is detected some time after its occurrence. This period is called *error latency*, and the average error latency time over a number of identical systems is called *mean time to detect* (MTTD). Figure 12.6 depicts the relationship of various reliability measures with the actual occurrences of faults.

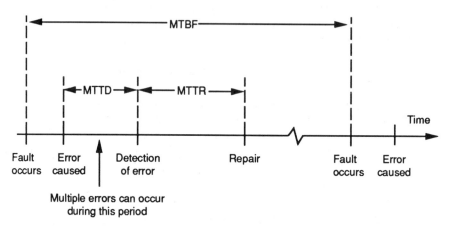

**Figure 12.6**   Occurrence of Events over Time

The fundamental principle employed in all fault tolerant system designs is that of providing *redundancy* in system components. Redundant components enable the effects of a faulty component to be compensated for. However, redundancy is not sufficient for fault tolerance. The additional and complementary fault tolerance principle is the *modularization* of the design. Each component of the system is implemented as a module with well-defined input and output interfaces with the other components. Modularization enables the isolation of faults within one component. It is therefore an important technique in both hardware and software systems.

These two concepts are utilized in typical systems by means of *fail-stop modules* and *process pairs*. A fail-stop module constantly monitors itself, and when it detects a fault, shuts itself down automatically [Schlichting and Schneider, 1983]. Another name given to such modules is *fail-fast* [Gray, 1985]. The implementation of fail-stop modules in hardware is beyond the scope of our discussion, but in software they can be implemented by defensive programming, where each software module checks its own state during state transitions. A further advantage of fail-stop software modules is a reduction in detection latency [Cristian, 1982].

Process pairs provide fault tolerance by duplicating software modules. The idea is to eliminate single points of failure by implementing each system service as two processes that communicate and cooperate in providing the service. One of these processes is called the *primary* and the other the *backup*. Both the primary and the backup are typically implemented as fail-stop modules that cooperate in providing a service. There are a number of different ways of implementing process pairs, depending on the mode of communication between the primary and the backup. The five common types are *lock-step*, *automatic checkpointing*, *state checkpointing*, *delta checkpointing*, and *persistent* process pairs. A detailed discussion of these alternative implementations is beyond the scope of this chapter. However, a review of them appears in [Gray, 1985]. Additional references are provided at the end of this chapter in Section 12.10.

Process pairs require communication between processes. An argument may be made for uniprocessor systems that for the sake of improved performance, the communication between processes may be implemented by means of shared memory. However, when designing a reliable software environment, it is important to implement an operating system that uses a message-based interprocess communication mechanism. Such an approach contributes to fault isolation since each process executes in its own address space, and an error that one of them might cause will not propagate to the other processes. We discuss interprocess communication mechanisms in more detail in Chapter 13.

Another important related concept is session-oriented communication between processes. Session-oriented communication delegates the responsibility of detecting and handling lost or duplicate messages to the message server of the operating system rather than to the application program. This not only facilitates a simpler application development environment but also enables the operating system to provide a reliable execution environment to application processes.

## 12.3  FAILURES IN DISTRIBUTED DBMS

Designing a reliable system that can recover from failures requires identifying the types of failures with which the system has to deal. In Section 12.2 we reviewed the major reasons for failures in distributed computer systems. That discussion, together with the termination conditions of transactions, covered in Chapter 10, indicates that a database recovery manager has to deal with four types of failures: transaction failures (aborts), site (system) failures, media (disk) failures, and communication line failures.

### 12.3.1  Transaction Failures

Transactions can fail for a number of reasons. Failure can be due to an error in the transaction caused by incorrect input data (e.g., Example 10.3) as well as the detection of a present or potential deadlock. Furthermore, some concurrency control algorithms do not permit a transaction to proceed or even to wait if the data that they attempt to access are currently being accessed by another transaction. This might also be considered a failure. The usual approach to take in cases of transaction failure is to *abort* the transaction, thus resetting the database to its state prior to the start of this transaction.

The frequency of transaction failures is not easy to measure. It is indicated that in System R, 3% of the transactions abort abnormally [Gray et al., 1981]. In general, it can be stated that (1) within a single application, the ratio of transactions that abort themselves is rather constant, being a function of the incorrect data, the available semantic data control features, and so on; and (2) the number of transaction aborts by the DBMS due to concurrency control considerations (mainly deadlocks) is dependent on the level of concurrency (i.e., number of concurrent transactions), the interference of the concurrent applications, the granularity of locks, and so on [Härder and Reuter, 1983].

### 12.3.2 Site (System) Failures

The reasons for system failure constituted the bulk of our discussion in Section 12.2. In short, it can be traced back to a hardware failure (processor, main memory, power supply, etc.) or to a software failure (bug in the operating system or in the DBMS code). The important point from the perspective of this discussion is that a system failure is always assumed to result in the loss of main memory contents. Therefore, any part of the database that was in main memory buffers is lost as a result of a system failure. However, the database that is stored in secondary storage is assumed to be safe and correct. In distributed database terminology, system failures are typically referred to as *site failures*, since they result in the failed site being unreachable from other sites in the distributed system.

We typically differentiate between partial and total failures in a distributed system. *Total failure* refers to the simultaneous failure of all sites in the distributed system; *partial failure* indicates the failure of only some sites while the others remain operational. As indicated in Chapter 1, it is this aspect of distributed systems that makes them more available.

### 12.3.3 Media Failures

*Media failures* refers to the failures of the secondary storage devices that store the database. Such failures may be due to operating system errors, as well as to hardware faults such as head crashes or controller failures. The important point from the perspective of DBMS reliability is that all or part of the database that is on the secondary storage is considered to be destroyed and inaccessible.

Duplexing of disk storage and maintaining archival copies of the database are common techniques that deal with this sort of catastrophic problem. Even though the data of Section 12.2 suggest that disk failures are quite common, the techniques described above enable us to assume that media failures do not have an impact more often than once or twice a year [Härder and Reuter, 1983].

Media failures are frequently treated as problems local to one site and therefore not specifically addressed in the reliability mechanisms of distributed DBMSs. We consider techniques for dealing with them in Section 12.4.5 under local recovery management. We then turn our attention to site failures when we consider distributed recovery functions.

### 12.3.4 Communication Failures

The three types of failures described above are common to both centralized and distributed DBMSs. Communication failures, however, are unique to the distributed case. There are a number of types of communication failures. The most common ones are the errors in the messages, improperly ordered messages, lost (or undeliverable) messages, and line failures. As discussed in Chapter 3, the first two errors are the responsibility of the computer network (specifically, the communication subnet, which consists of the physical, data link, and network layers of the ISO/OSI architectural model); we will not consider them further. Therefore, in our discussions of distributed DBMS reliability, we expect the underlying computer network hardware and software to ensure that two messages sent from a process at some originating site to another process at some destination site are delivered without error and in the order in which they were sent.

Lost or undeliverable messages are typically the consequence of communication line failures or (destination) site failures. If a communication line fails, in addition to losing the message(s) in transit, it may also divide the network into two or more disjoint groups. This is called *network partitioning*. If the network is partitioned, the sites in each partition may continue to operate. In this case, executing transactions that access data stored in multiple partitions becomes a major issue. Maintaining the mutual consistency of the database is a significant problem, especially if the database is replicated across these partitions.

Network partitions point to a unique aspect of failures in distributed computer systems. In centralized systems the system state can be characterized as all-or-nothing: either the system is operational or it is not. Thus the failures are complete: when one occurs, the entire system becomes nonoperational. Obviously, this is not true in distributed systems. As we indicated a number of times before, this is their potential strength. However, it also makes the transaction management algorithms more difficult to design.

If messages cannot be delivered, we will assume that the network does nothing about it. It will not buffer it for delivery to the destination when the service is reestablished and will not inform the sender process that the message cannot be delivered. In short, the message will simply be lost. We make this assumption because it represents the least expectation from the network and places the responsibility of dealing with these failures to the distributed DBMS. In Chapter 13 we address the issues that need to be considered to place this responsibility on the communication system.

One result of this assumption is that the responsibility of detecting that a message is undeliverable is left to the application program (in this case the distributed DBMS). The detection will be facilitated by the use of timers and a timeout mechanism that keeps track of how long it has been since the sender site has not received a confirmation from the destination site about the receipt of a message. This timeout interval needs to be set to a value greater than that of the maximum round-trip propagation delay of a message in the network. The term for the failure of the communication network to deliver messages and the confirmations within this period is *performance failure*. It needs to be handled within the reliability protocols for distributed DBMSs.

## 12.4  LOCAL RELIABILITY PROTOCOLS

In this section we discuss the functions performed by the local recovery manager (LRM) that exists at each site. These functions maintain the atomicity and durability properties of local transactions. They relate to the execution of the commands that are passed to the LRM, which are **begin_transaction, read, write, commit,** and **abort**. Later in this section we introduce a new command into the LRM's repertoire that initiates recovery actions after a failure. Note that in this section we discuss the execution of these commands in a centralized environment. The complications introduced in distributed databases are addressed in the upcoming sections.

### 12.4.1 Architectural Considerations

It is again time to use our architectural model (Figures 4.7 and 10.4) and discuss the specific interface between the LRM and the database buffer manager (BM). Remember that all acc sses to the database are via the database buffer manager. The detailed discussion of the algorithms that the buffer manager implements is deferred to Chapter 13. However, we can still specify the interface and its function, as depicted in Figure 12.7.[2]

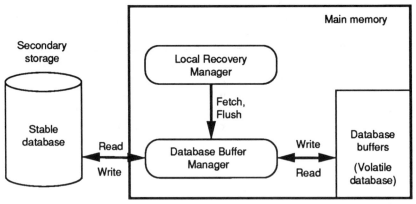

**Figure 12.7**   Interface Between the Local Recovery Manager and the Buffer Manager

In this discussion we assume that the database is stored permanently on secondary storage, which in this context is called the *stable storage* [Lampson and Sturgis, 1976]. The stability of this storage medium is due to its robustness to failures. A stable storage device would experience considerably less-frequent failures than would a nonstable storage device. In today's technology, stable storage is typically implemented by means of duplexed magnetic disks which store duplicate copies of data that are always kept mutually consistent. We call the version of the database that is kept on stable storage the *stable database*. The unit of storage and access of the stable database is typically a *page*.

The database buffer manager keeps some of the recently accessed data in main memory buffers. This is done to enhance access performance. Typically, the buffer is divided into pages that are of the same size as the stable database pages. The part of

---

[2]This architectural model is similar to that given in [Härder and Reuter, 1983] and [Bernstein et al., 1987].

the database that is in the database buffer is called the *volatile database*. It is important to note that the LRM executes the operations on behalf of a transaction only on the volatile database, which, at a later time, is written back to the stable database.

When the LRM wants to read a page of data[3] on behalf of a transaction—strictly speaking, on behalf of some operation of a transaction—it issues a **fetch** command, indicating the page that it wants to read. The buffer manager checks to see if that page is already in the buffer (due to a previous fetch command from another transaction) and if so, makes it available for that transaction; if not, it reads the page from the stable database into an empty database buffer. If no empty buffers exist, it selects one of the buffer pages to write back to stable storage and reads the requested stable database page into that buffer. There are a number of different algorithms by which the buffer manager may choose the buffer page to be replaced, and we discuss these in Chapter 13.

The buffer manager also provides the interface by which the LRM can actually force it to write back some of the buffer pages. This can be accomplished by means of the **flush** command, which specifies the buffer pages that the LRM wants to be written back. We should indicate that different LRM implementations may or may not use this forced writing. This issue is discussed further in subsequent sections.

### 12.4.2 Recovery Information

In this section we assume that only system failures occur. We defer the discussion of techniques for recovering from media failures until later. Since we are dealing with centralized database recovery, communication failures are not applicable.

When a system failure occurs, the volatile database is lost. Therefore, the DBMS has to maintain some information about its state at the time of the failure in order to be able to bring the database to the state that it was in when the failure occurred. We call this information the *recovery information*.

The recovery information that the system maintains is dependent on the method of executing updates. Two possibilities are in-place updating and out-of-place updating. *In-place updating* physically changes the value of the data item in the stable database. As a result, the previous values are lost. *Out-of-place updating*, on the other hand, does not change the value of the data item in the stable database but maintains the new value separately. Of course, periodically, these updated values have to be integrated into the stable database. We should note that the reliability issues are somewhat simpler if in-place updating is not used. However, most DBMSs use it due to its improved performance.

**In-place update recovery information.**    Since in-place updates cause previous values of the affected data items to be lost, it is necessary to keep enough information about the database state changes to facilitate the recovery of the database to a consistent state following a failure. This information is typically maintained in

---

[3]The LRM's unit of access may be in blocks which have sizes different than a page. However, for simplicity, we assume that the unit of access is the same.

a database log. Thus each update transaction not only changes the database but is also recorded in the *database log* (Figure 12.8). Before we discuss the contents of the log, let us first see why this information is necessary for the database to recover to a consistent state.

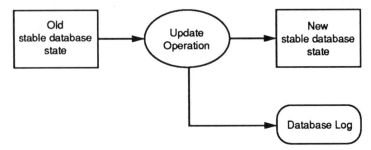

**Figure 12.8**  Update Operation Execution

Consider the following scenario. The DBMS began executing at time 0 and at time $t$ a system failure occurs. During the period $[0, t]$, two transactions (say, $T_1$ and $T_2$) pass through the DBMS, one of which ($T_1$) has completed (i.e., committed), while the other one has not (see Figure 12.9). The durability property of transactions would require that the effects of $T_1$ be reflected in the stable database. Similarly, the atomicity property would require that the stable database not contain any of the effects of $T_2$. However, special precautions need to be taken to ensure this.

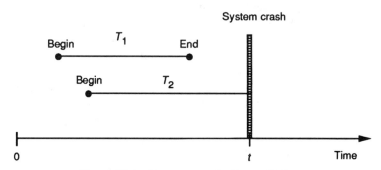

**Figure 12.9**  Occurrence of a System Failure

Let us assume that the LRM and buffer manager algorithms are such that the buffer pages are written back to the stable database only when the buffer manager needs new buffer space. In other words, the **flush** command is not used by the LRM and the decision to write back the pages into the stable database is taken at the discretion of the buffer manager. In this case it is possible that the volatile database pages that have been updated by $T_1$ may not have been written back to the stable database at the time of the failure. Therefore, upon recovery, it is important to be able to *redo* the operations of $T_1$. This requires some information to be stored in the database log about the effects of $T_1$. Given this information, it is possible to recover the database from its "old" state to the "new" state that reflects the effects of $T_1$ (Figure 12.10).

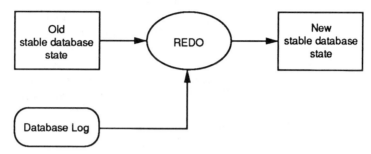

**Figure 12.10**    REDO Action

Similarly, it is possible that the buffer manager may have had to write into the stable database some of the volatile database pages that have been updated by $T_2$. Upon recovery from failures it is necessary to *undo* the operations of $T_2$.[4] Thus the recovery information should include sufficient data to permit the undo by taking the "new" database state that reflects partial effects of $T_2$ and recovers the "old" state that existed at the start of $T_2$ (Figure 12.11).

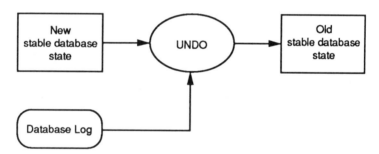

**Figure 12.11**    UNDO Action

We should indicate that the undo and redo actions are assumed to be idempotent. In other words, their repeated application to a transaction would be equivalent to performing them once. Furthermore, the undo/redo actions form the basis of different methods of executing the commit commands. We discuss this further in Section 12.4.3.

The contents of the log may differ according to the implementation. However, the following minimal information for each transaction is contained in almost

---

[4]One might think that it could be possible to continue with the operation of $T_2$ following restart instead of undoing its operations. However, in general it may not be possible for the LRM to determine the point at which the transaction needs to be restarted. Furthermore, the failure may not be a system failure but a transaction failure (i.e., $T_2$ may actually abort itself) after some of its actions have been reflected in the stable database. Therefore, the possibility of undoing is necessary.

all database logs: a begin_transaction record, the value of the data item before the update (called the *before image*), the updated value of the data item (called the *after image*), and a termination record indicating the transaction termination condition (commit, abort). The granularity of the before and after images may be different, as it is possible to log entire pages or some smaller unit.

Similar to the volatile database, the log is also maintained in main memory buffers (called *log buffers*) and written back to stable storage (called *stable log*) similar to the database buffer pages (Figure 12.12). The log pages can be written to stable storage in one of two ways. They can be written *synchronously* (more commonly known as *forcing a log*) where the addition of each log record requires that the log be moved from main memory to stable storage. It can also be written *asynchronously*, where the log is moved to stable storage either at periodic intervals or when the buffer fills up. When the log is written synchronously, the execution of the transaction is suspended until the write is complete. This adds some delay to the response-time performance of the transaction. On the other hand, if a failure occurs immediately after a forced write, it is relatively easy to recover to a consistent database state.

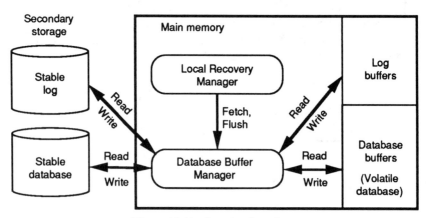

**Figure 12.12**   Logging Interface

Whether the log is written synchronously or asynchronously, one very important protocol has to be observed in maintaining logs. Consider a case where the updates to the database are written into the stable storage before the log is modified in stable storage to reflect the update. If a failure occurs before the log is written, the database will remain in updated form, but the log will not indicate the update that makes it impossible to recover the database to a consistent and up-to-date state. Therefore, the stable log is always updated prior to the updating of the stable database. This is known as the *write-ahead logging (WAL)* protocol [Gray, 1979] and can be precisely specified as follows:

1. Before a stable database is updated (perhaps due to actions of a yet uncommitted transaction), the before images should be stored in the stable log. This facilitates undo.

2. When a transaction commits, the after images have to be stored in the stable log prior to the updating of the stable database. This facilitates redo.

**Out-of-place update recovery information.**    As we mentioned above, the most common update technique is in-place updating. Therefore, we provide only a brief overview of the other updating techniques and their recovery information. Details can be found in [Verhofstadt, 1978] and the other references given earlier.

Typical techniques for out-of-place updating are *shadowing* ([Astrahan et al., 1979] and [Gray, 1979]) and *differential files* [Severance and Lohman, 1976]. Shadowing uses duplicate stable storage pages in executing updates. Thus every time an update is made, the old stable storage page, called the *shadow page*, is left intact and a new page with the updated data item values is written into the stable database. The access path data structures are updated to indicate that the shadow page contains the current data so that subsequent accesses are to this page. The old stable storage page is retained for recovery purposes (to perform undo).

Recovery based on shadow paging is implemented in System R's recovery manager [Gray et al., 1981]. This implementation uses shadowing together with logging.

The differential files approach was discussed in Chapter 6 within the context of integrity enforcement. In general, the method maintains each stable database file as a read-only file. In addition, it maintains a corresponding read-write differential file which stores the changes to that file. Given a logical database file $F$, let us denote its read-only part as $FR$ and its corresponding differential file as $DF$. $DF$ consists of two parts: an insertions part, which stores the insertions to $F$, denoted $DF^+$, and a corresponding deletions part, denoted $DF^-$. All updates are treated as the deletion of the old value and the insertion of a new one. Thus each logical file $F$ is considered to be a view defined as $F = (FR \cup DF^+) - DF^-$. Periodically, the differential file needs to be merged with the read-only base file.

Recovery schemes based on this method simply use private differential files for each transaction, which are then merged with the differential files of each file at commit time. Thus recovery from failures can simply be achieved by discarding the private differential files of noncommitted transactions.

There are studies that indicate that the shadowing and differential files approaches may be advantageous in certain environments. One study by [Agrawal and DeWitt, 1985] investigates the performance of recovery mechanisms based on logging, differential files, and shadow paging, integrated with locking and optimistic (using timestamps) concurrency control algorithms. The results indicate that shadowing, together with locking, can be a feasible alternative to the more common log-based recovery integrated with locking if there are only large (in terms of the base-set size) transactions with sequential access patterns. Similarly, differential files integrated with locking can be a feasible alternative if there are medium-sized and large transactions.

### 12.4.3  Execution of LRM Commands

Recall that there are five commands that form the interface to the LRM. These are the **begin_transaction, read, write, commit,** and **abort** commands. As we indicated in Chapter 10, some DBMSs do not have an explicit commit command. In this case the end (of transaction) indicator serves as the commit command. For simplicity, we specify commit explicitly.

In this section we introduce a sixth interface command to the LRM: **recover**. The **recover** command is the interface that the operating system has to the LRM. It is used during recovery from system failures when the operating system asks the DBMS to recover the database to the state that existed when the failure occurred.

The execution of some of these commands (specifically, **abort, commit**, and **recover**) is quite dependent on the specific LRM algorithms that are used as well as on the interaction of the LRM with the buffer manager. Others (i.e., **begin_transaction, read**, and **write**) are quite independent of these considerations.

The fundamental design decision in the implementation of the local recovery manager, the buffer manager, and the interaction between the two components is whether or not the buffer manager obeys local recovery manager's instructions as to when to write the database buffer pages to stable storage. Specifically, two decisions are involved. The first one is whether the buffer manager may write the buffer pages updated by a transaction into stable storage during the execution of that transaction, or it waits for the LRM to instruct it to write them back. We call this the *fix/no-fix* decision. The reasons for the choice of this terminology will become apparent shortly. Note that it is also called the steal/no-steal decision in [Härder and Reuter, 1983]. The second decision is whether the buffer manager will be forced to flush the buffer pages updated by a transaction into the stable storage at the end of that transaction (i.e., the commit point), or the buffer manager flushes them out whenever it needs to according to its buffer management algorithm. We call this the *flush/no-flush* decision. It is called the force/no-force decision in [Härder and Reuter, 1983].

Accordingly, four alternatives can be identified: (1) no-fix/no-flush, (2) no-fix/flush, (3) fix/no-flush, and (4) fix/flush. We will consider each of these in more detail. However, first we present the execution methods of the **begin_transaction, read**, and **write** commands, which are quite independent of these considerations. Where modifications are required in these methods due to different LRM and buffer manager implementation strategies, we will indicate them.

### Begin_transaction, read, and write commands

*Begin_transaction.* This command causes various components of the DBMS to carry out some bookkeeping functions. We will also assume that it causes the LRM to write a begin_transaction record into the log. This is an assumption made for convenience of discussion; in reality, writing of the begin_transaction record may be delayed until the first **write** to improve performance by reducing I/O.

*Read.* The **read** command specifies a data item. The LRM tries to read the specified data item from the buffer pages that belong to the transaction. If the data item is not in one of these pages, it issues a **fetch** command to the buffer manager in order to make the data available. Upon reading the data, the LRM returns it to the scheduler.

*Write.*  The **write** command specifies the data item and the new value. As with a read command, if the data item is available in the buffers of the transaction, its value is modified in the database buffers (i.e., the volatile database). If it is not in the private buffer pages, a **fetch** command is issued to the buffer manager, and the data is made available and updated. The before image of the data page, as well as its afterimage, are recorded in the log. The local recovery manager then informs the scheduler that the operation has been completed successfully.

**No-fix/no-flush.**    This type of LRM algorithm is called a redo/undo algorithm in [Bernstein et al., 1987] since it requires, as we will see, performing both the redo and undo operations upon recovery. It is called steal/no-force in [Härder and Reuter, 1983].

*Abort.*  As we indicated before, abort is an indication of transaction failure. Since the buffer manager may have written the updated pages into the stable database, abort will have to undo the actions of the transaction. Therefore, the LRM reads the log records for that specific transaction and replaces the values of the updated data items in the volatile database with their before images. The scheduler is then informed about the successful completion of the abort action. This process is called the *transaction undo* or *partial undo*.

An alternative implementation is the use of an *abort list*, which stores the identifiers of all the transactions that have been aborted. If such a list is used, the abort action is considered to be complete as soon as the transaction's identifier is included in the abort list.

Note that even though the values of the updated data items in the stable database are not restored to their before images, the transaction is considered to be aborted at this point. The buffer manager will write the "corrected" volatile database pages into the stable database at a future time, thereby restoring it to its state prior to that transaction.

*Commit.*  The **commit** command causes an end-of-transaction record to be written into the log by the LRM. Under this scenario, no other action is taken in executing a commit command other than informing the scheduler about the successful completion of the commit action.

An alternative to writing an end-of-transaction record into the log is to add the transaction's identifier to a *commit list*, which is a list of the identifiers of transactions that have committed. In this case the commit action is accepted as complete as soon as the transaction identifier is stored in this list.

*Recover.*  The LRM starts the recovery action by going to the beginning of the log and redoing the operations of each transaction for which both a begin-transaction and an end-of-transaction record is found. This is called *partial redo*. Similarly, it undoes the operations of each transaction for which a begin-transaction record is found in the log without a corresponding end-of-transaction record. This action is called *global undo*, as opposed to the transaction undo discussed above. The difference is that the effects of all incomplete transactions need to be rolled back, not one.

If commit list and abort list implementations are used, the recovery action consists of redoing the operations of all the transactions in the commit list and undoing the operations of all the transactions in the abort list. In the remainder of this chapter we will not make this distinction, but rather will refer to both of these recovery implementations as global undo.

**No-fix/flush.** The LRM algorithms that use this strategy are called undo/no-redo in [Bernstein et al., 1987] and steal/force in [Härder and Reuter, 1983].

*Abort.* The execution of **abort** is identical to the previous case. Upon transaction failure, the LRM initiates a partial undo for that particular transaction.

*Commit.* The LRM issues a **flush** command to the buffer manager, forcing it to write back all the updated volatile database pages into the stable database. The commit command is then executed either by placing a record in the log or by insertion of the transaction identifier into the commit list as specified for the previous case. When all of this is complete, the LRM informs the scheduler that the commit has been carried out successfully.

*Recover.* Since all the updated pages are written into the stable database at the commit point, there is no need to perform redo; all the effects of successful transactions will have been reflected in the stable database. Therefore, the recovery action initiated by the LRM consists of a global undo.

**Fix/no-flush.** In this case the LRM controls the writing of the volatile database pages into stable storage. The key here is not to permit the buffer manager to write any updated volatile database page into the stable database until at least the transaction commit point. This is accomplished by the **fix** command, which is a modified version of the **fetch** command whereby the specified page is fixed in the database buffer and cannot be written back to the stable database by the buffer manager. Thus any **fetch** command to the buffer manager for a write operation is replaced by a **fix** command.[5] Note that this precludes the need for a global undo operation and is therefore called a redo/no-undo algorithm in [Bernstein et al., 1987] and a no-force/no-steal algorithm in [Härder and Reuter, 1983].

*Abort.* Since the volatile database pages have not been written to the stable database, no special action is necessary. To release the buffer pages that have been fixed by the transaction, however, it is necessary for the LRM to send an **unfix** command to the buffer manager for all such pages. It is then sufficient to carry out the abort action either by writing an abort record in the log or by including the transaction in the abort list, informing the scheduler and then forgetting about the transaction.

*Commit.* The LRM sends an **unfix** command to the buffer manager for every volatile database page that was previously fixed by that transaction. Note that these

---

[5]Of course, any page that was previously fetched for read but is now being updated also needs to be fixed.

pages may now be written back to the stable database at the discretion of the buffer manager. The commit command is then executed either by placing a record in the log or by inserting the transaction identifier into the commit list as specified for the preceding case. When all of this is complete, the LRM informs the scheduler that the commit has been successfully carried out.

*Recover.* As we mentioned above, since the volatile database pages that have been updated by ongoing transactions are not yet written into the stable database, there is no necessity for global undo. The LRM, therefore, initiates a partial redo action to recover those transactions that may have already committed, but whose volatile database pages may not have yet written into the stable database.

**Fix/flush.** This is the case where the LRM forces the buffer manager to write the updated volatile database pages into the stable database at precisely the commit point—not before and not after. This strategy is called no-undo/no-redo in [Bernstein et al., 1987] and no-steal/force in [Härder and Reuter, 1983].

*Abort.* The execution of **abort** is identical to that of the fix/no-flush case.

*Commit.* The LRM sends an **unfix** command to the buffer manager for every volatile database page that was previously fixed by that transaction. It then issues a **flush** command to the buffer manager, forcing it to write back all the unfixed volatile database pages into the stable database.[6] Finally, the **commit** command is processed by either writing an end_of_transaction record into the log or by including the transaction in the commit list. The important point to note here is that all three of these operations have to be executed as an atomic action. One step that can be taken to achieve this atomicity is to issue only a **flush** command, which serves to unfix the pages as well. This eliminates the need to send two messages from the LRM to the buffer manager, but does not eliminate the requirement for the atomic execution of the flush operation and the writing of the database log. The LRM then informs the scheduler that the **commit** has been carried out successfully. Methods for ensuring this atomicity are beyond the scope of our discussion (see [Bernstein et al., 1987]).

*Recover.* The **recover** command does not need to do anything in this case. This is true since the stable database reflects the effects of all the successful transactions and none of the effects of the uncommitted transactions.

### 12.4.4 Checkpointing

In most of the LRM implementation strategies, the execution of the recovery action requires searching the entire log. This is a significant overhead because the LRM is

---

[6]Our discussion here gives the impression that two commands (*unfix* and *flush*) need to be sent to the BM by the LRM for each commit action. We have chosen to explain the action in this way only because of pedagogical simplicity. In reality, it is, of course, preferable to implement one command that instructs the BM to both unfix and flush. Using one command would reduce the message overhead between DBMS components.

trying to find all the transactions that need to be undone and redone. The overhead can be reduced if it is possible to build a wall which signifies that the database at that point is up-to-date and consistent. In that case, the redo has to start from that point on and the undo only has to go back to that point. This process of building the wall is called *checkpointing*.

Checkpointing is achieved in three steps [Gray, 1979]:

1. Write a begin_checkpoint record into the log.
2. Collect the checkpoint data into the stable storage.
3. Write an end_checkpoint record into the log.

The first and the third steps enforce the atomicity of the checkpointing operation. If a system failure occurs during checkpointing, the recovery process will not find an end_checkpoint record and will consider checkpointing not completed.

There are a number of different alternatives for the data that is collected in Step 2, how it is collected, and where it is stored. We will consider one example here, called *transaction-consistent checkpointing* ([Gray, 1979] and [Gray et al., 1981]). The checkpointing starts by writing the begin_checkpoint record in the log and stopping the acceptance of any new transactions by the LRM. Once the active transactions are all completed, all the updated volatile database pages are flushed to the stable database followed by the insertion of an end_checkpoint record into the log. In this case, the redo action only needs to start from the end_checkpoint record in the log. The undo action can go the reverse direction, starting from the end of the log and stopping at the end_checkpoint record.

Transaction-consistent checkpointing is not the most efficient algorithm, since a significant delay is experienced by all the transactions. There are alternative checkpointing schemes such as action-consistent checkpoints, fuzzy checkpoints, and others ([Gray, 1979] and [Lindsay, 1979]).

### 12.4.5 Handling Media Failures

As we mentioned before, the previous discussion on centralized recovery considered nonmedia failures, where the database as well as the log stored in the stable storage survive the failure. Media failures may either be quite catastrophic, causing the loss of the stable database or of the stable log, or they can simply result in partial loss of the database or the log (e.g., loss of a track or two).

The methods that have been devised for dealing with this situation are again based on duplexing. To cope with catastroptic media failures, an *archive* copy of both the database and the log is maintained on a different storage medium, which is typically the magnetic tape. Thus the DBMS deals with three levels of memory hierarchy: the main memory, random access disk storage, and magnetic tape (Figure 12.13). To deal with less catastrophic failures, having duplicate copies of the database and log may be sufficient.

When a media failure occurs, the database is recovered from the archive copy by redoing and undoing the transactions as stored in the archive log. The real question is

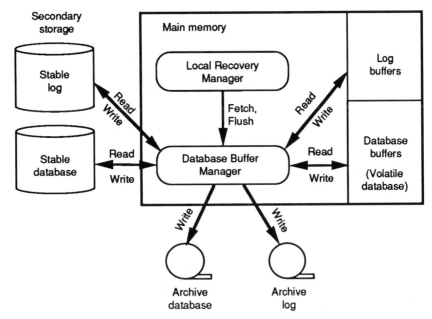

**Figure 12.13**    Full Memory Hierarchy Managed by LRM and BM

how the archive database is stored. If we consider the large sizes of current databases, the overhead of writing the entire database onto a magnetic tape medium is significant. Two methods that have been proposed for dealing with this are to perform the archiving activity concurrent with normal processing and to archive the database incrementally as changes occur so that each archive version contains only the changes that have occurred since the previous archiving.

## 12.5  DISTRIBUTED RELIABILITY PROTOCOLS

As with local reliability protocols, the distributed versions aim to maintain the atomicity and durability of distributed transactions that execute over a number of databases. The protocols address the distributed execution of the **begin_transaction, read, write, abort, commit**, and **recover** commands.

At the outset we should indicate that the execution of the **begin_transaction, read,** and **write** commands does not cause any significant problems. **Begin_transaction** is executed in exactly the same manner as in the centralized case by the transaction manager at the originating site of the transaction. The **read** and **write** commands are executed according to the ROWA rule discussed in Chapter 11. At each of these sites, the commands are executed in the manner described in Section 12.4.3. Similarly, abort is executed by undoing its effects.

To facilitate the description of the distributed reliability protocols, we resort to a commonly used abstraction. We assume that at the originating site of a transaction there is a process that executes its operations. This process is called the *coordinator*. The coordinator communicates with *participant* processes at the other sites which assist in the execution of the transaction's operations. Later we will return to our architectural model and discuss how the coordinator and participant processes can be implemented within that framework.

### 12.5.1 Components of Distributed Reliability Protocols

The reliability techniques in distributed database systems consist of commit, termination, and recovery protocols. Recall from the preceding section that the commit and recovery protocols specify how the commit and the recover commands are executed. Both of these commands need to be executed differently in a distributed DBMS than in a centralized DBMS. Termination protocols are unique to distributed systems. Assume that during the execution of a distributed transaction, one of the sites involved in the execution fails; we would like the other sites to terminate the transaction somehow. The techniques for dealing with this situation are called *termination protocols*. Termination and recovery protocols are two opposite faces of the recovery problem: given a site failure, termination protocols address how the operational sites deal with the failure, whereas recovery protocols deal with the procedure that the process (coordinator or participant) at the failed site has to go through to recover its state once the site is restarted. In the case of network partitioning, the termination protocols take the necessary measures to terminate the active transactions which execute at different partitions, while the recovery protocols address the establishment of mutual consistency of replicated databases following reconnection of the partitions of the network.

The primary requirement of commit protocols is that they maintain the atomicity of distributed transactions. This means that even though the execution of the distributed transaction involves multiple sites, some of which might fail while executing, the effects of the transaction on the distributed database is all-or-nothing. This is called *atomic commitment*. We would prefer the termination protocols to be *nonblocking*. A protocol is nonblocking if it permits a transaction to terminate at the operational sites without waiting for recovery of the failed site. This would significantly improve the response-time performance of transactions. We would also like the distributed recovery protocols to be *independent*. Independent recovery protocols determine how to terminate a transaction that was executing at the time of a failure without having to consult any other site. Existence of such protocols would reduce the number of messages that need to be exchanged during recovery. Note that the existence of independent recovery protocols would imply the existence of nonblocking termination protocols.[7]

### 12.5.2 Two-Phase Commit Protocol

Two-phase commit (2PC) is a very simple and elegant protocol that ensures the atomic commitment of distributed transactions. It extends the effects of local atomic commit

---

[7]The reverse implication is not true, however.

actions to distributed transactions by insisting that all sites involved in the execution of a distributed transaction agree to commit the transaction before its effects are made permanent. There are a number of reasons why such synchronization among sites is necessary. First, depending on the type of concurrency control algorithm that is used, some schedulers may not be ready to terminate a transaction. For example, if a transaction has read a value of a data item that is updated by another transaction that has not yet committed, the associated scheduler may not want to commit the former. Of course, strict concurrency control algorithms that avoid cascading aborts would not permit the updated value of a data item to be read by any other transaction until the updating transaction terminates. This is sometimes called the *recoverability condition* ([Hadzilacos, 1988] and [Bernstein et al., 1987]).

Another possible reason why a participant may not agree to commit is due to deadlocks that require a participant to abort the transaction. Note that in this case the participant should be permitted to abort the transaction without being told to do so. This capability is quite important and is called *unilateral abort.*

A brief description of the 2PC protocol that does not consider failures is as follows. Initially, the coordinator writes a begin_commit record in its log, sends a "prepare" message to all participant sites, and enters the WAIT state. When a participant receives a "prepare" message, it checks if it could commit the transaction. If so, the participant writes a ready record in the log, sends a "vote-commit" message to the coordinator, and enters READY state; otherwise, the participant writes an abort record and sends a "vote-abort" message to the coordinator. If the decision of the site is to abort, it can forget about that transaction, since an abort decision serves as a veto (i.e., unilateral abort). After the coordinator has received a reply from every participant, it decides whether to commit or to abort the transaction. If even one participant has registered a negative vote, the coordinator has to abort the transaction globally. So it writes an abort record, sends a "global-abort" message to all participant sites, and enters the ABORT state; otherwise, it writes a commit record, sends a "global-commit" message to all participants, and enters the COMMIT state. The participants either commit or abort the transaction according to the coordinator's instructions and send back an acknowledgment, at which point the coordinator terminates the transaction by writing an end_of_transaction record in the log.

Note the manner in which the coordinator reaches a global termination decision regarding a transaction. Two rules govern this decision, which, together, are called the *global commit rule*:

1. If even one participant votes to abort the transaction, the coordinator has to reach a global abort decision.

2. If all the participants vote to commit the transaction, the coordinator has to reach a global commit decision.

The operation of the 2PC protocol between a coordinator and one participant in the absence of failures is depicted in Figure 12.14, where the circles indicate the states and the dashed lines indicate messages between the coordinator and the participants. The labels on the dashed lines specify the nature of the message.

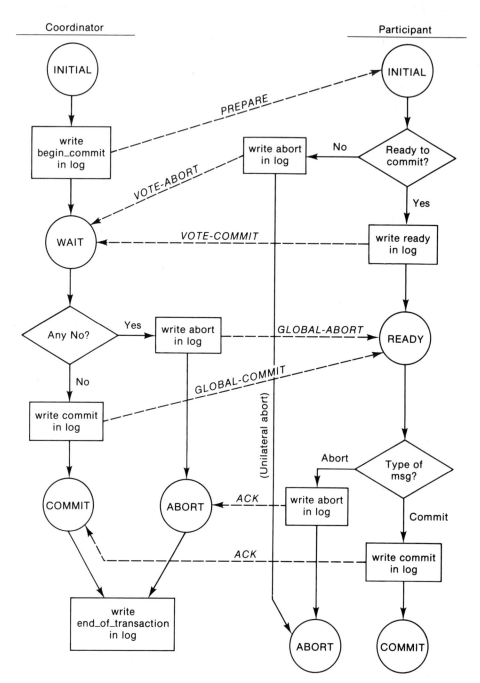

**Figure 12.14**   2PC Protocol Actions

A few important points about the 2PC protocol that can be observed from Figure 12.14 are as follows. First, 2PC permits a participant to unilaterally abort a transaction until it has decided to register an affirmative vote. Second, once a participant votes to commit a transaction, it cannot change its vote. Third, while a participant is in the READY state, it can move either to abort the transaction or to commit it, depending on the nature of the message from the coordinator. Fourth, the global termination decision is taken by the coordinator according to the global commit rule. Finally, note that the coordinator and participant processes enter certain states where they have to wait for messages from one another. To guarantee that they can exit from these states and terminate, timers are used. Each process sets its timer when it enters a state, and if the expected message is not received before the timer runs out, the process timeouts and invokes its timeout protocol (which will be discussed later).

There are a number of different communication paradigms that can be employed in implementing a 2PC protocol. The one discussed above and depicted in Figure 12.14 is called a *centralized 2PC* since the communication is only between the coordinator and the participants; the participants do not communicate among themselves. This communication structure, which is the basis of our subsequent discussions in this chapter, is depicted more clearly in Figure 12.15.

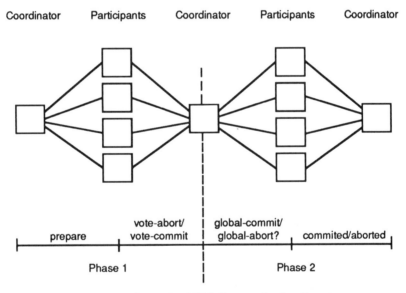

**Figure 12.15**   Centralized 2PC Communication Structure

Another alternative is *linear 2PC* (also called *nested 2PC* [Gray, 1979]) where participants can communicate with one another. There is an ordering between the sites in the system for the purposes of communication. Let us assume that the ordering among the sites that participate in the execution of a transaction are 1, ..., $N$, where the coordinator is the first one in the order. The 2PC protocol is implemented by a forward communication from the coordinator (number 1) to $N$, during which the first phase is completed, and by a backward communication from $N$ to the coordinator, during which the second phase is completed. Thus linear 2PC operates in the following manner.

The coordinator sends the "prepare" message to participant 2. If participant 2 is not ready to commit the transaction, it sends a "vote-abort" message (VA) to participant 3 and the transaction is aborted at this point (unilateral abort by 2). If, on the other hand, participant 2 agrees to commit the transaction, it sends a "vote-commit" message (VC) to participant 3 and enters the READY state. This process continues until a "vote-commit" vote reaches participant $N$. This is the end of the first phase. If $N$ decides to commit, it sends back to $N - 1$ "global-commit" (GC); otherwise, it sends a "global-abort" message (GA). Accordingly, the participants enter the appropriate state (COMMIT or ABORT) and propagate the message back to the coordinator.

Linear 2PC, whose communication structure is depicted in Figure 12.16, incurs fewer messages but does not provide any parallelism. Therefore, it suffers from low response-time performance. It may, however, be suitable for networks that do not have broadcasting capability.

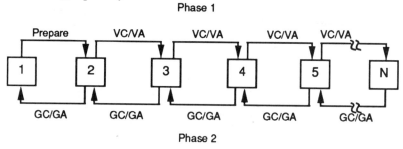

**Figure 12.16**   Linear 2PC Communication Structure. VC, vote.commit; VA, vote.abort; GC, global.commit; GA, global.abort.)

Another popular communication structure for implementation of the 2PC protocol involves communication among all the participants during the first phase of the protocol so that they all independently reach their termination decisions with respect to the specific transaction. This version, called *distributed 2PC*, eliminates the need for the second phase of the protocol since the participants can reach a decision on their own. It operates as follows. The coordinator sends the prepare message to all participants. Each participant then sends its decision to all the other participants (and to the coordinator) by means of either a "vote-commit" or a "vote-abort" message. Each participant waits for messages from all the other participants and makes its termination decision according to the global commit rule. Obviously, there is no need for the second phase of the protocol (someone sending the global abort or global commit decision to the others), since each participant has independently reached that decision at the end of the first phase. The communication structure of distributed commit is depicted in Figure 12.17.

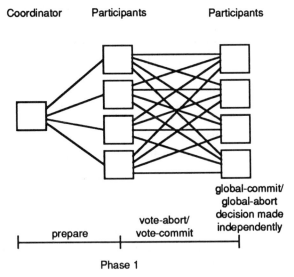

Figure 12.17    Distributed 2PC Communication Structure

One point that needs to be addressed with respect to the last two versions of 2PC implementation is the following. A participant has to know the identity of either the next participant in the linear ordering (in case of linear 2PC) or of all the participants (in case of distributed 2PC). This problem can be solved by attaching the list of participants to the prepare message that is sent by the coordinator. Such an issue does not arise in the case of centralized 2PC since the coordinator clearly knows who the participants are.

The algorithms for the execution of the 2PC protocol by the coordinator and the participants in a centralized communication structure are given in Algorithms 12.1 and 12.2, respectively. The algorithms show the handling of various messages between the coordinator and the participants.

**Algorithm 12.1**    *2PC-Coordinator*

**declare-var**
    $msg : Message$
    $ev : Event$
    $PL$ : List of participant {this list compiled prior to the start of 2PC protocol}
**begin**
    WAIT($ev$)
    **case of** $ev$                                    {possible events are $MsgArrival$ and $Timeout$}
        $MsgArrival$:
        **begin**
            Let the arrived message be in $msg$
            **case of** $msg$

```
        Commit:                           {commit command from scheduler}
        begin
            write begin_commit record in the log
            send "prepare" message to all the participants in PL
            set timer
        end
        Vote-Abort:                       {one participant has voted to abort}
        begin
            write abort record in the log
            send "global-abort" message to all the participants in PL
            set timer
        end
        Vote-Commit:
        begin
            update the list of participants who have answered
            if all the participants have answered then
            begin                         {all must have voted to commit}
                write commit in the log
                send "global-commit" to all the participants in PL
                set timer
            end
        end
        Ack:
        begin
            update the list of participants who have acknowledged
            if all the participants have acknowledged then
                write end_of_transaction in the log
            else
                send global decision to the unanswering participants
            end-if
        end
      end-case
    end
    Timeout:
    begin
        execute the termination protocol        {this will be discussed later}
    end
  end-case
end. {2PC-Coordinator}


Algorithm 12.2    2PC-Participant
declare-var
    msg : Message
    ev : Event
begin
```

```
WAIT(ev)
    case of ev                          {possible events are MsgArrival and Timeout}
        MsgArrival:
        begin
            Let the arrived message be in msg
            case of msg
                Prepare:
                begin
                    if ready to commit then
                    begin
                        write ready record in the log
                        send "vote-commit" message to the coordinator
                        set timer
                    end
                    else begin                                    {unilateral abort}
                        write abort record in the log
                        send "vote-abort" message to the coordinator
                        call local data processor to abort the transaction
                        end
                    end-if
                end
                Global-abort:
                begin
                    write abort record in the log
                    call local data processor to abort the transaction
                end
                Global-commit:
                begin
                    write commit record in the log
                    call local data processor to commit the transaction
                end
            end-case
        end
        Timeout:
        begin
            execute the termination protocol        {this will be discussed later}
        end
    end-case
end. {2PC-Participant}
```

## 12.5.3  Variations of 2PC

Two variations of 2PC have been proposed to improve its performance. This is accomplished by reducing (1) the number of messages that are transmitted between the coordinator and the participants, and (2) the number of times logs are written. These protocols are called *presumed abort* and *presumed commit* [Mohan and Lindsay, 1983; Mohan et al., 1986]. Presumed abort is a protocol that is optimized to handle read-only transactions as well as those update transactions, some of whose processes do not perform any updates to the database while the others do (called partially read-only). The presumed commit protocol is optimized to handle the general update transactions. We will discuss briefly both of these variations.

**Presumed abort 2PC protocol.**    In the presumed abort 2PC protocol the following assumption is made. Whenever a coordinator is inquired by a prepared participant about a transaction's outcome and there is no information in virtual storage about it, the response to the inquiry is to abort the transaction. This works since in the case of a commit, the coordinator does not forget about a transaction until all participants acknowledge, guaranteeing that they will no longer inquire about this transaction.

When this convention is used, it can be seen that the coordinator can forget about a transaction immediately after it decides to abort it. It can write an abort record and not expect the participants to acknowledge the abort command. The coordinator does not need to write an end_of_transaction record after an abort record.

The abort record does not need to be forced, because if a site fails before receiving the decision and then recovers, the recovery routine will check the log to determine the fate of the transaction. Since the abort record is not forced, the recovery routine may not find any information about the transaction, in which case it will ask the coordinator and will be told to abort it. For the same reason, the abort records do not need to be forced by the participants either.

Since it saves some message transmission between the coordinator and the participants in case of aborted transactions, presumed abort 2PC is expected to be more efficient.

**Presumed commit 2PC protocol.**    The presumed abort 2PC protocol improves performance by forgetting about transactions once a decision is reached to abort them. Since most transactions are expected to commit, it is reasonable to expect that it may be similarly possible to improve performance for commits. Hence the presumed commit 2PC protocol.

Presumed commit 2PC is based on the premise that if no information about the transaction exists, it should be considered committed. However, it is not an exact dual of presumed abort 2PC, since an exact dual would require that the coordinator forget about a transaction immediately after it decides to commit it, that commit records (also the ready records of the participants) not be forced, and that commit commands need not be acknowledged. Consider, however, the following scenario. The coordinator sends prepared messages and starts collecting information, but fails before being able to collect all of them and reach a decision. In this case, the participants will wait for a while and then turn the transaction over to their recovery routines. Since there is no information about the transaction, the recovery routines of each participant will commit the transaction. The coordinator, on the other hand, will abort the transaction when it recovers, thus causing inconsistency.

A simple variation of this protocol, however, solves the problem and that variant is called the *presumed commit 2PC*. The coordinator, prior to sending the prepare message, force-writes a collecting record, which contains the names of all the participants involved in executing that transaction. The participant then enters the COLLECTING state. It then sends the prepare message and enters the WAIT state. The participants, when they receive the prepare message, decide what they want to do with the transaction, write an abort record, or write a ready record and respond with either a "vote-abort" or a "vote-commit" message. When the coordinator receives decisions from all the participants, it decides to abort or commit the transaction. If the decision is to abort, the coordinator writes an abort record, enters the ABORT state, and sends a "global-abort" message. If it decides to commit the transaction, it writes a commit record, sends a "global-commit" command, and forgets the transaction. When the participants receive a "global-commit" message, they write a commit record and update the database. If they receive a "global-abort" message, they write an abort record and acknowledge. The participant, upon receiving the abort acknowledgment, writes an end record and forgets about the transaction.

## 12.6  DEALING WITH SITE FAILURES

In this section we consider the failure of sites in the network. Our aim is to develop nonblocking termination and independent recovery protocols. As we indicated before, the existence of independent recovery protocols would imply the existence of nonblocking recovery protocols. However, our discussion addresses both aspects separately. Also note that in the following discussion we consider only the standard 2PC protocol, not its two variants presented above.

Let us first set the boundaries for the existence of nonblocking termination and independent recovery protocols in the presence of site failures. It can formally be proven that such protocols exist when a single site fails. In the case of multiple site failures, however, the prospects are not as promising. An unfortunate result indicates that it is not possible to design independent recovery protocols (and, therefore, nonblocking termination protocols) when multiple sites fail [Skeen and Stonebraker, 1983]. We first develop termination and recovery protocols for the 2PC algorithm and show that 2PC is inherently blocking. We then proceed to the development of atomic commit protocols which are nonblocking in the case of single site failures.

### 12.6.1  Termination and Recovery Protocols for 2PC

**Termination protocols.**    The termination protocols serve the timeouts for both the coordinator and the participant processes. A timeout occurs at a destination site when it cannot get an expected message from a source site within the expected time period. In this section we consider that this is due to the failure of the source site.

The method for handling timeouts depends on the timing of failures as well as on the types of failures. We therefore need to consider failures at various points of 2PC execution. This discussion is facilitated by means of the state transition diagram of the 2PC protocol given in Figure 12.18. Note that the state transition diagram is a simplification of Figure 12.14. The states are denoted by circles and the edges represent the state transitions. The terminal states are depicted by concentric circles. The interpretation of the labels on the edges is as follows: the reason for the state transition, which is a received message, is given at the top, and the message that is sent as a result of state transition is given at the bottom.

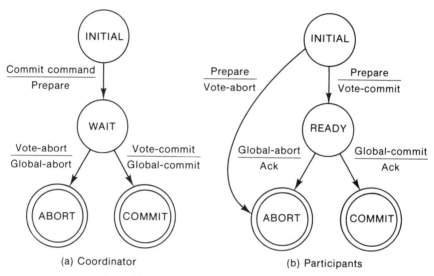

**Figure 12.18**   State Transitions in 2PC Protocol

*Coordinator Timeouts.*   There are three states in which the coordinator can timeout: WAIT, COMMIT, and ABORT. Timeouts during the last two are handled in the same manner. So we need to consider only two cases:

1. *Timeout in the WAIT state.* In the WAIT state, the coordinator is waiting for the local decisions of the participants. The coordinator cannot unilaterally commit the transaction since the global commit rule has not been satisfied. However, it can decide to globally abort the transaction, in which case it writes an abort record in the log and sends a "global-abort" message to all the participants.

2. *Timeout in the COMMIT or ABORT states.* In this case the coordinator is not certain that the commit or abort procedures have been completed by the local recovery managers at all of the participant sites. Thus the coordinator

repeatedly sends the "global-commit" or "global-abort" commands to the sites that have not yet responded, and waits for their acknowledgement.

*Participant Timeouts.*    A participant can timeout[8] in two states: INITIAL and READY. Let us examine both of these cases.

1. *Timeout in the INITIAL state.* In this state the participant is waiting for a "prepare" message. The coordinator must have failed in the INITIAL state. The participant can unilaterally abort the transaction following a timeout. If the "prepare" message arrives at this participant at a later time, this can be handled in one of two possible ways. Either the participant would check its log, find the abort record, and respond with a "vote-abort," or it can simply ignore the "prepare" message. In the latter case the coordinator would timeout in the WAIT state and follow the course we have discussed above.

2. *Timeout in the READY state.* In this state the participant has voted to commit the transaction but does not know the global decision of the coordinator. The participant cannot unilaterally make a decision. Since it is in the READY state, it must have voted to commit the transaction. Therefore, it cannot now change its vote and unilaterally abort it. On the other hand, it cannot unilaterally decide to commit it since it is possible that another participant may have voted to abort it. In this case the participant will remain blocked until it can learn from someone (either the coordinator or some other participant) the ultimate fate of the transaction.

Let us consider a centralized communication structure where the participants cannot communicate with one another. In this case the participant that is trying to terminate a transaction has to ask the coordinator for its decision and wait until it receives a response. If the coordinator has failed, the participant will remain blocked. This is undesirable.

If the participants can communicate with each other, a more distributed termination protocol may be developed. The participant that timeouts can simply ask all the other participants to help it make a decision. Assuming that participant $P_i$ is the one that timeouts, all the other participants $P_j$ respond in the following manner:

1. $P_j$ is in the INITIAL state. This means that $P_j$ has not yet voted and may not even have received the "prepare" message. It can therefore unilaterally abort the transaction and reply to $P_i$ with a "vote-abort" message.

2. $P_j$ is in the READY state. In this state $P_j$ has voted to commit the transaction but has not received any word about the global decision. Therefore, it cannot help $P_i$ to terminate the transaction.

---

[8]In some discussions of the 2PC protocol, it is assumed that the participants do not use timers and do not timeout. However, implementing timeout protocols for the participants solves some nasty problems and may speed up the commit process. Therefore, we consider this more general case.

3. $P_j$ is in the ABORT or COMMIT states. In these states, either $P_j$ has unilaterally decided to abort the transaction, or it has received the coordinator's decision regarding global termination. It can, therefore, send $P_i$ either a "vote-commit" or a "vote-abort" message.

Consider how the participant that timeouts ($P_i$) can interpret these responses. The following cases are possible:

1. $P_i$ receives "vote-abort" messages from all $P_j$. This means that none of the other participants had yet voted, but they have chosen to abort the transaction unilaterally. Under these conditions, $P_i$ can proceed to abort the transaction.
2. $P_i$ receives "vote-abort" messages from some $P_j$, but some other participants indicate that they are in the READY state. In this case $P_i$ can still go ahead and abort the transaction, since according to the global commit rule, the transaction cannot be committed and will eventually be aborted.
3. $P_i$ receives notification from all $P_j$ that they are in the READY state. In this case none of the participants knows enough about the fate of the transaction to terminate it properly.
4. $P_i$ receives "global-abort" or "global-commit" messages from all $P_j$. In this case all the other participants have received the coordinator's decision. Therefore, $P_i$ can go ahead and terminate the transaction according to the messages it receives from the other participants. Incidentally, note that it is not possible for some of the $P_j$ to respond with a "global-abort" while others respond with "global-commit" since this cannot be the result of a legitimate execution of the 2PC protocol.
5. $P_i$ receives "global-abort" or "global-commit" from some $P_j$, whereas others indicate that they are in the READY state. This indicates that some sites have received the coordinator's decision while others are still waiting for it. In this case $P_i$ can proceed as in case 4 above.

These five cases cover all the alternatives that a termination protocol needs to handle. It is not necessary to consider cases where, for example, one participant sends a "vote-abort" message while another one sends "global-commit." This cannot happen in 2PC. During the execution of the 2PC protocol, no process (participant or coordinator) is more than one state transition apart from any other process. For example, if a participant is in the INITIAL state, all other participants are in either the INITIAL or the READY state. Similarly, the coordinator is either in the INITIAL or the WAIT state. Thus all the processes in a 2PC protocol are said to be *synchronous within one state transition* [Skeen, 1981].

Note that in case 3 the participant processes stay blocked, as they cannot terminate a transaction. Under certain circumstances there may be a way to overcome this blocking. If during termination all the participants realize that only the coordinator site has failed, they can elect a new coordinator, which can restart the commit process.

There are different ways of electing the coordinator. It is possible either to define a total ordering among all sites and elect the next one in order [Hammer and Shipman, 1980], or to establish a voting procedure among the participants [Garcia-Molina, 1982]. This will not work, however, if both a participant site and the coordinator site fail. In this case it is possible for the participant at the failed site to have received the coordinator's decision and have terminated the transaction accordingly. This decision is unknown to the other participants; thus if they elect a new coordinator and proceed, there is the danger that they may decide to terminate the transaction differently from the participant at the failed site. It is clear that it is not possible to design termination protocols for 2PC that can guarantee nonblocking termination. The 2PC protocol is, therefore, a blocking protocol.

Since we had assumed a centralized communication structure in developing the 2PC algorithms in Algorithms 12.1 and 12.2, we will continue with the same assumption in developing the termination protocols. The portion of code that should be included in the timeout section of the coordinator and the participant 2PC algorithms is given in Algorithms 12.3 and 12.4, respectively.

**Algorithm 12.3**    *2PC-Coordinator-Terminate*

*Timeout:*
**begin**
   **if** in WAIT state **then**
   **begin**
      write abort record in the log
      send "global-abort" message to all the participants
   **end**
   **else begin**
      check for the last log record
      **if** last log record=abort **then**        {coordinator is in ABORT state}
         send "global-abort" to all the participants that have not responded
      **else**                  {coordinator is in COMMIT state}
         send "global-commit" to all the participants that have not responded
      **end-if**
      **end**
   **end-if**
   set timer
**end**

**Algorithm 12.4**    *2PC-Participant-Terminate*

*Timeout:*
**begin**
   **if** in INITIAL state **then**
      write abort record in the log

> **else**                                    {participant is in READY state}
>             send "vote-commit" message to the coordinator
>             reset timer
>     **end-if**
>  **end**

**Recovery protocols.**   In the preceding section we discussed how the 2PC protocol deals with failures from the perspective of the operational sites. In this section we take the opposite viewpoint: we are interested in investigating protocols that a coordinator or participant can use to recover their states when their sites fail and then restart. Remember that we would like these protocols to be independent. However, in general, it is not possible to design protocols that can guarantee independent recovery while maintaining the atomicity of distributed transactions. This is not surprising given the fact that the termination protocols for 2PC are inherently blocking.

In the following discussion we again use the state transition diagram of Figure 12.18. Additionally, we make two interpretive assumptions: (1) the combined action of writing a record in the log and sending a message is assumed to be atomic, and (2) the state transition occurs after the transmission of the response message. For example, if the coordinator is in the WAIT state, this means that it has successfully written the begin_commit record in its log and has successfully transmitted the "prepare" command. This does not say anything, however, about successful completion of the message transmission. Therefore, the "prepare" message may never get to the participants, due to communication failures, which we discuss separately. The first assumption related to atomicity is, of course, unrealistic. However, it simplifies our discussion of fundamental failure cases. At the end of this section we show that the other cases that arise from the relaxation of this assumption can be handled by a combination of the fundamental failure cases.

*Coordinator Site Failures.*   The following cases are possible:

1. *The coordinator fails while in the INITIAL state.* This is before the coordinator has initiated the commit procedure. Therefore, it will start the commit process upon recovery.

2. *The coordinator fails while in the WAIT state.* In this case the coordinator has sent the "prepare" command. Upon recovery, the coordinator will restart the commit process for this transaction from the beginning by sending the "prepare" message one more time.

3. *The coordinator fails while in the COMMIT or ABORT states.* In this case the coordinator will have informed the participants of its decision and terminated the transaction. Thus, upon recovery, it does not need to do anything if all the acknowledgments have been received. Otherwise, the termination protocol is involved.

*Participant Site Failures.*    There are three alternatives to consider:

1. *A participant fails in the INITIAL state.* Upon recovery, the participant should abort the transaction unilaterally. Let us see why this is acceptable. Note that the coordinator will be in the INITIAL or WAIT state with respect to this transaction. If it is in the INITIAL state, it will send a "prepare" message and then move to the WAIT state. Because of the participant site's failure, it will not receive the participant's decision and will timeout in that state. We have already discussed how the coordinator would handle timeouts in the WAIT state by globally aborting the transaction.

2. *A participant fails while in the READY state.* In this case the coordinator has been informed of the failed site's affirmative decision about the transaction before the failure. Upon recovery, the participant at the failed site can treat this as a timeout in the READY state and hand the incomplete transaction over to its termination protocol.

3. *A participant fails while in the ABORT or COMMIT state.* These states represent the termination conditions, so, upon recovery, the participant does not need to take any special action.

*Additional Cases.*    Let us now consider the cases that may arise when we relax the assumption related to the atomicity of the logging and message sending actions. In particular, we assume that a site failure may occur after the coordinator or a participant has written a log record but before it can send a message. For this discussion the reader may wish to refer to Figure 12.14.

1. *The coordinator fails after begin_commit record is written in the log but before the "prepare" command is sent.* The coordinator would react to this as a failure in the WAIT state (case 2 of the coordinator failures discussed above) and send the "prepare" command upon recovery.

2. *A participant site fails after writing the ready record in the log but before sending the "vote-commit" message.* The failed participant sees this as case 2 of the participant failures discussed before.

3. *A participant site fails after writing the abort record in the log but before sending the "vote-abort" message.* This is the only situation that is not covered by the fundamental cases discussed before. However, the participant does not need to do anything upon recovery in this case. The coordinator is in the WAIT state and will timeout. The coordinator termination protocol for this state globally aborts the transaction.

4. *The coordinator fails after logging its final decision record (abort or commit), but before sending its "global-abort" or "global-commit" message to the participants.* The coordinator treats this as its case 3, while the participants treat it as a timeout in the READY state.

5. *A participant fails after it logs an abort or a commit record but before it sends the acknowledgment message to the coordinator.* The participant can treat this as its case 3. The coordinator will handle this by timeout in the COMMIT or ABORT state.

### 12.6.2 Three-Phase Commit Protocol

The three-phase commit protocol (3PC) [Skeen, 1981] is designed as a nonblocking protocol. We will see in this section that it is indeed nonblocking when failures are restricted to site failures.

Let us first consider the necessary and sufficient conditions for designing nonblocking atomic commitment protocols. A commit protocol that is synchronous within one state transition is nonblocking if and only if its state transition diagram contains neither of the following:

1. No state that is "adjacent" to both a commit and an abort state
2. No noncommittable state that is "adjacent" to a commit state ([Skeen, 1981] and [Skeen and Stonebraker, 1983])

The term *adjacent* here means that it is possible to go from one state to the other with a single state transition.

Consider the COMMIT state in the 2PC protocol (see Figure 12.18). If any process is in this state, we know that all the sites have voted to commit the transaction. Such states are called *committable*. There are other states in the 2PC protocol that are *noncommittable*. The one we are interested in is the READY state, which is noncommittable since the existence of a process in this state does not imply that all the processes have voted to commit the transaction.

It is obvious that the WAIT state in the coordinator and the READY state in the participant 2PC protocol violate the nonblocking conditions we have stated above. Therefore, one might be able to make the following modification to the 2PC protocol to satisfy the conditions and turn it into a nonblocking protocol.

We can add another state between the WAIT (and READY) and COMMIT states which serves as a buffer state where the process is ready to commit (if that is the final decision) but has not yet committed. The state transition diagrams for the coordinator and the participant in this protocol are depicted in Figure 12.19. This is called the three-phase commit protocol (3PC) because there are three state transitions from the INITIAL state to a COMMIT state. The execution of the protocol between the coordinator and one participant is depicted in Figure 12.20. Note that this is identical to Figure 12.14 except for the addition of the PRECOMMIT state. Observe that 3PC is also a protocol where all the states are synchronous within one state transition. Therefore, the foregoing conditions for nonblocking 2PC apply to 3PC.

It is possible to design different 3PC algorithms depending on the communication topology. The one given in Figure 12.20 is centralized. It is also straightforward to design a distributed 3PC protocol. A linear 3PC protocol is somewhat more involved, so we leave it as an exercise.

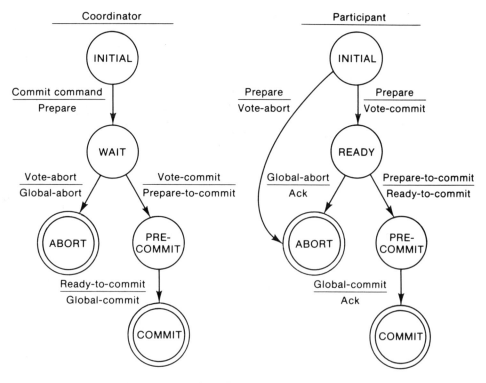

**Figure 12.19**    State Transitions in 3PC Protocol

**Termination protocol.**    As we did in discussing the termination protocols for handling timeouts in the 2PC protocol, let us investigate timeouts at each state of the 3PC protocol.

*Coordinator Timeouts.*    In 3PC, there are four states in which the coordinator can timeout: WAIT, PRECOMMIT, COMMIT, or ABORT.

1. *Timeout in the WAIT state.* This is identical to the coordinator timeout in the WAIT state for the 2PC protocol. The coordinator unilaterally decides to abort the transaction. It therefore writes an abort record in the log and sends a "global-abort" message to all the participants that have voted to commit the transaction.

2. *Timeout in the PRECOMMIT state.* The coordinator does not know if the nonresponding participants have already moved to the PRECOMMIT state. However, it knows that they are at least in the READY state, which means that they must have voted to commit the transaction. The coordinator can therefore go ahead and globally commit the transaction by writing a commit record in the log and sending a "global-commit" message to all the operational participants.

3. *Timeout in the COMMIT (or ABORT) state.* The coordinator does not know whether the participants have actually performed the commit (abort) com-

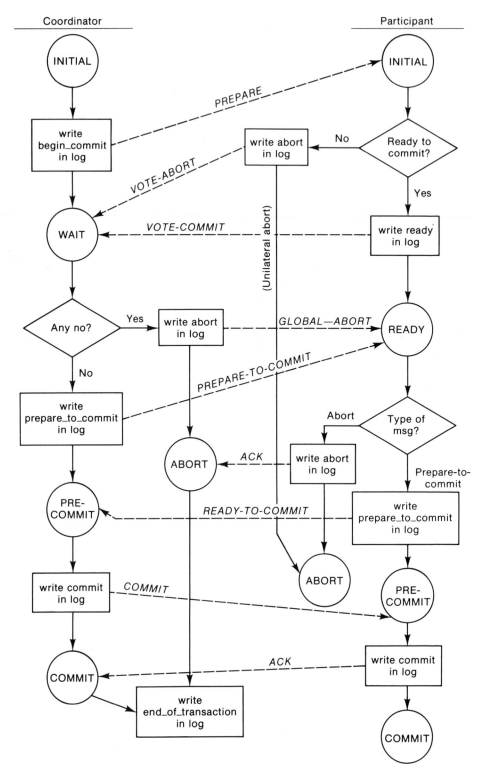

**Figure 12.20** 3PC Protocol Actions

mand. However, they are at least in the PRECOMMIT (READY) state (since the protocol is synchronous within one state transition) and can follow the termination protocol as described in case 2 or case 3 below. Thus the coordinator does not need to take any special action.

***Participant Timeouts.***  A participant can timeout in three states: INITIAL, READY, and PRECOMMIT. Let us examine all of these cases.

1. *Timeout in the INITIAL state.* This can be handled identically to the termination protocol of 2PC.
2. *Timeout in the READY state.* In this state the participant has voted to commit the transaction but does not know the global decision of the coordinator. Since communication with the coordinator is lost, the termination protocol proceeds by electing a new coordinator, as discussed earlier. The new coordinator then terminates the transaction according to a termination protocol that we discuss below.
3. *Timeout in the PRECOMMIT state.* In this state the participant has received the "prepare-to-commit" message and is awaiting the final "global-commit" message from the coordinator. This case is handled identically to case 2 above.

Let us now consider the possible termination protocols that can be adopted in the last two cases. There are various alternatives; let us consider a centralized one [Skeen, 1981]. We know that the new coordinator can be in one of three states: WAIT, PRECOMMIT, or ABORT. It sends its own state to all the operational participants, asking them to assume that state. Any participant who has proceeded ahead of the new coordinator (which is possible since it may have already received and processed a message from the old coordinator) simply ignores the new coordinator's message; others make their state transitions and send back the appropriate message. Once the new coordinator gets messages from the participants, it guides the participants toward termination as follows:

1. If the new coordinator is in the WAIT state, it will globally abort the transaction. The participants can be in the INITIAL, READY, ABORT, or PRECOMMIT states. In the first three cases, there is no problem. However, the participants in the PRECOMMIT state are expecting a "global-commit" message, but they get a "global-abort" instead. Their state transition diagram does not indicate any transition from the PRECOMMIT to the ABORT state. This transition is necessary for the termination protocol, so it should be added to the set of legal transitions that can occur during execution of the termination protocol.
2. If the new coordinator is in the PRECOMMIT state, the participants can be in the PRECOMMIT or COMMIT states. No participant can be in ABORT state. The coordinator will therefore globally commit the transaction and send a "global-commit" message.

3. If the new coordinator is in the ABORT state, at the end of the first message all the participants will have moved into the ABORT state as well.

The new coordinator is not keeping track of participant failures during this process. It simply guides the operational sites toward termination. If some participants fail in the meantime, they will have to terminate the transaction upon recovery according to the methods discussed in the next section. Also, the new coordinator may fail during the process; the termination protocol therefore needs to be reentrant in implementation.

This termination protocol is obviously nonblocking. The operational sites can properly terminate all the ongoing transactions and continue their operations. The proof of correctness of the algorithm is given in [Skeen, 1982b].

**Recovery protocols.**    There are some minor differences between the recovery protocols of 3PC and those of 2PC. We only indicate those differences.

1. *The coordinator fails while in the WAIT state.* This is the case we discussed at length in the earlier section on termination protocols. The participants have already terminated the transaction. Therefore, upon recovery, the coordinator has to ask around to determine the fate of the transaction.

2. *The coordinator fails while in the PRECOMMIT state.* Again, the termination protocol has guided the operational participants toward termination. Since it is now possible to move from the PRECOMMIT state to the ABORT state during this process, the coordinator has to ask around to determine the fate of the transaction.

3. *A participant fails while in the PRECOMMIT state.* It has to ask around to determine how the other participants have terminated the transaction.

One property of the 3PC protocol becomes obvious from this discussion. When using the 3PC protocol, we are able to terminate transactions without blocking. However, we pay the price that fewer cases of independent recovery are possible. This also results in more messages being exchanged during recovery.

## 12.7 NETWORK PARTITIONING

In this section we consider how the network partitions can be handled by the atomic commit protocols that we discussed in the preceding section. Network partitions are due to communication line failures and may cause the loss of messages, depending on the implementation of the communication subnet. A partitioning is called a *simple partitioning* if the network is divided into only two components; otherwise, it is called *multiple partitioning*.

The termination protocols for network partitioning address the termination of the transactions that were active in each partition at the time of partitioning. If one can develop nonblocking protocols to terminate these transactions, it is possible for the sites in each partition to reach a termination decision (for a given transaction) which is consistent with the sites in the other partitions. This would imply that the sites in each partition can continue executing transactions despite the partitioning.

Unfortunately, it is not in general possible to find nonblocking termination protocols in the presence of network partitions. Remember that our expectations regarding the reliability of the communication subnet are minimal. If a message cannot be delivered, it is simply lost. In this case it can be proven that no nonblocking atomic commitment protocol exists that is resilient to network partitioning [Skeen and Stonebraker, 1983]. This is quite a negative result since it also means that if network partitioning occurs, we cannot continue normal operations in all partitions, which limits the availability of the entire distributed database system. A positive counter result, however, indicates that it is possible to design nonblocking atomic commit protocols that are resilient to simple partitions. Unfortunately, if multiple partitions occur, it is again not possible to design such protocols [Skeen and Stonebraker, 1983].

In the remainder of this section we discuss a number of protocols that address network partitioning. Let us first indicate one important point, however. In our discussion of site failures in the preceding section, we did not make a distinction between replicated and nonreplicated databases. This separation is not necessary since the termination protocols are identical for both types of organization. However, the same is not true in the case of network partitioning. Recall from Chapter 11 that in the case of replicated databases, the replica control protocol has to be involved in mapping a read or a write on a logical data item to a read or a write on the physical data item copies. In the presence of network partitioning, the copies may be in different partitions and the replica control protocol has to be concerned with the management of network partitioning. In the presence of network partitioning of nonreplicated databases, on the other hand, the major concern is with the termination of transactions that were active at the time of partitioning. Any new transaction that accesses a data item that is stored in another partition is simply blocked and has to await the repair of the network. Concurrent accesses to the data items within one partition can be handled by the concurrency control algorithm. The significant problem, therefore, is to ensure that the transaction terminates properly. In short, in nonreplicated databases, the network partitioning problem is handled by the commit protocol, and more specifically, by the termination and recovery protocols, whereas in replicated databases it is the responsibility of the replica control protocol.

The absence of nonblocking protocols that would guarantee atomic commitment of distributed transactions points to an important design decision. We can either permit all the partitions to continue their normal operations and accept the fact that database consistency may be compromised, or we guarantee the consistency of the database by employing strategies that would permit operation in one of the partitions while the sites in the others remain blocked. This decision problem is the premise of a classification of partition handling strategies. We can classify the strategies as *pessimistic* or *optimistic* [Davidson et al., 1985]. Pessimistic strategies emphasize the consistency of the database, and would therefore not permit transactions to execute in a partition if there is no guarantee that the consistency of the database can be maintained. Optimistic approaches, on the other hand, emphasize the availability of the database even if this would cause inconsistencies.

The second dimension is related to the correctness criterion. If serializability is used as the fundamental correctness criterion, such strategies are called *syntactic* since the serializability theory uses only syntactic information. However, if we use a more abstract correctness criterion that is dependent on the semantics of the transactions or the database, the strategies are said to be *semantic*.

Consistent with the correctness criterion that we have adopted in this book (serializability), we consider only syntactic approaches in this section. The following two sections outline various syntactic strategies for nonreplicated and replicated databases.

### 12.7.1 Network Partitioning in Nonreplicated Databases

All the known termination protocols that deal with network partitioning in the case of nonreplicated databases are pessimistic. Since the pessimistic approaches emphasize the maintenance of database consistency, the fundamental issue that we need to address is which of the partitions can continue normal operations. We consider two approaches.

**Centralized protocols.**    Centralized termination protocols are based on the centralized concurrency control algorithms discussed in Chapter 11. Recall that these may be of two types: primary site and primary copy. In the case of primary site concurrency control algorithms, it makes sense to permit the operation of the partition that contains the primary site, since it manages the lock tables.

In the case of primary copy concurrency control algorithms, more than one partition may be operational for different queries. For any given query, only the partition that contains the primary copies of the data items that are in the write set of that transaction can execute that transaction.

Both of these are simple approaches that would work well, but they are dependent on the concurrency control mechanism employed by the distributed database manager. Furthermore, they expect each site to be able to differentiate network partitioning from site failures properly. This is necessary since the participants in the execution of the commit protocol react differently to the different types of failures.

**Voting-based protocols.**    Voting as a technique for managing concurrent data accesses has been proposed by a number of researchers. A straightforward voting with majority was first proposed in [Thomas, 1979] as a concurrency control method for fully replicated databases. The fundamental idea is that a transaction is executed if a majority of the sites vote to execute it.

The idea of majority voting has been generalized to voting with *quorums*. Quorum-based voting can be used as a replica control method (as we discuss in the next section), as well as a commit method to ensure transaction atomicity in the presence of network partitioning. In the case of nonreplicated databases, this involves the integration of the voting principle with commit protocols. We present next a specific proposal along this line [Skeen, 1982a].

Every site in the system is assigned a vote $V_i$. Let us assume that the total number of votes in the system is $V$, and the abort and commit quorums are $V_a$ and $V_c$, respectively. Then the following rules must be obeyed in the implementation of the commit protocol:

1. $V_a + V_c > V$, where $0 \leq V_a, V_c \leq V$.

2. Before a transaction commits, it must obtain a commit quorum $V_c$.

3. Before a transaction aborts, it must obtain an abort quorum $V_a$.

The first rule ensures that a transaction cannot be committed and aborted at the same time. The next two rules indicate the votes that a transaction has to obtain before it can terminate one way or the other.

The integration of these rules into the 3PC protocol requires a minor modification of the third phase. For the coordinator to move from the PRECOMMIT state to the COMMIT state, and to send the "global-commit" command, it is necessary for it to have obtained a commit quorum from the participants. This would satisfy rule 2. Note that we do not need to implement rule 3 explicitly. This is due to the fact that a transaction which is in the WAIT or READY state is willing to abort the transaction. Therefore, an abort quorum already exists.

Let us now consider the termination of transactions in the presence of failures. When a network partitioning occurs, the sites in each partition elect a new coordinator similar to the 3PC termination protocol in the case of site failures. There is a fundamental difference, however. It is not possible to make the transition from the WAIT or READY state to the ABORT state in one state transition, for a number of reasons. First, more than one coordinator is trying to terminate the transaction. We do not want them to terminate differently or the transaction execution will not be atomic. Therefore, we want the coordinators to obtain an abort quorum explicitly. Second, if the newly elected coordinator fails, it is not known whether a commit or abort quorum was reached. Thus it is necessary that participants make an explicit decision to join either the commit or the abort quorum and not change their votes afterward. Unfortunately, the READY (or WAIT) state does not satisfy these requirements. Thus we introduce another state, PREABORT, between the READY and ABORT states. The transition from the PREABORT state to the ABORT state requires an abort quorum. The state transition diagram is given in Figure 12.21.

With this modification, the termination protocol works as follows. Once a new coordinator is elected, it requests all participants to report their local states. Depending on the responses, it terminates the transaction as follows:

1. If at least one participant is in the COMMIT state, the coordinator decides to commit the transaction and send a "global-commit" message to all the participants.

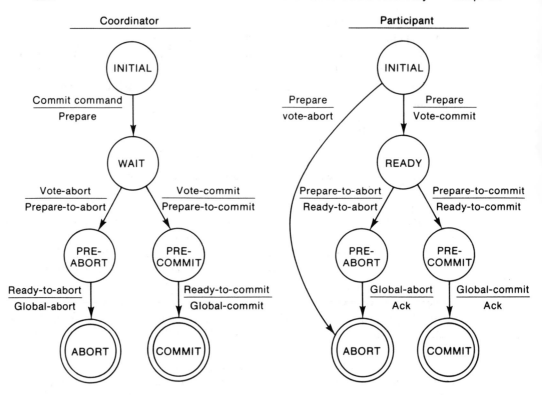

**Figure 12.21**   State Transitions in Quorum 3PC Protocol

2. If at least one participant is in the ABORT state, the coordinator decides to abort the transaction and sends a "global-abort" message to all the participants.

3. If a commit quorum is reached by the votes of participants in the PRECOMMIT state, the coordinator decides to commit the transaction and sends a "global-commit" message to all the participants.

4. If an abort quorum is reached by the votes of participants in the PREABORT state, the coordinator decides to abort the transaction and sends a "global-abort" message to all the participants.

5. If case 3 does not hold but the sum of the votes of the participants in the PRECOMMIT and READY states are enough to form a commit quorum, the coordinator moves the participants to the PRECOMMIT state by sending a "prepare-to-commit" message. The coordinator then waits for case 3 to hold.

6. Similarly, if case 4 does not hold but the sum of the votes of the participants in the PREABORT and READY states are enough to form an abort quorum, the coordinator moves the participants to the PREABORT state by sending a "prepare-to-abort" message. The coordinator then waits for case 4 to hold.

Two points are important about this quorum-based commit algorithm. First, it is blocking; the coordinator in a partition may not be able to form either an abort or a commit quorum if messages get lost or multiple partitionings occur. This is hardly surprising given the theoretical bounds that we discussed previously. The second point is that the algorithm is general enough to handle site failures as well as network partitioning. Therefore, this modified version of 3PC can provide more resiliency to failures.

The recovery protocol that can be used in conjunction with the above-discussed termination protocol is very simple. When two or more partitions merge, the sites that are part of the new larger partition simply execute the termination protocol. That is, a coordinator is elected to collect votes from all the participants and try to terminate the transaction.

### 12.7.2 Network Partitioning in Replicated Databases

As we discussed before, network partitioning in the case of replicated databases is addressed by the replica control protocol. In what follows we discuss only pessimistic protocols. We do not cover the optimistic approach to replica control [Davidson, 1984] because the assumptions of these methods are quite unrealistic for general transaction processing applications. A transaction is committed during failures subject to confirmation upon recovery. When recovery occurs, if the commit decision cannot be confirmed, the transaction has to be rolled back. Thus a transaction is committed, but its durability is not guaranteed. This is not appropriate for a large class of applications. In a banking application, for example, if money is dispensed to the customer as a result of a commit during failure, it may not be possible to claim it back. Even more seriously, if the application relates, for example, to a manufacturing operation where the transaction committing causes the equipment to perform an irreversible action (such as drilling a hole), the use of optimistic techniques is not appropriate.

Most of the pessimistic replica control protocols are based on some version of voting. Besides the initial algorithm by [Thomas, 1979], an early suggestion to use quorum-based voting for replica control is due to [Gifford, 1979]. Thomas's algorithm works on fully replicated databases and assigns an equal vote to each site. For any operation of a transaction to execute, it must collect affirmative votes from a majority of the sites. Gifford's algorithm, on the other hand, works with partially replicated databases (as well as with fully replicated ones) and assigns a vote to each copy of a replicated data item. Each operation then has to obtain a *read quorum* ($V_r$) or a *write quorum* ($V_w$) to read or write a data item, respectively. If a given data item has a total of $V$ votes, the quorums have to obey the following rules:

1. $V_r + V_w > V$
2. $V_w > V/2$

As the reader may recall from the preceding section, the first rule ensures that a data item is not read and written by two transactions concurrently (avoiding the read-write conflict). The second rule, on the other hand, ensures that two write operations from two transactions cannot occur concurrently on the same data item (avoiding write-write conflict). Thus the two rules ensure that one-copy serializability is maintained.

The difficulty with this approach is that transactions are required to obtain a quorum even to read data. This significantly and unnecessarily slows down read access to the database. We describe below another quorum-based voting protocol [Abbadi et al., 1985] that overcomes this serious performance drawback.

The protocol makes certain assumptions about the underlying communication layer and the occurrence of failures. The assumption about failures is that they are "clean." This means two things:

1. Failures that change the network's topology are detected by all sites instantaneously.
2. Each site has a view of the network consisting of all the sites with which it can communicate.

Based on the presence of a communication network that can ensure these two conditions, the replica control protocol is a simple implementation of the ROWA principle. When the replica control protocol attempts to read or write a data item, it first checks if a majority of the sites are in the same partition as the site at which the protocol is running. If so, it implements the ROWA rule within that partition: it reads any copy of the data item and writes all copies that are in that partition.

Notice that the read or the write operation will execute in only one partition. Therefore, this is a pessimistic protocol that guarantees one-copy serializability. When the partitioning is repaired, the database is recovered by propagating the results of the update to the other partitions.

The fundamental question with respect to implementation of this protocol is whether or not the failure assumptions are realistic. Unfortunately, they are not. Most network failures are not "clean." There is a time delay between the occurrence of a failure and its detection by a site. Because of this delay, it is possible for one site to think that it is in one partition when in fact subsequent failures have placed it in another partition. Furthermore, this delay may be different for various sites. Thus two sites that were in the same partition but are now in different partitions may proceed for a while under the assumption that they are still in the same partition. The violations of these two failure assumptions have significant negative consequences on the replica control protocol and its ability to maintain one-copy serializability.

The suggested solution is to build on top of the physical communication layer another layer of abstraction which hides the "unclean" failure characteristics of the physical communication layer and presents to the replica control protocol a communication service that has "clean" failure properties. This new layer of abstraction provides *virtual partitions* within which the replica control protocol operates. A virtual partition is a group of sites that have agreed on a common view of who is in that partition. Sites join and depart from virtual partitions under the control of this new communication layer, which ensures that the clean failure assumptions hold.

The advantage of this protocol is its simplicity. It does not incur any overhead to maintain a quorum for read accesses. Thus the reads can proceed as fast as they would in a nonpartitioned network. Furthermore, it is general enough so that the replica control protocol does not need to differentiate between site failures and network partitions.

## 12.8  ARCHITECTURAL CONSIDERATIONS

In previous sections we have discussed the atomic commit protocols at an abstract level. Let us now look at how these protocols can be implemented within the framework of our architectural model. This discussion involves specification of the interface between the concurrency control algorithms and the reliability protocols. In that sense, the discussions of this chapter relate to the execution of **commit** and **recover** commands.

Unfortunately, it is quite difficult to specify precisely the execution of these commands. The difficulty is twofold. First, a significantly more detailed model of the architecture than the one we have presented needs to be considered for correct implementation of these commands. Second, the overall scheme of implementation is quite dependent on the recovery procedures that the local recovery manager implements. For example, implementation of the 2PC protocol on top of a LRM that employs a no-fix/no-flush recovery scheme is quite different from its implementation on top of a LRM that employs a fix/flush recovery scheme. The alternatives are simply too numerous. We therefore confine our architectural discussion to three areas: implementation of the coordinator and participant concepts for the commit and replica control protocols within the framework of the transaction manager-scheduler-local recovery manager architecture, the coordinator's access to the database log, and the changes that need to be made in the local recovery manager operations.

One possible implementation of the commit protocols within our architectural model is to perform both the coordinator and participant algorithms within the transaction managers at each site. This provides some uniformity in executing the distributed commit operations. However, it entails unnecessary communication between the participant transaction manager and its scheduler; this is because the scheduler has to decide whether a transaction can be committed or aborted. Therefore, it may be preferable to implement the coordinator as part of the transaction manager and the participant as part of the scheduler. Of course, the replica control protocol is implemented as part of the transaction manager as well. If the scheduler implements a strict concurrency control algorithm (i.e., does not allow cascading aborts), it will be ready automatically to commit the transaction when the prepare message arrives. Proof of this claim is left as an exercise. However, even this alternative of implementing the coordinator and the participant outside the data processor has problems. First issue is database log management. Recall from Section 12.4 that the database log is maintained by the LRM and the buffer manager. However, implementation of the commit protocol as described here requires the transaction manager and the scheduler to access the log as well. One possible solution to this problem is to maintain a commit log [which could be called the *distributed transaction log* ([Bernstein et al., 1987] and [Lampson and Sturgis, 1976])] which is accessed by the transaction manager and is separate from the database log that the LRM and buffer manager maintain. The other alternative is to write the commit protocol records into the same database log. This second alternative has a number of advantages. First, only one log is maintained; this simplifies the algorithms that have to be implemented in order to save log records on stable storage. More important, the recovery from failures in a distributed database requires the cooperation of the local recovery manager and the scheduler (i.e., the participant). A single database log can serve as a central repository of recovery information for both these components.

A second problem associated with implementing the coordinator within the transaction manager and the participant as part of the scheduler has to be with integration with the concurrency control protocols. This implementation is based on the schedulers determining whether a transaction can be committed. This is fine for distributed concurrency control algorithms where each site is equipped with a scheduler. However, in centralized protocols such as the centralized 2PL, there is only one scheduler in the system. In this case, the participants may be implemented as part of the local recovery managers, requiring modification to both the algorithms implemented by the LRM and, possibly, to the execution of the 2PC protocol. We leave the details to exercises.

Storing the commit protocol records in the database log maintained by the LRM and the buffer manager requires some changes to the LRM algorithms. This is the third architectural issue we address. Unfortunately, these changes are dependent on the type of algorithm that the LRM uses. In general, however, the LRM algorithms have to be modified to handle separately the prepare command and global commit (or global abort) decisions. Furthermore, upon recovery, the LRM should be modified to read the database log and to inform the scheduler as to the state of each transaction, in order that the recovery procedures discussed before can be followed. Let us take a more detailed look at this function of the LRM.

The LRM first has to determine whether the failed site is the host of the coordinator or of a participant. This information can be stored together with the begin_transaction record. The LRM then has to search for the last record written in the log record during execution of the commit protocol. If it cannot even find a begin_commit record (at the coordinator site) or an abort or commit record (at the participant sites), the transaction has not started to commit. In this case the LRM can continue with its recovery procedure as we discussed in Section 12.4.3. However, if the commit process has started, the recovery has to be handed over to the coordinator. Therefore, the LRM sends the last log record to the scheduler.

## 12.9 CONCLUSION

In this chapter we discussed the reliability aspects of distributed transaction management. The studied algorithms (2PC and 3PC) guarantee the atomicity and durability of distributed transactions even when failures occur. One of these algorithms (3PC) can be made nonblocking, which would permit each site to continue its operation without waiting for recovery of the failed site. An unfortunate result that we presented relates to network partitioning. It is not possible to design protocols that guarantee the atomicity of distributed transactions and permit each partition of the distributed system to continue its operation under the assumptions made in this chapter with respect to the functionality of the communication subnet. The performance of the distributed commit protocols with respect to the overhead they add to the concurrency control algorithms is an interesting issue. Some studies have address this issue ([Dwork and Skeen, 1983], [Özsu and Koon, 1987], and [Wolfson, 1987]).

A final point that should be stressed is the following. We have considered only failures that are attributable to errors. In other words, we assumed that every effort was made to design and implement the systems (hardware and software), but that because of various faults in the components, the design, or the operating environment, they failed to perform properly. Such failures are called *failures of omission*. There is another class of failures, called *failures of commission*, where the systems may not have been designed and implemented so that they would work properly. The difference is that in the execution of the 2PC protocol, for example, if a participant receives a message from the coordinator, it treats this message as correct: the coordinator is operational and is sending the participant a correct message to go ahead and process. The only failure that the participant has to worry about is if the coordinator fails or if its messages get lost. These are failures of omission. If, on the other hand, the messages that a participant receives cannot be trusted, the participant also has to deal with failures of commission. For example, a participant site may pretend to be the coordinator and may send a malicious message. We have not discussed reliability measures that are necessary to cope with these types of failures. The techniques that address failures of commission are typically called *byzantine agreement*.

## 12.10 BIBLIOGRAPHIC NOTES

There are numerous books on the reliability of computer systems. These include [Anderson and Lee, 1981], [Anderson and Randell, 1979], [Avizienis et al., 1987], [Longbottom, 1980], [Gibbons, 1976], [Pradhan, 1986], [Siewiorek and Swarz, 1982], and [Shrivastava, 1985]. In addition, the survey paper [Randell et al., 1978] addresses the same issues. [Myers, 1976] specifically addresses software reliability. An important software fault tolerance technique that we have not discussed in this chapter is exception handling. This issue is treated in [Cristian, 1982], [Cristian, 1985], and [Cristian, 1987]. [Johnson and Malek, 1988] surveys the existing software tools for reliability measurement.

With respect to our discussion of process pairs, the lock-step process pair approach is implemented in the Stratus/32 systems ([Stratus, 1982] and [Kim, 1984]) for hardware processes. An automatic checkpointing process pairs approach is used in the Auras (TM) operating system for Aurogen computers ([Borg et al., 1983] and

[Gastonian, 1983]). State checkpointing has been used in earlier versions of the Tandem operating systems ([Bartlett, 1978] and [Bartlett, 1981]), which have later utilized the delta checkpointing approach [Borr, 1984]. The latest versions of the Tandem OS utilize persistent process pairs for fault tolerance.

More detailed material on the functions of the local recovery manager discussed in Section 12.4 can be found in [Verhofstadt, 1978] and [Härder and Reuter, 1983]. Implementation of the local recovery functions in System R is described in [Gray et al., 1981].

[Kohler, 1981] presents a general discussion of the reliability issues in distributed database systems. [Hadzilacos, 1988] is a formalization of the reliability concept. The reliability aspects of System R* is given in [Traiger et al., 1982], whereas [Hammer and Shipman, 1980] describe the same for the SDD-1 system.

The two-phase commit protocol is first described in [Gray, 1979]. Modifications to it are presented in [Mohan and Lindsay, 1983]. The definition of three-phase commit is due to Skeen ([Skeen, 1981] and [Skeen, 1982b]. Formal results on the existence of nonblocking termination protocols is due to [Skeen and Stonebraker, 1983].

Replica control protocols that deal with network partitioning are surveyed in [Davidson et al., 1985]. Besides the algorithm we have described here, others are given in [Davidson, 1984], [Eager and Sevcik, 1983], [Herlihy, 1987], [Minoura and Wiederhold, 1982], [Skeen and Wright, 1984], and [Wright, 1983].

Our discussion of checkpointing has been rather short. Further treatment of the issue can be found in [Bhargava and Lian, 1988], [Dadam and Schlageter, 1980], [Schlageter and Dadim, 1980], [Kuss, 1982], [Ng, 1988], and [Ramanathan and Shin, 1988]. Byzantine agreement is surveyed in [Strong and Dolev, 1983] and is discussed in [Babaoglu, 1987] and [Pease et al., 1980].

## 12.11 EXERCISES

**12.1**  Briefly describe the various implementations of the process pairs concept. Comment on how process pairs may be useful in implementing a fault-tolerant distributed DBMS.

**\*12.2**  Discuss the site failure termination protocol for 2PC using a distributed communication topology.

**\*12.3**  Design a 3PC protocol using the linear communication topology.

**\*12.4**  In our presentation of the centralized 3PC termination protocol, the first step involves sending the coordinator's state to all participants. The participants move to new states according to the coordinator's state. It is possible to design the termination protocol such that the coordinator, instead of sending its own state information to the participants, asks the participants to send their state information to the coordinator. Modify the termination protocol to function in this manner.

**\*\*12.5**  In Section 12.8 we claimed that a scheduler which implements a strict concurrency control algorithm will always be ready to commit a transaction when it receives the coordinator's "prepare" message. Prove this claim.

**\*\*12.6**  Assuming that the coordinator is implemented as part of the transaction manager and the participant as part of the scheduler, give the transaction manager, scheduler, and the local recovery manager algorithms for a nonreplicated distributed DBMS under the following assumptions.

(a)  The scheduler implements a distributed (strict) two-phase locking concurrency control algorithm.

(b)  The commit protocol log records are written to a central database log by the LRM when it is called by the scheduler.

(c)  The LRM may implement any of the protocols that have been discussed in Section 12.4.3. However, it is modified to support the distributed recovery procedures as we discussed in Section 12.8.

**\*12.7**  Write the detailed algorithms for the no-fix/no-flush local recovery manager.

**\*\*12.8**  Assume that

(a)  The scheduler implements a centralized two-phase locking concurrency control,

(b)  The LRM implements no-fix/no-flush protocol.  Give detailed algorithms for transaction manager, scheduler, and local recovery managers.

**12.9**  Consider data items $x$ and $y$ replicated across the sites as follows:

| Site 1 | Site 2 | Site 3 | Site 4 |
|--------|--------|--------|--------|
| $x$    | $x$    |        | $x$    |
|        | $y$    | $y$    | $y$    |

(a)  Assign votes to each site and give the commit and abort quorum.

(b)  Determine the possible ways that the network can partition and for each specify in which group of sites a transaction that updates (reads and writes) $x$ can be terminated and what the termination condition would be.

(c)  Repeat **(b)** for $y$.

**\*\*12.10**  Give the algorithm of a replica control protocol that implements the quorum-based voting protocol discussed in Section 12.7.1.

# 13

# Distributed Database Operating Systems

In previous chapters we discussed in considerable detail the functions performed by a DBMS. It is customary for a centralized or distributed DBMS to run as a user application on top of a host operating system (OS) and to use its functions. However, there is now significant evidence that such a mode of operation may not yield the best results in terms of the functionality and performance of DBMS software ([Gray, 1979], [Stonebraker, 1981], [Tanenbaum and Mullender, 1982], and [Christmann et al., 1987]). It has become clear that the functionality of the operating systems needs to be modified and enhanced considerably to satisfy the DBMS requirements. There is now a realization that the DBMS and OS perform both similar and complementary functions and that a better cooperation paradigm needs to be found.

This chapter is unique in its orientation, as its topic has not yet been fully researched and understood. The database community has restricted its research related to operating system support to basically two areas: buffer management and transaction support. Even though there are some research projects that address the more general architectural issues (e.g., [Özsu et al., 1988] and [Härder, 1988]), there is no clear understanding of how an operating system should be structured to provide adequate support for the DBMS functionality. In this chapter we discuss some of the relevant technical issues and point to new research problems involved.

Another way to look at this chapter is as a short introduction to the operating system issues for database researchers and specialists. We believe that this introduction is both necessary and long overdue. The two communities rarely cooperate to find the most suitable operating system and DBMS architectures. The isolated efforts have, unfortunately but understandingly, failed to produce reasonable solutions to date.

The outline of this chapter is as follows. In Section 13.1 we present the framework within which the above-mentioned issues arise. In Sections 13.2 to 13.5 we look at a number of issues that need to be resolved in distributed operating systems. The emphasis in these sections is on the special requirements of the distributed DBMS in terms of DOS services. Sections 13.6 and 13.7 review the issues of buffer management and operating system support for transactions. In Section 13.8 we discuss the architectural issues in distributed operating systems. The discussion addresses the architectural paradigm that should be used for the proper cooperation of the distributed operating system (DOS) and the distributed DBMS in providing the functionality that is addressed in previous sections.

## 13.1 FRAMEWORK

Traditionally, operating systems provide the following functions: (1) hardware management (i.e., handling interrupts), (2) process management, (3) resource allocation (scheduling), (4) storage management and access (I/O), (5) memory management, (6) file system service, and (7) protection of both the system and the user resources. In addition, the DOS provides additional functionality, such as (8) better reliability (survivability), (9) scaleability (expandability), (10) improved performance, and (11) support for hardware heterogeneity.

The DOS functionalities specified above are general and do not fully represent the requirements of centralized or distributed DBMSs. Indeed, DBMSs require additional functions (e.g., full transaction support, more complicated access methods) that are not provided by the file systems. Furthermore, they need different ways of handling numerous other problems (e.g., memory and cache buffer management, concurrency control). We discuss each of these issues in some detail in subsequent sections. For the time being, suffice it to say that the underlying issue in all these problems is that the functionalities provided by the operating system for database management are usually not satisfactory, and therefore the DBMS attempts to implement these services in its own workspace. This would not be a problem if the operating system actually provided the tools to build these services. Unfortunately, given that such tools are generally not provided, there is a duplication of functions.

The problems we address in this chapter have arisen with the development of relational DBMSs. The earlier DBMSs which support the hierarchical and network data models provide primitive record-at-a-time access to data. Thus the user writes a program to access the entire set of data items that need to be retrieved. The behavior of such a program may not be significantly different from that of other user programs and can therefore be supported by conventional operating systems. Relational DBMSs, on the other hand, have significantly different access behavior, due to the high-level access primitives with which users are provided.

In recent years the problem has become more severe as traditional DBMSs are fast approaching the limits of what they can provide for various new application areas. For example, engineering databases, real-time systems, and multimedia databases usually require new models and implementation methods (as we discuss in Chapter 15), whereas for applications such as on-line transaction processing, the performance needs to be improved significantly.

When the necessary functionality and performance is provided for new application areas, two bottlenecks can occur: the processor bottleneck and the database bottleneck.

1. The processor bottleneck is due mainly to limitations of the von Neumann computer architecture in supporting nonnumeric applications as well as the technological limitations, such as the I/O bandwidth restrictions. To overcome this problem, special-purpose computer architectures called *database machines* or *database computers* have been developed and are now commercially available. We can also count on new technologies, such as optical disks, more intelligent disk drivers, and multiprocessor computers, to assist us in the solution of these technical problems. We discuss database machines in distributed environments in Chapter 15. More information can be found in [Ozkarahan, 1986] and [Valduriez and Gardarin, 1989].

2. The database bottleneck occurs as a result of having to manage a large volume of data that is accessed by large numbers of users. Distributed database management is one of the alternative methods of solving this problem whereby the inherent parallelism of the distributed system is exploited to handle multiple accesses concurrently.

There are two approaches to integrating DBMSs with operating systems. One popular proposal has been to include the data management functions within the operating system kernel. A number of vendors have selected this approach, which leads to the design of special-purpose "database operating systems" where the DBMS practically serves as the operating system. Most of the OS functionality is implemented within the DBMS workspace. This approach, which we call the *tightly coupled design*, is a reasonable route to take in the case of database machines where the system is dedicated to the execution of one task and can therefore be tuned to best support that task. It is also a reasonable approach in cases where a system is tuned for a specific task, such as transaction processing. For general-purpose computing environments, however, this may not be particularly appealing since the operating system is supposed to provide functions that are required not only by the DBMS and its applications but also by the general-purpose computing tasks that are to be performed. This leads to *loosely coupled* systems, which are the focus of this chapter.

Let us turn to another issue that defines the emphasis of this chapter. In Chapter 4 we discussed various types of transparencies and those responsible for providing them. The issues of transparency are related to the abstraction levels that the system provides for its users. When one considers the data as they are stored on secondary storage and the view of the distributed DBMS user with respect to that stored data, the difference in the levels of abstraction is obvious. This is also commonly referred to as the *semantic gap* between representations. The various abstraction levels that exist between the two extreme views of data are depicted in Figure 13.1. Some of these abstractions are related to the distribution of data, whereas others have to do with its storage at each site.

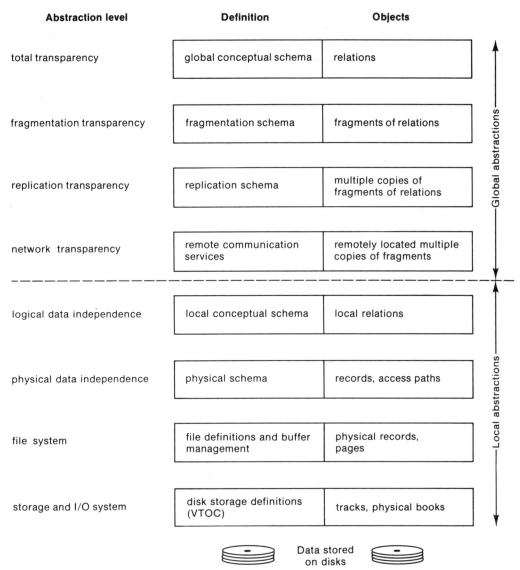

**Figure 13.1**    Abstraction Levels (Adapted from [Christmann et al., 1987].)

Obviously, from the viewpoint of providing easy and efficient access by users to the services of the distributed DBMS, one would desire to have full transparency, which involves all the types discussed in Chapter 4. The user would then see the database organized as a collection of relations as defined in the global conceptual schema of the distributed database. Thus there would not be any difference between the user's access to a centralized database and to a distributed one. This level of transparency may not be necessary for other distributed applications, but it is very important for database systems and their evolution from centralized to distributed applications. Inevitably, however, the level of transparency is an issue of compromises where the difficulty and overhead of providing high levels of transparency have to be balanced against the advantages due to ease of use.

An issue orthogonal to the transparencies has to do with operational considerations. In this context we are referring to issues related to concurrent access to system resources (of which data is only one) by multiple clients, maintenance of a consistent system state in the face of failures and recovery from them, protection of system resources, and so on.

Recall from Chapter 4 that we discussed the possibility of supporting transparencies at the language, operating system, or DBMS levels. Similar arguments can be made for the operational services listed above. In fact, most current DBMSs take over the provision of full-access transparency as well as the operational features. In earlier chapters we discussed techniques by which distributed DBMSs address these issues. There are programming systems that take over a number of these responsibilities as well. A notable example is the Argus [Liskov, 1988] system, which provides data abstraction and modularization, synchronization of concurrent accesses to system modules, and recovery (in the sense discussed in Chapter 12) from failures. The position that we take in this chapter is that these responsibilities should be shared between the operating system and the DBMS, and the issue is to find an architectural paradigm that lends itself easily to such coexistence.

Specifically, probably the data independence and the fragmentation transparencies are within the domain of the DBMS. However, the network and the replication transparencies can easily be provided by the distributed OS. If this can be achieved, various DBMS functions are simplified significantly. Furthermore, transparent access to the OS services are provided to the other applications as well as to the distributed DBMS. Most of the distributed OS research concentrates on the network transparency aspects of distributed computing, completely ignoring the replication transparency.

## 13.2 NAMING, ACCESS CONTROL, AND PROTECTION

The naming of OS services and other system entities (e.g., files, compilers, etc.) is a significant problem in distributed computing environments. The naming issue is commonly treated separately from the access control and protection problem. It is possible, however, to treat both issues uniformly by means of a powerful tool called a *capability*. In this section we first study both of these problems separately and then discuss how they can be addressed by capabilities.

### 13.2.1 Naming

A feature of the state-of-the-art DBMSs is the nonprocedural user interface that they provide for accessing the data. This provides the transparency of the data distribution and its structure, which we discussed above.

The fundamental means available to the operating system for providing transparent access to *all* system resources is the naming mechanism that it uses. The naming scheme should have the following features:

1. *Sharing of objects*. Multiple accesses to a system entity[1] from other entities should be permitted. For example, multiple users should be able to access a file just as they would a compiler.

2. *Replication support*. If there are replicas of a given entity, it is useful to be able to access any or a specific copy of that entity. Furthermore, it is important for the OS to support the updating and recovery of replicated entities.

3. *Fully transparent access*. The name resolution scheme should permit access to an entity only by its name, regardless of its location. The entity may be located (a) on the same machine and in the same directory as the one from which the access is made, or (b) on the same machine but in a directory different than the one from which the access is made, or (c) on another machine.

To support these features the operating systems implement two names for each entity: an *internal name* and an *external name*. Internal names are usually fixed-length binary numbers, whereas external names are user-defined character strings of arbitrary length. While users access objects via the external name, the OS operates on them using the internal name. The challenge is to find an external naming scheme that supports transparency, while the fixed-length internal name facilitates efficient manipulation of entities within the operating system [Saltzer, 1979].

We are talking, among other things, about the translation of external names for the database entities to internal names. Since the database entities, such as relations and fragments, are also treated as system entities, providing transparent access to them can be a service provided by the OS kernel.

A design decision relates to the manner and place of the name translation. Depending on the type of network and performance requirements, the name translation tables can be maintained centrally at one site or distributed to all the sites. Broadcasting local area networks with their high bandwidth may be more suitable for the latter, whereas star networks may appropriately employ centralized name translation. Furthermore, storing a separate name translation table at each site for those remote

---

[1] We use the term *entity* quite loosely here, referring to everything that needs to be named and addressed in a computer system. Even though these are usually files, we prefer to refer to them by their names. Thus the system entities are things such as users, files, programs, operating system service modules, and so on.

objects that have recently been invoked may reduce the name translation overhead considerably.

### 13.2.2 Access Control and Protection

Operating systems perform two protection functions: user authentication and authorization control. As we discussed in Chapter 6, *authorization control* deals with ensuring that only authorized users have access to computer resources. Furthermore, users should only have access to resources that are permitted to them. *Authentication*, on the other hand, is the process of guaranteeing that the users are indeed who they claim to be.

Traditionally, authentication is performed by means of user passwords. Highly reliable systems have used more elaborate mechanisms, such as fingerprint recognition. Authorization control, in most operating systems, is a function performed by the file system. Again, this is due to the fact that files are the only permanent objects. The file system enforces different access rights for different classes of users. For example, UNIX groups users of a file into three categories: the owner of the file, the group to which the owner belongs, and the rest of the world. For each class of users, a file may be accessible for reading, writing, execution, or any combination of these. The access rights can be modified by the owner of the file, who is, therefore, responsible for the protection of individual files.

### 13.2.3 Capabilities

As stated above, the protection mechanism used in most existing operating systems is disjoint from the naming scheme employed. It is, however, possible using capabilities to address both of these issues uniformly. Capabilities are indicators of the rights that an entity has for another entity. They serve as the fundamental building blocks for naming as well as for protection. To access an entity, it is necessary to have a capability for it.

For each entity that can be accessed in the system, there is at least one capability held by the creator of that entity. As access to that entity is permitted to others, the capability is duplicated. Capabilities can also be deleted, eventually resulting in an entity becoming useless (i.e., no capabilities being held for it).

The format of a capability (Figure 13.2) consists of a *rights field* and a *name field*. The rights field is a bit map where each bit defines one operation that can be performed on that entity. The name field of the entity contains the *internal name*, which is usually a binary number. The users can store capabilities by giving them names. The name that is given to a capability is the *external name* of the entity.

The use of capabilities is a convenient way of solving the transparent naming problem which reduces to mapping external names to internal names. Since the external names are assigned by individual users, it would be possible either to maintain the uniqueness of the external names or to adopt conventions that enable the choice of the appropriate capability. Site and storage information may be encoded in the

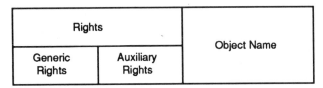

**Figure 13.2**    Capability Structure

internal name which is not accessible to the users. To provide transparent access, the operating system kernel has to simply implement a mechanism that maps an external name to an internal one. A recent distributed operating system that makes use of capabilities is Amoeba [Tanenbaum and Mullender, 1981].

Capabilities are useful in resolving access control issues as well. There are certain operations that can be performed on any capability for any type of entity. There are other operations that are specific to a given entity type. For example, copying the rights field of a capability is defined for all capabilities, whereas an operation called "read" may have been defined only for files. The rights field is divided into two sections to accommodate this distinction. The former is called the *generic rights* field and the latter is the *auxiliary rights* field [Cohen and Jefferson, 1975]. Auxiliary rights are defined by the creator of an entity according to the specific operations implemented for that entity. Generic rights are defined by the operating system for each type of entity.

Capabilities should be protected from being tampered with by users. There are a number of ways of achieving this. Hardware solutions involve the use of *tagged memory* or *partitioned memory* [Fabry, 1974]. In a system with tagged memory, each memory word has one or more tag bits associated with it which indicate whether or not the word contains a capability. In the case of partitioned memory, there are separate capability and data segments in memory. Only the capability segment—which can be accessed only by the OS kernel—contains capabilities.

Software-based approaches to capability protection involve encryption [Mullender and Tanenbaum, 1984], and hiding within the kernel [Lau, 1988]. In the former, the rights field of a capability is encrypted in a way known only to the server that issues the capability, and is checked every time an access is made. The capabilities can therefore be stored in each user's address space. In the latter approach, the capabilities are maintained inside the kernel, where only the OS kernel can access and modify them. The external names given to the capabilities are stored in the users' local address spaces and are mapped to the capabilities by the OS kernel.

## 13.3  SCHEDULING

A *process* is commonly defined as a program in execution. This is an acceptable definition as long as one does not lose sight of the fact that a program may execute as multiple processes. The important point is that a process is the smallest unit of work that may be scheduled for execution. In this section we deal with the scheduling of processes and process groups. We divide this discussion into two parts by first concentrating on individual processes, and then moving on to scheduling process groups in a distributed environment.

### 13.3.1 Local Process Management

An operating system performs the following functions related to process and processor management:

1.  *Low-level process control.* The typical operations that need to be implemented for this purpose are: to create a new process, to kill an existing process, to fork out a new process, and to join two processes, resulting in the destruction of one and the continuation of the other.
2.  *Dispatching.* This function involves the low-level scheduling of processes. A process is typically in one of three states: running, ready, and blocked. The dispatcher manages the movement of a process among these states.
3.  *Synchronization.* The concurrent execution of processes requires their synchronization. A typical synchronization technique is the use of semaphores. Semaphores can also be implemented as entities that can be created, destroyed, and initialized, as well as supporting the well-known P and V operations.
4.  *Deadlock management.* Concurrent execution of processes may cause deadlocks. To handle deadlocks, the well-known methods of prevention, avoidance, or detection and resolution may be used. We should indicate that the deadlock management function at this level deals with local deadlocks since only local processes are handled by the process manager.

As discussed in [Stonebraker, 1981], there are two ways of organizing a multiuser DBMS. One approach is to have one process per user, each sharing the code segment of the DBMS process as well as some common data segments, such as lock tables, buffers, and so on (Figure 13.3). The requirement for the process manager is to permit the sharing of data segments between processes. There are four problems with this approach:

1.  Creating a process for each user request can be expensive, especially when the processes are big and contain a significant amount of state information.
2.  Whenever a database process issues an I/O request, a context switch is performed. Again, the size of the process tends to make such switches inefficient.
3.  Scheduling of the database processes by the OS is troublesome. DBMSs usually implement their own semaphores to provide mutually exclusive access to DBMS resources such as lock tables and buffer pools. Since these

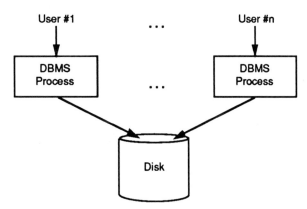

**Figure 13.3**  Process-per-User Approach (From: M. Stonebraker, OPERATING SYSTEM SUPPORT FOR DATABASE MANAGEMENT. COMM. ACM; July 1981; 24(7): 412–418.)

semaphores are implemented by the DBMS that runs at the user space, the OS does not know of these semaphores. If a DBMS process is deactivated by the OS scheduler (because of time slicing or I/O blocking) while holding one of these semaphores, other database processes that want to set this semaphore will be blocked. Soon this waiting queue will grow and form what is known as a *convoy* [Blasgen et al., 1979]. Convoys have been shown to have devastating effects on system performance and should therefore be prevented.

4. There is the limitation on the number of the database processes since the total cannot be more than the maximum number of OS processes permitted.

An alternative approach is to have a single DBMS server which receives requests from users and performs them on their behalf (Figure 13.4). This approach is gaining popularity among DBMS vendors. Such an approach has two requirements: (1) it should be able to do its own multitasking by scheduling the various requests, and (2) it should be possible to communicate efficiently between users and server in both directions. Thus the operating system should be flexible enough to permit the DBMS process to perform these functions. It is, of course, possible to have multiple server processes.

### 13.3.2 Distributed Scheduling

In the preceding section we discussed the local process scheduling issues on a single computer. In a distributed setting, one has to deal with an additional issue, the scheduling of processes to processors. A fundamental difference between process management in a centralized and a distributed OS is an issue that was raised in Chapter 1. In centralized systems, all the information about resources is easily maintained

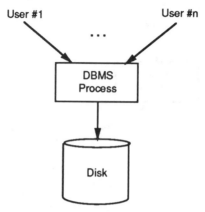

**Figure 13.4** Server DBMS Approach (From M. Stonebraker, OPERATING SYSTEM SUPPORT FOR DATABASE MANAGEMENT. COMM. ACM; July 1981; 24(7): 412–418.)

in system tables, providing immediate and up-to-date information about their status. In a distributed system, management of these tables is not that straightforward. If they are maintained independently by each local OS, no immediate information is available about the status of remote resources. If the system design involves the management of these tables centrally, reliability problems would arise since the tables would be unreachable as a result of the failure of a single site.

To separate the issues of local process management from distributed scheduling, let us introduce the concept of a *task*,[2] which includes the set of processes that run together (possibly on different computers) to execute a program.

Two operations need to be provided for the manipulation of a task: (1) scheduling a task, and (2) unscheduling a task by terminating its constituent processes. The discussion in this section relates to the design decisions regarding the semantics of these two operations. We will, however, only summarize the alternative techniques. These issues are the topics of much OS research and are discussed in OS texts that we cite in Section 13.10.

In a centralized OS, the scheduling function implements the policy decisions which determine the process that gets control of the single processor. This is achieved by a number of scheduling policies, such as first-come-first-served, round robin, shortest time first, prioritization, and so on. In a distributed OS, there are a number of additional functions related to scheduling, all of which are related to assigning processors to processes.

Given a set of processes and a set of processors, the scheduler is responsible for assigning the processes to processors. There are alternative means of performing this task. One method is to find the subsets of the processes in a given set and place members of each subset on different processors to make use of the parallelism. To

---

[2]This is not a standard term, but one that we are introducing here for convenience in discussing distributed scheduling issues.

avoid the delays in interprocess communication between the members of one subset, a technique called *coscheduling* [Osterhout, 1982] can be used, where each member of the subset is executed on a different processor but at the same time (i.e., during the same time slice). This ensures that processes do not have to wait for their remote counterparts to be active to be able to communicate with them.

An alternative distributed scheduling policy is to determine the subsets of processors as indicated above, but execute them concurrently on one processor. Obviously, such a strategy aims at minimizing the communication between remote processes, at the expense of parallel execution.

A third alternative distributed scheduling policy is to schedule a process to run on a processor with the least amount of load. These policies migrate processes from one processor to another in an attempt to balance the overall load. An obvious assumption that is made in these algorithms is that it is possible to run *any* process on *any* processor, which may be possible theoretically but difficult to maintain in practice.

A final related problem that the distributed scheduler has to address is that of distributed deadlock, since tasks that are located at different processors can interact with one another. Having discussed distributed deadlock management in detail in Chapter 11, we will not address it any further.

From the perspective of the distributed DBMS, the distributed scheduling issue is related strongly to problems of distributed query processing. Query processors are responsible for taking a high-level user query and developing an efficient distributed execution plan for that query. Thus the challenge in this area is to find suitable ways of enabling the cooperation of distributed query processors with distributed operating system schedulers.

## 13.4  REMOTE COMMUNICATION

Communication between processes in a traditional centralized OS is typically achieved by using primitives such as **signal** and **wait**. In a distributed OS, communication support needs to be provided for remote processes. It is possible to treat these issues uniformly by adopting a communication mechanism common to both local and remote processes.

The requirements for a communications service can be listed as follows:

1.  Access to remote resources should be the same, from the user's perspective, as access to local resources. This point brings up the issue of naming and transparency, which we have already discussed.

2.  The service should be efficient. Communication is probably the most important factor affecting the performance of distributed operating systems. It is not reasonable to expect remote communication to be as efficient as communication between two local processes; nevertheless, the design should emphasize the efficiency of this service.

3. The system users (of all kinds) should be provided with a flexible, easy-to-use, semantically rich, and consistent interface for communicating between system entities. The user interface for communication between local and remote entities should not be different.

4. Remote communication should be compatible with networking protocols. This enables delegation of a considerable amount of the communication responsibility to network services, with the OS communication manager providing a higher level of abstraction. We should point out that this is a controversial requirement not necessarily accepted by all researchers.

5. The service should be reliable. Recall from Chapter 12 that for reliable functioning of the DBMS in the presence of network partitioning as well as site failures, the OS can be of assistance. Specifically, the OS should provide session-based communication, thereby delegating the responsibility of dealing with lost and duplicate messages to the OS communication manager. It is therefore necessary to perform message buffering and handshaking to ensure reliable host-to-host delivery.

Two alternative approaches have been proposed for remote interprocess communication: *message passing* and *remote procedure calls* (RPC) ([Birrell, 1985] and [Birrell and Nelson, 1984]). Let us look at each alternative in some detail.

## 13.4.1 Message Passing

The discussion here is not on physical message passing between two nodes of a computer network, but on logical message passing between two processes regardless of whether they are located on the same machine or on two separate machines. Note that we dealt with the issues of physical message passing on a computer network in Chapter 3.

In the logical sense, a message is a text of variable length. There are two communication primitives: **send** and **receive**. The semantics of each primitive depends on a number of design decisions:

1. Is the message physically copied from the sender's address space to the receiver's?
2. Are the primitives blocking or nonblocking?
3. Are the primitives reliable or unreliable?
4. Are the primitives buffered or unbuffered?

Before we consider each of these issues, let us consider the simplest interpretation of the **send** and **receive** primitives. This will form the basis for the richer semantics, which we will add later. In its simplest form, the **send** indicates the destination process and the message that will be delivered. The process waiting for a message issues a **receive**, indicating from which process it is ready to receive a message.

Let us now consider each decision problem and its impact on the message passing operation. If the sender and receiver processes are on different machines, there is obviously no alternative but to transmit the message from the sender to the receiver. If, however, both processes are on the same machine, an alternative exists. Instead of copying the message from the sender's address space to the receiver's, the pointers to the message can be adjusted to permit the receiver process to access it. The advantage of this alternative is its efficiency, which explains why it is used in some systems (e.g., Pilot [Redell et al., 1980]). The disadvantage is the loss of fault tolerance due to memory sharing. Furthermore, local message passing is treated differently from remote message passing.

Both the **send** and the **receive** primitives may be made blocking or nonblocking. The semantics of a blocking **send** is such that the sender is blocked following the **send** until a reply (not an acknowledgment) is received. A nonblocking **send**, on the other hand, enables the sender to continue execution without waiting for a reply. We should note that a nonblocking **send** may be a sufficiently general primitive to use in an OS if a **wait** primitive is also provided. In that case a blocking send can be simulated by issuing a **wait** immediately following a **send**.

The **receive** primitive may also be blocking or nonblocking. A blocking **receive** will not permit the issuer to proceed until a message is received from the identified process.

The communication primitives can be reliable or unreliable depending on the guarantees they provide in terms of message delivery. This distinction is, obviously, meaningful only within the context of remote communication. An unreliable **send** simply promises to put the message on the network with no guarantees as to its delivery. In this case the issuer of the **send** has to take care of the end-to-end acknowledgments, retransmissions, and so on. This corresponds to what in computer networking parlance is commonly termed a *datagram* service. A reliable **send**, on the other hand, handles lost messages, retransmissions, and end-to-end acknowledgments. A reliable **receive** complements a reliable **send** by automatically acknowledging the receipt of a message.

Buffering of messages permits the **send** to continue to execute after the issuing of a **send**, since the OS will buffer the messages being delivered to the destination process. If there is a single message buffer, the sender has to wait for the receiver to remove the message from the buffer before issuing a second **send**. Obviously, this scheme can be generalized to allow the sender to issue multiple **sends** before a **receive** is issued. If there is no buffering, the sender is blocked until a **receive** is issued.

We should note that these decisions are not mutually independent. For example, an unbuffered **send** implies a blocking **send**. Similarly, a reliable **send** requires buffering.

### 13.4.2  Remote Procedure Call

The remote procedure call (RPC) mechanism for remote interprocess communication is an extension of the procedure call facility commonly used in programming languages. The caller issues a procedure call to the operation of the object with which it wishes to communicate. The semantics of a remote procedure call are identical to the semantics of a local procedure call: the caller is blocked, the callee is invoked, the parameter binding is performed, the callee executes, and upon its return the caller proceeds. Therefore, from the caller's viewpoint, it is identical to a blocking **send**. From the perspective of the callee, it is equivalent to a blocking **receive** and a non-blocking **send** at the end. The semantics of RPC also require that the calls and returns be reliable.

The implementation of an RPC facility can be achieved as follows (see Figure 13.5). The caller makes a regular procedure call which is trapped by a *caller stub* procedure (also called the *user stub* or *client stub*). In fact, the caller stub consists of a set of procedures, each corresponding to a remote call that the caller program makes. This procedure, which can be generated by the compiler for the language that the calling procedure is written in, is responsible for taking the parameters, putting them into one or more physical messages, and asking the low-level network communication mechanism to transmit the packets to the callee's site. The communication mechanism at the callee's site receives the packets, takes the actions required for reliable operations, and passes the packets to the *callee stub*. The callee stub then issues a normal procedure call to the callee. The reverse actions are performed when the callee executes a return. The details of implementation alternatives can be found in [Birrell and Nelson, 1984] and [Nelson, 1981].

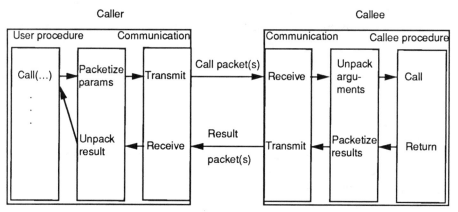

**Figure 13.5** Implementation of RPC (From: A.D. Birrell and B.J. Nelson, IMPLEMENTING REMOTE PROCEDURE CALLS. ACM Trans. Computer Sys.; February 1984; 2(1): 39–59.)

### 13.4.3 Comparison of Approaches

It is possible to compare the two approaches from a number of viewpoints. One possibility is to compare them with respect to control and data flow [Stankovic, 1982]. One can also compare them in terms of flexibility.

1. *Control flow.* An RPC mechanism enforces a master/slave type of control flow. The caller is the master to whom the callee is expected to respond at the completion of its execution. In the case of message passing, this is one of the three possible control flows. A second type of control that might be set up is a dialogue in which the link between the sender and the receiver is established temporarily. The receiver controls its own execution. The third possibility is the mail paradigm, where the sender sends a message even if the receiver has not yet issued a receive.

2. *Data flow.* In message transmission, the parameter passing is by value. The parameter values are copied into the message and transmitted. The RPC, on the other hand, can permit call by reference. The pointers that are transmitted may be simulated with capabilities, which we discussed in Section 13.2. It should be noted, however, that considerable overhead is associated with creating capabilities for primitive data types (integers, etc.) every time a procedure call is performed.

3. *Flexibility.* The above discussion on control flow has already touched on the flexibility issue. It is clear that the semantics of RPC can be provided by means of message-passing primitives. However, richer semantics can be provided for the **send** and **receive** primitives. Furthermore, quite useful physical message-passing concepts such as multicasting and broadcasting cannot easily be incorporated into RPC. The inclusion of these semantics into the **send** and **receive** primitives is straightforward.

### 13.4.4 Implementation Issues

A final point that we would like to discuss regarding remote communication has to do with the respective roles of the DOS and the networking protocols. An approach that has been adopted in distributed operating systems is to implement the communication mechanisms within the operating system, ignoring the network standardization efforts. A common reason for this approach is the performance of the remote communication. Thus the remote interprocess communication facilities are embedded within the kernel. Depending on the architectural model used, the problems of accommodating the two resource management functions may persist. One interesting approach to this issue is demonstrated in MOS [Barak and Litman, 1985], where the functionalities of the kernel are divided into an "upper kernel" and a "lower kernel," which is implemented as two modules, one to manage the network communication and the other to manage the hardware.

A fundamental problem associated with avoiding the standardization efforts is the two-track approach that is being followed. Since the DOS implements its own communication mechanism, porting it to different networking environments can result in major rework to accommodate the idiosyncrasies of each network architecture. Interfacing the OS with a network standard at a relatively high standardization level is essential for the OS to be portable and compatible with the developments in networking standards. On the other hand, it is certainly not easy to provide efficient communication if quite elaborate networking protocols are adopted. There is some work that addresses the design implementation issues in providing efficient general-purpose network protocols [Svobodova, 1986].

A strategy that might be helpful is to make use of the standard network protocols to handle the physical message passing at the communication subnet layer. In terms of the IEEE 802 standard, this involves the acceptance of the entire standard and interfacing with it at the logical link control level. In terms of the ISO/OSI protocol family, this means the adoption of the standard protocols at the physical, data link, and network layers. Such an approach is quite acceptable, since in the case of wide area networks, it translates into the acceptance of X.25 as the standard access to the network. For local area networks it simply defines what type of network services the OS expects. The remote communication service then builds on top of the network protocols to provide the primitives with the necessary semantics.

## 13.5 MANAGING PERSISTENT DATA

Databases store and manage persistent data which survive past the execution of the program that manipulates them. The traditional manner in which operating systems have dealt with persistent data is by means of file systems. Handling persistent and nonpersistent data within a programming language is an issue of significant research (see [Atkinson and Buneman, 1987] and [Atkinson et al., 1988]) and the proper operating system support for this functionality is not yet properly defined. It is quite likely that the OS requirements with respect to supporting persistent complex data are quite different from those that the current file systems provide. We will return to this issue in Chapter 15.

Even as traditional means of supporting secondary storage of data, current file systems are not suitable for DBMS use which have specific requirements regarding both the logical structure of files and their physical storage [Stonebraker, 1981]. The major issue regarding the file system is the management of memory buffers in accessing data files. This problem has attracted so much interest within the database community that we devote an entire section to it (Section 13.6). In this section we review briefly some of the other issues.

Since DBMSs store data in a structured manner, it is useful if the file system treats each file as a collection of structured records of fixed or variable length. Some operating systems, such as UNIX, consider files simply as streams of characters. Even though this treatment simplifies the file management, it also forces the DBMS to build its own structure on top of the character string structure. The challenge, in this case, is to be able to provide a file organization facility that supports files consisting of a collection of structured records.

The DBMS accesses the contents of a file in logical blocks (e.g., pages) and this access is not necessarily random. Therefore, the DBMS would improve its efficiency of access if the blocks that are logically next to one another were also physically stored contiguously. Most operating systems do not enforce physical contiguity, however, which results in the physical scattering of blocks on the secondary storage device.

One interesting suggestion related to the file system has been to map files into a user's virtual address space (see [Redell et al., 1980], [Diel et al., 1984] and [Traiger, 1982]). Thus the entire file (or parts of it) is resident in virtual memory during its processing. This approach is called *single-level storage* since it hides the memory hierarchy that exists in computer systems. The implication of such an implementation is to practically eliminate the need for a file system. A user does not need to "open" a file and issue a number of "read" instructions; it is sufficient to access the blocks of the file via virtual memory addresses. Proponents of this strategy recommend support for the single-level storage within a kernel that provides data management functionality. However, there are arguments against the idea, pointing out the problems that single-level storage would create for efficient transaction management [Stonebraker, 1984]. Furthermore, many current databases are larger than a typical virtual address space. We will not elaborate on these issues here since we believe it is still an open issue whether or not these problems can be overcome [Weikum, 1986].

## 13.6 BUFFER AND MEMORY MANAGEMENT

In relation to the OS support for database management operations, buffer management is the topic that has been studied most by the database researchers. It is because of this interest and the fundamental role that the buffer manager plays in controlling access to the database that we discuss the issue in this chapter even though it is not directly relevant to distributed systems. Earlier studies have concentrated on improving the classical buffer and memory management techniques. Recently, the emphasis has shifted to designing special-purpose buffer managers for database management. We discuss these research results in this section. However, we first give an overview of buffer management and its relationship to virtual memory management.

### 13.6.1 Buffer Management Functions

To facilitate reading data files from secondary storage, operating systems maintain buffers, which can be mapped either to virtual memory or to main (real) memory. The files in the secondary storage are divided into fixed-size pages that we will call *data pages*. The buffer space is also divided into pages of the same size, called *buffer pages*. Thus when a process attempts to read from a file, the buffer manager first searches the buffer pages for the specific data page. If it is found, it is made available to the requesting process for referencing. If the search is unsuccessful, there is a *buffer fault* which is serviced by bringing the data page from secondary storage and loading it into a buffer page [Fernandez et al., 1978]. By judiciously bringing data into the buffer, the OS attempts to improve the efficiency of file accesses (Figure 13.6).

From the foregoing discussion it is clear that a buffer manager has three responsibilities:

1. *Searching* the buffer pool for a given page
2. If it is not found in the buffer, *allocating* a free buffer page and *loading* the buffer page with a data page that is brought in from secondary storage

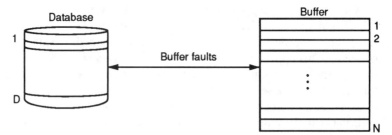

**Figure 13.6**   Use of Database Buffers

3. If no free buffer pages are available, choosing a buffer page for *replacement*

Commonly, the operating systems associate buffer pages with the processes that use them. However, if sharing of data pages among processes is to be permitted, the buffer manager searches the entire buffer directly every time a process refers to a file page.

Allocation of buffer pages is typically done dynamically. This means that the allocation of buffer pages to processes is performed as processes execute. The buffer manager tries to calculate the number of buffer pages needed to run the process efficiently and attempts to allocate that number of pages. The best known dynamic allocation method is the *working-set algorithm* ([Denning, 1968] and [Denning, 1980]).

A second aspect of allocation is fetching data pages. The most common technique is *demand paging*, where data pages are brought into the buffer as they are referenced. However, a number of operating systems prefetch a group of data pages that are in close physical proximity to the data page referenced. Buffer managers choose this route if they detect sequential access to a file.

In replacing buffer pages, the best known technique is the least recently used (LRU) algorithm that attempts to determine the *logical reference strings* [Effelsberg and Härder, 1984] of processes to buffer pages and to replace the page that has not been referenced for an extended period. The anticipation here is that if a buffer page has not been referenced for a long time, it probably will not be referenced in the near future.

The techniques discussed above are the most common. Other alternatives are discussed in [Effelsberg and Härder, 1984].

### 13.6.2 Problems with OS Buffer Management

There is considerable discussion in the literature against using the operating system buffer management functions in implementing database managers (see, e.g., [Stonebraker, 1981]). These problems can be listed as follows:

1. In dynamically allocating buffer pages, the OS buffer manager assumes that page references of processes are random and varying over time. Thus the

number of buffer pages that are allocated to a process can grow or shrink during its execution. However, it is possible for a DBMS to determine, with significant regularity, its reference pattern to data pages, which allows a more precise calculation of the buffer requirements [Chou, 1985].

2. Along the same lines, it may not be useful for the OS buffer manager to prefetch data pages when it detects sequential access. Since the DBMS knows its reference pattern, it is in a significantly better position to make that judgment. The reference string is known by the DBMS either as a result of query compilation (e.g., DB2 [Date, 1984]) or during execution "at (or very shortly after) the beginning of its examination of a block" [Stonebraker, 1981] (e.g., INGRES [Stonebraker et al., 1976]).

3. The LRU replacement algorithm, which performs nicely for general-purpose computing, fails to perform adequately in a number of cases. For example, in a nested-loop join, the buffer page that contains one data page of the outer relation is the least recently used if a replacement page is needed to bring in the last data page of the inner relation. However, if the outer relation buffer page is replaced, it will be read in again immediately, causing a buffer fault. Every page reference from then on will result in a buffer fault.

4. The LRU replacement algorithm writes the buffer pages to secondary storage when it needs a new buffer page. This is called *delayed writing* and corresponds to the no-fix/no-flush strategy described in Chapter 12. However, when the DBMS commits a transaction, it expects the log pages about the data items that the transaction has updated to be stored immediately on stable storage (i.e., disk). If the buffer manager keeps these buffer pages around, it may not be possible to guarantee the durability of transactions when failures occur.

For these reasons most DBMSs choose to implement their own buffer managers in the user space. We discuss these issues further in upcoming sections.

### 13.6.3 Relationship with Virtual Memory

Let us introduce one more complication into the scenario discussed in the preceding section. Most operating systems operate in a virtual memory environment. Therefore, the OS supports processes with address spaces that are larger than the available real memory. In this case each process is said to have its own *virtual address space*, the size of which is determined by the limitations of the hardware addressing mechanism and which is divided into fixed-size pages (called *virtual pages*). Thus the *virtual pages* of processes reside in secondary storage (called *paging* or *swapping device*). The main memory is also considered to be a collection of *page frames* of the same size as data pages. During process execution, any reference to a virtual address whose page is not currently in one of the page frames causes a *memory fault* (or *page fault*) which causes the virtual memory manager to fetch that page from the paging device to a main memory page frame. Note at this point that we have referred to four different types of pages: (1) data pages that store data and are part of the database, (2) buffer pages, (3) page frames that make up the main memory, and (4) virtual address pages.

If the DBMS is running in a virtual memory environment, its buffers are in its virtual address space. Therefore, accessing the buffers may not only cause buffer faults to bring in data pages, but may also cause memory faults since the buffer page may not be mapped to a page frame and there may not be any free frames. This phenomenon is commonly called the *double paging problem* [Chou and DeWitt, 1986]. Note that only a buffer fault can cause a double page fault. In this case, the buffer manager accesses the disk (secondary storage) where the database is located, and then maps the requested page onto a virtual buffer page which can invoke a memory fault if the selected virtual buffer page is not in real memory page frame (see Figure 13.7).

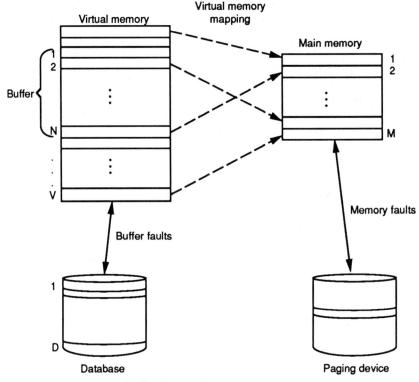

**Figure 13.7**  Buffer and Virtual Memory Management

Most of the earlier work ([Tuel, 1976], [Sherman and Brice, 1976], [Lang et al., 1977], and [Fernandez et al., 1978]) that dealt with database buffer management has actually concentrated on the double paging phenomenon and the ways of improving buffer management performance in such an environment. The results of these studies are summarized in [Teo, 1989].

An interesting issue related to buffer and memory size is discussed in [Gray and Putzolu, 1987]. The authors develop two rules regarding the size of buffer and memory space, based on the price/performance ratios of current computer systems. The two rules are as follows:

1. Data referenced every 5 minutes should be resident in memory (the *5-minute rule*).
2. It is economical to spend 10 bytes of main memory to save one instruction per second (the *10-byte rule*).

Both rules are derived by observing current disks and memory prices, CPU and I/O channel support costs, and the cost of one instruction per second. Their performance in terms of accesses per second which they can support is also observed. For the 5-minute rule, an assumption is made about the record size, and the break-even point is found where the cost of keeping this amount of data in memory is equal to the savings in disk accesses. For the 10-byte rule, the argument is similar but is based on how many instructions can be saved by using more memory. It should be noted that both of these rules are very technology dependent and are therefore subject to change over the years. As the authors point out, "Extrapolating these trends to 1996, the 5-minute rule will become the 5-hour rule—data used once every five hours will be main memory resident . . . . Similarly, the 10-byte rule is likely to become 100-byte rule—one will be willing to squander main memory in order to save a few instructions."

Regarding the performance of the DBMS, Lang, Wood, and Fernandez have also shown that the type of main memory replacement algorithm would also have a significant effect. In particular, an algorithm that takes the characteristics of a database application into account has a better performance. Although not surprising, this provides a basis for the comments made in the preceding section and a justification of our discussion in subsequent sections.

### 13.6.4 Database Buffer Managers

In this section we discuss further the three functions that are performed by DBMS buffer managers. Our emphasis is on buffer replacement algorithms that have been designed specifically for DBMS access. Most algorithms used by virtual memory OS for allocation and replacement of pages are based on the locality of references, since programs executing in this environment exhibit high locality. A program has a high locality of reference if the probability of reference for recently accessed pages is higher than the average reference probability. Although the reference pattern of a database string might be different from that of a program, it does, however, exhibit some form of locality [Effelsberg and Härder, 1984]. Thus, algorithms such as FIFO, LRU, CLOCK, and working set (WS) used by virtual memory operating systems can be applied to the allocation and replacement of database buffers. The details of these algorithms can be found in many OS books, and their application to database management is discussed in [Chou, 1985]. Instead of discussing them in the remaining two sections, we present two recent buffer management algorithms that have been developed specifically for database management.

At this point, recall from Chapter 12 that the local recovery managers may control page movement by the use of **fix/unfix** commands. In a database system, a **fix/unfix** interval is considered as one database page reference regardless of how many accesses are made to this page in the interval. Therefore, a "fixed" page cannot be a candidate for replacement. In fact, both the buffer allocation algorithm and the **fix/unfix** mechanism determine the set of candidates for replacement. In some systems there is no **fix/unfix** mechanism, but it is shown in [Effelsberg, 1983] that performance improvements are possible with such a mechanism.

**Hot set algorithm.**    The hot set model (HSM) [Sacco and Schkolnick, 1986] is a buffer allocation algorithm similar to the working set. It is designed to work in cooperation with an LRU page replacement mechanism. The fundamental idea is to determine, for each query, the necessary number of buffer pages and allocate that amount. This analysis is performed during query optimization. If the necessary number of buffer pages cannot be secured, the query should not even be scheduled. The fundamental difference of the HSM from the working set model is the former's static determination of the necessary buffer page amount. The term *hot set* is used to specify this amount.

*Calculation of Hot Points.*    To determine the hot set of a query, it is necessary to observe its buffer fault behavior as a function of buffer size. Figure 13.8 depicts the buffer fault behavior of a nested-loop join between two relations ($R_i$ and $R_j$) using sequential scan. Let us assume that $R_j$ is the inner relation. It is easy to observe that there are two *stable regions*, characterized by a constant number of buffer faults. *Unstable regions* are characterized by sudden increases in the number of buffer faults.

Let us analyze Figure 13.8 a little more carefully. If relation $R_j$ fits $P_j$ pages of buffer, a buffer size larger than $P_j$ will accommodate all of $R_j$ and some pages of the outer relation $R_i$. This will result in the minimum number of buffer faults. To understand this, consider the page reference string that will be generated by the join processor

$$p_1(R_i)p_1(R_j)p_2(R_j)\cdots p_{P_j}(R_j)p_2(R_i)p_1(R_j)\cdots p_{P_j}(R_j)\cdots p_{P_i}(R_i)p_1(R_j)\cdots p_{P_j}(R_j)$$

where $p_k(R_r)$ denotes page $k$ of relation $R_r$. Note that if the buffer size is $P_j + 1$, all the pages of the inner relation $R_j$ and the current page of the outer relation $R_i$ will fit into the buffer. Therefore, the page faults will occur only when a new page of the outer relation needs to be fetched.

If, on the other hand, only $P_j$ pages of buffer are allocated to this join, then only the following pages will fit in the buffer:

$$p_1(R_i)p_1(R_j)p_2(R_j)\cdots p_{P_{j-1}}(R_j)$$

Accessing the last page of the inner relation, $p_{P_j}(R_j)$, will cause $p_1(R_i)$ to be replaced, and the result in buffer contents will be[3]

---

[3]Here we are assuming a typical buffer manager that replaces buffers according to a local LRU algorithm.

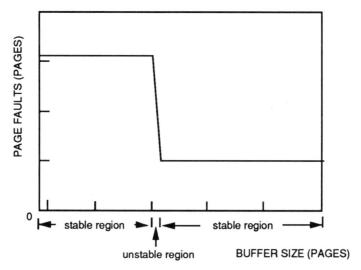

**Figure 13.8**  Determination of Hot Points (From: G.M. Sacco and M. Schkolnick, BUFFER MANAGEMENT IN RELATIONAL DATABASE SYSTEMS. ACM Trans. Database Sys.; December 1986; 11(4): 473–498.)

$$p_1(R_j)p_2(R_j)\cdots p_{P_j}(R_j)$$

However, the very next access of the join algorithm is another tuple of outer relation. This will cause $p_1(R_j)$ to be replaced with $p_1(R_i)$. Thus every page reference will cause a buffer fault. That is the reason for the sharp increase between $P_j$ and $P_{j+1}$ in Figure 13.8.

Note that it is possible to identify a stable region by the value of the fault function at the lower extremum of the region. This is called the *hot point* since it defines a buffer size where a change in the behavior of the buffer fault function occurs. Also note that even though in Figure 13.8 we have extended one of the stable regions to the point where the buffer size is 0, most systems need at least one page of buffer to operate. This is the *minimum hot point* for most DBMS operations. Therefore, the behavior of the nested-loop join using sequential scans can be characterized by two hot points: $hp_1 = 1$ and $hp_2 = P_j + 1$.

The example we discussed demonstrates a sharp increase within the unstable region. This behavior is representative of looping reusal. An alternative behavior is that the discontinuity within the unstable region may be smooth. This usually occurs in connection with indexed accesses. For example, Figure 13.9 depicts the buffer fault behavior of a nested-loop join where the access to the outer relation is by sequential scan, whereas the access to the inner relation is by a clustered index on the join attribute.

In case of smooth unstable regions, the behavior of the curve within this region needs to be analyzed more carefully. Note that the upper extremum for an unstable

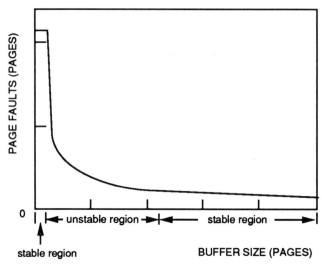

**Figure 13.9** Determination of Hot Points for Smooth Discontinuities (From: G.M. Sacco and M. Schkolnick, BUFFER MANAGEMENT IN RELATIONAL DATABASE SYSTEMS. ACM Trans. Database Sys.; December 1986; 11(4): 473–498.)

region is the lower extremum of a stable region. Therefore, the upper extremum of an unstable region is characterized by a hot point. The lower extremum of a smooth unstable interval is characterized by what is called a *cold point*. The only difference between a hot point and a cold point is that the buffer size represented by a cold point should never be chosen to execute a query. The reason is simple; the cold point also defines the upper extremum of a stable interval. Thus it is better to use the buffer size that corresponds to the lower extremum of that stable interval since the buffer faults are not going to be decreased with the use of more buffer pages. This is true since "buffer sizes inside a stable interval, and different from the hot point relative to that interval, do not produce any benefit in terms of fault reduction, while using more buffer resources" [Sacco and Schkolnick, 1986]. Sacco and Schkolnick describe how hot and cold points can be calculated for each primitive access path (simple reusal, loop reusal, unclustered index reusal, clustered index reusal) and discuss how they can be computed for each access strategy that is used by a DBMS.

*Buffer Management Algorithm Based on HSM.* The basic idea is to try to ensure that requests are run with an "effective" buffer size equal to their hot-set sizes. The buffer pool is organized so that separate LRU chains are maintained for each query. Each chain has a maximum size equal to the hot-set size for the request being serviced by that query. Buffer pages that are not associated with any concurrent queries are collected into a separate LRU list, called the *free list*. Associated with each LRU chain, two values are maintained: the number of buffer pages requested by the query (determined by the query optimizer), and the number of buffer pages actually allocated to the query. When a query requests a stack of size $p$, that number of free buffer pages are assigned to it from the free list, if possible. If fewer than $p$ buffer pages are given to the query (because the free list does not contain that many pages), the query is said to have a *deficient list*. A query can also have a deficient list if some of its pages are stolen by others, as we will see shortly.

When a query requests a page, the contents of the entire buffer are examined (by the hashing technique). If the page is found and it is also in the local LRU stack of the query, the local stack is updated. Then, the query fixes the page on which the reference count for the page is increased by one. When the query unfixes a page, the reference count is decreased by one.

If the page is not found, the least referenced unfixed page in the local stack, whose reference count is zero, is replaced by the requested page. If the query does not contain unfixed pages, a page from the free list or from another LRU stack (preferably an already deficient one) containing an unfixed page is obtained. Then the number of allocated pages is incremented by one.

When a query terminates, the pages of its stack are allocated to concurrent queries whose LRU stacks are deficient. It tries to satisfy deficient queries one by one. When all deficient queries have been given their deficient number of pages and there are still some left, they are returned to the free list.

**Query locality set model and DBMIN.** The approach that is taken in the hot-set model is to determine buffer requirements of each query according to a given buffer management policy. An alternative proposal made by Chou in his dissertation [Chou, 1985], and summarized in [Chou and DeWitt, 1986], is to (1) separate the modeling of the query behavior from the buffer management strategy, and (2) determine the behavior of the queries with respect to the file instances that they access. The query locality set model (QLSM) provides a framework for the classification of database operations according to their file access behavior. DBMIN is a general buffer management algorithm.

DBMIN has a finer grain of decomposition than that of the hot-set model. While the hot-set algorithm services a query, DBMIN services file instances of a query. It also uses a combination of replacement algorithms. Depending on the usage of the file instance, the replacement algorithm assigned to each file instance is different.

Associated with each file instance is a *locality set*, which defines the number of file pages that need to be in the buffers to carry out the operation on this file instance. The locality set is predetermined (as in the hot-set model) and, accordingly, buffers are assigned to the file instance.

Let us first consider how locality sets can be determined according to a taxonomy of the page reference behavior given by the QLSM. We then discuss the implementation of the DBMIN algorithm in some detail.

*QLSM Classification.* The QLSM classifies page reference patterns into three general classes: *sequential, random,* and *hierarchical references,* each of which are further subdivided.

1. *Sequential references.* Pages are referenced one after the other.

    (a) *Straight sequential* (SS). Each page is referenced only once, without looping. The locality set in this case is equal to a single buffer page. A requested page will always replace the page that is currently in the buffer.

    (b) *Clustered sequential* (CS). Pages are referenced sequentially with occasional backups. For example, in performing a merge-join, those pages of the inner relation that hold tuples with the same join attribute value will be accessed repeatedly for each tuple of the outer relation. In this case the locality set should be large enough to hold the records that are in the same cluster in the buffer. Suitable replacement policies are FIFO and LRU.

    (c) *Looping sequential* (LS). Pages are referenced repeatedly in a sequential manner. This is the reference pattern for the pages of the inner relation in a nested-loop join. In this case the locality set should be large enough to hold the entire set of pages in the buffer. If this cannot be satisfied, buffer pages should be replaced using the most recently used (MRU) replacement algorithm.

2. *Random references.* Pages are referenced randomly using some sort of index.

    (a) *Independent random* (IR). There is no specific pattern to accesses; the pages are accessed completely randomly. This is what occurs when an indexed scan is performed and the indexes are not clustered. The locality set in this case is a single buffer page, since every page can replace the preceding one.

    (b) *Clustered random* (CR). Random references exhibit a locality of reference. For example, unclustered indexes with nonunique index values will demonstrate a locality of reference in page references. The locality set behavior of such a reference pattern is similar to that of a clustered sequential reference pattern.

3. *Hierarchical references.* Page references traverse a hierarchical index from the root to the leaves.

    (a) *Straight hierarchical* (SH). The index is traversed only once from the root to the leaves. The locality set size is a single buffer page.

    (b) *Hierarchical with straight sequential* (H/SS). Following the index traversal, the leaf pages are scanned sequentially. The page reference behavior in this case is identical to that of a straight sequential reference.

    (c) *Hierarchical with clustered sequential* (H/CS). Following the tree traversal of index pages, the leaf data pages are not scanned sequentially but are accessed using a clustered access method. The page reference behavior in this case is identical to that of a clustered sequential reference.

> (d)   *Looping hierarchical* (LH). The hierarchical index structure is accessed repeatedly. This occurs, for example, when the inner relation in a join operation is indexed on the join field. The recommended locality set size in this case is one buffer page to keep the root page.

*DBMIN Algorithm.*   Two tables and a list are maintained. A global buffer table is maintained to allow data sharing among concurrent queries. For each file instance, a local table (i.e., locality set) keeps account of the pages currently used by it. A global free list is maintained to keep track of the free buffer pages. Note that a buffer page is free if it does not belong to any locality set. A page in the buffer can belong to at most one locality set.

Besides the buffer pool size (let us denote it by $N$), two additional values are maintained for each file instance accessed by a query:

$dl_{ij}$:   desired locality set size of file instance $j$ accessed by query $i$

$al_{ij}$ :   actual allocation of buffer pages to file instance $j$ accessed by query $i$

When a file is first opened by a query, its locality set and replacement policy are determined according to the access primitives already discussed. Subsequent page references by the query on that file cause a global search over the entire buffer. This permits sharing of pages among concurrent queries. Such a search may have three possible outcomes:

1. The page is found in both the global and local table for the query. In this case the only thing that needs to be done is to update the usage statistics.

2. The page is found in the global table but not in the local query table. If the page is in another query's locality set, the page is simply given to the requesting query. Otherwise, the page is added to the locality set of the file instance and $al$ is increased by one. If $al > dl$, a page chosen by the local replacement algorithm is released to the global free list. The usage statistics need to be updated as well.

3. The page is not in memory. In this case, a disk read is scheduled to bring it in from the disk into a buffer allocated from the global free list. Then the page is added to the locality set, $al$ is increased by one, and the usage statistics are updated.

To make sure that queries run efficiently, a load controller is activated as soon as a file is opened. The load controller checks if $\Sigma_i \Sigma_j dl_{ij} < N$ for all file instances $j$ accessed by all active queries $i$. In other words, the controller determines if it is safe (in terms of available buffers) to permit the query to proceed. If it is not, it is placed at the front of a waiting queue. When a file is closed, the buffer pages associated with its locality set are released back to the global free list. The load controller then activates the first query on the waiting queue if the system will still be in a safe state after the query's activation.

### 13.6.5 Concluding Remarks

If the DBMS runs in a virtual address space, the program code and DBMS buffers are paged by the OS memory manager. While the replacement of buffer pages is done by the DBMS according to logical references, paging of the main memory frames is performed by independent OS algorithms based on the addressing behavior of the processes. Therefore, the frequency of the various faults essentially determines whether or not the buffer manager becomes the bottleneck of the entire DBMS. This seems to point to DBMS having to interact more carefully with the OS. We should finally point out that most of the work on this topic has concentrated on the development of "better" buffer management algorithms. The significant question of how to support such a service on top of a virtual memory environment needs to be investigated further. A preliminary study along these lines is reported in [Teo, 1989].

## 13.7 TRANSACTION SUPPORT

We have discussed transaction management at length in Chapters 10 through 12. The transaction concept was originally developed by database researchers to allow application programmers to ignore the problems associated with concurrency and certain types of failures in multiuser environments. Remember that at the application level the programmers simply indicate the beginning and end of a transaction (either a commit point or an abort point), leaving the task of ensuring the atomicity, consistency, isolation, and durability of the transaction to the transaction manager.

In most commercially available database systems, the transaction manager is supported by the database system. Recently, there have been several proposals to make transactions part of normal OS services. This would permit the concept of a transaction to be used by any application that runs on the operating system in addition to the distributed DBMS. In this section we discuss some of the issues related to providing such a support.

### 13.7.1 Transaction Model Assumptions

Transaction managers typically perform three functions in order to support the ACIDity of transactions: concurrency control, commit, and recovery. As we have seen in Chapters 10 through 12, there are a multitude of techniques that could be used to perform these functions. Since it is quite difficult to present a general description that considers all the various combinations of techniques, let us first make certain realistic assumptions to facilitate the discussion.

Most DBMSs use locking as their concurrency control primitive, so we will assume the same in the following discussion. For atomicity, we will use the well-known two-phase commit protocol, and for recovery we will assume that the commit protocol can be implemented together with shadowing or logging.

## 13.7.2  Benefits of OS-Supported Transaction Management

Numerous technical problems need to be resolved in order to *efficiently* implement a *general* transaction manager as part of the OS. First let us review the potential benefits that can be gained if such a facility could be provided.

A commonly mentioned advantage of incorporating the transaction management function into the OS is that it avoids convoys, which we discussed in Section 13.3.1. Remember that one reason for the formation of convoys is the lack of OS knowledge regarding the DBMS semaphores and processes. If these DBMS actions are implemented by means of OS transactions, such a phenomenon can be eliminated.

Another argument in favor of OS transaction management is that hardware support can be used to reduce the overhead due to locking. Locking is obviously one of the most commonly used functions in a transaction system. If the instruction sequences for locking can be microcoded or if special hardware can be used to perform locking automatically on virtual memory pages, the costs of locking can be reduced significantly. Such low-level microcode and hardware management responsibility rightfully belongs to the operating system.

A further potential advantage of incorporating transaction management into the OS has to do with recovery. If an in-place update strategy is used, undo and redo records have to be written in the log. Recall from Chapter 12 that the write-ahead logging strategy requires that the log records be written out to stable storage before a transaction commits. This is one of the major I/O bottlenecks of log-based recovery techniques. Several strategies have been proposed to reduce the overhead: for example, chained I/O [Elhardt and Bayer, 1984] and grouped commit [DeWitt et al., 1984]. In the former, special channel facilities are used to decrease the I/O time to write the log records into stable storage. In the latter, commitment of transactions is deferred until a certain number of transactions can be committed together. As we indicated before, such low-level hardware manipulation should be the domain of the operating system.

If shadow paging is used, the updated pages are mapped into disk pages different from those from which they were fetched originally. At commit time, those disk pages are made the actual pages of the database. This mapping requires additional I/O to write the page onto a shadow disk page. The additional I/O has been cited as the major drawback of the shadow paging scheme [Gray et al., 1981]. If the approach discussed previously of mapping files into virtual memory is also used, additional I/O is eliminated, since there is no additional DBMS buffering. We have already mentioned the drawbacks of this idea. The implementation of the transaction manager as part of the OS may enable the use of low-level techniques such as the ones discussed for log files to improve the efficiency of shadow paging.

A final advantage is related to deadlock management. Since the distributed OS has to provide facilities for handling both local and global deadlocks, this service can be interfaced with the transaction manager to resolve deadlocks that are generated as a result of locking-based concurrency control mechanisms. Furthermore, the OS can make use of idle machine cycles to perform deadlock detection if that is the mechanism that is implemented.

### 13.7.3  Issues in OS Transaction Manager Design

As shown in the preceding section, providing support for transaction management at the OS level has many benefits. However, when designing such a system, several issues have to be considered. In this section we discuss these issues by searching for answers to two questions: Who implements the locking primitives? Where should the transaction manager be placed?

**Who implements the locking primitives?**   The "who" in this question refers to two OS components: the buffer manager and the transaction manager. The buffer manager may *physically* lock pages in the buffer, whereas the transaction manager may do *logical* locking on some unit of data, which might be smaller or bigger than a page. We will consider four possibilities.

1. *Transaction manager provides no locking/buffer manager provides no locking.* This is the trivial but unacceptable case. To enable concurrent access, applications are required to take special measures, which brings the reasons for the existence of the transaction manager into question.

2. *Transaction manager provides logical locking/buffer manager provides no locking.* If this alternative is to be used, the access to the buffer pages has to be implemented very carefully. Consider two transactions that would access two different sections of the same buffer page. The buffer manager simply fixes this page and permits the transaction manager to coordinate the concurrent accesses to it. If the logical locking granularity is less than a page, the transactions will update different parts of the page. If each transaction copies the buffer page into its own address space before it reads or writes to that page, each application will update different sections of the page, but one will overwrite the other when the page is committed to secondary storage [Bernstein et al., 1987].

3. *Transaction manager provides no locking/buffer manager provides page locking.* This strategy is quite inflexible and can be inefficient. As to inflexibility, the applications are forced to live with a single level of granularity for locks: the page. This is quite inconvenient if the DBMS wants to implement logical locking at a finer granularity (e.g., predicate locking). The potential inefficiency argument has to do with the way the buffer manager treats pages that contain metadata (e.g., the index table). Since it has no knowledge of the semantics of transactions, for each access to the index pages the buffer manager automatically locks the entire page. This can easily result in keeping other transactions from accessing any part of the database [Stonebraker et al., 1985], not because the corresponding data pages are locked, but because they cannot access the lock tables.

4. *Transaction manager provides logical locking/buffer manager provides page locking*. This is the most general and, obviously, the preferred alternative. However, it is also the most difficult to implement. First, unless special care is taken, the arguments that were made for case 3 hold here also. This is true if single-level transactions and single-mode locking are used. In this case, even though the transaction manager implements logical locking, the buffer manager has already locked the page, denying access to any other transaction. Therefore, the possibility of implementing nested transactions [Moss, 1985] with multilevel locking [Weikum, 1986] should be investigated. Furthermore, the coordination of the buffer manager and the transaction manager activities should receive special attention in this case.

**Where should the transaction manager be placed?**    There are two alternative ways of providing transaction support. It might be supported as part of the kernel services, or the transaction manager might be placed at the user level. This issue has more implications than merely deciding who provides the service and may influence how the OS is designed. Furthermore, it cannot be discussed in isolation, without considering the placement of the buffer manager. We deal with these issues systematically by considering several major alternatives. Others can easily be developed if desired.

1. *Placing the transaction manager in the OS kernel with the buffer manager also in the OS kernel*. If the transaction management is a kernel service, the concurrency and reliability of the operating system services can also be provided by means of transactions. For example, implementers of the OS can write the routines that manage system resources as transactions and can expect the OS kernel itself to provide the reliability of these services. Thus transaction management becomes a "low-level" kernel service that supports not only user processes but also operating system (kernel and nonkernel) service processes. Furthermore, since the buffer manager is also in the kernel, cooperation between the two can easily be established.

2. *Placing the transaction manager in the OS kernel with the buffer manager in the user level (DBMS)*. If the transaction manager resides inside the kernel and the locking primitives are implemented by the buffer manager that is at the user level, each **lock/unlock** request will cause a kernel process to send a message to a nonkernel process. Crossing the kernel boundaries for each such request is both cumbersome and inefficient.

3. *Placing the transaction manager in the OS (user level) with the buffer manager in the DBMS*. By placing the transaction manager at the user level, transactions are provided as reliable computing primitives for user services and user-level operating system services, but the OS kernel cannot make use of these primitives. Therefore, other reliability measures need to be taken for the kernel, or the kernel can be implemented as an unreliable piece of software. Thus if there is a system failure, we do a system restart without

expecting the kernel to recover transactions from the failure. Communication between the transaction manager and the buffer manager (which implements the locks) in this case requires efficient interprocess communication.

4. *Placing the transaction manager in the OS (user level) with the buffer manager in the OS kernel.* The issues are similar to case 3. In this case each **lock/unlock** request will cause two kernel calls.

### 13.7.4 Concluding Remarks

In this section we reviewed some of the transaction management issues that need to be addressed to provide OS support for the management of database transactions as well as to support the transaction concept as an OS primitive. In addition to the aspects discussed in this section, recall that distributed transaction management requires a reliable communication mechanism. We addressed that issue in Section 13.4.

There is an additional problem that we have not discussed. It has to do with the nature of the primitive operations of which a transaction is composed and the data on which these operations act. The theory of transaction management in DBMSs is based on the fact that the operations that make up transactions are simple reads and writes. Furthermore, the data that is manipulated by these operations is simple (i.e., files consisting of data items). When transactions are used to support general-purpose computing, neither of these two assumptions are true. The user applications may be manipulating complex data structures, and the user operations on them may be complicated. For example, a user may implement a B-tree manipulation application as a set of transactions. In this case the data structure and the operations that may be performed on such a data structure are quite complicated. It is well known that the efficient concurrency control algorithms for B-trees are quite different from the standard algorithms used in ordinary transactions.

The issue, then, is whether one can design and implement an efficient and generic transaction manager that can handle complex structures and complicated operations. Even though there are some early prototype systems (e.g., Camelot [Spector et al., 1987]; see also [Spector et al., 1985] and [Spector and Schwarz, 1983]), the state of the art in this area has not yet advanced to the point where this question can be answered. Work is ongoing on a number of fronts ([Schwarz and Spector, 1984] and [Weihl and Liskov, 1985]) and the pros and cons of supporting database transactions by means of an OS transaction manager are being hotly debated ([Stonebraker et al., 1985] and [Weikum, 1986]).

## 13.8 ARCHITECTURAL ISSUES

The issue that we address in this section is the appropriate architectural paradigm that needs to be adopted to provide a platform for efficient and meaningful cooperation between the distributed operating system and the distributed DBMS. Specifically, we are searching for ways of efficiently providing the required functionalities discussed in previous sections.

The first point to note is that the coupling of distributed database managers and distributed operating systems is not a binary integration issue. The communication network protocols also need to be considered, which adds to the complexity of the problem. Typically, distributed operating systems implement their own communication primitives, ignoring the standard services offered by communication protocols. However, as we discussed in Section 13.4.4, there are fundamental problems associated with avoiding standardization efforts. Thus the architectural paradigm has to accommodate distributed DBMS functions, distributed operating system services, and communication protocol standards such as the ISO/OSI or IEEE 802.

The architectural models can be characterized along two dimensions: the structuring paradigm and the implementation technology. Along the first dimension one can identify layered system models, monolithic systems, or client-server architectures. Along the second dimension, operating systems can be process-oriented or object-oriented. In the remainder of this chapter, we discuss some of the better known combinations of these alternatives and analyze their suitability as the paradigm of cooperation between distributed operating systems and distributed DBMSs.

### 13.8.1 Layered OS Architecture

A well-understood architectural framework for operating system development has been the layered approach (Figure 13.10), where each layer of the software provides a service to the higher layers. Thus each layer provides a *virtual machine* view to the higher layers.

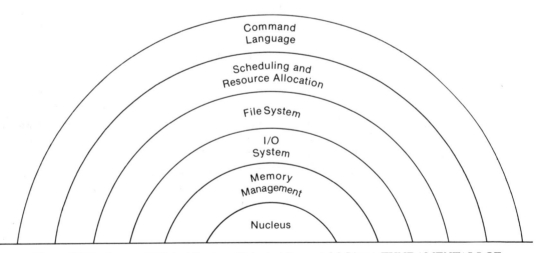

**Figure 13.10**   Layered OS Architecture (Adapted from: A.M. Lister, FUNDAMENTALS OF OPERATING SYSTEMS 3/E. New York, NY: Springer-Verlag; 1984.)

There is considerable difficulty, however, in applying this paradigm in a distributed environment, where two major physical resources rather than one need to be managed: the computer facility and the network. The functionality required of the lowest layers of the operating system is quite different for the two resources. As we discussed before, a separate set of protocols is required to manage the network for which standards are being developed.

One approach to resolving this architectural conflict is to extend one of the three participants (i.e., the DBMS, the OS, and the network protocols) to include the other two. One such proposal, due to [Bachman and Ross, 1982], extends the ANSI/SPARC DBMS architecture to include the communication mechanism and some OS functions (Figure 13.11). The architecture builds parallel layers of software to deal with networking protocols and storage and access of data, and layers on top of these which hide the duality of services.

Another proposal ([Denning and Brown, 1983] and [Brown et al., 1984]) extends the layered OS architecture to include the distributed system functionalities. The suggestion is to extend the six layers of Figure 13.10 to fifteen, where the lower eight layers implement a single-machine operating system, and the higher seven layers implement protocols to achieve a multimachine operating system. Figure 13.12 depicts the layers and the objects that are managed at each layer.

The single-machine layers are well understood and constitute the functions that are commonly available in most existing operating systems. These layers implement primitive OS objects such as processes, procedures, and instruction sets, as well as the essential functions to support the use of these objects (i.e., interrupts, storage and memory management, and capability support for access control and protection).

The communication between processes is the function of layer 9. The implementation details of the communication mechanism are hidden in this layer so that uniform access to local or remote resources is provided for the higher layers. It is important that this functionality be implemented efficiently to minimize the penalty of accessing remote resources.

Even though the layered software architecture has the advantages of being clear and well understood within the OS community, its extension to the distributed environment may suffer a performance penalty. The fact that user processes have to be implemented on top of 10 to 12 layers of software certainly has a performance cost.

Furthermore, architectural proposals treat the coupling of communication protocols with either the operating system or the distributed DBMS, but not both. From the distributed DBMS perspective, the algorithms are implemented as user processes at some $n$th level and are forced to live with the file system, virtual memory, and other services imposed by the OS. Extending the layered approach to provide full cooperation among all three components requires (more or less) the merging of the model proposed by Bachman and Ross with that of Denning and Brown's. Such an approach results in even more increase in the number of layers of software, causing further performance degradation.

The difficulty that both of these extensions face is in their attempt to extend an architectural paradigm that was originally designed to manage a single resource

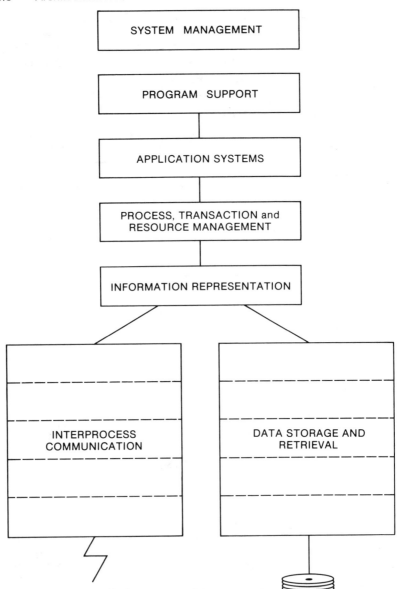

**Figure 13.11**   Reference Model as an Extension of ISO/OSI

(i.e., the computer system) to an environment where there are two major physical resources (computer and network). The functionality required of the lowest layers of the operating system is quite different for management of these resources. A separate set of protocols, for which standards are being developed, is required to manage the network.

| Level | Name | Object | Example Operations |
|-------|------|--------|--------------------|
| 15 | Shell | User programming environment scalar data, array data | statements in shell language |
| 14 | Directories | Directories | create, destroy, attach, detach search, list |
| 13 | User processes | User process | fork, quit, kill, suspend, resume |
| 12 | Stream I/O | Streams | open, close, read, write |
| 11 | Devices | External devices and peripherals such as printer, display, keyboard | create, destroy, open, close, read, write |
| 10 | File systems | Files | create, destroy, open, close, read, write |
| 9 | Communications | Pipes | create, destroy, open, close, read, write |
| 8 | Capabilities | Capabilities | create, validate, attenuate |
| 7 | Virtual Memory | Segments | read, write, fetch |
| 6 | Local Secondary Store | Block of data, device channels | read, write, allocate, free |
| 5 | Primitive Processes | Primitive process, semaphores, ready list | suspend, resume, wait, signal |
| 4 | Interrupts | Fault handler programs | invoke, mask, unmask, retry |
| 3 | Procedures | Procedure segments, Call stack, display | mark_stack, call, return |
| 2 | Instruction Set | Evaluation stack, microprogram interpreter | load, store, un_op, bin_op, branch, array_ref, etc. |
| 1 | Electronic Circuits | Registers, gates, buses, etc. | clear, transfer, complement, activate, etc. |

**Figure 13.12**    A Layered DOS Proposal (From: P.J. Denning and R.L. Brown, SHOULD DISTRIBUTED SYSTEMS BE HIDDEN; Workshop on Comp. Sys. Org., ©1983 IEEE.)

## 13.8.2 Monolithic (All-Kernel) OS Architecture

Another quite popular architectural model is characterized by a large kernel that includes almost all OS services. A prime example of this architecture is UNIX, where

the only nonkernel OS routines are the system utilities (Figure 13.13) [Bach, 1986].
In the subsequent discussion we use UNIX as a vehicle to clarify the concepts.

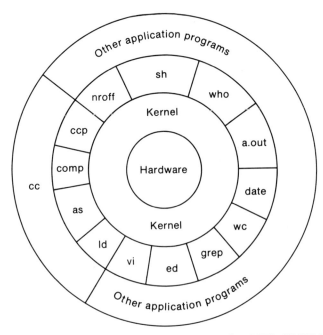

**Figure 13.13**    UNIX Architecture (Maurice Bach, *The Design Of The UNIX Operating System,*
©1986, p. 5. Reprinted by permission of Prentice-Hall, Inc., Englewood Cliffs, NJ.)

At this point we should define what we mean by a kernel. In this context the term
refers to the part of the OS (i.e., routines) that run in the privileged mode (called "kernel mode" in UNIX). Thus the term *kernel* as we use it here is different from the term
*nucleus* that is sometimes used [Lister, 1984]. The latter refers only to the hardware
handlers and low-level process handlers; the nucleus is therefore part of the kernel.
The UNIX kernel is not layered in the same sense as depicted in Figure 13.10, but
consists of components that interact with one another to perform the services (Figure
13.14). These modules, however, are not separated from one another as clearly as the
figure suggests.

Despite its popularity, an architectural model that includes all the services inside
the kernel is not very suitable for DBMS integration. The reason for this is exactly as
discussed in the preceding section. Even though the user applications (distributed
DBMS is one) do not access the operating system services at the topmost "layer,"
access is still at a fairly high "level" since the kernel is tightly closed. This makes it difficult for the distributed DBMS to implement alternative modes of providing services
at the user level.

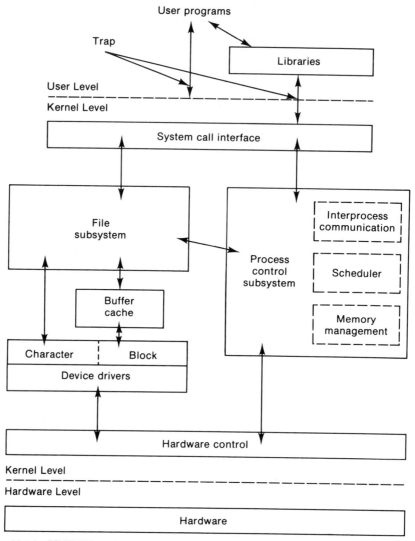

**Figure 13.14** UNIX Kernel Architecture (Maurice Bach, *The Design Of The UNIX Operating System,* © 1986, p. 5. Reprinted by permission of Prentice-Hall, Inc., Englewood Cliffs, NJ.)

A solution that has been tried is to modify the kernel and implement alternative services within it. This has been done in the case of INGRES and UNIX [Stonebraker et al., 1983a], enabling the distributed DBMS to make use of these alternative services. However, there are two problems with this approach. One of them is that the operating system kernels are typically resident in memory (most of UNIX is). This is to improve the performance of the system by not paging the kernel code. However, any OS with a large kernel requires a large real memory. The implementation of additional services inside the kernel only adds to the problem by increasing the size of the kernel.

A second issue is flexibility. It is necessary to recompile and reinstall the kernel each time the modules that implement the alternative distributed DBMS functionally within the kernel need to be modified. This is not an infrequent occurrence, because the policy modules are actually built into the kernel. Neither the OS implementers nor the system programmers who have to maintain the system find it appealing to have to reinstall the operating system every time the distributed DBMS implementers find a new and better way to perform a known task or to include a new functionality within the distributed DBMS.

There has been some recognition of the problems related to large kernels. The specific problems associated with developing INGRES on top of UNIX are well documented [Stonebraker, 1981]. Several research projects also implement small kernels (e.g., V-kernel [Cheriton, 1984] and [Cheriton, 1988]; Clouds [Dasgupta and LeBlanc, 1985]; Eden [Lazowska et al., 1981]). Some attempts were even aimed at modifying UNIX by reducing the kernel and providing some OS services in the user space. A noteworthy example of this work is the Mach Operating System development at the Carnegie-Mellon University [Jones and Rashid, 1986].

### 13.8.3  Client-Server Model

The *client-server* model has been used in the design of distributed operating systems mainly to model the communication between the servers in a distributed system (e.g., file servers, print servers, etc.) and the clients who use these services. In this model, the OS consists of a set of server modules with clean interfaces through which services can be accessed (Figure 13.15). It is possible to extend this approach beyond its initial framework to structure the components of operating systems. In other words, the operating system can be organized as a group of modules, each of which performs a specific function.

An important feature of the client-server model is the abstraction of the OS services. Each server can be implemented as an abstract module that provides a given service to clients through a series of operations that it implements. One method of achieving this abstraction is with the object-oriented system implementation. We consider the role of object orientation in OS design further in the next section.

Another important aspect of this approach is its replacement by a *dynamic layering* of the more traditional *static layering*, imposed by the layered OS architectures discussed in Section 13.8.1. In other words, as a software module requests the services of another module, which, in turn, can request the services of some other module, a layering in terms of service messages (or system calls) is established. However, layering occurs temporarily during the execution of the program and is specific to the requirements of that program. The user and system software can then use only those functions of the operating system which are necessary, without having to accommodate all the other functionalities. For example, if the DBMS does not need the services of a file system (which is possible under this architecture, since the DBMS can imple-

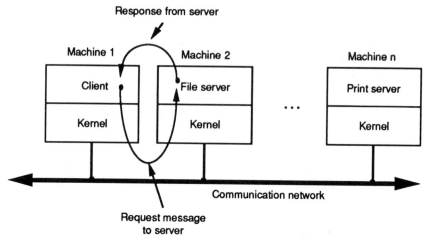

**Figure 13.15**   Client-Server Model

ment its own storage manager), the file system does not exist as part of the operating system as far as the DBMS is concerned.

A fundamental principle in such a design is to keep the kernel small and to implement the OS functionality with user-level modules. This can be achieved by using a design principle that separates the *policies* employed by the operating system from the *mechanisms* that support these policies. Such a separation was first argued for in Hydra [Levin et al., 1975] and should be adopted as a useful operating system design principle. This principle can easily be supported in the client-server model. The kernel implements only the low-level mechanisms (e.g., process management, page management) which provide support for the definition of policies (e.g., file system, scheduling, memory management) at the user level.

What should go into the kernel is a topic of much discussion and differs from system to system. This is also the fundamental difficulty with the client-server model. System performance can be adversely affected if the kernel functions are improperly chosen. The challenge is to find new and efficient ways of interacting the nonkernel routines with the kernel routines.

The important aspect of this architecture is the flexibility that it provides for applications. As long as the kernel implements the very fundamental mechanisms, it is possible to develop a DBMS that uses these kernel services but implements all the policy decisions in its own workspace. For example, it is possible to implement a file server specific to the database management requirements, and another one that emulates, for example, the UNIX file system. This allows the DBMS to use only those nonkernel OS services it can use efficiently and bypass others, allowing it to grow without being impeded by OS policy restrictions, while normal OS services can also be provided to other computing tasks.

### 13.8.4 Object-Oriented Operating Systems

The development paradigm of the object-oriented system has something to offer to all the architectural approaches discussed so far. We would therefore like to talk about the general ideas and how they would be useful in operating system design. Object orientation, as a DBMS implementation approach, is discussed further in Chapter 15.

The object model of systems was first investigated for programming languages but has since been adapted to OS design [Jones, 1979] and that of DBMSs [Dittrich and Dayal, 1986]. In the object-oriented approach to software development, the application is developed as a collection of modules where each module implements an object, which can be a system resource, a data structure, or anything similar. The important properties of objects are as follows:

1. *Information hiding*. The internal representation of objects is not available to those that may want to access a particular object. The object is accessed only by a set of operations that are encapsulated with the object. The internal structure can be modified only by these operations.
2. *Types*. Each object belongs to a given class which determines the type of the object. Individual objects are therefore instances of some type. For example, "xyz.abc" may be an instance of an object of type "file." Two objects are of the same type if they have the same set of operations defined on them.
3. *Integrity*. The set of operations defines the possible behavior of an object. The object cannot exhibit a behavior that is not defined by the semantics of at least one of these operations.
4. *Composition*. It is possible to define *composite* (or *extended-type*) objects, which consist of other objects.
5. *Inheritance*. A hierarchy of object classes may be defined which enables an object to inherit the properties (operations) of its parent class or classes. Furthermore, inherited properties can be modified to provide different services based on services previously defined. All classes in the system can be considered to be descendents of a class called "object" that is implemented inside the kernel [Wulf et al., 1981].

Depending on the architecture of the operating system, the object-oriented software development approach can be useful. In layered and all-kernel architectures, providing support for the creation of user-level objects may present advantages. Thus the operating system can provide better tools and facilities for reliable software development. This is done, for example, in Eden [Lazowska et al., 1981], which is a layered OS.

The object-oriented approach is especially suitable for the client-server model. Each "service module" we have referred to implements an OS object, which may be a process, file, peripheral device, and so on. The operating system services can therefore be viewed as the union of the functions provided by each module. This perspective permits the system and user applications to use only those functionalities of the operating system that they need, without having to go through a layered software architecture where the applications have almost no flexibility as to whether or not to utilize the lower-layer services.

To demonstrate the use of object orientation in OS design, let us assume that we would like to implement a kernel that supports the client-server architecture. The first thing is to determine what primitive objects need to be supported within the kernel. This list includes the following: (1) peripherals, (2) memory pages, (3) processes, (4) semaphores, and (5) messages. Accordingly, the kernel consists of several modules which implement the type manager[4] for one of the objects listed above. In addition, the kernel provides support for the concept of an object (via the object manager), permitting the creation of user-level objects.

There are two possible ways of designing such a system. One way is to have each kernel module implement a primitive object. This provides the facilities for creating user-level objects, but the OS kernel does not internally contain the concept of an object. The second way is to have the OS kernel itself be implemented as a collection of objects. In this case, the nucleus of the system has to implement the object support facilities (i.e., subsume object manager functions).

There are, of course, advantages and disadvantages to each of the foregoing alternatives. The latter, which can be called pure object orientation, provides a uniform design principle. In such a system, since everything is an object, it is easier to handle concerns about reliability, security, and so on. On the other hand, such systems usually incur a high performance overhead because of the extensive communication between objects. The first alternative is a *hybrid* architecture which requires a dual development strategy. For example, the reliability of user-level objects can be achieved by means of the fault isolation properties of objects. However, an entirely different mechanism has to be employed to guarantee the reliability of the OS kernel. On the positive side, the performance overheads of hybrid architectures are not as high as those of pure architectures, primarily because of the tighter integration of functions that can be achieved within the kernel.

As a system design and implementation technique, the object model offers several important advantages for OS designers:

1. Each OS service module can implement an OS object with clear interfaces. Therefore, services are provided to the other system and user modules without requiring that they get involved in the implementation details.

2. The system can be made easily extensible. The operating system is designed as a collection of small modules that provide certain services. If modifications or additions to these services are required, a module can be developed that uses (or contains) one of these OS modules. Developing systems in this manner has been called the "software IC" approach [Cox, 1986].

3. It is easy to provide alternative services with similar functions. Since the kernel supports certain primitive objects, the other OS services can be de-

---

[4]The term *type manager* corresponds to a "class" implementation in object-oriented systems. The term *object manager* is used more commonly in the OS literature.

fined as user-level objects built from primitive objects. Therefore, it is relatively easy to implement, for example, two file systems with different functionalities based on a common kernel.

4. Since each module is self-contained with well-defined interfaces to the outside world, it is easier to develop reliable software. The possibility of modules corrupting one another is almost nonexistent if the object-based system kernel does not permit one module to modify the implementation details of another module.

## 13.9  CONCLUSION

In this chapter we accomplished several things. First we discussed various architectural models and compared them with respect to their flexibility in accommodating the distributed DBMS requirements. A second task has been to critically review the research that has been going on within the database OS communities. It is clear that the effort has focused on buffer management more than anything else. General-purpose transaction management has received considerable attention lately, but there is still much that we do not know. The architectural aspects of cooperation between a distributed DBMS and a DOS are not very well understood either. Finally, the discussion in this chapter indicates a number of future research directions. Work to investigate these issues is going on within both the database and OS communities.

## 13.10  BIBLIOGRAPHIC NOTES

The content of this chapter is based on [Özsu, 1988], which is an extended treatment of the same issues; Section 13.8 is based on [Özsu, 1989]. For those readers who may not be familiar with the functions performed by operating systems, there are numerous excellent textbooks on operating systems (e.g., [Tanenbaum, 1987], [Lister, 1984], and [Peterson and Silberschatz, 1985]). The specific issues related to the design of distributed operating systems are covered in [Maekawa et al., 1987] and [Lorin, 1980] as well as in [Tanenbaum and van Renesse, 1985], an excellent overview.

A number of operating system designs have some of the features that we discussed in this chapter. The early work on object-oriented operating systems goes back to Hydra [Wulf et al., 1981] and STAROS [Jones et al., 1979]. One sees the effects of these systems on almost all of the more recent operating systems that support objects.

Among the more recent work, we have already mentioned Mach [Jones and Rashid, 1986], which is an implementation of UNIX that provides a small kernel and supports user-level objects. Another example is the V-kernel [Cheriton, 1984], which provides a small, minimal kernel that acts as a communication medium between processes. Amoeba [Tanenbaum and Mullender, 1981] implements a small capability-based kernel that provides support for objects, and follows the "separation of policy and mechanism" policy. However, none of these has special support for DBMS functions. Operating systems such as LOCUS [Popek and Walker, 1985] and GENESIS [Page et al., 1985] have some support for transactions. However, they are based on UNIX and therefore have the problems discussed in [Stonebraker, 1981] in implementing distributed DBMSs on top of them. Another OS that provides transaction support is QuickSilver [Haskin et al., 1988]. Eden [Lazowska et al., 1981] and Clouds [Dasgupta and LeBlanc, 1985] are two operating system designs that resemble the architecture we discussed here. They both have small kernels and support nested transactions. A more complete comparison of these systems can be found in [Tanenbaum and van Renesse, 1985]. FLEX [Özsu et al., 1988] is an experimental distributed operating system that specifically addresses the issues related to the integration of distributed operating systems with distributed database managers. The PRIMA project [Härder, 1988] addresses many of the issues discussed in this chapter as well.

# 14

# Distributed Multidatabase Systems

Up to this point we have considered technical issues related to distributed database systems. As we discussed in Chapter 4, these systems are logically integrated and provide a single image of the database even though they are physically distributed. In this chapter we concentrate on distributed multidatabase systems. The topics addressed in this chapter are threefold: global conceptual schema design (Section 14.1), query processing (Section 14.2), and transaction management (Section 14.3). The presentation of these topics will be based on the related concepts that were developed for distributed DBMSs. In discussing data model integration, distribution is secondary since the fundamental aim is the design of the global conceptual schema. Therefore, in Section 14.1 we will not deal with issues that arise due to data distribution.

## 14.1 DATABASE INTEGRATION

*Database integration* involves the process by which information from participating databases can be conceptually integrated to form a single cohesive definition of a multidatabase; in other words, it is the process of designing the global conceptual schema. Recall from Chapter 4 that not all multidatabase architectures actually require the definition of this integrated view. Thus the discussions in this section are relevant only for those architectures that specify a global conceptual schema.

Recall from Chapter 5 that the design process in multidatabase systems is bottom-up. In other words, the individual databases actually exist, and designing the global conceptual schema involves integrating these databases (which we will call *local*) into a multidatabase. Database integration can occur in two steps (Figure 14.1): *schema translation* (or simply *translation*) and *schema integration*. In the first step, the participating local database schemas are translated to a common intermediate ($InS_1$, $InS_2$, ..., $InS_n$) canonical representation. Clearly, this translation is necessary only if the databases are heterogeneous and each local schema may be defined using a different data model. The choice of a canonical representation facilitates the translation process. It is quite time consuming to write schema translators; estimates range from three to six months to write a translator between two schemas [Elmagarmid and Helal, 1986]. In addition, time is needed to fine-tune for real-life databases. The use of a canonical representation reduces the number of translators that need to be written.

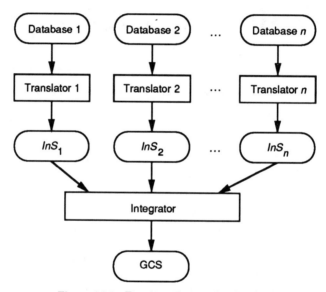

**Figure 14.1**    Database Integration Process

In the second step, each intermediate schema is integrated into a global conceptual schema. In some methodologies local external schemas are considered for integration rather than local conceptual schemas, since it may not be desirable to incorporate the entire local conceptual schema in the multidatabase.

**Example 14.1**

To facilitate our discussion of global schema design in multidatabase systems, we will use an example that is an extension of the engineering database we have been using throughout the book. To demonstrate both phases of the database integration process, we introduce some data model heterogeneity into our example.

Consider three organizations, each with its own database definition. One of these organizations is our engineering company, with its relational definition of its database. We
repeat that definition in Figure 14.2 for completeness. The attributes underscored are
the keys of the associated relations. We have made one modification in the J relation
by including attributes LOC and CNAME. LOC is the location of the project whereas
CNAME is the name of the client for whom the project is carried out. The second organization has an employee database that is defined according to the CODASYL network
data model as given in Figure 14.3. The third organization is another engineering company which defines its database according to the entity-relationship (E-R) data model
[Chen, 1976] as depicted in Figure 14.4.

E(<u>ENO</u>, ENAME, TITLE)

J(<u>JNO</u>, JNAME, BUDGET, LOC, CNAME)

G(<u>ENO, JNO</u>, RESP, DUR)

S(<u>TITLE</u>, SAL)

**Figure 14.2**    Relational Engineering Database Representation

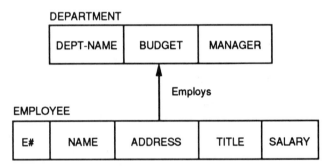

**Figure 14.3**    CODASYL Network Definition of the Employee Database

We assume that the reader is familiar with the CODASYL network and the entity-relationship data models. Therefore, we will not describe the formalisms. However, the semantics of the last two models need some explanation. The employee database of Figure 14.3
is a simple employee database that shows departments and the employees that work in
that department. The directed arc from the EMPLOYEE *record type* to the DEPART-
MENT record type represents what is called a *DBTG set* and corresponds to a relationship between the two record types that it links. In this case the DBTG set is named "Employs" and indicates a many-to-one relationship in the direction of the arrow. In other
words, a department may employ many employees, but a given employee can belong to
a single department.

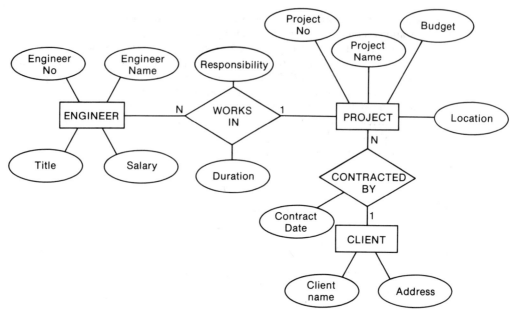

**Figure 14.4**   Entity-Relationship Database

The third database shown in Figure 14.4 is similar to the relational engineering database definition of Figure 14.2, with one significant difference. In addition to the same information, it keeps track of the clients for whom the projects are conducted. The rectangular boxes in Figure 14.4 represent the entities modeled in the database, and the diamonds indicate a relationship between the entities to which they are connected. The type of relationship is indicated around the diamonds. For example, the CONTRACTED-BY relation is a many-to-one from the PROJECT entity to the CLIENT entity (e.g., each project has a single client but each client can have many projects). Similarly, the WORKS-IN relationship indicates a many-to-many relationship between the two connected relations. The attributes of entities and the relationships are shown as elliptical circles.

### 14.1.1  Schema Translation

Schema translation is the task of mapping from one schema to another. This requires the specification of a target data model for the global conceptual schema definition. Schema translation may not be necessary in a heterogeneous database if it can be accomplished during the integration stage. Combining the translation and integration steps [Brzezinski et al., 1984] provides the integrater with all the information about the entire global database, at one time. Obviously, the integrater can make trade-offs between the different local schemas to determine which representation should be given precedence when conflicts arise. This requires that the integrater have knowledge of all the various trade-offs that must be made among several different schemas and their semantics, which may be different.

The two data models that have been studied most as candidate target formalisms have been the relational and the entity-relationship data models. It is now commonly accepted that a data model which is expressively more powerful than the relational is needed for this purpose. In that sense the E-R model is more popular and we concentrate on translations to the E-R model to demonstrate the process.

CODASYL network to E-R translation is relatively straightforward. It is accomplished essentially by mapping each record type in the CODASYL schema to an entity and each DBTG set to a relationship.

**Example 14.2**

The employee database in Figure 14.3 can be translated to an E-R equivalent by creating one entity for each record type and one relationship for each link defined in the network schema. A straightforward translation creates the entities EMPLOYEE and DEPARTMENT with the associated attributes and the keys defined. The "Employs" DBTG set becomes a many-to-one relationship from the EMPLOYEE entity to the DEPARTMENT entity. The final model is depicted in Figure 14.5.

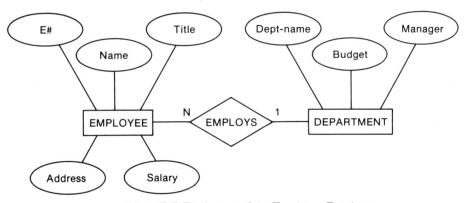

**Figure 14.5**   E-R Equivalent of the Employee Database

The translation of Example 14.2 is a relatively simple one because it contains only a binary many-to-one relationship which has a direct representation in both the network and the E-R model. However, if the relationship is more complex (e.g., many-to-many), the mapping is not that trivial. The CODASYL model uses dummy records in its representation of many-to-many relationships that need to be recognized during mapping.

**Example 14.3**

Assume that the relationship between the EMPLOYEE and DEPARTMENT record types are many-to-many. This would be represented in the CODASYL network by the inclusion of a dummy record type WORK, which has a many-to-one relationship to both EMPLOYEE and the DEPARTMENT record types (Figure 14.6a[1]). The direct trans-

---

[1] To simplify the figures, we omit the attributes of the record and entity types.

lation of this schema into E-R formalism would result in Figure 14.6b. Clearly, this is not an optimal E-R model since the ability to represent many-to-many relationships is not utilized. Figure 14.6c demonstrates an alternative structure that makes use of this capability and represents the same schema with one less entity and one less relationship.

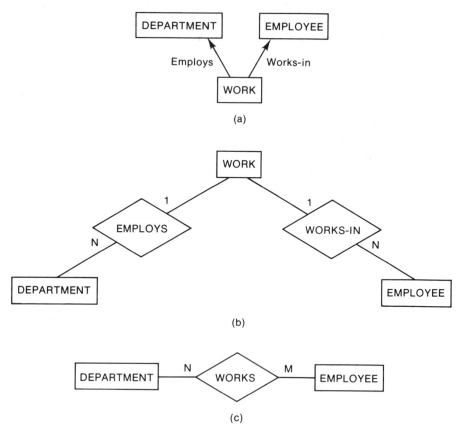

**Figure 14.6** Mapping of a More Complicated CODASYL Schema to E-R Model

Translation of relational schemes to an E-R model requires consideration of each relation's role. The first difficulty is the determination of relations that represent entities versus those that represent relationships. In certain cases this information may be easy to identify if there are specific relations that represent relationships as well as entities. Otherwise, these relationships may be identified from the foreign keys defined for each relation. Once this determination is made, the mapping is straightforward: relations that represent entities are modeled as entities, and relations that represent relationships are modeled as relationships.

A second difficulty relates to the nature of the relationships. Identification of the type of relationship (e.g., many-to-many) and relationship constraints requires that semantic information be known about the relational implementation, since these are not intrinsic to the relational model. This typically requires consulting the system directory.

**Example 14.4**

The relational model of the engineering database (see Figure 14.2) consists of four relations, three of which (E and J) clearly correspond to entities whereas one (G) corresponds to a relationship. The ENO and JNO attributes of G are foreign keys, which indicates that G is a relationship between E and J. The type of relationship that G represents cannot be discerned from the relational schema definition. From our knowledge of the semantics of the database, we know it to be many-to-many.

The handling of relation S is more difficult. It can be treated as an entity, in which case it is necessary to establish a relationship between it and one of the other entities, probably E. Even though no such relation exists in Figure 14.2, it is possible to create a many-to-one relationship from S to E (Figure 14.7a). The relationship needs to be many-to-one since each employee can have one salary, but a salary can belong to two employees who happen to have the same title. Another alternative would be to treat salary as an attribute of an engineer entity (Figure 14.7b). This provides a cleaner E-R model but does not explicitly specify the relationship between the employee titles and their salaries.

## 14.1.2  Schema Integration

Schema integration follows the translation process and generates the global conceptual schema by integrating the intermediate schemas. Schema integration is the process of *identifying* the components of a database which are related to one another, *selecting* the best representation for the global conceptual schema, and finally, *integrating* the components of each intermediate schema. Two components can be related as equivalent, one contained in the other one, or disjoint [Sheth et al., 1988a].

Integration methodologies can be classified as binary and *n*ary mechanisms [Batini et al., 1986] (Figure 14.8). Binary integration methodologies involve the manipulation of two schemas at a time. These can occur in a stepwise (ladder) fashion (Figure 14.9a) where intermediate schemas are created for integration with subsequent schemas [Pu, 1988], or in a purely binary fashion (Figure 14.9b), where each schema is integrated with one other, creating an intermediate schema for integration with other intermediate schemas ([Batini and Lenzirini, 1984] and [Dayal and Hwang, 1984]).

*N*ary integration mechanisms integrate more than two schemas at each iteration. One-pass integration (Figure 14.10a) occurs when all schemas are integrated at once, producing the global conceptual schema after one iteration. Benefits of this approach include the availability of complete information about all databases at integration time. There is no implied priority for the integration order of schemas, and the trade-offs, such as the best representation for data items or the most understandable structure, can be made between all schemas rather than between a few. Difficulties with this approach include increased complexity and difficulty of automation.

Iterative *n*ary integration (Figure 14.10b) offers more flexibility (typically, more information is available) and is more general (the number of schemas can be var-

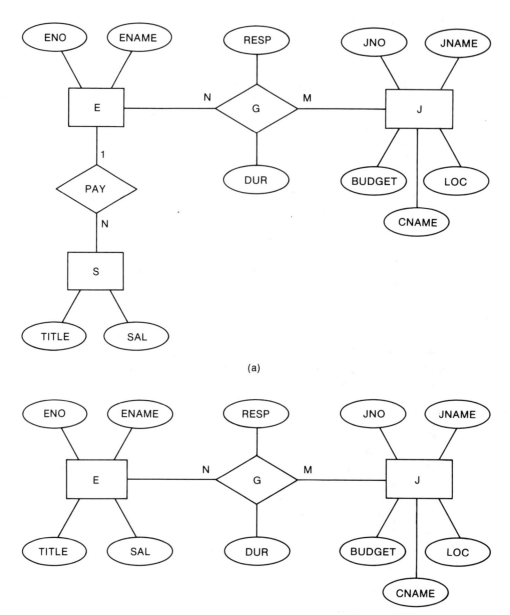

(a)

**Figure 14.7**   E-R Equivalent of the Engineering Database

ied depending on the integrater's preferences). Binary approaches are a special case of iterative $n$ary but decrease the potential integration complexity and lead toward automation techniques since the number of schemas to be considered at each step

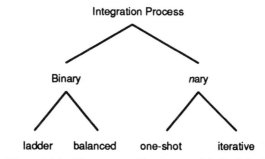

**Figure 14.8**    Taxonomy of Integration Methodologies

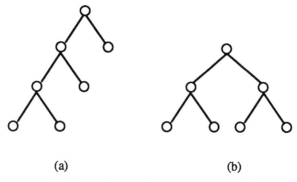

(a)                                            (b)

**Figure 14.9**    Binary Integration Methods

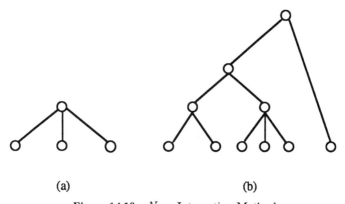

(a)                                            (b)

**Figure 14.10**    $N$ary Integration Methods

is more manageable. Integration by an $n$ary process enables the integrater to perform the operations on more than two views. For practical reasons, the majority of
systems utilize binary methodology, but a number of researchers prefer the one-shot
approach because complete information is available ([Elmasri et al., 1987] and [Yao

et al., 1982b]). Tools have started to be developed to aid in this integration process (see, e.g., [Sheth et al., 1988a]).

Schema integration occurs in a sequence of four steps: preintegration, comparison, conformation, and merging and restructuring. Each stage will be described below with reference to the example we have been considering.

**Preintegration.** Preintegration is required to establish the "rules" of the integration process before actual integration occurs. Initially, an integration method must be selected and the schema integration order defined. The order of schema integration implicitly defines priorities.

Candidate keys in each schema are identified to enable the integrater to determine dependencies implied by the schemas. Potentially equivalent domains of attributes [Larson et al., 1989] must be described in terms of mappings from one representation to another. For example, degrees Celsius in one schema may be represented in degrees Fahrenheit in another. Therefore, the mapping or transformation rules should be described before integration begins.

**Example 14.5**

In the example that we are considering, integration will be performed on intermediate schemas in E-R notation. The intermediate schemas are depicted in Figures 14.4, 14.5, and 14.7b, which we will refer to as $InS_1$, $InS_2$, and $InS_3$, respectively.

The first decision that we will need to make is with respect to the integration method. Without loss of generality, let us decide to use a ladder-type binary integration method. Let us further fix the order of integration as follows: (1) integrate $InS_1$ with $InS_3$ first, then (2) integrate the schema generated in step (1) with $InS_2$.

We next have to determine the identifiers (keys) of each entity in the intermediate schemas. In $InS_1$ these are

> ENGINEER entity: Engineer No.
> PROJECT entity: Project No.
> CLIENT entity: Client name

for $InS_2$ they are

> EMPLOYEE entity: E#
> DEPARTMENT entity: Dept-name

and for $InS_3$ they can be specified as

> E entity: ENO
> J entity: JNO

**Comparison.** During this phase both the naming and structural conflicts are identified. The fundamental naming problem is that of *synonyms* and *homonyms*. Two identical entities that have different names are synonyms, and two different entities that have identical names are homonyms. For example, ENGINEER in Figure 14.4 and E in 14.7b are synonyms; they both refer to an engineer entity. On the other hand, the Address attribute in the EMPLOYEE entity in Figure 14.5 and the Address attribute of the CLIENT entity in Figure 14.7 may be homonyms if one represents the full street address and the other indicates the city. The detection and resolution of homonyms is the easier of the two conflicts. A straightforward way of resolving them is to prefix the homonyms by the schema or model name [Elmasri et al., 1987].

**Example 14.6**

The synonyms in the example intermediate databases exist only between $InS_1$ and $InS_3$. These are depicted in Figure 14.11, where the corresponding entries on the same row are synonyms (e.g., Salary and SAL). The only homonym is the title attribute that exists in all three intermediate schemas. In $InS_1$ and $InS_3$, the attribute refers to the title of engineers, so its domain is engineering titles, whereas in $InS_2$ it refers to the titles of all employees, and therefore has a larger domain. Thus the title attributes in $InS_1$ and $InS_2$ form a homonym since the same attribute name is used to mean two different things. Similarly, the title attributes in $InS_3$ and $InS_2$ also form homonyms.

| $InS_1$ | $InS_3$ |
|---|---|
| ENGINEER | E |
| Engineer No | ENO |
| Engineer Name | ENAME |
| Salary | SAL |
| WORKS IN | G |
| Responsibility | RESP |
| Duration | DUR |
| PROJECTS | J |
| Project No | JNO |
| Project Name | JNAME |
| Location | LOC |

**Figure 14.11**    Synonyms in the Intermediate Schemas

The determination of synonyms and homonyms, as well as the identification of structural conflicts, requires specification of the relationship between the intermediate schemas. Two schemas can be related in four possible ways: they can be identical to one another, one can be a subset of the other, some components from one may occur in the other while retaining some unique features, or they could be completely different with no overlap. Determination of the type of relationship is essential in GCS design. For example, equivalence of the schemas is important in determining if two schemas represent the same information, so that the most appropriate schema can be used for the representation [Jajodia et al., 1983]. Unfortunately, the identification of these relationships cannot be done entirely syntactically; the semantics of each schema have to be considered. Recall, for example, our discussion above with respect to the address attribute in two intermediate schemas. To determine whether one attribute is identical to the other requires knowledge about the "meaning" of the information captured by that attribute. A further complication may be that an attribute in one schema may represent the same information as an entity in another one. Discussion of formal specification of these relationships is beyond our scope (see [Barker and Özsu, 1988]) and we present the resolution of such conflicts by means of an example.

**Example 14.7**

Considering the three intermediate schemas, the following relationships can be determined:

1. $InS_3$ (Figure 14.7b) is a subset of $InS_1$ (Figure 14.4).
2. Some parts of $InS_1$ and $InS_3$ occur in $InS_2$ (Figure 14.5). The part that is common is that the ENGINEER (and E) entity instances occur as part of the EMPLOYEE entity instances. However, the EMPLOYEE entity has many other instances. In terms of the E-R relationships, we state that there is an IS-A relationship between the ENGINEER (and E) entity and the EMPLOYEE entity [i.e., ENGINEER (and E) IS-A EMPLOYEE]. Another way of thinking about this relationship is to treat ENGINEER as a *specialization* or a *subclass* of the EMPLOYEE entity. This means that instances of the ENGINEER entity type comprise a subset of the EMPLOYEE entity type. Therefore, ENGINEER entities *inherit* the attributes of the EMPLOYEE entity. Figure 14.12 depicts the relationship. Notice that we use a circle to indicate the specialization and the subset ($\subset$) sign to indicate which entity type is a subclass of the other. In specialization relationships, the attributes of the EMPLOYEE entity type are inherited by the ENGINEER entity (*attribute inheritance*). These inherited attributes are not depicted in the figure.

Structural conflicts occur in four possible ways: as *type conflicts, dependency conflicts, key conflicts,* or *behavioral conflicts* [Batini et al., 1986]. Type conflicts occur when the same object is represented by an attribute in one schema and by an entity in another schema. Dependency conflicts occur when different relationship modes (e.g., one-to-one versus many-to-many) are used to represent the same thing in different schemas. Key conflicts occur when different candidate keys are available and different primary keys are selected in different schemas. Behavioral conflicts are implied by the modeling mechanism. For example, deleting the last item from one database may cause the deletion of the containing entity (i.e., deletion of the last employee causes the dissolution of the department).

**Example 14.8**

We have two structural conflicts in the example we are considering. The first is a type conflict involving clients of projects. In the schema of Figure 14.4, the client of a project is modeled as an entity. In the schema of Figure 14.7b, however, the client is included as an attribute of the J entity.

The second structural conflict is a dependency conflict involving the WORKS_IN relationship in Figure 14.4 and the G relationship in Figure 14.7b. In the former, the relationship is many-to-one from the ENGINEER to the PROJECT, whereas in the latter, the relationship in many-to-many. The resolution of these conflicts is the subject of the next section.

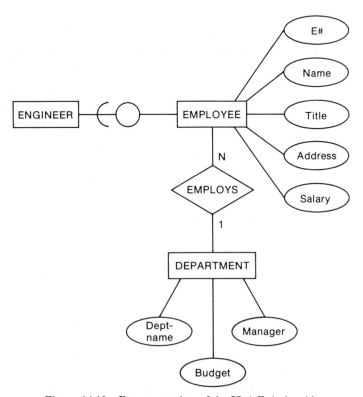

**Figure 14.12**    Representation of the IS-A Relationship

**Conformation.**    Conformation is the resolution of the conflicts that are determined at the comparison phase. Naming conflicts are resolved simply by renaming conflicting ones. In the case of homonyms, the simplest way of handling them is to prefix each attribute by the name of the entity to which it belongs and to prefix each entity by the name of the schema to which it belongs.

**Example 14.9**

The naming conformations in our example involve renaming of the entities, attributes, and relationships in the schemas of Figures 14.4 and 14.7b. For simplicity, we will rename the schema of Figure 14.7b to conform to the naming of Figure 14.4. We will also rename the homonym title attribute in the manner described above.

Transforming entities/attributes/relationships among one another is a tool for handling structural conflicts ([Batini and Lenzirini, 1984] and [Batini et al., 1986]). One can accomplish these transformations on an instance-by-instance basis. Figure 14.13 depicts the possible atomic transformation scenarios. The dashed lines indicate that a given attribute is an identifier (key) of the associated entity.

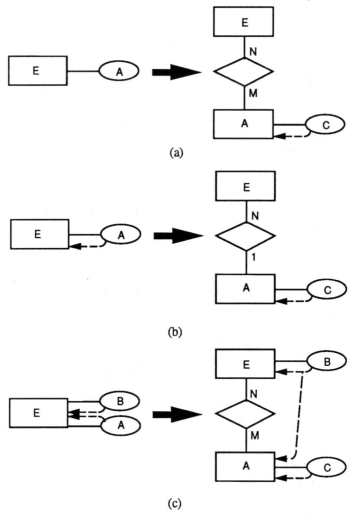

(a)

(b)

(c)

**Figure 14.13**  Atomic Conformation Alternatives. (Adapted from: C. Batini, M. Lenzerini, and S.B. Navathe, *Comparison Of Methodologies For Database Scheme Integration.* ACM Comp. Surveys; December 1986; 18(4): 323–364.)

A nonkey attribute can be transformed into an entity by creating an intermediate relationship connecting the new entity and a new attribute to represent it. Figure 14.13a depicts such a transformation of a nonkey attribute A of entity E to a separate entity that is related to E by a many-to-many relationship and is uniquely identified by a new key attribute, C. Figure 14.13b illustrates a key attribute translation where a key attribute is transformed into an entity that has an identifier C. C becomes the identifier of both the new entity A and the entity E because the relationship between E and A is many-to-one. Figure 14.13c demonstrates the case where identifier A is only a part of the complete identifier which requires the nonstandard reference back to the originating entity.

**Example 14.10**

In the example we are considering, there is one case where such a transformation would be necessary. In Figure 14.7b the attribute CNAME is represented as an attribute and needs to be converted to an entity using the technique demonstrated in Figure 14.13a. The result is depicted in Figure 14.14.

Recall that there is a dependency conflict between the two schemas as well. In this example we will resolve the conflict by choosing to accept the more general many-to-many relationship between the ENGINEER and PROJECT entities. Note that this is a design decision which reflects alternative semantics of integration and results in the loss of the more restricting one-to-many constraint between ENGINEER and PROJECT.

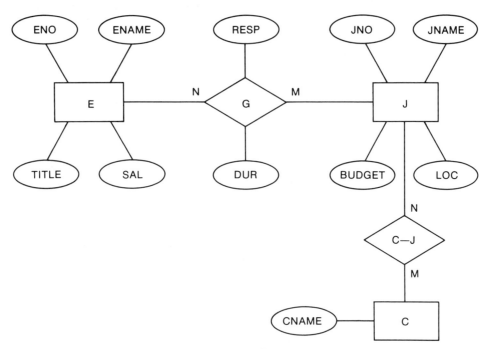

**Figure 14.14**   Attribute-to-Entity Transformation

Unfortunately, the conformation stage is virtually an art rather than a science. Clearly, semantic knowledge about all intermediate schemas is required, which makes automation of this process very difficult. No method has yet been shown to be complete in the sense of being able to handle every possible conformation activity.

**Merging and restructuring.**   If conformation is an art form, restructuring is a black art. Clearly, all schemas must be merged into a single database schema and then restructured to create the "best" integrated schema. Merging requires that the information contained in the participating schemas be retained in the integrated schema.

**Example 14.11**

In our example we decided in the preintegration stage that we were first going to integrate intermediate schema $InS_1$ (Figure 14.7b) with schema $InS_3$ (Figure 14.4). We had previously shown that the information in $InS_1$ is fully contained in $InS_3$. Merging these two schemas should therefore be trivial; we can simply accept the more general schema (i.e., $InS_3$) as the final one. However, after the conformation stage, this relationship may no longer be true. Consider the CONTRACTED_BY relationship in $InS_3$. It is many-to-one from the PROJECT entity to the CLIENT entity. However, the same relationship in $InS_1$ is many-to-many (Figure 14.14), which is more general. This conflict did not manifest itself before, because it arose due to the resolution of a type conflict during the confirmation stage. Therefore, merging these two schemas can be accomplished by accepting $InS_3$ as the result provided that the CONTRACTED_BY relationship is converted to a many-to-many relationship. Merging the employee database (Figure 14.5) with this can be accomplished by means of the previously established IS-A relationship between the ENGINEER and EMPLOYEE entities. The result of the merging step is given in Figure 14.15.

Three dimensions of merging and restructuring can be defined: *completeness, minimality,* and *understandability* [Batini et al., 1986]. Merging is *complete* if all the information from all the schemas is integrated into the common schema. To accomplish a complete merging, one may use *subsetting* a technique that describes one entity in terms of another. The well-known concepts of generalization and specialization are special cases of subsetting. It is possible to devise special operators for this purpose [Motro and Buneman, 1981].

A merging is *nonminimal* when redundant relationship information is retained in an integrated schema because of a failure to detect containment where part of one intermediate schema may be included within another intermediate schema. Nonminimal schemas can also result from the translation process, due to the production of an intermediate schema which itself is not minimal.

*Understandability* is the final dimension for determining the best schema. Once all the elements are merged, the restructuring should facilitate an understandable schema. Unfortunately, quantifying exactly what makes something easily understandable is usually not possible since the concept itself is highly subjective. It may be necessary to make trade-offs between minimality and understandability, provided that the resulting merged and restructured schema is complete.

## 14.2 QUERY PROCESSING

Query processing techniques in multidatabase systems are not significantly different from query processing in distributed database systems. Recall from Chapter 7 that we characterized distributed query processing in four steps: query decomposition, data localization, global optimization, and local optimization. This is a generalization of the local query processing steps in centralized DBMSs, which include decomposition, optimization, and execution [Gardarin and Valduriez, 1989]. The nature of multi-

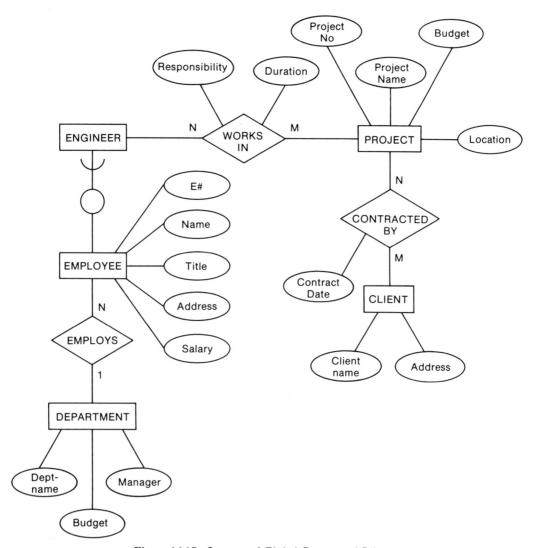

**Figure 14.15**  Integrated Global Conceptual Schema

database systems requires slightly different steps, but the fundamental techniques remain the same.

The first thing to remember in this discussion is the nature of the multi-DBMS.
In Chapter 4 (specifically in Figure 4.10) we indicated that the multi-DBMS is a layer
of software that runs on top of individual DBMSs. Each DBMS has its own query
processors, which execute queries according to the three steps listed above. In the
case of distributed multi-DBMSs, there is a multi-DBMS layer at each site (Figure

14.16). Therefore, execution of distributed queries in a distributed multi-DBMS involves cooperation among the various local multi-DBMSs.

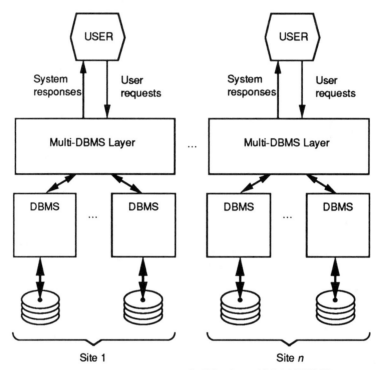

**Figure 14.16**   Structure of a Distributed Multi-DBMS

Query processing in a multidatabase system is more complex than in a distributed DBMS, for the following reasons [Sheth, 1989]:

1. The capability of individual DBMSs may be different, which prevents uniform treatment of queries across multiple DBMSs and sites.
2. Similarly, the cost of processing queries may be different on different DBMSs. This increases the complexity of the cost functions that need to be evaluated.
3. There may be difficulties in moving data between DBMSs since they may differ in their ability to read "moved" data.
4. The local optimization capability of each DBMS may be quite different.

The architecture depicted in Figure 14.16 points to an additional complexity in distributed multi-DBMSs. In distributed DBMSs, query processors have to deal only with data distribution across multiple sites. In a distributed multi-DBMS environment, on the other hand, data is distributed not only across sites but also across multiple databases, each managed by an autonomous DBMS. Thus while there are two parties that cooperate in the processing of queries in a distributed DBMSs (the control site and local sites), the number of parties increases to three in the case of a distributed multi-DBMS: the multi-DBMS layer at the control site, which receives the global query; the multi-DBMS layers at the sites, which participate in processing the query; and the individual DBMSs, which ultimately optimize and execute the query.

### 14.2.1 Query Processing Layers in Distributed Multi-DBMSs

With this structure in mind, we can now discuss the various steps involved in query processing in distributed multi-DBMSs (Figure 14.17). When a query is received at a site, the first thing that needs to be done is to "split" it into subqueries based on data distribution across multiple sites. At this step it is only necessary to worry about the placement of data across the sites, rather than its storage across various databases. Therefore, the only information that is required is the typical data allocation information that is stored in a global directory. The site that receives the query and performs the splitting, called the *control site*, is ultimately responsible for successful completion of the task.

Each subquery is then sent to the site where it is to be processed. The multi-DBMS layer at each site further "fragments" the query for each DBMS that it controls. At this stage the information within the directory is used. Each subquery is then translated into the language of the respective DBMS. Extensive information about the global query language and the individual languages used by the DBMSs needs to be maintained to facilitate translation. Even though this information can be kept within the directory, it is common to store it as an *auxiliary database* [Landers and Rosenberg, 1982].

The queries submitted to the individual DBMSs are processed following decomposition, optimization, and execution steps. The decomposition step involves the simplification of a user query that is specified in some relational calculus and its translation to an equivalent relational algebra query over the conceptual schema. The optimization step involves the reordering of relational algebra operations as well as determination of the best access paths to data. The resulting schedule is then executed by the run-time support processor.

### 14.2.2 Global Dictionary/Directory and Auxiliary Databases

As indicated above, specific translation information is stored in a separate auxiliary database. There is no overriding principle that dictates separation of the global directory from the auxiliary database. In fact, there are prototype heterogeneous systems (such as OMNIBASE [Rusinkiewicz et al., 1988], COSYS [Adiba and Portal, 1978], ADDS [Breitbart and Paolini, 1985], and MRDSM [Wong and Bazek, 1985]) that combine the two pieces of information into one database. We have separated them to highlight their different functionalities and to facilitate the incremental definition of the two databases. This separation serves to emphasize the distinction between distributed databases and distributed multidatabase systems.

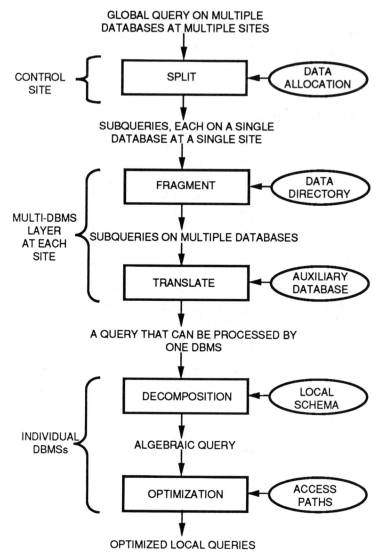

**Figure 14.17**   Query Processing Steps in Multidatabase Systems

The auxiliary database contains information describing how mappings from/to participating schemas and global schema can be performed. It enables conversions between components of the database in different ways. For example, if the global schema represents temperatures in Fahrenheit degrees but a participating database uses Celsius degrees, the auxiliary database must contain a conversion formula to provide the proper presentation to the global user and the local databases. If the conversion is across types and simple formulas cannot perform the translation, complete mapping tables could be located in the auxiliary database, as illustrated in the age category relations above.

## 14.3  TRANSACTION MANAGEMENT

Transaction management is probably the major open question in multidatabase systems. The challenge is to permit concurrent global updates to the underlying databases without violating their autonomy. Most current prototypes either do not permit updates to the local databases or execute updates off-line and in batch mode.

In this context, transaction management can be viewed in two dimensions: autonomy and heterogeneity. Autonomy requires that the global transaction management functions be performed independent of the local transaction execution functions. In other words, the individual DBMSs (more specifically, their transaction managers) are not modified to accommodate global updates. Heterogeneity has the additional implication that the transaction managers of each DBMS may employ different concurrency control and commit protocols (this is called *design autonomy* in [Du and Elmagarmid, 1989]). Intuitively, heterogeneity adds further difficulty since it becomes difficult to make uniform assumptions about the functionality provided by individual DBMSs. However, if techniques can be found that enable concurrent and recoverable (i.e., reliable) access to local databases with minimal assumptions about their functionality, these two dimensions converge into one.

In this section we review the existing work in the literature while providing directions for research that should lead to some form of transaction management in heterogeneous systems. First we discuss a transaction and computation model and then present an extension to the serializability theory that accommodates multidatabase systems.

### 14.3.1  Transaction and Computation Model

Let us first elaborate on the architectural aspects of multidatabase transaction processing. As described in Chapter 4 (specifically in Figure 4.10), the MDBS architecture involves a number of DBMSs, each with its own transaction manager (called *local transaction managers* or LTMs) and a multi-DBMS layer on top. The transaction manager of the multi-DBMS layer is called the *global transaction manager* (GTM) since it manages the execution of global transactions. Furthermore, in a distributed multi-DBMS, the architecture of Figure 4.10 exists at each site. Thus our architectural model can be further abstracted as in Figure 14.18 for the purposes of distributed transaction management.

In a multidatabase system, there are two types of transaction: *local* transactions, which are submitted to each DBMS, and *global* transactions, which are submitted to the multi-DBMS layer. Local transactions execute on a single database, whereas global transactions access multiple databases. A global transaction is divided into a set of *global subtransactions*, each of which execute on one database. For a global trans-

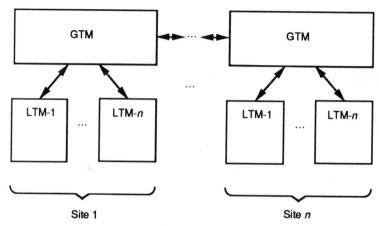

**Figure 14.18**   Distributed Multi-DBMS Transaction Management

action $GT_i$, its global subtransaction, which executes on database $j$, will be denoted as $GST_{ij}$. For a distributed transaction $GT_i$ (which by definition has to be global), the global subtransaction that executes at site $k$ is denoted as $GST_i^k$.

**Example 14.12**

Consider the three databases that we designed in Section 14.1 (Figures 14.2 through 14.4). In this example we ignore distribution for simplicity and without loss of generality. Let us denote the relational engineering database as 1, the CODASYL employee database as 2, and the E-R engineering database as 3 and assume that all these databases reside at the same site. Assume that a global transaction updates the salary of "J. Doe" by 15%. Let us denote this transaction as $GT_1$. First note that $GT_1$ may be specified on the global conceptual schema (if one is defined) which is specified in Example 14.11 (Figure 14.15). This global transaction will be subdivided into three subtransactions, each executing on one of the databases. Below we specify them using a self-descriptive algorithmic notation.

$GST_{11}$:   read(E.TITLE) into *temp*1 where E.ENAME = "J.Doe"
      if *temp*1 is empty then
        abort
      else begin
        read(S.SAL) into *temp*2 where S.TITLE = *temp*1
        S.SAL ← *temp*2 ∗ 1.15
        write(S.SAL)
        commit
      end

$GST_{12}$:   read(EMPLOYEE.SAL) into *temp*
        where EMPLOYEE.ENAME = "J.Doe"
      if *temp* is empty then
        abort
      else begin

> EMPLOYEE.SAL ← $temp * 1.15$
> write(EMPLOYEE.SAL)
> commit
> end

$GST_{13}$:    read(ENGINEER.Salary) into $temp$
   where ENGINEER.Name = "J.Doe"
 if $temp$ is empty then
  abort
 else begin
  ENGINEER.Salary ← $temp * 1.15$
  write(ENGINEER.Salary)
  commit
 end

There could be other transactions that may have been submitted directly to the individual DBMSs. For example, the following local transactions $LT_1$ and $LT_2$ update, respectively, the salaries of all electrical engineers in database 1 by 50% and update the budgets of maintenance projects by $50,000 in database 3.

$LT_1$:    read(S.SAL) into $temp$ where S.TITLE = "Elect. Eng."
 if $temp$ is empty then
  abort
 else begin
  S.SAL ← $temp * 1.5$
  write(S.SAL)
  commit
 end

$LT_2$:    read(PROJECT.Budget) into $temp$
   where PROJECT.Name = "Maintenance"
 if $temp$ is empty then
  abort
 else begin
  PROJECT.Budget ← $temp + 50000$
  write(PROJECT.Budget)
  commit
 end

The execution of these transactions on the architectural model of Figure 14.18 is depicted in Figure 14.19.

In such an execution environment it is necessary to discuss the responsibilities of the local and global transaction managers. A series of conditions have been defined that specify when global transactions can safely update a multidatabase system ([Gligor and Popescu-Zeletin, 1986] and [Gligor and Luckenbaugh, 1984]). These conditions are helpful in determining the minimal functionality required of the various transaction managers.

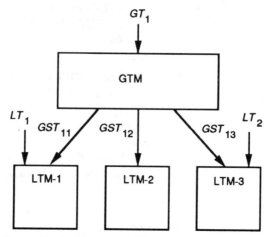

**Figure 14.19**   Transaction Execution Model Example

The first condition for providing global concurrency control is to have the individual database managers guarantee local synchronization atomicity. This means that the local transaction managers are simply responsible for the correct execution of the transactions on their respective databases. If serializability is the correctness criterion used, each local transaction manager is responsible for maintaining that its schedule is serializable and recoverable. These schedules are made up of global subtransactions as well as local ones. The fundamental point to watch out for here is that the local DBMSs accept a transaction and execute it until its termination (either abort or commit).

The second condition requires that each LTM maintain the relative execution order of the subtransactions determined by the GTM. The global transaction manager, then, is responsible for coordinating the submission of the global subtransactions to the local transaction managers and coordinating their execution. If serializability is the correctness criterion used, the global transaction manager is responsible for the serializability of the global transaction execution schedules. Furthermore, it is responsible for dealing with global deadlocks that occur among global transactions. Obviously, if the GTM awaits the result of one subtransaction before submitting the next, this ordering can be maintained.

In a distributed multi-DBMS, the global transaction manager is also responsible for the coordination of the distributed execution of global transactions. This involves a different execution paradigm than the one used in distributed DBMSs. In the latter, the transaction manager at the site where the transaction is submitted (called the *coordinating transaction manager*) can communicate directly with schedulers at its site and at other sites. In distributed multi-DBMSs, however, this is not possible, for two reasons. First, individual DBMSs do not necessarily know how to communicate in a distributed environment. The earlier discussion on the functionality of the local transaction managers, together with our architectural discussions in Chapter 4, indicates that each individual DBMS only knows how to communicate with an application program that executes on the same machine as itself. Second, global transaction managers usually have difficulty in scheduling transactions across multiple sites, so that it may not be feasible for them to get even more involved with transaction scheduling across multiple DBMSs at one site. This would mean that a global transaction manager would send a global subtransaction to another global transaction manager at another site and expect it to coordinate the execution of the global subtransaction. The global transaction manager at the other site may then further decompose the transaction into global subtransactions, depending on the organization of the local databases at its site. The condition that governs the execution of global transactions states that a global transaction should have only one global subtransaction executing at any one site.

**Example 14.13**

Consider the following transaction, which, among other things, accesses two data items $x$ and $y$ stored at site 2.

$$GT_1: \quad \text{read}(x)$$
$$\vdots$$
$$\text{write}(x)$$
$$\vdots$$
$$\text{read}(y)$$
$$\vdots$$
$$\text{write}(y)$$
$$\text{commit}$$

Since $GT_1$ accesses, among others, two data items that are stored in site 2, it may be tempting (but incorrect, as we will demonstrate) for the coordinating global transaction manager to split it into the following two global subtransactions to be submitted to the global transaction manager of site 2:

$$GST_{11}^2: \quad \text{read}(x)$$
$$\vdots$$
$$\text{write}(x)$$
$$\text{commit}$$

and

$$GST_{12}^2: \quad \text{read}(y)$$
$$\vdots$$
$$\text{write}(y)$$
$$\text{commit}$$

Now consider a local transaction $LT_1$ that conflicts with either $GST_{11}^2$ or $GST_{12}^2$ (e.g., reading $x$ or $y$). Then serializability of the global transaction $GT_1$ and the local transaction $LT_1$ would require that either $GT_1 \prec LT_1$ or $LT_1 \prec GT_1$. In terms of the sub-transactions, this would mean that $GST_{11}^2 \prec GST_{12}^2 \prec LT_1$ or $LT_1 \prec GST_{11}^2 \prec GST_{12}^2$. However, it is possible to have an execution schedule, as, for example, $GST_{11}^2 \prec LT_1 \prec GST_{12}^2$. Certainly, this schedule is not serialiazable with respect to the local and global transactions.

## 14.3.2  Multidatabase Serializability

Our earlier discussion of distributed transaction scheduling brings up an interesting point. The careful reader will have noticed that the schedule $GST_{11}^2 \prec LT_1 \prec GST_{12}^2$ may not necessarily be wrong, even though it is not serializable. For example, if $LT_1$ conflicts with $GT_1$ by reading $x$, and if $GST_{12}^2$ never accesses $x$, the database would be consistent at the end of the execution schedule above even though it may not be serializable. This is actually a known property of serializability theory: serializable schedules are only a subset of the correct execution schedules. Thus serializability is quite conservative in the schedules it allows. In multidatabase systems this becomes even more significant. A corollary of the third condition that we discussed above is that a global subtransaction of a distributed transaction should not be split further by the global transaction manager at the site to which it is submitted.

### Example 14.14

Consider the same transaction $GT_1$ that we considered in Example 14.13, but this time assume that $x$ and $y$ are stored in different databases at the same site (say, site 2). $GT_1$ can be split into a number of global subtransactions, one of which is submitted to the global transaction manager at site 2 as follows:

$$GST_1^2: \quad \text{read}(x, y)$$
$$\vdots$$
$$\text{write}(x)$$
$$\text{write}(y)$$
$$\text{commit}$$

Since $x$ and $y$ are in different databases, the global transaction manager itself may split $GST_1^2$ into $GST_{11}^2$ and $GST_{12}^2$ as defined in Example 14.13. Again notice that if there is a local transaction $LT_i$ that conflicts with either of these subtransactions, we would have a schedule that is not serializable but is correct.

This restriction is quite severe in multidatabase systems since it makes it very difficult to find a computation model for executing transactions. Again considering the example above, where $x$ and $y$ are stored in different databases, to maintain serializability, the global transaction manager at site 2 has to hold exclusive access rights to data items at one local database (say, $x$) long after the transaction that accesses the data item (in this case, $GST_{11}^2$) may have completed.

This realization has caused some researchers to argue that serializability theory as it is defined for distributed database systems is unsuitable for distributed multidatabase systems [Du et al., 1988]. The outcome is a modification of the serializability theory such that the resulting class of schedules is a superset of the serializable schedules ([Du and Elmagarmid, 1989], and [Breitbart and Silberschatz, 1988], and [Barker and Özsu, 1990]).

Since these theories are still in their infancy and will take a considerable amount of research to mature, we will not embark on a detailed description of them. The generalizations are based on identification of the problems of maintaining serializability as we have described them here, and the realization that two levels of schedules are involved in a multidatabase system: local schedules at each local DBMS and global schedules at the multidatabase level. In distributed multi-DBMSs, there is a third level of distributed global schedule. Thus it is natural to expect that the concurrency control algorithms that satisfy these modified serializability theories would be multilevel in nature.

It should be noted here that the development of the necessary correctness theory for synchronization is the simpler problem. The real difficulty comes with the reliability issues. Integrating reliability theory at the detail of [Hadzilacos, 1988] proves to be significantly more difficult. It is then that the autonomy of the local DBMSs become a significant obstacle. The work in this area has not yet matured to provide a full theoretical framework for multidatabase transaction processing.

## 14.4  CONCLUSION

In this chapter we have surveyed the issues and some of the work performed to date in the area of distributed multidatabase systems. The emphasis in this discussion has been on highlighting the major research areas.

Fundamental to any other work in the area is a determination of the need for a global conceptual schema and its meaning. The existence or lack of the GCS reflects on the user view of the multidatabase as well as the manner in which some of the issues are handled. If a GCS is to exist, its design is a problem that needs to be tackled. Even though the issues are well understood, automated tools are hard to design. Probably a fully automated design tool is not a realistic expectation. Currently, no such tool exists. However, an automated interactive tool to assist the designer in the translation and integration process would be useful.

Query processing is fairly well understood. The major difference between the multidatabase environment and the distributed DBMS is the addition of translators. Real-time query translators need to be written in such a way that they function very efficiently. Research intended to discover the characteristics of a "good" translator that would minimize overhead should produce a significant step forward. A second open problem in the area is that of query optimization in a heterogeneous distributed database. Since the translation of queries and results imposes some overhead, research into optimization requirements is required to determine if the traditional database optimization techniques are sufficient in the heterogeneous case.

Transaction management offers numerous research opportunities. Since little work has been done in the area, some fundamental problems need to be addressed. It is important to determine the amount of autonomy, if any, that needs to be sacrificed to permit transaction management on multidatabase systems. This is an issue of determining the proper computation model in a distributed database. The model will, undoubtedly, influence the theoretical framework that is developed. If the current extensions to the serializability theory are successful in including recoverability as well, one needs to develop scheduling and recovery algorithms that would provide "correct" schedules according to this criterion. Otherwise, a more relaxed correctness criterion may have to be adopted. A candidate may be the semantic transaction processing approaches espoused in [Garcia-Molina, 1983] and [Farrag and Özsu, 1989]. Then the issues to be investigated will be systems related, emphasizing the development of practical and efficient multidatabase transaction management systems.

## 14.5 BIBLIOGRAPHIC NOTES

Interest in heterogeneous database systems has a long history. There are some good tutorial papers on the topic. This chapter is structured after [Barker and Özsu, 1988]. Other good introductory papers are [Sheth and Larson, 1990], [Litwin, 1988], and [Gligor and Luckenbaugh, 1984].

A large number of prototype multidatabase implementations exist. Some of the more interesting ones are SIRIUS-DELTA ([Litwin et al., 1982] and [Ferrier and Stangret, 1982]), Multibase ([Smith et al., 1981], [Landers and Rosenberg, 1982], and [Dayal and Hwang, 1984]), MERMAID [Templeton et al., 1987], DDTS [Dwyer and Larson, 1987], ADDS [Breitbart and Tieman, 1985], and OMNIBASE [Rusinkiewicz et al., 1988].

As already indicated, most of the early work concentrated on global schema design, specifically on data translation. A good review of some of the earlier work on translation can be found in [Han and Fisher, 1983], [Schneiderman and Thomas, 1982] and [Larson, 1983]. The entire topic of schema integration is covered in [Batini et al., 1986], which also forms the basis of the presentation in Section 14.1. We should indicate that some of the definitions provided in that paper (which are also included in our discussion) are not universally accepted. This controversy over terminology (as well as methodology) reflects the unsettled nature of the topic and makes it quite difficult to compare discussions in the literature. [Sheth, 1987] discusses a methodology for building multidatabase systems consisting of heterogeneous and autonomous databases. [Sheth et al., 1988a] describes a tool developed for integrating schemas in an extended E-R model.

Most of the work on multidatabase query processing is reported in general system description papers (e.g., [Brill et al., 1984], [Dayal and Hwang, 1984], and [Landers and Rosenberg, 1982]). Some interesting work specifically addressing query processing in multidatabase systems includes [Czejdo et al., 1989], [Rusinkiewicz et al., 1989], [Czejdo et al., 1987], [Rusinkiewicz and Czejdo, 1987], and [Rusinkiewicz and Czejdo, 1985].

Transaction management is still an open problem. In addition to the papers referred to in Section 14.3, other important work is the following. Some early work (e.g., [Motro and Buneman, 1981]) treated the multidatabase layer as a "superview" (see

Chapter 6 for a discussion of views). Thus the update problem in multidatabase systems reduces to the update problem of views. The superview approach is also used for schema integration [Motro, 1987]. [Pu, 1988] defines "superdatabases" as hierarchical structures whose leaves consist of individual databases. The global transactions are managed by the super-DBMS at the lowest level that covers the individual databases affected. This approach assumes that a super-DBMS at one level is aware of all the local transactions submitted to its constituent DBMSs. The model described in Section 14.3.1 is from [Özsu and Barker, 1990]. Concurrency control proposals are given in [Alonso et al., 1987], [Breitbart et al., 1987], [Sugihara, 1987], [Elmagarmid and Helal, 1986] [Du and Elmagarmid, 1989], and [Barker and Özsu, 1990].

With respect to transaction processing, a final note is in order. The computational model that we presented in Section 14.3.1 is only one alternative. Other models, such as an object-oriented view of multidatabase systems, are also available (see, e.g., [Manola, 1989]). The model that we have presented is similar to the one used in the InterBase project [Elmagarmid and Du, 1990]. This computational model also did not discuss value dependency between data items stored across multiple databases. A discussion of the issues can be found in [Elmagarmid and Du, 1989].

## 14.6 EXERCISES

**14.1**  Distributed database systems and distributed multidatabase systems represent two different approaches to systems design. Find three real-life applications for which each of these approaches would be more appropriate. Discuss the features of these applications that make them more favorable for one approach or the other.

**14.2**  Some architectural models favor the definition of a global conceptual schema, whereas others do not. What do you think? Justify your selection with detailed technical arguments.

**\*14.3**  Give algorithms to convert:

   **(a)**  From a CODASYL network model to an entity-relationship model.

   **(b)**  From a relational model to an entity-relationship model.

**\*\*14.4**  Consider the three databases given in Figures 14.20 through 14.22 and described below. Design a global conceptual schema as a union of the three databases by first translating them into the E-R model. Use the methodology discussed in Section 14.1.

Figure 14.20 describes a relational race database used by organizers of road races; Figure 14.21 describes a network database used by a government agency to grant and distribute licenses; and Figure 14.22 describes an entity-relationship database used by a shoe manufacturer. The semantics of each of these database schemas is discussed below. Figure 14.20 describes a relational road race database with the following semantics:

**DIRECTOR** is a relation that defines race directors who organize races; we assume that each race director has a unique name (to be used as the key), a phone number, and an address.

**LICENSES** is required because all races require a governmental license, which is issued by a CONTACT in a department who is the ISSUER, possibly contained within another govern-

DIRECTOR(<u>NAME</u>, PHONE_NO, ADDRESS)
LICENSES(<u>LIC_NO</u>, CITY, DATE, ISSUES, COST, DEPT, CONTACT)
RACER(<u>NAME, ADDRESS</u>, MEM_NUM)
SPONSOR(<u>SP_NAME</u>, CONTACT)
RACE(<u>R_NO</u>, LIC_NO, DIR, MAL_WIN, FRM_WIN, SP_NAME)

**Figure 14.20**    Road Race Database

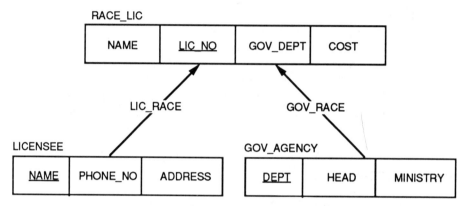

**Figure 14.21**    Government Database

ment department DEPT; each license has a unique LIC_NO (the key), which is issued for use in a specific CITY on a specific DATE with a certain COST.

**RACER** is a relation that describes people who participate in a race. Each person is identified by NAME, which is not sufficient to identify them uniquely, so a compound key formed with the ADDRESS is required. Finally, each racer may have a MEM_NUM to identify him or her as a member of the racing fraternity but not all competitors have membership numbers.

**SPONSOR** indicates which sponsor is funding a given race. Typically, one sponsor funds a number of races through a specific person (CONTACT), and a number of races may have different sponsors.

**RACE** uniquely identifies a single race which has a license number (LIC_NO), and race number (R_NO) (to be used as a key since a race may be planned without acquiring a license yet); each race has a winner in the male and female groups (MAL_WIN and FEM_WIN) and a race director (DIR).

Figure 14.21 describes a network governmental database that is able to grant licenses for (among other things) road races with the following semantics.

**GOV_AGENCY** defines a government agency able to grant licenses for road races; each government department has a supervisor represented by the HEAD field, and each government agency may be contained within another ministry of government (e.g., another government department).

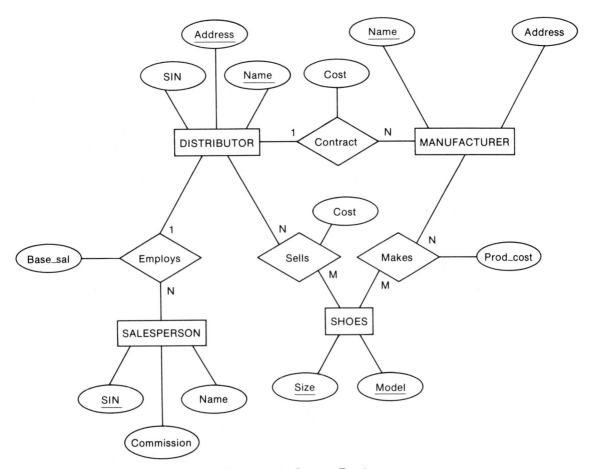

**Figure 14.22**  Sponsor Database

**LICENSEE** is the relation that defines who is granted a license since race licenses are given to an individual (NAME) who has a PHONE_NO and an ADDRESS.

**RACE_LIC** race licenses have a certain COST, and once granted, a special identifier (LIC_NO) will be used to identify the race to the government's database.

**LIC_HOLDERS** is an owner-coupled set where each LICENSEE may hold a number of licenses. This enables one person to hold more than one license.

**DEPT_LIC** is an owner-coupled set whereby a single GOV_AGENCY may grant a number of distinct race licenses for different races.

Figure 14.22 illustrates an entity-relationship schema used by the sponsor's database system with the following semantics:

**SHOES** are produced by sponsors of a certain MODEL and SIZE, which forms the key to the entity.

**MANUFACTURER** is identified uniquely by NAME and resides at a certain ADDRESS.

**DISTRIBUTOR** is a person that has a NAME and an ADDRESS (which are necessary to form the key) and SIN number for tax purposes.

**SALESPERSON** is a person (entity) who has a NAME, earns a COMMISSION, and is uniquely identified by his or her SIN number (the key).

**Makes** is a relationship that has a certain fixed production cost (PROD_COST) and indicates that a number of different shoes are made by a manufacturer and that different manufacturers' produce the same shoe.

**Sells** is a relationship that indicates the wholesale COST to a distributor of shoes and indicates that each distributor sells more than one type of shoe and that each type of shoe is sold by more than one distributor.

**Contract** is a relationship whereby a distributor purchases for a COST exclusive rights to represent a manufacturer. Note that this does not preclude the distributor from selling different manufacturers' shoes.

**Employs** indicates that each distributor hires a number of salespeople to sell the shoes; each earns a BASE_SALARY.

**\*\*14.5** Logic (first-order logic, to be precise) has been suggested as a uniform formalism for schema translation and integration. Discuss how logic can be useful for this purpose.

**\*\*14.6** Can any type of global optimization be performed on global queries in a multidatabase system? Discuss and formally specify the conditions under which such optimization would be possible.

**\*14.7** Consider three prototype multidatabase systems (e.g., MULTIBASE, SIRIUS, ADDS, MERMAID) and discuss their query processing strategies with respect to their functionalities.

**\*\*14.8** Can every transaction be subdivided into a set of subtransactions such that the third condition specified by Gligor and Popescu-Zeletin will be satisfied? (See Section 14.3.1 for a definition of the condition.) Formally specify the conditions under which such splitting may be possible.

**\*\*14.9** As stated in Section 14.3, recovery poses an especially difficult problem in concurrent updates of multidatabase systems. A fundamental difficulty is with the definition of the commit point of global transactions.

    **(a)** How would you define the commit point of a global transaction in a multidatabase system?

    **(b)** What type of computational model that specifies the execution of global transactions between the global transaction manager and the local ones can be developed to support this definition?

**14.10** State an algorithm to detect global deadlocks in a multidatabase system without violating the autonomy of the individual DBMSs.

# 15

# Current Trends in Distributed Databases

In the preceding chapters, the presentation of distributed database technology has been facilitated by three important assumptions. First, each site in the computer network is a general-purpose computer that executes both application programs and distributed database management functions. Second, the computer network is either a wide area network or a local network. Third, database management is based on the relational data model. These assumptions are satisfied by most of today's distributed databases. However, the recent advances in computer architecture and database technology have initiated new trends in which these assumptions may be relaxed.

The most significant impact of computer architecture on distributed databases stems from the recent availability of powerful workstations and parallel computers. The integration of workstations in a distributed environment enables a more efficient function distribution in which application programs run on workstations, called *application servers*, while database functions are handled by dedicated computers, called *data servers*. This leads to the present trend in distributed system architecture, where sites are organized as specialized servers rather than as general-purpose computers. To improve performance and data availability, for example, a data server can be implemented on a parallel computer and take advantage of the parallelism in data management [Boral, 1988a]. The relaxation of the second assumption leads to another trend—using of distributed database technology in implementing parallel data servers.

Database technology is rapidly evolving toward the support of new applications. Relational databases have proven to be very successful at supporting business data processing applications. However, there are now important types of applications that exhibit pressing needs for database management. Examples include computer-aided design (CAD), office information systems (OIS), and artificial intelligence (AI). These application types require the introduction of new capabilities that can be divided in two main areas: *knowledge bases* and *object-oriented databases*. Therefore, the relaxation of the third assumption may lead to two new research areas, such as distributed object-oriented databases and distributed knowledge bases.

These new trends pose challenging problems for which active research is ongoing. In this chapter we pursue each of these trends and present the new problems they introduce. When appropriate, we indicate potential solutions to these problems. However, research in these areas has not yet matured.

This chapter is organized as follows. In Section 15.1 we present the objectives of the data server approach and of the integration of data servers and application servers in a distributed database. In Section 15.2 we show the application of distributed database technology in the implementation of a parallel data server and focus on data placement and parallel algorithms for database operations. In Section 15.3 we introduce the topic of knowledge bases and their implementation in a parallel environment to process deductive queries efficiently. In Section 15.4 we introduce object-oriented databases and the new problems posed by their integration in a parallel environment; the main issue is the management of distributed complex objects.

## 15.1 DATA SERVERS

In this section we introduce the data server approach, which enables distributed applications to access a remote data server. Although this approach is often used as an alternative to distributed databases, a promising alternative is the use of data servers as sites of a distributed database.

### 15.1.1 Data Server Approach

Typically, a DBMS runs as a system program on a computer, which is shared by other system and application programs. This traditional approach has several shortcomings. As a result of the recent advances in database theory and technology, the size of the databases and the variety of applications have significantly increased. Nowadays, some databases have several gigabytes. Their management by a general-purpose computer may result in poor utilization of computer resources shared between applications and other complex software programs with different requirements. For example, the DBMS can easily congest the main memory with useless data and saturate the central processor when selecting the relevant data. As shown in Chapter 13 this approach is inefficient because the general-purpose operating system does not satisfy the particular requirements of database management. This situation stems from the excessive centralization of data and application management functions in the same computer.

A solution to that problem appeared in the early 1970s [Canaday et al., 1974]. The idea is to offload the central processor by isolating the database management functions from the main computer and grouping them in another computer dedicated to their execution. The main computer executing the application programs is often termed the *host computer*; the dedicated computer is called the *database machine*, *database computer*, or *backend computer*. We will use, instead, the more recent terms *application server* for the host computer and *data server* for the dedicated computer. Figure 15.1 illustrates a simple view of the data server approach, with one application server connected to one data server via a communication channel. This follows the architectural model of Figure 4.7, with the user processor and data processor functions performed by the application server and data server, respectively. The application server manages the user interface, parses the user queries to be submitted to the data server, and manages the interface and communication with the data server for sending commands and receiving results. The application server may also run other system and application programs. The data server manages the interface and communication with the application server and performs the database functions.

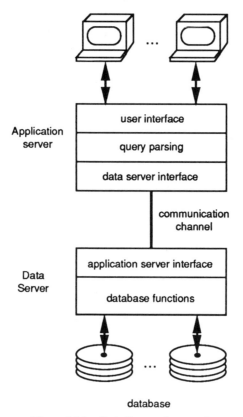

Figure 15.1   Data Server Approach

The data server approach has several potential advantages. First, the single focus on database data makes possible the development of specific techniques for increasing data reliability and availability. Second, the overall performance of database management can be significantly enhanced by the tight integration of the database system and a dedicated database operating system. These two first advantages were discussed extensively in Chapter 13. They are demonstrated successfully in Britton Lee's Intelligent Database Machine [Epstein and Hawthorn, 1980]. Third, a data server fits naturally in a modern distributed environment, as we shall see in the next section. Finally, a data server can also exploit recent hardware architectures, such as multiprocessor computers to enhance both performance and data availability. This last aspect has been the most studied by database researchers ([Boral and Redfield, 1985], [DeWitt and Hawthorn, 1981] and [Valduriez and Gardarin, 1989]) and is discussed in Section 15.2 in the context of highly parallel data server architectures.

Although these advantages are significant, they can be offset by the overhead introduced by the additional communication between the application and the data servers. For example, accessing the data server one record at a time may incur a prohibitive communication cost since at least two messages must be exchanged for each record that is useful to the application program. The communication cost can be amortized only if the server interface is sufficiently high level to allow the expression of complex queries involving intensive data processing. The relational model, which favors set-oriented manipulation of data, has therefore been the natural data model supported by the data server approach. As a result, all commercial data servers today are relational.

### 15.1.2 Servers and Distributed Databases

The original data server approach, shown in Figure 15.1, typically connects a data server to a single application server that supports multiple users. A decade ago this approach was motivated by the necessity of having the MIPS power[1] of a mainframe to execute application programs. Since then, the situation has changed dramatically. Personal workstations with a power of 3 to 10 MIPS and fast communication networks are becoming common and this trend will accelerate in the near future. Bit-mapped workstations significantly enhance end-user productivity through better human interfaces. Therefore, economics will force the replacement of cheap terminals by workstations acting as application servers.

The need to integrate a variety of workstations connected by a local network with a data server [Taylor, 1987] has resulted in a new and popular organization of computer resources that could be termed the *centralized server organization* (see Figure 15.2). This organization favors a clean separation of labor which minimizes communication between the workstation and the data server. The processing power of a workstation is best utilized for the user interface and most data controls. The user interface on a workstation can be very sophisticated, typically with pull-down menus, as well as

---

[1]MIPS power is a commonly used measure to model the raw processing units. It corresponds to 1 million instructions per second.

multiple windows and forms. These user interface commands must be mapped into data server interface commands. To avoid communication overhead, the commands sent to the data server should ideally be error free. This can be achieved by performing most semantic data control operations, such as authorization, view management, and semantic integrity controls, on the workstation rather than on the data server. For instance, locally performing type checking enables efficient interactive data entry. However, data directory information (e.g., data types and rules) must be available on the workstation to enable those controls. The simplest solution is to have the data directory managed by the data server and accessed by the workstation in read-only mode when needed (e.g., at session initiation). In this case directory data is updated only by the central data server.

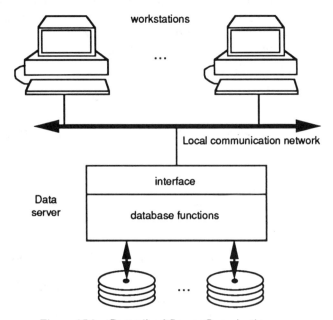

**Figure 15.2**    Centralized Server Organization

With such an organization, the data server may have to support a large number of users (e.g., several hundred), making the performance issue more critical. An initial solution to the data server efficiency is software oriented and consists of implementing the DBMS code on a database operating system exploiting a traditional uniprocessor architecture. This solution has already proven to be cost-effective. Another solution is more hardware oriented and tries to achieve a high degree of parallelism using a multiprocessor architecture. This approach can provide higher benefits than the software-oriented approach. It is the topic of Section 15.2.

The centralized server approach enables distributed applications to access a single data server efficiently. It is often a cost-effective alternative to distributed databases, whereby all the difficult problems of distributed database management disappear at the local data server level. However, this centralized approach is likely to suffer from the traditional limitations of centralized databases. The addition of new application servers in a local network is technically easy but may require the expansion of the data server's processing power and storage capacity. Furthermore, the access to a single data server from geographically distant application servers is inefficient because communication over a wide area network is relatively slow.

The natural solution to these problems is to combine the data server and distributed database technologies in what could be termed *distributed server organization*. Figure 15.3 shows a simple example of this organization, in which each data server is extended with a distributed DBMS component. The distributed server organization can accommodate a large variety of configurations, each being application dependent. For example, in a geographically distributed distributed database whose sites are connected by a wide area network, each site can consist of a single data server connected by a local network to a cluster of workstations. Any workstation could access the data at any data server through either the local network (local access) or the wide area network (remote access).

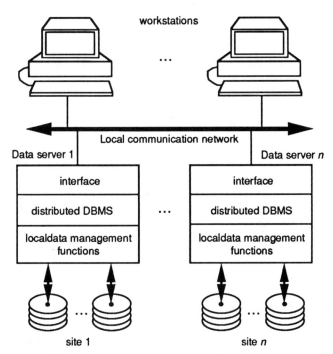

**Figure 15.3**   Distributed Server Organization

The application servers may remain unchanged from the centralized data server approach. In this case a database query is always submitted to the local server, which is in charge of all distributed query processing. An alternative is to have the distributed query processor and the data directory operational at each application server. This avoids the systematic access to a single data server in order to retrieve from a remote data server. Although more complex, this solution more efficiently supports configurations where several data servers are connected by a local network, as in Figure 15.3.

In the distributed server organization, each data server is fully dedicated to distributed and centralized database management. Therefore, a first solution to improve performance is to implement the DBMS and distributed DBMS modules on top of a distributed database operating system running on a traditional (von Neumann) computer. The advantages of this approach have been discussed at length in Chapter 13. Another solution is to have the distributed database operating system exploiting special computer architectures (e.g., multiprocessor). The combination of dedicated software and hardware should provide higher performance than the general-purpose solution. However, as we will see in the next section, a lot of open design issues remain.

## 15.2  PARALLEL DATA SERVERS

In this section we show the value of parallel architectures for efficient database management. We emphasize one class of data server architecture which makes an interesting use of distributed database technology. The critical performance issues for such architectures are data placement and parallel algorithms for database operations. The solutions to these issues are more involved than in traditional distributed databases because the number of nodes may be very high.

### 15.2.1  Architectures

Hardware progress has greatly influenced the design of data server architectures. The uniprocessor von Neumann computer architecture model, designed primarily for the efficient execution of numerical operations, has been dominant until recently. However, the maximum performance of this model is limited by its sequential operating mode. This architectural model is not suitable for database management, for two main reasons. First, it cannot exploit the parallelism inherent in many applications. As we have seen in previous chapters, relational database management provides several opportunities for parallelism. *Interquery parallelism* enables the parallel execution of multiple queries. *Intraquery parallelism* makes the parallel execution of multiple operations possible within the same query. Finally, with *intraoperation parallelism*, the same operation can be executed as many suboperations. The set-oriented mode of relational languages provides many opportunities for intraoperation parallelism. For example, the performance of the join operation can be increased significantly by parallel processing.

Second, the performance of database management on a von Neumann computer is hurt by the so-called I/O bottleneck [Boral and DeWitt, 1983], induced by high disk I/O time, which is more than 1000 times slower than main memory access time. An immediate and simple solution to the I/O bottleneck is to maintain the entire database in stable main memory [Leland and Roome, 1985]. This completely eliminates the I/O bottleneck. However, the high cost of making main memory stable restricts this approach to small databases. All technology forecasts indicate that magnetic disks will remain the main type of repository for medium and large databases. Furthermore, as disk bandwidth increases at a much lower rate than either processor or main memory bandwidth, the I/O bottleneck problem will be accentuated in the near future. The main solution to the I/O bottleneck is to increase the I/O bandwidth through parallelism [Du, 1984]. Instead of having the entire database residing on a few high-capacity disk units, many smaller disks are employed so that disk accesses can be done in parallel. Thus disk access time can be divided by the number of disk units.

A common solution to these problems is to have multiple independent hardware components interconnected through some fast communication medium. This can be achieved by using recent multiprocessor architectures. A multiprocessor architecture naturally supports interquery, intraquery, and intraoperation parallelism by assigning queries, operations, or suboperations to different processing elements. Multiprocessor architectures can range between two extremes, the *shared-everything* and the *shared-nothing* architectures. In what follows we discuss both of these architectures, although we focus on the shared-nothing architecture because it relies heavily on distributed database technology.

In a shared-everything architecture (see Figure 15.4), any processor has access to any main memory module or disk unit through a fast interconnect (e.g., cross-bar switch). A tightly coupled multiprocessor (see Figure 1.3) is a particular instance of shared-everything design. Several new mainframe designs such as the Sequent machine [Sequent, 1986] are based on a shared-everything architecture. Examples of shared-everything data servers include XPRS [Stonebraker et al., 1988] and to some extent, the SABRE data server [Gardarin et al., 1983]. Since every single access to a data item requires access to the common interconnect, such architectures may suffer from a communication bottleneck caused by contention for the interconnect. One way to solve the problem is to have a limited number of powerful processors. In general, writing application software such as database management is not very different for these machines than for von Neumann computers, since meta-information (directory) and control information (e.g., lock table) can be shared by all processors. However, the main difference with a centralized DBMS is that database operations can be processed in parallel. As shown in [Bhide and Stonebraker, 1988], shared-everything architectures can provide high performance for database management.

In a shared-nothing architecture [Stonebraker, 1986], each processor has exclusive (nonshared) access to one or more memory modules and one or more disk units. A typical shared-nothing architecture is illustrated in Figure 15.5. Each node[2] includes a processor, a local cache memory, and a disk unit on which resides a local database.

---

[2]In the multiprocessor context, we use the generic term *node* in a way similar to *site* in a distributed system.

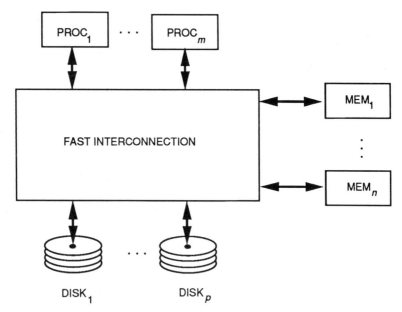

**Figure 15.4**   Shared-Everything Architecture

Diskless nodes may be used to interface with application servers or to process intermediate relations in parallel. The term *shared-nothing* refers to the fact that there is no sharing of main memory or disks by the nodes. The only shared resource is the network, with which the nodes can exchange messages.

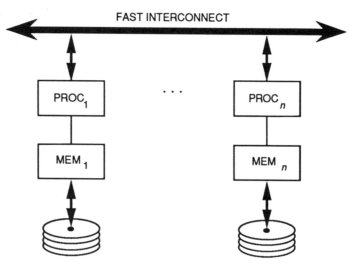

**Figure 15.5**   Shared-Nothing Architecture

A switch-based multiprocessor (see Figure 1.5) is a particular instance of shared-nothing design. Examples of shared-nothing architectures are Bubba ([Boral, 1988b], [Boral et al., 1990]) the Teradata DBC/1012 [Neches, 1985], GAMMA [DeWitt et al., 1986], MBDS [Demurjian et al., 1986], and the Tandem NonStop SQL [Tandem, 1987]. This approach can be viewed as a particular implementation of a distributed database system. The main idea is that a powerful computer may be built out of several smaller and less powerful ones. One similarity with the distributed database approach is that each node can be managed by the same local system. Therefore, each node must implement solutions to global data directory, distributed data definition and control, distributed query processing, and distributed transaction management. However, the major difference with a distributed database system is that a node of the multiprocessor is not a site at which a user can run an application program. Application programs run typically on an application server and interface the multiprocessor system through a specific network.

Shared-nothing architectures are more able than other architectures to achieve two important objectives: performance and extensibility. Increased performance can be achieved in the context of a high-speed interconnect by exploiting parallel processing. The ideal performance goal is to provide high *throughput*, typically defined as the number of transactions per second [Anon, 1985]. Since this is linear in the number of nodes across which the data is fragmented, doubling the number of nodes should result in doubling the throughput. Performance improvement is obtained by using two complementary solutions. First, data should be carefully fragmented across many nodes so that parallelism is maximized when processing a distributed query. Second, distributed data management should be efficiently supported by a distributed database operating system. The main difficulties are to place the data so that most of the queries get processed in parallel, and to develop efficient parallel algorithms for performing database operations. Solutions to these problems are introduced below.

Extensibility is the ability to smoothly increment the growth of the system by adding new nodes. Similar to homogeneous distributed databases, a shared-nothing architecture is uniform and thus extensible. Furthermore, the same architecture and same system can be used for a large range of database sizes, from small to very large. For example, the DBC/1012 data server can be configured with a number of nodes ranging from a few to a thousand.

### 15.2.2 Data Placement

Data placement in a highly parallel shared-nothing data server architecture exhibits similarities with data fragmentation in distributed databases (see Chapters 5 and 8). An obvious similarity is that fragmentation can be used to increase parallelism. Furthermore, fragmentation in a highly parallel architecture favors load balancing, meaning that the load is equally distributed among all the nodes. In what follows, similar to [Livny et al., 1987], we use the term *declustering* instead of *horizontal fragmentation*, in contrast to the alternative strategy, which consists of *clustering* a relation at a single node. Vertical fragmentation can also be used to increase parallelism and load balancing much as in distributed databases. Another similarity is that since data is much larger than programs, programs should be executed as much as possible where the data resides [Khoshafian and Valduriez, 1987]. However, there are two important differences with the distributed database approach. First, there is no need to maximize local processing since users are not associated with particular nodes. Second, load balancing is much more difficult to achieve in the presence of a large number of nodes. The main problem is to avoid resource contention, which may result in thrashing the entire system (e.g., one node ends up doing all the work while the others remain idle). Since programs are executed where the data resides, data placement is a critical performance issue.

Data placement must be done to maximize system performance, which can be measured by combining the total amount of work done by the system and the response time of individual queries. In Chapter 9 we have seen that maximizing response time (through intraquery parallelism) results in increased total work due to communication overhead. For the same reason, interquery parallelism results in increased total work. On the other hand, clustering all the data necessary to a program minimizes communication and thus the total work done by the system in executing that program. In terms of data placement, we have the following trade-off. Maximizing response time or interquery parallelism leads to declustering, whereas minimizing the total amount of work leads to clustering. As we have seen in Chapter 5, this problem is addressed in distributed databases in a rather static manner. The database administrator is in charge of periodically examining fragment reference frequencies, and when necessary, must move and reorganize fragments.

An alternative solution to data placement is *full declustering*, whereby each relation is horizontally fragmented across *all* the disk nodes in the system. Full declustering is used in the DBC/1012, GAMMA, and NonStop SQL. To ensure uniform data distribution, relations are fragmented via a hash function applied to some attribute. This strategy allows exact-match queries on the selection attribute to be processed by exactly one node and all other queries to be processed by all the nodes in parallel. In [Livny et al, 1987], the performance of full declustering is compared to that of clustering the relations on a single disk. The results indicate that for a wide variety of multiuser workloads, declustering is consistently better. However, clustering may dominate in processing complex queries (e.g., joins). In [Tandem, 1987], the throughput of a system running debit-credit transaction workload [Anon, 1985] in the presence of full declustering is shown to increase linearly with the number of nodes for up to 32 nodes.

Although full declustering has obvious performance advantages, high parallel execution might cause a serious performance overhead for complex queries involving joins. For example, in a 1024-node architecture, the worst-case number of messages for a binary join (without select) would be 10,242. Furthermore, full declustering is not appropriate for small relations that span a few disk blocks. These drawbacks suggest that a compromise between clustering and full declustering (i.e., *variable declustering*), needs to be found.

In [Copeland et al., 1988], a solution to data placement by variable declustering is proposed. The degree of declustering, in other words, the number of nodes over which a relation is fragmented, is a function of the size and access frequency of the relation. This strategy is much more involved than either clustering or full declustering because changes in data distribution may result in reorganization. For example, a relation initially placed across eight nodes may have its cardinality doubled by subsequent insertions, in which case it should be placed across 16 nodes.

In a highly parallel system with variable declustering, reorganizations for load balancing are essential and should be frequent unless the workload is fairly static and experiences only a few updates. Such reorganizations should remain transparent to compiled programs that run on the data server. In particular, programs should not be recompiled because of reorganization. Therefore, the compiled programs should remain independent of data location, which may change rapidly. Such independence can be achieved if the run-time system supports associative access to distributed data. This is different than in a traditional distributed database system, where associative access is achieved at compile time by the query processor using the data directory.

One solution to associative access is to have a global index mechanism replicated on each node [Khoshafian and Valduriez, 1987]. The global index indicates the placement of a relation onto a set of nodes. Conceptually, the global index is a two-level index with a major clustering on the relation name and a minor clustering on some attribute of the relation. This global index supports variable declustering, where each relation has a different degree of declustering. The index structure can be based on hashing or on a B-tree like organization [Bayer and McCreight, 1972]. In both cases, exact match queries can be processed efficiently with a single node access. However, with hashing, range queries are processed by accessing all the nodes that contain data from the relation queried. Using a B-tree index (usually much larger than a hashed index) enables more efficient processing of range queries, where only the nodes containing data in the specified range are accessed.

**Example 15.1**

Figure 15.6 provides an example of a global index based on the engineering database example we have been using in this book. Recall that this database consists of the following relations:

    E(ENO, ENAME, DEPT, TITLE)
    S(TITLE, SAL)
    J(JNO, JNAME, BUDGET)
    G(ENO, JNO, RESP, DUR)

Suppose that we want to locate the elements in relation E with ENO value "E5". The first-level index on set name maps the name E onto the index on attribute ENO for relation E. Then the second-level index further maps the cluster value "E5" onto node number $j$. A local index within each node is also necessary to map a relation onto a set of disk blocks within the node. The local index has two levels, with a major clustering on relation name and a minor clustering on some attribute. The minor clustering attribute for the local index is the *same* as that for the global index. Thus *associative routing* is improved

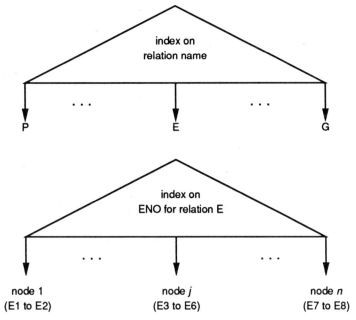

**Figure 15.6**    Example of Global Index

from one node to another based on <relation name, cluster value>. Figure 15.7 provides an example of a local index for the same node $j$ in Figure 15.6. The first-level index on relation name maps the name E onto the index on attribute ENO for the E relation just as was done for the global index. This second-level index further maps the cluster value "E5" onto block number 91.

[Copeland et al., 1988] provides experimental results for variable declustering of a workload consisting of a mix of short transactions (debit-credit like) and complex ones. The results indicate that as declustering is increased, throughput continues to increase for short transactions. However, for complex transactions involving several large joins, further declustering reduces throughput because of communications overhead.

### 15.2.3  Parallel Processing

Declustered data placement is the basis for the parallel execution of database queries. Given a declustered data placement, an important issue is the design of parallel algorithms for an efficient processing of database operations (i.e., relational algebra operations) and database queries which combine multiple operations. This issue is difficult because a good trade-off between parallelism and communication cost must be reached. Parallel algorithms for relational algebra operations are the building blocks necessary for parallel query processing. In this section we introduce algorithms for parallel operation processing and parallel query processing.

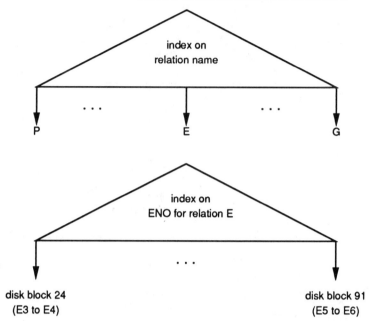

**Figure 15.7**   Example of Local Index (within node $j$)

**Parallel operation processing.**   Parallel operation processing should exploit intraoperation parallelism. Similar to Chapter 9, we concentrate our presentation of parallel algorithms for database operations on the select and join operations, since all other binary operations (such as union) can be handled very much like join [Bratbersengen, 1984]. The processing of the select operation in a declustered data placement context is identical to that in a fragmented distributed database. Depending on the select predicate, the operation may be executed at a single node (in the case of an exact match predicate) or in the case of arbitrary complex predicates at all the nodes over which the relation is declustered. If the global index is organized as a B-tree-like structure (see Figure 15.6), a select operation with a range predicate may be executed only by the nodes storing relevant data.

The parallel processing of join is significantly more involved than that of select. The distributed join algorithms designed for high-speed networks (see Chapter 9) can be applied successfully in a declustered database context. However, the availability of a global index at run time provides more opportunities for efficient parallel execution. In the following pages we introduce three basic parallel join algorithms for declustered databases: the parallel nested loop (PNL) algorithm, the parallel associative join (PAJ) algorithm, and the parallel hash join (PHJ) algorithm. We describe each using a pseudo-concurrent programming language with three main constructs: **do-in-parallel, send,** and **receive. Do-in-parallel** specifies that the following block of actions is executed in parallel. For example,

```
for i from 1 to n do in parallel action A
```

indicates that the action $A$ is to be executed by $n$ nodes in parallel. **Send** and **receive** are the basic communication primitives to transfer data between nodes. **Send** enables data to be sent from one node to one or more nodes. The destination nodes are typically obtained from the global index. **Receive** gets the content of the data sent to a particular node. In what follows we consider the join of two relations $R$ and $S$ that are declustered over $m$ and $n$ nodes, respectively. For the sake of simplicity, we assume that the $m$ nodes are distinct from the $n$ nodes. A node at which a fragment of $R$ (respectively, $S$) resides is called an $R$-node (respectively, $S$-node).

The parallel nested loop algorithm [Bitton et al., 1983] is the simplest one and the most general. It basically composes the Cartesian product of the relations $R$ and $S$ in parallel. Therefore, arbitrarily complex join predicates may be supported. This algorithm has been introduced in Chapter 9 in the context of Distributed INGRES. It is more precisely described in Algorithm 15.1, where the join result is produced at the $S$-nodes. The algorithm proceeds in two phases.

> **Algorithm 15.1**    *PNL*
>
> **input:**    $R_1, R_2, \ldots, R_m$: fragments of relation $R$;
>            $S_1, S_2, \ldots, S_n$: fragments of relation $S$;
>            $JP$: join predicate
> **output:** $T_1, T_2, \ldots, T_n$: result fragments
> **begin**
>     **for** $i$ **from 1 to** $m$ **do in parallel**          {send $R$ entirely to each $S$-node}
>       send $R_i$ to each node containing a fragment of $S$
>     **end-for**
>     **for** $j$ **from 1 to** $n$ **do in parallel**          {perform the join at each $S$-node}
>     **begin**
>       $R \leftarrow \bigcup_{i=1}^{m} R_i$ {receive $R_i$ from $R$-nodes; $R$ is fully replicated on each
>                                                        node of $S$}
>       $T_j \leftarrow \text{JOIN}(R, S_j, JP)$                    {JOIN is a generic function}
>     **end-for**
> **end.** {PNL}

In the first phase, each fragment of $R$ is sent and replicated at each node containing a fragment of $S$ (there are $n$ such nodes). This phase is done in parallel by $m$ nodes and is efficient if the communication network has a broadcast capability. In this case each fragment of $R$ can be broadcast to $n$ nodes in a single transfer, thereby incurring a total communication cost of $m$ messages. Otherwise, $(m * n)$ messages are necessary.

In the second phase, each $S$-node $j$ receives relation $R$ entirely, and locally joins $R$ with the fragment $S_j$. This phase is done in parallel by $n$ nodes. The local join can be done as in a centralized DBMS. Depending on the local join algorithm, join processing may or may not start as soon as data is received. In the first case (e.g., with the nested loop join algorithm), join processing can be done in a pipelined fashion as soon as a tuple of $R$ arrives. In the latter case (e.g., with the sort merge join algorithm), all the data must have been received before the join of the sorted relations begins.

To summarize, the parallel nested loop algorithm can be viewed as replacing the operation $R \bowtie S$ by

$$\bigcup_{i=1}^{n} (R \bowtie S_i)$$

**Example 15.2**

Figure 15.8 shows the application of the parallel nested loop algorithm with $m = n = 2$.

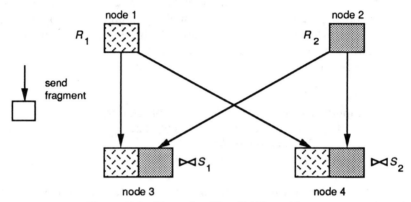

**Figure 15.8** Example of Parallel Nested Loop

The parallel associative join algorithm, shown in Algorithm 15.2, applies only in the case of equijoin with one of the operand relations declustered according to the join attribute. To simplify the description of the algorithm, we assume that the equijoin predicate is on attribute $A$ from $R$, and $B$ from $S$. Furthermore, relation $S$ is declustered according to the hash function $h$ applied to join attribute $B$, meaning that all the tuples of $S$ that have same value for $h(B)$ are placed at the same node. No knowledge of how $R$ is declustered is assumed. The application of the parallel associative join algorithm will produce the join result at the nodes where $S_i$ exists (i.e., the $S$-nodes).

**Algorithm 15.2** *PAJ*

    **input:**   $R_1, R_2, \ldots, R_m$: fragments of relation $R$;
              $S_1, S_2, \ldots, S_n$: fragments of relation $S$;
              $JP$: join predicate
  **output:** $T_1, T_2, \ldots, T_n$: result fragments
  **begin**   {we assume that $JP$ is $R.A = S.B$ and relation $S$ is fragmented
                              according to the function $h(B)$}
    **for** $i$ **from** 1 **to** $m$ **do in parallel** {send $R$ associatively to each $S$-node}
    **begin**
        $R_{ij} \leftarrow$ apply $h(A)$ to $R_i$ $(j = 1, \ldots, n)$

     **for** $j$ **from** 1 **to** $n$ **do**
      send $R_{ij}$ to the node storing $S_j$
     **end-for**
    **end-for**
    **for** $j$ **from** 1 **to** $n$ **do in parallel** {perform the join at each $S$-node}
    **begin**
     $R_j \leftarrow \bigcup_{i=1}^{m} R_{ij}$     {receive only the useful subset of $R$}
     $T_j \leftarrow \text{JOIN}(R_j, S_j, JP)$
    **end-for**
   **end.** {PAJ}

  The algorithm proceeds in two phases. In the first phase, relation $R$ is sent associatively to the $S$-nodes based on the function $h$ applied to attribute $A$. This guarantees that a tuple of $R$ with hash value $v$ is sent only to the $S$-node that contains tuples with hash value $v$. The first phase is done in parallel by $m$ nodes where $R_i$'s exist. Unlike the parallel nested loop algorithm, the tuples of $R$ get distributed but not replicated across the $S$-nodes. In the second phase, each $S$-node $j$ receives in parallel the relevant subset of $R$, (i.e., $R_j$), and joins it locally with the fragments $S_j$. Local join processing can be done as in the parallel nested loop join algorithm.

  To summarize, the parallel associative join algorithm replaces the operation $R \bowtie S$ by

$$\bigcup_{i=1}^{n} (R_i \bowtie S_i)$$

**Example 15.3**

Figure 15.9 shows the application of the parallel associative join algorithm with $m = n = 2$. The squares that are hatched with the same pattern indicate fragments whose tuples match the same hash function.

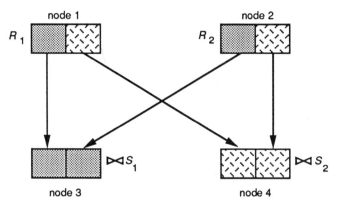

**Figure 15.9** Example of Parallel Associative Join

The parallel hash join algorithm, shown in Algorithm 15.3, can be viewed as a generalization of the parallel associative join algorithm. It also applies in the case of equijoin but does not require any particular declustering of the operand relations. The basic idea is to partition relations $R$ and $S$ into the same number $p$ of mutually exclusive sets (fragments) $R_1, R_2, \ldots, R_p$, and $S_1, S_2, \ldots, S_p$, such that

$$R \bowtie S = \bigcup_{i=1}^{p} (R_i \bowtie S_i)$$

**Algorithm 15.3    *PHJ***

**input:**    $R_1, R_2, \ldots, R_m$: fragments of relation $R$;
$S_1, S_2, \ldots, S_n$: fragments of relation $S$;
$JP$: join predicate
**output:** $T_1, T_2, \ldots, T_n$: result fragments
**begin**         {we assume that $JP$ is $R.A = S.B$ and $h$ is a hash function
                                                          that returns an element of $[1, p]$}
   **for** $i$ **from 1 to** $m$ **do in parallel**         {hash $R$ on the join attribute}
   **begin**
      $R_{ij} \leftarrow$ apply $h(A)$ to $R_i$ $(j = 1, \ldots, p)$
      **for** $j$ **from 1 to** $p$ **do**
         send $R_{ij}$ to node $j$
      **end-for**
   **end-for**
   **for** $i$ **from 1 to** $n$ **do in parallel**         {hash $S$ on the join attribute}
   **begin**
      $S_{ij} \leftarrow$ apply $h(B)$ to $S_i$ $(j = 1, \ldots, p)$
   **for** $j$ **from 1 to** $p$ **do**
      send $S_{ij}$ to node $j$
   **end-for**
   **end-for**
   **for** $j$ **from 1 to** $p$ **do in parallel**      {perform the join at each $S$-node}
   **begin**
      $R_j \leftarrow \bigcup_{i=1}^{p} R_{ij}$                          {receive from $R$-nodes}
      $S_j \leftarrow \bigcup_{i=1}^{p} S_{ij}$                          {receive from $S$-nodes}
      $T_j \leftarrow \text{JOIN}(R_j, S_j, JP)$
   **end-for**
**end.** {PAJ}

As in the parallel associative join algorithm, the partitioning of $R$ and $S$ can be based on the same hash function applied to the join attribute. Each individual join ($R_i \bowtie P_i$) is done in parallel, and the join result is produced at $p$ nodes. These $p$ nodes may actually be selected at run time based on the load of the system. The main difference with the parallel associative join algorithm is that partitioning of $S$ is necessary and the result is produced at $p$ nodes rather than at $n$ $S$-nodes. Variations of this algorithm for specific multiprocessor architectures are given in [Valduriez and Gardarin, 1984] and [DeWitt and Gerber, 1985].

**Example 15.4**

Figure 15.10 shows the application of the parallel hash join algorithm with $m = n = 2$. We assumed that the result is produced at nodes 1 and 2. Therefore, an arrow from node 1 to node 1 or node 2 to node 2 indicates a local transfer.

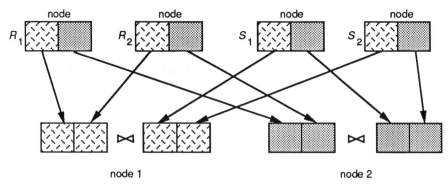

**Figure 15.10**   Example of Parallel Hash Join

These parallel join algorithms apply and dominate under different conditions. Join processing is achieved with a degree of parallelism of either $n$ or $p$. Since each algorithm requires moving at least one of the operand relations, a good indicator of their performance is total cost. To compare these algorithms, we now give a simple analysis of cost, defined in terms of total communication cost, denoted by $C_{COM\#}$ and processing cost, denoted by $C_{PRO}$. The total cost of each algorithm is therefore

$$Cost(Alg.) = C_{COM}(Alg.) + C_{PRO}(Alg.)$$

For simplicity, $C_{COM}$ does not include control messages, which are necessary to initiate and terminate local tasks. We denote by $msg(\#tup)$ the cost of transferring a message of $\#tup$ tuples from one node to another. Processing costs (total I/O and CPU cost) will be based on the function $C_{LOC}(m, n)$ which computes the local processing cost for joining two relations of cardinalities $m$ and $n$. We assume that the local join algorithm is the same for all three parallel join algorithms. Finally, we assume that the amount of work done in parallel is uniformly distributed over all nodes allocated to the operation.

Without broadcasting capability, the parallel nested loop algorithm incurs a cost of $m * n$ messages, where a message contains a fragment of $R$ of size $card(R)/m$. Thus we have

$$C_{COM}(PNL) = m * n * msg\left(\frac{card(R)}{m}\right)$$

Each of the $S$-nodes must join all of $R$ with its $S$ fragments. Thus we have

$$C_{PRO}(PNL) = n * C_{LOC}(card(R), card(S)/n)$$

The parallel associative join algorithm requires that each $R$-node partitions a fragment of $R$ into $n$ subsets of size $card(R)/(m * n)$ and sends them to $n$ $S$-nodes. Thus we have

$$C_{COM}(PAJ) = m * n * msg\left(\frac{card(R)}{m * n}\right)$$

and

$$C_{PRO}(PAJ) = n * C_{LOC}(card(R)/n, card(S)/n)$$

The parallel hash join algorithm requires that both relations $R$ and $S$ be partitioned across $p$ nodes in a way similar to the parallel associative join algorithm. Thus we have

$$C_{COM}(PHJ) = m * p * msg\left(\frac{card(R)}{m * p}\right) + n * p * msg\left(\frac{card(S)}{n * p}\right)$$

and

$$C_{PRO}(PHJ) = n * C_{LOC}(card(R)/n, card(S)/n)$$

Let us first assume that $p = n$. In this case the join processing cost for the PAJ and PHJ algorithms is identical. However, it is higher for the PNL algorithm because each $S$-node must perform the join with $R$ entirely. From the equations above, it is clear that the PAJ algorithm incurs the least communication cost. However, the least communication cost between the PNL and PHJ algorithms depends on the values of relation cardinality and degree of declustering. If we now choose $p$ so that it is smaller than $n$, the PHJ algorithm may well incur the least communication cost but at the expense of increased join processing cost. For example, if $p = 1$, the join is processed in a purely centralized way.

In conclusion, the PAJ algorithm is most likely to dominate and should be used when applicable. Otherwise, the choice between the PNL and PHJ algorithms requires estimation of their total cost with the optimal value for $p$. The choice of a parallel join algorithm can be summarized by the procedure CHOOSE_JA shown in Algorithm 15.4.

**Algorithm 15.4**    *CHOOSE_JA*

**input:** $prof(R), prof(S)$: relation profiles; $JP$: join predicate
**output:** $JA$: join algorithm
**begin**
    **if** $JP$ is equijoin **then**
        **if** one relation is declustered according to the join attribute **then**

$$JA \leftarrow PAJ$$
**else if** $Cost(PNL) < Cost(PHJ)$ **then**
$$JA \leftarrow PNL$$
    **else**
$$JA \leftarrow PHJ$$
    **end-if**
  **end-if**
**else**
$$JA \leftarrow PNL$$
**end-if**
**end.** {CHOOSE_JA}

**Parallel query processing.**    Parallel query processing designates query processing in a parallel data server and exhibits similarities with distributed query processing. Parallel query processing should minimize both intraoperation parallelism (using the algorithms described above) and interoperation parallelism. This second objective can be achieved using some of the techniques devised for distributed databases. A good example is the exhaustive search approach [Selinger and Adiba, 1980], in which all possible execution strategies are enumerated. Although this approach can select the optimal strategy to execute a query in a highly parallel data server, additional criteria must be considered to exploit interoperation and intraoperation parallelism. Key criteria are the number of temporary relations that can be produced in parallel and the optimal number of nodes to participate in the execution of an operation. These additional criteria make the solution space larger, and thus the cost of optimization prohibitive, for queries involving several joins. A solution to avoid the prohibitive exhaustive search approach is to rely on heuristics. The approach in Distributed INGRES [Epstein et al., 1978] employs heuristics but is also dynamic, meaning that optimization is done at run time. A heuristic approach in which optimization is done at compile time is the pivot algorithm ([Khoshafian et al., 1987] and [Khoshafian et al., 1988b]), which is specifically designed for declustered databases in highly parallel systems.

We now summarize the features of the basic pivot algorithm for select-project-join queries. The physical schema assumed by the algorithm distinguishes between three kinds of physical relations: base relations, secondary indexes, and join indexes. A base relation is a direct mapping of a conceptual relation with the addition of a tuple identifier (TID) and the replacement of each foreign key attribute by the corresponding tuple identifier. It is clustered on its TID. A secondary index is a binary relation associating attribute values with the tuple identifiers of tuples matching that value. It is clustered on the attribute value. A join index [Valduriez, 1987] is a binary relation associating the TIDs of two relations that match a join predicate. It is clustered on one of the TIDs. If the join index captures a foreign key link [i.e., of the form (foreign TID, base relation TID)], it is clustered on the foreign TID to provide direct access to the base relation (clustered on its TID).

The algorithm consists of four phases: *select, pivot, value materialization,* and *composition.*

1. The select phase performs all the select operations before the joins and returns relations containing the tuple identifiers of the tuples selected. This phase achieves significant interoperation parallelism (because all selects are done in parallel) and some intraoperation parallelism (depending on how much the selected relations are declustered).

2. The pivot phase performs the main $m$-way join of the query, incorporating the TIDs of the selected tuples as well as those of the tuples needed to produce the final result using the relevant join indexes. The join ordering can be determined using a conventional technique (see Chapter 9). The output of this phase is a collection of binary relations, each associating a common TID, called *pivot TID*, with the TID of a tuple whose attributes are projected in the result. With the parallel join algorithms described above, this phase can achieve considerable intraoperation parallelism, and some interoperation parallelism depending on the join ordering that is chosen. Furthermore, the operands that are moved between nodes (i.e., binary relations) are small. This minimizes the message size and thus the communication cost.

3. For each binary relation, the value materialization replaces each nonpivot TID by the corresponding projected attributes. This is done by joining each binary relation with the projected relation on its TID. This phase achieves much interoperation parallelism because all joins can be done concurrently and much intraparallelism using the parallel join algorithms.

4. The composition phase joins all relations produced in the previous phase on the pivot TID. This phase can also achieve significant intraoperation parallelism using parallel join algorithms.

In conclusion, the pivot algorithm leads to high inter and intraoperation parallelism. In addition, other heuristics can be easily incorporated to avoid accessing a relation more than once [Khoshafian et al., 1988a].

**Example 15.5**

We consider the following physical schema of the engineering database. Clustering attributes are indicated in boldface type. Each physical relation is clustered on the first attribute, which is its TID. The base relations are

E(**EID**, ENO, ENAME, SID)
G(**GID**, EID, JID, RESP, DUR)
J(**JID**, JNO, JNAME, BUDGET)
S(**SID**, TITLE, SAL)

The secondary indexes are

G-RESP(**RESP**, GID)
J-JNAME(**JNAME**, JID)

The join indexes are

EG(**EID**, GID)
JG(**JID**, GID)

We consider the following SQL query:

```
SELECT   ENAME, DUR
FROM     E, G, J
WHERE    E.ENO = G.ENO
AND      G.PNO = J.JNO
AND      RESP = ''Manager''
AND      JNAME = ''Instrumentation''
```

whose answer is the tuple <J. Doe, 12 >.

The application of the pivot algorithm for that query is shown by the relational algebra tree in Figure 15.11. The chosen pivot TID is EID. Note that since the joins are always on a clustered attribute, the parallel associative join algorithm is likely to be the best one. Note also that relation G is accessed in both the pivot and value materialization phases of the algorithm.

## 15.2.4  Concluding Remarks

A shared-nothing parallel data server can provide high performance at lower cost than can a general-purpose computer, by exploiting declustered data placement as well as parallel operation and query processing. As in a distributed database, it provides two major advantages: smooth incremental growth by the addition of new nodes, and high data availability through hardware/software and data replication. Two examples of successful products based on a shared-nothing architecture are the Tandem NonStop SQL and the Teradata DBC.

Although parallelism for data management is now better understood [Boral, 1988a], there are a number of open problems. The major ones are query processing, recovery, and data reorganization. The difficulty with parallel query processing is to maximize inter and intraoperation parallelism while avoiding the high optimization cost of the exhaustive search approach. Recovery is of major importance in the presence of a large number of nodes since the probability of node failure is high. The problem is to make recovery fast. Data reorganization, critical to load balancing, should be very dynamic to accommodate changes in application workloads.

## 15.3  DISTRIBUTED KNOWLEDGE BASES

Intuitively, a *knowledge base* supplements a database with the capability of deducing new information from existing information. Its functionality is far superior to that

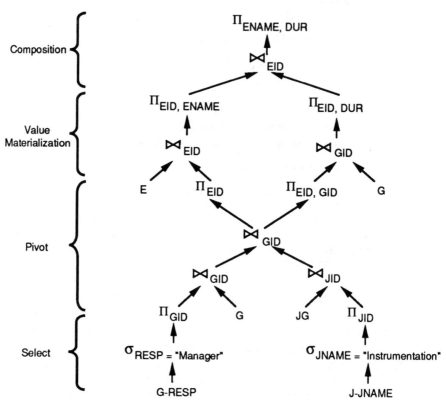

**Figure 15.11**   Pivot Algorithm Applied to Relational Schema

of a relational database, for instance. Challenging issues face the design of knowledge bases (see Chapter 10 of [Gardarin and Valduriez, 1989] for a thorough tutorial). In particular, queries to a knowledge base have expressive power much higher than relational calculus, thereby making performance of query processing of utmost importance. In this section we briefly introduce the objectives of knowledge bases. We concentrate our presentation on those based on mathematical logic, also called *logic databases* or *deductive databases* [Gallaire et al., 1984], given that they can be viewed as extensions of relational databases. We also discuss the important problem of recursive query processing, which is peculiar to this context. Then, to bridge the gap between a distributed system and a knowledge base system, we illustrate how a parallel data server can efficiently support knowledge base management through parallel execution techniques. We assume that the reader is somewhat familiar with mathematical logic (see [Kowalski, 1979]) and logic programming as exemplified by PROLOG [Clocksin and Mellish, 1981].

### 15.3.1  Knowledge Bases

A database is a collection of data representing facts. In a relational database, facts are modeled by tuples. Relational query languages (e.g., relational algebra) enable a user to retrieve tuples and combine them in new (result) tuples. These new tuples do not provide more information than that stored explicitly in the database. Rather, they present the existing information the way the user wants.

A database system lacks reasoning capabilities to infer new facts from existing facts. Examples of applications requiring such capabilities are data analysis and planning, or more generally expert systems that deal with lots of facts [Wiederhold, 1984]. These applications are generally built using a programming language interfacing the database to retrieve facts. Reasoning is based on knowledge, typically more abstract than data. For example, the assertion "John is human" is a fact, whereas the assertion "all humans are mortal" is knowledge, from which the new fact "John is mortal" may be deduced. Having knowledge embedded in application programs makes it difficult to share knowledge among users and creates the problem of knowledge being redundantly stored in many programs.

The knowledge base approach overcomes these problems by factoring out common knowledge in much the same way that the database approach factors out schema information. A simple definition of a knowledge base is as a union of an *intensional database* that stores common knowledge and an *extensional database* that stores facts, that is, the extension of knowledge. The extensional database is therefore a traditional one, for example, a relational database. The interface to a knowledge base system is such that user queries against the extensional database implicitly use the knowledge stored in the intensional database. User queries may be expressed in a concise and simple way, and enriched with the knowledge to become more complex and powerful. Some analogy can be made with relational queries enriched with semantic data control information (see Chapter 6), which constitutes some rudimentary knowledge. The knowledge in an intensional database is essentially more general than semantic data control information. Supporting an intensional database enables better sharing, control, and management of knowledge while minimizing the size and complexity of application programs. Many believe that knowledge base systems will be useful to new database applications (e.g., large expert systems) and traditional data processing applications (e.g., business) as well.

The design and implementation of a knowledge base system present difficult and new problems. The most important problems are related to knowledge representation, knowledge consistency, and knowledge base query processing. As with a conceptual data model, a *knowledge model* is needed to represent and manipulate knowledge independent of its physical representation in a computer. Associated with this model is a knowledge manipulation language which enables a *knowledge administrator* to manage the intensional database. As more knowledge is acquired, the intensional database needs to be updated, however, much less frequently than the extensional database. Updates that do not preserve knowledge consistency should be rejected automatically by a mechanism typically more involved than semantic integrity control.

Finally, the processing of knowledge base queries requires an inferential process to derive new facts from known facts. In the presence of a large number of facts, the efficiency of the inferential process is crucial to the performance of the knowledge base system. The foregoing problems have been addressed in the context of artificial intelligence and some solutions have been developed. However, these solutions are applicable to only small numbers of facts. Knowledge base technology attempts to solve these problems for large extensional databases. It is therefore a cross-point between artificial intelligence and database technologies, and a step toward intelligent or expert database systems [Kerschberg, 1987].

In artificial intelligence, four types of knowledge representation are predominant [Barr et al., 1981]: production rules, frames, semantic nets, and mathematical logic. Mathematical logic, more specifically first-order logic [Manna, 1974], provides the best foundation for knowledge bases for two reasons. First, relational calculus languages are based on first-order logic (see Chapter 2). Thus a knowledge base system could be built as an extension of a relational database system. Second, logic provides the inference mechanism necessary to derive new facts from known facts. This mechanism is used in artificial intelligence to prove theorems, that is, to derive new formulas from known formulas (the axioms). In the remainder of this section, we discuss knowledge bases implemented using logic, called *logic databases* or *deductive databases*, which best illustrate the state of the art in knowledge bases. Our objective here is not to give a formal tutorial on logic databases but to provide enough motivation for the subsequent sections. We refer to [Gallaire et al., 1984], [Gardarin and Valduriez, 1989], and [Ullman, 1988] for a more complete discussion.

In Chapter 2 we briefly introduced first-order logic formulas and illustrated their use in relational calculus languages. A special form of formula, called a *Horn clause*, is the basis for logic databases. A Horn clause is a formula of the form

$$A \vee \neg B_1 \vee \neg B_2 \vee \cdots \vee \neg B_n$$

in which $A$ and $B_1, B_2, \ldots, B_n$ are *positive atomic formulas*, that is, predicates of the form $P(t_1, t_2, \ldots, t_n)$, which are implicitly universally quantified. Using logical implication ($\rightarrow$), a Horn clause is generally written as

$$A \leftarrow B_1 \wedge B_2 \wedge \cdots \wedge B_n$$

A Horn clause corresponds to a *rule*. $A$ is called the *head* of the rule, while the conjunction of $B_i$'s is called the *body* of the rule. A *ground clause* is a rule with an empty body. A *fact* is a ground clause with no variables. A logic database can be defined as a set of rules, where the predicate names are relation names or function names and the constants are attribute values. A logic database is interpreted by associating each predicate with a set of tuples that satisfy it. Therefore, we can use the terms *relation* and *predicate* in an equivalent way. Predicate variables range over domains in a way similar to the domain relational calculus. A query to a logic database is simply a predicate whose name is used in the head of some rule. The answer to a query is the set of tuples that make the query predicate true. The rules whose body is not empty enable the derivation of new tuples. They can be viewed as a generalization of the view derivation rules (see Chapter 6). An important kind of rule, called a *recursive rule*, is one where the same predicate (the recursive predicate) appears in both the head and body of the rule. A rule is said to be *linearly recursive* if the recursive predicate appears only once in the body of the rule.

In the following two examples of logic databases, variables are denoted in *italic* letters, predicate names are denoted in **bold** and constants are in lowercase letters. Queries are denoted by a predicate prefixed by "?".

**Example 15.6**

The classical example of a logic database is based on the parent and the ancestor predicates:

> **parent** (john, ann)
> **parent** (cathy, john)
> **parent** (michael, john)
> **parent** (sarah, cathy)
> **parent** (juliette, cathy)
> **ancestor** $(D, A) \leftarrow$ **parent** $(D, A)$
> **ancestor** $(D, A) \leftarrow$ **parent** $(D, P)$, **ancestor** $(P, A)$

This logic database contains five facts defining the **parent** relation (or **parent** predicate), and two rules defining the **ancestor** relation (or **ancestor** predicate). The parent relation associating a child (first attribute) with the parent (second attribute) constitutes the extensional database. For instance, the presence of the tuple (cathy, john) in the parent relation can be interpreted as the **parent** predicate being true for the pair (cathy, john), meaning that john is the parent of cathy. The **ancestor** relation of schema (descendant, ascendant) is a derived relation and constitutes the intensional database. For instance, the linearly recursive rule

> **ancestor** $(D, A) \leftarrow$ **parent** $(D, P)$, **ancestor** $(P, A)$

can be interpreted as follows. If there are three terms $D$, $P$, and $A$ such that **parent**$(D, P)$ is true and **ancestor**$(P, A)$ is true, then **ancestor**$(D, A)$ is also true. The two rules defining the **ancestor** relation take the **parent** relation as input to derive the **ancestor** relation. We now illustrate some queries with their answers.

> ?**parent** (cathy, $P$)      returns (cathy, john)
> ?**parent** (cathy, bill)      returns false
> ?**parent** ($C, P$)       returns {(john, ann), (cathy, john),
>                  (michael, john), (sarah, cathy), (juliette, cathy)}
> ?**ancestor** (cathy, $A$)     returns {(cathy, john), (cathy, ann)}
> ?**ancestor** (juliette, $A$)    returns {(juliette, cathy),
>                     (juliette, john), (juliette, ann)}

**Example 15.7**

We consider the relation

> part(pname, weight, support_pname)

in which pname and support_pname are of the same domain, and weight is the individual weight of the part pname. Support_pname is the name of another part which is mounted on part pname (i.e., "pname" supports "support_pname"). If part $p_1$ supports part $p_2$, the total weight of $p_1$ is the sum of the individual weights of $p_1$ and $p_2$. An example of logic database is (null values are denoted by *null*)

> **part** $(p_1, 30, p_2)$
> **part** $(p_2, 20, p_3)$
> **part** $(p_3, 10, null)$
> **part** $(p_4, 10, null)$
> **total_part** $(P, W, S) \leftarrow$ **part** $(P, W, S)$
> **total_part** $(P, W, S) \leftarrow$ **total_part** $(P, W_1, P_1)$, **total_part** $(P_1, W_2, S)$,
>                            **sum** $(W, W_1, W_2)$

The extensional database consists of the **part** relation (four facts). The intensional database consists of a derived relation of the same schema, which gives the total weight of each part. **Sum**$(W, W_1, W_2)$ is a predicate that is true if $W$ is the sum of $W_1$ and $W_2$. The recursive rule enables one to deduce all the parts that are transitively supported by a part. For instance, we have

> ?**part** $(p_2, W, S)$      returns $(p_2, 20, p_3)$
> ?**total_part** $(p_2, W, S)$      returns $\{(p_2, 20, p_3), (p_2, 30, null)\}$
> ?**total_part** $(p_1, W, null)$      returns $(p_1, 60, null)$

Horn clauses have been used as the basis for the popular PROLOG programming language. However, PROLOG is not a pure implementation of first-order logic and cannot be considered a logic database for two reasons. First, PROLOG is essentially procedural since the ordering of the rules in a PROLOG program is left to the programmer, who is responsible for ensuring optimization and correct program termination. Second, the PROLOG inference mechanism does not distinguish between facts and rules, which must all reside in main memory, thereby limiting its usefulness to small intensional databases.

A better language for logic databases is DATALOG ([Ullman, 1985] and [Maier and Warren, 1988]), a pure Horn clause-based language. It is a language for nonprocedural defining rules. Therefore, the responsibility for the efficient program execution and correct program termination can be shifted to the system.

Logic query processing is typically more involved than relational query processing and is addressed in the next section. Other difficult issues not reported here are the support of updates, negation, and sets, in DATALOG [Tsur and Zaniolo, 1986].

### 15.3.2 Logic Query Processing

In this section we discuss the processing of logic queries expressed in a DATALOG-like language. Since DATALOG is a superset of relational calculus, the experience gained with relational query optimization is beneficial but not sufficient. In particular, efficient support for queries involving recursive rules, called *recursive queries*, is a new and difficult problem which has been studied thoroughly within the last few years (see [Bancilhon and Ramakrishnan, 1986] and [Gardarin and Valduriez, 1989] for good surveys).

There are many different techniques for efficiently evaluating logic queries. In what follows we limit ourselves to the discussion of a technique, called *bottom-up evaluation*, which starts from the facts and applies the rules necessary to derive the answer to the query. This technique is chosen since with it one is able to make use of relational query optimization at query compile time. We concentrate the discussion on query optimization, ignoring aspects of correct program termination [Zaniolo, 1986].

The intensional database can be viewed as a set of parameterized queries, each defined by a predicate appearing in the head of the rule. A query on a logic database is a predicate with actual parameter values which bind variables to constants. The bottom-up processing of a logic query has two major steps:

1. The query is merged with the relevant rules, the ones whose head or body use the query predicate. The rapid access to the relevant rules can be achieved using some form of index, called predicate connection graph [McKay and Shapiro, 1981]. The bindings given in the query can be propagated in the rule bodies. This first step produces a rule program with bindings.

2. The rule program is translated into an optimized program in the internal language of the logic database system. To make use of relational query optimization techniques, a good candidate for the internal language is a relational algebra enriched with control constructs such as "while do" and "if then."

**Example 15.8**

Consider the engineering database presented in Chapter 2 and the query "Find the employees working on the CAD/CAM project," which can be expressed in SQL as

```
SELECT    ENAME, JNAME
FROM      E, G, J
WHERE     E.ENO = G.ENO
AND       G.PNO = J.JNO
AND       JNAME = ''CAD/CAM''
```

One rule is necessary for abstracting this query (_ denotes don't care):

$$\mathbf{R}\,(ENAME, JNAME) \quad \leftarrow \quad E\,(ENO, ENAME, \_), G\,(ENO, JNO, \_, \_),$$
$$J(JNO, JNAME, \_)$$

The query can be expressed as

$$?\mathbf{R}\,(ENAME, \text{"CAD/CAM"})$$

The first step of query processing yields

$$\mathbf{R}\,(ENAME, \text{"CAD/CAM"}) \quad \leftarrow \quad E\,(ENO, ENAME, \_), G\,(ENO, JNO, \_, \_),$$
$$J(JNO, \text{"CAD/CAM"}, \_)$$

which can be translated in the second step into the relational algebra program

$$\Pi_{ENAME, JNAME}(((\sigma_{JNAME = \text{"CAD/CAM"}}(J)) \bowtie_{JNO} G) \bowtie_{ENO} E)$$

In the example above, logic query processing reduces to relational query processing. This is not true for recursive queries, as they cannot be directly mapped into pure relational algebra, which has no recursive or iterative operators.

With bottom-up evaluation, there is a simple technique to process recursive queries using an iterative "while do" operator and relational algebra. This technique, called *naive evaluation* [Bancilhon, 1986], iteratively applies the rules to derived tuples until no more new tuples can be produced. The naive evaluation method may be sketched as in Algorithm 15.5, where $T$ is a relation derived by a recursive rule, $R$ is a relation stored in extension, and $f(T)$ is a function that produces new tuples by applying a relational algebra expression to $T$ corresponding to the body of the rule.

**Algorithm 15.5   *NAIVE***

   **input:** $R$: operand relation
   **output:** $T$: output relation
   **begin**
      $T \leftarrow R$
      **while** $T$ is not empty **do**
         $T \leftarrow T \cup f(R)$
   **end.** {NAIVE}

**Example 15.9**

Consider the logic database of Example 15.6 and the query

$$?\text{ancestor}(D, A)$$

which computes all the pairs (descendant, ascendant). The naive evaluation of the ancestor relation is expressed as

   $T \leftarrow$ parent
   **while** $T$ is not empty **do**
      $T \leftarrow \bigcup \Pi_{p.child, T.par} (\text{parent} \bowtie_{par=child} T)$

where $p.child$ denotes the first attribute from the parent relation and $T.par$ denotes the second attribute from the $T$ relation. The first iteration joins the parent relation with itself, which yields

$$R_1 = \text{parent} \cup \{ \text{(cathy, ann), (michael, ann), (juliette, john), (sarah, john)} \}$$

and the second iteration produces

$$R_2 = R_1 \cup \{ \text{(juliette, ann), (sarah, ann)} \}$$

The main shortcoming of the naive evaluation method is that it performs redundant work. Since the function $f(R)$ is applied to the tuples derived previously, the inferencing of derived tuples is repeated at each iteration. In Example 15.9 the four tuples produced in the first iteration are also produced in the second.

*Seminaive evaluation* [Bancilhon, 1986] eliminates this problem by considering at each iteration only the tuples derived from the preceding one. The main idea is to use a differential relation, denoted by $DR$, that stores the new tuples produced by one iteration, and to replace $f(T)$ by $df(T, DR)$, $df$ being the differential of $f$ where $DR$ replaces $T$. The seminaive evaluation method is described in Algorithm 15.6.

**Algorithm 15.6    *SEMINAIVE***

**input:** $R$: operand relation
**output:** $T$: output relation
**declare**
   $DR$: relation
**begin**
   $DR \leftarrow R$
   $T \leftarrow R$
   **while** $DR$ is not empty **do**
   **begin**
      $DR \leftarrow df(R, DR)$
      $T \leftarrow T \cup DR$
   **end-while**
**end.** {SEMINAIVE}

**Example 15.10**

The seminaive evaluation of the ancestor relation is expressed as

$DR \leftarrow$ parent
$T \leftarrow$ parent
**while** $DR$ is not empty **do**
**begin**
   $DR \leftarrow \Pi_{p.child, DR.par}$ (parent $\bowtie_{par=child} DR$)
   $T \leftarrow T \cup DR$
**end**

Compared to Example 15.9, the join operation is applied to parent and $DR$ instead of $R$.

### 15.3.3  Parallel Recursive Query Processing

The performance of knowledge base management can be improved significantly by combining knowledge base and distributed database technologies into *distributed knowledge bases*. In this section we illustrate this aspect by considering a logic database implemented on a shared-nothing data server. In this context the difficulty of parallel query processing is magnified by the presence of recursive queries. In the following we concentrate on the problem of parallel recursive query processing and view the transitive closure of a database relation as a paradigm to study this problem.

    As advocated by many researchers ([Valduriez and Boral, 1986], [Ioannidis, 1986], [Lu et al., 1987] and [Agrawal and Jagadish, 1987]) the transitive closure operator is central to the optimization of recursive queries. One reason is that relational database languages may be easily augmented with a transitive closure operator to provide a simple deductive capability [Zloof, 1975]. Another reason is that a large class of logic queries, the linearly recursive queries, can be translated into a transitive closure possibly preceded and followed by relational algebra operations [Jagadish et al., 1987]. In Examples 15.6 and 15.7 the queries involving the ancestor and total_part predicates (respectively) are linearly recursive.

In a uniprocessor architecture, efficient implementations of the transitive closure operator consist of optimizing the main memory utilization using a compact representation of the operand relation (matrix, list, join index). A few parallel transitive closure algorithms have been proposed as a method of finding the connected components of an undirected graph in a shared memory architecture model [Quinn and Deo, 1984].

In the rest of this section we first present two basic algorithms for transitive closure: the *iterative transitive closure* (ITC) and *transitive closure of transitively closed relations* (TCCR). Then we briefly describe two parallel transitive closure algorithms: the *transitive closure with parallel operations* (TCPO) algorithm and the *transitive closure with parallel programs* (TCPP) algorithm.

Transitive closure is more difficult to parallelize in a shared-nothing architecture. In what follows we present two parallel algorithms for evaluating the transitive closure of a relation in a shared-nothing data server. These algorithms can be viewed as a parallel version of the iterative algorithm [Valduriez and Boral, 1986], which basically performs seminaive evaluation. The base relation is declustered across many nodes to favor the parallel execution of database operations.

**Iterative transitive closure algorithm.** We describe the ITC algorithm on a binary relation $R$ having attributes $A$ and $B$ defined on the same domain. The extension to a relation with more than two attributes is straightforward. Relation $R$ can be viewed as a set of edges in a directed graph, in which an edge from node $a$ to node $b$ indicates the tuple $(a, b)$ of $R$. We call the depth of $R$, noted $depth(R)$, the length of the longest path in the graph as measured by the number of edges. The transitive closure of $R$, denoted $R^+$, is equivalent to the transitive closure of the corresponding graph; in other words, the tuple $(x, y)$ is in $R^+$ if and only if there is a path of nonzero length from $x$ to $y$. Let $\bullet$ denote the composition of two binary relations $R(A, B)$ and $P(B, C)$, where all attributes are defined over the same domain

$$R \bullet P = \{(a, c) \mid \exists b \ (a, b) \in R \ and \ (b, c) \in P\}$$

and let $R^i$ be the $i$th power of relation $R$, that is, $R^1 = R$ and $R^i = R^{i-1}R$. Then $R^+$ is

$$R^+ = \bigcup_{i > 0} R^i$$

$R \bullet P$ can be implemented by a join with projection as

$$R \bullet P = \Pi_{A,C}(R \bowtie_B P)$$

Note that the binary composition is not commutative, that is, $R \bullet P \neq P \bullet R$.

**Example 15.11**

Figure 15.12 shows the graph corresponding to the parent relation and the parent[+] relation corresponding to the transitive closure of that graph.

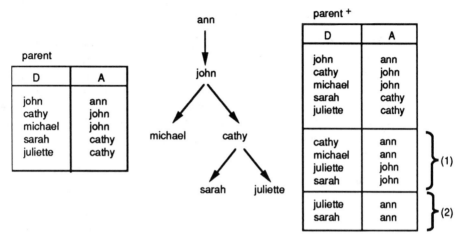

**Figure 15.12**    Transitive Closure of the Parent Relation

Although the ITC algorithm works for cyclic relations [e.g., with a cycle of three tuples $(a, b)$, $(b, c)$ and $(c, a)$], we assume that $R$ is acyclic for simplicity.[3] The algorithm can be expressed using relational algebra extended with assignment and iteration, as shown in Algorithm 15.7. The correctness of this algorithm is given in [Ioannidis, 1986]. ITC is a direct implementation of seminaive evaluation using the differential relation DR.

**Algorithm 15.7    *ITC***

**input:** $R$: operand relation
**output:** $T$: output relation
**declare**
    $DR$: relation
**begin**
    $DR \leftarrow R$
    $T \leftarrow R$
    **while** $DR$ is not empty **do**
    **begin**
        $DR \leftarrow DR \bullet R$
        $T \leftarrow T \cup DR$

---

[3]A cyclic relation essentially poses a termination problem which can be solved with a simple extension to the algorithm [Valduriez and Boral, 1986].

**end-while**
**end.** {ITC}

**Example 15.12**

Since ITC is an implementation of the seminaive method, it is well illustrated by Example 15.9. The subsets (1) and (2) of the parent in Figure 15.12 are produced, respectively, at the first and second iterations of the application of ITC.

**Transitive closure of transitively closed relations.**    A transitively closed relation is a relation in which no new tuple can be generated by transitive closure of the corresponding graph. Given a relation $R$ partitioned into $R_1$ and $R_2$ (that is, $R = R_1 \cup R_2$) the transitive closure of the transitively closed relations $R_1^+$ and $R_2^+$ computes $R^+$. A straightforward way of computing $R^+$ consists of performing ITC($R_1^+ \cup R_2^+$). However, this solution also recalculates $R_1^+$ and $R_2^+$, and therefore does redundant work. For instance, the first iteration of algorithm ITC computes

$$(R_1^+ \cup R_2^+) \bullet (R_1^+ \cup R_2^+) = (R_1^+ \bullet R_1^+) \cup (R_1^+ \bullet R_2^+) \cup (R_2^+ \bullet R_1^+) \cup (R_2^+ \bullet R_2^+)$$

and recalculates $R_1^+ = (R_1^+ \bullet R_1^+)$ and $R_2^+ = (R_2^+ \bullet R_2^+)$.

The TCCR algorithm performs the transitive closure of two transitively closed relations without redundant work. The algorithm (shown in Algorithm 15.8) and its correctness are detailed in [Valduriez and Khoshafian, 1988a]. It computes the transitive closure of $R_1^+ \cup R_2^+$ by producing only alternating composition sequences, that is, sequences of $R_1$ such that $(R_1 \bullet R_1)$ or $(R_2 \bullet R_2)$ never occur. Since alternating composition sequences never contain redundant compositions, the TCCR algorithm does not perform redundant work.

**Algorithm 15.8    TCCR**
    **input:** $R_1, R_2$: operand relations
    **output:** $T$: output relation
    **declare**
        $DR_1, DR_2$: relation
    **begin**
        $DR_1 \leftarrow R_1 \bullet R_2$
        $DR_2 \leftarrow R_2 \bullet R_1$
        $T \leftarrow R_1 \cup R_2 \cup DR_1 \cup DR_2$
        **while** $DR_1$ is not empty **or** $DR_2$ is not empty **do**
        **begin**
            $DR_1 \leftarrow (DR_1 \bullet R_1) \cup (DR_1 \bullet R_2)$
            $DR_2 \leftarrow (DR_2 \bullet R_1) \cup (DR_2 \bullet R_2)$
        **end-while**
        $T \leftarrow T \cup DR_1 \cup DR_2$
    **end.** {TCCR}

**Example 15.13**

We illustrate the TCCR algorithm on the parent relation of Example 15.6. We assume that parent is partitioned in $parent_1$ and $parent_2$ as follows:

$parent_1$:    {(john, ann), (sarah, cathy), (juliette, cathy)}
$parent_2$:    {(cathy, john), (michael, john)}.

Relations $DR_1$ and $DR_2$ are initialized with the following new tuples:

$DR_1$:    {(sarah, john), (juliette, john)}
$DR_2$:    {(cathy, ann), (michael, ann)}.

The first iteration of the algorithm produces the new tuples

$DR_1$:    {(sarah, ann), (juliette, ann)}
$DR_2$ is empty

Finally, the second iteration produces no more new tuples and the algorithm terminates.

**Transitive closure with parallel operations.**    The TCPO algorithm [Valduriez and Khoshafian, 1988b] computes in parallel the operations of the transitive closure on a relation $R$ declustered across $n$ nodes. It is a parallel version of the ITC algorithm in which the join operation of the composition is implemented by the parallel hash join algorithm. The union operation can be achieved locally as partial unions. This minimizes the internode communications required by a global union. However, the final result may contain tuples replicated at different nodes, therefore requiring a duplicate elimination operation to complete the transitive closure.

To simplify the description of the TCPO algorithm, we assume that the composition operation iteratively applied to relations $R$ and $DR$, both having attributes $A$ and $B$, is

$$R \bullet DR = \Pi_{R.A, DR.B}(R \bowtie_{B=A} DR)$$

Furthermore, we call $partition(R, A)$ the function that partitions relation $R$ over $n$ nodes by applying a hash function to attribute $A$. The TCPO algorithm can be described by three subsequent phases: the initialization phase, the processing phase, and the result phase. In the initialization phase, the operation $partition(R, B)$ distributes relation $R$ across $n$ nodes according to a hash function on $B$. Relations $T$ (output relation) and $DR$ are also initialized to $R$. The processing phase is a loop of a parallel join operation (for the composition) and local union operations. Since $R$ is partitioned by hashing on attribute $B$, the parallel join operation includes the operation $partition(DR, A)$, so that the tuples of $DR$ are moved to the nodes of $R$ with matching tuples. The distribution of $DR$ tuples over $n$ nodes is done at each pass of the loop. The loop terminates when $DR$ is empty. Since $DR$ is distributed over $n$ nodes, the termination test must be done by a centralized controller (e.g., one of the $n$ nodes) which combines the individual boolean values "is $DR$ empty?" transmitted by each node $i$ ($i = 1, \ldots, n$). When all $DR_i$'s are empty, the processing phase terminates. The result relation $T$ is distributed across $n$ nodes and may contain the same new tuples at different nodes. The result phase eliminates these duplicate tuples. This can be achieved by a parallel hash-based algorithm. $T$ is first partitioned across $n$ nodes by hashing on one attribute, say $A$, and the operation can complete as $n$ parallel duplicate elimination operations. Again, the result of the operation is distributed over $n$ nodes.

**Example 15.14**

Figure 15.13 illustrates the initialization and processing phases of the TCPO algorithm with $n = 4$. The processing phase has two passes. The arrows show the communication between the nodes at each pass. This example exhibits the constant degree of parallel execution.

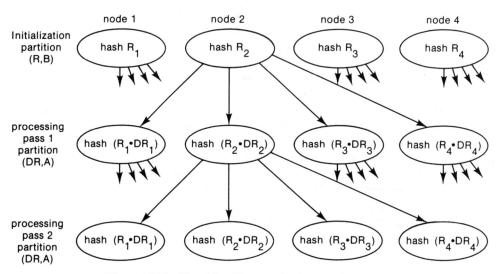

**Figure 15.13**    Transitive Closure with Parallel Operations

**Transitive closure with parallel programs.**    The TCPP algorithm [Valduriez and Khoshafian, 1988a] decomposes the transitive closure operation into a series of parallel programs, each executing the ITC algorithm or the TCCR algorithm. The algorithm consists of two phases: initialization and processing phases. The ITC algorithm is used in the initialization phase to produce transitively closed relations in which the TCCR algorithm can work in the processing phase. Contrary to the TCPO algorithm, the TCPP algorithm does not achieve a constant degree of parallelism. However, it minimizes internode communication. The degree of parallelism in the initialization phase is $n$ (the degree of declustering of relation $R$) and is divided by 2 at each pass of the processing phase until a single node terminates the operation.

The TCPP algorithm proceeds as follows. For simplicity, we assume that $n$ is a power of 2. The initialization phase computes in parallel $n$ partial transitive closures, each using the ITC algorithm. These $n$ transitively closed relations are combined in the processing phase by a two-way merge-type operation, in which the $n$ nodes are arranged as a binary tree. Therefore, the processing phase has $log_2 n$ passes, each pass corresponding to one level of the tree. At pass $i$, $n/2^i$ nodes receive two transitively closed relations produced either at the initialization phase (if $i = 1$) or at pass $i - 1$

(if $i > 1$), and apply the TCCR algorithm to them. The processing phase terminates when a single node applies the TCCR algorithm to the two transitively closed relations produced at pass $log_2 n - 1$.

**Example 15.15**

Figure 15.14 illustrates the TCPP algorithm with $n = 4$ and two passes of the processing phase. The arrows show the communication between the nodes. To minimize internode communication, the arrangement of nodes in a binary tree uses at each pass every other node employed at the immediately preceding pass. This example shows that the degree of parallel execution is divided by 2 at each pass.

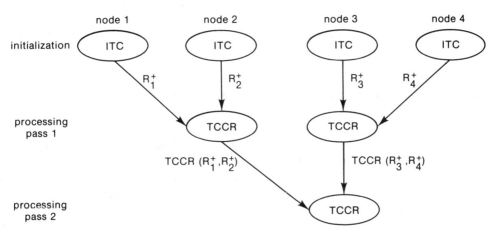

**Figure 15.14**    Transitive Closure with Parallel Programs

**Performance comparisons.**    In [Valduriez and Khoshafian, 1988a] and [Valduriez and Khoshafian, 1988b] the performance of the parallel transitive closure algorithms is compared with the centralized algorithm that moves all operand data to a single node where the operation is completed. The performance comparisons indicate that these parallel algorithms can provide significant performance improvement over the centralized algorithm. The improvement factor is best (between one and two orders of magnitude) with a high number of nodes (more than 16) and when the transitive closure produces a large number of new tuples. The response time of the algorithm TCPO (with parallel operations) is generally superior to the algorithm TCPP (with parallel programs). The reason is that TCPO achieves a constant degree $n$ of parallelism, whereas, that of TCPP is divided by 2 at each pass. The best response-time improvement over the centralized algorithm is one order of magnitude for TCPP and two orders of magnitude for TCPO. However, TCPP provides a better compromise than TCPO between response time and total cost. A generalization of the algorithms above can be found in [Agrawal and Jagadish, 1988].

### 15.3.4 Concluding Remarks

Query processing, in particular recursive query processing, is probably the major issue that distinguishes knowledge bases that use logic from relational databases. Therefore, it has recently received much attention from database researchers. We have discussed how the parallelism of a shared-nothing data server can be exploited to improve the performance of recursive query processing. Because knowledge bases based on logic are extensions of relational databases, most of the technology presented in previous chapters can be used successfully.

There are a number of important open issues for both centralized and distributed knowledge bases. One is the extension of DATALOG's expressive power, for example, to support complex updates, negation, and sets [Tsur and Zaniolo, 1986]. This requires new compilation techniques, which may significantly affect query processing. Another issue is efficient access to a large rule base which is particularly difficult if it is distributed.

## 15.4 DISTRIBUTED OBJECT-ORIENTED DATABASES

An object-oriented database is a database that supports object-oriented features. In particular, it uses an "object" as the fundamental modeling primitive. In Chapter 13 we have introduced the object-oriented system approach and shown its value in the design of distributed operating systems. The object-oriented paradigm has been used primarily in programming languages such as Smalltalk [Goldberg and Robson, 1983] and more recently, C++ [Stroustrup, 1986]. Object-oriented databases stem from integration of the object-oriented programming language and database technologies, and bring several definite advantages.

First, the modeling power and flexibility of the object-oriented approach facilitates the design of complex database applications such as CAD and office information systems, which are not well supported by the relational model. Second, users of object-oriented programming languages may benefit from database features such as persistent data, set-oriented processing, and transaction management. Third and most important, complex database applications may be written entirely in a single object-oriented database programming language [Atkinson and Buneman, 1987]. This avoids the impedance mismatch [Copeland and Maier, 1984] of the embedded query language solution, in which the concepts and types of the query language (e.g., SQL), typically set at a time, do not match with those of the programming language (e.g., COBOL), which are typically record at a time. These essentially functional advantages augment programmer productivity. The main issue in object-oriented databases is to provide such functionality with acceptable performance. In the rest of this section we briefly introduce the object-oriented database approach. For a more complete discussion of the concepts, we refer the reader to [Bancilhon, 1988], [Kim and Lochovsky, 1989] and [Ullman, 1988], and for details of specific systems, to [Lochovsky, 1985]. To focus on the performance-related issues of object-oriented databases, we discuss object management, which is made difficult by the desire to support large or complex objects. Finally, we deal with the more difficult problem of object management in a database distributed for performance or availability reasons.

### 15.4.1  Object-Oriented Databases

Contrary to knowledge bases, there is no accepted definition of an object-oriented database. A simple way to introduce object-oriented databases is by describing the essential object-oriented capabilities added to those traditionally found in databases. These capabilities are: objects, abstract data types, and inheritance. This list is not exhaustive, and there are other object-oriented features (e.g., versions) that might be incorporated to an object-oriented database.

**Objects.**    An important property of relational databases is that they deal with data values in a uniform fashion. Attribute values are the atoms with which structured values (tuples and relations) may be constructed. In a value-based data model such as the relational model, data is identified by values. A relation is identified by a name, and a tuple is identified by a key, a combination of values. This way of identifying data leads to several problems. One major problem is that the modeling of relationships among data leads to data redundancy (introduction of foreign keys) whose automatic management requires the support of integrity constraints (referential integrity). This also makes it hard to model complex structures (e.g., deep hierarchies or complex networks). Another important problem is the lack of precise semantics for updates. To talk about a single attribute value change (e.g., increase John's salary) in relational algebra, one needs to use set difference and union to produce the new employee relation. The difficulty of handling updates through views is also due to the fact that updates involve data copies rather than the data itself. This complicates the integration of a relational query language into an imperative programming language in which data modification is simply done through pointers.

The foregoing problems disappear in the context of an object-based model. In order to discuss the differences between value-based and object-based models, we use the following simple definition for object semantics [Lecluse et al., 1988] (a more precise definition is given in Section 15.4.2). An *object* is a pair (OID, state) in which OID is the object identity and the corresponding state is either an atomic value or a constructed value (e.g., tuple or set). Object identity [Khoshafian and Copeland, 1986] is an essential property which permanently distinguishes an object from all other objects regardless of its state. The OID can be considered the unique name of the object. Two objects are said to be *identical* if they have the same OID, and *equal* if they have the same state.

**Example 15.16**

We let [ ] and { } denote tuple and set constructors, respectively. As a particular case, a relation can be constructed as a set of tuples. Although attribute names are normally stored with types in the schema, we put them within tuple values for pedagogical purpose. Let us consider the following objects:

$(i_1, 231)$

$(i_2, \text{J. Doe})$

$(i_3, [\text{JNO: J1, JNAME: Instrumentation, BUDGET: 15000}])$

$(i_4, \{1,2,3\})$

$(i_5, [\text{ENO: E1, ENAME: J. Doe, TITLE: Elect. Eng., PROJECT: } i_3])$

Objects $i_1$ and $i_2$ are atomic objects and the others are constructed objects. Object $i_5$ references object $i_3$. By considering object identifiers (e.g., $i_3$) as values in the object model, arbitrarily complex objects may be constructed.

Contrary to values, objects support a well-defined update operation that changes the object state without changing the object identity. This is analogous to updates in imperative programming languages in which object identity is implemented by main memory pointers. However, object identity is more general (than pointers) in the sense that it persists following the program termination. Another implication of object identity is that objects may be shared without incurring the problem of data redundancy.

**Example 15.17**

Let us consider the following objects:

$(i_1, \text{Advanced Development})$

$(i_2, [\text{NAME: John, DEPT: } i_1])$

$(i_3, [\text{NAME: Mary, DEPT: } i_1])$

John and Mary share the object denoted by DEPT (they work in the same department). Changing the value of object $i_1$ from "Advanced Development" to "Applied Research" is automatically seen by both objects $i_2$ and $i_3$. Note that in the relational model, the tuples John and Mary should both be updated.

The main advantages of an object-based model are the natural integration with object-oriented programming languages made possible by object identity, and the capability of modeling arbitrarily complex data structures. However, these advantages pose the difficult problems of object management, significantly more expensive than the management of flat relations. Because it is a performance-related issue, we discuss it in more detail in Section 15.4.2.

**Abstract data types.**    Abstract data types (ADTs) have long been used in programming languages [Guttag, 1977], and more recently in relational databases ([Stonebraker et al., 1983b], [Osborn and Heaven, 1986] and [Gardarin and Valduriez, 1989]). To introduce abstract data types, we use the general term *data* to indicate either object or value [Danforth and Valduriez, 1989]. An ADT describes the type of data by providing a domain of data with the same structure, as well as operations (also called methods) applicable to elements of that domain. The abstraction capability of ADTs, commonly referred to as *encapsulation*, hides the implementation details of the operations, which can be written in a general-purpose programming language. This is similar to the primitive operations (e.g., addition) associated with primitive types (e.g., integer) provided by the programming language. In general, several standard ADT operations, such as conversion for input-output, are mandatory. The user of the ADT only sees the interface data structure and the interface operation names with their associated input and output types.

**Example 15.18**

Let us consider the ADT "money" with the interface type:

money_amount = [currency: string, amount: float]

and operations:

convert(s: string): money_amount
exchange(m: money_amount, currency: string): money_amount

The first operation converts an input string, for example, "$90,000.99," into a money_-amount. The second operation exchanges a given money_amount to another one in the specified currency. The user of the ADT money does not need to know how foreign exchange is implemented.

The interface data structure of an ADT may be arbitrarily complex or large. For example, the employee relation can be modeled as an ADT with associated operations hire_employee and raise_salary. Similarly, a long document with a complex internal structure may be defined as an ADT with operations specific to document manipulation. ADTs provide two major advantages. First, the primitive types provided by the system can easily be extended with user-defined types. Since there are no inherent constraints on the notion of relational domain, such extendibility can be incorporated in the context of the relational model [Osborn and Heaven, 1986]. Second, ADT operations capture parts of the application programs which are more closely associated with data. Therefore, an object model with ADTs allows modeling of both data and operations at the same time. This does not imply that operations are stored with the data. Rather, they are stored in an operation library, similar to the data directory.

**Inheritance.**    Object-oriented programming enables types (or ADTs) to be organized as a hierarchy so that common data structures and operations may be shared among objects. The root of the hierarchy is the most general *type* and the leaves are the most specialized types. All the children of a type node, called *subtype*, have the data structures and operations of that node in common and may have more specific attributes or operations not in common with their siblings or ancestors. The concept of type hierarchy enables one to model the common properties and differences among types in a concise manner. It has therefore been applied in the database context for conceptual schema modeling and led to semantic data models [Borgida, 1985], which are much richer than the relational model to capture semantic relationships among data.

*Inheritance* is a powerful capability for exploiting the type hierarchy. It enables all descendants of a type to inherit the data structures and operations associated with that type. The immediate advantage is that operations of a type are applicable to objects of a descendant type.

**Example 15.19**

Let us consider the type hierarchy with the type person and subtypes employee and student.

person = [NAME: string, AGE: int]
employee = [NAME: string, AGE: int, ENO: int, TITLE: string]
student = [NAME: string, AGE: int, SNO: int, DEGREE: string]

Employee and student have the type person in common. The specific attributes of an employee are the employee number and the title, while the specific attributes of a student are a student number and the desired degree. Depending on the type language, the attributes of persons may not need to be repeated for employee and student. Let us assume that the type person has the operations

age(name: string): int
display(name: string)

The operation age implemented for person may be used for students and employees and does not have to be implemented for the student and employee types. The display operation prints the person attributes on the screen.

Inheritance essentially eliminates code redundancy and improves program modularity, thus facilitating maintenance. However, it is not always desired to use the operation of an ancestor type, even if the functionality should be the same. For example, we may wish to display all the attributes of a student, not only the name and age. A simple way to handle this is to define the operation with a different name, for example, display_student. However, this approach requires the programmer to deal with different operation names for doing the same thing on different types. Object-oriented programming provides the capability of *overriding* an operation implementation by another one without having to use a different name. Therefore, the same operation display may be used to display objects of different types.

It is customary to group all objects of the same type into a *class*. Similar to the type hierarchy, there can be a class hierarchy. For instance, the class employee, which contains all the employee instances, is a subclass of the class person, meaning that an employee also belongs to the class person. Whereas a type describes all possible instances of a class, the class contains only the instances present in the system. There is an obvious similarity between relation and class.

### 15.4.2 Object Management

By merging the database capabilities with object-oriented programming, object-oriented databases bring definite functional advantages. From a data modeling point of view, an object-based model combines the advantages of the relational model (e.g., associative access), and the network model (e.g., support of graph structures). As a result, the language for an object-based model may be nonprocedural: for instance, an extension of SQL ([Carey et al., 1988] and [Valduriez and Danforth, 1989a]). Nonprocedural languages are highly desirable because they enable the system to perform query optimization. This is probably the salient feature that has made the success of relational database systems [Valduriez and Gardarin, 1989]. Although the earlier languages for object-oriented databases were very procedural (similar to network database languages), they are all evolving toward more declarative languages.

The functional advantages of object-oriented databases incur a price to pay: performance. Since data is uniformly stored within objects, which may be large and complex, the efficiency of object management is, in our opinion, the main issue for object-oriented databases. In particular, when used for business applications, object-oriented database systems should be as efficient as relational database systems. An object-based model is essentially conceptual and can provide high physical data independence—even higher than the relational model. Thus there is some freedom in choosing the underlying physical model, which can be constrained by application performance requirements. To focus on object management, we first precisely define an object model for the conceptual level. For simplicity, this is done independent of the type hierarchy. Since efficient object management is an ongoing research area, we discuss the potential solutions to the storage of objects at the physical level and the implications on object query processing.

**Object model.**    The terms *object* or *complex object* are used extensively in the database literature with different definitions. We can distinguish roughly between two different contexts of use: value-based models in extensions of relational databases, and object-based models in object-oriented databases. In a value-based model, complex objects refer to nonflat tuples ([Zaniolo, 1985] and [Bancilhon and Khoshafian, 1986]) as opposed to relational tuples. The rationale for such complex objects is to generalize the relational model while keeping the advantages, so that nonflat relations may be modeled. A related area of research addresses the support of *nested relations* [Özsoyoglu et al., 1987]. A nested relation, also called a non-first normal form (NFNF) relation, is a relation in which attribute values may themselves be relations. The complex objects of [Bancilhon and Khoshafian, 1986] support nested relations and nested tuples, tuples with tuple-valued attributes. Nested relations avoid the excessive decomposition into flat first-normal-form relations and therefore can significantly reduce the number of foreign key joins that would be required to reconstruct hierarchical data. As extensions of the relational model, nested relation models offer such advantages as normalization for schema design [Özsoyoglu et al., 1987] and algebra for query optimization ([Abiteboul and Bidoit, 1984] and [Schek and Scholl, 1986]).

### Example 15.20

In Figure 15.15 the engineering database defined in Chapter 2 is shown using nested relations. Relations S and J are still in third normal form, while relations E and G have been combined in a single nested relation, where relation G is nested within each tuple of relation E. Compared to the normalized database of Figure 2.4, this database eliminates the need to join relations E and G. Since join is an expensive operation, this can improve performance significantly.

E

| ENO | ENAME | TITLE | G | | |
| | | | JNO | RESP | DUR |
|-----|-------|-------|-----|------|-----|
| E1 | J. Doe | Elect. Eng. | J1 | Manager | 12 |
| E2 | M. Smith | Syst. Anal. | J1 | Analyst | 24 |
| | | | J2 | Analyst | 6 |
| E3 | A. Lee | Mech. Eng. | J3 | Consultant | 10 |
| | | | J4 | Engineer | 48 |
| E5 | B. Casey | Syst. Anal. | J4 | Manager | 24 |

S

| TITLE | SAL |
|-------|-----|
| Elect. Eng. | 40000 |
| Syst. Anal. | 34000 |
| Mech. Eng. | 27000 |

J

| JNO | JNAME | BUDGET |
|-----|-------|--------|
| J1 | Instrumentation | 150000 |
| J2 | Database Develop. | 135000 |
| J3 | CAD/CAM | 250000 |
| J4 | Maintenance | 310000 |

**Figure 15.15**   Engineering Database with Nested Relations

Contrary to a value-based model, an object-based model relies on the notion of object identity. This enables referential object sharing [Khoshafian and Valduriez, 1987], which is the basis for supporting graph structures. It also makes clear the semantics of updates. To describe what an object-based model is, we define objects based on the notion of domain and values. Let $D$ be the union of the system-defined domains (e.g., domain of integers) and of user-defined ADT domains, let $I$ be the domain of identifiers used to name objects, and let $A$ be the domain of attribute names. A *value* is defined as follows:

1. An element of $D$ is a value, called an *atomic value*.
2. $[a_1 : v_1, \ldots, a_n : v_n]$, in which $a_i$ is an element of $A$ and $v_i$ is either a value or an element of $I$, is a value, called a *tuple value*.
3. $\{v_1, \ldots, v_n\}$, in which $v_i$ is either a value or an element of $I$, is a value, called a *set value*.

Similar to pointers in many programming languages (e.g., C), object identifiers are treated as values. Set and tuple are data constructors that we consider essential for database applications. Other constructors, such as list or array, could also be added to increase the modeling power.

An *object* is simply a pair $(oid, v)$, in which $oid$ is an element of $I$ and $v$ is a value. The object is an atomic object if $v$ is atomic, a tuple object if $v$ is a tuple value, and a set object if $v$ is a set value. An object whose value includes identifiers of other objects is a *complex object*. An object whose identifier appears in the value of another object $o$ is a *subobject*, of $o$.

Following the FAD data model [Danforth and Valduriez, 1989], the inherent difference between value and object is that only objects can be shared and updated. As in value-based models, values can be used in a functional manner to produce new values. Furthermore, they are the basis for constructing objects. In most object-based models, for example, the $O_2$ model [Lecluse et al., 1988], all data must be modeled as objects. FAD is a notable exception since data can be modeled as either objects or values. The rationale for the focus on objects and values as well is to provide the respective benefits of both value-based and object-based models.

### Example 15.21

An example of a subset of the engineering database using the object-based model is shown in Figure 15.16. All foreign keys have disappeared and been replaced by the correspond- ing object identifiers. For instance, in an object $g_i$, JNO (which was present in relation G) has been replaced by the corresponding identifier $p_j$, thereby allowing direct access from $g_i$ to the attributes of the project identified by $p_j$. The set object identified by E is object-based modeling of the nested relation E in Figure 15.15. $e_1$ is an example of a complex object, which has objects $s_1$ and $g_1$ as subobjects.

The language for an object-based model can be navigational, as in CODASYL databases, or nonprocedural, as in relational databases. In the latter and more inter- esting case, associative access to set values or set objects can be similar to that of the relational languages. However, since values may contain object identifiers, referenc- ing of subobjects is required. This is typically provided by a path syntax based on a dot notation ([Copeland and Maier, 1984] and [Carey et al., 1988]). The dot notation is used in SQL to denote attribute names by $<R.att>$, where $R$ is either a variable ranging over a relation or a relation name. In an object-based model, the path syntax is generalized to include more than one attribute name along the path. The general syntax is $R.att_1.att_2 \ldots att_n$, where $att_i$ is an attribute of a constructed object which can be accessed from $att_{i-1}$. In a SQL-like language for an object-based model, paths may be used in the project or select parts of a query. Compared to a pure relational language, paths avoid the specification of foreign key joins.

### Example 15.22

The following two queries are expressed on the object database of Figure 15.16 in an SQL-based version of the language described in [Carey et al., 1988]. The following query retrieves the employee name and salary of employee with ENO = E5:

```
SELECT   E.ENAME, E.S.SAL
FROM     E
WHERE    E.ENO = ''E5''
```

S, $(\{s_1, s_2, s_3\})$
$(s_1,$ [TITLE: Elect. Eng., SAL: 40000])
$(s_2,$ [TITLE: Syst. Anal., SAL: 34000])
$(s_3,$ [TITLE: Mech. Eng., SAL: 27000])

$(J, \{j_1, j_2, j_3, j_4\})$
$(j_1,$ [JNO: J1, JNAME: Instrumentation, BUDGET: 150000])
$(j_2,$ [JNO: J2, JNAME: Database Develop., BUDGET: 135000])
$(j_3,$ [JNO: J3, JNAME: CAD/CAM, BUDGET: 1250000])
$(j_4,$ [JNO: J4, JNAME: Maintenance, BUDGET: 310000])

$(G, \{g_1, g_2, g_3, g_4, g_5, g_6\})$
$(g_1,$ [J: j1, RESP: Manager, DUR: 12])
$(g_2,$ [J: j1, RESP: Analyst, DUR: 24])
$(g_3,$ [J: j2, RESP: Analyst, DUR: 6])
$(g_4,$ [J: j3, RESP: Consultant, DUR: 10])
$(g_5,$ [J: j4, RESP: Engineer, DUR: 48])
$(g_6,$ [J: j2, RESP: Manager, DUR: 24])

$(E, \{e_1, e_2, e_3, e_4\})$
$(e_1,$ [ENO: E1, ENAME: J. Doe, S: $s_1$, G: $\{g_1\}$])
$(e_2,$ [ENO: E2, ENAME: M. Smith, S: $s_2$, G: $\{g_2, g_3\}$])
$(e_3,$ [ENO: E3, ENAME: A. Lee, S: $s_3$, G: $\{g_4, g_5\}$])
$(e_4,$ [ENO: E5, ENAME: B. Casey, S: $s_2$, G: $\{g_6\}$])

**Figure 15.16**    Object-based Engineering Database

The path E.S ranges over the salary information of the employee. It avoids the specification of join between relations E and S that would be needed in a relational database. The following query retrieves the name of the employees who are analysts in some project.

```
SELECT   E.ENAME
FROM     E
WHERE    E.G.RESP = ''Analyst''
```

The path E.G ranges over the G information of the employee and avoids the join specification of the join between relations E and G.

**Object storage.** The object model described in the preceding section is purely conceptual, as it does not suggest how objects should be stored on either disk or main memory. Object storage at the physical level affects the efficiency of object management and is therefore crucial to the viability of object-oriented databases. The system module responsible for object storage and access is generally called the *object man-*

*ager*. The object manager mainly performs two related functions: physical clustering of objects and localization of objects. In general, the object manager is also responsible for transaction management (see Chapters 10 through 12). Object clustering is the grouping of objects in the same memory extent, according to common properties, for example, the same value of an attribute or subobjects of the same object. By minimizing the number of memory extents to examine, fast access to clustered objects can be provided. Object localization gives the location of an object based on its identifier or content (e.g., an attribute value). It exploits object clustering information, possibly augmented with some form of indexing.

Relational databases are efficient at managing simple objects. The problem is made significantly more difficult in object-oriented databases by large atomic objects and complex objects. Large atomic objects are quite frequent in new database applications. For instance, a digitized image in an image database can require a few megabytes of storage. The object manager should be able to deliver only useful portions of a large atomic object to the application program or ADT operation that needs it. Complex objects may also be large because objects can be nested within each other using set and tuple constructors to an arbitrary degree. The typical example, from CAD applications, is a VLSI chip object that consists of several sections (e.g., 10), each consisting of many cells (e.g., 100), each containing more than 1000 transistors. Although the number of atomic objects of a VLSI chip (cells) is small (e.g., 100 bytes), the complex object may require several megabytes of storage. The object manager must be able to access an object and its subobjects rapidly if the entire complex object is needed. It must also provide efficient access to collections of subobjects without having to read the large complex object. The management of complex objects is also made difficult by object sharing, which permits each subobject to have more than one parent.

An important design decision for an object manager is the implementation of object identity. The objects manipulated by a program include *persistent objects*, the disk-resident objects concurrently shared by all users, and *transient objects*, the main-memory-resident objects local to a program execution. Implementation of the identity of persistent objects generally differs from that of transient objects, since only the former must provide global uniqueness. In particular, transient object identity can be implemented more efficiently.

The implementation of persistent object identity has two common solutions, based on either physical or logical identifiers, with their respective advantages and shortcomings. The physical identifier approach equates the OID with the physical address of the corresponding object. The address can be a disk page address and an offset from the base address in the page. The advantage is that the object can be obtained directly from the OID. The drawback is the need to update all parent objects and indexes when an object is moved to a different page. The logical identifier approach consists of allocating a systemwide unique OID (i.e., a surrogate) per object. Since OIDs are invariant, there is no overhead due to object movement. This is achieved by an OID table associating each OID with the physical object address, at the expense of one table look-up per object access. To avoid the overhead of OIDs for small objects that are not referentially shared, both approaches can consider the object value as its identifier. The earlier hierarchical and network database systems used the physical identifier approach. Object-oriented database systems tend to prefer the logical identifier approach that better supports dynamic environments.

The implementation of transient object identity involves the techniques used in programming languages. As for persistent object identity, identifiers can be physical or logical. The physical identifier can be the real address or virtual address of the object, depending on whether virtual memory is provided. The physical identifier approach is the most efficient but requires that objects not move. The logical identifier approach, promoted by object-oriented programming, treats objects uniformly through an indirection table local to the program execution. This table associates a logical identifier, called an *object oriented pointer* (OOP) in Smalltalk, to the physical identifier of the object. Object movement is provided at the expense of one table look-up per object access.

The dilemma for an object manager is a trade-off between generality and efficiency. The general support of the object model incurs a certain overhead. For example, object identifiers for small objects can make the OID table quite large. By limiting the support of the object model—for example, by not providing object sharing directly, and by relying on higher levels of system (e.g., the compiler of the database language) for that support—more efficiency may be gained. In the remainder of this section we discuss three main approaches to object storage: persistent object storage for programming languages, extension of relational database storage techniques, and complex object storage.

Persistent object storage is a new concept in programming languages [Atkinson and Morrison, 1985]. As we indicated in Chapter 13, in a traditional programming language such as C or Pascal, the only way to make objects persist after program execution is by embedding implicit commands to the file system in the program. This is typically achieved by making persistent the objects of a specific variable type, such as file. Objects of other types can be made persistent by explicitly copying into an object of the file type. In a persistent programming language such as PS-Algol [Atkinson et al., 1983], persistent object storage is independent of object type and size. In other words, variables of any type and size can persist without explicit commands. Object storage in persistent programming must therefore treat all objects uniformly. The common solution is the logical identifier approach with an OID table, as illustrated in Figure 15.17. During program execution, this table can be viewed conceptually as the union of two tables: one for persistent objects and one for transient objects. In the LOOM system [Kaehler and Krasner, 1983], a persistent version of Smalltalk, the OID table is implemented as the map table of an object-based virtual memory. Distinguishing between transient and persistent objects requires a special identifier at the root of the persistent space. This identifier is accessible within a program by a reserved name (e.g., *db* in FAD [Bancilhon et al., 1987]). Only the objects accessible from the root of the persistent space are persistent. A transient object becomes persistent simply by being made a subobject of a persistent object.

**25**

| ENO | ENAME | S | G |
|-----|-------|-----|-----|
| E1 | J. Doe | $s_1$ | $g_1$ |

**32**

| JNO | JNAME | BUDGET |
|-----|-------|--------|
| J1 | Instrumentation | 150000 |

OID Table

| OID | Memory Address |
|-----|----------------|
| $s_1$ | 110 |
| $j_1$ | 32 |
| $g_1$ | 241 |
| $e_1$ | 25 |

**110**

| TITLE | SAL |
|-------|-----|
| Elect. Eng. | 40000 |

**241**

| J | RESP | DUR |
|---|------|-----|
| $j_1$ | Manager | 12 |

**Figure 15.17**   OID Table

Since all objects are treated uniformly, the programming languages need not be changed to become persistent. Such generality implies a large OID table, which must itself be paginated and organized as a hierarchical data structure for fast look-up (e.g., based on hashing on OID). This approach has two serious limitations. First, the OID table is a highly contented resource in a multiuser environment. Second, it is difficult to cluster complex objects, which must be accessed one component at a time.

Storage techniques for relational databases may well be extended to support complex objects. The philosophy of this approach is to retain as much of the relational model and its underlying technology as possible. It applied initially to System

R for CAD application support [Lorie and Plouffe, 1983] and more recently to POST-GRES [Stonebraker and Rowe, 1986], an extension of INGRES. With the relational model, complex objects are decomposed into tuples (the subobjects). By treating tuple identifiers as attribute values, the object manager can maintain the links between the subobjects composing an object. An atomic object can be stored as a tuple <TID, atomic value>. The nesting of a tuple $t_1$ within a tuple $t_p$ is represented by storing the identifier of $t_1$ as an attribute of $t_p$. The nesting of a set of tuples $\{t_1, t_2, \ldots, t_n\}$ within a tuple $t_p$ can be represented by a binary relation containing the pairs <TID of $t_p$, TID of $t_i$ >, with $i = 1, \ldots, n$. This binary relation corresponds to the concept of a join index [Valduriez, 1987] that captures the links between two relations. This can be generalized to hierarchical join indices [Valduriez et al., 1986] to cope with more than two relations organized as a hierarchy.

**Example 15.23**

The storage of the object-based engineering database of Figure 15.16 could be done with the following relations:

E(**EID**, ENO, ENAME, SID)
G(**GID**, RESP, DUR)
GE(**GID**, EID)
GJ(**GID**, JID)
J(**JID**, JNO, JNAME, BUDGET)
S(**SID**, TITLE, SAL)

The attribute SID in relation E replaces a nested tuple. Relation GE links relations G and E, while relation GJ links relations G and J.

This storage approach brings out the benefits of the relational model. The access to subobjects stored in the same relation can be efficient if the clustering is appropriate. Furthermore, traditional indexing on attribute values is possible. However, access to an entire complex object requires joins on tuple identifiers. Finally, this approach is less general than the preceding one since object identity is restricted to tuples and atomic objects. Therefore, sharing of set objects at the conceptual level is difficult to map at the physical level.

Complex object storage must provide the capability of storing a complex object with its subobjects in the same memory extent. The early hierarchical and network database systems partially provided this capability. In CODASYL, restrictions are that a complex object must fit in a page and that records can only be shared using their physical identifiers (called database pointers). These techniques have recently been generalized to support nested relations and object-based models [Khoshafian et al., 1988b]. Special attention has also been paid to the storage of atomic objects of arbitrary size. In EXODUS [Carey et al., 1988], an atomic object is a long byte sequence, which can be accessed in parts through a byte index. The storage of arbitrarily complex objects is more involved because of object sharing. A complex object may be stored directly in the same address space as a large tuple of a nested relation [Paul et al., 1987]. Similar to the previous approach, object identifiers should be considered attribute values at the physical level. The problem is to provide rapid access from an object identifier to a shared object while avoiding the overhead of the OID table. A good solution proposed in [Khoshafian et al., 1988b] is to store the object value together with one parent and give the other parents a direct path to the parent storing the shared subobject. Note that a path is a sequence of object identifiers and attribute names. Set identifiers are followed by "@" and tuple identifiers are followed by ".". For instance, $S@t.A$ is a path denoting the attribute of the object tuple identified by $t$ in the set $S$.

**Example 15.24**

An example of complex object storage for the objects corresponding to relations E and S is given in Figure 15.18. The tuple S is physically nested within each tuple of E, whereas the sets of G are only identifiers to tuples of G. The objects J and G could be exactly as in Example 15.23. The object $s_2$ is shared by both objects $e_2$ and $e_4$. Since it is shared with the object $e_2$, $e_4$ has a path to $e_2$.

E

| EID | ENO | ENAME | S | | | G |
| --- | --- | --- | --- | --- | --- | --- |
| | | | SID | TITLE | SAL | |
| $e_1$ | E1 | J. Doe | $s_1$ | Elect. Eng. | 40000 | $\{g_1\}$ |
| $e_2$ | E2 | M. Smith | $s_2$ | Syst. Anal. | 34000 | $\{g_2, g_3\}$ |
| $e_3$ | E3 | A. Lee | $s_3$ | Mech. Eng. | 27000 | $\{g_4, g_5\}$ |
| $e_4$ | E5 | B. Casey | $E@e_2.SID$ | | | $\{g_6\}$ |

**Figure 15.18**    Complex Object Storage

The main difficulty of complex object storage with sharing is when the parent containing a shared object is deleted. In this case, the shared subobject must be relocated with another parent, which can be an expensive operation. A simpler solution would be to use the relational storage approach whenever objects are shared. In Figure 15.18 this would lead to storing relation S separately from E. Another difficulty with this approach is indexing in order to access entire objects or subobjects, since objects may be nested within other objects. A solution is to have path indexes [Maier and Stein, 1986] that associate attribute values with paths to the objects.

**Example 15.25**

Figure 15.19 illustrates an example of path index that associates the attribute E.G.RESP (which is really a path to the attribute value) with the path to the corresponding E object.

**Object query processing.**    The notion of query for an object-based model exhibits similarities and differences with relational queries [Banerjee et al., 1988]. The similarity comes from the fact that the language for complex objects can be an extension of relational calculus or algebra (see Example 15.20). Operators such as select,

| E.G. RESP | EID |
|-----------|-----|
| Analyst | $e_2$ |
| Consultant | $e_3$ |
| Engineer | $e_3$ |
| Manager | $\{ e_1 , e_4 \}$ |

**Figure 15.19**   Path Index

project, and join of complex objects can be defined [Schek and Scholl, 1986]. When the objects are flat sets, these operators reduce to the traditional ones, described in Chapter 2. However, because there is not yet a common definition for such operators, we use such notions intuitively, which is sufficient when focusing on object query processing. The difference with relational query processing is that the selection predicates may involve attributes at any nesting level of complex objects, and that nested objects are indicated by a dot notation.

Defining operators such as join and project imply that new objects can be created as a result of querying the object-oriented database. An alternative algebra specification is to define operators with the property that objects that are accessed as a result of a query are already in the database. Operators that follow the former approach are called *object creating* while those that obey the second alternative are called *object preserving* [Scholl and Schek, 1990]. Object algebra definitions that provide object creating operators are given in [Kim, 1989], [Shaw and Zdonik, 1989] and [Osborn, 1988]. The advantages of an object creating algebra is the uniform treatment of views. The relational model permits views to be defined as queries as follows

**create view** $<$ *name* $>$ **as** $<$ *query* $>$

The same approach can be easily adopted in object creating algebras since they allow creation of new objects as views.

On the other hand, the disadvantage of object creating algebras is that they allow objects to be disassembled and the components to be reassembled into new objects. This violates the encapsulation property of objects since the internal structure of an object is visible to the outside world. Such operations, it is believed, should be performed by the methods (operations) that are defined for a specific class of objects by the creator of those objects rather than by the operators of a general purpose query language. Thus, these algebras define only object preserving operators [Straube and Özsu, 1990a].

The strong similarities with relational query processing enable the compiler of the language for complex objects to use relational query optimization techniques with some changes [Valduriez and Danforth, 1989b]. As in a relational system, the compiler transforms a query on conceptual objects into a lower-level query on physical (stored) objects. In what follows we illustrate object query processing in the cases of relational database storage and complex object storage.

With relational database storage, complex objects are mapped into relations, and the links between subobjects are materialized by attribute values. Object query processing is rather simple here. The conceptual query is first mapped into a relational query, which is expressed on the stored relations by replacing path expressions with the corresponding joins. The relational query can then be optimized using any relational query optimization technique.

**Example 15.26**

We consider the conceptual query of Example 15.22:

```
SELECT   E.ENAME
FROM     E
WHERE    E.G.RESP = ''Syst. Anal.''
```

This query can be rewritten into the following relational query on the relations of Example 15.23:

```
SELECT   E.ENAME
FROM     E
WHERE    E.EID = GE.EID
AND      GE.GID = G.GID
AND      G.RESP = ''Syst. Anal.''
```

With complex object storage, complex objects may be mapped more directly at the physical level so that an object and its subobjects may be clustered in the same memory extent. In this case the conceptual query is mapped into a query expressed on the stored objects in the algebra for complex objects (e.g., a combination of joins, selects, and projects on stored objects). The query processing algorithm could be similar to the exhaustive search approach by commuting all joins of stored objects, and for each one, selecting the best access method to the stored object. The only difference here is in the choice of the best access method in the complex object. Since the access to a complex object may involve path expressions and predicates on nested objects, the availability of path indexes is critical for efficiency.

**Example 15.27**

The conceptual query of Example 15.22 would be transformed into a complex select operation in order to access the complex object of Figure 15.18. The best method to access object E is to use the index of Figure 15.19, whose first entry provides the identifier of the relevant object. Compared to the relational storage model, the processing of this query does not require any joins (compared to three joins in Example 15.26).

## 15.4.3  Distributed Object Management

Object-oriented databases and distributed databases are two orthogonal concepts which may well be combined to produce a distributed object-oriented database. Although still in their infancy, we believe that distributed object-oriented databases will be very important in the near future for three reasons. First, as in relational databases, it is likely that object-oriented databases will need distributed database amenities for high availability and increased performance (e.g., by implementation on a shared-nothing data server). Second, applications that require object-oriented database capabilities are generally highly distributed. For example, a large CASE application typically involves many cooperating designers and distributed computing facilities. Third, the information-hiding capability makes object-oriented databases a natural candidate to support heterogeneous databases, which tend to be distributed.

The design of distributed object-oriented databases will benefit from the experience gained with both distributed relational databases and object-oriented databases, since many issues are orthogonal. For example, some of the techniques for distributed transaction management could be used. As in centralized object-oriented databases, the main issue that affects performance is the efficient distribution of object management functions. However, the fact that objects are distributed and can migrate from one node to another makes object identity and object sharing difficult to support. In particular, the full support of these functions may hurt system performance. In the remainder of this section we discuss potential solutions to the storage of a distributed database and object query processing in a distributed database.

**Distributed object storage.**   The *distributed object manager* is the system module responsible for distributed object storage and access. It can be viewed as an extension of an object manager to deal with physical clustering and localization of objects in a distributed environment. In particular, physical clustering and localization of local objects could use the complex object storage approach described in Section 15.4.2. Making efficient and transparent object distribution is the complicating factor. Most object-oriented systems designed for a distributed environment simplify the problem by making the programmer aware of object location [Caplinger, 1987]. The application program typically runs at a single node and performs remote access to obtain nonlocal objects. This approach is not feasible in distributed object-oriented databases because location transparency and distributed program execution, two essential functions for high performance and availability, would be precluded. As in distributed relational databases, set objects can be fragmented or declustered so that a transaction executes a program in parallel where the data is located [Khoshafian and Valduriez, 1988]. Declustering sets of complex objects can be based on top-level attribute values or object identifiers of the complex objects. A global directory can capture persistent object distribution information in a traditional way. The main problems addressed by the distributed object manager remain the support of global object identity and object sharing.

Global identity for persistent objects is equivalent to the generation of globally unique file names in a distributed environment [Leach et al., 1982]. A popular approach is to implement global object identity through surrogates [Khoshafian and Copeland, 1986], which can be implemented by a concatenation of the object birth site number and a number produced by a site counter. Global identity for transient objects is more involved. The main problem is that a distributed system or shared-nothing architecture does not provide a physical address space that is global to all nodes. Therefore, the approaches used in centralized object management do not apply. We discuss below two possible solutions to that problem.

The first solution is based on a global indirection table per transaction for transient objects [Frank, 1987]. The indirection table is distributed across all the sites where the transaction executes. Transient OIDs are made globally unique within the transaction by concatenating the object birth site and a number produced by a site counter initialized to zero at the start of the transaction. The indirection table associates each transient object identifier to its physical identifier. Each site at which the transaction executes has an indirection table which initially contains only those OIDs generated locally. When a transient object migrates from one site to another, it carries its OID. As objects arrive from other sites, the indirection table is updated to include their OIDs with their new physical identifier. It may be the case that a transient object arrives several times at the same site following different paths. For instance, object $o$ is first sent to sites 1 and 2, and then sent by sites 1 and 2 to site 3. Thus object $o$ arrives twice at site 3. The introduction of foreign OIDs in the indirection table therefore requires duplicate elimination of OIDs. This can be accomplished efficiently if the table is hashed on OID for fast look-up. This is required anyway to access transient objects rapidly.

This approach is general since objects can be moved during transaction execution. However, it suffers from problems similar to those of persistent storage in programming languages. First, the indirection table may become quite large. If used for small objects, it can well double the size of the space needed for transient objects. Second, it is impossible to cluster complex transient objects in main memory, as objects in it must be accessed one at a time. Third, the support of object sharing may, in the presence of updates, lead to inconsistencies.

**Example 15.28**

Let us consider an object $o_1$ shared by objects $o_2$ and $o_3$. We assume that object $o_3$ is moved (together with its subobject $o_1$) to site 2 and changes the value of $o_1$. Then we have two different values of the same object at two different sites. Site 1 has the original value, and site 2 has the new value of $o1$. This contradicts the basic definition of an object. If both values of $o_1$ are subsequently used in parallel at sites 1 and 2, inconsistencies may be produced.

One way of solving the foregoing problem is to propagate updates of shared objects automatically during program execution. After being updated, the new value of object $o_1$ could be sent to site 1. However, this poses the problem of synchronizing the programs executed at sites 1 and 2 since the program at site 1 should not use the old value of object $o_1$ after it has been updated at site 2 but not yet sent to site 1. Another way to solve the problem is to avoid the movement of a shared object that might be updated. This is detailed in what follows.

The second solution avoids the overhead associated with managing an indirection table. Object identity for transient objects is based on physical identifiers, and object migration is restricted by the compiler of the database language. This solution has been designed to compile the FAD database programming language ([Bancilhon et al., 1987] and [Danforth et al.,1987]) to run on Bubba, a parallel shared-nothing data server [Boral, 1990]. As pointed out in Section 15.4.2, the focus of the FAD data model is on objects as well as values. In particular, objects (and complex objects) can be copied into values and then manipulated with a relational-algebra-like language. Since OIDs are not considered values in FAD, graph structures resulting from object sharing are copied into tree structures by replicating the values of the shared objects. Therefore, complex values include nested sets and nested tuples but no sharing. For example, Figure 15.20 shows the complex value copied from the complex object in Figure 15.18. Conversely, a value can be converted into a new object or can replace an existing object value.

E

| ENO | ENAME | S | | G | | |
|-----|-------|---------|-------|-----|------------|-----|
| | | TITLE | SAL | JNO | RESP | DUR |
| E1 | J. Doe | Elect. Eng. | 40000 | J1 | Manager | 12 |
| E2 | M. Smith | Syst. Anal. | 34000 | J1 | Analyst | 24 |
| | | | | J2 | Analyst | 6 |
| E3 | A. Lee | Mech. Eng. | 27000 | J3 | Consultant | 10 |
| | | | | J4 | Engineer | 48 |
| E5 | B. Casey | Syst. Anal. | 34000 | J4 | Manager | 24 |

**Figure 15.20**   Complex Value Storage

Because values cannot be shared or updated, they are much easier to handle than objects in a distributed environment. Like the advantage of distributed relational databases, no restriction concerning value migration between sites is necessary. In the FAD context, objects are used locally (within one site) to allow updates and sharing of persistent and transient data. The functionality in terms of object manipulation is that of a centralized object-oriented database. Values are used locally to manipulate efficiently (with no overhead for OIDs) transient and persistent data that need not be shared or updated. Values are also used to exchange data between sites.

The problem of avoiding object migration is solved by a parallelizing compiler ([Hart et al., 1988] and [Hart et al., 1989]). This compiler transforms a FAD program expressed on conceptual objects into an optimized FAD program with communication operations expressed on physical (distributed) objects. The FAD language can be seen as a superset of relational algebra for complex objects. When the use of FAD is reduced to relational algebra, the tasks achieved by the compiler are similar to the query decomposition, data localization, and optimization phases (see Figure 7.3) detailed in Chapters 7 through 9. The main difference with a relational query compiler is that object migration must be avoided. This is achieved by data flow analysis of the input FAD program to detect the possibility that a shared object may be updated. Shared objects that are not updated can be converted easily to values and therefore can migrate to remote sites. Shared objects that may be updated must be processed locally. This implies the prohibition of some parallel query optimizations which would require moving such shared objects.

This approach provides a compromise between the efficiency of value-based systems and the functionality of object-based systems. For example, complex retrieval programs or simple update programs (e.g., debit-credit operations) can be performed efficiently in parallel. Compared to the previous approach, clustering of complex structures (objects or values) is easily supported. However, parallelism for complex update programs may be more restricted.

**Distributed object query processing.**    Distributed object query processing deals with the efficient processing of queries against a distributed object-oriented database. Since it is a completely new research area, very little information is available on the subject. The pivot algorithm [Khoshafian et al., 1988a] is a notable exception since it handles complex hierarchical objects in a parallel context. When set objects are fragmented across the sites of a distributed system, distributed query optimization techniques for relational databases can be used with minor changes. In what follows we discuss distributed object query processing in the case of relational database storage and complex object storage.

Similar to the centralized case (see Section 15.4.2), distributed object query processing with relational database storage is rather simple. After the conceptual query on objects is mapped into a relational query on distributed relations, the problem becomes identical to that of distributed query processing in relational databases. The relational query can then be mapped into an optimized fragment query, as shown in Figure 7.3.

In the case of complex object storage, the query processing algorithm can be based on the exhaustive search approach used in R* (see Section 9.4.2), where the only difference is in the choice of the access methods to complex objects. The problem with using an extension of the R* algorithm is that it generates relational algebra trees which are linear; in other words, the input to a binary operation (e.g., join) has at most one transient object. Therefore, different select and join operations cannot be done in parallel; rather, they are serialized. In Section 15.2.3 we have seen that the pivot algorithm provides significant inter and intraoperation parallelism in the context of relational databases. The algorithm also works with base relations that are hierarchical, as in Figure 15.20. The main modification to the basic algorithm for dealing with complex objects is in the pivot phase. Instead of choosing a single-pivot TID, one-pivot TID is necessary for each nesting level of the answer. If the answer is not hierarchical (flat), a single-pivot TID is sufficient. Another modification is that the algorithm may use path indexes as secondary indexes. Compared to the original pivot algorithm for relations, it generates fewer joins because of complex objects.

**Example 15.29**

We consider the following hierarchical physical schema of the engineering database. Each physical relation is clustered on the first attribute (in boldface font). The base relations are

E(**EID**, ENO, ENAME, SID, G(**GID**, JID, RESP, DUR))
J(**JID**, JNO, JNAME, BUDGET)
S(**SID**, TITLE, SAL)

The main difference with the schema of Example 15.5 is that relation G is nested within relation E. The secondary and join indexes and the SQL query are as in Example 15.5.

The application of the pivot algorithm for that query is shown by the relational algebra tree in Figure 15.21. Since the answer to that query is a flat relation, one-pivot TID is sufficient. The one chosen is EID. The select phase is identical to that of Example 15.5. The pivot phase is similar to that of Example 15.5 except that a single relation (instead of two) is produced. This is because a single join with relation E (which contains attributes ENAME and DUR) is necessary to produce the final result. Since a single relation is accessed in the value materialization phase, there is no composition phase. Compared to Example 15.5, two joins are avoided, although the same interoperation and intraoperation parallelism is provided.

### 15.4.4  Concluding Remarks

In distributed object-oriented databases, object management and object query processing are critical issues for performance. Unlike query processing in knowledge bases, very few research results are available at the moment.

There are several other research issues that deserve attention. The major one in object-oriented databases is the lack of theoretical foundation. Contrary to relational databases, there is no object-based model commonly accepted by database professionals. This makes it hard to define or compare object-oriented database systems, which tend to be application specific.

There are also practical issues. When the conceptual language of an object-oriented database is a database programming language, the combination of general-purpose compilation with distributed query optimization techniques becomes a completely new problem. Other issues are related to the addition of functionality required by new applications such as CAD: long-lived transactions, dynamic schema evolution, and versions of objects. The incorporation of these functions in a distributed object-oriented database will hurt performance, which remains the main issue.

## 15.5  CONCLUSION

In this chapter we have illustrated three major directions toward which distributed technology is rapidly evolving: parallel data servers, distributed knowledge bases, and distributed object-oriented databases. These trends stem from new application re-

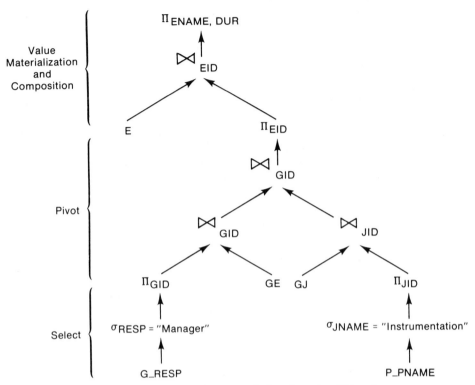

**Figure 15.21**    Pivot Algorithm Applied to Complex Object Storage

quirements expressed in terms of higher functionality and performance. We have discussed how distributed database technology, as presented in this book, can be used and extended to support such requirements.

Each of these trends comes with a number of challenging open issues for the research community. Common to all of them is the need to efficiently exploit the parallelism provided by highly distributed systems. Significant progress has been made in understanding parallelism and data management [Boral, 1988a] in the relational database context. However, much remains to be done in the context of knowledge bases and object-oriented databases. Since their languages may exhibit general-purpose programming capabilities, they face the more general parallel processing problem [Filman and Friedman, 1984].

At the moment, knowledge bases and object-oriented databases are considered two separate and sometimes antagonistic areas. However, because they each solve a subset of the problems presented by the new database applications, it is likely that they will be more and more integrated in the future in order to combine their respective benefits. This would be similar to trends in programming languages where logic and object-oriented programming paradigms are combined in a natural fashion. The main issue for such integration is the definition of a theoretically sound data/object model.

## 15.6 BIBLIOGRAPHIC NOTES

The earlier proposal of the idea of a data server or database machine is given in [Canaday et al., 1974]. A comprehensive survey of database machines is provided in [Valduriez and Gardarin, 1989], [Ozkarahan, 1986] and [Su, 1988]. Other survey papers are [Boral and Redfield, 1985] and [DeWitt and Hawthorn, 1981]. Experiences and lessons learned from data server applications are discussed in [Taylor, 1987].

Parallel data server architectures are discussed in [Stonebraker, 1986] and compared using a simple simulation model in [Bhide and Stonebraker, 1988]. Examples of parallel data servers are presented in [Neches, 1985], [Demurjian et al., 1986], [DeWitt et al., 1986], and [Tandem, 1987]. A good discussion of the issues facing the design of parallel data servers is provided in [Boral, 1988a]. Data placement in a parallel data server is treated in [Livny et al., 1987] and [Copeland et al., 1988]. The section on parallel operation processing is inspired by our work in [Valduriez and Gardarin, 1984]. The section on parallel query processing is based on our work reported in [Khoshafian and Valduriez, 1987] and [Khoshafian et al., 1988a].

A general discussion on knowledge base management can be found in [Wiederhold, 1984]. Thorough tutorials on logic databases appear in [Gallaire et al., 1984], [Gardarin and Valduriez, 1989], and [Ullman, 1988]. The first mentioning of the DATALOG language is given in a early version of [Maier and Warren, 1988]. An example of a DATALOG-like language is LDL [Tsur and Zaniolo, 1986]. Recursive query processing is surveyed at length in [Bancilhon and Ramakrishnan, 1986] and [Gardarin and Valduriez, 1989]. The naive and seminaive evaluation methods are presented in [Bancilhon, 1986]. The importance of the transitive closure operator for recursive query processing is advocated in [Valduriez and Boral, 1986], [Ioannidis, 1986], [Lu et al., 1987], and [Agrawal and Jagadish, 1987]. The section on parallel recursive query processing is based on our work reported in [Valduriez and Khoshafian, 1988a] and [Valduriez and Khoshafian, 1988b]. More recent work on the topic is given in [Agrawal and Jagadish, 1988].

The case for object-oriented database systems is made in [Bancilhon, 1988]. A discussion on object-oriented databases is available in [Ullman, 1988]. However, in that reference, hierarchical and network systems are considered object-oriented database systems, which is unusual since they lack many object-oriented features. A recent book on the subject is [Kim and Lochovsky, 1989]. An early example of object-oriented database system is described in [Copeland and Maier, 1984]. Other examples appear in [Lochovsky, 1985]. A thorough survey of database programming languages is in [Atkinson and Buneman, 1987]. Examples of object-based models are given in [Bancilhon et al., 1987], [Lecluse et al., 1988], and [Danforth and Valduriez, 1989].

Our discussion on the object model is based on the latter reference. [Ullman, 1987] provides a personal critique of object-based versus value-based models. The use of abstract data types in databases is best described in [Osborn and Heaven, 1986].

Examples of nested relation and complex object models are given in [Zaniolo, 1985], [Abiteboul and Bidoit, 1984], [Bancilhon and Khoshafian, 1986], [Schek and Scholl, 1986], and [Özsoyoglu et al., 1987]. [Khoshafian and Copeland, 1986] argues for the support of object identity in the conceptual model. [Khoshafian and Valduriez, 1987] discusses sharing, persistence, and object orientation in a database framework.

Solutions to the management of complex objects appear in [Lorie and Plouffe, 1983], [Carey et al., 1988], [Maier and Stein, 1986], [Valduriez et al., 1986], and [Khoshafian et al., 1988b]. Object query processing in a centralized context is discussed in [Banerjee et al., 1988], [Straube and Özsu, 1990a], [Straube and Özsu, 1990b], and [Straube and Özsu, 1989]. Distributed object management is dealt with in [Caplinger, 1987], [Frank, 1987], and [Hart et al., 1988]. A solution to object query processing in a distributed context is given in [Khoshafian et al., 1988a].

## 15.7 EXERCISES

**\*15.1**  Consider the centralized server organization of Figure 15.2. Also assume that each application server stores a subset of the data directory which is fully stored on the data server. Assume also that the local data directories at different application servers are not necessarily disjoint. What are the implications on data directory management and query processing if the local data directories can be updated by the application servers rather than the data server?

**\*\*15.2**  Propose an architecture for a parallel shared-memory data server and provide a qualitative comparison with shared-nothing architecture on the basis of expected performance, software complexity (in particular, data placement and query processing), extensibility, and availability.

**15.3**  Specify the parallel hash join algorithm for the parallel shared-memory data server architecture proposed in Exercise 15.2.

**\*15.4**  Explain the problems associated with clustering and full declustering in a parallel shared-nothing data server. Propose several solutions and compare them.

**\*15.5**  Propose a parallel semijoin algorithm for a parallel shared-nothing data server. How should the parallel join algorithms be extended to exploit this semijoin algorithm?

**\*\*15.6**  In Example 15.5 the application of the pivot algorithm leads to access relation G twice. Incorporate heuristics to the pivot algorithm so that relations are accessed only once.

**15.7**  Apply the seminaive evaluation algorithm to the query  ?total_part $(p_2, W, S)$ on the knowledge base defined in Example 15.7.

**\*\*15.8**  Specify the TCPO and TCPP algorithms in terms of the partition function and the constructs used in the description of the parallel algorithms in Section 15.2.3.

**\*15.9**  The TCPO algorithm may incur significant communication cost with a large number of nodes. Modify the algorithm so that internode communication is reduced, possibly at the expense of higher local execution cost.

**15.10**   Model the entire relational database of Figure 2.4 using the object model defined in Section 15.4.2. Propose a corresponding physical schema using the complex object storage technique.

**\*\*15.11**   Provide a qualitative comparison of the various implementation techniques of object identity in centralized and distributed systems. Propose a uniform solution for transient and persistent identity in a distributed system and evaluate it with respect to existing ones.

**\*\*15.12**   Express the query "List the names and salaries of the employees who are or have been programmers in the database development project" in SQL extended with dot notation on the conceptual database of Example 15.24. Transform it into a query on the physical database proposed in Exercise 15.10 and apply the pivot algorithm to it.

# Bibliography

[Abbadi et al., 1985] A. E. Abbadi, D. Skeen, and F. Cristian. An Efficient, Fault–Tolerant Protocol for Replicated Data Management. In *Proc. 4th ACM SIGACT–SIGMOD Symp. on Principles of Database Systems*, Portland, Oreg., March 1985, pp. 215–229.

[Abiteboul and Bidoit, 1984] S. Abiteboul and N. Bidoit. Non First Normal Form Relations to Represent Hierarchically Organized Data. In *Proc. 3rd ACM SIGACT–SIGMOD Symp. on Principles of Database Systems*, Waterloo, Ontario, Canada, March 1984, pp. 191–200.

[Abramson, 1973] N. Abramson. The ALOHA System. In *Computer Communication Networks*; N. Abramson and F. F. Kuo (eds.); Englewood Cliffs, N.J.: Prentice-Hall, 1973.

[Adiba, 1981] M. Adiba. Derived Relations: A Unified Mechanism for Views, Snapshots and Distributed Data. In *Proc. 7th Int. Conf. on Very Large Data Bases*, Cannes, France, September 1981, pp. 293–305.

[Adiba and Lindsay, 1980] M. Adiba and B. G. Lindsay. Database Snapshots. In *Proc. 6th Int. Conf. on Very Large Data Bases*, Montreal, Quebec, Canada, October 1980, pp. 86–91.

[Adiba and Portal, 1978] M. Adiba and D. Portal. A Cooperation System for Heterogeneous Data Base Management Systems. *Inf. Syst.* (1978), 3: 209–215.

[Adiba et al., 1978] M. Adiba, J. C. Chupin, R. Demolombe, G. Gardarin, and J. LeBihan. Issues in Distributed Data Base Management Systems: A Technical Overview. In *Proc. 4th Int. Conf. on Very Large Data Bases*, West Berlin, September 1978, pp. 89–110.

[Agrawal and DeWitt, 1985] R. Agrawal and D. J. DeWitt. Integrated Concurrency Control and Recovery Mechanisms. *ACM Trans. Database Syst.*, (December 1985), 10(4): 529–564.

[Agrawal and Jagadish, 1988] R. Agrawal and H. V. Jagadish. Multiprocessor Transitive Closure Algorithms. In *Proc. Int. Symp. on Databases in Parallel and Distributed Systems*, Austin, Texas, December 1988, pp. 56–67.

[Agrawal and Jagadish, 1987] R. Agrawal and H. V. Jagadish. Direct Algorithms for Computing the Transitive Closure of Database Relations. In *Proc. 13th Int. Conf. on Very Large Data Bases*, Brighton, England, September 1987, pp. 255–266.

[Agrawal et al., 1987] R. Agrawal; M. J. Carey and M. Livny. Concurrency Control Performance Modeling: Alternatives and Implications. *ACM Trans. Database Syst.* (December 1987), 12(4): 609–654.

[Allchin and McKendry, 1983] J. E. Allchin and M. S. McKendry. Synchronization and Recovery of Actions. In *Proc. ACM Int. Symp. on Principles of Distributed Computing*, Montreal, Quebec, Canada, August 1983, pp. 31–44.

[Alonso et al., 1987] R. Alonso, H. Garcia-Molina, and K. Salem. Concurrency Control and Recovery for Global Procedures in Federated Database Systems. *IEEE Quart. Bull. Database Eng.* (September 1987), 10(3): 5–11.

[Alsberg and Day, 1976] P. A. Alsberg and J. D. Day. A Principle for Resilient Sharing of Distributed Resources. In *Proc. 2nd Int. Conf. on Software Engineering*, San Fransisco, 1976, pp. 562–570.

[Anderson and Lee, 1985] T. Anderson and P. A. Lee. Software Fault Tolerance Terminology Proposals. In [Shrivastava, 1985], pp. 6–13.

[Anderson and Lee, 1981] T. Anderson and P. A. Lee. *Fault Tolerance: Principles and Practice*. Englewood Cliffs, N.J.: Prentice-Hall, 1981.

[Anderson and Randell, 1979] T. Anderson and B. Randell (eds.). *Computing Systems Reliability*. Cambridge: Cambridge University Press, 1979.

[Anon, 1985] Anon. A Measure of Transaction Processing Power. *Datamation* (April 1985), 31(7): 112–118.

[ANSI, 1986] American National Standard for Information Systems. *Database Language SQL*. ANSI X3.135-1986, October 1986.

[Apers, 1981] P. M. G. Apers. Redundant Allocation of Relations in a Communication Network. In *Proc. 5th Berkeley Workshop on Distributed Data Management and Computer Networks*, Berkeley, Calif., 1981, pp. 245–258.

[Apers et al., 1983] P. M. G. Apers, A. R. Hevner, and S. B. Yao. Optimization Algorithms for Distributed Queries. *IEEE Trans. Software Eng.* (1983), 9(1): 57–68.

[Armstrong, 1974] W. W. Armstrong. Dependency Structures of Data Base Relationships. In *Information Processing '74*, Stockholm, 1974, pp. 580–583.

[Aspnes et al., 1988] J. Aspnes, A. Fekete, N. Lynch, M. Merritt, and W. Weihl. A Theory of Timestamp–Based Concurrency Control for Nested Transactions. In *Proc. 14th Int. Conf. on Very Large Data Bases*, Los Angeles, August 1988, pp. 431–444.

[Astrahan et al., 1979] M. M. Astrahan et al. System R: A Relational Database Management System. *Computer* (May 1979), 12(5): 43–48.

[Astrahan et al., 1976] M. M. Astrahan, M. W. Blasgen, D. D. Chamberlin, K. P. Eswaran, J. N. Gray, P. P. Griffith, W. F. King, R. A. Lorie, P. R. McJones, J. W. Mehl, G. R. Putzolu, I. L. Traiger, B. W. Wade, and V. Watson. System R: A Relational Approach to Database Management. *ACM Trans. Database Syst.* (June 1976), 1(2): 97–137.

[Atkinson and Buneman, 1987] M. P. Atkinson and O. P. Buneman. Types and Persistence In Database Programming Languages. *ACM Comput. Surv.* (June 1987), 19(2): 105–190.

[Atkinson and Morrison, 1985] M. P. Atkinson and R. Morrison. First Class Persistent Procedures. *ACM Trans. Prog. Lang. Syst.* (October 1985), 7(4): 539–559.

[Atkinson et al., 1988] M. P. Atkinson, P. Buneman, and R. Morrison (eds.). *Data Types and Persistence.* New York: Springer-Verlag, 1988.

[Atkinson et al., 1983] M. P. Atkinson, P. J. Bailey, K. J. Chrisholm, K. J. Cockshott, and R. Morrison. An Approach to Persistent Programming. *Comput. J.* (November 1983), 26(4): 360–365.

[Avizienis, 1977] A. Avizienis. Fault-Tolerant Computing: Progress, Problems, and Prospects. In *Information Processing '77*, Toronto, Ontario, Canada, 1977, pp. 405–420.

[Avizienis, 1976] A. Avizienis. Fault-Tolerant Systems. *IEEE Trans. Comput.* (December 1976), C-25(12): 1304–1312.

[Avizienis et al., 1987] A. Avizienis, H. Kopetz, and J. C. Laprie (eds.). *The Evolution of Fault-Tolerant Computing.* Vienna: Springer–Verlag, 1987.

[Babaoglu, 1987] Ö. Babaoglu. On the Reliability of Consensus-Based Fault-Tolerant Distributed Computing Systems. *ACM Trans. Comput. Syst.* (November 1987), 5(3): 394–416.

[Bach, 1986] M. J. Bach. *The Design of the UNIX Operating System.* Englewood Cliffs, N.J.: Prentice–Hall, 1986.

[Bachman and Ross, 1982] C. W. Bachman and R. G. Ross. Toward a More Complete Reference Model of Computer-Based Information Systems. *Comput. & Stand.* (1982), 1(1): 35–48.

[Badal, 1979] D. Z. Badal. Correctness of Concurrency Control and Implications in Distributed Databases. In *Proc. COMPSAC Conf.*, November 1979, pp. 588–593.

[Badrinath and Ramamritham, 1988] B. R. Badrinath and K. Ramamritham. Synchronizing Transactions on Objects. *IEEE Trans. Comput.* (May 1988), C-37(5): 541–547.

[Ball and Hardie, 1967] M. O. Ball and F. Hardie. *Effects and Detection of Intermittent Failures in Digital Systems.* Internal Report 67-825-2137. IBM, 1967. Cited in [Siewiorek and Swarz, 1982].

[Balter et al., 1982] R. Balter, P. Berard, and P. Decitre. Why Control of Concurrency Level in Distributed Systems Is More Important Than Deadlock Management. In *Proc. ACM SIGACT–SIGOPS Symp. on Principles of Distributed Computing*, Ottawa, Ontario, Canada, August 1982, pp. 183–193.

[Bancilhon, 1988] F. Bancilhon. Object-Oriented Database Systems. In *Proc. 7th ACM SIGACT–SIGMOD–SIGART Symp. on Principles of Database Systems*, Austin, Tex., March 1988, pp. 152–162.

[Bancilhon, 1986] F. Bancilhon. Naive Evaluation of Recursively Defined Relations. In *On Knowledge Base Management Systems: Integrating Database and AI Systems*, M. Brodie and J. Mylopoulos (eds.), New York: Springer-Verlag, 1986, pp. 165–178.

[Bancilhon and Khoshafian, 1986] F. Bancilhon and S. Khoshafian. A Calculus for Complex Objects. In *Proc. 5th ACM SIGACT–SIGMOD–SIGART Symp. on Principles of Database Systems*, Portland, Oreg., March 1986, pp. 53–59.

[Bancilhon and Ramakrishnan, 1986] F. Bancilhon and R. Ramakrishnan. An Amateur's Introduction to Recursive Query Processing Strategies. In *Proc. ACM SIGMOD Int. Conf. on Management of Data*, Washington, D.C., May 1986, pp. 16–52.

[Bancilhon and Spyratos, 1981] F. Bancilhon and N. Spyratos. Update Semantics of Relational Views. *ACM Trans. Database Syst.* (December 1981), 6(4): 557–575.

[Bancilhon et al., 1987] F. Bancilhon, T. Briggs, S. Khoshafian, and P. Valduriez. FAD: A Powerful and Simple Database Language. In *Proc. 13th Int. Conf. on Very Large Data Bases*, Brighton, England, September 1987, pp. 97–106.

[Banerjee et al., 1988] J. Banerjee, W. Kim, and K. C. Kim. Queries in Object-Oriented Databases. In *Proc. 4th Int. Conf. on Data Engineering*, Los Angeles, February 1988, pp. 31–38.

[Barak and Litman, 1985] A. Barak and A. Litman. MOS: A Multicomputer Distributed Operating System. *Software Pract. Experience* (August 1985), 15(8): 725–737.

[Barker and Özsu, 1990] K. Barker and M. T. Özsu. Concurrent Transaction Execution in Multidatabase Systems, In *Proc. COMPSAC'90*, Chicago, Illinois, October 1990, pp. 282–288.

[Barker and Özsu, 1988] K. Barker and M. T. Özsu. *A Survey of Issues in Distributed Heterogeneous Database Systems*. Technical Report TR88-9, Edmonton, Alberta, Canada: Department of Computing Science, University of Alberta, 1988.

[Barr et al., 1981] A. Barr, P. R. Cohen, and E. F. Feigenbaum. *The Handbook of Artificial Intelligence,* Volumes 1–3, San Mateo, Calif.: Morgan Kaufmann, 1981.

[Bartlett, 1981] J. Bartlett. A NonStop Kernel. In *Proc. 8th ACM Symp. on Operating System Principles*, Pacific Grove, Calif., December 1981, pp. 22–29.

[Bartlett, 1978] J. Bartlett. A NonStop Operating System. In *Proc. 11th Hawaii Int. Conf. on System Sciences*, Honolulu, 1978, pp. 103–117.

[Batini and Lenzirini, 1984] C. Batini and M. Lenzirini. A Methodology for Data Schema Integration in Entity-Relationship Model. *IEEE Trans. Software Eng.* (November 1984), SE-10(6): 650–654.

[Batini et al., 1986] C. Batini, M. Lenzirini, and S. B. Navathe. A Comparative Analysis of Methodologies for Database Schema Integration. *ACM Comput. Surv.* (December 1986), 18(4): 323–364.

[Bayer and McCreight, 1972] R. Bayer and E. McCreight. Organization and Maintenance of Large Ordered Indexes. *Acta Inf.* (1972), 1: 173–189.

[Beeri et al., 1989] C. Beeri, P. A. Bernstein, and N. Goodman. A Model for Concurrency in Nested Transaction Systems. *J. ACM* (April 1989), 36(2): 230–269.

[Bernstein and Blaustein, 1982] P. A. Bernstein and B. Blaustein. Fast Methods for Testing Quantified Relational Calculus Assertions. In *Proc. ACM SIGMOD Int. Conf. on Management of Data*, Orlando, Fla., June 1982, pp. 39–50.

[Bernstein and Chiu, 1981] P. A. Bernstein and D. M. Chiu. Using Semi–joins to Solve Relational Queries. *J. ACM* (January 1981), 28(1): 25–40.

[Bernstein and Goodman, 1985] P. A. Bernstein and N. Goodman. Serializability Theory for Replicated Databases. *J. Comput. Syst. Sci.* (December 1985), 31(3): 355–374.

[Bernstein and Goodman, 1984] P. A. Bernstein and N. Goodman. An Algorithm for Concurrency Control and Recovery in Replicated Distributed Databases. *ACM Trans. Database Syst.* (December 1984), 9(4): 596–615.

[Bernstein and Goodman, 1981] P. A. Bernstein and N. Goodman. Concurrency Control in Distributed Database Systems. *ACM Comput. Surv.* (June 1981), 13(2): 185–222.

[Bernstein et al., 1987] P. A. Bernstein, V. Hadzilacos, and N. Goodman. *Concurrency Control and Recovery in Database Systems*. Reading, Mass.: Addison-Wesley, 1987.

[Bernstein et al., 1981] P. A. Bernstein, N. Goodman, E. Wong, C. L. Reeve, and J. B. Rothnie, Jr. Query Processing in a System for Distributed Databases (SDD-1). *ACM Trans. Database Syst.* (December 1981), 6(4): 602–625.

[Bernstein et al., 1980a] P. A. Bernstein, B. Blaustein, and E. M. Clarke. Fast Maintenance of Semantic Integrity Assertions Using Redundant Aggregate Data. In *Proc. 6th Int. Conf. on Very Large Data Bases*, Montreal, Quebec, Canada, October 1980, pp. 126–136.

[Bernstein et al., 1980b] P. A. Bernstein, D. W. Shipman, and J. B. Rothnie. Concurrency Control in a System for Distributed Databases (SDD-1). *ACM Trans. Database Syst.* (March 1980), 5(1): 18–51.

[Bhargava, 1987] B. Bhargava (ed.). *Concurrency Control and Reliability in Distributed Systems*. New York: Van Nostrand Reinhold, 1987.

[Bhargava and Lian, 1988] B. Bhargava and S.-R. Lian. Independent Checkpointing and Concurrent Rollback for Recovery in Distributed Systems: An Optimistic Approach. In *Proc. 7th Symp. on Reliable Distributed Systems*, Columbus, Ohio, October 1988, pp. 3–12.

[Bhide, 1988] A. Bhide. An Analysis of Three Transaction Processing Architectures. *ACM SIGMOD Int. Conf. on Management of Data*, Chicago, June 1988, pp. 339–350.

[Bhide and Stonebraker, 1988] A. Bhide and M. Stonebraker. A Performance Comparison of Two Architectures for Fast Transaction Processing. In *Proc. 4th Int. Conf. on Data Engineering*, Los Angeles, February 1988, pp. 536–545.

[Birrell, 1985] A. D. Birrell. Secure Communication Using Remote Procedure Calls. *ACM Trans. Comput. Syst.* (February 1985), 3(1): 1–14.

[Birrell and Nelson, 1984] A. D. Birrell and B. J. Nelson. Implementing Remote Procedure Calls. *ACM Trans. Comput. Syst.* (February 1984), 2(1): 39–59.

[Bitton et al., 1983] D. Bitton, H. Boral, D. J. DeWitt, and W. K. Wilkinson. Parallel Algorithms for the Execution of Relational Database Operations. *ACM Trans. Database Syst.* (September 1983), 8(3): 324–353.

[Blakeley et al., 1986] J. A. Blakeley, P.-A. Larson, and F. W. Tompa. Efficiently Updating Materialized Views. *Proc. ACM SIGMOD Int. Conf. on Management of Data*, San Francisco, May 1986, pp. 61–71.

[Blasgen et al., 1979] M. W. Blasgen, J. N. Gray, M. Mitoma, and T. G. Price. The Convoy Phenomenon. *ACM Oper. Syst. Rev.* (1979), 13(2): 20–25.

[Blaustein, 1981] B. Blaustein. *Enforcing Database Assertions: Techniques and Applications*. Ph.D. thesis, Cambridge, Mass.: Harvard University, August 1981.

[Bochmann, 1983] G. von Bochmann. *Concepts for Distributed Systems Design*. Berlin: Springer-Verlag, 1983.

[Boral, 1988a] H. Boral. Parallelism and Data Management. In *Proc. 3rd Int. Conf. on Data and Knowledge Bases*, Jerusalem, June 1988, pp. 362–373.

[Boral, 1988b] H. Boral. Parallelism in Bubba. In *Proc. Int. Symp. on Database in Parallel and Distributed Systems*, Austin, Tex., December 1988, pp. 68–71.

[Boral and DeWitt, 1983] H. Boral and D. J. DeWitt. Database Machines: An Idea Whose Time Has Passed? A Critique of the Future of Database Machines. In *Proc. 3rd Int. Workshop on Database Machines*, Munich, September 1983, pp. 166–187.

[Boral and Redfield, 1985] H. Boral and S. Redfield. Database Machine Morphology. In *Proc. 11th Int. Conf. on Very Large Data Bases*, Stockholm, August 1985, pp. 59–71.

[Boral et al., 1990] H. Boral, W. Alexander, L. Clay, G. Copeland, S. Danforth, M. J. Franklin, B. Hart, M. Smith, and P. Valduriez. Prototyping Bubba, A Highly Parallel Database System. *IEEE Trans. Knowl. and Data Eng.* (March 1990), 2(1): 4–24.

[Borg et al., 1983] A. Borg, J. Baumbach, and S. Glazer. A Message System Supporting Fault Tolerance. In *Proc. 9th ACM Symp. on Operating System Principles*, Bretton Woods, N.H., October 1983, pp. 90–99.

[Borgida, 1985] A. Borgida. Features of Languages for the Development of Information Systems at the Conceptual Level. *IEEE Software* (January 1985), 2(1): 63–72.

[Borr, 1988] A. Borr. High Performance SQL through Low-Level System Integration. In *Proc. ACM SIGMOD Int. Conf. on Management of Data*, Chicago, June 1988, pp. 342–349.

[Borr, 1984] A. Borr. Robustness to Crash in a Distributed Database: A Non Shared-Memory Multiprocessor Approach. In *Proc. 10th Int. Conf. on Very Large Data Bases*, Singapore, August 1984, pp. 445–453.

[Bratbersengen, 1984] K. Bratbergsengen. Hashing Methods and Relational Algebra Operations. In *Proc. 10th Int. Conf. on Very Large Data Bases*, Singapore, August 1984, pp. 323–333.

[Breitbart and Paolini, 1985] Y. Breitbart and P. Paolini. The Multidatabase Session Chairmen's Report. In *Distributed Data Sharing Systems*, F. A. Schreiber and W. Litwin (eds.), Amsterdam: North-Holland, 1985, pp. 3–6.

[Breitbart and Silberschatz, 1988] Y. Breitbart and A. Silberschatz. Multidatabase Update Issues. In *Proc. ACM SIGMOD Int. Conf. on Management of Data*, Chicago, June 1988, pp. 135–142.

[Breitbart and Tieman, 1985] Y. Breitbart and L. Tieman. ADDS: Heterogeneous Distributed Database System. In *Distributed Data Sharing Systems*, F. A. Schreiber and W. Litwin (eds.), Amsterdam: North-Holland, 1985, pp. 7–24.

[Breitbart et al., 1987] Y. Breitbart, A. Silberschatz, and G. Thompson. An Update Mechanism for Multidatabase Systems. *IEEE Q. Bull. Database Eng.* (September 1987), 10(3): 12–18.

[Brill et al., 1984] D. Brill, M. Templeton, and C. Yu. Distributed Query Processing Strategies in MERMAID: A Front-end to Data Management Systems. In *Proc. First Int. Conf. on Data Engineering*, Los Angeles, 1984, pp. 211–218.

[Brodie and Schmidt, 1982] M. K. Brodie and J. W. Schmidt. Final Report of the ANSI/X3/SPARC DBS-SG Relational Database Task Group. *ACM SIGMOD Rec.* (July 1982), 12(4): i1–i62.

[Brown et al., 1984] R. L. Brown, P. J. Denning, and W. F. Tichy. *Levels of Abstraction in Operating Systems*. RIACS TR 84.5, Research Institute for Advanced Computer Science, Moffatt Field, Calif.: NASA Ames Research Center, July 1984.

[Brzezinski et al., 1984] Z. Brzezinski, J. Getta, J. Rybnik, and W. Stepniewski. Unibase: An Integrated Access to Database. In *Proc. 10th Int. Conf. on Very Large Data Bases*, Singapore, August 1984, pp. 388–400.

[Bucci and Golinelli, 1977] G. Bucci and S. Golinelli. A Distributed Strategy for Resource Allocation in Information Networks. In *Proc. Int. Computing Symp.*, 1977, pp. 345–356.

[Bux et al., 1983] W. Bux, F. Closs, K. Kummerle, H. Keller, and H. Mueller. Architecture and Design of a Reliable Token-Ring Network. *IEEE J. Sel. Areas Commun.* (November 1983), SAC-1(5): 756–765.

[Canaday et al., 1974] R. H. Canaday, R. D. Harrisson, E. L. Ivie, J. L. Rydery, and L. A. Wehr. A Back-End Computer for Data Base Management. *Commun. ACM* (October 1974), 17(10): 575–582.

[Caplinger, 1987] M. Caplinger. An Information System Based on Distributed Objects. In *Proc. Int. Conf. on OOPSLA*, Orlando, Fl., October 1987, pp. 126–137.

[Cardenas, 1987] A. F. Cardenas. Heterogeneous Distributed Database Management: HD–DBMS. *Proc. IEEE* (May 1987), 75(5): 588–600.

[Carey and Livny, 1988] M. J. Carey and M. Livny. Distributed Concurrency Control Performance: A Study of Algorithms, Distribution and Replication. In *Proc. 14th Int. Conf. on Very Large Data Bases*, Los Angeles, August 1988, pp. 13–25.

[Carey and Stonebraker, 1984] M. J. Carey and M. Stonebraker. The Performance of Concurrency Control Algorithms for Database Management Systems. In *Proc. 10th Int. Conf. on Very Large Data Bases*, Singapore, August 1984, pp. 107–118.

[Carey et al., 1988] M. J. Carey, D. J. DeWitt, and S. L. Vandenberg. A Data Model and Query Language for EXODUS, In *Proc. ACM SIGMOD Int. Conf. on Management of Data*, Chicago, June 1988, pp. 413–423.

[Casey, 1972] R. G. Casey. Allocation of Copies of a File in an Information Network. In *Proc. Spring Joint Computer Conf.*, Atlantic City, N.J., 1972, pp. 617–625.

[CCA, 1982] Computer Corporation of America. *An Architecture for Database Management Standards*. NBS Special Publication 500–86, January 1982.

[CCA, 1980] Computer Corporation of America. *A Component Architecture for Database Management Systems*. NBS-GCR-81-340, June 1980.

[Cellary et al., 1988] W. Cellary, E. Gelenbe and T. Morzy. *Concurrency Control in Distributed Database Systems*. Amsterdam: North–Holland, 1988.

[Ceri and Navathe, 1983] S. Ceri and S. B. Navathe. A Methodology for the Distribution Design of Databases. In *Digest of Papers – COMPCON*, 1983, pp. 426–431.

[Ceri and Owicki, 1982] S. Ceri and S. Owicki. On the Use of Optimistic Methods for Concurrency Control in Distributed Databases. In *Proc. 6th Berkeley Workshop on Distributed Data Management and Computer Networks*, Berkeley, Calif., February 1982, pp. 117–130.

[Ceri and Pelagatti, 1984] S. Ceri and G. Pelagatti. *Distributed Databases: Principles and Systems*. New York: McGraw-Hill, 1984.

[Ceri and Pelagatti, 1983] S. Ceri and G. Pelagatti. Correctness of Query Execution Strategies in Distributed Databases. *ACM Trans. Database Syst.* (December 1983), 8(4): 577–607.

[Ceri and Pelagatti, 1982] S.Ceri and G. Pelagatti. A Solution Method for the Non-additive Resource Allocation Problem in Distributed System Design. *Inf. Process. Lett.* (October 1982), 15(4): 174–178.

[Ceri and Pernici, 1985] S. Ceri and B. Pernici. DATAID–D: Methodology for Distributed Database Design. In *Computer-Aided Database Design*, A. Albano, V. de Antonellis, and A. di Leva (eds.), Amsterdam: North-Holland, 1985: pp. 157–183.

[Ceri et al., 1987] S. Ceri, B. Pernici, and G. Wiederhold. Distributed Database Design Methodologies. *Proc. IEEE* (May 1987), 75(5): 533–546.

[Ceri et al., 1986] S. Ceri, G. Gottlob, and G. Pelagatti. Taxonomy and Formal Properties of Distributed Joins. *Inf. Syst.* (1986), 11(1): 25–40.

[Ceri et al., 1983] S. Ceri, S. B. Navathe, and G. Wiederhold. Distribution Design of Logical Database Schemes. *IEEE Trans. Software Eng.* (July 1983), SE-9(4): 487–503.

[Ceri et al., 1982a] S. Ceri, M. Negri, and G. Pelagatti. Horizontal Data Partitioning in Database Design. In *Proc. ACM SIGMOD Int. Conf. on Management of Data*, Orlando, Fla., June 1982, pp. 128–136.

... 

[Ceri et al., 1982b] S. Ceri, G. Martella, and G. Pelagatti. Optimal File Allocation in a Computer Network: A Solution Method Based on the Knapsack Problem. *Comput. Networks* (1982), 6: pp. 345–357.

[Chamberlin et al., 1975] D. D. Chamberlin, J. N. Gray, and I. L. Traiger. Views, Authorization and Locking in a Relational Database System. In *Proc. National Computer Conf.*, Anaheim, Calif., 1975, pp. 425–430.

[Chang and Cheng, 1980] S. K. Chang and W. H. Cheng. A Methodology for Structured Database Decomposition. *IEEE Trans. Software Eng.* (March 1980), SE-6(2): 205–218.

[Chang and Liu, 1982] S. K. Chang and A. C. Liu. File Allocation in a Distributed Database. *Int. J. Comput. Inf. Sci.* (1982), 11(5): 325–340.

[Chen, 1976] P. P. S. Chen. The Entity-Relationship Model: Towards a Unified View of Data. *ACM Trans. Database Syst.* (March 1976), 1(1): 9–36.

[Cheriton, 1988] D. R. Cheriton. The V Distributed System. *Commun. ACM* (March 1988), 31(3): 314–333.

[Cheriton, 1984] D. R. Cheriton. The V Kernel: A Software Base for Distributed Systems. *IEEE Software* (February 1984), 1(2): 19–43.

[Chiu and Ho, 1980] D. M. Chiu and Y. C. Ho. A Methodology for Interpreting Tree Queries into Optimal Semi-join Expressions. In *Proc. ACM SIGMOD Int. Conf. on Management of Data*, Santa Monica, Calif., May 1980, pp. 169–178.

[Chou, 1985] H. T. Chou. *Buffer Management of Database Systems*. Ph.D. dissertation, Madison, Wis.: Department of Computer Science, University of Wisconsin, 1985.

[Chou and DeWitt, 1986] H. T. Chou and D. J. DeWitt. An Evaluation of Buffer Management Strategies for Relational Database Systems. *Algorithmica* (1986), 1(3): 311–336.

[Christmann et al., 1987] P. Christmann, Th. Härder, K. Meyer-Wegener, and A. Sikeler. Which Kinds of OS Mechanisms Should Be Provided for Database Management. In *Experiences with Distributed Systems*, J. Nehmer (ed.), New York: Springer-Verlag, 1987: pp. 213–251.

[Chu, 1976] W. W. Chu. Performance of File Directory Systems for Data Bases in Star and Distributed Networks. In *Proc. National Computer Conf.*, New York, 1976, pp. 577–587.

[Chu, 1973] W. W. Chu. Optimal File Allocation in a Computer Network. In *Computer Communication Networks*, N. Abramson and F. F. Kuo (eds.), Englewood Cliffs, N.J.: Prentice-Hall, 1973, pp. 82–94.

[Chu, 1969] W. W. Chu. Optimal File Allocation in a Multiple Computer System. *IEEE Trans. Comput.* (October 1969), C-18(10): 885–889.

[Chu and Nahouraii, 1975] W. W. Chu and E. E. Nahouraii. File Directory Design Considerations for Distributed Databases. In *Proc. First Int. Conf. on Very Large Data Bases*, Framingham, Mass., September 1975, pp. 543–545.

[Civelek et al., 1988] F.N. Civelek, A. Dogac, and S. Spaccapietra. An Expert System Approach to View Definition and Integration. In *Proc. 7th Int'l. Conf. on Entity-Relationship Approach*; Rome, Italy, November 1988.

[Clocksin and Mellish, 1981] W. F. Clocksin and C. S. Mellish. *Programming in PROLOG*. New York, Springer-Verlag, 1981.

[CODASYL, 1971] CODASYL Programming Committee. *CODASYL Data Base Task Group April 1971 Report*. New York: Association for Computing Machinery, 1971.

[CODASYL, 1969] CODASYL Programming Committee. *Data Base Task Group Report to the CODASYL Programming Language Committee.* New York: Association for Computing Machinery, October 1969.

[Codd, 1982] E. F. Codd. Relational Databases: A Practical Foundation for Productivity, *Commun. ACM* (February 1982), 25(2): 109–117.

[Codd, 1979] E. F. Codd. Extending the Database Relational Model to Capture More Meaning. *ACM Trans. Database Syst.* (December 1979), 4(4): 397–434.

[Codd, 1974] E. F. Codd. Recent Investigations in Relational Data Base Systems. In *Information Processing '74*, Stockholm, 1974, pp. 1017–1021.

[Codd, 1972] E. F. Codd. Relational Completeness of Data Base Sublanguages. In *Data Base Systems*, R. Rustin (ed.), Englewood Cliffs, N.J.: Prentice–Hall, 1972, pp. 65–98.

[Codd, 1970] E. F. Codd. A Relational Model for Large Shared Data Banks. *Commun. ACM* (October 1970), 13(6): 377–387.

[Cohen and Jefferson, 1975] E. Cohen and D. Jefferson. Protection in the HYDRA Operating System. In *Proc. ACM Symp. on Operating System Principles*, 1975, pp. 141–160.

[Copeland and Maier, 1984] G. Copeland and D. Maier. Making SmallTalk a Database System. In *Proc. ACM SIGMOD Int. Conf. on Management of Data*, Boston, June 1984, pp. 316–325.

[Copeland et al., 1988] G. Copeland, W. Alexander, E. Bougherty, and T. Keller. Data Placement in Bubba. In *Proc. ACM SIGMOD Int. Conf. on Management of Data*, Chicago, May 1988, pp. 99–108.

[Cox, 1986] B. Cox. *Object-Oriented Programming.* Englewood Cliffs, N.J.: Prentice–Hall, 1986.

[Cristian, 1987] F. Cristian. *Exception Handling.* Technical Report RJ 5724, San Jose, Calif., IBM Almaden Research Laboratory, 1987.

[Cristian, 1985] F. Cristian. A Rigorous Approach to Fault–Tolerant Programming. *IEEE Trans. Software Eng.* (January 1985), SE-11(1): 23–31.

[Cristian, 1982] F. Cristian. Exception Handling and Software Fault Tolerance. *IEEE Trans. Comput.* (June 1982), C-31(6): 531–540.

[Czejdo et al., 1989] B. Czejdo, D. W. Embley and M. Rusinkiewicz. Query Transformation in a Multidatabase Environment Using a Universal Symbolic Manipulation System. In *Proc. 17th Annual ACM Computer Science Conf.*, Louisville, KY., 1989, pp. 46–53.

[Czejdo et al., 1987] B. Czejdo, D. W. Embley and M. Rusinkiewicz. An Approach to Schema Integration and Query Formulation in Federated Database Systems. In *Proc. 3rd Int. Conf. on Data Engineering*, Los Angeles, February 1987, pp. 477–484.

[Dadam and Schlageter, 1980] P. Dadam and G. Schlageter. Recovery in Distributed Databases Based on Non-synchronized Local Checkpoints. In *Information Processing '80*, 1980, pp. 457–462.

[DAFTG, 1986] Database Architecture Framework Task Group. Reference Model for DBMS Standardization. *ACM SIGMOD Rec.* (March 1986), 15(1): 19–58.

[Danforth and Valduriez, 1989] S. Danforth and P. Valduriez. The Data Model of FAD: A Database Programming Language. *Inf. Sci.*, to appear.

[Danforth et al., 1987] S. Danforth, S. Khoshafian, and P. Valduriez. *FAD: A Database Programming Language.* Technical Report DB-151-85, Rev. 2, Austin, Tex.: Microelectronics and Computer Corporation, September 1987.

[Dasgupta and LeBlanc, 1985] P. Dasgupta and R. J. LeBlanc Jr. *Clouds: A Support Architecture for Fault Tolerant, Distributed Systems.* Atlanta, Ga.: School of Information and Computer Science, Georgia Institute of Technology, 1985.

[Date, 1987] C. J. Date. *A Guide to the SQL Standard.* Reading, Mass.: Addison-Wesley, 1987.

[Date, 1986] C. J. Date. *An Introduction to Database Systems,* Volume 1 (4th edition). Reading, Mass.: Addison-Wesley, 1986.

[Date, 1984] C. J. Date. *Guide to DB2.* Reading, Mass.: Addison-Wesley, 1984.

[Date, 1983] C. J. Date. *An Introduction to Database Systems,* Volume 2. Reading, Mass.: Addison-Wesley, 1983.

[Davenport, 1981] R. A. Davenport. Design of Distributed Data Base Systems. *Comput. J.* (1981), 24(1): 31–41.

[Davidson, 1984] S. B. Davidson. Optimism and Consistency in Partitioned Distributed Database Systems. *ACM Trans. Database Syst.* (September 1984), 9(3): 456–481.

[Davidson et al., 1985] S. B. Davidson, H. Garcia-Molina, and D. Skeen. Consistency in Partitioned Networks. *ACM Comput. Surv.* (September 1985), 17(3): 341–370.

[Dawson, 1980] J. L. Dawson. A User Demand Model for Distributed Database Design. In *Digest of Papers – COMPCON,* 1980, pp. 211–216.

[Dayal and Bernstein, 1978] U. Dayal and P. A. Bernstein. On the Updatability of Relational Views. In *Proc. 4th Int. Conf. on Very Large Data Bases,* West Berlin, September 1978, pp. 368–377.

[Dayal and Hwang, 1984] U. Dayal and H. Hwang. View Definition and Generalization for Database Integration in MULTIBASE: A System for Heterogeneous Distributed Database. *IEEE Trans. Software Eng.* (November 1984), SE-10(6): 628–644.

[Demurjian et al., 1986] S. Demurjian, D. K. Hsiao, and J. Menon. A Multi-backend Database System for Performance Gains, Capacity Growth and Hardware Upgrade. In *Proc. 2nd Int. Conf. on Data Engineering,* Los Angeles, February 1986, pp. 542–554.

[Denning, 1980] P. J. Denning. Working Sets: Past and Present. *IEEE Trans. Software Eng.* (January 1980), SE-6(1): 64–84.

[Denning, 1968] P. J. Denning. The Working Set Model for Program Behavior. *Commun. ACM* (May 1968), 11(5): 323–333.

[Denning and Brown, 1983] P. J. Denning, and R. L. Brown. Should Distributed Systems Be Hidden? In *Proc. Int. Workshop on Computer System Organization,* 1983, pp. 49–60.

[DeWitt and Gerber, 1985] D. J. DeWitt and R. H. Gerber. Multi Processor Hash-Based Join Algorithms. In *Proc. 11th Int. Conf. on Very Large Data Bases,* Stockholm, August 1985, pp. 151–164.

[DeWitt and Hawthorn, 1981] D. J. DeWitt, P. B. Hawthorn. A Performance Evaluation of Database Machine Architectures. In *Proc. 7th Int. Conf. on Very Large Data Bases,* Cannes, France, September 1981, pp. 199–213.

[DeWitt et al., 1986] D. J. DeWitt, R. H. Gerber, G. Graek, M. L. Heytens, K. B. Kumar, and M. Muralikrishna. GAMMA: A High Performance Dataflow Database Machine. In *Proc. 12th Int. Conf. on Very Large Data Bases,* Kyoto, Japan, August 1986, pp. 228–237.

[DeWitt et al., 1984] D. J. DeWitt, R. H. Katz, F. Olken, L. D. Shapiro, M. Stonebraker, and D. Wood. Implementation Techniques for Main Memory Database Systems. In *Proc. ACM SIGMOD Int. Conf. on Management of Data,* Boston, June 1984, pp. 1–8.

[Diel et al., 1984] H. Diel, G. Kreissig, and N. Lenz. Data Management Facilities of an Operating System Kernel. In *Proc. ACM SIGMOD Int. Conf. on Management of Data*, Boston, June 1984, pp. 58–69.

[Diffie and Hellman, 1976] W. Diffie and M. E. Hellman. New Directions in Cryptography. *IEEE Trans. Inf. Theory* (November 1976), IT–22(6): 644–654.

[Dittrich and Dayal, 1986] K. Dittrich and U. Dayal (eds.). *Proc. 1986 Int. Workshop on Object-Oriented Database Systems*, Pacific Grove, Calif., September 1986.

[Dogac and Ozkarahan, 1980] A. Dogac and E. A. Ozkarahan. A Generalized DBMS Implementation on a Database Machine. In *Proc. ACM SIGMOD Int. Conf. on Management of Data*, Santa Monica, Calif., May 1980, pp. 133–143.

[D'Oliviera, 1977] C. R. D'Oliviera. *An Analysis of Computer Decentralization*. Technical Memo TM-90, Cambridge, Mass.: Laboratory for Computer Science, Massachusetts Institute of Technology, 1977.

[Dowdy and Foster, 1982] L. W. Dowdy and D. V. Foster. Comparative Models of the File Assignment Problem. *ACM Comput. Surv.* (June 1982), 14(2): 287–313.

[Du, 1984] H. C. Du. Distributing a Database for Parallel Processing Is NP-Hard. *ACM SIGMOD Rec.* (March 1984), 14(1): 55–60.

[Du and Elmagarmid, 1989] W. Du and A. K. Elmagarmid. Quasi-serializability: A Correctness Criterion for Global Concurrency Control in InterBase. In *Proc. 15th Int. Conf. on Very Large Data Bases*, Amsterdam, August 1989, pp. 347–355.

[Du et al., 1989] W. Du, A. K. Elmagarmid, Y. Leu, and S. Ostermann. Effects of Local Autonomy on Global Concurrency Control in Heterogeneous Distributed Database Systems. In *Proc. Int. Conf. on Data and Knowledge Management for Manufacturing and Engineering*, Gaithersburg, MD., 1989, pp. 113–120.

[Dwork and Skeen, 1983] C. Dwork and D. Skeen. The Inherent Cost of Nonblocking Commitment. In *Proc. 2nd ACM SIGACT–SIGOPS Symp. on Principles of Distributed Systems*, August 1983, pp. 1–11.

[Dwyer and Larson, 1987] P. Dwyer and J. L. Larson. Some Experiences with a Distributed Database Testbed System. *Proc. IEEE* (May 1987), 75(5): 633–648.

[Dwyer et al., 1986] P. Dwyer; K. Kasravi and M. Pham. *A Heterogeneous Distributed Database Management System (DDTS/RAM)*. Technical Report CSC-86-7:8216, Golden Valley, Minn.: Honeywell Corporate Research Center, 1986.

[Eager and Sevcik, 1983] D. L. Eager and K. C. Sevcik. Achieving Robustness in Distributed Database Systems. *ACM Trans. Database Syst.* (September 1983), 8(3): 354–381.

[Effelsberg, 1983] W. Effelsberg. Fixing Pages in a Database Buffer. *ACM SIGMOD Rec.* (January 1983), 13(2): 52–59.

[Effelsberg and Härder, 1984] W. Effelsberg and T. Härder. Principles of Database Buffer Management. *ACM Trans. Database Syst.* (December 1984), 9(4): 560–595.

[Eisner and Severance, 1976] M. J. Eisner and D. G. Severance. Mathematical Techniques for Efficient Record Segmentation in Large Shared Databases. *J. ACM* (October 1976), 23(4): 619–635.

[Elhardt and Bayer, 1984] K. Elhardt and R. Bayer. A Database Cache for High Performance and Fast Restart in Database Systems. *ACM Trans. Database Syst.* (December 1984), 9(4): 503–525.

[Elkind, 1982] S. A. Elkind. Reliability and Availability Techniques. In [Siewiorek and Swarz, 1982], pp. 63–181.

[Elmagarmid, 1986] A. K. Elmagarmid. A Survey of Distributed Deadlock Detection Algorithms. *ACM SIGMOD Rec.* (September 1986), 15(3): 37–45.

[Elmagarmid and Du, 1990] A. K. Elmagarmid and W. Du. A Paradigm for Concurrency Control in Heterogeneous Database Systems. In *Proc. 6th Int. Conf. on Data Engineering*, Los Angeles, February 1990, pp. 347–355.

[Elmagarmid and Du, 1989] A. K. Elmagarmid and W. Du. *Value Dependency for Nested Transactions in InterBase*. Technical Report CSD-TR-886, West Lafayette, Ind.: Department of Computer Sciences, Purdue University, June 1989.

[Elmagarmid and Helal, 1986] A. K. Elmagarmid and A. A. Helal. *Heterogeneous Database Systems*. Technical Report TR-86-004, University Park, Pa.: Program of Computer Engineering, Pennsylvania State University, 1986.

[Elmagarmid et al., 1988] A. K. Elmagarmid, N. Soundararajan, and M. T. Liu. A Distributed Deadlock Detection and Resolution Algorithm and Its Correctness Proof. *IEEE Trans. Software Eng.* (October 1988), 14(10): 1443–1452.

[Elmasri and Navathe, 1989] R. Elmasri and S. B. Navathe. *Fundamentals of Database Systems*. Menlo Park, Calif.: Benjamin-Cummings, 1989.

[Elmasri et al., 1987] R. Elmasri, J. L. Larson, and S. B. Navathe. *Integration Algorithms for Database and Logical Database Design*. Technical Report, Golden Valley, Minn.: Honeywell Corporate Research Center, 1987.

[Enderton, 1972] H. B. Enderton. *A Mathematical Introduction to Logic*. New York: Academic Press, 1972.

[Epstein and Hawthorn, 1980] R. Epstein and P. B. Hawthorn. Design Decisions for the Intelligent Database Machine. In *Proc. National Computer Conf.*, 1980, pp. 237–241.

[Epstein and Stonebraker, 1980] R. Epstein and M. Stonebraker. Analysis of Distributed Data Base Processing Strategies. In *Proc. 5th Int. Conf. on Very Large Data Bases*, Montreal, Quebec, Canada, October 1980, pp. 92–101.

[Epstein et al., 1978] R. Epstein, M. Stonebraker, and E. Wong. Query Processing in a Distributed Relational Database System. In *Proc. ACM SIGMOD Int. Conf. on Management of Data*, Austin, Tex., May 1978.

[Eswaran, 1974] K. P. Eswaran. Placement of Records in a File and File Allocation in a Computer Network. In *Information Processing '74*, Stockholm, 1974, pp. 304–307.

[Eswaran et al., 1976] K. P. Eswaran, J. N. Gray, R. A. Lorie, and I. L. Traiger. The Notions of Consistency and Predicate Locks in a Database System. *Commun. ACM* (November 1976), 19(11): 624–633.

[Fabry, 1974] R. S. Fabry. Capability-Based Addressing. *Commun. ACM* (July 1974), 17(7): 403–412.

[Fagin, 1979] R. Fagin. Normal Forms and Relational Database Operators. In *ACM SIGMOD Int. Conf. on Management of Data*, Boston, May 1979, pp. 153–160.

[Fagin, 1978] R. Fagin. On an Authorization Mechanism. *ACM Trans. Database Syst.* (December 1978), 3(4): 310–320.

[Fagin, 1977] R. Fagin. Multivalued Dependencies and a New Normal Form for Relational Databases. *ACM Trans. Database Syst.* (September 1977), 2(3): 262–278.

[Fagin and Vardi, 1984] R. Fagin and M. Y. Vardi. *The Theory of Data Dependencies: A Survey*. Research Report RJ 4321 (47149), San Jose, Calif.: IBM Research Laboratory, June 1984.

[Farrag, 1986] A. A. Farrag. *Concurrency and Consistency in Database Systems*. Ph.D. thesis, Edmonton, Alberta, Canada: Department of Computing Science, University of Alberta, 1986.

[Farrag and Özsu, 1989] A. A. Farrag and M. T. Özsu. Using Semantic Knowledge of Transactions to Increase Concurrency. *ACM Trans. on Database Syst.* (December 1989), 14(4): 503–525.

[Farrag and Özsu, 1987] A. A. Farrag and M. T. Özsu. Towards a General Concurrency Control Algorithm for Database Systems. *IEEE Trans. Software Eng.* (October 1987), 13(10): 1073–1079.

[Farrag and Özsu, 1985] A. A. Farrag and M. T. Özsu. A General Concurrency Control for Database Systems. In *Proc. National Computer Conf.*, Chicago, July 1985, pp. 567–573.

[Fekete et al., 1989] A. Fekete, N. Lynch, M. Merritt, and W. Weihl. *Commutativity-Based Locking for Nested Transactions*. Technical Memo MIT/LCS/TM-370b, Cambridge, Mass.: Massachusetts Institute of Technology, July 1989.

[Fekete et al., 1987a] A. Fekete, N. Lynch, M. Merritt, and W. Weihl. *Nested Transactions and Read/Write Locking*. Technical Memo MIT/LCS/TM-324, Cambridge, Mass.: Massachusetts Institute of Technology, April 1987.

[Fekete et al., 1987b] A. Fekete, N. Lynch, M. Merritt, and W. Weihl. *Nested Transactions, Conflict-Based Locking, and Dynamic Atomicity*. Technical Memo MIT/LCS/TM-340, Cambridge, Mass.: Massachusetts Institute of Technology, September 1987.

[Fernandez et al., 1981] E. B. Fernandez, R. C. Summers, and C. Wood. *Database Security and Integrity*. Reading, Mass.: Addison-Wesley, 1981.

[Fernandez et al., 1978] E. B. Fernandez, T. Lang, and C. Wood. Effect of Replacement Algorithms on a Paged Buffer Database System. *IBM J. Res. Dev.* (March 1978), 22(2): 185–196.

[Ferrier and Stangret, 1982] A. Ferrier and C. Stangret. Heterogeneity in the Distributed Data Management System SIRIUS-DELTA. In *Proc. 8th Int. Conf. on Very Large Data Bases*, Mexico City, September 1982, pp. 45–53.

[Filman and Friedman, 1984] R. Filman and D. Friedman. *Coordinated Computing*. New York: McGraw-Hill, 1984.

[Fisher and Hochbaum, 1980] M. K. Fisher and D. S. Hochbaum. Database Location in Computer Networks. *J. ACM* (October 1980), 27(4): 718–735.

[Fisher et al., 1980] P. S. Fisher, P. Hollist, and J. Slonim. A Design Methodology for Distributed Data Bases. In *Digest of Papers – COMPCON*, 1980, pp. 199–202.

[Florentin, 1974] J. J. Florentin. Consistency Auditing of Databases. *Comput. J.* (1974), 17(1): 52–58.

[Foster and Browne, 1976] D. V. Foster and J. C. Browne. File Assignment in Memory Hierarchies. In *Modelling and Performance Evaluation of Computer Systems*, E. Gelenbe (ed.), Amsterdam: North-Holland, 1976: pp. 119–127.

[Frank, 1987] D. Frank. *A Proposal for Global Object Identity in Bubba*. Internal Report, Austin, Tex.: Microelectronics and Computer Corporation, August 1987.

[Gallaire et al., 1984] H. Gallaire, J. Minker, and J.-M. Nicolas. Logic and Databases: A Deductive Approach. *ACM Comput. Surv.* (June 1984), 16(2): 153–186.

[Garcia-Molina, 1983] H. Garcia-Molina. Using Semantic Knowledge for Transaction Processing in a Distributed Database. *ACM Trans. Database Syst.* (June 1983), 8(2): 186–213.

[Garcia-Molina, 1982] H. Garcia-Molina. Elections in Distributed Computing Systems. *IEEE Trans. Comput.* (January 1982), C-31(1): 48–59.

[Garcia-Molina, 1979] H. Garcia-Molina. *Performance of Update Algorithms for Replicated Data in a Distributed Database.* Ph.D. thesis, Stanford, Calif.: Department of Computer Science, Stanford University, 1979.

[Garcia-Molina and Wiederhold, 1982] H. Garcia-Molina and G. Wiederhold. Read-Only Transactions in a Distributed Database. *ACM Trans. Database Syst.* (June 1982), 7(2): 209–234.

[Gardarin and Valduriez, 1989] G. Gardarin and P. Valduriez. *Relational Databases and Knowledge Bases.* Reading, Mass.: Addison–Wesley, 1989.

[Gardarin et al., 1983] G. Gardarin, P. Bernadat, N. Temmerman, P. Valduriez, and Y. Viemont. Design of a Multi Processor Relational Database System. In *Information Processing '83*, Paris, September 1983, pp. 363–367.

[Gastonian, 1983] R. Gastonian. The Auragen System 4000. *IEEE Q. Bull. Database Eng.* (June 1983), 6(2).

[Gavish and Pirkul, 1986] B. Gavish and H. Pirkul. Computer and Database Location in Distributed Computer Systems. *IEEE Trans. Comput.* (July 1986), C-35(7): 583–590.

[GE, 1976] General Electric Research and Development Center. *MADMAN User Manual.* Schenectady, N.Y.: General Electric Company, 1976.

[Gelenbe and Gardy, 1982] E. Gelenbe and D. Gardy. The Size of Projections of Relations Satisfying a Functional Dependency. In *Proc. 8th Int. Conf. on Very Large Data Bases*, Mexico City, September 1982, pp. 325–333.

[Gelenbe and Sevcik, 1978] E. Gelenbe and K. Sevcik. Analysis of Update Synchronization for Multiple Copy Databases. In *Proc. 3rd Berkeley Workskop on Distributed Data Management and Computer Networks*, Berkeley, Calif., August 1978, pp. 69–88.

[Gibbons, 1976] T. Gibbons. *Integrity and Recovery in Computer Systems.* Manchester, England, NCC Publications, 1976.

[Gifford, 1979] D. K. Gifford. Weighted Voting for Replicated Data. In *Proc. 7th ACM Symp. on Operating System Principles*, Pacific Grove, Calif., December 1979, pp. 150–159.

[Gligor and Luckenbaugh, 1984] V. D. Gligor and G. L. Luckenbaugh. Interconnecting Heterogeneous Database Management Systems. *IEEE Computer* (January 1984), 17(1): 33–43.

[Gligor and Popescu-Zeletin, 1986] V. Gligor and R. Popescu-Zeletin. Transaction Management in Distributed Heterogeneous Database Management Systems. *Inf. Syst.* (1986), 11(4): 287–297.

[Goldberg and Robson, 1983] A. Goldberg and D. Robson. *SmallTalk-80: The Language and Its Implementation.* Reading, Mass.: Addison-Wesley, 1983.

[Goldman, 1987] K. J. Goldman. *Data Replication in Nested Transaction Systems.* Technical Report MIT/LCS/TR-390, Cambridge, Mass.: Massachusetts Institute of Technology, May 1987.

[Goodman et al., 1983] N. Goodman, R. Suri, and Y. C. Tay. A Simple Analytic Model for Performance of Exclusive Locking in Database Systems. In *Proc. 2nd ACM SIGACT–SIGMOD Symp. on Principles of Database Systems*, Atlanta, Ga., March 1983, pp. 203–215.

[Grant, 1984] J. Grant. Constraint Preserving and Lossless Database Transformations. *Inf. Syst.* (1984), 9(2): 139–146.

[Grapa and Belford, 1977] E. Grapa and G. G. Belford. Some Theorems to Aid in Solving the File Allocation Problem. *Commun. ACM* (November 1977), 20(11): 878–882.

[Gray, 1987] J. N. Gray. *Why Do Computers Stop and What Can Be Done About It.* Tutorial Notes, CIPS (Canadian Information Processing Society) Edmonton '87 Conf., Edmonton, Alberta, Canada, November 1987.

[Gray, 1985] J. N. Gray. *Why Do Computers Stop and What Can Be Done About It.* Technical Report 85-7, Cupertino, Calif.: Tandem Computers, 1985.

[Gray, 1983] J. N. Gray. A Discussion of Distributed Systems. In *Advances in Distributed Processing Management,* Volume 2, P. S. Fisher, J. Slonim, and E. A. Unger (eds.), Chichester, West Sussex, England: Wiley, 1983: pp. 1–14.

[Gray, 1981] J. N. Gray. The Transaction Concept: Virtues and Limitations. In *Proc. 7th Int. Conf. on Very Large Data Bases*, Cannes, France, September 1981, pp. 144–154.

[Gray, 1979] J. N. Gray. Notes on Data Base Operating Systems. In *Operating Systems: An Advanced Course*, R. Bayer, R. M. Graham, and G. Seegmüller (eds.), New York: Springer-Verlag, 1979, pp. 393–481.

[Gray and Putzolu, 1987] J. N. Gray and F. Putzolu. The 5 Minute Rule for Trading Memory for Disc Accesses and the 10 Byte Rule for Trading Memory for CPU Time. In *Proc. ACM SIGMOD Int. Conf. on Management of Data*, San Francisco, May 1987, pp. 395–398.

[Gray and Reuter, 1987] J. N. Gray and A. Reuter. *Transaction Processing: Version 1.* Tutorial Notes, 1987.

[Gray et al., 1981] J. N. Gray, P. McJones, M. W. Blasgen, B. G. Lindsay, R. A. Lorie, T. G. Price, F. Putzolu, and I. L. Traiger. The Recovery Manager of the System R Database Manager. *ACM Comput. Surv.* (June 1981), 13(2): 223–242.

[Gray et al., 1976] J. N. Gray, R. A. Lorie, G. R. Putzolu, and I. L. Traiger. Granularity of Locks and Degrees of Consistency in a Shared Data Base. In *Modelling in Data Base Management Systems*, G. M. Nijssen (ed.), Amsterdam: North-Holland, 1976, pp. 365–394.

[Griffiths and Wade, 1976] P. P. Griffiths and B. W. Wade. An Authorization Mechanism for a Relational Database System. *ACM Trans. Database Syst.* (September 1976), 1(3): 242–255.

[Guttag, 1977] J. Guttag. Abstract Data Types and the Development of Data Structures. *Commun. ACM* (June 1977), 20(6): 396–404.

[Hadzilacos, 1988] V. Hadzilacos. A Theory of Reliability in Database Systems. *J. ACM* (January 1988), 35(1): 121–145.

[Hadzilacos and Yannakakis, 1986] V. Hadzilacos and M. Yannakakis. Deleting Completed Transactions. In *Proc. 5th SIGACT–SIGMOD Symp. on Principles of Database Systems*, Cambridge, Mass., March 1986, pp. 43–47.

[Haessig and Jenny, 1980] K. Haessig and C. J. Jenny. *An Algorithm for Allocating Computational Objects in Distributed Computing Systems*. Research Report RZ 1016, Zurich: IBM Research Laboratory, June 1980.

[Halici and Dogac, 1989] U. Halici and A. Dogac. Concurrency Control in Distributed Databases through Time Intervals and Short-Term Locks. *IEEE Trans. Software Eng.* (August 1989), 15(8): 994–995.

[Halsall, 1988] F. Halsall. *Data Communications, Computer Networks and OSI* (2nd edition). Wokingham, Berkshire, England: Addison-Wesley, 1988.

[Hammer and Niamir, 1979] M. Hammer and B. Niamir. A Heuristic Approach to Attribute Partitioning. In *Proc. ACM SIGMOD Int. Conf. on Management of Data*, Boston, May 1979, pp. 93–101.

[Hammer and Shipman, 1980] M. Hammer and D. W. Shipman. Reliability Mechanisms for SDD-1: A System for Distributed Databases. *ACM Trans. Database Syst.* (December 1980), 5(4): 431–466.

[Han and Fisher, 1983] M. J. Han and P. S. Fisher. The Problems of Data Structure and Application Software Conversion in a Heterogeneous Environment. In *Advances in Distributed Processing Management,* Volume 2, P. S. Fisher, J. Slonim, and E. A. Unger (eds.), Chichester, West Sussex, England: Wiley, 1983, pp. 145–178.

[Härder, 1988] T. Härder (ed). *The PRIMA Project.* Technical Report 26/88 - SFB 124, Kaiserslautern, West Germany: University of Kaiserslautern, March 1988.

[Härder and Reuter, 1983] T. Härder and A. Reuter. Principles of Transaction-Oriented Database Recovery. *ACM Comput. Surv.* (December 1983), 15(4): 287–317.

[Hart et al., 1989] B. Hart, P. Valduriez, and S. Danforth. Parallelizing FAD Using Compile Time Analysis Techniques. *IEEE Q. Bull. Database Eng.* (March 1989), 12(1): 9–15.

[Hart et al., 1988] B. Hart, S. Danforth, and P. Valduriez. Parallelizing FAD: A Database Programming Language. In *Proc. Int. Symp. on Databases in Parallel and Distributed Systems*, Austin, Tex., December 1988, pp. 72–79.

[Haskin et al., 1988] R. Haskin, Y. Malachi, W. Sawdon, and G. Chan. Recovery Management in QuickSilver. *ACM Trans. Computer Syst.* (February 1988), 6(1): 82–108.

[Heimbigner and McLeod, 1985] D. Heimbigner and D. McLeod. A Federated Architecture for Information Management. *ACM Trans. Office Inf. Syst.* (July 1985), 3(3): 253–278.

[Herlihy, 1987] M. Herlihy. Concurrency versus Availability: Atomicity Mechanisms for Replicated Data. *ACM Trans. Comput. Syst.* (August 1987), 5(3): 249–274.

[Herman and Verjus, 1979] D. Herman and J. P. Verjus. An Algorithm for Maintaining the Consistency of Multiple Copies. In *Proc. First Int. Conf. on Distributed Computing Systems*, Huntsville, Ala., 1979, pp. 625–631.

[Hevner and Schneider, 1980] A. R. Hevner and G. M. Schneider. An Integrated Design System for Distributed Database Networks. In *Digest of Papers – COMPCON*, 1980, pp. 459–465.

[Hevner and Yao, 1979] A. R. Hevner and S. B. Yao. Query Processing in Distributed Database Systems. *IEEE Trans. Software Eng.* (March 1979), 5(3): 177–182.

[Hoffer, 1975] J. A. Hoffer. *A Clustering Approach to the Generation of Subfiles for the Design of a Computer Data Base.* Ph.D. dissertation, Ithaca, N.Y.: Department of Operations Research, Cornell University, January 1975.

[Hoffer and Severance, 1975] H. A. Hoffer and D. G. Severance. The Use of Cluster Analysis in Physical Data Base Design. In *Proc. First Int. Conf. on Very Large Data Bases*, Framingham, Mass., September 1975, pp. 69–86.

[Hoffman, 1977] J. L. Hoffman. *Model Methods for Computer Security and Privacy*, Englewood Cliffs, N.J.: Prentice-Hall, 1977.

[Hsiao and Özsu, 1981] D. K. Hsiao and M. T. Özsu. *A Survey of Concurrency Control Mechanisms for Centralized and Distributed Databases.* Technical Report 81-1, Columbus, Ohio: Department of Computer and Information Science, Ohio State University, 1981.

[Hunt and Rosenkrantz, 1979] H. B. Hunt and D. J. Rosenkrantz. The Complexity of Testing Predicate Locks. In *Proc. ACM SIGMOD Int. Conf. on Management of Data*, Boston, May 1979, pp. 127–133.

[Ibaraki and Kameda, 1984] T. Ibaraki and T. Kameda. On the Optimal Nesting Order for Computing $N$-Relation Joins. *ACM Trans. Database Syst.* (September 1984), 9(3): 482–502.

[IEEE, 1985a] Institute of Electrical and Electronics Engineers. *ANSI/IEEE Standard 802.2 Logical Link Control*, New York: IEEE, 1985.

[IEEE, 1985b] Institute of Electrical and Electronics Engineers. *ANSI/IEEE Standard 802.3 CSMA/CD Bus Access Method*, New York: IEEE, 1985.

[IEEE, 1985c] Institute of Electrical and Electronics Engineers. *ANSI/IEEE Standard 802.2 Token–Passing Bus Access Method*, New York: IEEE, 1985.

[IEEE, 1985d] Institute of Electrical and Electronics Engineers. *ANSI/IEEE Standard 802.2 Token Ring Access Method*, New York: IEEE, 1985.

[Ioannidis, 1986] Y. E. Ioannidis. On the Computation of the Transitive Closure of Relational Operators. In *Proc. 12th Int. Conf. on Very Large Data Bases*, Kyoto, Japan, August 1986, pp. 403–411.

[Irani and Khabbaz, 1982] K. B. Irani and N. G. Khabbaz. A Methodology for the Design of Communication Networks and the Distribution of Data in Distributed Computer Systems. *IEEE Trans. Comput.* (May 1982), C-31(5): 419–434.

[Isloor and Marsland, 1980] S. S. Isloor and T. A. Marsland. The Deadlock Problem: An Overview. *Computer* (September 1980), 13(9): 58–78.

[ISO, 1983] International Standards Organization. *Information Processing Systems – Open Systems Interconnection – Basic Reference Model*. ISO 7498, 1983.

[Jacobs et al., 1978] I. M. Jacobs, R. Binder, and E. V. Hoversten. General Purpose Packet Satellite Networks. *Proc. IEEE* (1978), 6(11): 1448–1467.

[Jagadish et al., 1987] H. V. Jagadish, R. Agrawal, and L. Ness. A Study of Transitive Closure as a Recursion Mechanism. In *Proc. ACM SIGMOD Int. Conf. on Management of Data*, San Francisco, May 1987, pp. 331–344.

[Jajodia et al., 1983] S. Jajodia, P. A. Ng, and F. N. Springsteel. The Problem of Equivalence for Entity-Relationship Diagrams. *IEEE Trans. Software Eng.* (September 1983), SE-9(5): 617–629.

[Jarke and Koch, 1984] M. Jarke and J. Koch. Query Optimization in Database Systems. *ACM Comput. Surv.* (June 1984), 16(2): 111–152.

[Johnson and Malek, 1988] A. M. Johnson, Jr., and M. Malek. Survey of Software Tools for Evaluating Reliability, Availability and Serviceability. *ACM Comput. Surv.* (December 1988), 20(4): 227–269.

[Jones, 1979] A. K. Jones. The Object Model: A Conceptual Tool for Structuring Software. In *Operating Systems: An Advanced Course*, R. Bayer, R. M. Graham, G. Seegmüller (eds), New York: Springer-Verlag, 1979: 7–16.

[Jones and Rashid, 1986] M. B. Jones and R. F. Rashid. Mach and Matchmaker: Kernel and Language Support for Object-Oriented Distributed Systems. In *Proc. Int. Conf. on OOP-SLA*, Portland, Oreg., September 1986, pp. 67–77.

[Jones et al., 1979] A. K. Jones, R. J. Chandler, I. E. Durham, K. Schwans, and S. Vegdahl. STAROS: A Multi Processor Operating System for Implementing Task Forces. In *Proc. ACM Symp. on Operating System Principles*, 1979: pp. 117–129.

[Kaehler and Krasner, 1983] T. Kaehler and G. Krasner. LOOM: Large Object Oriented Memory for SmallTalk-80 Systems. In *SmallTalk-80: Bits of History, Words of Advice*, G. Krasner (ed.), Reading, Mass.: Addison-Wesley, 1983.

[Kambayashi et al., 1982] Y. Kambayashi, M. Yoshikawa, and S. Yajima. Query Processing for Distributed Databases Using Generalized Semi-joins. In *Proc. ACM SIGMOD Int. Conf. on Management of Data*, Orlando, Fla., June 1982, pp. 151–160.

[Kangassalo, 1983] H. Kangassalo. *On the Selection of the Approach for the Development of the Reference Model for DBMS Standards*. ISO/TC 97/SC 5/WG 5 Document N104, 1983.

[Keller, 1982] A. M. Keller. Update to Relational Databases through Views Involving Joins. In *Proc. 2nd Int. Conf. on Databases: Improving Usability and Responsiveness*, P. Scheuerman (ed.), Jerusalem, June 1982, pp. 363–384.

[Kerschberg, 1987] L. Kerschberg (ed.). *Proc. First Int. Conf. on Expert Database Systems*. Menlo Park, Calif., Benjamin-Cummings, 1987.

[Kerschberg et al., 1982] L. Kerschberg, P. D. Ting, and S. B. Yao. Query Optimization in Star Computer Networks. *ACM Trans. Database Syst.* (December 1982), 7(4): 678–711.

[Khoshafian and Copeland, 1986] S. Khoshafian and G. Copeland. Object Identity. In *Proc. Int. Conf. on OOPSLA*, Portland, Oreg., September 1986, pp. 406–416.

[Khoshafian and Valduriez, 1988] S. Khoshafian and P. Valduriez. Parallel Execution Strategies for Declustered Databases. In *Database and Knowledge Base Machines*, N. Kitswegawa and H. Tanaka (eds.), Norwell, Mass.: Kluwer Academic, 1988, pp. 458–471.

[Khoshafian and Valduriez, 1987] S. Khoshafian and P. Valduriez. Sharing Persistence and Object-Orientation: A Database Perspective. In *Int. Workshop on Database Programming Languages*, Roscoff, France, September 1987, pp. 181–205.

[Khoshafian et al., 1988a] S. Khoshafian, P. Valduriez, and G. Copeland. Parallel Query Processing of Complex Objects. In *Proc. 4th Int. Conf. on Data Engineering*, Los Angeles, February 1988, pp, 202–209.

[Khoshafian et al., 1988b] S. Khoshafian, M. J. Franklin, and M. J. Carey. *Storage Management for Persistent Complex Objects*. Technical Report ACA-ST-118-88. Austin, Tex.: Microelectronics and Computer Corporation, April 1988.

[Khoshafian et al., 1987] S. Khoshafian, H. Boral, G. Copeland, T. Jagodits, and P. Valduriez. A Query Processing Algorithm for the Decomposed Storage Model. In *Proc. 3rd Int. Conf. on Data Engineering*, Los Angeles, February 1987, pp. 636–643.

[Kim, 1989] W. Kim. A Model of Queries for Object-Oriented Databases. In *Proc. 15th Int. Conf. on Very Large Data Bases*, Amsterdam, August 1989, pp. 423–432.

[Kim, 1984] W. Kim. Highly Available Systems for Database Applications. *ACM Comput. Surv.* (March 1984), 16(1): 71–98.

[Kim and Lochovsky, 1989] W. Kim and F. H. Lochovsky (ed.). Object-Oriented Concepts, Databases, and Applications. Reading, Mass.: Addison-Wesley, 1989.

[Kim et al., 1985] W. Kim, D. S. Reiner, and D. S. Batory (eds.). *Query Processing in Database Systems*. New York: Springer-Verlag, 1985.

[Knapp, 1987] E. Knapp. Deadlock Detection in Distributed Databases. *ACM Comput. Surv.* (December 1987), 19(4): 303–328.

[Kohler, 1981] W. H. Kohler. A Survey of Techniques for Synchronization and Recovery in Decentralized Computer Systems. *ACM Comput. Surv.* (June 1981), 13(2): 149–183.

[Kollias and Hatzopoulos, 1981] J. G. Kollias and M. Hatzopoulos. Criteria to Aid in Solving the Problem of Allocating Copies of a File in a Computer Network. *Comput. J.* (1981) 24(1): 29–30.

[Koon and Özsu, 1986] T. M. Koon and M. T. Özsu. Performance Comparison of Resilient Concurrency Control Algorithms for Distributed Databases. In *Proc. 2nd Int. Conf. on Data Engineering*, Los Angeles, February 1986, pp. 565–573.

[Korth and Silberschatz, 1986] H. Korth and A. Silberschatz. *Database System Concepts*. New York: McGraw-Hill, 1986.

[Kowalski, 1979] R. Kowalski. *Logic for Problem Solving*. Amsterdam: North Holland, 1979.

[Krishnamurthy et al., 1986] R. Krishnamurthy, H. Boral, and C. Zaniolo. Optimization of Non-recursive Queries. In *Proc. 11th Int. Conf. on Very Large Data Bases*, Kyoto, Japan, August 1986, pp. 128–137.

[Kung and Papadimitriou, 1979] H. T. Kung and C. H. Papadimitriou. An Optimality Theory of Concurrency Control for Databases. In *Proc. ACM SIGMOD Int. Conf. on Management of Data*, Boston, May 1979, pp. 116–125.

[Kung and Robinson, 1981] H. T. Kung and J. T. Robinson. On Optimistic Methods for Concurrency Control. *ACM Trans. Database Syst.* (June 1981), 6(2): 213–226.

[Kuss, 1982] H. Kuss. On Totally Ordering Checkpoint in Distributed Data Bases. In *Proc. ACM SIGMOD Int. Conf. on Management of Data*, Orlando, Fla., June 1982, 174–174.

[LaChimia, 1984] J. LaChimia. Query Decomposition in a Distributed Database System Using Satellite Communications. In *Proc. 3rd Seminar on Distributed Data Sharing Systems*, Parma, Italy, 1984, pp. 105–118.

[Lacroix and Pirotte, 1977] M. Lacroix and A. Pirotte. Domain-Oriented Relational Languages. In *Proc. 3rd Int. Conf. on Very Large Data Bases*, Tokyo, October 1977, pp. 370–378.

[Lam and Yu, 1980] K. Lam and C. T. Yu. An Approximation Algorithm for a File Allocation Problem in a Hierarchical Distributed System. In *Proc. ACM SIGMOD Int. Conf. on Management of Data*, Santa Monica, Calif., May 1980, pp. 125–132.

[Lampson and Sturgis, 1976] B. Lampson and H. Sturgis. *Crash Recovery in Distributed Data Storage System*. Technical Report, Palo Alto, Calif.: Xerox Palo Alto Research Center, 1976.

[Landers and Rosenberg, 1982] T. Landers and R. L. Rosenberg. An Overview of MULTI-BASE. In *Distributed Data Bases*; H.-J. Schneider (ed.), Amsterdam: North-Holland, 1982, pp. 153–184.

[Lang et al., 1977] T. Lang, C. Wood, and E. B. Fernandez. Database Buffer Paging in Virtual Storage Systems. *ACM Trans. Database Syst.* (December 1977), 2(4): 339–351.

[Larson, 1983] J. L. Larson. Bridging the Gap between Network and Relational Database Management Systems. *Computer* (September 1983), 16(9): 82–92.

[Larson et al., 1989] J. L. Larson, S. B. Navathe, and R. Elmasri. A Theory of Attribute Equivalence in Databases with Applications to Schema Integration. *IEEE Trans. Software Eng.* (April 1989), SE-15(4): 449–463.

[Lau, 1988] C. Lau. *Object Management, Access Control and Scheduling in FLEX.* M.Sc. thesis, Edmonton, Alberta, Canada: Department of Computing Science, University of Alberta, 1988.

[Lazowska et al., 1981] E. F. Lazowska, H. M. Levy, G. T. Almes, M. J. Fisher, R. J. Fowler, and S. C. Vestal. The Architecture of the Eden System. In *Proc. ACM Symp. on Operating System Principles*, Pacific Grove, Calif., 1981, pp. 148–159.

[Leach et al., 1982] P. J. Leach, B. L. Stumpf, J. A. Hamilton, and P. H. Levine. UIDS As Internal Names in a Distributed File System. In *Proc. ACM Int. Symp. on Principles of Distributed Computing*, Ottawa, Ontario, Canada, August 1982, pp. 34–41.

[Lecluse et al., 1988] C. Lecluse, P. Richard, and F. Velez. $O_2$: An Object-Oriented Data Model. In *Proc. ACM SIGMOD Int. Conf. on Management of Data*, Chicago, June 1988, pp. 424–433.

[Leland and Roome, 1985] M. D. P. Leland and W. D. Roome. The Silicon Database Machine. In *Proc. 4th Int. Workshop on Database Machines*, Grand Bahama Island, March 1985, pp. 169–189.

[Leung and Lai, 1979] J. Y. Leung and E. K. Lai. On Minimum Cost Recovery From System Deadlock. *IEEE Trans. Comput.* (September 1979), 28(9): 671–677.

[Levin and Morgan, 1975] K. D. Levin and H. L. Morgan. Optimizing Distributed Data Bases: A Framework for Research. In *Proc. National Computer Conf.*, 1975, pp. 473–478.

[Levin et al., 1975] R. Levin, E. Cohen, W. Corwin, F. Pollack, and W. A. Wulf. Policy/Mechanism Separation in Hydra. In *Proc. ACM Symp. on Operating System Principles*, 1975, pp. 132–140.

[Li, 1987] V. O. K. Li. Performance Models of Timestamp-Ordering Concurrency Control Algorithms in Distributed Databases. *IEEE Trans. Comput.* (September 1987), C-36(9): 1041–1051.

[Lin, 1981] W. K. Lin. Performance Evaluation of Two Concurrency Control Mechanisms in a Distributed Database System. In *Proc. ACM SIGMOD Int. Conf. on Management of Data*, Ann Arbor, Mich., April 1981, pp. 84–92.

[Lin and Nolte, 1983] W. K. Lin and J. Nolte. Basic Timestamp, Multiple Version Timestamp, and Two-Phase Locking. In *Proc. 9th Int. Conf. on Very Large Data Bases*, Florence, Italy, October–November 1983, pp. 109–119.

[Lin and Nolte, 1982] W. K. Lin and J. Nolte. Performance of Two Phase Locking. In *Proc. 6th Berkeley Workshop on Distributed Data Management and Computer Networks*, Berkeley, Calif., February 1982, pp. 131–160.

[Lindsay, 1979] B. Lindsay. *Notes on Distributed Databases.* Technical Report RJ 2517, San Jose, Calif.: IBM San Jose Research Laboratory, 1979.

[Liskov, 1988] B. Liskov. Distributed Programming in Argus. *Commun. ACM* (March 1988), 31(3): 300–312.

[Lister, 1984] A. M. Lister. *Fundamentals of Operating Systems* (3rd edition). New York: Springer-Verlag, 1984.

[Litwin, 1988] W. Litwin. From Database Systems to Multidatabase Systems: Why and How. In *Proc. British National Conference on Databases (BNCOD 6)*, W. A. Gray (ed), Cambridge: Cambridge University Press, 1988, pp. 161–188.

[Litwin and Abdellatif, 1987] W. Litwin and A. Abdellatif. An Overview of the Multidatabase Manipulation Language – MDL. *Proc. IEEE.* (May 1987), 75(5): 621–631.

[Litwin and Abdellatif, 1986] W. Litwin and A. Abdellatif. Multidatabase Interoperability. *Computer* (December 1986), 19(12): 10–18.

[Litwin et al., 1982] W. Litwin, J. Baudenant, C. Esculier, A. Ferrier, A. M. Glorieux, J. La Chimia, K. Kabbaj, C. Moulinoux, P. Rolin, and C. Stangret. SIRIUS Systems for Distributed Data Management. In *Distributed Data Bases*, H.-J. Schneider (ed.), Amsterdam: North-Holland, 1982, pp. 311–366.

[Livny et al., 1987] M. Livny, S. Khoshafian and H. Boral. Multi-disk Management. In *Proc. ACM SIGMETRICS Conf. on Measurement and Modeling of Computer Systems*, Banff, Alberta, Canada, 1987, pp. 69–77.

[Lochovsky, 1985] F. H. Lochovsky (ed.). Special Issue on Object-Oriented Database Systems. *IEEE Q. Bull. Database Eng.* (December 1985), 8(4).

[Locke, 1982] P. W. Locke. A Guide to DBMS Standardization Activities. *Comput. & Stand.* (1982), 1: 169–187.

[Lohman and Mackert, 1986] G. M. Lohman and L. F. Mackert. R* Optimizer Validation and Performance Evaluation for Distributed Queries. In *Proc. 11th Int. Conf. on Very Large Data Bases*, Kyoto, Japan, August 1986, pp. 149–159.

[Lohman et al., 1985] G. M. Lohman, C. Mohan, L. Haas, D. J. Daniels, B. Lindsay, P. Selinger, and P. Wilms. Query Processing in R*. In [Kim et al., 1985], pp. 31–47.

[Longbottom, 1980] R. Longbottom. *Computer System Reliability*. Chichester, West Sussex, England: Wiley, 1980.

[Lorie and Plouffe, 1983] R. A. Lorie and W. Plouffe. Complex Objects and Their Use in Design Transactions. In *Proc. IEEE Databases for Engineering Design Applications*, San Jose, Calif., May 1983, pp. 115–121.

[Lorin, 1980] H. Lorin. *Aspects of Distributed Computer Systems*. New York: Wiley, 1980.

[Lu and Carey, 1985] H. Lu and M. J. Carey. Some Experimental Results on Distributed Join Algorithms in a Local Network. In *Proc. 10th Int. Conf. on Very Large Data Bases*, Stockholm, August 1985, pp. 292–304.

[Lu et al., 1987] H. Lu, K. Mikkilineni, and J. P. Richardson. Design and Analysis of Algorithms to Compute the Transitive Closure of a Database Relation. In *Proc. 3rd Int. Conf. on Data Eng.*, Los Angeles, Calif., February 1987, pp. 112–119.

[Lynch, 1983a] N. Lynch. Concurrency Control for Resilient Nested Transactions. In *Proc. 2nd ACM SIGACT–SIGMOD Symp. on Principles of Database Systems*, Atlanta, Ga., March 1983, pp. 166–181.

[Lynch, 1983b] N. Lynch. Multilevel Atomicity: A New Correctness Criterion for Database Concurrency Control. *ACM Trans. Database Syst.* (December 1983), 8(4): 484–502.

[Lynch and Merritt, 1986] N. Lynch and M. Merritt. *Introduction to the Theory of Nested Transactions*. Technical Report MIT/LCS/TR-367, Cambridge, Mass.: Massachusetts Institute of Technology, July 1986.

[Mackert and Lohman, 1986] L. F. Mackert and G. M. Lohman. R* Optimizer Validation and Performance Evaluation for Local Queries. In *Proc. ACM SIGMOD Int. Conf. on Management of Data*, Washington, D.C., May 1986, pp. 84–95.

[Maekawa et al., 1987] M. Maekawa, A. E. Oldehoeft and R. R. Oldehoeft. *Operating Systems: Advanced Concepts*. Menlo Park, Calif.: Benjamin-Cummings, 1987.

[Mahmoud and Riordon, 1976] S. A. Mahmoud and J. S. Riordon. Optimal Allocation of Resources in Distributed Information Networks. *ACM Trans. Database Syst.* (March 1976), 1(1): 66–78.

[Maier and Stein, 1986] D. Maier and J. Stein. Indexing in an Object-Oriented DBMS. In *Proc. Int. Workshop on Object-Oriented Database Systems*, Pacific Grove, Calif., September 1986, pp. 171–182.

[Maier and Warren, 1988] D. Maier and D. S. Warren. *Computing with Logic: Logic Programming with Prolog.* Menlo Park, Calif: Benjamin–Cummings, 1988.

[Manna, 1974] L. Manna. *Mathematical Theory of Computation.* New York: McGraw-Hill, 1974.

[Manola, 1989] F. Manola. Applications of Object-Oriented Database Technology in Knowledge-Based Integrated Information Systems. In *Notes for CRAI School on Recent Techniques for Integrating Heterogeneous Databases*, Venice: Venezia University, April 1989.

[Martin, 1985] J. Martin. *Fourth Generation Languages.* Englewood Cliffs, N.J.: Prentice-Hall, 1985.

[Martin and Chapman, 1989] J. Martin and K. K. Chapman. *Local Area Networks: Architectures and Implementations.* Englewood Cliffs, N.J.: Prentice-Hall, 1989.

[McConnel and Siewiorek, 1982] S. McConnel and D. P. Siewiorek. Evaluation Criteria. In [Siewiorek and Swarz, 1982], pp. 201–302.

[McCormick et al., 1972] W. T. McCormick, P. J. Schweitzer, and T. W. White. Problem Decomposition and Data Reorganization by a Clustering Technique. *Oper. Res.* (1972), 20(5): 993–1009.

[McKay and Shapiro, 1981] D. McKay and S. Shapiro. Using Active Connection Graphs for Reasoning with Recursive Rules. In *Proc. 7th Int. Joint Conf. on Artificial Intelligence*, Vancouver, British Columbia, Canada, 1981, pp. 368–374.

[Menasce and Muntz, 1979] D. A. Menasce and R. R. Muntz. Locking and Deadlock Detection in Distributed Databases. *IEEE Trans. Software Eng.* (May 1979), SE-5(3): 195–202.

[Menasce and Nakanishi, 1982a] D. A. Menasce and T. Nakanishi. Optimistic versus Pessimistic Concurrency Control Mechanisms in Database Management Systems. *Inf. Syst.* (1982), 7(1): 13–27.

[Menasce and Nakanishi, 1982b] D. A. Menasce and T. Nakanishi. Performance Evaluation of a Two-Phase Commit Based Protocol for DDBS. In *Proc. First ACM SIGACT–SIGMOD Symp. on Principles of Database Systems*, Los Angeles, Calif., 1982, pp. 247–255.

[Merrett and Rallis, 1985] T. H. Merrett and N. Rallis. An Analytic Evaluation of Concurrency Control Algorithms. In *Proc. CIPS (Canadian Information Processing Society) Congress '85*, Montreal, Quebec, Canada, June 1985, pp. 435–439.

[Minoura and Wiederhold, 1982] T. Minoura and G. Wiederhold. Resilient Extended True-Copy Token Scheme for a Distributed Database System. *IEEE Trans. Software Eng.* (May 1982), SE-8(3): 173–189.

[Mohan, 1979] C. Mohan. *Data Base Design in the Distributed Environment.* Working Paper WP-7902, Austin, Tex.: Department of Computer Sciences, University of Texas at Austin, May 1979.

[Mohan and Lindsay, 1983] C. Mohan and B. Lindsay. Efficient Commit Protocols for the Tree of Processes Model of Distributed Transactions. In *Proc. 2nd ACM SIGACT–SIGMOD Symp. on Principles of Distributed Computing*, 1983, pp. 76–88.

[Mohan and Yeh, 1978] C. Mohan and R. T. Yeh. Distributed Data Base Systems: A Framework for Data Base Design. In *Distributed Data Bases, Infotech State-of-the-Art Report*, London: Infotech, 1978.

[Mohan et al., 1989] C. Mohan, D. Haderle, B. Lindsay, H. Pirahesh and P. M. Schwarz. *ARIES: A Transaction Recovery Method Supporting Fine-Granularity Locking and Partial Rollbacks Using Write-Ahead Logging*. Research Report RJ 6649, San Jose, Calif.: IBM Almaden Research Center, January 1989.

[Mohan et al., 1986] C. Mohan, B. Lindsay, and R. Obermarck. Transaction Management in the R* Distributed Database Management System. *ACM Trans. Database Syst.* (December 1986), 11(4): 378–396.

[Morgan and Levin, 1977] H. L. Morgan and K. D. Levin. Optimal Program and Data Location in Computer Networks. *Commun. ACM* (May 1977), 20(5): 315–322.

[Moss, 1985] E. Moss. *Nested Transactions*. Cambridge, Mass.: MIT Press, 1985.

[Motro, 1987] A. Motro. Superviews: Virtual Integration of Multiple Databases. *IEEE Trans. Software Eng.* (July 1987), SE-13(7): 785–798.

[Motro and Buneman, 1981] A. Motro and P. Buneman. Constructing Superviews. *ACM SIGMOD Int. Conf. on Management of Data*, Ann Arbor, Mich., April 1981, pp. 56–64.

[Mourad and Andres, 1985] S. Mourad and D. Andres. The Reliability of the IBM/XA Operating System. In *Proc. 15th Annual Int. Symp. on Fault-Tolerant Computing Systems*, Ann Arbor, Mich., 1985, pp. 93–98.

[Mullender and Tanenbaum, 1984] S. J. Mullender and A. S. Tanenbaum. Protection and Resource Control in Distributed Operating Systems. *Comput. Networks* (1984), 8: 421–432.

[Muro et al., 1985] S. Muro, T. Ibaraki, H. Miyajima and T. Hasegawa. Evaluation of File Redundancy in Distributed Database Systems. *IEEE Trans. Software Eng.* (February 1985), SE-11(2): 199–205.

[Muro et al., 1983] S. Muro, T. Ibaraki, H. Miyajima, and T. Hasegawa. File Redundancy Issues in Distributed Database Systems. In *Proc. 9th Int. Conf. on Very Large Data Bases*, Florence, Italy, October-November 1983, pp. 275–277.

[Myers, 1976] G. J. Myers. *Software Reliability: Principles and Practices*. New York: Wiley, 1976.

[Navathe et al., 1984] S. B. Navathe, S. Ceri, G. Wiederhold, and J. Dou. Vertical Partitioning of Algorithms for Database Design. *ACM Trans. Database Syst.* (December 1984), 9(4): 680–710.

[NBS, 1977] U. S. Department of Commerce/National Bureau of Standards. *Data Encryption Standard*. Federal Information Processing Standards Publication 46, January 1977.

[Neches, 1985] P. M. Neches. The Anatomy of a Data Base Computer System. In *Digest of Papers — COMPCON*, San Francisco, February 1985, pp. 252–254.

[Nelson, 1981] B. J. Nelson. *Remote Procedure Calls*. Ph.D. dissertation, Pittsburgh, Pa.: Department of Computing Science, Carnegie Mellon University, 1981.

[Newton, 1979] G. Newton. Deadlock Prevention, Detection and Resolution: An Annotated Bibliography. *ACM Oper. Syst. Rev.* (April 1979), 13(2): 33–44.

[Ng, 1988] P. Ng. A Commit Protocol for Checkpointing Transactions. In *Proc. 7th. Symp. on Reliable Distributed Systems*, Columbus, Ohio, October 1988, pp. 22–31.

[Niamir, 1978] B. Niamir. *Attribute Partitioning in a Self-Adaptive Relational Database System*. Technical Report 192, Cambridge, Mass.: Laboratory for Computer Science, Massachusetts Institute of Technology, 1978.

[Nicolas, 1982] J. M. Nicolas. Logic for Improving Integrity Checking in Relational Data Bases. *Acta Inf.* (1982), 18: 227–253.

[Obermarck, 1982] R. Obermarck. Deadlock Detection for All Resource Classes. *ACM Trans. Database Syst.* (June 1982), 7(2): 187–208.

[Osborn, 1988] S. L. Osborn. Identity, Equality and Query Optimization. In *Advances in Object-Oriented Database Systems*, K. Dittrich (ed.), New York: Springer-Verlag, 1988, pp. 346–351.

[Osborn and Heaven, 1986] S. L. Osborn and T. E. Heaven. The Design of a Relational Database System with Abstract Data Types for Domains. *ACM Trans. Database Syst.* (September 1986), 11(3): 357–373.

[Osterhout, 1982] J. K. Osterhout. Scheduling Techniques for Concurrent Systems. In *Proc. 3rd Int. Conf. on Distributed Computing Systems*, Miami, Fla., 1982, pp. 22–30.

[Ozkarahan, 1986] E. A. Ozkarahan. *Database Machines and Database Management*. Englewood Cliffs, N. J.: Prentice-Hall, 1986.

[Özsoyoglu and Zhou, 1987] Z. M. Özsoyoglu and N. Zhou. Distributed Query Processing in Broadcasting Local Area Networks. In *Proc. 20th Hawaii Int. Conf. on System Sciences*, Kailua-Kona, Hawaii, January 1987, pp. 419–429.

[Özsoyoglu et al., 1987] G. Özsoyoglu, M. Z. Özsoyoglu, and V. Matos. Extending Relational Algebra and Relational Calculus with Set-Valued Attributes and Aggregate Functions. *ACM Trans. Database Syst.* (December 1987), 12(4): 566–592.

[Özsu, 1989] M. T. Özsu. Architectural Models for Distributed Database Operating Systems. In *Computing and Information*, R. Janicki and W. W. Koczkodaj (eds.), Amsterdam: North-Holland, 1989, pp. 343–349.

[Özsu, 1988] M. T. Özsu. *Distributed Database Operating Systems*. Technical Report TR88-2, Edmonton, Alberta, Canada: Department of Computing Science, University of Alberta, February 1988.

[Özsu, 1985a] M. T. Özsu. Performance Comparison of Distributed vs Centralized Locking Algorithms in Distributed Database Systems. In *Proc. 5th Int. Conf. on Distributed Computing Systems*, Denver, Colo., May 1985, pp. 254–261.

[Özsu, 1985b] M. T. Özsu. Modeling and Analysis of Distributed Concurrency Control Algorithms Using an Extended Petri Net Formalism. *IEEE Trans. Software Eng.* (October 1985), SE-11(10): 1225–1240.

[Özsu and Barker, 1990] M. T. Özsu and K. Barker. Architectural Classification and Transaction Execution Models of Multidatabase Systems. In *Proc. Int. Conf. on Computing and Information*, Niagara Falls, Canada, May 1990.

[Özsu and Koon, 1987] M. T. Özsu and T. M. Koon. Evaluation of the Reliability Mechanisms in Distributed Database Systems. In *Proc. CIPS (Canadian Information Processing Society) Edmonton '87 Conf.*, Edmonton, Alberta, Canada, 1987, pp. 246–255.

[Özsu et al., 1988] M. T. Özsu, C. Lau, Y. Li and M. F. Teo. *The Architecture of FLEX: A Distributed Database Operating System Testbed*. Technical Report TR88-4, Edmonton, Alberta, Canada: Department of Computing Science, University of Alberta, April 1988.

[Page and Popek, 1985] T. W. Page and G. J. Popek. Distributed Data Management in Local Area Networks. In *Proc. ACM SIGACT–SIGMOD Symp. on Principles of Database Systems*, Portland, Oreg., March 1985, pp. 135–142.

[Page et al., 1985] T. W. Page Jr, M. J. Weinstein, and G. J. Popek. Genesis: A Distributed Database Operating System. In *Proc. ACM SIGMOD Int. Conf. on Management of Data*, Austin, Tex., May 1985, pp. 374–387.

[Papadimitriou, 1986] C. H. Papadimitriou. *The Theory of Concurrency Control*. Rockville, Md.: Computer Science Press, 1986.

[Papadimitriou, 1979] C. H. Papadimitriou. Serializability of Concurrent Database Updates. *J. ACM* (October 1979), 26(4): 631–653.

[Papadimitriou and Kanellakis, 1984] C. Papadimitriou and P. Kanellakis. On Concurrency Control by Multiple Versions. *ACM Trans. Database Syst.* (December 1984), 9(1): 89–99.

[Paul et al., 1987] M.-B. Paul, H.-J. Schek, M. H. Scholl, G. Weikum, and U. Deppisch. Architecture and Implementation of the Darmstadt Database Kernal System. In *Proc. ACM SIGMOD Int. Conf. on Management of Data*, San Francisco, Calif., May 1987, pp. 196–207.

[Pease et al., 1980] M. Pease, R. Shostak, and L. Lamport. Reaching Agreement in the Presence of Faults. *J. ACM* (April 1980), 27(2): 228–234.

[Peterson and Silberschatz, 1985] J. L. Peterson and A. Silberschatz. *Operating System Concepts* (2nd edition). Reading, Mass.: Addison-Wesley, 1985.

[Piatetsky and Connell, 1984] G. Piatetsky-Shapiro and C. Connell. Accurate Estimation of the Number of Tuples Satisfying a Condition. In *Proc. ACM SIGMOD Int. Conf. on Management of Data*, Boston, Mass., June 1984, pp. 256–276.

[Popek and Walker, 1985] G. Popek and B. J. Walker. *The LOCUS Distributed System Architecture*. Cambridge, Mass.: MIT Press, 1985.

[Potier and LeBlanc, 1980] D. Potier and P. LeBlanc. Analysis of Locking Policies in Database Management Systems. *Commun. ACM* (October 1980), 23(10): 584–593.

[Pradhan, 1986] D. K. Pradhan (ed.) *Fault-Tolerant Computing: Theory and Techniques,* Volume 2. Englewood Cliffs, N.J.: Prentice-Hall, 1986.

[Pu, 1988] C. Pu. Superdatabases for Composition of Heterogeneous Databases. In *Proc. 4th Int. Conf. on Data Engineering*, Los Angeles, Calif, February 1988, pp. 548–555.

[Quinn and Deo, 1984] M. J. Quinn and N. Deo. Parallel Graph Algorithms. *ACM Comput. Surv.* (September 1984), 16(3): 319–348.

[Rahimi, 1987] S. Rahimi. *Reference Architecture for Distributed Database Management Systems*. Tutorial Notes, 3rd Int. Conf. on Data Engineering, 1987.

[Ramamoorthy and Wah, 1983] C. V. Ramamoorthy and B. W. Wah. The Isomorphism of Simple File Allocation. *IEEE Trans. Comput.* (March 1983), C-23(3): 221–231.

[Ramanathan and Shin, 1988] P. Ramanathan and K. G. Shin. Checkpointing and Rollback Recovery in a Distributed System Using Common Time Base. In *Proc. 7th Symp. on Reliable Distributed Systems*, Columbus, Ohio, October 1988, pp. 13–21.

[Randell et al., 1978] B. Randell, P. A. Lee and P. C. Treleaven. Reliability Issues in Computing System Design. *ACM Comput. Surv.* (June 1978), 10(2): 123–165.

[Redell et al., 1980] D. D. Redell, Y. K. Dalal, T. R. Horsley, H. C. Lauer, W. C. Lynch, P. R. McJones, H. G. Murray, and S. C. Purcell. Pilot: An Operating System for a Personal Computer. *Commun. ACM* (February 1980), 24(2): 81–92.

[Rivest et al., 1978] R. L. Rivest, A. Shamir, and L. Adelman. A Method for Obtaining Digital Signatures and Public-Key Cryptosystems. *Commun. ACM* (February 1978), 21(2): 120–126.

[Roesler and Burkhard, 1988] M. Roesler and W. A. Burkhard. Semantic Lock Models in Object-Oriented Distributed Systems and Deadlock Resolution. In *Proc. ACM SIGMOD Int. Conf. on Management of Data*, Chicago, Ill., June 1988, pp. 361–370.

[Rosenkrantz and Hunt, 1980] D. J. Rosenkrantz and H. B. Hunt. Processing Conjunctive Predicates and Queries. In *Proc. 6th Int. Conf. on Very Large Data Bases*, Montreal, Quebec, Canada, October 1980, pp. 64–72.

[Rosenkrantz et al., 1978] D. J. Rosenkrantz, R. E. Stearns, and P. M. Lewis. System Level Concurrency Control for Distributed Database Systems. *ACM Trans. Database Syst.* (June 1978), 3(2): 178–198.

[Ross, 1986] R. E. Ross. FDDI – A Tutorial. *IEEE Commun.* (1986), 24(5): 10–17.

[Roth et al., 1967] J. P. Roth, W. G. Bouricius, E. C. Carter, and P. R. Schneider. *Phase II of an Architectural Study for a Self-Repairing Computer*. Report SAMSO-TR-67-106, El Segundo, Calif.: U. S. Air Force Space and Missile Division, 1967. Cited in [Siewiorek and Swarz, 1982].

[Rothermel and Mohan, 1989] K. Rothermel and C. Mohan. ARIES/NT: A Recovery Method Based on Write-Ahead Logging for Nested Transactions. In *Proc. 15th Int. Conf. on Very Large Data Bases,* Amsterdam, August, 1989, pp. 337–346.

[Rothnie and Goodman, 1977] J. B. Rothnie and N. Goodman. A Survey of Research and Development in Distributed Database Management. In *Proc. 3rd Int. Conf. on Very Large Data Bases*, Tokyo, Japan, 1977, pp. 48–62.

[Rusinkiewicz and Czejdo, 1987] M. Rusinkiewicz and B. Czejdo. An Approach to Query Processing in Federated Database Systems. In *Proc. 20th Hawaii Int. Conf. on System Sciences*, Kailua-Kona, Hawaii: January 1987, pp. 430–440.

[Rusinkiewicz and Czejdo, 1985] M. Rusinkiewicz and B. Czejdo. Query Transformation in Heterogeneous Distributed Database Systems. In *Proc. 5th Int. Conf. on Distributed Computing Systems*, Denver, Colo., May 1985, pp. 300–307.

[Rusinkiewicz et al., 1989] M. Rusinkiewicz, R. Elmasri, B. Czejdo, D. Georgakopulos, G. Karabatis, A. Jamoussi, K. Loa, and Y. Li. Query Processing in a Heterogeneous Multidatabase Environment. In *Proc. First Annual Symp. Parallel and Distributed Computing*, Dallas, Tex., 1989, pp. 162–169.

[Rusinkiewicz et al., 1988] M. Rusinkiewicz, R. Elmasri, B. Czejdo, D. Georgakopulos, G. Karabatis, A. Jamoussi, K. Loa, Y. Li, J. Gilbert, and R. Musgrove. *Query Processing in OMNI-BASE – A Loosely Coupled Multi-Database System*. Technical Report UH-CS-88-05, Houston, Tex.: Department of Computer Science, University of Houston, February 1988.

[Sacca and Wiederhold, 1985] D. Sacca and G. Wiederhold. Database Partitioning in a Cluster of Processors. *ACM Trans. Database Syst.* (October 1985), 10(1): 29–56.

[Sacco and Schkolnick, 1986] G. M. Sacco and M. Schkolnick. Buffer Management in Relational Database Systems. *ACM Trans. Database Syst.* (December 1986), 11(4): 473–498.

[Sacco and Yao, 1982] M. S. Sacco and S. B. Yao. Query Optimization in Distributed Data Base Systems. In *Advances in Computers*, Volume 21, M.C. Yovits (ed.), New York: Academic Press, 1982, pp. 225–273.

[Saltzer, 1979] J. H. Saltzer. Naming and Binding of Objects. In *Operating Systems: An Advanced Course*, R. Bayer, R. M. Graham, and G. Seegmüller (eds.), New York: Springer-Verlag, 1979, pp. 99–208.

[Schek and Scholl, 1986] H.-J. Schek and M. H. Scholl. The Relational Model with Relation-Valued Attributes. *Inf. Syst.* (1986), 11(2): 137–148.

[Schlageter, 1978] G. Schlageter. Process Synchronization in Database Systems. *ACM Trans. Database Syst.* (September 1978), 3(3): 248–271.

[Schlageter and Dadam, 1980] G. Schlageter and P. Dadam. Reconstruction of Consistent Global States in Distributed Databases. In *Distributed Data Bases*, C. Delobel and W. Litwin (eds.), Amsterdam: North-Holland, 1980, pp. 191–200.

[Schlichting and Schneider, 1983] R. D. Schlichting and F. B. Schneider. Fail-Stop Processors: An Approach to Designing Fault-Tolerant Computing Systems. *ACM Trans. Comp. Syst.* (August 1983), 1(3): 222–238.

[Schmidt, 1977] J. W. Schmidt. Some High Level Language Constructs for Data of Type Relation. *ACM Trans. Database Syst.* (September 1977), 2(3): 247–261.

[Schneiderman and Thomas, 1982] B. Schneiderman and G. Thomas. Automatic Database System Conversion: Schema Revision, Data Translation and Source-to-Source Program Transformation. In *Proc. National Computer Conf.*, 1982, pp. 579–587.

[Scholl and Schek, 1990] M. H. Scholl and H.-J. Schek. A Relational Object Model. In *Proc. 3rd Int. Conf. on Database Theory*, S. Abiteboul and P.C. Kanellakis (eds.), Berlin: Springer-Verlag, 1990, pp. 89–105.

[Schreiber, 1977] F. Schreiber. A Framework for Distributed Database Systems. In *Proc. Int. Computing Symposium*, 1977, pp. 475–482.

[Schwarz and Spector, 1984] P. M. Schwarz and A. Z. Spector. Synchronizing Shared Abstract Types. *ACM Trans. Comp. Syst.* (August 1984), 2(3): 223–250.

[Selinger and Adiba, 1980] P. G. Selinger and M. Adiba. Access Path Selection in Distributed Data Base Management Systems. In *Proc. First Int. Conf. on Data Bases*, Aberdeen, Scotland, 1980, pp. 204–215.

[Selinger et al., 1979] P. G. Selinger, M. M. Astrahan, D. D. Chamberlin, R. A. Lorie and T. G. Price. Access Path Selection in a Relational Database Management System. In *Proc. ACM SIGMOD Int. Conf. on Management of Data*, Boston, Mass., May 1979, pp. 23–34.

[Sequent, 1986] Sequent Computers. *Balance Guide to Parallel Programming*. Sequent, June 1986.

[Sevcik, 1983] K. C. Sevcik. Comparison of Concurrency Control Methods Using Analytic Models. In *Information Processing '83*, 1983, pp. 847–858.

[Severence and Lohman, 1976] D. G. Severence and G. M. Lohman. Differential Files: Their Application to the Maintenance of Large Databases. *ACM Trans. Database Syst.* (September 1976), 1(3): 256–261.

[Shaw and Zdonik, 1989] G. Shaw and S. Zdonik. An Object-Oriented Query Algebra. *IEEE Quart. Bull. Database Eng.* (September 1989), 12(3): 29–36.

[Sherman, 1985] K. Sherman. *Data Communications: A User's Guide* (2nd edition). Reston, Va.: Reston Publishing Co. , 1986.

[Sherman and Brice, 1976] S. W. Sherman and S. S. Brice. Performance of a Database Manager in a Virtual Memory System. *ACM Trans. Database Syst.* (December 1976), 1(4): 317–343.

[Sheth, 1989] A. Sheth. *Heterogeneous Distributed Databases: Issues in Integration.* Tutorial Notes, 5th Int. Conf. on Data Engineering, 1989. Also presented at the 3rd Int. Conf. on Data Engineering, 1987, and at ACM SIGMOD Int. Conf. on Management of Data, 1989.

[Sheth, 1987] A. Sheth. Building Federated Database Systems. *IEEE Dist. Comput. Tech. Commun. Newsl.* (November 1988), 10(2): 50–58.

[Sheth and Larson, 1990] A. Sheth and J. L. Larson. Federated Databases: Architectures and Integration. *ACM Comput. Surv.*, Special Issue on Heterogeneous Databases, A. El-magarmid and C. Pu (eds.), 1990.

[Sheth et al., 1988a] A. Sheth, J. L. Larson, A. Cornellio, and S. B. Navathe. A Tool for Integrating Conceptual Schemas and User Views. In *Proc. 4th Int. Conf. on Data Engineering*, Los Angeles, Calif., February 1988, pp. 176–183.

[Sheth et al., 1988b] A. Sheth, J. L. Larson, E. Watkins. TAILOR, A Tool for Updating Views. In *Advances in Database Technology – EDBT '88*, J. W. Schmidt, S. Ceri, and M. Missikoff (eds.), Berlin: Springer-Verlag, 1988, pp. 190–213.

[Shrivastava, 1985] S. K. Shrivastava (ed.). *Reliable Computer Systems*. Berlin: Springer-Verlag, 1985.

[Siegel, 1987] M. D. Siegel. *A Survey of Heterogeneous Database Systems*. BUCS Technical Report 87-011, Boston, Mass.: Boston University, October 1987.

[Siewiorek and Swarz, 1982] D. P. Siewiorek and R. S. Swarz. *The Theory and Practice of Reliable System Design*. Bedford, Mass.: Digital Press, 1982.

[Simon and Valduriez, 1987] E. Simon and P. Valduriez. *Design and Analysis of a Relational Integrity Subsystem*. Technical Report DB-015-87, Austin, Tex.: Microelectronics and Computer Corporation, January 1987.

[Simon and Valduriez, 1986] E. Simon and P. Valduriez. Integrity Control in Distributed Database Systems. In *Proc. 19th Hawaii Int. Conf. on System Sciences*, Honolulu, January 1986, pp. 622–632.

[Simon and Valduriez, 1984] E. Simon and P. Valduriez. Design and Implementation of an Extendible Integrity Subsystem. In *Proc. ACM SIGMOD Int. Conf. on Management of Data*, Boston, Mass., June 1984, pp. 9–17.

[Sinha et al., 1985] M. K. Sinha, P. D. Nanadikar and S. L. Mehndiratta. Timestamp Based Certification Schemes for Transactions in Distributed Database Systems. In *Proc. ACM SIGMOD Int. Conf. on Management of Data*, Austin, Tex., May 1985, pp. 402–411.

[Skeen, 1982a] D. Skeen. A Quorum-Based Commit Protocol. In *Proc. 6th Berkeley Workshop on Distributed Data Management and Computer Networks*, Berkeley, Calif., February 1982, pp. 69–80.

[Skeen, 1982b] D. Skeen. *Crash Recovery in a Distributed Database Management System*. Ph.D. thesis, Berkeley, Calif.: Department of Electrical Engineering and Computer Science, University of California at Berkeley, 1982.

[Skeen, 1981] D. Skeen. Nonblocking Commit Protocols. *Proc. ACM SIGMOD Int. Conf. on Management of Data*, Ann Arbor, Mich., April–May 1981, pp. 133–142.

[Skeen and Stonebraker, 1983] D. Skeen and M. Stonebraker. A Formal Model of Crash Recovery in a Distributed System. *IEEE Trans. Software Eng.* (May 1983), SE-9(3): 219–228.

[Skeen and Wright, 1984] D. Skeen and D. Wright. Increasing Availability in Partitioned Networks. In *Proc. 3rd ACM SIGACT–SIGMOD Symp. on Principles of Database Systems*, Waterloo, Ontario, Canada, April 1984, pp. 290–299.

[Smith and Chang, 1975] J. M. Smith and P. Y. Chang. Optimizing the Performance of a Relational Algebra Database Interface. *Commun. ACM* (1975), 18(10): 568–579.

[Smith et al., 1981] J. M. Smith, P. A. Bernstein, U. Dayal, N. Goodman, T. Landers, K. Lin, and E. Wong. MULTIBASE: Integrating Heterogeneous Distributed Database Systems. In *Proc. National Computer Conf.*, May 1981, pp. 487–499.

[SPARC, 1975] ANSI/X3/SPARC Study Group on Data Base Management Systems. Interim Report. *ACM FDT Bull.* (1975), 7(2).

[Spector and Schwarz, 1983] A. Z. Spector and P. M. Schwarz. Transactions: A Construct for Reliable Distributed Computing. *ACM Oper. Syst. Rev.* (April 1983), 17(2): 18–35.

[Spector et al., 1987] A. Z. Spector, D. Thompson, R. Pausch, J. L. Eppinger, D. J. Duchamp, R. Draves, D. J. Daniels, and J. Bloch. *Camelot: A Distributed Transaction Facility for Mach and the Internet — An Interim Report*. Technical Report CMU-CS-87-129, Pittsburg, Pa.: Department of Computer Science, Carnegie Mellon University, June 1987.

[Spector et al., 1985] A. Z. Spector, J. Butcher, D. S. Daniels, D. J. Duchamp, J. L. Eppinger, C. E. Fineman, A. Heddaya, and P. M. Schwarz. Support for Distributed Transactions in the TABS Prototype. *IEEE Trans. Software Eng.* (June 1985), SE-11(6): 520–530.

[Stallings, 1988] W. Stallings. *Data and Computer Communications* (2nd edition). New York: Macmillan, 1988.

[Stallings, 1986] W. Stallings. A Totorial on the IEEE 802 Local Network Standard. In *Local Area and Multiple Access Networks*, R. L. Pickholtz (ed.), Rockville, Md.: Computer Science Press, 1986, pp. 1–30.

[Stallings, 1984] W. Stallings. *Local Networks: An Introduction*. New York: Macmillan, 1984.

[Stankovic, 1982] J. A. Stankovic. Software Communication Mechanisms: Procedure Calls versus Messages. *IEEE Comput.* (April 1982), 15(4): 19–25.

[Stearns et al., 1976] R. E. Stearns, P. M. Lewis, II and D. J. Rosenkrantz. Concurrency Controls for Database Systems. In *Proc. 17th Symp. on Foundations of Computer Science*, 1976, pp. 19–32.

[Steel, 1982] T. B. Steel, Jr. International Standardization and Distributed Data Bases. In *Distributed Data Bases*, H.-J. Schneider (ed.), Amsterdam: North-Holland, 1982, pp. 1–7.

[Stoll, 1963] R. R. Stoll. *Set Theory and Logic*. San Fransisco, Calif.: W.H. Freeman, 1963.

[Stonebraker, 1988] M. Stonebraker. *Readings in Database Systems*. San Mateo, Calif.: Morgan Kaufmann, 1988.

[Stonebraker, 1986] M. Stonebraker. The Case for Shared Nothing. *IEEE Q. Bull. Database Eng.* (March 1986), 9(1): 4–9.

[Stonebraker, 1984] M. Stonebraker. Virtual Memory Transaction Management. *ACM Oper. Syst. Rev.* (April 1984), 18(2): 8–16.

[Stonebraker, 1981] M. Stonebraker. Operating System Support for Database Management. *Commun. ACM* (July 1981), 24(7): 412–418.

[Stonebraker, 1975] M. Stonebraker. Implementation of Integrity Constraints and Views by Query Modification. In *Proc. ACM SIGMOD Int. Conf. on Management of Data*, San Jose, Calif., May 1975, pp. 65–78.

[Stonebraker and Neuhold, 1977] M. Stonebraker and E. Neuhold. A Distributed Database Version of INGRES. In *Proc. 2nd Berkeley Workshop on Distributed Data Management and Computer Networks*, Berkeley, Calif., May 1977, pp. 9–36.

[Stonebraker and Rowe, 1986] M. Stonebraker and L. A. Rowe. The Design of POSTGRES. In *Proc. ACM SIGMOD Int. Conf. on Management of Data*, Washington, D.C., May 1986, pp. 340–355.

[Stonebraker et al., 1988] M. Stonebraker, R. Katz, D. Patterson and J. Ousterhout. The Design of XPRS. In *Proc. 14th Int. Conf. on Very Large Data Bases*. Los Angeles, Calif., September 1988, pp. 318–330.

[Stonebraker et al., 1985] M. Stonebraker, D. DuBourdieux, and W. Edwards. Problems in Supporting Data Base Transactions in an Operating System Transaction Manager. *ACM Oper. Syst. Rev.* (January 1985), 19(1): 6–14.

[Stonebraker et al., 1983a] M. Stonebraker, J. Ranstrom, M. Murphy, M. Meyer, and E. Allman. Performance Enhancements to a Relational Database System. *ACM Trans. Database Syst.* (June 1983), 8(2): 167–185.

[Stonebraker et al., 1983b] M. Stonebraker, B. Rubenstein and A. Guttman. Application of Abstract Data Types and Abstract Indices to CAD Databases. In *Proc. Annual Meeting Database Week*, San Jose, Calif., May 1983, pp. 107–115. Also in M. Stonebraker (ed.). *The INGRES Papers: Anatomy of a Relational Database System*. Reading, Mass.: Addison-Wesley, 1986, pp. 317–333.

[Stonebraker et al., 1976] M. Stonebraker, P. Kreps, W. Wong, and G. Held. The Design and Implementation of INGRES. *ACM Trans. Database Syst.* (September 1976), 1(3): 198–222.

[Stratus, 1982] Stratus Computers. *Stratus/32 System Overview*. Natick, Mass: Stratus, 1982.

[Straube and Özsu, 1990a] D. D. Straube and M. T. Özsu. Queries and Query Processing in Object-Oriented Database Systems, *ACM Trans. on Inf. Syst.*, (October 1990), 8(4): 387–430.

[Straube and Özsu, 1990b] D. D. Straube and M. T. Özsu. *Access Plan Generation for an Object Algebra*. Technical Report TR90-20, Edmonton, Alberta, Canada: Department of Computing Science, University of Alberta, June 1990.

[Straube and Özsu, 1989] D. D. Straube and M. T. Özsu. *Query Transformation Rules for Object-Oriented Databases*. Technical Report TR89-23, Edmonton, Alberta, Canada: Department of Computing Science, University of Alberta, August 1989.

[Strong and Dolev, 1983] H. R. Strong and D. Dolev. Byzantine Agreement. In *Digest of Papers — COMPCON*, San Fransisco, Calif., March 1983, pp. 77–81.

[Stroustrup, 1986] B. Stroustrup. *The C++ Programming Language*. Reading, Mass.: Addison-Wesley, 1986.

[Su, 1988] S. Y. W. Su. *Database Computers: Principles, Architectures and Techniques*. New York: McGraw-Hill, 1988.

[Sugihara, 1987] K. Sugihara. Concurrency Control Based on Cycle Detection. In *Proc. 3rd Int. Conf. on Data Engineering*, Los Angeles, Calif., February 1987, pp. 267–274.

[Svobodova, 1986] L. Svobodova. Communication Support for Distributed Processing: Design and Implementation Issues. In *Networking in Open Systems*, G. Müller and R. P. Blanc (eds.), Berlin: Springer-Verlag, 1986, pp. 176–192.

[Tandem, 1988] The Tandem Performance Group. A Benchmark of NonStop SQL on the Debit Credit Transaction. In *Proc. ACM SIGMOD Int. Conf. on Management of Data*, Chicago, Ill., June 1988, pp. 337–341.

[Tandem, 1987] The Tandem Database Group. NonStop SQL – A Distributed High-Performance, High-Availability Implementation of SQL. In *Proc. Int. Workshop on High Performance Transaction Systems*, Asilomar, Calif., September 1987.

[Tanenbaum, 1988] A. S. Tanenbaum. *Computer Networks* (2nd edition). Englewood Cliffs, N.J.: Prentice-Hall, 1988.

[Tanenbaum, 1987] A. S. Tanenbaum. *Operating Systems: Design and Implementation*. Englewood Cliffs, N.J.: Prentice-Hall, 1987.

[Tanenbaum and Mullender, 1982] A. S. Tanenbaum and S. J. Mullender. Operating System Requirements for Distributed Data Base Systems. In *Distributed Data Bases*, H.-J. Schneider (ed.), Amsterdam: North-Holland, 1982, pp. 105–114.

[Tanenbaum and Mullender, 1981] A. S. Tanenbaum and S. J. Mullender. An Overview of the Amoeba Distributed Operating System. *ACM Oper. Syst. Rev.* (July 1981), 15(3): 51–64.

[Tanenbaum and van Renesse, 1985] A. S. Tanenbaum and R. van Renesse. Distributed Operating Systems. *ACM Comput. Surv.* (December 1985), 17(4): 419–470.

[Taylor, 1987] R. W. Taylor. Data Server Architectures: Experiences and Lessons. In *Proc. CIPS (Canadian Information Processing Society) Edmonton '87 Conf.*, Edmonton, Alberta, Canada, 1987, pp. 334–342.

[Taylor and Frank, 1976] R. W. Taylor and R. L. Frank. CODASYL Data-Base Management Systems. *ACM Comput. Surv.* (March 1976), 8(1): 67–103.

[Templeton et al., 1987] M. Templeton, D. Brill, S. K. Dao, E. Lund, P. Ward, A. L. P. Chen, and R. MacGregor. Mermaid – A Front-End to Distributed Heterogeneous Databases. *Proc. IEEE* (May 1987), 75(5): 695–708.

[Teo, 1989] M. F. Teo. *Experiments with Virtual Memory Implementation of Database Buffer Managers*. M.Sc. thesis, Edmonton, Alberta, Canada: Department of Computing Science, University of Alberta, 1989.

[Thomas, 1979] R. H. Thomas. A Majority Consensus Approach to Concurrency Control for Multiple Copy Databases. *ACM Trans. Database Syst.* (June 1979), 4(2): 180–209.

[Traiger, 1982] I. L. Traiger. Virtual Memory Management for Data Base Systems. *ACM Oper. Syst. Rev.* (October 1982), 16(4): 26–48.

[Traiger et al., 1982] I. L. Traiger, J. N. Gray, C. A. Galtieri, and B. G. Lindsay. Transactions and Recovery in Distributed Database Systems. *ACM Trans. Database Syst.* (September 1982), 7(3): 323–342.

[Tsichritzis and Klug, 1978] D. C. Tsichritzis and A. Klug. The ANSI/X3/SPARC DBMS Framework Report of the Study Group on Database Management Systems. *Inf. Syst.* (1978), 1: 173–191.

[Tsichritzis and Lochovsky, 1981] D. C. Tsichritzis and F. H. Lochovsky. *Data Models*. Englewood Cliffs, N.J.: Prentice-Hall, 1981.

[Tsichritzis and Lochovsky, 1977] D. C. Tsichritzis and F. H. Lochovsky. *Data Base Management Systems*. New York: Academic Press, 1977.

[Tsichritzis and Lochovsky, 1976] D. C. Tsichritzis and F. H. Lochovsky. Hierarchical Data-Base Management: A Survey. *ACM Comput. Surv.* (March 1976), 8(1): 105–123.

[Tsuchiya et al., 1986] M. Tsuchiya, M. P. Mariani, and J. D. Brom. Distributed Database Management Model and Validation. *IEEE Trans. Software Eng.* (April 1986), SE-12(4): 511–520.

[Tsur and Zaniolo, 1986] S. Tsur and C. Zaniolo. LDL: A Logic-Based Data Language. In *Proc. 12th Int. Conf. on Very Large Data Bases*, Kyoto, Japan, 1986, pp. 33–41.

[Tuel, 1976] W. G. Tuel, Jr. An Analysis of Buffer Paging in Virtual Storage Systems. *IBM J. Res. Dev.* (September 1976), 20(5): 518–520.

[Ullman, 1988] J. D. Ullman. *Principles of Database and Knowledge Base Systems*, Volume 1. Rockville, Md.: Computer Science Press, 1988.

[Ullman, 1987] J. D. Ullman. Database Theory: Past and Future. In *Proc. 6th ACM SIGACT–SIGMOD–SIGART Int. Symp. on Principles of Database Systems*, San Diego, Calif., March 1987, pp. 1–10.

[Ullman, 1985] J. D. Ullman. Implementation of Logical Query Languages for Databases. *ACM Trans. Database Syst.* (September 1985), 10(3): 289–321.

[Ullman, 1982] J. D. Ullman. *Principles of Database Systems* (2nd edition). Rockville, Md.: Computer Science Press, 1982.

[Valduriez, 1987] P. Valduriez. Join Indices. *ACM Trans. Database Syst.* (June 1987), 12(2): 218–246.

[Valduriez, 1986] P. Valduriez. Optimization of Complex Queries Using Join Indices. *IEEE Q. Bull. Database Eng.* (December 1986), 9(4): 10–16.

[Valduriez, 1982] P. Valduriez. Semi-Join Algorithms for Distributed Database Machines. In *Distributed Data Bases*, J.-J. Schneider (ed.), Amsterdam: North-Holland, 1982, pp. 23–37.

[Valduriez and Boral, 1986] P. Valduriez and H. Boral. Evaluation of Recursive Queries Using Join Indices. In *Proc. First Int. Conf. on Expert Database Systems*, Charleston, S C., 1986, pp. 197–208.

[Valduriez and Danforth, 1989a] P. Valduriez and S. Danforth. Functional SQL (FSQL), A SQL Upward Compatible Database Programming Language. *Information Science, An International Journal* (to appear).

[Valduriez and Danforth, 1989b] P. Valduriez and S. Danforth. Query Optimization in Database Programming Languages. In *Proc. Int. Conf. on Deductive and Object-Oriented Databases*, Kyoto, Japan, December 1989, pp. 516–534.

[Valduriez and Gardarin, 1989] P. Valduriez and G. Gardarin. *Analysis and Comparison of Relational Database Systems*. Reading, Mass.: Addison-Wesley, 1989.

[Valduriez and Gardarin, 1984] P. Valduriez and G. Gardarin. Join and Semi-join Algorithms for a Multi Processor Database Machine. *ACM Trans. Database Syst.* (March 1984), 9(1): 133–161.

[Valduriez and Khoshafian, 1988a] P. Valduriez and S. Khoshafian. Transitive Closure of Transitively Closed Relations. In *Proc. 2nd Int. Conf. on Expert Database Systems*, L. Kerschberg (ed.), Menlo Park, Calif., Benjamin–Cummings, 1988, pp. 377–400.

[Valduriez and Khoshafian, 1988b] P. Valduriez and S. Khoshafian. Parallel Evaluation of the Transitive Closure of a Database Relation. *Int. J. Parallel Prog.* (February 1988), 12(1): 19–42.

[Valduriez et al., 1986] P. Valduriez, S. Khoshafian, and G. Copeland. Implementation Techniques of Complex Objects. In *Proc. 11th Int. Conf. on Very Large Databases*, Kyoto, Japan, August 1986, pp. 101–109.

[Verhofstadt, 1978] J. S. Verhofstadt. Recovery Techniques for Database Systems. *ACM Comput. Surv.* (June 1978), 10(2): 168–195.

[Wah and Lien, 1985] B. W. Wah and Y. N. Lien. Design of Distributed Databases on Local Computer Systems. *IEEE Trans. Software Eng.* (July 1985), SE-11(7): 609–619.

[Weihl, 1989] W. Weihl. Local Atomicity Properties: Modular Concurrency Control for Abstract Data Types. *ACM Trans. Prog. Lang. Syst.* (April 1989), 11(2): 249–281.

[Weihl, 1988] W. Weihl. Commutativity-Based Concurrency Control for Abstract Data Types. *IEEE Trans. Comput.* (December 1988), C-37(12): 1488–1505.

[Weihl and Liskov, 1985] W. Weihl and B. Liskov. Implementation of Resilient, Atomic Data Types. *ACM Trans. Prog. Lang. Syst.* (April 1985), 7(2): 244–269.

[Weikum, 1986] G. Weikum. Pros and Cons of Operating System Transactions for Data Base Systems. In *Proc. Fall Joint Computer Conf.*, Dallas, Tex., 1986, pp. 1219–1225.

[Wiederhold, 1984] G. Wiederhold. Knowledge and Database Management. *IEEE Software* (1984), 1(1): 63–74.

[Wiederhold, 1982] G. Wiederhold. *Database Design* (2nd edition). New York: McGraw-Hill, 1982.

[Williams et al., 1982] R. Williams, D. Daniels, L. Haas, G. Lapis, B. Lindsay, P. Ng, R. Obermarck, P. Selinger, A. Walker, P. Wilms, and R. Yost. R*: An Overview of the Architecture. In *Proc. 2nd Int. Conf. on Databases*, Jerusalem, Israel, June 1982, pp. 1–28.

[Wilms and Lindsay, 1981] P. F. Wilms and B. G. Lindsay. *A Database Authorization Mechanism Supporting Individual and Group Authorization.* Research Report RJ 3137, San Jose, Calif.: IBM Research Laboratory, May 1981.

[Wolf et al., 1979] J. J. Wolf, M. T. Liu, B. W. Weide and D. P. Tsay. Design of a Distributed Fault-Tolerant Loop Network. In *Proc. 9th Int. Symp. on Fault-Tolerant Computing Systems*, Madison, Wis., 1979, pp. 17–23.

[Wolfson, 1987] O. Wolfson. The Overhead of Locking (and Commit) Protocols in Distributed Databases. *ACM Trans. Database Syst.* (September 1987), 12(3): 453–471.

[Wong, 1977] E. Wong. Retrieving Dispersed Data from SDD-1. In *Proc. 2nd Berkeley Workshop on Distributed Data Management and Computer Networks*, Berkeley, Calif., 1977, pp. 217–235.

[Wong and Bazek, 1985] K. K. Wong and P. Bazek. MRDSM: A Relational Multidatabase Management System. In *Distributed Data Sharing Systems*, F. A. Schreiber and W. Litwin (eds.), Amsterdam: North-Holland, 1985, pp. 77–85.

[Wong and Youssefi, 1976] E. Wong and K. Youssefi. Decomposition: A Strategy for Query Processing. *ACM Trans. Database Syst.* (September 1976), 1(3): 223–241.

[Wright, 1983] D. D. Wright. *Managing Distributed Databases in Partitioned Networks.* Technical Report TR83-572, Ithaca, N.Y.: Department of Computer Science, Cornell University, September 1983.

[Wulf et al., 1981] W. A. Wulf, R. Levin, and S. P. Harbison. *HYDRA/C. mmp: An Experimental Computer System.* New York: McGraw-Hill, 1981.

[Yao et al., 1982a] S. B. Yao, S. B. Navathe, and J-L. Weldon. An Integrated Approach to Database Design. In *Data Base Design Techniques I: Requirements and Logical Structures*, Lecture Notes in Computer Science 132, New York: Springer-Verlag, 1982, pp. 1–30.

[Yao et al., 1982b] S. B. Yao, V. Waddle and B. Housel. View Modeling and Integration Using the Functional Data Model. *IEEE Trans. Software Eng.* (November 1982), SE-8(6): 544–554.

[Yeager, 1987] D. A. Yeager. 5ESS™ Switch Performance Metrics. In *Proc. Int. Conf. on Communications, Volume 1*, Seattle, Wa., June 1987, pp. 46–52.

[Yormark, 1977] B. Yormark. The ANSI/SPARC/DBMS Architecture. In *ANSI/SPARC DBMS Model*, D. A. Jardine (ed.), Amsterdam: North-Holland, 1977, pp. 1–21.

[Yoshida et al., 1985] M. Yoshida, K. Mizumachi, A. Wakino, I. Oyake, and Y. Matsushita. Time and Cost Evaluation Schemes of Multiple Copies of Data in Distributed Database Systems. *IEEE Trans. Software Eng.* (September 1985), SE-11(9): 954–958.

[Yu and Chang, 1984] C. T. Yu and C. C. Chang. Distributed Query Processing. *ACM Comput. Surv.* (December 1984), 16(4): 399–433.

[Zaniolo, 1986] C. Zaniolo. Safety and Compilation of Non-Recursive Horn Clauses. In *Proc. First Int. Conf. on Expert Database Systems*, Charleston, N.C., April 1986, pp. 237–252.

[Zaniolo, 1985] C. Zaniolo. The Representation and Deductive Retrieval of Complex Objects. In *Proc. 11th Int. Conf. on Very Large Data Bases*, Stockholm, August 1985, pp. 458–469.

[Zloof, 1977] M. M. Zloof. Query-by-Example: A Data Base Language. *IBM Syst. J.* (1977), 16(4): 324–343.

[Zloof, 1975] M. M. Zloof. *Query-by-Example: Operations on the Transitive Closure.* Research Report RC 5526, Yorktown Heights, N.Y.: IBM Research Laboratory, 1975.

[Zobel, 1983] D. D. Zobel. The Deadlock Problem: A Classifying Bibliography. *ACM Oper. Syst. Rev.* (October 1983), 17(2): 6–15.

# Index

553

Programming-in-the-small, 66
Projection operation, 27–28
Projection-join dependency, 21, 23
Projection-join normal form, 25
Prolog, 480, 484
Protection, 384, 386
PS-Algol, 504
Pu, C., 431, 453, 543
Purcell, S.C., 393, 397, 543
Putzolu, F., 333, 341, 346, 378, 401, 409, 533
Putzolu, G.R., 161, 216, 266, 520, 533

QBE, 36
QUEL, 35, 81, 213
Query
  analysis, 191–93
  decomposition, 183–84, 188–89
  graph, 191
  language, 26
  locality set model, 405
  modification, 150
  optimization, 174, 210, 216
  processing, 173
  processor, 15, 173
  simplification, 159
  substitution, 214
Quinn, M.J., 488, 543
Quorum, 370
  based voting protocol, 373
Quotient operation, 27

R*, 69, 224, 230, 254, 298, 315, 513
R*-QOA algorithm, 221, 235–36
Rahimi, S., 93, 543
Rallis, N., 320, 540
Ramakrishnan, R., 484, 516, 521
Ramamoorthy, C.V., 144, 543
Ramamritham, K., 320, 521
Ramanathan, P., 378, 543
Randell, B., 323, 377, 520, 543
Ranstrom, J., 418, 548
Rashid, R.F., 419, 423, 535
Read
  lock, 285
  quorum, 373
  set, 262
  timestamp, 299
Read-before-write transaction, 271
Read-once/write-all protocol, 282
Read-write conflict, 277
Reconstruction, 103
  program, 185
Recovery, 14, 258, 408
  protocol, 348, 362
Recursive
  query, 484
  rule, 483
Redell, D.D., 393, 397, 543
Redfield, S., 460, 516, 523
Redo, 338, 341, 409
Redo/no-undo, 344
Reducer, 224, 226
Reduction technique, 199
Redundancy, 322

elimination, 189, 192–93
Reeve, C.L., 182, 230, 239, 241, 254, 523
Reference architecture, 66
Referential integrity, 25, 121
Register insertion ring, 58
Reiner, D.S., 187, 536, 539
Relation, 18
  cardinality, 18
  degree, 18
  fragment, 188
  instance, 19
  key, 18
  scheme, 18
Relational
  algebra, 18, 27
  algebra query, 189
  algebra tree, 194–95
  calculus, 18, 26, 34
  calculus query, 189
  database, 17–18
Relevant simple predicate, 111
Reliability, 9, 13, 15, 322–23, 327, 451
Remote
  communication, 391
  procedure call, 392–93
  user authentication, 157
Renesse, R.v., 154, 414, 423, 549
Repetition anomaly, 19
Replica control protocol, 282, 369
Replicated database, 12
Replication, 15
  transparency, 69, 383
Resiliency, 258
Response time, 177, 211–12
  optimization, 177
Restricted transaction, 271
  two-step transaction, 271
Reuter, A., 16, 275, 334, 336, 342–45, 378, 534
Richard, P., 495, 501, 516, 538
Richardson, J.P., 487, 516, 539
Ring network, 56, 62
Riordon, J.S., 145, 540
Rivest, R.L., 154, 543
Robinson, J.T., 307–9, 537
Robson, D., 494, 532
Roesler, M., 320, 544
Rolin, P., 452, 539
Rollback, 261
Roome, W.D., 464, 538
Rosenberg, R.L., 87, 443, 452, 537
Rosenkrantz, D.J., 190, 200, 208, 271, 313, 535, 544, 547
Ross, R.E., 212, 544
Ross, R.G., 414, 521
Roth, J.P., 329, 544
Rothermel, K., 320, 544
Rothnie, J.B., 16, 139, 182, 230, 239, 241, 254, 306, 523, 544
Round robin, 390
Routing, 53
ROWA rule, 282, 298, 347, 374
Rowe, L.A., 506, 547
Rubenstein, B., 496, 548
Run-time support processor, 86
Rusinkiewicz, M., 443, 452, 527, 544

Rybnik, J., 428, 524
Rydery, J.L., 459, 516, 524

SABRE, 464
Sacca, D., 122, 139, 145, 544
Sacco, G.M., 16, 177, 179, 187, 245, 249, 253, 402–4, 544
Salem, K., 453, 520
Saltzer, J.H., 385, 544
Sawdon, W., 424, 534
Schedule, 277, 279
  serial schedule, 280
  serializable schedule, 281
Scheduler, 272
Scheduling, 381, 387
Schek, H.-J., 499, 506, 508, 512, 543, 545
Schema, 35
  definition, 67
  integration, 426, 431
  translation, 426, 428
Schkolnick, M., 402–4, 544
Schlageter, G., 320, 378, 527, 545
Schlichting, R.D., 332, 545
Schmidt, J.W., 37, 92, 524, 545
Schneider, F.B., 332, 545
Schneider, G.M., 146, 534
Schneider, P.R., 329, 544
Schneiderman, B., 452, 545
Scholl, M.H., 499, 506, 508, 517, 543, 545
Schreiber, F., 79, 92, 545
Schwans, K., 423, 536
Schwarz, P.M., 320, 412, 541, 545, 547
Schweitzer, P.J., 126, 540
SDD-1, 230, 254
SDD-1-QOA algorithm, 239, 241
Secondary index, 477, 479, 513
Security
  constraint, 148
  control, 148
Selection, 27
  predicate, 28
  selectivity, 214
Selectivity factor, 214
Selinger, P.G., 69, 152, 180–82, 211–12, 214–15, 220, 230, 235, 253–54, 477, 539, 545, 551
Semantic
  data control, 148
  data controller, 83
  integrity constraint, 148, 158
  integrity control, 148, 158, 481
  net, 482
Semantically incorrect query, 190
Semiautonomous systems, 80
Semijoin, 27, 31
  semijoin program, 227
  semijoin selectivity, 215
SEMINAIVE algorithm, 487
Seminaive evaluation, 486
Sequent, 464, 545
SERIAL algorithm, 247
Serializability, 277, 279, 281, 445
  conflict-based serializability, 277
  serializability graph testing algorithm, 317–18